THE WAR OF 1812

1

FORGOTTEN
SOLDIERS

IN THE NORTH

Blue Coats – American infantry, 1813

In this fine painting by H.C. McBarron, American infantry in the uniform current
in the autumn of 1813 prepare to meet the enemy. Brave but not well trained,
they were hard put to defeat a tough opponent at the battle of Crysler's Farm.
(Courtesy, Parks Canada)

Other titles by Donald E. Graves

BOOKS

South Albertas: A Canadian Regiment at War
(Robin Brass Studio, 1998)

Where Right and Glory Lead! The Battle of Lundy's Lane, 1814
(Robin Brass Studio, 1997)

Redcoats and Grey Jackets: The Battle of Chippawa, 1814
(Dundurn Press, 1994)

(with Michael Whitby) *Normandy 1944: The Canadian Summer*
(Art Global, 1994)

EDITED MEMOIRS

Soldiers of 1814: American Enlisted Men's Memoirs of the Niagara Campaign
(Old Fort Niagara Press, 1996)

*Merry Hearts Make Light Days: The War of 1812 Memoirs
of Lieutenant John Le Couteur, 104th Foot*
(Carleton University Press, 1993)

1885. Experiences of the Halifax Battalion in the North-West
(Museum Restoration Service, 1985)

MONOGRAPHS

Editor, *De Scheel's Treatise on Artillery, 1800*
(Museum Restoration Service, 1984)

Sir William Congreve and the Rocket's Red Glare
(Museum Restoration Service, 1989)

Field of Glory

THE BATTLE OF CRYSLER'S FARM, 1813

DONALD E. GRAVES

Foreword by
John R. Elting
Colonel, United States Army (Ret.)

Maps by
Christopher Johnson

*A List of the Crysler's Farm and
Châteauguay Medal Recipients by*
Stephen Pallas

Marine Art by
Peter Rindlisbacher

ROBIN BRASS STUDIO
Toronto

Published 1999 by Robin Brass Studio Inc.
10 Blantyre Avenue, Toronto, Ontario M1N 2R4, Canada
Fax: (416) 698-2120 • e-mail: rbrass@total.net •
www.rbstudiobooks.com

Distributed in the United States of America by
Midpoint Trade Books
27 West 20th St., Suite 1102
New York, NY 10011
Fax: 212-727-0195 • e-mail: midpointny@aol.com

Printed and bound in Canada by AGMV-Marquis,
Cap-Saint-Ignace, Quebec

Canadian Cataloguing in Publication Data

Graves, Donald E. (Donald Edward)
    Field of glory : the Battle of Crysler's Farm, 1813

Includes bibliographical references and index
ISBN 1-896941-11-7 (bound) ISBN 1-896941-10-9 (pbk.)

1. Crysler's Farm, Battle of, Ont., 1813.* 2. Châteauguay, Battle of,
Quebec, 1813. 3. Canada – History – War of 1812.* 4. United States
– History – War of 1812. I. Title.

FC446.C57G72 1999   971.03'4   C99-930808-4
E355.4.G72 1999

For Dianne, My English Rose
Who exchanged the comfort of the Home Counties
for the inclement weather, pestiferous insects
and impolite animals of the North American woods
and, in doing so, taught me that courage
can sometimes come in a softer package.

Contents

MAPS

Foreword

BY JOHN R. ELTING, COLONEL,
UNITED STATES ARMY (RET.)

To both the United States Army and American military historians the 1813 battle of Crysler's Farm has always been regarded as an unmitigated disgrace, the absolute nadir of the history of the American regular army.[1] In truth, it is a daunting tale: approximately 3,000 American regulars attacked some 1,200 British and Canadians and were driven off in disorder, suffering twice the casualties they inflicted. If the action is considered at all, it is only briefly for its obvious "what not to do next time" lessons and then consigned to oblivion.

Those lessons *were* many and blunt. The American soldiers at Crysler's Farm might have been regulars, but they were poorly trained and too often officered by civilians-in-uniform whose only qualification for a commission was their unswerving loyalty to the governing Democratic-Republican party.[2] One prime example was Thomas M. Randolph, whom President James Madison appointed colonel of the 20th Infantry Regiment directly from civilian life since the president felt he "could do no less than give the public the benefit" of the man's talents. (Said talents, if any, seem to have been confined to the study of botany.) A few months service on the northern frontier had Randolph pleading for a return to the comforts of Monticello, the residence of his father-in-law, Thomas Jefferson, and left the unfortunate 20th Infantry reduced to a skeleton by hardship and his incompetence. The senior American general, that strange creature James Wilkinson, was too sick to exercise command at the battle, and so stayed snug abed through the bloody fiasco that his shortage of such basic military qualities as patriotism, valour and ability had done so much to create.[3] As if this was not bad enough, the American plan of campaign was adventuresome to an extreme, and the campaign itself was launched on the very edge of winter, far too late.

Now, in *Field of Glory*, Donald Graves has for the first time told the complete story of this disastrous campaign and told it well. His research – wide, deep, and well directed – has covered its intricacies from a teenage American drummer cutting up his extra blanket to improvise a pair of trousers to the perplexities of President James Madison and Sir George Prevost, the British commander-in-chief. The assessment that emerges of the American command system is close to devastating: President Madison, decent, well-meaning, vacillating, and wholly unmilitary; Secretary of War John Armstrong, almost competent, ambitious, but careless of detail and lacking the ultimate toughness to force balking generals to do what should be done, and do it promptly. The senior commanders were Wilkinson, facing his first active campaign and desperate to get his "old carcass" out of it undamaged; and Wade Hampton, stiff-necked, touchy, arrogant, justly contemptuous of Wilkinson, ready enough to lead his army into battle, but utterly lacking comprehension of what to do with it when he got there. Under them was a shaky stratum of other political appointees: Morgan Lewis, failed Army quartermaster general, tactically timid, sickly, and ignorant of everything military; Robert Swartout, another quartermaster who yearned to be a hero, but possessed none of the necessary qualifications; John Boyd, an adventurer who had been a competent enough regimental commander but quickly proved his promotion to general unjustified.

Yet among and under these politically correct failures were others, ready, willing, and able to train and care for their commands *and* to slug it out with any enemy. There was Leonard Covington (whom Graves has rescued from undeserved obscurity), unfortunately mortally wounded at Crysler's Farm; Alexander Macomb, the first general who had been trained at the United States Military Academy at West Point;[4] Jacob Brown, ex-militiaman and instinctive warrior; Winfield Scott, originally a political appointee but since self-converted into a dedicated professional; and a goodly sprinkling of other officers who combined courage and a determination to learn and do their duty.

Graves's coverage of the defenders of Canada in 1813 is equally thorough, from harassed Sir George Prevost down to buck privates and their "camp women," and he contrasts the iron discipline and tactical proficiency of British infantry and gunners at Crysler's Farm with the harum-scarum and poorly directed American attacks. Equally, he compares the calm professional competence of the senior British officers, Lieutenant Colonels Joseph Morrison and Thomas Pearson; with the muddled American leadership. (The Americans, British officers agreed, showed valour in the action, but lacked the training and discipline necessary to manoeuvre effectively under fire.) As usual in his work, Graves explains the weapons and tactics of that period in detail, and the logistical problems involved in the movement of men and supplies through what was still a good deal of a wilderness. Especially jolting is the author's description of the care of the sick and wounded – an everlasting shame for

Americans. Finally, Graves completes his tale with a review of the subsequent fortunes/misfortunes of the participants of the battle and of the battlefield itself.

One puzzle – so far unsolved by any historian of this campaign – remains. The American naval commander on Lake Ontario, Commodore Isaac Chauncey, had superiority over the opposing British squadron at this time. Yet he failed to prevent the British from sending Morrison, with an escort of gunboats, down the St. Lawrence River to overtake Wilkinson. An able organizer and administrator, Chauncey had previously – and would again – abandon American armies rather than risk his fleet in combat. His negligence here converted the probable failure of Wilkinson's reluctant offensive against Montreal to a certainty. Yet Chauncey never exhibited the least concern or responsibility for his own share in this defeat.

In summation, in this book – well written and containing a sufficiency of first-rate maps – Graves presents Crysler's Farm as a grievous American defeat, but also (along with the hardships of their subsequent winter encampment at French Mills) as a screening process that would eventually strengthen the American Army. Armstrong was at last able, one way or another, to purge it of Wilkinson, Hampton, and other aging bumblers and to promote those younger officers who wanted to fight and knew how. (It was possibly his major service to the United States, ensuring competent military leadership for the next half-century – and it made him no friends whatever in Washington.) Other unqualified officers such as Thomas Randolph removed themselves from the hazards of short rations, bad weather, and shots fired in anger. The results, as Don Graves has told in his earlier War of 1812 titles, *Red Coats and Grey Jackets* and *Where Right and Glory Lead*, would be clearly evident in 1814 at Chippawa, Lundy's Lane, Fort Erie and Plattsburgh.

JOHN R. ELTING
Colonel USA (Ret.)

Notes to Foreword

1. Certain incidents early in the Korean War may possibly rival it.
2. Which exists today, not too much changed, as the modern Democratic party.
3. Even stranger, while an officer of the U.S. Army, Wilkinson had solicited and enjoyed a pension and extra bribes from Spain and there is evidence that he had treasonous correspondence with British authorities in Canada during Wayne's Fallen Timbers campaign, 1790-1795. A disloyal subordinate to Wayne, Wilkinson took no care of his men's health but did cheat them of their rations.
4. The author states that Macomb was a graduate of West Point. In actual fact, he had been commissioned from civil life as a cavalry second lieutenant in 1799; he was a first lieutenant, when ordered to West Point c. 1803 as a student, remaining until 1805, but is not technically considered a graduate.

Preface

On a cold, raw day in March 1994 I was among those bystanders who witnessed a unique event take place at Fort Niagara near Youngstown, New York. As American and Canadian military units paraded to the music of their bands, Baroness Strange of Megginch formally returned to the United States the garrison flag, measuring 24 by 28 feet, captured in December 1813 when British troops stormed the fort in a daring night-time assault. It had been presented to the baroness's ancestor, Lieutenant General Sir Gordon Drummond, then commanding in Upper Canada, and his descendants had preserved it carefully, through fires and other hazards, at the family estate in Scotland for nearly two centuries. It had now come home.

The fall of Fort Niagara and the capture of that flag, with its fifteen stars and fifteen stripes, was the last act in the American campaign against Canada in the autumn of 1813. *Field of Glory* is the story of the central event of that campaign, the battle of Crysler's Farm, an obscure military action almost unknown outside the country in which it was fought (and not that well remembered inside it). This is perhaps understandable given the battle's timing and outcome. From the British perspective, Crysler's Farm was a minor engagement overshadowed by larger events in Europe that year when the Duke of Wellington led his troops to victory at Vittoria, the Pyrenees, Nivelle and the Nive. From the American point of view, Crysler's Farm marked the lowest point reached by the United States Army during the War of 1812 – and no army likes to dwell on its defeats.

The neglect of this battle and the campaign of which it was part may be understandable but it is also unfortunate. The autumn offensive of 1813 represented the most serious attempt by the United States to conquer British North America. More regular American troops were committed to this operation than in any other offensive of the War of 1812 – in fact, in numbers of regular troops deployed, this offensive was possibly the largest military operation mounted by the United States before 1861. More importantly, these troops were committed against crucial strategical objectives, the city of Montreal and the St. Lawrence River lifeline between Upper and Lower Canada and at no time during the war did senior British commanders express so much concern at the possibility that the republic to the south would prevail. British victory in 1813, based on success at Crysler's Farm and on a parallel triumph at Châteauguay, preserved Canada's independence from its aggressive neighbour.

The results, while not as happy for the United States, were no less significant. For eighteen months prior to the offensive, the republic had tried to wage war with half-trained troops led by green officers, the whole commanded by a collection of politicians and relics of the Revolutionary War. The failure of the American northern army in 1813 was so catastrophic it was beneficial for it swept away much of the senior ranks of the officer corps, permitting the promotion of younger, more aggressive and professional men. If the Crysler's Farm campaign of 1813 represents the nadir of the United States Army's fortunes during the war, it also prepared the way for that army's fine performance in the Niagara campaign of the following year. I have written about the long and bloody summer of 1814 elsewhere and *Field of Glory* is intended as the "prequel" (to use a word much favoured by Hollywood) to *Where Right and Glory Lead*, my study of the battle of Lundy's Lane.

One aspect of the battle of Crysler's Farm will be of interest mainly to Canadians, who live in a nation, it has been remarked, with one foot in the grave of the language issue and the other on the banana peel of the next constitutional crisis. They will be interested and hopefully pleased to learn that in 1813 English- and French-speaking Canadians fought side by side with warriors of the First Nations to defend their soil against a common enemy, a situation all too rare in the history of this country.

Field of Glory is my third book-length study of a War of 1812 battle, and for me, writing about Crysler's Farm has been like going home again. This is because I can trace my personal interest in that obscure conflict to a childhood excursion to Upper Canada Village, the historic site near Morrisburg, Ontario. After pestering the student guide in the battlefield memorial with questions about the organization of the American army he was unable to answer, I remember standing in awe in front of the magnificent mural of the action. A seed was planted at that moment and from such seeds mighty obsessions can grow – they certainly did in my case.

I now have the necessary but pleasant task of thanking those who have helped me over the four years it has taken to research and write this book. Any author who has undertaken a serious work of history knows that he or she is dependent on the generosity of colleagues, particularly concerning specialized subjects. This was certainly the case with *Field of Glory*, a book that could not have been written without the contributions of the following people.

First, I owe a great debt to three Toronto historians. Stuart Sutherland answered many questions about individual British officers, and I am glad that his comprehensive work on the officer corps of the War of 1812, *His Majesty's Gentlemen*, which I have cheerfully plundered for years, will soon be available to a wider public. William Gray, author of *Soldiers of the King: The Militia of Upper Canada*, provided similar information from his field of expertise, and finally, Dr. Carl Benn, author of a fine new study, *The Iroquois in the War of 1812*, was helpful in matters relating to the First Nations.

My idea to list the names of the recipients of the medals and clasps awarded for the battles of Crysler's Farm and Châteauguay was fine in theory but soon proved a quagmire for an author not all that knowledgeable about this specialized subject. Fortunately I was extracted from this morass by Cameron Ward of Hamilton and Professor Graham Neale and Stephen Pallas of Ottawa, who lent me their expert advice. Stephen Pallas also compiled the list of the recipients contained in Appendix G and to him belongs the credit for this labour.

Soldiers' songs have always been a subject of fascination to me and my wish to include a selection of what is, after all, the poetry of the lower ranks was only made possible through the labours of Brian Dunnigan and John Harrigan of the Clements Library at the University of Michigan, who helped me collect them. In a similar vein, Michael Putnam of Dundas and Nicko Elliott of Hamilton, Canada, provided me with information on military drumming in the War of 1812.

On the naval side of things I am indebted to Lieutenant Commander (Retd.) Pat Whitby, RCN, and Mike Whitby, captain and first mate respectively of the 29-foot *Amaranth*, who tolerated my presence on board during a voyage in September 1995 that traced Wilkinson's route from Grenadier Island to French Creek, and to Robert Malcomson, author of *Lords of the Lake: The Naval War on Lake Ontario, 1812-1814*, who did his best to explain to a confirmed landlubber the apparently critical difference between a futtock and a clew garnet.

Back on dry land I must acknowledge the aid of Robert Henderson, historian of the Canadian Fencibles, who put at my disposal *all* his research on Crysler's Farm and answered many minor and, what must have been to him, annoying questions. Ian Bowering of Cornwall and Paul Fortier of Prescott were helpful concerning matters of local history on the St. Lawrence, while two former professionals from the St. Lawrence Parks Commission, and experts on the battle in their own right, rendered excellent support: Jack Schechter, former archivist-librarian at Upper Canada Village, pointed out likely sources and Brigadier General (Retd.) William Patterson, former director of the St. Lawrence Parks Commission and biographer of Joseph Wanton Morrison, cast a very critical eye over my drafts.

In Britain I wish to thank Sir Christopher Prevost of London for giving me permission to quote from the wartime journal kept by Sir George Prevost's daughter, Anne Elinor, and Mr. Simon Bendall, also of London and late of 52 ("Niagara") Battery, Royal Artillery, for identifying its present day designation. I must not forget Doug Hendry, who offered advice on the complexities of the Public Record Office in Britain.

My thanks also go to John Fredriksen who provided manuscripts concerning the 1813 campaign; Jon Jouppien of St. Catharines who assisted in matters of architectural history; and René Chartrand, Derek Cooke, Ron Dale, Mike McNorgan and Joe Thatcher who advised me on illustrations. I must acknowledge the expert assistance given me by Donald S. Richan and his staff at the Queen's University archives in Kingston, particularly George Henderson, which allowed me to do twice the research in half the time.

I was very fortunate to make the acquaintance of Dr. Traer Van Allen of New York and Morrisburg whose family owned much of the Crysler's Farm battlefield for nearly a century. Thanks to Dr. Van Allen's efforts to preserve the visual and documentary history of his family and their property, I am able to include in *Field of Glory* rare photographs of a battlefield that has long disappeared.

Once again, four good friends and fellow 1812 historians went into the breach on my behalf. Dr. John Morris of Garretsville, Ohio, put at my disposal his research on the St. Lawrence campaign gathered for his long overdue biography of Jacob Brown which is shortly to be published as *Sword of the Border: Major General Jacob Jennings Brown, 1775-1828*. Professor Joseph Whitehorne of Front Royal, author of *The Battle of Baltimore, 1814*, read my drafts and laboured long and hard to make me understand the complexities of the lineage of the United States Army. Patrick Wilder of Oswego lent me books from his personal library and material gathered for his own study on the battle of Sackets Harbor. Last, but certainly not least, Colonel (Retd.) John Elting of Cornwall-on-the-Hudson, N.Y., acted as a sounding board for many ideas and shared his expertise (becoming all too rare) on the care and handling of the military horse.

I am only responsible for the text of *Field of Glory* – its attractive jacket, maps and presentation are the work of three professionals. Peter Rindlisbacher of Amherstburg, Ontario, *the* artist of the naval War of 1812, generously agreed to take time from a busy schedule to do the wonderful painting that graces its cover and the fine sketches inside, while Christopher Johnson of Newcastle laboured hard to translate my arcane hieroglyphics into intelligent and legible maps. Finally, Robin Brass took it all, shook it up, and poured out the pleasing result that follows.

In closing, I must be careful not to forget those close to me lest I come home one night to find the locks changed. I will begin with Belle the dog, whose habit of getting sprayed by skunks abruptly jerked me back from 1813 to a noxious present on a number of occasions, and the late Wally the cat, a mighty garden hunter, who contributed two frogs, two chipmunks, a half dozen birds, a fish and countless mice to assist me in my labours, many of which were dropped (some still wriggling) beside my desk. Finally, there is she who must be obeyed, Dianne, chief among whose many virtues (including her skill with a camera) is the simple fact that she puts up with me.

DONALD E. GRAVES
St. George's Day, 1999
Almonte, Canada

A NOTE TO THE READER

During the War of 1812 both the British and American armies used numerical designations for their infantry units. To avoid confusion I have used figures for British units and words for American units – thus the British 49th Regiment of Foot but the American Thirty-Third Infantry Regiment.

The terms "battalion" and "regiment" need clarification. In the British army and most Commonwealth armies, the word regiment has nothing to do with a military unit's organization but is instead part of its formal title. In 1813 the infantry of the British army consisted of 104 regiments, each having at least one and some as many as six battalions, and each headed by a colonel. These colonels, however, held only honorary and financial appointments, *not* command appointments – the basic infantry administrative and tactical unit was the battalion, commanded by a lieutenant colonel. If this is confusing to readers unversed in the subtleties of the British military mind, they would be best to substitute "battalion" when "regiment" comes up in a British context. Generally speaking, a British infantry battalion and an American infantry regiment were the same thing, permanently organized military units of between 500 and 1,000 men at full strength.

That is the general rule, but unfortunately there are some perverse exceptions. In the spring of 1812 the American army raised a number of two-battalion infantry regiments, an organization done away with shortly after the war started but still retained in 1813 by some American units that feature in *Field of Glory*, notably the Tenth and Eleventh Infantry. As if this is not bad enough, the word "battalion" also had two additional meanings in the United States Army of the period. It could mean an *ad hoc* grouping of two or more infantry companies, sometimes from different regiments, commanded by an officer of the rank of major and above, and it was also used in the expression "to form battalion", that is to deploy for battle. Incredible and confusing as it may seem, in 1813 an American *battalion* (used in the sense of an *ad hoc* grouping) composed of two companies from one infantry regiment and a third from a *battalion* (used in the sense of a sub-unit of a regiment organized on the two-battalion structure) from another infantry regiment, might "form *battalion*" (used in the sense of deploying for action). It all depends, as do so many things, on the context.

Happily, we can now move on to geography, which in this book is fairly straightforward. The military operations discussed below largely take place along the St. Lawrence River and some readers may not be familiar with this major waterway, which flows northeast from the Great Lakes to where it joins the gulf of the same name. "Down," "downstream" or "down river" on the St. Lawrence is northeast towards Quebec City while "up," "up river" or "upstream" is southwest towards Kingston, Ontario. The "head" of the river is at Kingston, the "foot" below Quebec City. In the area of the St. Lawrence over which the armies moved in 1813, the "left" or northern bank was Canadian while the "right" or southern bank was American. For no other reason than that I have grown weary of trying to divine the correct version of the many variants of the name of that little village in upstate New York, I have called it Sackets Harbor throughout except in quoted text.

Last, we come to that always puzzling question, the measurement of time in an age before regulated time zones existed. In 1813 watches were set according to a locally agreed time which might vary within a few miles, and this resulted in British and American accounts often differing as to the time of an event. Very generally, British time seems to have been about an hour behind that used by the American army. There is no easy way to get around this problem, which can reduce an historian to despair, and wishing to avoid that, the times for events stated below are a consensus based on all available information.

D.E.G.

A Miserable Night
in November 1813

Michael Cook had seen more welcome visitors to his tavern. Their coming was no surprise because news travels fast along the river, and besides, the American advance guard had passed through that morning, riflemen in green coats and blue-uniformed dragoons, the rain-soaked white falls of their leather helmets pressed flat on their necks, riding what Cook, a good judge of horseflesh, thought were runty mounts. Still, it was an impressive sight when the main body arrived, as in a matter of minutes his fields were covered with blue-coated infantry and boats – hundreds of boats – were beached on the river bank. Michael Cook had been operating a log tavern in Williamsburgh Township on the Canadian shore of the St. Lawrence River for nine years when these unwanted customers landed on his doorstep and their arrival did not gladden him because Cook, a Loyalist born in Philadelphia forty-eight years before, was no friend of the Yankees.[1]

Neither was his wife, Abigail, pleased. And who could blame her, with nine of the couple's eleven children at home and foreign invaders in her kitchen. She quickly ordered the older girls, eight-year-old Abigail and twelve-year-old Elizabeth, to look after the little ones, five-year-old George, three-year-old Catharine and two-year-old Elias (who was always a handful) while she minded the baby. The older boys, sixteen-year-old Michael Mason, ten-year-old Abraham and nine-year-old David, were told to help their father and stay out of trouble.[2]

The Cooks needn't have worried. The Americans were not unfriendly and those who made purchases paid in silver, which was better currency than the military scrip tendered by the British army – in fact a man couldn't get better. The problem was that many Americans did not bother to pay for what they took and they took a lot. Fence rails disappeared to feed large bonfires as the invaders tried to dry clothing soaked by the rain that had been falling throughout the day. The rails were shortly followed by Cook's wheat, oats,

1

peas, corn, hay, sheep, beehives, honey, potatoes, a yearling calf, half a bushel of salted sausages, and all the farm poultry. There was little Michael Cook could do – he had fought his war against the Yankees thirty years or more before and the simple fact was that he was badly outnumbered.[3]

All in all, with the exception of the looting, much of which was understandable as the Americans appeared to be very hungry, the intruders behaved reasonably well. The Cooks could not help, however, but compare their appearance to that of the well-turned-out British and Canadian troops who had camped many times on their fields while moving up or down the St. Lawrence. The American enlisted men were dirty, unkempt, many with ragged uniforms and they appeared to have little wet-weather gear, since some wore scraps of waterproof coverings stripped off provision and ammunition containers in an attempt to shield themselves from the rain. The officers made a better impression, particularly the dashing young staff officers ("stafflings" they called themselves), who found a pretext to enter the tavern hoping to catch a glimpse of "the fair."[4] In that they were disappointed because thirty-nine-year-old Abigail Cook with her baby and flock of toddlers, wide-eyed faces pressed into her skirts, was not quite what these military Lotharios had in mind.

By evening the invaders had made themselves comfortable, the more fortunate feasting on the Cooks' sheep, poultry and calf, the less fortunate subsisting on their rations. There was much traffic between the shore and the two boats in the river where the senior generals ("Big Bugs" said the staff officers) of the army lay ill. Sentries were posted and the last of Cook's dwindling stock of fence rails were heaped on fires ringed about by wet and miserable soldiers. Without even trying to, Michael and Abigail overheard snatches of their conversation. There had been fighting that day and much marching to and fro with little result; there was concern about running the Long Sault rapids which lay below and many complaints about the weather but their guests were generally confident they would spend the coming winter in Montreal – in comfort. Gradually, the talking and the movement died away as Major General James Wilkinson's army settled down for the night.[5]

Two miles to the west, the sentry outside the front door of John Crysler's brightly lit farmhouse facing the King's highway on the bank of the St. Lawrence was cursing his luck. It was bad enough to be on duty on a rotten night such as this with its rain and sleet; worse luck still to be assigned to this post because the farmhouse was serving as headquarters, and that meant senior officers coming and going and an anxious sergeant of the guard on the prowl. The traffic had been heavy this Godforsaken evening; many times already he had gone through the ten separate motions required to bring his musket off his left shoulder and present arms, the prescribed salute for an officer of major's rank and above. Bemoaning the day he said farewell to Enniscorthy to join His Britannic Bloody Majesty's British Bloody Army, the sentry eased his neck inside his tight leather stock, cursed this foreign, heathen land with its awful weather, shifted his weight from foot to foot, damned and double-damned all kings, officers, sergeants and corporals twice over, spat to see how far the wind would carry it, and continued to do his duty.

Inside the farmhouse, Nancy Crysler, always the good hostess, smiled bravely as she watched her spotless floors despoiled by muddy boots and water-soaked riding cloaks. Lamps and candles were called for, and their light picked out the glint of the metal buttons and the bullion and braid adorning the uniforms of the dozen or so officers crowded into her parlour. Most wore the scarlet of the British army, their regiments and corps distinguished by the colour of the facings or trim on their coats: the green of Lieutenant Colonel Charles Plenderleath of the 49th Foot, the black of Major Miller Clifford of the 89th and the dark blue of the staff officers, Lieutenant Colonels Thomas Pearson and John Harvey. Captain Henry Jackson, the gunner, in blue with red facings, and Major Frederick Heriot, in the rifle green with black cords of an officer of the Canadian Voltigeurs, presented a pleasant contrast, while Captain William Mulcaster of the Royal Navy stood out in the simplicity of his sailor's plain dark blue coat and trousers.[6]

The eyes of these officers were on the man who had called this orders group. Lieutenant Colonel Joseph Wanton Morrison was young, just thirty years old, with round, even features and thinning dark brown hair. For two days his British and Canadian force had been shadowing Wilkinson's much larger American army down the St. Lawrence. That day there had been some desultory fighting but Morrison had not pressed the issue because the Americans had the better position. They had obligingly withdrawn late in the afternoon and given Morrison the ground he wanted and his small army of just under twelve hundred men now occupied it. That was the good news; the bad was that Morrison had received an order from his superior at Kingston to break off the pursuit and return there. The decision before him was whether to obey this order and let the Americans go without hindrance, or disobey it, stand his ground, and see what the morrow brought.[7]

The officers present that night may have discussed the consequences of either choice but they knew the final decision belonged to Morrison as the responsibility for the result would be his alone. While his officers waited for him to make up his mind, their men made camp on the grounds and in the buildings of militia Captain John Crysler's prosperous farm. His fence rails, like Michael Cook's, disappeared to fuel their fires and the forage in the barns was appropriated for the horses of the artillery teams. Anything edible by humans was consumed including fifty bushels of potatoes, twenty bushels of apples, pigs, sheep and the honey from Crysler's beehives. As it was in the American camp, so it was in the British – the lucky ones got the fresh food, the less fortunate had to make do with salt pork and hardtack but all welcomed the tot of thick Demerara ration rum – good insulation on a wretched night such as this.[8]

Back in the Crysler parlour Morrison had made up his mind. He did so without dramatics, for dramatics were not the style of this man. The army would not return to Kingston but would hold its present position – tomorrow might see a battle but there would be no withdrawal, and if the Americans moved down the river to Montreal he would follow and continue to harass them. Messages were dispatched and, probably after some further talk about dispositions, the officers were dismissed to make their way back to their commands.

As they passed the sentry outside the front door, the man came alert and presented arms. When the last officer had disappeared into the wet gloom of the night, the soldier returned to his reveries and his curses as the rain continued to fall, its spatter drowning out the gentle sound of the St. Lawrence flowing by a few hundred feet away.

PART I

The Background

Rough passage on Lake Ontario, October 1813
Throughout September 1813, shortage of water transport and the presence of the
British naval squadron on Lake Ontario delayed the movement of the American division
in the Niagara to Sackets Harbor, New York, for the operation against Montreal. When
it finally set out at the beginning of October, autumn storms on the lake caused a
rough and dangerous passage, as shown in this sketch by marine artist Peter
Rindlisbacher.

CHAPTER 1

"Hark, now the drums beat up again"

ORIGINS OF A CAMPAIGN, JUNE 1812-JUNE 1813

Hark, now the drums beat up again,
For all true soldier gentlemen,
Then let us 'list and march, I say,
Over the hills and far away.

>*Over the hills and o'er the main,*
>*To Flanders, Portugal and Spain*
>*King George commands and we'll obey,*
>*Over the hills and far away.*

Over rivers, bogs and springs,
We all shall live as great as kings,
And plunder get both night and day
When over the hills and far away.

>*Over the hills and o'er the main ...*

We then shall lead more happy lives,
By getting rid of brats and wives,
That scold on, both night and day,
When o'er the hills and far away.[1]

Everyone wanted to look his best on the morning of 4 September 1813. Word had come to the American army occupying Fort George in Upper Canada that a new general was at Fort Niagara on the river bank opposite and would shortly arrive to assume command. This same message also contained "a hint, that no salutes were desired on this occasion, whose noise might blab to the enemy." This precaution was realistic as there were British advance posts not a thousand yards from the most outlying pickets of the camp, but it offended the sensibilities of the senior officers. Determined to start off on the

right foot, they decided a "hint" was not "sufficient to supersede the regulations" and "the artillery should speak out, whoever might be the wiser for it."
At the appointed time, therefore, the gunners were standing by their 6-pdr.
field pieces ready to render the fifteen-gun salute requisite to the stature of a
major general of the United States Army.

The army at Fort George had known of the coming of this new commander
– the "Big Bug from the south" they called him – for some time. During the
past summer, one officer remembered, his progress north "made a great noise
through the country, and rumour trumpeted in our ears sometime before official information could reach the same point." As the stipulated hour for the
"Big Bug's" appearance drew nigh, the senior officer at Fort George, Brigadier
General John Parker Boyd, and his staff, dressed in their best uniforms and occasionally checking their pocket watches, gathered in the bastion of the fort
offering the best view across the Niagara River. A barge was duly "sent over,
with flag flying, to receive the distinguished comer" and "was followed by
every eye to the landing on the other side, and glasses were put in requisition
to inspect the crowd collected there, and mark the movement when the great
man should settle on the handsome cushion, which had been arranged in the
stern-sheets for his especial accommodation."

Nobody paid much attention to a small boat coming the other way that
passed the barge in midstream and landed at the wharf below the bastion. Nor
did they pay much heed to the single passenger who disembarked and walked
up the road to the fort because, in his "sort of box coat" and large slouch hat,
he looked like one of the local civilians "who were daily importuning the commanding officer on a thousand and one accounts." When word came that this
caller wished to see Boyd, the general "felt no inclination to quit his lookout
point at that interesting moment," so dispatched an aide to deal with the interruption. This officer, "vexed at such an unseasonable call," curtly demanded
"without any prefatory civility" what the man wanted. The stranger "taking off
his slouched hat, and showing a fine bald head," and, "with an expression of
the eye that had much good-humour as rebuke in it, very gently answered:
'you will please to inform your General, that General Wilkinson wishes to
speak with him.'"

The aide was aghast – the box-coated individual before him was the "Big
Bug" himself. Boyd was hurriedly sent for and had just begun making his
apologies when some vigilant artillery officer, learning that the long-awaited
visitor had arrived, gave the order and the 6-pdrs. began to boom out making
such a noise as to leave the two generals "nothing better to do than to look at
each other in silence."[2]

The train of events that brought Major General James Wilkinson to Fort George on a September morning had begun fifteen months before in Washington. On 18 June 1812, President James Madison signed a declaration of war against Britain and plunged his nation into the most desperate venture of its brief history. This act was the outcome of nearly three decades of tension between America and Britain, tension that had been increased by fallout from the great struggle Britain had been waging since 1793 against revolutionary, and then imperial France. Forbidden by both these warring powers to trade with the other, the United States had become enmeshed in a conflict that did not concern it and its government's attempts to avoid entanglements by passing legislation restricting its citizens from engaging in commerce with the two belligerents had little effect on either Britain and France but did much harm to the American economy.

Of the two European powers, the United States regarded Britain as the source of most of her troubles, and there was little love lost between the two English-speaking nations. In the view of the United States, Britain had not lived up to the terms of the 1783 Treaty of Paris, which had established the independence of her former colonies, because British garrisons remained on American soil for more than a decade after it was signed. Americans also suspected that the British Crown was behind the resistance offered by the Indian nations on the northwest frontier which blocked white settlement and, when these troubles flared up again in 1811, many citizens of the republic became convinced that the Northwest would only be secure if adjacent British territory came under their flag. Worst of all, perhaps, were the depredations of

Reluctant warrior – President James Madison (1751-1836)

A humane man of principles, James Madison saw war as the only way to resolve his nation's problems with Great Britain. He soon discovered that declaring a war was much simpler than fighting one. (Portrait by Gilbert Stuart, courtesy of the Virginia Historical Society and the U.S. Naval Historical Center, NH-48047)

British warships which entered the territorial waters of the United States with impunity, stopped and searched her merchant vessels at will and forcibly impressed her sailors into the Royal Navy. In the decade preceding the declaration of war, Britain, preoccupied with what was a global conflict, paid little heed to increasing American frustration, her statesmen displaying, at one and the same time, a masterful combination of arrogance, stupidity and shortsightedness in their relations with the young republic. The result was that by the spring of 1812 President Madison and his cabinet had decided the only option left was a military one.

It was not a popular choice in the United States, a fact that was brought to the attention of the government by men such as Lieutenant Colonel Alexander Macomb, who remarked that war "seems to be the determination of the administration and they are astonished when I tell them that the people in New York & Jersey do not believe as they do."[3] But soldiers, like Lieutenant Colonel Daniel Bissell, while acknowledging the contrary mood of many Americans, thought they should "subscribe to the soldiers' creed, viz. not to ask why or wherefore they are to fight – it is the will of Government, and I think absolutely necessary."[4] The vote on the war measure reflected the uncertainty in the country – it passed Congress only by a very narrow margin but it did pass, and on 18 June 1812 America went to war.

The problem was how the United States was to fight this war. The American navy was a very professional service but had only sixteen warships, not nearly enough to challenge the more than five hundred vessels the Royal Navy had in commission. War against Britain would therefore have to be land war, and that meant war against the British colonies in North America. Senior government officials were sure that their conquest would be a stroll. It certainly looked easy on the map. The colonies which were the main object of attack, Lower Canada (modern Quebec) and Upper Canada (modern Ontario), had about one tenth the population of the United States. Because Upper Canada was nearly surrounded by American territory, it was particularly exposed, as was its lifeline to the lower province, the St. Lawrence River, and if this waterway was cut, Upper Canada must fall. Montreal, the commercial capital and largest city of the Canadas, lay open to attack from either the St. Lawrence or from Lake Champlain. As American strategy evolved in the spring of 1812, it called for a major offensive against Montreal, but political considerations required that a second thrust be made in the Northwest to preserve that area against possible attack from the native peoples. In its final version, the plan of campaign envisaged two major offensives, one from the Northwest across the Detroit River into Upper Canada and another from the Lake Champlain area against

Montreal, with subsidiary attacks against the Niagara Peninsula and Kingston.[5]

It was a good plan, but in its eagerness to draw the sword James Madison's government overlooked a basic factor – logistics. Logistics has been defined as the administrative and transport means by which armies are "supplied with subsistence and materiel in order to accomplish their strategic and tactical aims."[6] To conquer the Canadas, the United States would have to wage war in a semi-wilderness area where the climate curtailed the campaigning season and where armies would be unable to forage locally; they could not live off the land but would have to rely on supplies transported over terrible roads from coastal cities hundreds of miles away. The primitive communication network not only dramatically increased the difficulty and cost of providing timely logistical support to these armies; it also limited the amount of that support and thus restricted the size of armies and the operations they could undertake.[7]

The logistical problems were not insurmountable They might have been partly overcome by careful planning, preparation and co-ordination but all three were lacking in Washington in June 1812. Even had they been present, though, it was nearly impossible, given the distances involved, for the American government to co-ordinate offensives against British North America. Since it took as much as a week for a message from Washington to reach the northern frontier, the result was that the secretary of war, the official primarily concerned with the direction of military effort, was too often ignorant of the actual state of affairs on the frontier while the generals in the field were unsure of his intentions or what support they could expect from him. As events would show, it proved difficult to direct separate operations of poorly supplied armies based on plans drawn up using inaccurate maps in Washington. The conquest of the Canadas was not an impossible task, but it would have strained the resources of a military power far stronger than the United States in 1812.[8]

The fact was that the army of the republic was manifestly unprepared for war, particularly an offensive war. The tiny prewar force was dispersed across the nation guarding the coasts, garrisoning the western frontier, enforcing the unpopular embargo acts and occupying territories recently acquired in Louisiana. It had also been neglected since the governing Republican party had never favoured a professional military establishment; Madison's cabinet at first planned to carry out operations mainly with non-regular troops and, in the late spring of 1812, issued a call for thirty thousand volunteers. The incentives offered, particularly the 160 acres of land that each volunteer would receive at the end of his service, were regarded as too modest for a man, as one

American remarked, "to turn out and get himself killed."[9] In a remarkably modern sentiment (or perhaps things have not changed all that much) the same commentator added that he wished "every member of Congress had 160 acres of land stuffed up his XXXX instead of receiving $6.00 per day."[10]

When the volunteers did not come forward, the government belatedly turned to increasing the size of the regular army. On paper this force had an authorized strength in June 1812 of 35,603 men, organized in twenty-five regiments of infantry, four of artillery, two of cavalry and one of riflemen, but actual numbers were far fewer: the most reliable figure is that there were 13,000 regular troops under arms and more than two-thirds of them were raw recruits. Recruiting for what was in many areas an unpopular war suffered from competition from civilian employers and from state and volunteer militias which offered shorter terms of enlistment and less rigorous discipline. Moreover, everything needed to arm, equip, train and supply the newly-raised units was lacking, including the proper paperwork; when Congress asked the War Department in June 1812 to provide the number of men enlisted in the previous three months, the best estimate the department could make was about five thousand, based on the uniforms issued, because there was no more reliable source of information.[11]

Numbers and shortages were only part of the problem – from top to bottom the army lacked leadership. Secretary of War William Eustis was a pedant obsessed with bureaucratic minutiae and quickly proved incapable of handling the demands of his office. Moreover, of the seventeen generals appointed in 1812 to command the wartime army, thirteen were older veterans of the Revolutionary War while only seven of the total had experience in the prewar regular force, and their *average* age was fifty-five, much too old for active service. At the middle level, there were not enough experienced regular officers to command the newly raised units and regimental commanders had to be appointed (many as a result of political connections) directly from civilian life. The junior officers were no better. Hundreds of commissions were handed out, and for every man like Mordecai Myers, who had not only served six years in the militia but had attended a private military school at his own expense, there were dozens of captains and lieutenants totally ignorant of their new profession.[12]

In the summer and autumn of 1812 this army of untrained and poorly equipped recruits commanded by generals well past their best years and by a varied collection of political hacks and raw civilians moved north to the border to campaign against a very professional enemy.

That enemy was commanded by Lieutenant General Sir George Prevost. Born in New Jersey in 1767, the son of a Swiss officer in British service, Prevost had entered the army in 1779. He saw action in the West Indies in the 1790s and in 1804 was appointed governor of Dominica, beginning the civil side of his career which progressed in tandem with the military until it culminated in his appointment in 1811 as governor-general of British North America.[13]

Prevost was in a difficult position. Britain could not easily reinforce him as, by 1812, that nation had reached a crisis point in its twenty-year struggle against France. Napoleon's closure of European ports to British ships had adversely affected the nation's export trade; the pound sterling had declined 20 per cent in value over the previous two years and there was massive unemployment and unrest in the manufacturing industries. Nearly every nation in Europe was either controlled by or allied to France, and Britain was spending vast amounts of money (£14 million by 1811) to subsidize her few allies and maintain Wellington's army in the Iberian Peninsula. After two decades of warfare, the British army was an experienced force, but it was not strong in numbers, for Britain had never resorted to conscription for overseas service. About half the British regulars enlisted for universal or overseas service were with Wellington in 1812, but they numbered only about 40,000, and from the remainder had to be found garrisons for India, North America, the West Indies, Ireland, India and the Mediterranean, and replacements for casualties. The Royal Navy, with 102 line-of-battleships in commission, was the strongest navy in the world but those ships were spread along the coasts of Europe

**Defender of the Canadas —
Lieutenant General Sir George Prevost
(1767-1816)**
The commander-in-chief, British North America, Prevost faced the unenviable task of defending the Canadas against an opponent far superior in numbers. Throughout the war, his strategy was basically defensive and although he provided sound overall direction, he was often failed by his subordinate generals. (Courtesy, Château Ramezay Museum, Montreal)

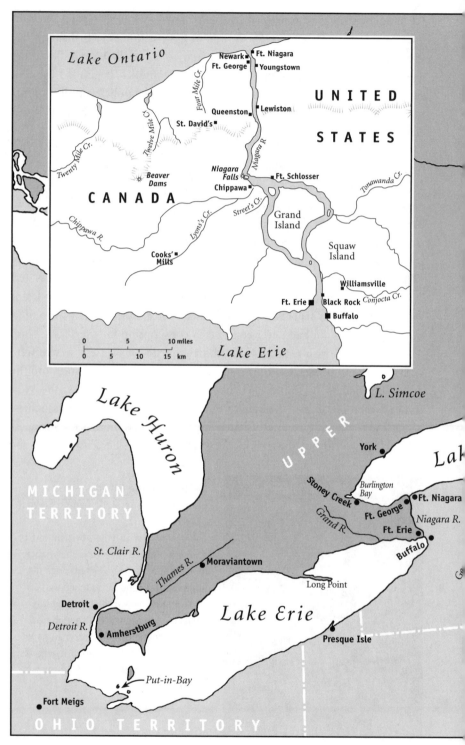

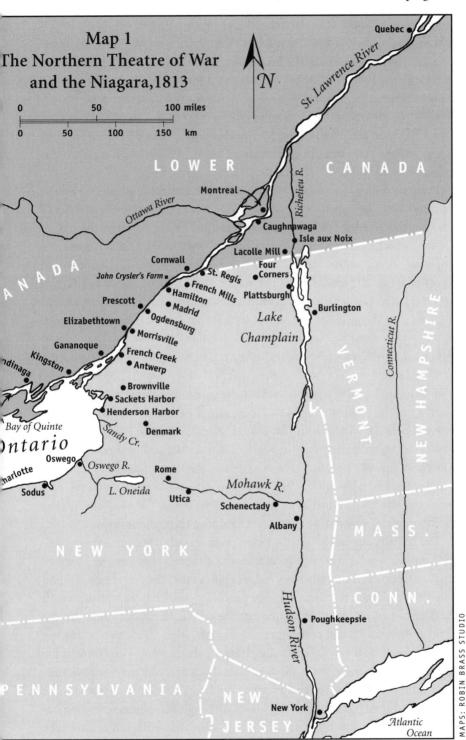

Map 1
The Northern Theatre of War
and the Niagara, 1813

N

| 0 | 50 | 100 miles |
| 0 | 50 | 100 | 150 | km |

Quebec

St. Lawrence River

LOWER   CANADA

Ottawa River

Montreal

Richelieu R.

Caughnawaga

Isle aux Noix

Lacolle Mill

Cornwall   Four
                Corners
John Crysler's Farm ▪   St. Regis

A N A D A   French Mills   Plattsburgh

Hamilton

Prescott   Madrid

Elizabethtown   Ogdensburg   Burlington

Gananoque   Morrisville   Lake

ndinaga   French Creek   Champlain

Kingston   Antwerp

                Brownville   VERMONT

                Sackets Harbor   NEW HAMPSHIRE

                Henderson Harbor

Bay of Quinte   Sandy Cr.   Connecticut R.

Ontario   Denmark

harlotte   Oswego

Oswego   Oswego R.   Rome

Sodus   L. Oneida   Mohawk R.

                Utica   Schenectady

                                Albany   MASS.

NEW   YORK

                                                CONN.

Hudson River

                                Poughkeepsie

PENNSYLVANIA   NEW

                                New York   Atlantic
JERSEY   Ocean

MAPS: ROBIN BRASS STUDIO

15

enforcing a blockade that had been in place without pause for nine years. It was also facing an increasing threat from Napoleon, who, after years of intensive construction, had built the French fleet up to a strength of eighty battleships and had also cut off the Royal Navy's supplies of timber from the Baltic nations, restricting construction of both warships and commercial vessels. The one positive aspect of this situation for Britain was that, six days after James Madison signed the American declaration of war, Napoleon invaded Russia with 600,000 men, beginning the campaign that would ultimately lead to his downfall.[14]

Prevost's only option was to adopt a defensive strategy and hang on as best he could until the situation improved. As he saw it, the key to the defence of the Canadas was the "only permanent Fortress" in the country, the city of Quebec, and he believed that to that object "every other Military operation ought to become subservient."[15] Because an American invading force would have to approach Quebec by land, he stationed the bulk of his forces south of Montreal, since that city would have to be taken first. Here he was prepared to fight a major defensive action, and if he lost that, "the retreat of the Troops upon Quebec must be the primary consideration." Prevost would fight and fight hard, to retain Montreal and Quebec, but he was quite ready, if necessary, to abandon everything to the west, particularly exposed Upper Canada. Thanks to American newspapers, which also gave him detailed, accurate information on U.S. troop strengths and movements, he was well informed of the internal political situation in the United States, and knew the war was unpopular in many parts of the republic. He therefore resolved not to attack American territory lest such an action create "the least tendency to unite the people of America" because, when "disunion" prevails "among them, their attempts on the British American provinces will be feeble."[16] Prevost's basic posture was defensive and it would remain so almost throughout the war.

The British commander did, however, possess assets. He commanded 8,500 well-trained regular troops in June 1812, and although they were scattered in small garrisons along hundreds of miles of border they formed the cadre upon which local military resources could be based. He enjoyed better relations with the Indian nations, particularly the nations of the Northwest, than did the United States and could count on their support, which, although it was not strong enough to seriously affect the military balance, would supplement the British war effort and distract the American. The Royal Navy gave secure communications with Britain, and Prevost could expect reinforcements in due course or at least replacements for losses. Although his internal communications along the St. Lawrence and the Great Lakes were vulnerable, since they

Capital of the Canadas – Quebec during the War of 1812
Retaining Quebec, the capital of British North America and the only permanent
fortress in the Canadas, was the key to British strategy. In this 1814 watercolour by
H.T. Davies, the anchorage below the city is crowded with naval and merchant
shipping. (National Archives of Canada, C-138099)

ran near the border, they were also mostly water-borne and would allow him
to shift forces rapidly. To do so, he had the Provincial Marine, a small but viable naval service on Lakes Ontario and Erie whose presence also denied the
use of those waters to the United States. His final, but not least, advantage was
that he did not intend to mount major offensive operations – his logistical
problems were difficult but not nearly as difficult as those of the United
States.[17]

Prevost also had disadvantages. He had a much smaller population to draw
on, and there were problems with segments of this population. Many of the
people of Upper Canada were recent immigrants from the United States
whose loyalty in time of war could only be regarded as dubious, and the support of the *Canadiens*, the French-speaking inhabitants of Lower Canada, was
also uncertain. Prevost could not expect, nor could he ask for, major reinforcements from Britain while the great conflict in Europe raged but would have to
depend on his own resources. Despite his problems, the British commander-
in-chief worked hard in the months preceding the war to place Upper and
Lower Canada in the best possible state of defence.

Given the logistical problems inherent in the United States waging war on
its northern border, the quality and number of the forces at its disposal
and the quality of its enemy, it was almost predictable that it would fail in 1812.

Brigadier General William Hull made a halfhearted invasion of western Upper Canada in July but, becoming concerned about his lengthy supply lines, withdrew to Detroit. He then surrendered his entire army to the aggressive British Major General Isaac Brock, who used the Provincial Marine to transfer his forces and attack Detroit with a much smaller force. This ended one of the two planned major thrusts; the other, directed against Montreal, foundered when the senior American general on the northern frontier, Major General Henry Dearborn, tried to carry it out with untrained troops and state militia who refused to cross the border. A timid attempt to move into Canadian territory was brought to a halt in a confusing skirmish at Lacolle Mill in November 1812 while the planned secondary attacks against Kingston and Niagara were never mounted because the generals responsible simply did not possess the resources to accomplish them. A second, more serious, attempt to invade the Niagara in October was repulsed at the battle of Queenston Heights, and cost the United States much of another army, although the British and Canadians lost the aggressive Brock. For America, the first six months of hostilities were a succession of disasters mitigated only by the superb performance of her navy in a series of single-ship engagements.

One positive outcome of these misfortunes, however, was the government's realization of the need to provide naval forces on the lakes. In September 1812 Commodore Isaac Chauncey, USN, was sent north with instructions to establish a base at Sackets Harbor on Lake Ontario and construct a squadron to control that lake and a subsidiary squadron on Lake Erie. Another positive outcome was that Major General William H. Harrison, a former governor of Kentucky and an experienced campaigner in the Northwest, assumed command in the latter area and began to prepare for an offensive to retake Detroit. The third positive outcome was the replacement of the incompetent Secretary of War William Eustis.

Congressional pressure forced Eustis to resign on 3 December 1812 and his duties were temporarily assumed by Secretary of State James Monroe. Finding a permanent replacement for Eustis proved more difficult, since many of the leading candidates were either unacceptable to Madison or were not interested in a post that came with small chance of gaining distinction and much of attracting disgrace – particularly Monroe, who had presidential ambitions. Almost by default, therefore, Madison was forced to consider John Armstrong of New York, a man whom he disliked but whose appointment would bring certain political advantages. The president tendered the post to Armstrong in mid-January 1813 and the offer was immediately accepted.[18]

Fifty-four years old when he took over the War Department, John Arm-

The politician who wanted to be a general – Secretary of War John Armstrong (1758-1843)
Armstrong drew up the plans for the 1813 offensive against the Canadas. Although he was capable of selecting the correct objective, he proved incapable of maintaining the chosen aim. An armchair general who fancied himself a strategist, Armstrong went north in August 1813 to coordinate the attack on Montreal. (Portrait by J.W. Jarvis, courtesy of the National Portrait Gallery, NPG 72.12)

strong had had a varied career. A native of Pennsylvania, he was studying at Princeton when the Revolution broke out and was a volunteer in the unsuccessful attempt to capture Quebec in 1775-1776 before serving in a variety of staff positions. By the end of the war in 1783, Armstrong was a major in the main camp of the Continental army at Newburgh, New York, and it was here he gained notoriety by writing a number of unsigned "addresses" that urged the officers of the army, disgruntled because Congress had made no financial provision for them, to take matters into their own hands. The unrest reached such a level that Washington was forced to personally appeal to his officers not "to open the flood gates of civil discord."[19] Following his return to civilian life, Armstrong dabbled briefly in Pennsylvania politics until marriage into the powerful Livingston clan of New York caused him to shift his focus to that state. A committed Republican, he was elected to Congress from New York in 1802 and, in 1804, appointed minister to France. Armstrong held the latter position for five years, which were marked by some controversy, but, on his return to the United States in 1809, devoted his energies to his 728-acre estate, "La Bergerie," at Red Hook on the Hudson River.[20]

When war broke out, Armstrong's connections ensured his appointment as a brigadier general in the regular army and command of the defences of New York City. Although his military background was not all that extensive, Madison's administration regularly consulted him on questions of strategy, and his reputation as an expert in the field was enhanced in July 1812 when he published a work entitled *Hints to Young Generals by an Old Soldier*. This seventy-one-page booklet, which Armstrong later confessed he had written in only four days, was largely cribbed from the writing of the Swiss theorist Antoine-Henri Jomini, and followed that author's emphasis on concentration of force as the primary principle of strategy.[21] A man of "known talents," who possessed "a degree of military information which might be useful," Armstrong was a logical candidate as secretary of war, but his was an appointment Madison made only with reluctance, for this ambitious man had a reputation for being arrogant and difficult and was an outspoken critic of the Virginians who dominated the cabinet. Balanced against this, however, was the fact that Armstrong's appointment would bring political advantages as it would increase support for the war in New York state, which was facing a crucial gubernatorial election in April 1813.[22]

Armstrong assumed his new office on 4 February 1813. Displaying impressive energy, he worked hard to bring order into the disarray left by Eustis. He reorganized the military staff and ordered publication of much-needed "Rules and Regulations" for the army that set out the duties and responsibilities of officers and departments. He increased the number of general officers and secured the promotion of deserving younger men who had made their mark during the campaigns of the previous year. But he could do nothing about the senior generals already in service because he had no power to remove them – "I have to execute other men's plans and fight with other men's weapons," he complained.[23]

The new secretary soon discovered he had three major problems: an inefficient logistical apparatus; a shortage of trained regular troops; and, most worrisome, a serious shortage of funds. No less than three separate organizations existed to supply the army in the field. The purchasing department procured and distributed arms, clothing and equipment; the quartermaster's department purchased horses, wagons and forage; the commissary of subsistence and civilian contractors supplied food. In 1812 this clumsy arrangement had broken down completely and although Armstrong laboured mightily to make it work, he was never able to ensure that American troops in the field would be adequately armed, clothed and fed. Equally serious was the problem of troop strengths – the army had entered the war with an authorized paper strength of 35,000, but this figure had never been reached, and in February 1813 the army listed only 18,495 men on its rolls. Monroe had earlier obtained congressional authorization to increase the size of the regular force to 57,351, but this increase, which consisted of twenty infantry regiments enlisted for one year only, would not be ready until early summer and even then recruiting lagged to such an extent that by the end of 1813 the army would possess only 34,325 men.[24]

Problems of supply and recruiting, however, paled beside the shortage of money. The governing Republican party had never favoured the idea of a national bank or central financial institution that would underwrite government activities, and rather than pay for the war through increased taxation, Madison's government relied on private loans. It had borrowed more than $5 million in 1812, but so unattractive were the rates of interest offered that when Secretary of the Treasury Albert Gallatin tried in early 1813 to obtain further loans totalling $16 million, he had such a lack of success that he warned Madison the United States "had hardly enough money to last until the end of the month" and that all military operations might have to be cancelled.[25] Fortunately for the government, three wealthy financiers bailed it out and the $16 million was raised, and of this the War Department was allotted $13,320,000, but Armstrong was told that his expenditures were not to exceed $1,480,000 per month. When Major General Dearborn, the senior commander on the northern frontier, complained about insufficient funds, the secretary told him that "economy must be your alpha & omega as well as mine."[26]

When Armstrong turned to drawing up plans for an 1813 offensive against Canada, shortage of supplies, men and money forced him to cut his coat according to his cloth. It was the secretary's belief, most likely based on a careful reading of his mentor, Jomini, that military resources must be applied to "a single stroke" that would be "creditable to our arms" and he had no doubt where that stroke should fall. More than a year previously, Armstrong had advised Eustis that in planning offensive strategy against the Canadas, British possessions "separated from the rest of the empire by an ocean, and having to this but one outlet," the St. Lawrence River, this river "forms your true object or point of attack."[27] When he presented his campaign plan to the cabinet on 8 February, Armstrong informed them that the United States would not possess the strength at the outset to mount an attack on Montreal in 1813 and had to "choose between a course of entire inaction, because [we are] incompetent to the main attack, or one secondary, but still an important object."[28] He urged the secondary objective, "the reduction of Upper Canada," and called for initial attacks against the line of the St. Lawrence near Kingston to sever that province from Montreal, followed by subsidiary attacks on the provincial capital of Upper Canada at York (modern Toronto) and in the Niagara area. The cabinet registered its approval on 10 February and that day Armstrong ordered Dearborn to begin massing troops at Sackets Harbor, the major naval base on Lake Ontario, for an attack on Kingston in conjunction with Chauncey's naval squadron as soon as Lake Ontario was free of ice.[29]

It was a sound and logical plan, but having issued the orders, Armstrong immediately began to fiddle with them. On 15 February he suggested to Dearborn he divert part of his force to Ogdensburg, New York, to confuse the enemy and nine days later proposed that Dearborn make an overland dash by sleigh against Kingston to compel the British to reinforce it and weaken the defences of Montreal. But these were only "hints" he wrote Dearborn on 4 March, mere suggestions for Dearborn's "consideration," as that officer must "choose between alternatives."[30] It is easy to see why Dearborn began to believe the secretary was not firmly committed to the campaign plan. In late February, when Dearborn learned that Prevost had arrived at Kingston, he interpreted this to mean that a large British army was massing there to attack Sackets Harbor. The American general could not have been reassured when, having informed Armstrong of his belief, the secretary told him it might not be a bad thing as the bulk of the British forces were now drawn westward to a country where their subsistence would be difficult.[31]

By March Dearborn had convinced himself that the British garrison at Kingston was 6,000 men – a strength that could "effectually oppose the movements contemplated on our part."[32] Seizing on a fatal phrase in a letter written by the secretary on 4 March that allowed him to "choose between alternatives," Dearborn, with Chauncey's agreement, decided to change the objective and informed the secretary that York should be attacked in preference to Kingston since its capture "will give us the complete command of the lake."[33] His army would then be employed against the British forts in the Niagara area and only after taking them would it move against Kingston. Armstrong reluctantly agreed but was careful to put the responsibility on Dearborn by noting that if Prevost had "assembled at Kingston a force of six or eight thousand men, as stated by you", it was too strong to be assailed by the means at Dearborn's disposal. If this was true, the secretary conceded, then the "alteration in the plan of campaign so as to make Kingston the last object instead of making it the first, would appear to be necessary, or at least proper."[34]

Dearborn's offensive got off to an auspicious start on 27 April when his army took York in a successful amphibious landing, although it cost him Brigadier General Zebulon M. Pike, one of his best generals. His force remained there a few days before sailing to Fort Niagara to join the troops Armstrong had concentrated at that place. On 27 May, under cover of the guns of Chauncey's squadron, Dearborn's troops made a successful amphibious landing on the British side of the Niagara River and captured Fort George, forcing the British commander, Brigadier General John Vincent, to withdraw to Burlington Bay at the head of Lake Ontario (modern Hamilton, Ontario). Within a few days, the entire Canadian bank of the Niagara River, including

Fort Erie, was in American hands, and these victories ensured the re-election of New York Governor Daniel D. Tompkins, a supporter of the administration.

But this was the high point, and thereafter things began to go off the rails. An attempt by two brigades to push toward Vincent's position was turned back in a hard-fought night action at Stoney Creek on 6 June. A few weeks later, another American force was surrounded by a smaller British force composed largely of native warriors and persuaded to surrender at the battle of Beaver Dams. Dearborn's response was to withdraw his army to the immediate vicinity of Fort George and not attempt any further offensive movement. Armstrong was not happy about these setbacks and acidly commented that "some strange fatality seems to attend our efforts," as "battles are not gained when an inferior and broken army is not destroyed."[35]

Disappointments in the Niagara were to some extent offset by success to the west. Armstrong was no supporter of Major General Harrison, whom he regarded as unaggressive: by June 1813, after ten months in the field, Harrison had neither retaken Detroit nor attacked the British base at Amherstburg but had instead retreated to a defended position at Fort Meigs, near the Maumee rapids in Ohio. Harrison's luck began to change when he withstood an attack on Fort Meigs on 28 July by British Major General Henry Procter's forces. Even more promising was the fact that the American capture of Fort Erie had released vessels blockaded in the Niagara River to join the main USN squadron on Lake Erie at Presque Isle, Pennsylvania. This, coupled with an intensive construction programme by the naval commander there, Master Commandant Oliver Hazard Perry, which his British counterpart, Commander Robert H. Barclay, could not match, threatened to challenge British control of that body of water.

The naval situation on Lake Ontario, where the opposing commanders, Commodores Sir James Yeo, RN, and Isaac Chauncey, USN, were also engaged in a competition to get hulls into the water, was somewhat different. In May and June Yeo was strong enough to seriously contest the control of that lake, which convinced Armstrong that nothing further could be accomplished either in the Niagara or against Kingston until Chauncey dominated Lake Ontario. This being the case, he turned to other matters, but he managed to persuade Madison that the aging and sickly Henry Dearborn would have to be replaced, and on 6 July that officer was informed it was the president's orders that he retire from his command until his "health be re-established."[36] Temporary command in the Niagara went to the next senior officer, Brigadier General John Boyd, whom Armstrong instructed to "pay the utmost attention to the instruction and disciplining of the troops and engage in no affair with the enemy that can be avoided."[37] For the time being, the campaign against the Canadas was stalled.

In the early summer of 1813, Lieutenant General Sir George Prevost had reason to be satisfied with his situation. The American offensive of April and May had petered out in the Niagara while, in the west, Procter was deep in enemy territory. Prevost was aware that the czar of Russia had offered to negotiate a peace settlement of the war and that American representatives had travelled to St. Petersburg in May to discuss this proposal. He was also aware from his reading of American newspapers of the dissatisfaction on the part of many Americans about the way the war was being conducted by Madison's government. "That I might not diminish the internal causes," Prevost reported to his superior, Lord Bathurst, the Secretary for War and the Colonies, which would "compel the American government to seek for peace before the ensuing winter," he had "carefully avoided any offensive movement upon the territory of the United States which was not considered a just and necessary retaliation," thereby hoping "to increase the unpopularity of the war and to add to the depression of their public credit."[38]

While Prevost had been doing his best to defend the Canadas with limited resources, the course of the great war against France had taken a positive turn. Napoleon's invasion of Russia had ended with the loss of most of his army, Prussia had allied herself with Russia and Britain, and Austria and Sweden were about to join the coalition which would ultimately put an end to the French dictator's ramshackle empire. In Spain, Wellington's victory at Vittoria in June caused rejoicing throughout Europe and sent the French armies in that country scrambling for their border. Prevost had deliberately refrained from asking for major reinforcements because he knew that the main theatre was Spain and this forbearance was noted and approved by his superiors, who were only able to promise him a few new units before the winter and more in the spring of 1814. Until the war in Europe was brought to a successful conclusion, British North America would have to look to its own devices.

Prevost would get few troops but he would get new generals. This was good news because he had been experiencing difficulties with his senior commanders. Brock, his best subordinate, had been killed at Queenston Heights in October 1812, and Brock's successor, Major General Roger Sheaffe, had been a disappointment. In June Prevost replaced him with Major General Francis de Rottenburg, a fifty-six-year-old veteran who had served in the French and Polish armies before joining the British service in 1795. De Rottenburg was experienced but somewhat past his prime, and Prevost was pleased when he learned that two younger officers, Lieutenant General Gordon Drummond and Major General Phineas Riall, were on their way to North America.[39]

The British commander did, however, receive naval reinforcements. In April, Commodore Sir James Lucas Yeo had arrived at Kingston from Britain with a detachment of Royal Navy officers and men to take over the Provincial Marine. In late May, while Chauncey was preoccupied with supporting Dearborn's offensive in the Niagara peninsula, Yeo's squadron had transported Prevost and a small force to make a pre-emptive attack on the American naval base at Sackets Harbor. The assault was a very near thing which, had it succeeded, would have tipped the naval balance on the Great Lakes irretrievably in favour of Britain because the latest and largest American warship, the *General Pike*, was on the stocks when the attackers landed. A combination of bad weather, bad luck, stiff resistance and Prevost's hesitation at the critical moment defeated this venture and the expedition withdrew, having accomplished little.

This had been the British commander's only major setback. Otherwise he had reason to be proud of the efforts of his soldiers and sailors during the first year of the war, as, with the exception of a few thousand square yards in and around Fort George, Canadian soil was free from American troops.

CHAPTER 2

"How uncomfortably like a civil war it seemed"

THE LONG SUMMER OF 1813

To Anacreon in Heaven, where he sat in full glee,
A few sons of Harmony sent a petition,
That He their Inspirer and Patron would be:
When this answer arrived from the Jolly Old Grecian
"Voice, Fiddle, and Flute, no longer be mute,
I'll lend you my Name and inspire you to boot,
And, besides, I'll instruct you like me to entwine
The Myrtle of Venus with Bacchus's Vine."

Ye sons of Anacreon, then, join Hand in Hand;
Preserve Unanimity, Friendship, and Love!
'Tis your's to support what's so happily plann'd;
You've the Sanction of Gods, and the Fiat of Jove.
While thus we agree, Our Toast let it be
May our club flourish happy, united and free!
And long may the Sons of Anacreon intwine
The myrtle of Venus with Bacchus's Vine.[1]

James Wilkinson, the general who arrived without ceremony at Fort George in September 1813, was one of the most notorious men in American public life. The son of a wealthy Maryland family, Wilkinson was an eighteen-year-old medical student when the Revolution broke out in 1775 and he joined the insurgent forces besieging Boston as a captain. He participated in the ill-fated Quebec expedition of 1775-1776, fought at the battles of Trenton, Princeton and Saratoga the following year and enjoyed meteoric promotion – by November 1777 he was a brigadier general. Appointed secretary of the board of war, he was removed after he joined the "Conway cabal" of officers trying to depose Washington. He was then made clothier-general of the army but had to vacate this position after audits revealed serious irregularities in his financial records.[2]

Wilkinson's blemished career was saved by his fortunate marriage into the powerful and wealthy Biddle family of Philadelphia. This connection served him well between 1784 and 1791, when he spent a term in the Pennsylvania legislature, but devoted most of his considerable energies to land speculation and trading ventures in Kentucky and Louisiana, the latter at that time a Spanish territory. Wilkinson's relations with the Spanish were always profitable – for a number of years he received an annual pension of $2,000 from Spain for supporting that country's interests in the western territories. This lucrative but treasonable arrangement was typical of James Wilkinson for as one historian has written about the man, "the only word that adequately describes his character is 'slippery'" because Wilkinson preferred "the oblique direction, the devious method, in pursuing his objective," and if caught in the trammels of his actions, he would seek "to the utmost of his not inconsiderable ability to shift responsibility for any misfortunes to other shoulders."[3]

In 1791 Wilkinson's financial ventures collapsed but his connections secured him a commission as a lieutenant colonel in the regular army. Six months later he was promoted brigadier general and became the senior officer on the death of his only superior in 1796, and remained as such for the next twelve years. Still the recipient of a Spanish pension Wilkinson was transferred to the southern frontier, where he engaged in schemes that aroused government suspicion. In 1803 he assumed command of the newly acquired Louisiana Territory and became involved in Aaron Burr's plot to create a separate nation west of the Mississippi River. However, when this scheme was exposed, Wilkinson served as the chief witness against Burr in the trial that followed and only narrowly avoided indictment himself. His relationship with Burr led to him becoming the subject of a military court of inquiry but no charges resulted. Strangely, President Thomas Jefferson, who had his own suspicions about Wilkinson, ordered him back to Louisiana, where he again busied himself in intrigues to enhance his personal wealth, intrigues that led to a Congressional inquiry in 1810. Once again, Wilkinson emerged unscathed.[4]

The lengthy tenure of Wilkinson as its senior officer had a disastrous effect on the peacetime army. Many officers disliked and distrusted Wilkinson but there was little they could do as their promotion and careers depended on retaining his favour. In 1808, an expansion of the army brought a new general, Wade Hampton, into service, and Hampton and Wilkinson quickly became enemies, causing the officer corps to divide into two camps, a larger group supporting (but not liking) Wilkinson and a smaller one supporting Hamp-

Notorious figure – Major General James Wilkinson (1757-1826)
One of the most disreputable men in American public life, Wilkinson was a born intriguer and the paid spy of a foreign government who saw his appointment as the senior general on the northern frontier as a chance to redeem a badly tarnished reputation. (Portrait by unknown artist, courtesy of the National Portrait Gallery, NPG 75.15)

ton. By 1810 Hampton was complaining to Secretary of War Eustis that the "intrigue" had "grown to so great a height, in the army and out of it," that he needed assurances of the government's confidence.[5]

Hampton got those assurances in 1811 when President Madison ordered Wilkinson to appear before a court martial on charges of "treason, conspiracy with Colonel Burr, corruption with the Spanish governor of Louisiana" and "disobedience of orders, neglect of duty, etc."[6] Among the specifications under the charge of "neglect of duty" was Wilkinson's responsibility for the death by disease of nearly a thousand soldiers (about one-fifth of the enlisted strength of the army) at the notorious Terre-aux-Boeufs camp in Louisiana during the winter of 1809-1810. The court discovered many "queer transactions of a political and mercantile character," but no act of treason or conspiracy was proven and Wilkinson was restored to command in Louisiana.[7]

James Wilkinson was one of the problems John Armstrong inherited when he took over the War Department. Armstrong knew him well (they had served together during the Revolutionary War) and also knew Wilkinson was not popular in the south; indeed, the two senators from Louisiana had recently requested he be transferred away from their area. Armstrong's solution to the problem was to send Wilkinson north to serve under Dearborn. On 10 March, he ordered him to "proceed with the least possible delay" to Dearborn's headquarters and followed this two days later with a conciliatory note asking Wilkinson why he should "remain in your land of *cypress*, when *patriotism*, and *ambition*, equally invite, to one where grows the *laurel?*" Urging him to "come to the north, and come quickly," the secretary sweetened the proposition with an offer of immediate promotion to major general.[8]

Unfortunately, due to faulty mails and Wilkinson's absence from his head-quarters, he did not read these communications until 19 May. They must have given him pause as, following the death of his wife in 1807, he had married a much younger woman and was devoted to her. Balanced against this was the fact that he was aware of the feeling against him in Louisiana and there was also the question of his vanity for this might be the fifty-six-year-old Wilkinson's last chance to win fame and restore a badly stained reputation. He decided to go and wrote Armstrong on 23 May, using the orotund style that would become familiar, to accept the promotion, however "injurious it may prove, to my domestic concerns," as "it may furnish me, a more favourable opportunity, than I can find elsewhere, to testify to the world, my readiness to offer my best faculties, and to lay down my life for the honour and independence of our country."[9]

On 10 June, accompanied by his pregnant wife, Wilkinson left New Orleans and made a leisurely journey north. By 6 July he was at Milledgeville, Georgia, and took the time to write to Major General Morgan Lewis, a personal friend then commanding at Sackets Harbor. Wilkinson had just learned of the death of Brigadier General Pike during the attack on York, and although he acknowledged that death "on the field of battle in a good cause, such as ours is," was certainly a fine ending, he cautioned Lewis to remember that a "general officer does not expose his person, but in the last resort" as "to mingle in the conflict, is to abandon the power of direction."[10]

Wilkinson reached Washington on 31 July 1813. Five days later, Armstrong showed him the plan of campaign which had recently been approved by the cabinet. As Armstrong saw it, it was essential to join the forces now at Fort

"Old Hickory" – Major General Wade Hampton (1751 or 1752-1835)
Wade Hampton from South Carolina (shown here as a colonel of light dragoons in 1809) possessed a boundless sense of his own self-importance. He and Wilkinson hated each other but Hampton's appointment as the commander in the Lake Champlain area meant the two would have to cooperate. A stern disciplinarian, Hampton's penchant for caning miscreant soldiers earned him the nickname of "Old Hickory." (Miniature by Memin, courtesy National Portrait Gallery, NPG 74/38, Dexter 23)

George and Sackets Harbor and, once concentrated, the choice was between renewing the offensive in the Niagara or attacking Kingston. Armstrong thought the first option would bear only limited results and in any case might well be accomplished by Harrison moving east from the Michigan Territory. His preference was Kingston but in choosing this objective he suggested that, in conjunction, an attack also be made on Montreal from the Lake Champlain area – if the British reinforced Kingston, they would weaken Montreal and vice versa. Armstrong had mentioned Montreal before in his strategical assessments but it had always been a distant goal, to be accomplished after other objectives had been taken; now, for the first time, he moved it up the priority list. The proposal involved some risk but the secretary knew that Madison's administration, whose conduct of the war was not popular, "needed a spectacular achievement to redeem itself."[11] All operations, however, were contingent on Chauncey gaining naval superiority on Lake Ontario and, although Armstrong was confident this would shortly come to pass, he had advised the cabinet that the commanding general should be left the choice, to be determined by circumstances, "between the two plans suggested."[12] That commanding general was now James Wilkinson.

Wilkinson did not like the plan. He agreed that if naval superiority was gained on Lake Ontario, a concentration at Sackets Harbor for an attack on Kingston was the best alternative, but if the combined force was not powerful enough to carry that place, he thought it better to concentrate all available forces in the Niagara, "cut up the British in that quarter; destroy the Indian establishments and (should General Harrison fail in his object) march a detachment and capture Malden [Amherstburg, Ontario]." These objectives accomplished, the army could "descend like lightning with our whole force on Kingston, and having reduced that place and captured both garrison and shipping, go down the St. Lawrence." For his part, Wilkinson had no objections against a "bold feint or provisional attack on Montreal" from Lake Champlain because it would "call Sir George Prevost to that place" and "he may carry his best troops with him from Kingston." "These operations," he concluded, "spring from my desire to hazard as little as possible in the outset and to secure infallibly whatever may be attempted, with the intention to increase our own confidence, to diminish that of the enemy and *to popularize the war*." Wilkinson was also aware of the prevailing political breezes.[13]

In response, Armstrong emphasized that the goal must be Kingston, for any offensive west of there only "wounds the tail of the lion, and, of course, is not calculated to hasten the termination of the war." Kingston was "the great depot of his [the enemy's] resources," the secretary noted, "and so long as he retains this, and keeps open his communication with the sea, he will not want the means of multiplying his naval and other defences, and of reinforcing or re-newing the war in the west." Kingston had to be taken "on grounds of policy, as of military principle" because it presented "the first, and great object of the campaign." There were two ways of going about it, Armstrong reasoned, "by direct or indirect attack: by breaking down the enemy's battalions, and forcing his works; or by seizing and obstructing the line of his communication, and thus drying up the sources by which he is nourished and maintained." If Wil-kinson could not mount a direct attack on Kingston, Armstrong advised that, if he were in command, he would collect his "force at the head of St. Lawrence, make every demonstration of attacking Kingston, proceed rapidly down the river, seize the northern bank at the village of Hamilton [modern Wadding-ton, New York], leave a corps to fortify and hold it," and then move on Mon-treal, joining the army coming from Lake Champlain "and take a position, which shall enable you to secure what you gain." Kingston must be the "pri-mary object" but the secretary left it to Wilkinson to "choose (as circum-stances may warrant) between a direct and indirect attack on that post."[14]

Any operation that included the division stationed on Lake Champlain was not welcome news to Wilkinson because that formation was commanded by his most implacable enemy – Major General Wade Hampton. Either sixty-one or sixty-two (sources vary) in 1813, Hampton was a native of South Carolina. By the time of the Revolutionary War, he was a successful farmer and planter. In 1780 Hampton declared himself a loyal subject of the Crown but the follow-ing year joined the partisan forces of General Thomas Sumter and served with great distinction. Through shrewd investment and speculation, using funds fuelled by his choice of cotton as a staple crop, Hampton became one of the largest landowners in South Carolina and Mississippi and also one of the larg-est slave-owners. He served two terms in Congress, but having military aspira-tions, got a commission as a colonel in the army in 1808 and the following year was promoted brigadier general. A vain and arrogant man, possessed of a boundless sense of his self-importance, Hampton had been angered by Wilkinson's acquittal in 1811 and withdrew to his estates to sulk but in Novem-ber 1812 had a change of heart and wrote Madison asking for an appointment in order "to avoid the imputation of being thought unworthy of commanding of my own corps, and of sharing their dangers and honors."[15] He was assigned to the defences of Norfolk, Virginia, and spent the winter there, but in the late spring of 1813 requested a transfer to serve with Dearborn on Lake Ontario.[16]

Armstrong, having already ordered Wilkinson to join Dearborn, knew he could not place these inveterate enemies in close proximity. He therefore offered Hampton the command of the division on Lake Champlain and Hampton accepted, but with certain important conditions. Wade Hampton was aware (because it was common knowledge) that Wilkinson was going north and he negotiated the terms of his employment with a view to being as independent of Dearborn (and thus Wilkinson) as possible. His was to be a "separate and distinct command," even though it operated in Military District No. 9, which Dearborn commanded. Moreover, Hampton stipulated that his orders were to come directly from Armstrong but graciously allowed that if the two forces joined, seniority would prevail, and in that case only, he would accept orders directly from his superior officer. Armstrong agreed to these conditions, and on 3 July Hampton assumed command of the division on Lake Champlain with his headquarters at Burlington, Vermont.[17]

Dearborn's retirement upset this carefully balanced command apple cart as Wilkinson was now Hampton's superior officer. The two most bitter enemies in the army now held the two most important commands in that service and, what was worse, if the campaign against the Canadas was to go forward, these two generals would have to co-operate closely. As there was little chance of that, Armstrong decided he too would go north to ensure the rivals worked together.

Wilkinson was quick to grasp the implications of the situation. Before he left Washington, he had asked for assurances that no "improper communications" would be permitted between his subordinates and the secretary.[18] Armstrong replied that Hampton's instructions "go only to assemble and organize his division at Burlington" and it was "intended that he shall operate contemporarily with you, and under your orders, in prosecution of the plan of campaign, which has been given to you."[19] As for Wilkinson's subordinates communicating directly with Washington, the secretary added, he would forbid "all improper communications, and particularly such as may bear any color of insubordination."

Thus reassured, Wilkinson departed for Sackets Harbor on 11 August. Five days later, he wrote a curt letter to Hampton which informed him that since President Madison had "thought proper to confer on me the chief command" of Military District No. 9, he requested complete strength returns of Hampton's division and, since this information was "essential to our effectual co-operation in the common cause of our country, I beg to receive it as promptly as may be … with any additional information you may deem essential to the public service."[20] In a separate message dated the same day, Wilkinson suggested that Hampton start shifting his units from Burlington across Lake Champlain to Plattsburgh, New York, "as soon as you can … without hazarding the public interest."[21]

These communications infuriated Hampton. Wilkinson was within his rights to ask for information regarding his nominal subordinate's strength and to make suggestions on the conduct of operations but, given the tension between the two and the complicated nature of the command structure, it would have been better if he had not attempted to exert his authority so soon. Not surprisingly, Hampton made no reply, causing Wilkinson to observe to Armstrong that if Hampton intended "to take the stud ... we can do without him, and he should be sent home."[22] After two weeks went by with no response from Hampton, Wilkinson sent copies of his letters to Armstrong with the comment "that if I am authorized to Command, he is bound to obey, and if he will not respect the obligation, he should be turned out of the Service."[23]

As it happened, Wade Hampton decided to turn himself out of the service. He complained to Armstrong on 23 August that, if Wilkinson's letters had been authorized by the government then the nature of his appointment had changed and his only option was to request from the president his "immediate discharge from the army."[24] Armstrong, attempting to soothe ruffled feelings, informed Hampton that the planned operation created a situation where seniority must apply and that although he enjoyed a "separate and distinct" command, it was not an independent command.[25] The secretary went on to reassure the touchy South Carolinian that he was coming north to "be with you throughout this campaign, & pledge to you my honor as a soldier, that your rights shall not be invaded." This did not mollify Hampton, who retorted that the secretary's words had "locked the door upon me" and his only choice was "*to throw away the scabbard*" as the "close of the campaign must open me a passage should I not find a shorter route in the course of it."[26] Wade Hampton would go through the forthcoming operation, but if he was not killed in action, he would resign at its end.

Having established his authority, in his own mind at least, James Wilkinson continued on his way north.

Impatiently awaiting his arrival were the officers and men of the two divisions at Sackets Harbor and Fort George. They had not seen any major action since early summer and the troops in the Niagara had had the worst of it, as they were kept under a loose but effective British blockade throughout July and August. David R. Williams (nicknamed "Thunder and Lightning" from his favourite oath), a senator with delusions of military glory who had obtained a brigadier general's commission, arrived at the fort in July and quickly complained to Armstrong that service there was "exceedingly hard owing to the great detail for the piquet & camp guards, for fatigue and forage

parties."[27] "We are alarmed almost every night and are under arms a considerable portion of each," the newly minted general protested, and "I have not
slept without my clothes on, since my arrival within His Majesty's dominion."
Williams managed to stick it for just six weeks before exchanging his martial
ambitions for the comforts of Washington. Writing about the same time, Brigadier General Peter B. Porter of the New York militia was scathing: "we have had
an army at Ft. George for two months past which, at any moment of this time,
might be a vigorous & well directed exertion of 3 or 4 days, have prostrated the
whole of the enemy's face in this division of the country."[28] Instead, Porter continued, that army "lies panic-struck – shut up, and whipped in by a few hundred
miserable Savages, leaving the whole of this frontier, excepting the mile in extent
which they occupy, exposed to the inroads & depredations of the enemy."

It was a long summer for the troops at Fort George and it was a sickly season. Given the sanitary standards of the time, it was inevitable that the "soldier's disease," dysentery, would make its appearance, and in early June more
than five hundred were on the sick list while in August nearly a third of the
division, 1,200 men, were suffering from one ailment or another. Doctor James
Mann, the senior medical officer, attributed the high incidence of illness to the
unhealthy location, lack of proper sanitary precautions (even as they were understood in 1813), constant alarms and frequent inebriation. The weather ag-
gravated the situation; June and July were unusually cold and rainy while August was hot, humid and very oppressive. Mann thought that the strain of
dysentery on the frontier was "very obstinate" and "the prostration of strength
as usual most dangerous."[29] He noted it could be controlled "by obliging the
men to cook their food in the form of soup" and treated by diet, particularly
milk and vegetables as milk "is the grand restorative of convalescents, and vegetables generally are useful, in combatting that putrid tendency to which all
hospital patients are so liable." Most army doctors preferred the use of ipecac
and opium "in doses of half a grain each, or to a grain of Opium at night &
half a grain in the morning without the ipecac," which Surgeon William
Beaumont recorded, "were generally sufficient to carry off the disease."[30] This
treatment cured the symptoms at least, but by this time the afflicted soldier
was usually so weak and dehydrated he had to spend a period in the hospital
where he often contracted another disease, usually "lake" or intermittent fevers. This brought him more opium, followed by bleeding and then massive
doses of emetics, for Surgeon General James Tilton was a firm believer that "a
vomit" was "of excellent use, by opening and squeezing of all the glands of the
body, and thus shaking from the nervous system, the contaminating poison
before its impressions are fixed."[31]

Not surprisingly, these conditions resulted in a decline in the soldiers' morale – and their appearance. An inspecting officer reported that the enlisted personnel in the Niagara "are more durty [sic] and filthy than any set of Men I have ever seen, in Service" and many soldiers "perhaps from want and very likely from laziness wear their Shirts & pantaloons, without washing until they fall to peaces off their bodies."[32]

There was much frustration at Fort George and it vented itself on forty-nine-year-old Brigadier General John Parker Boyd, the commander there throughout most of the summer. A native of Massachusetts, Boyd had a somewhat unusual background – he had apparently served as a lieutenant in the regular army from the end of the Revolutionary War to 1789, but then resigned to become a mercenary in India and for nineteen years was employed by the rulers of several small native states to train and lead their forces. He re-entered the United States Army in 1808 as a colonel and commander of the Fourth Infantry Regiment and led this unit in action against the Indian nations of the Northwest at the battle of Tippecanoe in 1811. This earned him a promotion to brigadier general at the outbreak of war.[33]

Most of those who had dealings with John Boyd did not have a high opinion of the man. His superior on the northern frontier, Major General Morgan Lewis, described him as a "compound of ignorance, vanity and petulance, with nothing to recommend him, but that species of bravery in the field, which is vaporing, boisterous, stifling reflection, blinding observation and better adapted to the Bully of a Brothel than the Soldier."[34] Colonel Winfield Scott of the Second Artillery was more kind and thought Boyd "courteous, amiable, and respectable, as a subordinate; but vacillating and imbecile, be-

The mercenary – Brigadier General John Boyd (1764-1830)

A native of Boston and a former mercenary in the service of Indian potentates, John Boyd joined the American army as a colonel shortly before the war began and was promoted brigadier general in 1812. He had a reputation as a brave but stupid officer who followed his orders to the letter and his mental abilities garnered him the nickname of "Tippy Canoe." (Benson Lossing, *Pictorial Field Book of the War of 1812*)

yond all endurance as a chief under high responsibilities."[35] Junior officers, not realizing Boyd was under orders restricting his actions, decided he must be a coward, although Captain John Walworth of the Sixth Infantry was a bit more generous and described his general as a "brave man, but [one who] has not capability to plan an enterprize."[36] There seems to have been a general consensus in the northern army that Boyd was not particularly intelligent – soldiers' nicknames for their generals can be very telling and Boyd's nickname, in a play upon his most notable action, was "Tippecanoe" (as in "tippy-canoe").[37]

It was hard for the troops at Fort George to comprehend why they were being kept inactive for so long and there was much speculation about the motives of the senior generals, the so-called "Big Bugs," and the "Big Article" himself, Secretary of War Armstrong.[38] "We shall be ruined if there is not some change in our affairs," wrote twenty-one-year-old Second Lieutenant Matthew Hughes of the Twelfth Infantry to his parents in early July, because everything "is going wrong in my opinion but a platoon officer has no right to think."[39] When reflecting "on the generalship of our armies," Captain Arthur Sinclair of the navy had lost all "patience with those who have the direction" as "it appears to me that everything like energy, enterprise and judgement had forsaken them or that they never possest either."[40] "We had better make peace than carry on the war as we have done," was his conclusion. By mid-summer there was concern that the campaign season was slipping away without any action and chagrin that the army's reputation must be low in the eyes of the public. "We still remain here doing nothing, nor do I know when we shall move," lamented Lieutenant Patrick Macdonogh of the Second Artillery in early August. "If things go no better than they have done I shall be ashamed to return to Philadelphia next winter" as soldiers "must rank mighty low there."[41]

In the meantime, they did their best to keep their spirits high. An anonymous young aide-de-camp, who left a marvellously witty and informative account of the 1813 campaign, recalled that "having little to do, the officers naturally endeavored to shake off the hours that hung heavy on their hands, by being much together in order to talk, and laugh, and scold, and visit the sins of the campaign on those who were responsible for them."[42] He and his tentmates had a cask of wine which they only resorted to on rare occasions as they were determined to drink the last glasses from it in Montreal, but sometimes it all just got a bit much and so a modicum was consumed for therapeutic reasons and more than a few verses intoned of "Old King Twine," their name for a popular drinking song also known as "Anacreon in Heaven" or the "Anacreontic Song." About a year later, a lawyer from Baltimore would put new words to the melody and the result would be called "The Star-Spangled Banner."[43]

The veteran – Brigadier General Moses Porter (1756-1822)
A hard-bitten veteran of the Revolutionary War and the senior artillery officer on the northern frontier, Moses Porter delighted younger officers with his considerable vocabulary of profanity, which he trotted forth at any opportunity, a social grace that earned him the nickname of "Old Blow Hard." (From the *Danvers Herald,* 1927)

"It was a season for waggery," remembered the aide-de-camp and the best purveyor of waggery at Fort George was a jovial lieutenant from Virginia enjoying the appellation of the "Chickahominy wag" who was generous with whatever came his way, including drink, delicacies, cigars and a good quip. Chickahominy was renowned for his extensive vocabulary of profanity but all agreed that in this respect the camp champion was fifty-nine-year-old Colonel Moses Porter, the senior officer of artillery and a hard-bitten Revolutionary War veteran whose penchant for swearing long and loud had earned him the nickname of "Old Blowhard."[44]

One day, the Chickahominy wag decided to put the matter to a test. While an appreciative audience of fellow officers loitered about and Porter was within earshot, he began to chew out some hapless private for a minor offence. This luckless individual must have thought that "the vehemence of the reprimand was greatly disproportionate to the offence" but Porter walked by without stopping. The Virginian, however, was just warming up and soon got into his stride, working "himself up into a fine fit of frenzy" as he "began to curse and swear with a fluency and variety" that brought a spellbound Porter to a halt until a stream of "the most horrible and astounding execrations announced the finale of the piece." "Old Blowhard" continued on his way shaking his head but was so impressed that he actually refrained from profanity himself for a few days, which everyone remarked made his conversation rather dull as, besides oaths, Moses Porter was a man of remarkably few words.[45]

Things were not so amusing on the perimeter of the camp. The American position at Fort George backed onto the Niagara River, its left anchor the fort itself and its right an entrenched battery, the whole extent of about a mile being protected by a ditch and an earthwork. Six pickets of between fifty and a hundred men were posted outside the main camp from a half to three-quarters of a mile in every direction to prevent enemy scouts from approaching the main position and give warning in the event of a surprise attack. There was frequent skirmishing at these outposts, particularly at night, when British-allied warriors would creep in close and wait for the American sentries to challenge, then, "guided by the sound of the voice, fire, and sometimes hit a man."[46]

Captain Mordecai Myers of the Thirteenth Infantry, one of the better company officers in the northern army, came up with a solution to this problem. A native of New York City and friend of such influential men as Morgan Lewis and state governor Daniel Tompkins, the thirty-three-year-old Myers had studied "Military Tactics, etc." in 1810-1812 at a private military school run by an expatriate French officer. In the spring of 1812, with war threatening, Myers had requested and obtained a captain's commission although, as he commented, it was a "rank far beneath what I might have had, as my friend, Governor Tompkins, told me, if I had asked for the assistance of my friends." Myers thought his rank as high as it should be as he wanted to gain promotion by his own merits, but Tompkins warned him that he "would find very many above me who would be more fit to obey than command" and so it was, for as Myers remarked, a "great ignorance of military tactics prevailed in the new army, and the old [peacetime] one was not far beyond us in field duty."[47]

Myers's solution to the night-time sniping was simple but effective. He instructed his sentries "to strike once on the cartridge box when they heard an approach instead of challenging" and "instructed the rounds, relief, and grand rounds when they heard a sentinel strike his cartridge box to answer by striking twice and to advance." In his opinion, this innovation "saved many lives." Myers also positioned a 6-pdr. field gun "loaded with grape" at his picket. Attacked one morning at 4 A.M., he "touched off the gun" – the enemy warriors "set up a shout like that of a thousand devils, and were off."[48]

Heavier fighting occasionally took place when the British tried to cut off and capture an entire picket. If this occurred, a column would be dispatched from the main camp to support the picket, and one captain who specialized in such alarm work drilled his company to move at the trot so that they could rush to any threatened sector. On 8 July the enemy launched a serious attack against Picket No. 3 and a detachment commanded by Lieutenant Joseph Eldridge of the Thirteenth Infantry was sent to its assistance. The firing continued heavy and the entire Thirteenth was ordered to Eldridge's support, only to find that he had rebuffed the attackers and then followed them into the woods, where the British warriors had turned and killed or captured thirty-seven of his men. The regiment reached the scene to find the dead and

The young American officer – Captain Mordecai Myers, Thirteenth Infantry (1786-1871

Portrayed here in the uniform of the New York militia, Mordecai Myers was representative of the better type of company officer in the northern army. He served with distinction throughout the summer and autumn of 1813 and was twice wounded at the battle of Crysler's Farm. (Portrait by J.W. Jarvis, courtesy of the Toledo Museum of Art)

wounded had been "utterly stripped, and scalped, and mangled and maimed in a way that looked as it there had been a sort of sportive butchery among the dead and the dying."[49] Eldridge, "a young man of great promise, and much beloved by his fellow officers," was not among the corpses and a message inquiring about his fate was sent across to the British lines.[50]

This message was received and inquiries duly made among the British native contingent. The warriors who had fought Eldridge were a group of between two and three hundred from the Delaware, Onondaga, Cayuga, Mohawk, Ottawa, Chippawa and Mississauga nations, and they were led by one of the most competent and aggressive native leaders serving the Crown – John Norton or the Snipe, a war chief of the Mohawks. On 8 July Norton had set an ambush "with the design of allowing them [the Americans] to pass before we should assail them" and that is exactly what happened.[51] His warriors "were just on their backs, when they perceived us, – they fell into such confusion, that they were instantly routed, & pursued in all directions." At that moment, one of Norton's subordinates reported that he had seen "one of my young Warriors shot by an officer with a Pistol, while he seemed to be standing unsuspicious of harm, the Warriors who followed instantly killed the officer and two Soldiers who were in his Company."[52] The officer was Lieutenant Joseph Eldridge.

The "Nitchies," as British soldiers called their native allies, were very effective in this type of warfare which called for field craft, cunning and stealth – "no surprises with Nitchie on the look out" was how Lieutenant John Le Couteur of the 104th Foot put it.[53] But they could commit excesses in the heat of battle which upset British sensibilities, and this was particularly true of those warriors from the Northwest nations who had been fighting the Americans for

War chief – John Norton, or the Snipe
Half Cherokee, half Scot, John Norton was the war chief of the Mohawk peoples and one of the most effective British native leaders during the war. He commanded the warriors who sealed the American army in their defensive position at Fort George throughout most of the summer of 1813. (Oil portrait by Thomas Philips, reproduced by gracious permission of the Duke of Northumberland)

years. Ten days after Eldridge was killed a council was held between the officers of the British Indian Department and the native contingent serving with the blockading force. One of the white officers asked Black Bird, chief of the Ottawa, for information about Eldridge's death and admonished him for the mutilation of the dead in the action. Black Bird denied his people had mutilated bodies but talked plain to the white man about why they might be capable of such acts:

> At the foot of the Rapids last spring we fought the Big Knives, and we lost some of our people there. When we retired the Big Knives got some of our dead. They were not satisfied with having killed them, but cut them into small pieces. This made us very angry. My words to my people were: "As long as the powder burnt, to kill and scalp," but those behind us came up and did mischief.
>
> ...... If the Big Knives, after they killed people of our colour, leave them without hacking them to pieces, we will follow their example. They have themselves to blame. The way they treat our killed, and the remains of those that are in their graves in the west, makes our people mad when they meet the Big Knives.
>
> ...... We thought white people were Christians. They ought to show us a better example.[54]

As for Eldridge, the chief continued, "the officer that we killed you have spoken to us before about," and "I now tell you again, he fired and wounded one of our colour; another fired at him and killed him." The Ottawa warriors "wished to take him prisoner, but the officer said 'God damn,' and fired, when he was shot." "That is all I have to say," concluded Black Bird. A message was sent into Fort George that Eldridge had been killed while trying to escape.[55]

The British warriors dominated the American perimeter until 17 August when they encountered a new enemy. John Norton was in the advance that day and saw some warriors approaching at a run, which he thought to be friendly Chippawa "retiring in consequence of having seen a band of enemies too formidable to attack." However, "their appearance soon undeceived us – I suspected them to be the Indians of the opposite side of the Water [the Niagara River]." Norton "was about to challenge them when I saw them level and fire" and his warriors "returned their fire, & retreated on a more advantageous position about one hundred paces in our rear." "This was the first time," the Mohawk war chief added, "that we had met that part of the Five Nations which remain within the Boundary of the United States," and it "spread no small Dismay" among his men, who respected these nations "for their ancient celebrity in arms." The arrival of a contingent of the Iroquoian peoples of New York state led by their chief, Farmer's Brother, effectively put a stop to the harassment of the American outposts.[56]

Life for the British and Canadian troops and native warriors in the Niagara during the summer of 1813 was no happier than it was for the Americans – a compound of boredom, fatigue, illness and occasional action. The British force consisted of Norton's warriors, whose numbers fluctuated between two and three hundred, backed up by about 2,000 regulars. They did not like the Niagara, which Lieutenant John Le Couteur regarded as a place "where only misery, wretchedness, Broken heads and no honour or credit can be met with."[57] There was also a high rate of illness – nearly a third of the troops were on the sick list in August – and at the end of that month conditions were so bad that Prevost and Major General Francis de Rottenburg, the commander in Upper Canada, seriously considered abandoning their forward positions and falling back to some healthier place.[58]

For John Le Couteur, a light infantry officer, the high points of that long and dreary summer were the times when he was sent under a flag of truce to the American lines. He was always halted at one of the outlying pickets and allowed no further but when news of his arrival reached the main camp, American officers "would ride out from Fort George to chat to me." The eighteen-year-old native of Jersey thought it "strange indeed" to "find so many names, 'familiar household words,' as enemies – the very names of Officers in our own army."[59] "How uncomfortably like a civil war it seemed," he mused, "when we were in good-humoured friendly converse – far less animosity than between the Cavaliers and Roundheads." On another occasion, a visit to the enemy re-

The young British officer – Lieutenant John Le Couteur, 104th Foot (1794-1875) Le Couteur served in the Niagara throughout the summer of 1813 and left a literate and witty memoir of his wartime experiences. He often visited the outlying pickets of the American position at Fort George under a flag of truce and was struck by the similarities between the two armies, musing that it all seemed uncomfortably like a civil war. (Oil portrait, c. 1812, courtesy of the Société Jersiaise, St. Helier, Jersey).

sulted in a fine repast. Le Couteur had been instructed to escort two American ladies to Fort George, but when the forward sentry refused to let him approach, Le Couteur told him to fetch the officer on duty. One soon appeared and the two young men "got to be friends in a Jiffy for I talked to Him as if He had been of our mess, asked Him how He liked it, how He roughed it and was so friendly that we both forgot the Ladies and walked pleasantly on."[60]

"His dinner came," Le Couteur remembered, "a better one than I had smelt since I dined with Gen[eral] Vincent – Capital beef steaks, Potatoes, and bottle of excellent brandy.

"You'll picnic with me?" asked the young American.

"With the greatest of pleasure!" replied Le Couteur.

But such occasions were few and far between – mostly it was boredom and fatigue for the young officer and his comrades and they too questioned the intelligence of the "Big Wigs," their name for their generals.

What both armies were waiting for that summer was the naval action that would decide who would control Lake Ontario; until that issue was settled, neither one could undertake prolonged operations. After the abortive British attack on his base at Sackets Harbor in May, Chauncey spent all of June and most of July there waiting for his latest warship, the *General Pike*, to be completed before re-emerging onto the lake. This gave Yeo a free run for nearly six weeks, and he took the opportunity to harass the American shore and lend active support to the British army in the field. The *Pike* was ready on 20 July and the following day Chauncey sailed for the Niagara where he picked up a small force under Colonel Winfield Scott and raided York on 31 July. Yeo came out of Kingston in response and on 7 August the two squadrons came in sight. For three days they snapped at each other, Chauncey trying to get the weather gauge to run down on Yeo, while Yeo, whose armament had a shorter range, tried to avoid that very thing. Chauncey lost two schooners to a storm and two to the British but this was no great disadvantage because he still possessed larger ships with heavier armament. For the rest of August both naval commanders cruised the lake seeking the best situation for an engagement but never finding it.[61]

Prevost was disappointed in the outcome of the action of 7 August but, like everyone else, he could do nothing but wait. In the meantime he decided to take a closer look at the situation in the Niagara and travelled there late in the month to find "2000 British soldiers on an extended line cooping up in Fort George an American force exceeding 4000 men."[62] Wanting accurate information about the strength and extent of the enemy position, Prevost ordered his troops to drive in the American pickets on 24 August, and they actually penetrated into the village of Newark beside the fort. This reconnaissance was so successful that many of the unit commanders involved wished to convert it into a full-scale assault and were only reined back by their commander's positive orders. Prevost was "satisfied that Fort George is not to be reduced, strengthened and supported as it is by Fort Niagara, without more troops, the co-operation of the fleet and a battering train," but as he explained to Bathurst, his "resources and means do not allow me to contemplate so glorious a termination to the campaign in Upper Canada."[63]

That same day the British commander-in-chief received news of the arrival at Sackets Harbor "of the American Secretary of War, General Armstrong, accompanied by Genl. Wilkinson" and "concentration at that place of a very considerable force."[64] This could only mean that Kingston was threatened and Prevost immediately headed for that place.

Prevost's information was not accurate. Armstrong was indeed on his way to Sackets Harbor but he had stopped off in Albany to confer with New York Governor Daniel Tompkins. Wilkinson meanwhile had pushed on north but became so sick at Utica that he had to be bled, and he only arrived at the Harbor on 20 August, almost five months since he had been ordered north from Louisiana. Waiting to greet him were his senior subordinates, Major General Morgan Lewis and Brigadier Generals Jacob Brown, Leonard Covington and Robert Swartout.[65]

Morgan Lewis was a fifty-nine-year-old native of New York who had served during the Revolutionary War as a quartermaster. He then pursued a legal career but his marriage into the influential Livingston clan guaranteed him a role in state politics and Lewis served as attorney general of New York and a chief justice. He was elected governor in 1804 but was defeated by Tompkins in

Amiable but ineffective – Major General Morgan Lewis (1754-1844)
A former governor of New York, wealthy Morgan Lewis (shown in the uniform of the New York militia) was fifty-nine years old in 1813 when he served as Wilkinson's second-in-command during the offensive against Montreal. He proved a disaster as a general. (Courtesy, New York States Office of Parks, Recreation and Preservation, Mills Museum Historic Site, ML. 1974.267)

1807 and returned to politics as a state senator. In the spring of 1812 his connections procured him a commission as brigadier general and the appointment of quartermaster general. Lewis was never too enthusiastic about his duties in this department, which he carried on while continuing his political career, and when Judge Ambrose Spencer, the kingmaker of New York politics, became tired of his "political stupidity" in the state senate, he secured Lewis a promotion to major general and a command appointment on the northern frontier.[66]

Lewis had served under Dearborn during the assault on Fort George on 27 May but his caution allowed the beaten British to escape, much to the fury of his subordinates. Morgan Lewis was also a general who believed war should be waged in comfort. Brigadier General Peter Porter commented that, although "General Lewis is brave & capable … he is no *veni, vidi, vici* man – and be assured that he will never overrun the wilderness of Canada" because "he could not go 16 miles to fight the enemy – not because his force was too small – but because *he had not waggons to carry tents & camp kettles for his army*."[67] The former governor's "own baggage moves in two stately waggons, one drawn by two & the other by 4 horses carrying the various furniture of a Secretary of State's office, a lady's dressing chamber, an alderman's dining room, & the contents of a grocer's shop."[68] In June 1813 Dearborn sent Lewis to command at Sackets Harbor and he had remained there throughout the summer, holding a watching brief over military affairs in the north. A kindly man known for his generosity, Morgan Lewis was basically an amiable nonentity but Wilkinson would have to be careful not to cross him as Lewis happened to be John Armstrong's brother-in-law.

Robert Swartout, thirty-five years of age, was a merchant from New York city and a leading Republican in state politics. He had been a colonel in the state militia before being commissioned a brigadier general in the regular service in the spring of 1813, replacing Lewis as quartermaster general although Swartout hankered after an active command in the line. He was no friend of James Wilkinson because his brother, Samuel, had been implicated in the Burr conspiracy and had challenged Wilkinson to a duel after the general had testified against him. A few days after his arrival at Sackets Wilkinson took Lewis aside to tell him that, in the "necessity of harmony and confidence" he and Swartout should agree to put aside their differences. Lewis carried these sentiments to Swartout, who found them "very liberal" and "expressed his cordial assent."[69]

The other two generals, Jacob Brown and Leonard Covington, were much different men. Brown, a thirty-eight-year-old native of Pennsylvania, came to northern New York in 1799 to open up the Black River country just east of Sackets Harbor. He had established the town of Brownville and had worked hard for more than a decade to build up this and the surrounding communities, cutting roads, building bridges and mills and acting as a magistrate and local militia commander. His activities during the Embargo period had earned him the nickname of "Smuggler," but Brown's loyalty was steadfast, and shortly before war broke out he was appointed a brigadier general in the New York militia with responsibility for guarding the frontier between the Harbor and Ogdensburg. He had carried out this task well, repulsing a British attack on Ogdensburg in October 1812 and playing a prominent role in defeating the attack on Sackets Harbor in May 1813. Brown so impressed senior regular officers that they pressed Armstrong to bring him into the army and he was duly commissioned a brigadier general in July 1813. Jacob Brown was a natural leader who exhibited decisiveness, determination and tempered aggression. He also possessed what many American generals lacked – first-hand knowledge of local conditions and what was required to wage war on the northern frontier. Colonel Joseph Swift, Wilkinson's chief engineer and a good judge of military character, liked Brown, whom he described as a "self-taught, active, and highly intelligent officer."[70]

Leonard Covington was a prewar regular. A native of Maryland, he had been commissioned in the cavalry in 1792 and had fought with "Mad Anthony" Wayne during that general's campaigns in the Northwest, where he had played a prominent part in the battle of Fallen Timbers in 1794. He left the army as a captain the following year to manage his property, but he also had an interest in politics and served two terms in the Maryland House of Delegates before being elected to Congress in 1805. When the army was expanded in 1808, Covington received a colonel's commission and was posted to the Mississippi Territory, where he ac-

Sword of the Border – Brigadier General Jacob Brown (1775-1828) A former militia officer, Jacob Brown quickly proved the most capable of Wilkinson's subordinates as he was one of the few senior officers who understood the difficulties of campaigning on the northern frontier. (National Archives of Canada, C-100390)

quired much property. In the early summer of 1813 he had been ordered north and on 1 August was promoted brigadier general. It was somewhat ironic that Brown, who had less military experience, was senior in rank but the forty-four-year-old Covington, a professional soldier, did not complain.[71]

Wilkinson's first step after arriving at Sackets Harbor was to issue a general order informing his new command that his

> orders will be few & those as concise as possible, he will require from no one (relative rank & functions considered) that which he will not be ready himself to perform, it will be his pride to participate, toil, hazard, peril & glory with those he commands, but his orders & arrangements must be properly executed, be implicitly obeyed; He will cherish harmony, Union & a Manly fraternal Spirit, as the precursor of triumph & fame, but should Intrigue & faction, those demons of discord, ever shew their Heads within the limits of command it will be his duty to strangle them in the Birth.[72]

This order was followed on 24 August by a review of the garrison. The division at Sackets Harbor was not in good case: nearly a third of the troops were on the sick list; many units were only fragments separated from their regiments in the Niagara, and their training had suffered because Lewis was not the most conscientious commanding officer. Wilkinson was complimentary about the men's appearance, but noted deficiencies and his opinion was echoed by Covington, who regarded the troops at the Harbor as being "in bad order and under sorry discipline."[73] A naval officer, Captain Arthur Sinclair, who was familiar with the garrison expressed a harsher view (although perhaps jaundiced by a little interservice rivalry):

> There are about 3000 effective men – but they really make me sick at the stomache to look at them. They remind me very much of the water street Hogs of Norfolk well fed and lazy and muddy as the devil. Really I never saw such looking troops in any Country. Figure to yourself the dirtiest and most slovenly looking blackguards you ever have seen, and you have our army, generally, in your own mind's eye. The fittest of the army, *if they have any*, is the worst in the world. I believe the men are brave but they want officers and discipline.[74]

Wilkinson discovered that the state of training was so bad that the sentries did not know how to walk their posts. Things obviously needed tightening up and he issued the necessary orders, putting an emphasis on drill and weapons handling, insisting that the troops "must be instructed in the expert use of their arms, and an uniformity of pace in every movement; to form the column, and to display it with celerity and correctness; to change front to the right and left by battalions and brigades with promptitude and good order, and to preserve the line in the front march." If these evolutions were mastered, Wilkinson believed, his men "will, under God, enable this army to beat the enemy, when, and wherever they may be met."[75]

Nobody in the division minded the extra work, because officers and men were confident that the arrival of Wilkinson meant something big was in the works. Captain Rufus McIntire of the Third Artillery was enthusiastic about

The regular – Brigadier General Leonard Covington (1768-1813)
Leonard Covington appears here as a young cavalry officer in this 1795 portrait. Covington served with distinction throughout the campaign although he had personal doubts about the operation. (From *Memoir of Leonard Covington*, 1928)

his new commander who "infused new spirit into the troops at this post" and "inspired a degree of confidence in every officer and soldier that I never saw equalled."[76]

Sackets Harbor was not the best place to serve in 1813. One officer thought it "most contemptible" with "no respectable looking houses & many sheds & slight temporary habitations erected by the [camp] followers & sutlers of the army," while the "street, for there is but one, is muddy & contains all the filth which is collected within the buildings that stand upon it & which is daily discharged into it."[77] But it was a bustling location: another officer was amazed at the "astonishing activity in building ships, rigging, hauling great guns, anchors, cables, cannon balls, grape and canister shot, bar shot, etc., from day light til dark" and "the *yo heave ho* of the sailors, the hammering of carpenters … sweetened with drums and fifes, bugle horns, etc."[78] He noted, however, that these activities were "interrupted several times each day with the solemn knell of funerals attended with honors of war."

There were indeed many, too many, military funerals at the Harbor in 1813. With its large military and civilian population, poor facilities, crowded lodgings and inadequate sanitation, the village was a breeding ground for disease. In early September, 681 soldiers, about one fifth of the garrison, were on the sick list, the greatest number suffering "dysenteries" followed by jaundice, fever, and rheumatism. Medical officers attributed the high rate of illness to a combination of bad water, poor sanitation and above all the bread issued with the rations. On 18 September the senior medical officer, Doctor James Ross, reported that the bread, the staple of a soldier's diet, was "made from the flour of sprouted or grown wheat and damaged flour, in which from negligence, lime, soap, and other extraneous and even feculent ingredients, have been discovered."[79] Ross was horrified to discover that the army's bakers were drawing their water from the lake near where the "camp sinks" or latrines drained into it, and that that water was "impregnated with, and contains a diffusion of excrementious matter." The result was predictable – Covington recorded: "We bury hundreds."[80]

As commander of Military District No. 9, which stretched from Vermont to the Pennsylvania line on Lake Erie, Wilkinson had three divisions under his command. Boyd's in the Niagara consisted of 4,600 men; Lewis's at Sackets mustered 3,200; while Hampton had a 3,500-strong division at Burlington, Vermont – a total strength of 9,300 men but of these nearly 2,500 (more than a quarter) were on the sick list in August 1813. To decide how this force was to be employed, Wilkinson convened a council of war six days after his arrival which was attended by Brown, Chauncey, Lewis and Swartout. He opened the discussion by stating that the "conquest of the province of Upper Canada comprises the instructions of the executive" and "the reduction of Kingston, by a direct attack or indirect movement, embraces the primary objects of these instructions."[81]

Noting that "the season is slipping by rapidly, and the honour and interests of the nation imperiously demand that a deadly blow should be struck somewhere," he placed four options before them:

1. Await the outcome of the naval struggle on Lake Ontario before making any offensive moves.

2. Resume the offensive in the Niagara peninsula, secure that area and then, with Hampton's division, mount a major attack on Kingston.

3. While Hampton made a feint on Montreal from Burlington, Boyd's division would be shifted from the Niagara to Sackets Harbor to join with Lewis's division to attack Kingston and, "should the season permit," move against Montreal.

4. Shift Boyd to the Harbor, make a feint on Kingston with the combined force, then slip down the St. Lawrence and, in concert with Hampton, attack Montreal.

The third and fourth options were, of course, Armstrong's "direct" and "indirect" attacks. The council approved the fourth option, reserving the "feint on Kingston" for future consideration.[82]

Wilkinson next announced he was going to the Niagara to expedite the transfer of Boyd's division to the east end of Lake Ontario. His presence there

Dashing blades – American staff officers, 1813
"Stafflings" they called themselves and these dashing young officers thought the whole business a great lark, according to one of their number who left a witty account of the 1813 campaign. (Drawing by H.C. McBarron, courtesy of the Company of Military Historians).

might also give the enemy the false impression that the main effort would be made in that area and draw off British strength. While he made that journey, all possible preparations were to be made for the forthcoming operation. Lewis being forced to take a month's leave because of poor health, the burden of this work fell on Brown, who assumed command at the Harbor, and Swartout, whose department was primarily responsible. Wilkinson handed these two officers an impressive shopping list: horses for the cavalry, who needed them as well as supply wagons and teams and the necessary forage; boats sufficient to move 7,000 men with 12 of the craft to be fitted as gunboats; 300-400 river pilots to be engaged; 20 siege guns with 300 rounds per gun and 40 field pieces with 150 rounds per gun to be assembled; two months' provisions packed ready to be embarked; and due proportions of winter clothing, entrenching tools, small arms and medical stores. Enough water transport to carry 5,000 men was to be at Fort George by 10 September, the remainder to be available at the Harbor five days later. Everything else was to be ready by 22 September, less than a month away. Finally, Brown was ordered to "have the troops trained for action" with "redoubled industry."[83] "My machinery is in motion," Wilkinson crowed to Armstrong on 21 August.[84]

But what of Hampton's machinery? Wilkinson relayed his orders for Hampton through Armstrong. The crucial thing was to co-ordinate the movements of the troops on Lake Ontario and those on Lake Champlain, and Wilkinson was concerned that Hampton not advance on Montreal too early and give the game away. On 21 August, Wilkinson advised the secretary that Hampton "must not budge until everything is matured in this quarter and we have either possession of Kingston or have cut its communication with Montreal," and he promised to give Hampton "seasonable advice" at Plattsburgh, New York, where Wilkinson expected that general to concentrate, "completely equipped for forward movement," by 20 September.[85]

Everything, however, still depended on the outcome of the naval struggle for control of Lake Ontario. When news came on 29 August that Yeo had left the shelter of Kingston and sailed westward, Chauncey's warships raised anchor the next day and followed. All now depended on the navy. "God! what an eventful moment for us all," Wilkinson wrote to Armstrong while making his way by boat to the Niagara, but "Chauncey will triumph, and if I am not opposed by storms and tempests, the rest will follow."[86]

And so Major General James Wilkinson, the "Big Bug from the South," complete with box coat and slouch hat, arrived at Fort George on 4 September 1813 to stare at an embarrassed John Boyd while the echoes of a fifteen-gun salute died away across Lake Ontario.

CHAPTER 3

"Two heads on the same shoulders make a monster"

ORDER, COUNTER-ORDER, DISORDER, SEPTEMBER–OCTOBER 1813

Fifty I got for selling me coat,
Fifty for selling me blanket.
If ever I 'lists for a sodger again,
The Divil shall be me sergeant
Poor old sodger, poor old sodger

Twice tried for selling me coat,
Three times tried for desertion.
If ever I be a sodjer again,
May the Divil promote me sergeant.
Poor old sodger, poor old sodger[1]

On 5 September 1813, the day after Wilkinson was greeted with unwanted military honours at Fort George, Secretary of War John Armstrong arrived at Sackets Harbor. He brought with him a large retinue that included the chief engineer of the army, the acting adjutant general and inspector general, the surgeon general, the commissary general of ordnance, and their staffs. For nearly two months the War Department would be located in this humble upstate New York village, which by now had become the largest military and naval base in the republic.

All eyes were on the lake for, in Armstrong's words, "the pivot is if Chauncey beats Yeo."[2] On 8 September, the opposing squadrons hove in view of each other near the mouth of the Niagara River. Watching from their respective parts of the shore were the men of the two armies, including Le Couteur of the 104th Foot, who thought the warships were "very exciting to behold, they

51

American naval commander – Commodore Isaac Chauncey, USN (1772-1840) Chauncey suffered much from the constantly changing plans of Secretary of War John Armstrong and his senior generals. Before the St. Lawrence campaign could begin, it was necessary that his squadron gain naval superiority on Lake Ontario but Chauncey was cautious – a defeat on the lake would mean not just the loss of a battle but British supremacy on Ontario for the remainder of the war. (Courtesy, Toronto Reference Library, T-15206)

looked so trim and wary of each other like two grim Bull dogs eyeing each other askance."[3]

Yeo and Chauncey paralleled each other's course north across the lake to York and then back again, until on the morning of 11 September they were near the mouth of the Genesee River on the south shore. At that moment the wind died and Chauncey, whose squadron was armed with more long-range guns, had the advantage and made full use of it, bombarding the British vessels, which could make no effective reply, for nearly ninety minutes. Fortunately for Yeo, the wind picked up and he was able to extricate himself from this perilous situation and sail for Kingston in the late afternoon, licking his wounds. Prevost, who had been hoping for a British victory, complained to Bathurst that he felt "some disappointment at the return of our squadron after being so many days in sight of the enemy's squadron without having obtained a decided advantage."[4]

While he waited for the outcome of the naval contest, Armstrong coordinated the forthcoming offensive. Since his two senior generals were not on speaking terms, the secretary acted as the relay between them. To Hampton, Armstrong expressed Wilkinson's wish that he cross to the New York side of Lake Champlain and move by water to attack the fortified British post at Isle aux Noix, on the Richelieu River north of the border. In response, Hampton consulted Master Commandant Thomas Macdonough, the commander of the small naval squadron on Lake Champlain. Macdonough had recently lost two of his vessels, the *Eagle* and the *Growler*, to the British and did not believe he had the strength to support this operation. Hampton reported this information to Armstrong on 7 September and stated that he would instead push forward to Isle aux Noix by land and would commence this movement on 20 September but, he warned the secretary, "too much must not be expected" from his command.[5]

Major General Wade Hampton had some reason for this negative assessment for his division was very green. The best units in the Lake Champlain area had been transferred west in the spring of 1813 and only a scratch force consisting of a battalion of the Eleventh Infantry, two companies of the Second Dragoons and an under-strength company of artillery had remained behind. In the late spring and early summer, however, new troops had marched into the cantonment at Burlington, and by August Hampton commanded eight infantry units: the Fourth Infantry, the battalion of the Eleventh, the Twenty-Ninth, Thirtieth, Thirty-First and Thirty-Third Infantry, and two regiments of United States Volunteers from Maine and New Hampshire. This was an impressive force on paper but these troops were not of a quality to inspire confidence. The best of them, the small four-company battalion of the Eleventh, had been under arms for nearly a year but had seen little action while the Fourth Infantry, nominally part of the prewar regular establishment, was actually a new unit recruited over the winter to replace the regiment of the same number surrendered at Detroit in 1812. The Twenty-Ninth, Thirtieth, Thirty-First and Thirty-Third Infantry were one-year regiments, authorized in January 1813 and raised in March through May, as were the two regiments of volunteers. A good-quality battalion of the Tenth Infantry from Virginia was on the march from the south but could not be expected to arrive much before the end of September.[6]

Hampton did what he could with such fresh military clay. He instituted a rigorous training programme, starting with a daily officers' drill from which "no officer of any Corps will be excused" without "written dispensation."[7] When the officers had learned the basics, they were set to work teaching their men through six hours of company and regimental drill each day. Progress

British naval commander – Commodore Sir James Lucas Yeo (1782-1818)
Possessing a distinguished combat record, Yeo assumed command of the British squadron on Lake Ontario in 1813. He was at first aggressive but later grew cautious as he became aware that a lost engagement would cost more than a few ships; it would mean American domination of the lake for the rest of the war. (Engraving after a painting by A. Buck, courtesy, Toronto Reference Library, T-15241).

was apparently made because by the end of July Hampton was able to manoeuvre his infantry in brigade formations. But, as one of his senior officers
remarked, the division "was composed principally of recruits who had been
but a short time in service" and, although they had "been taught various
evolutions, a spirit of subordination was foreign to their views."[8]

Good officers make good soldiers, but there is considerable evidence, both
from the orders Hampton issued at Burlington and from the behaviour of his
officers during the subsequent campaign that they, particularly the junior
ones, had failed to grasp that their basic responsibility was to the men under
their command and not to their own gratification. Indeed, these officers do
not seem to have been an inspiring lot – Private A.G. Cogswell of the Eleventh
Infantry regarded his immediate superiors as "ignorant, wilful, and ugly-
natured puppies."[9] An extreme but not unusual case was Lieutenant Jackson
Durant of the Fourth Infantry, who was dismissed from the service after a
court martial for "ungentlemanlike & unofficerlike conduct" produced evidence that he was not only often "intoxicated while on duty" but in the "habit
of frequenting the sutlers' shops" (suttlers were private merchants who sold
liquor and other items to the troops) and "there drinking with the noncom-
missioned officers & privates."[10]

To curb such excesses Hampton imposed harsh discipline. Forbidden from
using flogging because it had been abolished by the government at the outbreak of war, he proved ingenious in finding satisfactory and painful substi-
tutes. One private found guilty of minor offences was sentenced "to ride a
wooden horse one hour every Sunday for 2 months, with a hangman's cap on,
a 4 lb. shot tied to each foot and a label placed upon him designating his
crime."[11] A common punishment was "running the gauntlet" and, as Private
Joseph Penley of the Maine Volunteers recorded, it was not a pretty sight:

> All the troops, excepting those on guard, etc., were drawn up in a double
> rank, that is, in two lines about six feet apart, facing each other, every man
> being furnished with a small bundle of birch twigs. The prisoner was then
> brought on to the ground, the drums beating and fifes playing the "Rogue's
> March," and placed in an open space between the files, and marched
> through one regiment, an officer holding the point of a drawn sword at his
> breast and a file of men with charged bayonets at this back, at a slow pace,
> every man giving him a switch on his bare back, and blood was drawn upon
> it at every blow. They flogged him to their hearts content before he came to
> me, and glad I was.[12]

"Cobbing" or caning was also frequently used, so much so that Hampton's men nicknamed him "Old Hickory" because of his preference for this punishment above all else.[13]

The men in the division did not know what to make of this patrician from South Carolina. "The outlines of his character," remembered an officer who served with Hampton, "were sharp and well defined" and he was "vigorous, prompt, intrepid, sagacious; but of irritable nerves, consequently, often harsh, and sometimes unjust."[14] Lieutenant Eleazar Williams, the commander of Hampton's native scouts, thought him "in the main" a "brave, and good officer" but one who "lacked judgement."[15] Moreover, Williams considered it strange "that the Government should appoint Southern men to such responsible stations in the North." Many of the troops at Burlington would have agreed and, as most came from the northern states where the "peculiar institution" of slavery was not well regarded, they noted with distaste Hampton's retinue of black personal servants from the slave population on his plantations.[16]

Hampton did, however, obey his orders. On 8 September he began transferring his division of 4,000 across Lake Champlain to Cumberland Head near Plattsburgh. This movement took nearly a week but on 19 September (one day earlier than promised) Hampton started his drive north. Covered by Macdonough's squadron, the army again moved by boat down the lake to Chazy Landing and then to Champlain on the border, which it reached at midnight. Here the troops disembarked and crossed the international boundary into Lower Canada heading for Odelltown, a difficult march as the roads had been blocked by fallen trees and the bridges burned. Close to Odelltown there was a brisk action with the enemy but Hampton pushed on into the village and made camp. Hampton was not impressed with his soldiers' behaviour in their first action and complained to Armstrong that the "perfect rawness" of his troops, "with the exception of not a single platoon, has been the source of much solicitude to the best informed among us." They had done everything they were supposed to do "but not in that style which the example of a Snelling, a Hamilton [officers of his division] &c. ought to have inspired. We want a little more mercury in the ranks at least."[17]

Hampton now examined the situation. It would be difficult to proceed north down the Richelieu to Isle aux Noix for not only were the cart tracks that crossed a large hemlock swamp in his front barricaded and defended but a recent drought had dried up the wells, leaving a shortage of fresh water. He convened his senior officers in a council of war and proposed abandoning the Richelieu line and swinging west to the Châteauguay River, which emptied into the St. Lawrence west of Montreal. If ordered to attack that city, he could

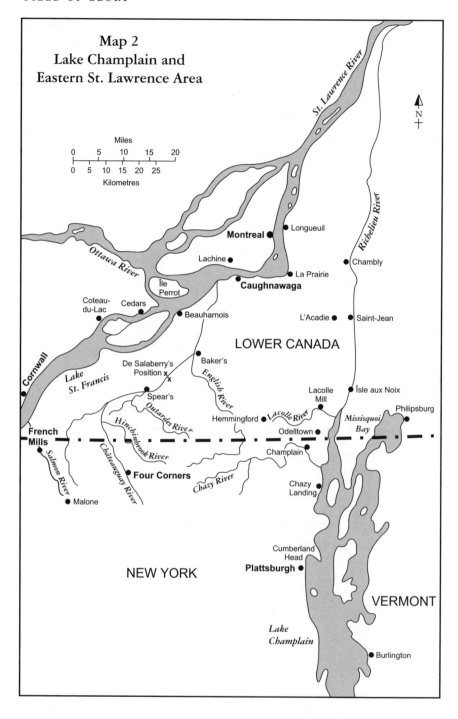

Map 2
Lake Champlain and
Eastern St. Lawrence Area

use this watercourse as his route with the ultimate objective of Caughnawaga across the river from Montreal. Agreement was unanimous and on 21 September the division fell back to Chazy and the following day struck out west.[18]

It was a nightmare trek through very rough country. One brigade commander, Colonel Robert Purdy, complained that the "whole of this march, a distance of more than seventy miles, was very disagreeable; the officers were not permitted to take with them the necessaries; much less the conveniences of life." However, they "forebore complaint, enduring every privation, presuming the commanding officer had sufficient reasons for his conduct, and concluding it was pro bono public."[19]

It took the division four days to reach its destination, the hamlet of Chateaugay Four Corners, New York, near the head of the Châteauguay River. From this location, four roads (hence the name) radiated: down the Châteauguay River to Montreal, to Malone and French Mills on the St. Lawrence, to Plattsburgh and to Sackets Harbor. Hampton established a defended camp and set his troops to work strengthening his logistical situation by improving the road back to Plattsburgh. This task took nine days, and although Hampton boasted the result was a "perfect turnpike," an officer who travelled it complained that it was littered with stumps and rocks and "assuredly as bad a road as can be."[20]

Hampton reported his movements to Armstrong in a letter of 23 September. In response, the secretary instructed him not to advance until he "had advice of our movement."[21] Armstrong approved the shift westward but emphasized Hampton was not to move any further as the "position you have taken is better calculated to keep up the enemy's doubts with regard to your real point of attack than any other." He was to *Hold it fast till we approach you*" because "we ought to run no risks by *separate* attacks when *combined* ones are practicable and sure."[22]

As it turned out, Hampton's division would have a lengthy wait because Boyd's division did not leave Fort George for the Harbor until the first days of October.

It was not planned that way. Immediately after his arrival at Fort George on 4 September Wilkinson had ordered that all attention be given to acquiring and preparing transport for the movement down the lake. He had hoped there would be enough boats from the flotilla Dearborn had used for his assault on Fort George in May, but an inspection revealed that these craft, which had been neglected on a beach for more than three months, "wanted caulking and repairing" and were "small, inconvenient, and unsafe."[23] Swartout at the Harbor received orders to procure and send watercraft to Fort George, for the repair of those craft on hand and for all local resources to be checked. "Boats! Boats! was all the cry," commented the aide-de-camp, until every "harbor, creek, and nook" within miles of the American camp "had been ransacked for its craft, and where purchase, or hire, was out of the question, the strong hand of military necessity cut short the business by a summary acquisition."[24]

Boyd's division was in somewhat better case than the troops at the Harbor – an inspection found it to be "decent in clothing; the arms were good" but the "organization defective, and discipline loose" and orders were issued to tighten things up.[25] Unfortunately, three days after he landed, Wilkinson fell victim to "lake fever" and, "feeble to childhood," took to his bed, where he remained for nearly two weeks, although he continued to exercise intermittent command.[26] "He was so much indisposed," Boyd later commented, "that in any other service he would have perhaps been superseded in his command."[27] Armstrong, however, would not hear of it, and although he wrote Madison that the northern climate "seems very unfriendly to our commanding generals," the secretary was determined the ailing Wilkinson would lead the offensive against the Canadas.[28] He is said to have remarked about this time that "I would feed the old man pap sooner than leave him behind."[29]

While Wilkinson lay sick abed, the squadrons on Lake Ontario met in the inconclusive action of 7 to 11 September. The naval situation was on Wilkinson's mind when on 16 September, "having escaped from my pallet, and with a giddy head and trembling hand," he wrote Armstrong that he was without word from Chauncey and that because of delays the "season, I fear, will be lost."[30] He therefore suggested that since his presence at Fort George appeared to have attracted the bulk of the British forces in Upper Canada, he "make a sweep of them" in the Niagara, an operation he contemplated would take about three weeks. It was only a suggestion, he added, and since it might "lead to the abandonment of the chief design," he requested Armstrong to "give me your advice without delay." Two days later Wilkinson expanded on his suggestion. He did not want to turn Fort George over to a force of militia who might not be able to hold it and asked the secretary: "Shall I attack the enemy here and bog us down or should I come up to Sackets Harbor?"[31] At about the same time Wilkinson held a council of war of his senior officers, who unanimously decided that if the regular army left Fort George, it "should be razed and abandoned."[32]

In response, Armstrong brought Wilkinson back yet again to the objective, Kingston, which he told him on 18 September was held only by De Watteville's Regiment, a foreign unit in British service composed of various nationalities and "completely disaffected." If Kingston fell, the secretary emphasized, "all

Fort George, from Fort Niagara, c. 1805
Located directly across from Fort Niagara, Fort George was held by the United States throughout the summer of 1813 and American possession of the two mutually supporting posts was an important asset. The wharf to the left of the vessel in the river is where Wilkinson landed on Canadian soil in September 1813. (Watercolour by Edward Walsh, National Archives of Canada, C-000026)

above perishes, because the tree is then girdled." If the enemy was strong in the Niagara, they must be weak at Kingston, even though it now appeared that, due to delays, no operation could be mounted against that place until mid-October. Armstrong concluded that "nothing forbids and everything invites to a prompt and steady prosecution of the plan of operations already prescribed to you," which was to concentrate "as speedily as possible the two divisions at the harbour and, in conjunction with the fleet," assault the British naval base.[33]

For Armstrong, this was fairly strong language, and Wilkinson knew he would have to obey. It seems clear that Wilkinson was reluctant to undertake an operation in the autumn of 1813 against Kingston or down the St. Lawrence because of the state of his health and the lateness of the season, and perhaps also because it might mean shifting his headquarters to Sackets Harbor, where he would be in close proximity to the secretary of war. Now, however, he had to undertake such an offensive, but during the preparations for it he vacillated on almost a daily basis, swinging between reckless abandon and extreme caution. On 20 September he wrote Brown that, "in taking the leap we are about to, too much caution cannot be mingled with a dauntless resolution, for we must succeed or die to a man."[34] But when Brown expressed confidence, Wilkinson swayed the other way: "Pardon me! but I fear you have the sort of mania which impels military men, to undervalue the force of the Enemy and to treat Him with contempt."[35]

Wilkinson received good news on 22 September when he learned of Perry's triumph twelve days before in the naval battle at Put-In-Bay, which resulted in the capture of the entire British squadron on Lake Erie and American control of that body of water. Armstrong immediately wrote to Major General William Henry Harrison to move east to the Niagara because it was more important "to expel the enemy from the country lying between the two lakes, Erie and Ontario, than to pursue the Indians into their woody and distant recesses."[36] If Harrison came east, Wilkinson's concerns about defending Forts George and Niagara in the absence of regulars would be groundless.[37]

By the last week in September, having assembled the necessary number of watercraft, Wilkinson issued orders that the units preparing for embarkation were "not to leave a man behind capable of pushing a bayonet," and on 25 September the first wave launched in a somewhat motley collection of Durham boats, batteaux, skiffs and smaller craft.[38] Adverse winds forced them to turn back, and when they were about to try again two days later, Yeo's squadron came in sight, halting all movement on the lake.

Chauncey was also out, and at first light on 28 September the two squadrons met each other near Burlington Bay and cruised southward, each commodore trying to get the most favourable position. At midday, the flagships, Yeo's *Wolfe* and Chauncey's *Pike*, engaged as the men of both armies watched from the shore. John Le Couteur "climbed into a tree with a good spy glass and reported to Col[onel] Harvey what was going on" but when he saw "the *Wolfe's* Main and mizzen top Masts fall inboard and several of her Guns silent," he "nearly fell out of the tree from agitation at the sight!"[39]

American spectators were thrilled by the same event and confident that "Sir James was under the Commodore's thumb and we felt assured that common wriggling would not enable him to escape from that predicament."[40] Yeo was saved when one of his captains, William Howe Mulcaster, interposed his own ship between the *Wolfe* and *Pike* and managed to hold off the American vessel long enough for Yeo's crew to get their ship battleworthy. The two squadrons then engaged in a day-long manoeuvre, later termed "the Burlington Races," as Chauncey vainly endeavoured to bring the retreating British squadron into action but did manage to scoop up a half dozen little British troop transports. He could now provide cover for the movement of the troops from Fort George to Sackets Harbor.[41]

Boyd's units therefore embarked on 1 October 1813. Their immediate destination was Henderson Harbor, a sheltered bay southwest of Sackets, where they would rendezvous before moving in conjunction with Lewis's division at Sackets to Grenadier Island, near the head of the St. Lawrence, the final staging point for the attack on Kingston. The aide-de-camp and his comrades pushed off for parts unknown as it "did not seem to be known, even at the embarkation, what our destination was; nor was it until just at the moment of casting loose, that Henderson's harbour was specified as the point of rendezvous." The location of that place was a mystery, "not two men, among the three or four thousand on board the boats, had ever heard of this place, and we turned down the Lake without any absolute certainty that we were on the right track." "It was quite a picturesque sight," the aide remembered, to see "hundreds of boats" as "full of soldiers as if they had been stowed in bulk."[42]

Wilkinson and his staff did not leave until 2 October because he had to finalize plans for the defences of the Niagara area. Governor Tompkins and prominent local citizens had expressed concern that if the army left Niagara, the two forts would fall to the British and the American side of the river would be exposed. In response, Armstrong had ordered that the incompetent commanding officer of Fort Niagara, Captain Nathaniel Leonard, be replaced and a regular garrison left at Fort George, which was not to be razed as Wilkinson planned but put in a state of defence to allow it to withstand an assault. Command of the post went to the twenty-seven-year-old Colonel Winfield Scott and his Second Artillery Regiment, and the choice was a good one as Scott, one of the most aggressive soldiers in the northern army, had participated in almost every major action in the Lake Ontario theatre since the war had begun. At six feet five inches, he was also one of the tallest men in that army, although as the aide-de-camp quipped, Scott "had not been selected so much because his head was on the top of a maypole, and therefore enabled him to keep a good look-out" but "because it was thought he had the obstinate sort of gallantry which was deemed necessary to defend the point of honour left so much exposed to the enemy by the departure of the main army."[43] Scott would be reinforced by a brigade of New York militia and Wilkinson gave him discretionary orders allowing him to follow the main army should the British withdraw from their position before the fort. These arrangements complete, Wilkinson departed for the Harbor after writing a note to Armstrong that concluded: "Oh! if it may please God to favor us with this breeze, we shall soon be near you; but it is in his power, by adverse winds, to delay, and, by tempests, to destroy us."[44]

The Deity was not on Wilkinson's side. Heavy weather set in and the journey from the Niagara to Henderson Harbor (which could be done in as little as thirty hours) was much delayed by winds and storms. Few of Boyd's units made it in less than a week – Second Lieutenant Joseph Dwight of the Thirteenth Infantry took fifteen days and Captain Mordecai Myers of the same regiment twenty. Myers remembered that his boat travelled "in continual gales, making ports for shelter as often as possible." Sometimes they "would land on the beach where no inlet was to be seen; a hundred men with spades would soon remove a bar of sand thrown up by the surf, and open a passage to a commodious bay." It was a rough and dangerous passage as his unit was "much scattered during the descent; many of our boats were stranded."[45] A few lucky units took passage on Chauncey's squadron but for the majority it was a hard journey to an ultimate destination no one could guess. "I think the object is to make a decent [sic] on Montreal," wrote Captain Richard Goodell of the Twenty-Third Infantry to his father, "some think it Kingston but let it be where it may, I will write you as soon as we secure an independent post in the Enemy's country, should my life be spared."[46]

Wilkinson arrived at Sackets Harbor on 3 October. During his five-week absence, Swartout and Brown had been busy – Swartout later confessed so busy "that he did not know the day of the month, or the week."[47] Starting with a nucleus of three small schooners, four Durham boats and eight batteaux capable of transporting about a thousand men, they had constructed, purchased or requisitioned enough watercraft (including those in use by the division moving from the Niagara) to carry between seven and eight thousand, their arms, provisions, ammunition and stores. This miniature armada, numbering just over three hundred vessels, consisted mainly of Durham boats and batteaux. The former had a rounded bow and a square stern, a rudder and mast, and depending on size, could transport between sixty and seventy-five men plus stores. The smaller and flat-bottomed batteau had a pointed bow and stern, was also furnished with a mast but had no rudder, and again depending on its size could carry between twenty-five and fifty men. The armada also included eleven gunboats, each mounting a 6-pdr. or 12-pdr. gun, twelve scows to carry the artillery and several small schooners to transport the senior staff and invalids. Between three and four hundred civilian boatmen had been engaged to man these craft, and Brown and Swartout had not been too choosy about whom they hired for their numbers included Canadians and enemy deserters.[48]

Horses had been procured for the artillery and two light dragoon regiments, as had ammunition, equipment and medical supplies. The stockpile of provisions was impressive. At Armstrong's orders, the contractor's agents had placed on board the watercraft 235,392 lb. of hardtack, 14,000 lb. of soap, 10,195 gallons of whisky, 5,100 lb. of candles, 2,915 gallons of vinegar, 1,391 barrels of pork and 35 barrels of salt. The two generals had been able to accomplish this work so quickly because of the knowledge of local resources possessed by Brown and his brother, Samuel, a major in the quartermaster's department.[49]

Despite all his preoccupations, Jacob Brown was in good spirits. His work was approved by his superiors, and as he wrote a correspondent, Lewis (who had resumed command at the Harbor on 24 September) was "kind and gentlemanly," otherwise his position as a general officer with major responsibilities but little professional experience would not have been "very pleasant."[50] Wilkinson had also treated Brown "with marked attention and politeness" and in "the situation in which I am placed know well his views."[51] It was the new general's opinion that his superior was "no common Man" but a commander who "views things as they really are and I do not doubt but that with the smile of heaven something will yet be done worthy of the American nation."

What this uncommon man was going to do was still not settled, at least in his own mind. On 4 October, the day after his arrival, Wilkinson met with Armstrong, in the company of Lewis and Brown, and, according to the secretary, protested "freely and warmly against making an attack on Kingston, urging the propriety of passing that post and of going directly to Montreal." Armstrong "differed from General Wilkinson in opinion" but agreed to a formal council the following day when the matter would be settled – once and for all.[52]

At the meeting Wilkinson presented his views in a memorandum drafted by his staff. He admitted that an attack on Kingston would "demolish a stronghold of the enemy" and "destroy his naval depot and magazines of every variety." This would not only place the British forces in the Niagara "in great difficulty" but also result in American control of Lake Ontario for the indefinite future. Set against this, however, was that such an operation might take more time "than we calculate on," encumber the army with sick and wounded and possibly not result in the destruction of Yeo's squadron, which might elude Chauncey and "overtake us on the St. Lawrence." The result, Wilkinson concluded, would in "the first place, from the lateness of the season, the loss of a few days may expose us to the autumnal rains, and jeopard the chief object of the campaign." Second, he continued, "our own force will be diminished and our movements retarded; and in the third place, the chief object of the campaign, *the capture of Montreal*, will be utterly defeated, and our own army subjected to great difficulties, losses and perils."[53]

Armstrong responded that the weather was improving, the lake was navigable by Wilkinson's transport, and since the enemy's main force was in the

Niagara as was the British squadron, Kingston must be weakly defended. It should therefore be possible to seize the high ground east of the town, and if that happened, the "time necessary to reduce the place will not exceed a single day, and of course will not materially interfere, on that account, with our object below." The advantages of taking the British base were manifest: "you sever the enemy's line of communication and you expel him from his only secure harbor." In Armstrong's opinion, the "only safe decision" was to attack Kingston if – but the secretary added some qualifications as he always did – "the British fleet shall not escape Commodore Chauncey, and get into Kingston harbour; if the garrison of that place be not largely reinforced; and if the weather be such as will allow us to navigate the lake securely." If all or some of these variables remained in American favour, "Kingston shall be our first object"; otherwise, the secretary concluded, "we shall go directly to Montreal."[54]

These discussions marked the beginning of a rift between Armstrong and Wilkinson. Colonel Joseph Swift, who was to act as Wilkinson's chief of staff throughout the forthcoming campaign, thought their relations became "too formal for that ease which is desirable for the interchange of opinion among chieftains."[55] The result, in Swift's opinion, was "an inactivity that, as it seemed to me arose, from some doubts as to who was in command, General Armstrong or General Wilkinson." Wilkinson had worried about just such a situation when Armstrong informed him in Washington of his intention to go north and he had then asked the secretary not to "interfere with my arrangements or give orders within the district of my command but to myself, because it would impair my authority and distract the public service." "Two heads on the same shoulders," he cautioned, "make a monster."[56]

That very circumstance had now come to pass, with the added complication that the two men were becoming suspicious of each other's motives. Swift was alarmed about the widening breach and also about Wilkinson's attitude toward Hampton:

> In my interviews with General Wilkinson his expressions implied a strong dislike of the interference of the War Department, and in fact the presence of the Secretary did lessen the influence of General Wilkinson. The contemplated junction with Hampton was a subject of discourse, and General Wilkinson indulged in a too public expression of his dislike to General Hampton, which, on one occasion gave me a fair opportunity of saying to General Wilkinson that his remarks tended to revive the feuds and party feelings of the army that had been described before [Wilkinson's] court martial at Fredericksburg in 1811.[57]

Wade Hampton's attitude was no better. Colonel John Walbach, Wilkinson's adjutant general, who visited Burlington, Vermont, returned to the Harbor with some of the returns Wilkinson had requested in August and reported to Wilkinson that Hampton had handed them over with the comment that he could "inform General Wilkinson, *that, in case of necessity,* I should feel no dislike, to co-operate with him; notwithstanding, I understood when I left Washington, that I was to have a separate and independent command."[58]

Hampton was still waiting at the Four Corners for orders to advance into Lower Canada. By 12 October he had become anxious about the lack of them and complained to Armstrong that his need "to know your progress, and the real state of the *grand army* is extreme," and asked to "be constantly informed" as "implicit faith, cordiality and concert ought to unite our efforts."[59] Hampton's biggest concern was the proposed junction point with Wilkinson as his division would need to start earlier and he had to "judge the obstacles on the way."

While Hampton marked time, Wilkinson continued his preparations at the Harbor. His intention to concentrate on Grenadier Island would need the support of Chauncey's squadron and on 9 October Armstrong queried Wilkinson if he and the commodore had a "clear and distinct understanding on the subject of our plan of operations, and the kind and degree of assistance [Chauncey] will be able to give to its execution?" After some discussion, the two respective commanders agreed that the navy would protect the army if it landed above Kingston or moved down the St. Lawrence. Satisfied, Wilkinson told Armstrong that he and Chauncey "understood each other perfectly & I think we shall harmonize to the End."[60]

On 11 October, Wilkinson sent a senior aide, Major Henry Lee, to the secretary to tell him that he had now decided that Kingston must be attacked but that the attack should be made from the west, as suggested by Chauncey, not from the east, as proposed by Armstrong. It was Wilkinson's opinion that "the possession, or demolition of Kingston, was a necessary preliminary, to the conquest of Upper Canada" and "his mind was so resolved on this course of action, that nothing short of an official direction from the secretary of war" would "cause him to refrain from it; or to adopt any other, which had been proposed to him." After trying to avoid doing so for more than two months, James Wilkinson had finally grasped the nettle and Lee recorded that the secretary naturally "expressed his agreement."[61]

The operation seemed to be on the right path at last, but three factors combined to derail all plans. First, the troops' slow progress from Fort George to Henderson Harbor – it was not until 15 October that Boyd's command was complete at the latter place. Second, on 5 October Wilkinson "was assailed by a violent ague, followed by a fever" that confined him to his bed for nearly two weeks although he continued to transact business. According to Wilkinson, he told the secretary at this time that "due to my incapacity to command," Armstrong should propose that "I retire from it." The secretary replied that there was no officer who could take Wilkinson's place, he "could not be spared" and therefore "must accompany the expedition."[62]

The third factor was the weather, which remained boisterous. Boyd recalled that his troops at Henderson Harbor experienced "one of the worst storms that was ever witnessed" and that "it was a matter of curiosity to see twenty or thirty large trees blown down by it."[63] Wilkinson had planned to begin the movement to Grenadier Island on 5 October but this operation was delayed until Chauncey's squadron had returned. The squadron anchored late on 6 October, but the following day was consumed dealing with the two hundred prisoners the commodore had taken on board from the British transport vessels captured on the lake. On the 8th, the weather turned bad as autumnal gales swept in and remained bad, blowing and variable, for much of the next two weeks. Not until 16 October did the first units start embarking for Grenadier.[64]

Despite the lengthy wait and the uncertainty, the officers and men of the northern army were in good fettle. Captain Rufus McIntire regarded the confusion about their ultimate destination as a matter of security and praised his general for throwing "a mystery over our army" as "manoeuvres and future intentions that are impenetrable" are "highly necessary when so near the enemy and where everything that can be known is immediately communicated to the enemy."[65] Brown, who knew more than most, remained confident: "I am very willing to stake my Fortune upon the success of the Campaign as now laid out," he wrote a correspondent, "if the plan is firmly and steadily adhered to," but "what the plan is, is none of your Business."[66] The aide-de-camp, the Chickahominy wag and the rest of their merry crew took it all in their stride. While waiting for the weather to clear and the "Big Bugs" to make up their minds, they polished off the cask of wine from which they had intended to drink the last glasses in triumph in Montreal but "inactivity and delays had postponed the conquest of that place" and "the outpourings of a tapped cask, like the course of time and tide, are not easily restrained."[67]

CHAPTER 4

"God knows when we shall set out"

LAST-MINUTE PLANS AND PREPARATIONS
OCTOBER 1813

Come all ye bold Canadians,
I'd have you lend an ear
Unto a short ditty
Which will your spirits cheer,
Concerning an engagement
We had at Detroit town,
The pride of those Yankee boys
So bravely we took down.

The Yankees did invade us,
To kill and to destroy,
And to distress our country,
Our peace for to annoy,
Our countrymen were filled
With sorrow, grief and woe,
To think that they should fall
By such an unnatural foe.

Come all ye bold Canadians,
Enlisted in the cause,
To defend your country,
And to maintain your laws;
Being all united,
This is the song we'll sing:
Success unto Great Britain
And God save the King![1]

The delay on the part of the American commanders had one positive result: it totally confused their British counterparts. In late August, after learning that Armstrong and Wilkinson had arrived at Sackets Harbor, Sir George Prevost had hurried from the Niagara to Kingston fully expecting the enemy would attack that place, but when nothing happened, he and his subordinates began to wonder what was brewing.

By September, Major General Francis de Rottenburg, the commander in Upper Canada, had become heartily sick of maintaining the blockade around Fort George. His forces were wasting away from disease, and the situation was so grave that de Rottenburg received permission from Prevost to withdraw the troops "to a more healthy situation" at Burlington Bay.[2] He was reluctant to do so because if he fell back de Rottenburg knew he would "lose all resources of the fertile country in my rear." The inconclusive naval engagements on the lake gave him no comfort – "the hostile fleets have been distressing us with scientific manoeuvres," he complained to Prevost and warned that if he did not receive "fresh troops the country will be lost for want of hands to defend it."[3]

On 16 September things got worse for de Rottenburg when he learned of Perry's victory on Lake Erie and the retreat of Major General Procter's army east from Amherstburg toward Lake Ontario. He wanted to pull back from Fort George but reluctantly decided to hold on in the hope that the question of naval superiority on the lake would be settled in Yeo's favour. Confessing to Prevost on 28 September that his movements "must now depend on the issue of this [the naval] action," de Rottenburg steeled himself for the worst, "prepared to meet disaster with fortitude" and promised that "any retrograde movement I may be compelled to make shall be done deliberately and without precipitation" as the fate of Upper Canada "must be decided in a few days."[4]

In fact it was not, as that same day the two squadrons met south of York and fought another inconclusive action. De Rottenburg was disappointed but soon had more pressing problems for news reached him a few days later about the American movement from Fort George. He began to fear for the security of Kingston and warned Brigadier General Duncan Darroch, the commander there, to be on his guard. He contemplated withdrawing his troops from the Niagara to Kingston but was pinned in place by his need to remain until Procter's retreating army joined him. He decided instead to shift a considerable part of his force to Kingston in small boats and go there himself. Command of the forces in the Niagara now devolved on Major General John Vincent, who was ordered to concentrate his troops, hold on in front of Fort George as long as possible to keep contact with Procter, but ultimately to withdraw to Burlington Bay.[5]

John Le Couteur and his comrades "thoroughly rejoiced" at getting out of the Niagara. The 104th and 49th Foot, together with three companies of the Canadian Voltigeurs, were "embarked in boats and pushed on with the greatest of haste." Reaching Burlington Bay, they "passed through the fleet and gave them three Jolly cheers" and the "Men-of-War returned the Compliment by manning their yards." The little flotilla made better progress than its American counterpart on the south shore of the lake, reaching York at midnight on 5 October, "wet and miserable," and started out again at daybreak, "cold and cheerless." That day, Le Couteur recalled, the waves were "so high that in our fleet, when two were in the trough of the Sea, the Crews entirely lost sight of each other," and more than once someone in his boat would see a massive wave approach and shout, "Here comes our finisher!" Finally, at 1 A.M. on 7 October they reached Kingston and a very tired eighteen-year-old stretched himself out "on the carpet near the Stove at Thibodo's Hotel" because "there was no bed to be had."[6]

The arrival of these reinforcements, amounting to about 1,100 men who, Darroch noted, "do not look overwell," was the cause of much rejoicing.[7] As the Kingston *Gazette* put it:

> By all accounts we understand that the Americans are on the eve of attacking this place. It is our province to observe that their intentions have been completely anticipated and every necessary preparation has been made to give them a warm reception. ...... [The arrival of these] three gallant Regiments together with our brave Militia who are pouring in from all quarters and have already assembled in considerable numbers will be a sufficient reinforcement and with our present respectable garrison will be able to repel any force which the enemy may be able to bring against us. ...... We are glad to observe that every piece of artillery is most advantageously posted and we must really congratulate our fellow citizens on the formidable appearance of every defensible position in the vicinity of this town.[8]

German veteran – Major General Francis de Rottenburg (1757-1832)
A German officer serving in the British army, de Rottenburg was the commanding general in Upper Canada during the summer and autumn of 1813. He was competent but, at age 55, somewhat past his prime. De Rottenburg was a light infantry specialist, the author of a standard manual on rifle and light infantry tactics, and the patron of Lieutenant Colonel Charles de Salaberry, who would perform well during the forthcoming campaign. (*Journal of the Society for Army Historical Research*, 1931)

69

The two senior officers in eastern Upper Canada, Darroch at Kingston and Lieutenant Colonel Thomas Pearson at Prescott on the St. Lawrence, enjoyed a steady stream of information from various sources. When they first learned of the enemy movement from the Niagara, Darroch was convinced that the American objective was Kingston but Pearson thought his own post was the American target. On 6 October Darroch sent a spy over to the Harbor and a few days later, provided with up-to-date intelligence from this man, warned Prevost that Montreal might be the real enemy objective. Prevost, who had returned to that city at the end of September, agreed and took steps to strengthen the defences of Lower Canada. The British commander-in-chief was aware that he would shortly face a major enemy offensive. As he confessed to Bathurst, the force "now assembled by the enemy at different points for the purpose of invading these provinces is greater than at any other period during the war." Prevost was particularly concerned about Hampton's position at the Four Corners, which forced him to "concentrate a considerable body of troops to protect" Montreal while at the same time Hampton "has it in his power to molest the communication with the Upper Province and impede the progress of the stores required there for the navy and army."[9]

British bewilderment increased, however, when Hampton appeared to be nailed to the Four Corners, although Pearson became more and more convinced that the Americans were going to attack Montreal. On 12 October he forwarded intelligence from spies that nobody at Sackets Harbor "believes Kingston to be the point of attack, but all agree that Prescott and Montreal are the destined objects." Pearson was prepared to act "according to the movements of the enemy," and if the enemy ignored him at Prescott, he would "instantly follow" and "considerably annoy him on his descent down the river." "Whenever the enemy does appear," he concluded, "I hope to God we shall be able to get some account of him."[10]

Prevost thought any enemy movement down the St. Lawrence – a fairly risky business for the Americans – might present some good tactical opportunities, and commented to de Rottenburg he would "be disappointed should the enemy commit his vessels and small craft encumbered with troops in the narrow waters without sustaining a complete defeat."[11] He ordered de Rottenburg, now back at Kingston, to form a small "corps of observation" to follow any such attempt and directed it be placed in "the hands of an active and intelligent officer," suggesting Lieutenant Colonel Joseph Morrison of the 89th Foot, in whom he had "great confidence."[12] He also issued a rare direct order to Yeo to position his smaller vessels and gunboats at the east end of Wolfe Island at the head of the St. Lawrence while the larger warships took station in front

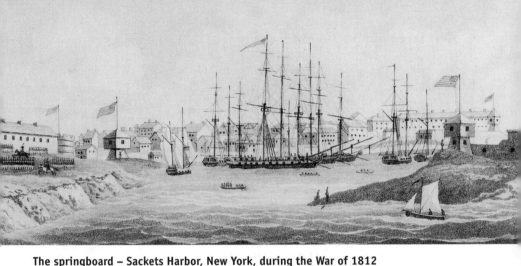

The springboard – Sackets Harbor, New York, during the War of 1812
By 1813 this little hamlet had become the major military and naval base in the United States and served as the campaign headquarters of both Armstrong and Wilkinson. It was also a very unhealthy place. (From the *Naval Chronicle*, 1818, courtesy of the U.S. Naval Historical Center, NH-1696)

of Kingston, expressing the belief that if the Americans entered the St. Lawrence it would afford the British naval commander an "opportunity of using your vessels and gunboats to the greatest advantage and enable you to defeat and distress either of these operations beyond measure."[13] In response, Yeo promised to make "every effort" but he was not pleased about dividing his squadron, warning that "nothing but your Excellency's pointed Instructions on that head could have induced me to it."[14]

As British commanders puzzled and prepared in the first weeks of October, disaster struck. On 5 October Harrison's army caught up with Procter's division near the hamlet of Moraviantown on the Thames River. The British force was swept away in a matter of minutes, and Tecumseh, the great Shawnee leader, was killed. The division disintegrated into a flood of refugees heading east for Burlington Bay, and one of the first survivors to reach that place spread such a tale of woe as to inspire a near panic in Major General John Vincent. On hearing the grim news, de Rottenburg took it upon himself to cancel Prevost's orders about the deployment of Yeo's squadron and, instead, sent the commodore to Burlington Bay to succour Procter, a task "of greater importance than any other on which the squadron can be employed."[15] Vincent ordered a withdrawal by forced march from Fort George to the Twelve-Mile Creek and was anxious to continue to Burlington Bay "without delay" but feared that a rapid movement would require him to leave his sick, stores and baggage. He managed to get the sick away but abandoned almost everything else – Commissary Thomas Gibbs Ridout remembered the retreat, which took

The key – Kingston, Upper Canada, during the War of 1812
The British equivalent of Sackets Harbor, the village of Kingston and the Royal Dockyard (in the centre of the engraving) were Armstrong's prime objectives in 1813. If Kingston fell, all British territory to the west would be in jeopardy. (From Ronald Way, "The Day of Crysler's Farm," *Canadian Geographical Magazine*, 1961).

place on 9 October, as a "most dreadful time" with more than "300 men … straggling upon the road, and waggons loaded with miserable objects stuck fast in mudholes, broken down and unable to ascend the hills, and the men too ill to stir hand or foot."[16]

Arriving at Burlington Bay, Vincent next requested permission to fall back to Kingston, abandoning western and central Upper Canada, but he gradually calmed down after more accurate reports revealed that Procter's situation was not as bad as first feared. Both his superiors were annoyed with his conduct: de Rottenburg thought the retreat was "effected in a most shameful manner and with unnecessary precipitation," and although he granted permission for Vincent to withdraw to York if he thought necessary, he ordered him to then leave a strong rear guard at Burlington Bay.[17] Prevost was furious – he informed de Rottenburg that Vincent's panicky and bungled withdrawal "stamps that officer in my mind as one incapable of performing an arduous task," and in a not very subtle reference to the fact that new senior officers were on their way from Britain, warned the commander in Upper Canada that "I shall have generals enough soon."[18]

Secretary of War Armstrong learned of the British reinforcement of Kingston on 16 October. He immediately about-faced, telling Madison that as the British were no longer "naked and napping," an attack on that place was not viable and, moreover, although it might be possible to bring Hampton's division across to increase Wilkinson's strength, such a movement would cause further delay and "compel us to abandon the other and better object below," meaning Montreal.[19] In public, Armstrong continued to behave as if that objective was attainable and on 19 October wrote Hampton that the plan "is lost so far as regards Kingston" even if the importance of that objective "may, however, justify the means" – which must have left Hampton scratching his head to divine the secretary's meaning.[20] If the main army moved on Montreal, Armstrong wanted Hampton to march to "the mouth of the Chateauguay or other point which shall favor our junction and hold the enemy in check," adding that Hampton's "vigilance and skill" made it "unnecessary to suggest any measures of precaution against the enterprises of the enemy while you remain within stroke of him." John Armstrong had assumed command.

It is evident, however, from his private correspondence and his postwar comments that the secretary now had serious doubts that Wilkinson or Hampton, or both, would reach Montreal in 1813. In later years he wrote that he suspected "early in October, from the lateness of the season, the inclemency of the weather, and the continued indisposition of the commanding general, that the campaign then in progress would terminate" with "the disgrace of doing nothing, but without any material diminution of physical power."[21] He appears to have reached that decision on 16 October because that day he issued an order to Brigadier General Robert Swartout, the quartermaster of the northern army, to establish a winter camp, which might be construed as an admission that the operation was over. Armstrong's instructions were:

> To be prepared against contingencies, as to winter quarters, you will dispatch an active intelligent assistant to the Chateaugay river, who will report to General Hampton, and take his directions. With regard to the place of hutting an army, of ten thousand men, the views which should govern in

The storekeeper who would be a general – Brigadier General Robert Swartout (1778-1831)
A merchant and former militia officer, Swartout was appointed to succeed Morgan Lewis as quartermaster general in the spring of 1813. Dissatisfied with his duties in that office, he hankered to command troops in battle and, against Wilkinson's better judgement, Armstrong granted Swartout his wish. (From *American Historical Register*, 1896)

making the selection, are healthiness and military strength of position; fa-
cility of supply; future and prompt operations against the enemy; and the
government of the cantonment and its environs, by martial law exclusively.
This last will necessarily carry it, within the limits of Canada.[22]

If the winter camp was located on the territory of the United States, civil
law would prevail immediately outside its perimeter, so Armstrong wanted it
in Canadian territory, where stricter martial law would discourage desertion.
He later commented to Madison that this order "showed only wisdom and
foresight" because the "failure of the enterprize was a possible event & being
such was guarded against." "If we got to Montreal," he concluded, "we but lost
the labor," but "if we did not get to the city – a covering for the army was provided." It was a sensible precaution, but Armstrong did not see fit to give Wilkinson a copy of this order.[23]

Wilkinson, meanwhile, had taken the opportunity of the latest delays to re-
organize his army. This task was necessary because many of his regiments had
been split over the summer into separate detachments at Sackets Harbor or
the Niagara and because a new brigade had to be formed for Swartout. The
quartermaster had appealed directly to Armstrong for a command in the line
and Wilkinson had acceded to the secretary's wish despite the fact that Swartout had no experience. This resulted in the rearrangement of the infantry
from three to four brigades (see Appendix D). Each brigade – Boyd's First,
Brown's Second, Covington's Third and Swartout's Fourth – was given three
infantry regiments, while Colonel Alexander Macomb assumed command of
a Reserve brigade (later renamed the "Elite") which consisted of the Third Artillery acting as infantry, a strong detachment of the Rifle Regiment, the
Albany Volunteers and the First and Second Regiments of Light Dragoons.
The artillery, which consisted of between twenty and thirty-five weapons
ranging from light field guns to heavy siege pieces, was under the command of
the recently promoted Brigadier General Moses Porter. Other units were on
their way and it was hoped they would join at Grenadier Island. Wilkinson's
total strength was between 7,300 and 7,500 men but many were sick.[24]

Wilkinson's relationship with Armstrong continued to deteriorate. On 16
October they had another brush over their respective authority when Armstrong, without informing Wilkinson, ordered Chauncey to take the squadron
and pick up some reinforcements at the mouth of the Genesee River. Since this
would leave the movement to Grenadier Island unguarded, Wilkinson was
rightfully furious and informed the naval commander that, as "this arrangement was made without my knowledge or approval" he was "not responsible

for its consequences."[25] Two days later, Wilkinson requested Armstrong to revoke the order the secretary had issued Hampton to advance to the mouth of the Châteauguay and instead direct him to move to Morrisville (modern Morristown, New York) on the St. Lawrence "as rapidly as may be consistent with the health of his troops."[26] This change of plan, the general explained, was because of the high rate of sickness in the main army, the uncertain weather and the frequent delays, and it was "founded on the presumption that we make the reduction of Kingston and the conquests of the upper province the first objects of our operations."[27]

Armstrong did not agree. On 19 October, three days after he had made up his mind that Montreal could not be taken, he informed Wilkinson that he would not order Hampton to Morrisville nor did he now advise an attack on Kingston as such an operation would "surround us with the embarrassments of a Canadian winter, and extinguish the other, the safer and the greater object below."[28] If, however, Wilkinson should think those same "embarrassments" ruled out an attack on Montreal, the secretary was willing to listen to arguments but he had to insist that Wilkinson move against that city in accordance with a plan "which, besides the approbation of the President, has received the sanction of a [cabinet] council of war." Again, Armstrong made no mention of the order he had issued to construct winter quarters for both Wilkinson and Hampton's troops.

Wilkinson received this communication just as he was about to embark for Grenadier Island. Since it affected all his plans he immediately replied, summarizing the arguments in favour of attacking Kingston put forward over the past three months (mainly by Armstrong) and although "personal considerations would make me prefer a visit to Montreal to the attack of Kingston," warning the secretary that changing objectives at this late date might prove disastrous. "Having passed Kingston," he cautioned, "the fortifications at Prescott may present such an obstacle to our further progress, as to compel us to land and reduce it by force – an operation which might consume more time than can be spared at this advanced season." And even "should we surmount every obstacle in descending the river, we shall advance upon Montreal ignorant of the force arrayed against us, and in case of misfortune, having no retreat, the army must surrender at discretion." Plainly, Wilkinson's confidence in the forthcoming operation and his superior had evaporated and he was beginning to think about the consequences of failure. He therefore informed Armstrong that it was necessary "*to my justification*" that the secretary "should by the *authority of the President*, direct the operations of the army under my command, *particularly against Montreal*."[29]

75

Armstrong sidestepped an obvious trap. He pointed out that Wilkinson's original instructions made Kingston "the principal object" and that he had been left the choice to accomplish it by a direct or indirect attack. As Kingston was now reinforced, a direct attack was out of the question but an indirect attack, via Montreal, might still be viable – in other words, by attacking Montreal Wilkinson would be carrying out his original orders to take Kingston. They therefore needed no further elaboration or confirmation on the secretary's part as they neither infringed Wilkinson's "right of choice" nor "*lessened his responsibility.*" As for issuing additional written orders, the secretary did not feel "at liberty to change the ground" of the earlier instructions since the "only effect of this would be to substitute my opinion for yours." Concluding that these were "the best thoughts I can offer," Armstrong warmly added "to them my best wishes for your army and yourself" and, a few days later, rode out of Sackets Harbor with his entourage, leaving Wilkinson with the impression he was going to follow him down the St. Lawrence by land.[30]

This latest exchange demonstrates, as one historian has written, that Wilkinson "believed Armstrong to be trying to evade responsibility, as Armstrong believed Wilkinson to be trying to shirk it."[31] Both men knew that the operation was over, for all practical purposes, but neither dared speak that thought aloud as "there would have inevitably been embarrassing questions asked about the abandonment of a campaign before it had ever started."[32] Washington expected results and Republican newspapers throughout the nation were reprinting an editorial from the Philadelphia *Aurora* which boasted that "the general of the enemy has found his superior in the field and been completely outgeneralled" as the "war minister [Armstrong] and his commander-in-chief concur in the opinion that in order to fell the tree, we must not begin at the top branches but strike at the stump."[33] The offensive would go forward, not because it had any chance of success but because to cancel it at this late date would make things difficult for the secretary of war and his senior general. Like it nor not, Wilkinson was going to have to make a try for Montreal, an operation that would require his army leaving a "hostile fleet and fortresses" in their rear and running "past every fortified position" on the St. Lawrence" only to arrive "in the heart of a comparably well populated country, held by a force greater than their own" while having "no certain base of supplies, reinforcements, or path of escape."[34] All this and a Canadian winter coming on.

Incredibly, however, neither Armstrong nor Wilkinson saw fit to inform Chauncey of the change in objective, leaving the naval commander under the impression that the troops moving to Grenadier would shortly be headed for Kingston. "The weather for the last three days," he reported to Secretary of the

Navy William Jones on 27 October, "has been so boisterous that I have not had communication" with Wilkinson and "consequently, am ignorant" just "when the army intends to move for its ulterior destination."[35] Becoming concerned, he visited Wilkinson on Grenadier on 29 October and only then learned the army was going to Montreal. Furious, he complained to Jones that he "was much disappointed and mortified to find that the General had taken his determination to descend the St. Lawrence and attack Montreal in preference to Kingston" despite the fact that, "in all our consultations upon this subject for the last four weeks, Kingston was fixed upon as the point to be first attacked; and when I parted with the Secretary of War on the 16th [of October] I understood that it was his decided opinion that Kingston should be first reduced."[36] He was the angrier because his squadron would now be "used as a mear [sic] attendant upon the Army for the purpose of Transport and protection" and then, with "the Season too far advanced to cruise in the Lake with safety," it would be "left to protect itself [at Sackets Harbor] in the best manner it can, without the possibility of participating in any enterprize against the enemy this season."

Chauncey was not the only senior officer with doubts. The night before his brigade embarked for Grenadier Island, Leonard Covington drafted a memorandum to Morgan Lewis, his immediate superior. Covington regarded the order "to embark upon the watery, unstable Element" as "highly inauspicious" because "his transports are leaky & unsound, much crowded & entirely exposed to the weather & secondly because we lack the proper Navigators, Charts & pilots to conduct us with safety, being unacquainted with the waters over which we are to pass." It was his "solemn duty," Covington concluded, to apprise Lewis of these dangers "which may destroy the lives of hundreds" in "the melancholy event of disaster."[37]

G renadier Island is situated at the eastern end of Lake Ontario about a mile off the headland at Gravelly Point, New York, near the confluence of the lake and the St. Lawrence. Lying midway between Sackets Harbor and Kingston, Grenadier was an ideal staging point, within easy distance of both the Harbor and the St. Lawrence and with enough sea-room for Chauncey's ships to protect it. The island consists of about a thousand very fertile acres and there is a spacious bay at its southeastern tip, Basin Harbor, which formed a good anchorage for the flotilla of boats transporting the army.[38]

The first units embarked for Grenadier on 16 October. They made a quick and safe passage and two days later Boyd and Brown embarked their brigades, followed over the next four days by the remaining troops. This latter movement, however, ran into serious trouble as high winds from the west combined with squalls and storms to cause rough seas. Many boats and some larger vessels were blown ashore on the mainland or stranded on other islands, and when Morgan Lewis embarked in the late afternoon of 21 October he saw bonfires lit by marooned parties along the entire lake shore from Sackets Harbor to Grenadier. One of the artillery scows was lost with its cargo, and two small schooners, carrying two hundred sick men, ran aground on a rocky ledge about a mile from shore and were about to founder when Captain Mordecai Myers of the Thirteenth Infantry volunteered to rescue those on board. With three boats and thirty men, he managed to reach the wrecks with great difficulty as they were "lying on the rocks with the sails blowing in every direction and the breakers making a full sweep over them."[39] Boarding the schooners, Myers found them full of ill and terrified soldiers but could discover no sign of the crews until he came across the captain of one of the vessels "in an upper berth in the forecastle," which he refused to leave. Myers used the flat of his sword to encourage the man to do his duty, and after his party had transported thirteen boatloads of sick men to safety, the young officer left the vessels just before they disintegrated.[40]

When Wilkinson arrived at Grenadier in the naval schooner *Lady of the Lake* on 23 October, he assessed the damage. The news was bad. Of the 340,000 rations (one ration being enough food to feed a soldier for a day), no fewer than 150,000, nearly half the army's provisions, had been lost in transit, while the ordnance and medical supplies and ammunition had also suffered heavy loss or damage. There was, moreover, great difficulty establishing just what was lost because apparently no master cargo lists had been kept of what stores had been placed in each boat, so that in order to find an article, all the craft had to be searched. Almost all the heavily laden craft were being used as troop transports, but the infantry and artillery officers in charge of them saw no reason they should be responsible for what was, after all, the property of the quartermaster's department, and they permitted wet and shivering soldiers to strip the painted, waterproof covers off the casks of provisions and use them as makeshift rain gear, leaving the contents to spoil. Not that the quartermaster's department seemed all that concerned. When one artillery officer complained at the Harbor that his scow was so full of entrenching tools, medical supplies and other stores that he might have to toss them overboard in a heavy sea, a quartermaster told him he "might throw them to the devil" for all he cared.[41] Just to complete the disagreeables, about one-third of the army's water transport had been lost or severely damaged, either in transit, or at Grenadier Island, where many of the boats that did arrive dragged their anchors in the high seas and ran onto the rocks, stove in other craft or disappeared out on the lake.[42]

This disaster, coupled with the scattering of his units on passage, inflicted yet more delay as Wilkinson tried to sort out the mess. Orders were issued to repair all boats that could be repaired and military artificers were brought from the Harbor to supervise this work. Marooned and delayed units straggled into Basin Harbor for days after the main army landed; according to Lewis, it was not until 3 November that the last regiment showed up. Finding that much of the winter clothing had been left at Sackets, Wilkinson ordered it brought forward to Grenadier for distribution. It was needed, for ten inches of snow fell on 27-28 October, and mixed with the snow was almost continuous rain – one officer recalled that the troops on the island were "pelted daily with the inexhaustible rains, which seem to be collected and poured upon us from all the lakes and swamps between this and Lake Superior."[43]

While he waited, Wilkinson made his final preparations. Swift and some assistants were dispatched down the American side of the St. Lawrence to examine Prescott and "obtain the best plan of it; measure the width of the river, at that place, determine the nature and strength of the currents; the position of the shoals in the neighbourhood; and generally to find the best landing places, and procure pilots for the rapids; with a view to the flotilla passing Prescott."[44] Wilkinson also tried to co-ordinate his movements with those of the secretary of war. He was under the impression that Armstrong would be joining him at Ogdensburg but soon learned this would not be the case. The secretary wrote on 27 October from the hamlet of Antwerp, midway between Sackets Harbor and Ogdensburg, that he had been taken ill, and should his "fever continue, I shall not be able to approach you as I had intended." Instead, he advised Wilkinson to send a copy of any communications to Washington, where Armstrong was about to head. "Adieu," wrote the secretary, "all kinds of prosperity attend you."[45]

Wilkinson had not yet received this communication when he wrote Armstrong the following day to inform him of the delay occasioned by the storm and of his intention to slip the army by detachments into the St. Lawrence to rendezvous at French Creek (modern Clayton, New York). As time was running short, he had decided not to attack Prescott but to bypass it under cover of darkness. Leaving this enemy position in his rear was "no matter," he confidently assured the secretary, as "our Bayonets and Sabres shall remove all impediments."[46] In reply, Armstrong approved this decision but explained that although he had planned to meet Wilkinson near Ogdensburg, "bad roads, worse weather, and a considerable degree of illness," prevented him from travelling further from Washington, where the press of official business demanded his urgent return. "It remains with you," he cheerfully informed his senior general, "to sweep the rest of the line before you. Montreal taken, what are Prescott and Kingston?" But the important thing, the secretary noted, was for Wilkinson to give Hampton "timely notice of your approach and of the place and hour of junction."[47]

Although conditions on Grenadier Island were often miserable, the army's morale remained good. After nearly five months of inactivity and stagnation, the troops knew that something big was afoot and that was enough to lift their spirits. Captain John Walworth of the Sixth Infantry wrote that "we have had a very boisterous time of it in our open Boats" as it "had rained almost all the time since we started [from Fort George]" and the "wind has been extremely heavy."[48] Despite this, Walworth was excited, for great "preparations have been made to do something brilliant before the close of the campaign and unless some unforseen accident takes place," he was confident "this Army will winter in Montreal." The aide-de-camp and his companions did not overly concern themselves about such matters. In their tent, "the joke was cracked" and "Old King Twine" was "encored many a time and oft, until we all had caught sufficient of the merry strain to join in the general chorus."[49]

During the intermittent periods of good weather, life was not unpleasant on Grenadier. There were a number of farms under cultivation and there was one young woman on the island who immediately became the "object of more interest and admiration than often falls to the lot of the most dominant city belle." Her officer admirers christened her the "Lady of the Lake" but the "unexpected incense thus offered up to her few charms almost turned her head." She was "suddenly converted, by some military magic, from a Cinder-breech into a Cinderella, and flaunted about in her linsey-woolsey gown and checked apron, with more airs than many a lady feels authorized to assume, even when arrayed in lame and tulle" and "would not speak to a colonel, would hardly look at a captain, and would almost spit in the face of a subaltern, who hazarded a side-long glance of admiration."[50]

Being only fourteen years old, Drummer Jarvis Hanks of the Eleventh Infantry was more interested in food than girls and recalled with satisfaction how his comrades came across an unexpected bonanza. A nearby farmer "had still in the ground a number of hundreds of bushels of potatoes" and the owner "was offered fifty cents a bushel for them, if he would dispose of as many as were wanted for that price" but this proposition was refused by the farmer, who added "with an air of triumph, and self complacence," that he "could get a dollar a bushel for them in Kingston." When word of this spread, "it was decided that he would be saved the trouble and expense of digging his potatoes, and of transporting them to market," and the army "relieved him of the burden." When the outraged farmer "applied to the officers to remunerate him for his loss, they gave him no encouragement, or consolation, in the premises, and he retired, lamenting his unwise decision."[51]

By the last days of the month, Wilkinson's army was as ready as it would ever be. On 27 October, Brown managed to leave Basin Harbor with his Second Brigade to establish the rendezvous point at French Creek. The rest of the army embarked the next day; rain, snow and severe winds forced them back and they had to wait another two days before making a second try, but again heavy winds and high seas caused a cancellation of the movement. "God knows when we shall set out from hence," Morgan Lewis wrote his wife, if "we do not in a few days we may as well abandon our expedition, for the winter will soon begin here."[52]

E ighteen miles directly across Lake Ontario from Lewis, Lieutenant John Le Couteur had discovered that soldiering sometimes has its rewards. On his return to Kingston the young officer had been afflicted with boils on his legs (probably brought on by poor diet in the Niagara), which restricted him to the house of the elderly widow where he boarded. His many lady friends, however, sent him novels to pass the time, and as he fondly recalled in later years, "some of these I read aloud of an evening, to a coterie of sweet girls, three or four, whom the old Lady permitted to listen to me."[53] Le Couteur was confident about the outcome of any attack on Kingston – as he wrote a friend in England: "We shall give them a warm and spirited reception as they have no right or pretension whatever in attacking and disturbing the peaceable inhabitants" of the city. He was so annoyed at the Americans that he paid "the rascals" his supreme insult: "They are worse than Frenchmen."[54]

While the young light infantryman rested on his laurels, his "Big Wigs," Sir George Prevost, Major General Francis de Rottenburg and other senior officers, continued to puzzle over American intentions. It was clear from the enemy concentrations at Grenadier Island and Four Corners, New York, that an attack was imminent but the target – Kingston, Prescott or Montreal – remained unknown. In the third week of October de Rottenburg actually became convinced York might be the enemy objective and gave Vincent permission to retreat there, but later cooled down and countermanded that order. De Rottenburg also continued to fear for Kingston, and throughout October the garrison worked hard to improve its defences. There were now five battalions of regular troops with part of a sixth in the village, a company of the Royal Artillery to man the fifty-five artillery pieces in the batteries defending the harbour, and a troop of regular cavalry. In addition, several regiments of local militia had been mobilized in response to orders to turn out – no one expected them to do any serious fighting, but they would be useful for labour and logistical tasks. Commodore James Yeo had the six warships of his squadron, mounting ninety-one guns, standing by, and over the summer eight gunboats, each about 60 feet in length and mounting a gun and a carronade, had been constructed. On 11 October their number was reduced when Gunboat No. 1 strayed too close to Gravelly Point near Grenadier Island and was captured.[55]

The most exposed position along the border was that of Lieutenant Colonel Thomas Pearson. He had about one thousand regulars and militia under command to hold Prescott, situated on the river 1,800 yards across from Ogdensburg. To gain information about enemy dispositions and intentions, Pearson sent local men into the United States and the most effective at this business was the thirty-eight-year-old militia Captain Reuben Sherwood from Elizabethtown (modern Brockville, Ontario), the son of a prominent Loyalist officer and the deputy land surveyor for Upper Canada. Sherwood had worked on the American side of the river, and his knowledge of the St. Lawrence country and its people was unparalleled. He was an intelligent, aggressive and ingenious man whom one British officer regarded as the "best qualified" for "superintending and organizing the procuring of secret intelligence."[56] Sherwood moved through American territory with ease and, leading a small group of militia, he so harried Swift when the engineer tried to survey the river and the defences of Prescott that Swift and his assistants were forced to do their scouting early in the morning and move from place to place under cover of darkness. On 17 October, after Sherwood informed Pearson of an isolated vedette of American dragoons at Red Mills on the American side of the St. Lawrence a few miles below Ogdensburg, Pearson organized a raid that crossed over and captured an officer and seven men. Information garnered by Sherwood and other scouts was sent to de Rottenburg at Kingston or Prevost at Montreal by means of a dragoon express established along the line of the St. Lawrence, with relays of riders every eight miles. This ability to communicate quickly gave British commanders a decided advantage over their American counterparts.[57]

For his part, Prevost was convinced that Montreal was the American target and throughout October took steps to improve its defences. The city had no permanent fortifications and the Americans would therefore have to be stopped before they reached it, but since Prevost had sent most of his regular troops to the upper province, he could count on the immediate services of only three troops of cavalry, two companies of artillery, three battalions of regular infantry and parts of two others – about three thousand men in total. There were two fine battalions of Royal Marines on the way from Quebec but, if the enemy moved down the St. Lawrence, Prevost would still need reinforcements to hold Montreal and stressed to de Rottenburg that the "corps of observation" organized at Kingston on his orders must be sent to his aid – "You will not fail in affording me the reinforcement I require the Moment the Enemy's Object is unquestionably ascertained" and de Rottenburg promised that "every exertion" would be made to do so.[58]

In Lower Canada, Prevost's second line of defence was the provincial militia and here he could call on numbers if not quality. The militia of Lower Canada had a two-tiered organization. The sedentary militia comprised all males from sixteen to sixty, organized into units by parish and district, and from this mass, bachelors aged eighteen to twenty-five were drafted by ballot for varying periods into six battalions of Select Embodied Militia. Uniformed, armed, equipped and trained as regulars, the Select Embodied units provided a useful addition to Prevost's strength. In the early days of the war there had been some doubts whether the *Canadiens* would take up arms for the Crown, and these doubts were not allayed after riots broke out when the first Embodied battalions were drafted for service in June 1812. This unrest, however, eventually settled down and the Lower Canada militia had rendered loyal service since that time.[59]

To reinforce the patriotism of the *Canadiens* and leave no doubts the situation was serious, on 18 October Prevost issued a proclamation appealing to their "loyalty, courage, and patriotism" and asking them to "be prepared to manifest the most determined devotion in resisting" an attack. "The history of the world," he confidently asserted, "abundantly proves that an united nation cannot easily be overcome," and "if with one heart and soul you are cheerfully and promptly united for their preservation, you need not fear what hosts may be opposed to you.[60]

Preparations were made to call out the sedentary militia in the Montreal area *en masse*, with each man to receive "forty Rounds of Ball Cartridge and one flint and two days Provisions ready Cooked."[61] When the "Tocsin and other Signals of Alarm" were "sounded in every Parish within fifty Miles of Montreal all Militia without exception are to assemble with Arms and those who are not possessed of Arms, with Axes, Spades and pick-axes and repair with the least possible delay to Montreal." Nearly 8,000 sedentary militia were ready for a general call-out, although only 2,000 had muskets and ammunition; the remainder would assist with the transport and supply requirements of the 3,000 regulars and the five battalions, 2,400 strong, of the Select Embodied Militia moving into position to defend the city.[62]

Prevost deployed to counter an attack on Montreal either by Hampton from the Châteauguay or one by Wilkinson down the St. Lawrence. A forward

The prize – Montreal, c. 1830
The wealthiest and most populous city in the Canadas, Montreal was the centre of the fur trade, the largest commercial activity in North America in 1813. It was not defended by permanent fortifications and British troops would have to defeat an American invasion attempt before the enemy reached the city. (Ink sketch by R.A. Sproule, National Archives of Canada, C-100559)

position was created on the Châteauguay River under Major General Louis de Watteville, a Swiss officer in British service, to guard the line of the frontier opposite Hampton, while a reserve force was built up along a cordon immediately south of the city. There was considerable troop movement in October as the various units took up their assigned positions – Lieutenant Charles Pinguet de Vaucour of the Canadian Fencibles recorded that his company spent three weeks marching across the province from one location to another but always being ordered to keep going until they finally arrived at the forward position on the Châteauguay. Meanwhile, the sedentary militia in the most threatened areas was mustered and responded with enthusiasm.[63]

As October passed and the defenders of Upper and Lower Canada completed their preparations, the people in both provinces were apprehensive. "The times are so gloomy," wrote Thomas Ridout from Burlington to his father at York, "that I know not what to say."[64] In Lower Canada, Prevost's eighteen-year-old daughter, Anne Elinor, remembered her mother being "tortured with anxiety" as "the Province was called to Arms."[65] There was not much longer to wait. On the evening of 21 October 1813 a messenger arrived at de Watteville's headquarters at Baker's house on the Châteauguay River with the information that the Americans had crossed the border and attacked an advanced picket. The invasion had begun.[66]

PART II

The Invasion

21 OCTOBER–10 NOVEMBER 1813

Shooting the rapids, November 1813
To reach Montreal by descending the St. Lawrence River, Wilkinson's flotilla of more than 300 craft of various types had to traverse the five rapids of the St. Lawrence. They formed a dangerous obstacle, as shown in this sketch by marine artist Peter Rindlisbacher.

CHAPTER 5

"Le diable au corps"

THE CHÂTEAUGUAY CAMPAIGN

Le matin, dès le point du jour,
On entend ce maudit tambour,
Maudit tambour et maudit exercice,
Toi, pauvr' soldat, tu en as d'la fatigue.

Ils nous font mettre dans les rangs,
Les officiers et les sergents,
L'un dit: recule et l'autre dit: avance!
Toi, pauvr' soldat, t'en faut de la patience.

Nos sergents et nos officiers
Sont bien traites dan leurs quartiers,
Nos capitain' boiv' le vin et la bière
Toi, pauvr' soldat, va boire à la rivière.

Qu'en a composé la chanson
C'est un tambour du bataillon
C'est un tambour en battant sa retraite
Toujours regrettant sa joli' mâitresse.[1]

After weeks of inactivity, Major General Wade Hampton's men had become fed up with Four Corners, New York. Private Charles Fairbanks of the New Hampshire Volunteers recalled that their camp was "in great danger from Indians," which meant a constant state of alert for everybody.[2] The weather was turning cooler but the division was still wearing summer clothing. Corporal Richard Bishop of the Twenty-Ninth Infantry wrote in his diary on 11 October that "it snows a little and it is very cold, the soldiers complain of cold fingers" and "wish to hear the news to go to winter quarters," and he was pleased when the troops were issued blue wool winter pants and flannel shirts a few days later.[3] There were frequent parades to witness punishments ranging from cobbing to executions, but despite such spectacles there were disciplinary problems in the camp. Bishop noted that as soon as the enlisted men were paid, they spent their money on liquor at the sutlers, and as a corporal he was constantly arresting men and escorting them to the guardhouse. "The money of the soldiers goes free," he commented, "for we keep seven or eight under guard continually for drinking – Cobb them in the morning and before night some will be under guard again, such work as stealing money and getting drunk is very familiar in the army."[4] Bishop was no more impressed with his officers and noted that three lieutenants were court-martialled for selling liquor to their own men.

Hampton was also unhappy. His communication with Armstrong at Sackets Harbor was slow and infrequent and he had no clear idea of what was happening with Wilkinson's force. To improve matters he established a dragoon express from the Four Corners to Ogdensburg, where he stationed an officer to act as liaison with the secretary and ensure the rapid transmission of orders and intelligence, but it still took considerable time to get messages to and from the main army. Deserters and spies brought information of enemy strength and movements, and Hampton attempted to draw away some of the British forces defending Montreal by "kicking up dust on the lines" or mounting diversionary raids on the Lake Champlain frontier.[5] These raids were carried out by militia, who on 12 October attacked the little village of Missisquoi just over the border and took about a hundred *Canadien* militia prisoner. This expedition caused British concern but did not have the result Hampton hoped, for Prevost did not rise to the bait and divert large numbers of troops to the Lake Champlain area.[6]

Even worse for Hampton, his own camp at Four Corners was "smartly attacked" by the enemy on 1 October although they were repulsed with the loss of two Americans killed. A week later, Hampton learned that the British forces between him and Montreal consisted of 2,100 men, of whom a third were militia, and that they were beginning to construct defensive positions along the Châteauguay River. He wrote Armstrong that his "solicitude to know your progress and the real state of the *grand army* is extreme," and, since the road down the Châteauguay required much work to be usable for troops and artillery, requested advance warning of any move on Wilkinson's part so that his division would be able to join that general before Montreal. On 16 October, Hampton actively began to prepare for such a move by issuing his men six days rations, checking their ammunition and making sure their weapons were in good order.[7]

Competent but cautious – Brigadier General George Izard (1776-1828)
One of the best-educated officers in the United States Army and a wealthy man in his own right, George Izard (shown here in the uniform of a colonel of artillery) assumed command of a brigade in Hampton's division shortly before the invasion of Canada in October 1813. Intelligent but cautious, he and Brown were the only American generals to emerge from the 1813 campaign with any credit. (Courtesy, Arkansas History Commission)

That same day he received a new senior officer when Brigadier General George Izard arrived at the Four Corners. A thirty-seven-year-old native of New York and the son of a wealthy family, George Izard had more professional military education than any other officer in the United States Army. After graduating from Columbia University at the age of fifteen in 1792, he had spent five years attending private military schools in England and Germany before becoming the first foreigner to study at the prestigious French *École du Génie* at Metz. Izard returned to the United States in 1797 to serve as a captain in the engineers but resigned in 1802 to spend the next decade as a gentleman of leisure and learning in Philadelphia. When war was declared, he was commissioned a colonel and briefly commanded the Second Artillery Regiment before being promoted brigadier general in early 1813 and succeeding Armstrong at New York City. Izard was an intelligent and well-educated but essentially very cautious officer.[8]

Hampton gave Izard his Second Brigade comprising a newly arrived battalion of the Tenth Infantry, the combined Eleventh/Twenty-Ninth Infantry and the combined Thirtieth/Thirty-First Infantry. Hampton's First Brigade, with the Fourth Infantry, the Thirty-Third Infantry and the combined Maine and New Hampshire Volunteers, was commanded by Colonel Robert Purdy, a prewar regular with nearly twenty years of service. The division was rounded out by Captain Henry Hall's squadron of the Second Light Dragoons and Major William McRee's three companies of artillery with one 12-pdr. gun, eight 6-pdr. guns and one 5$\frac{1}{2}$-inch howitzer. The total strength was about four thousand men (see Appendix B).[9]

On 18 October a deserter brought Hampton word that the enemy on the lower Châteauguay numbered only sixteen hundred, of which nearly half was said to be militia. This information, revealing "the present weakness of the enemy and rendering probable his increasing strength if left undisturbed," convinced Hampton it was "his duty to break him down without loss of time."[10] If he pushed down the Châteauguay and Prevost "was unable from want of force to check his movement, there had arisen that condition of things" which "permitted, if it did not enjoin, an attack on Montreal." About this time, Hampton received Armstrong's letter of 16 October which directed him, if Wilkinson moved down the St. Lawrence, to "approach the mouth of the Chateauguay or other point which shall favor our junction and hold the enemy in check."[11] The two things became fused in Hampton's mind – he wanted to move down the Châteauguay and the secretary of war wanted him to do the same, so advance he would. What Hampton overlooked was that Armstrong had qualified that direction by making it dependent on Wilkinson ignoring Kingston in favour of an attack on Montreal and at this point Hampton had no concrete information to that effect. By proceeding independently, he was about to do exactly what Armstrong had feared and put the two American armies in the position of making "*separate* attacks when *combined* ones are practicable and sure."[12] None the less, the orders were issued and the division prepared to break camp and move "down the Chateauguay for the purpose," Hampton later stated, "of placing itself in a situation which would enable it to fulfil its part of the proposed combined operations on the St. Lawrence."[13]

It was not going to be an easy march as the road along the Châteauguay River was a rough cart track that ran through an "extensive wood of eleven or twelve miles" blocked by "felled timber, and covered by Indians and light troops of the enemy."[14] As this wood formed "a serious impediment," Hampton ordered Izard to take an *ad hoc* force and move along a track that paralleled the river road a few miles to the southeast, bypass the obstacle and seize the open ground which lay beyond the wood. Izard took the Thirtieth/Thirty-First Infantry Regiment from his own brigade, Hall's squadron of light dragoons and the "Elite," or light infantry corps. This latter unit, which consisted of nine companies drawn from all the regiments in the division, had a total strength of seven hundred men organized in three detachments commanded by competent young majors, Josiah Snelling, John Wool and John McNeil.[15]

Thursday, 21 October 1813, the day the army set out, was very cold and Corporal Bishop recorded that the ground was "white with snow."[16] Izard got away at first light, followed by the rest of the division a few hours later. Morale was high: "our troops were in the best of spirits," wrote Bishop.[17] Sergeant Alexander Neef of the Fourth Infantry remembered that "every countenance was bright, each soldier appeared to feel as men ought to feel on such occasions" and nothing "but opportunity was wanted to add fresh laurels to the splendour of American arms."[18] The camp at Four Corners was left in the hands of a New York militia brigade who were not constitutionally required to cross the international border.

Unencumbered by artillery or wagons, Izard made quick progress and by late afternoon his advance guard was in the woods overlooking the cleared fields of a farmer named Spear, at the junction of the Châteauguay and Outardes rivers. The farmhouse was abandoned but a fire was still burning so Izard formed his troops in the fields and sent Snelling with his light infantry to reconnoitre some houses on the river bank. Snelling came across a picket of enemy militia and native warriors who, unaware of the swift American advance, were peacefully cooking their dinner. A firefight broke out and Izard recorded the result in his diary:

Snelling's reconoitering party … surprises a company of 60 to 80 Indians – 2 killed on the spot, a number wounded – the whole fled, some into the wood, others swim the river – probably several will die for their tracks are very bloody. We find 115 blankets 30 to 40 muskets & fusils, cartridges, powder, 2 kegs of rum, waumpum belts, tobacco pouch, etc.

Expecting "skirmishing in the night," Izard ordered his troops to make large fires, but all was quiet.[19]

The main force moved more slowly, making only two miles on 21 October because of the very bad condition of the track over which it marched. The following day Hampton joined Izard at Spear's while the main column laboured along the river road. The next two days, 23 and 24 October, were devoted to "completing the road and getting up the artillery and stores" to Spear's house.[20] Between two and three hundred men were put to work, including Private Fairbanks of the Volunteers, who recorded that they

cut the trees out of the road the British had felled in, and rebuild the bridges they had destroyed. The roads were soft and miry, and often the wheels of the baggage wagons cut up the road so we had to lay logs across for miles; we often had to wade in the river up to our knees, or above them, lugging logs and timber. Such is the work of the poor soldier on half rations.[21]

Conditions were generally bad. On 23 October it began to rain and continued to do so intermittently for the next two days. There were only a limited number of tents so the troops were ordered to build shelters of branches. Corporal Bishop had just started his when he was ordered on a baggage guard and by the time he returned it was dark and the "commissary refusing to issue provisions so late in the day … we had to return to camp and lye down in the wet rain all night."[22] "At night," another soldier recalled,

> we had to take our blankets out of our knapsacks, roll ourselves up in them, and with our knapsacks for a pillow, lie down on the frozen ground, often times with a storm of hail or sleet driving down upon us; we could not stop to pitch our tent every day. The Indians would often be seen in the woods near us, so that we were always compelled to sleep with our guns by our side.[23]

Many of the men, required to do heavy manual labour, quickly ran through the provisions they had been issued. As Fairbanks complained, "We received six or eight days rations at a time, and a day before our time was out, our rations would be out, no matter how closely we hoarded the scanty allowance, and then we had nothing to eat."[24] His comrades on the working party rejoiced when they "found some corn buried" which "was eaten about as quick as so many hogs would have eaten it." Finally, "after many of us had nothing to eat for a day or two," Fairbanks and his companions received more food, but it was not inviting fare, being salt beef, so they "cut it on a board in about one half pound pieces and each man was allowed to take a piece; we would cut it in slices, stick them on the end of a stick, and hold them in the blaze of the fire, which would draw out the salt, then put it in water." They were so hungry they ate it "with a grand relish" and "*that* was to give us courage to fight."

By 25 October, after three days of hard work, the entire division was concentrated at Spear's – they were now nineteen miles from their objective, Caughnawaga, across the St. Lawrence from Montreal.[25]

Throughout this period, patrols of dragoons and light infantry went out to ascertain the enemy's position and strength to supplement the reports brought in by spies and deserters. On 22 October Izard noted in his diary that a cavalry patrol chasing some warriors through the woods had discovered "from 5 to 600 men in red uniforms in line about six miles below."[26] From the intelligence brought in by these patrols Hampton was gradually able to form a picture of the enemy's strength and position. He knew that in front of him were about seven miles of open country beyond which was a wood "which had been … filled by a succession of wooden breastworks, the rearmost of which were well supplied with ordnance." Hampton had received no communications from either Armstrong or the main army, which "was a cause of regret," but since he believed "the enemy was hourly adding to his strength," he decided that "an effort was necessary to dislodge him" as, if successful, his army would "be in possession of a position which we could hold as long as any doubts remained of what was passing above [on the St. Lawrence] and of the real part to be assigned us."[27]

On 25 October, Wade Hampton made the decision to attack and he was confident as he had four thousand men and also accurate information that the "enemy's entire force" immediately in front of him "did not exceed three hundred and fifty combattants altogether, [French] Canadian and Indian" commanded by some "militia colonel" named de Salaberry.[28]

Lieutenant Colonel Charles-Michel d'Irumberry de Salaberry was no amateur militia officer and he was a dangerous man to underestimate. He was the scion of a well-established and respected *Canadien* family with a long tradition of service – his grandfather had been a naval officer prominent in the defence of New France during the Seven Years War while his father had fought for the Crown during the Revolutionary War and had been badly wounded at the battle of Saratoga in 1777. The elder de Salaberry had survived to become one of the leading public figures in Lower Canada, active in politics, law, agriculture and military affairs, and his personal friendship with the Duke of Kent, a son of George III, led to Charles and his three brothers receiving commissions in the British army. Two died from fever in the East Indies while a third was killed leading one of Wellington's forlorn hopes at the siege of Badajoz in Spain in March 1812.

Charles de Salaberry joined the 60th Regiment of Foot at Martinique as a sixteen-year-old ensign in 1794. He served there, except for one summer of leave in Lower Canada, for a decade and saw combat in a number of "island-hopping" campaigns against the French, managing to avoid death from yellow fever and also from a fellow officer who challenged him to a duel – it ended when de Salaberry cut the man nearly in half. In 1805 he was posted to England as a captain in the 5th Battalion of the 60th, commanded by Lieutenant Colonel Francis de Rottenburg, who was training it to be the first regular rifle unit in the British army. De Rottenburg's instruction was based on his own book, *Regulations for the Exercise of Riflemen and Light Infantry and Instructions for Their Conduct in the Field*, which was to become a standard manual. De Salaberry and de Rottenburg saw action together in the Walcheren campaign of 1809, and when the older officer was promoted brigadier general and posted to Lower Canada in 1810, he took his protégé along as an aide.[29]

De Salaberry was a major on the staff in the spring of 1812 when Prevost,

The professional (1) – Lieutenant Colonel Charles-Michel d'Irumberry de Salaberry, the devil in person (1778-1829)
The commanding officer of the Canadian Voltigeurs, a light infantry unit composed of *Canadiens*, de Salaberry commanded a British detachment which defeated Hampton's vastly superior force. This engraving, made after the war when de Salaberry was 48, portrays him in his Voltigeur uniform wearing the gold medal he was awarded for the action and his companionship in the Order of the Bath. (Sketch by Anson Dickinson, engraving by A.B. Durand, National Archives of Canada, C-9226)

desperate to increase his trained manpower, accepted his proposal to raise a *Canadien* light infantry unit. Popularly known as the Canadian Voltigeurs, this eight- and later ten-company battalion was composed of volunteers who engaged to serve during the war and it was armed, equipped, trained and disciplined as a regular unit. Not surprisingly, de Salaberry turned out to be a very strict commander and a relentless taskmaster who was as hard on his officers as he was on his men – one of the former, his own brother-in-law, became so disgusted with the endless drill and duty he requested a transfer to another unit. His men may not have liked de Salaberry but they respected him and, as soldiers do in such cases, boasted about his toughness in song: *C'est notre Major qu'a le diable au corps, qui nous donn'ra la mort* ("there's our major who's the devil in person, he'll be the death of us yet").[30]

In the autumn of 1812 the Voltigeurs were sent to the frontier of Lower Canada when de Salaberry took charge of the defences of the border area. It was de Salaberry who commanded the force of Voltigeurs and other units that blunted Dearborn's timorous invasion attempt at Lacolle Mill in November 1812; it was de Salaberry who had defended Odelltown against Hampton in September; and it was de Salaberry who commanded the abortive raid on the American camp at Four Corners on 1 October. Following this action, he was assigned the task of defending the lower Châteauguay under the direct command of de Watteville, whose headquarters was at Baker's house at the junction of the Châteauguay and English rivers. Described as "a big man – a little above average height, broad shouldered, strong and stern," thirty-five-year-old Charles de Salaberry was one of the most experienced light infantry officers in the British army in North America.[31]

He also enjoyed the advantage of knowing the ground he had to defend. After his attack on Hampton's camp, he had withdrawn down the Châteauguay and spotted a wooded and swampy area where a series of gullies or ravines intersected the river at right angles. When word arrived during the evening of 21 October that the Americans were advancing down the river, de Salaberry began to turn this site into a strong defensive position, employing skilled axemen from the local sedentary militia. On the gullies they

established four lines of defence, the one after the other. The first three lines were upon an average, at the distance of about two hundred yards from each other; the fourth line was about a half a mile in the rear, and commanded a ford to the right bank of the river, which it became important to defend, to protect his left flank. Upon each of these lines, he caused a breastwork to be thrown up, extending some distance into the woods, so as to guard his right.

All the bridges between four and five miles in advance were destroyed and a formidable abatis, an obstacle formed by trees felled for the purpose, was constructed about a mile in front of the first defence line. It extended from the river bank some hundreds of yards into the woods where it joined a swamp. De Salaberry had a very strong position.[32]

To hold the line of the Châteauguay, his superior, Major General Louis de Watteville, could count on about eighteen hundred troops, a polyglot mixture of regulars, Canadian Voltigeurs, Select Embodied and sedentary militia and the greater part of them *Canadiens*. Despite the Lower Canada militia's good behaviour during some of the skirmishes that had taken place along the border in the previous year, British officers were still somewhat uncertain about how willing these people would be to fight for the Crown. As one remarked about the *Canadiens*, the war "did not affect them much," as "winter still brought its enjoyments – perhaps some near the large towns, or on the immediate frontier, might have found a little difference but they were governed by their old laws; they followed their own [Catholic] religion," and "if their troublesome [English-speaking] neighbours could not agree it was no great fault of theirs." But, he concluded, although the *Canadiens* "perhaps did not like the English government or people," they "loved the Americans less," and if their country was directly threatened by invasion, they would fight and fight hard.[33]

British commanders need not have worried. When summoned in October 1813, the sedentary militia of Lower Canada turned out in great numbers, displaying that light-hearted attitude to life that is the hallmark of the *Canadien*

95

Defenders of the Canadas – Canadian Voltigeurs and warrior ally
The Voltigeurs, a light infantry unit, was raised and trained by Charles de Salaberry, himself a student of Francis de Rottenburg, one of the foremost light infantry and rifle specialists in the British army during the Napoleonic Wars. Clothed in drab grey uniforms, they specialized as skirmishers and often served with their native allies. (Painting by G.A. Embleton, courtesy Parks Canada)

in general and the *Canadien* soldier in particular but which is often a source of puzzlement to their more dour English-speaking fellow citizens. A British officer who encountered a column of these men marching to the frontier that autumn remembered they had a "serviceable effective appearance," having been "pretty well drilled" and "were in perfectly good order," with "capots and trowsers of home-spun stuff, and their blue *tuques* (night caps) were all of the same cut and color, which gave them an air of uniformity that added much to their military look." "They marched merrily along to the music of their voyageur songs," he fondly recalled, "and as they perceived our [scarlet] uniform as we came up, they set up the Indian War-whoop, followed by a shout of *Vive le Roi* along the whole line."[34]

It was men like this who composed the units under de Salaberry's command at his forward position. With him (see Appendix C) he had two companies of his own Voltigeurs, the light company of the Canadian Fencible Regiment, a company of the Select Embodied Militia, two companies of sedentary militia and a small detachment of warriors from the Abenaki and Nipissing nations. In immediate reserve was an *ad hoc* battalion of Select Embodied Militia, 600 strong, led by another veteran light infantryman, Lieutenant Colonel George Macdonell.[35]

"Red George" Macdonell had been commissioned an ensign in the army in 1796 at the age of sixteen and had come to North America in 1808 as a captain in the 8th Foot. Shortly before the war, he had been made a major in the Glengarry Light Infantry, a fencible regiment (a regular unit recruited for service in North America only) raised from mainly Scots immigrants. Clothed as British rifle units in green uniforms but equipped with muskets, the Glengarries had quickly established a reputation as very able skirmishers. In early 1813 Macdonell received the local rank of lieutenant colonel and command of the Prescott area, where in February he had mounted a successful raid against Ogdensburg. The following June he was appointed to command a light battalion composed of the flank companies of the 2nd, 3rd and 5th Select Embodied Militia battalions, which was stationed at Kingston. On 20 October, when information came about Hampton's advance over the border, he received orders to move as quickly as possible to the Châteauguay area.[36]

It took nearly twenty-four hours to procure the requisite number of boats, and because there were few pilots to be had, Macdonell acted as his own navigator. The battalion headed down the St. Lawrence on 21 October and Macdonell managed to get his convoy safely through the rapids and across Lake St. Francis west of Montreal "in the teeth of a very heavy gale of wind." Arriving at the Beauharnois shore at last light on 24 October, the battalion then made a twenty-mile forced march to reach the bank of the Châteauguay just before daylight the following morning, having moved 210 miles by water and by land in just three days. Macdonell reported immediately to Prevost, who had come down to inspect the area, and the British commander-in-chief, deciding that Macdonell had hurried down the St. Lawrence without his unit, began a "very severe reprimand" which "soon changed into most complimentary terms of astonishment" when Macdonell "proudly pointed to his 600 exhausted soldiers sleeping on the ground, *not one man absent.*" After they had taken a well-deserved rest, his light battalion began to construct a new series of defence works to the rear of those put in place by de Salaberry.[37]

De Salaberry was aware of the American patrols scouting his position and, believing the enemy would soon move to the attack, he kept working parties of the local militia busy improving the abatis "to render it still more formidable."[38] He protected these parties with detachments of his own unit, and on the morning of 26 October 1813 Lieutenants Louis Guy and William David Johnson of the Voltigeurs set out a picket line in front of the abatis. Around 10 A.M. their men spotted blue-coated troops approaching along the river road and opened fire.[39]

Wade Hampton was well informed of de Salaberry's position but local guides had assured him that there was a "practicable fording place opposite the lower flank of the enemy's defences." If Hampton took this ford, he could bypass de Salaberry's defence lines and be in his rear before the enemy recovered from the shock. He therefore decided to send Purdy's First Brigade across the Châteauguay to push down the right bank through a wooded area "that was practicable for the passage of troops" and seize the ford. While Purdy accomplished this task, Izard's Second Brigade would attack the main position, which "might be carried before the enemy's distant troops could be brought to his support," and that being done it would only be a question of mopping up and moving on to Montreal. It was a good but somewhat risky

The professional (2) – Lieutenant Colonel George Macdonell, the fiery Scot (1780-1870)
Known as "Red George," Macdonell was an aggressive light infantry officer who raided Ogdensburg, New York, in February 1813 and made a journey of 200 miles with his battalion in three days to support de Salaberry on the Châteauguay. (National Archives of Canada, C-19719)

plan, for it meant that Hampton would not only be dividing his division in the face of the enemy but also placing the two parts on opposite sides of a river that was about 100 feet wide and five or six deep at this point.[40]

At last light on 25 October 1813, Purdy moved out under a drizzle. With him were the three units of his First Brigade – the Fourth and Thirty-Third Infantry and the combined Volunteer Regiment – plus the Elite, or light infantry force, of the division, a total of about 2,300 men. Ahead lay a difficult night march through more than ten miles of marshy ground and thick undergrowth, and it quickly became obvious the guides "knew nothing of the country having never been that way," since the column got into the middle "of a thick cedar growth or swamp on the bank of the river" from which they "knew not how to extricate us." Purdy later claimed these guides had insisted to Hampton "that they were not acquainted with the country and were not competent to direct such an expedition" and Hampton had promised that he would send Purdy a more knowledgeable local man, which "he neglected to do." It was a terrible march, "very dark and rainy," the brigade commander recorded, through thickets and bogs, and dawn found the First Brigade floundering around somewhere on the right bank of the Châteauguay.[41]

Hampton may have changed his mind about sending Purdy a better guide after returning to his headquarters the previous night. Waiting for him was an officer with Armstrong's order of 16 October "respecting the building of huts for the army on the Châteauguay below the line." "This paper," he later stated, "sunk my hopes and raised serious doubts of receiving that efficacious support which had been anticipated" from the main army. It now appeared as though the operation against Montreal was over, and Hampton considered calling Purdy back, but "the darkness of the night rendered it impracticable." As he later remarked, the only option was to "go forward," and at first light on 26 October Hampton ordered Izard to advance with his brigade along the left bank of the river against the main British position and "attract the enemy's notice while Purdy gets in the rear." Izard was on the move quickly and marched down the river road to Baird's house, about a mile and half from the abatis, where he left the Eleventh/Twenty-Ninth and Thirty/Thirty-First Infantry and pushed forward with the Tenth Infantry and Hall's dragoons. At about 10 A.M., the enemy fired on his advance guard and killed two dragoon horses.[42]

De Salaberry was at the first defence line when Guy and Johnson's men opened up at Izard's lead element. He immediately moved forward to the abatis with two companies of his own Voltigeurs, the light company of the Canadian Fencibles, a company of Beauharnois sedentary militia, a total of

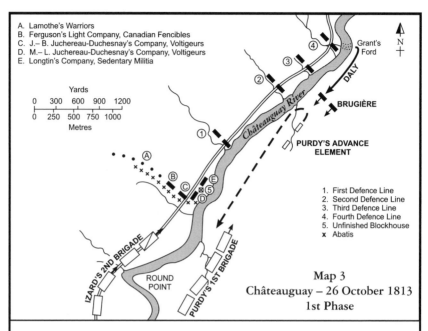

A. Lamothe's Warriors
B. Ferguson's Light Company, Canadian Fencibles
C. J.– B. Juchereau-Duchesnay's Company, Voltigeurs
D. M.– L. Juchereau-Duchesnay's Company, Voltigeurs
E. Longtin's Company, Sedentary Militia

Yards
0   300   600   900   1200
0   250   500   750   1000
Metres

Grant's Ford

BRUGIÈRE

PURDY'S ADVANCE ELEMENT

1. First Defence Line
2. Second Defence Line
3. Third Defence Line
4. Fourth Defence Line
5. Unfinished Blockhouse
x Abatis

ROUND POINT

IZARD'S 2ND BRIGADE

PURDY'S 1ST BRIGADE

Map 3
Châteauguay – 26 October 1813
1st Phase

1. Izard encounters Guy and Johnson's pickets and then the troops de Salaberry moves forward from the rearward defence lines. De Salaberry's men at first take post in front of the abatis but later move behind it. Izard demonstrates with the 10th Infantry alone but later moves up his other units.

2. Purdy, on the right bank of the river, orients himself by the sound of the firing on the left and advances on the ford. His lead elements, two companies in single file, which are well in advance, are hit by Brugière's company. Both sides fall back: the Americans to their main body, the Canadians to Daly's company sent across the river by Macdonell.

just over three hundred men, and twenty-two Abenaki warriors. Guy and Johnson, who had withdrawn near the abatis for cover, reported the situation and de Salaberry deployed for action. The Fencibles and one Voltigeur company were placed in a skirmish line in front of the abatis and the warriors pushed out into the woods on his right. The other Voltigeur company and a company of Beauharnois sedentary militia were posted slightly to the rear facing the river, where they could protect the left flank as well as fire across the Châteauguay at the American force suspected to be working its way down the right bank. Macdonell, also alerted by the firing, moved some of his companies forward to take over the positions on the first and second defence lines vacated by de Salaberry and dispatched two more companies over the ford to the right bank. Having given his orders, de Salaberry "placed himself in the

Vive le canadien! – Lower Canada sedentary militiaman, 1813
Wearing his standard garb of tuque, blanket coat and leggings, the sedentary militiaman of Lower Canada rendered good service during the invasion of 1813. (Painting by G.A. Embleton, courtesy Parks Canada)

Near regular – Lower Canada Select Embodied militiaman, 1813
Uniformed, armed, and trained as regular troops, the six battalions of Select Embodied Militia formed a useful auxiliary to the British army defending Lower Canada. (Painting by G.A. Embleton, courtesy Parks Canada)

centre of the front line" as Captain Joseph-Marie Longtin, commanding the company of Beauharnois militia, knelt down with his men" and "said a short prayer in his own good way."[43] This necessary prelude to battle observed, Longtin told his company that, as "they had done their duty to their God," he now "expected they would also to their duty to their King."[44]

The *Canadiens* had just got into position when a "strong column of infantry advanced thro' the plain in front of the abattis" and de Salaberry, "perceiving that this column had laid itself open to a front and flank fire ... himself fired the first shot which was seen to bring down a mounted officer." This "strong column" was actually Izard's advance guard and the mounted officer probably one of Hall's dragoons.[45]

Hampton, "on hearing the firing below," had asked Izard if he had "any objection to proceeding with the 10th [Infantry] alone" as the rest of the brigade was more than a mile in the rear. "Of course I go," recorded Izard, and moved forward with the Tenth Infantry, about 250 strong, and deployed into line in a cleared area in front of the abatis. Izard remembered that on "the brink of a deep ravine, within a hundred yards of a thick wood, we are met by a volley of musketry." He experienced some confusion "in forming the 10th in line, but at last succeed[ed]."[46]

On seeing the Americans deploy, de Salaberry ordered his bugler "to sound for commence firing" and a brisk little action took place. Lieutenant Michael O'Sullivan, serving as an aide to the Voltigeur commander, recalled that a "spirited and well-directed fire from the companies in front checked for a few minutes the advance of the enemy, they remained motionless for some time and then wheeled to the left into line, in which position they fired several volleys."[47] The exchange was "brisk for about 20 minutes," Izard remembered, and then it died down as the Tenth began to run low on ammunition.[48]

On the right bank of the river, meanwhile, Purdy was able to orient himself by the noise of this firing. At about 11 A.M. his two advance companies, moving in single file considerably ahead of the main body, were nearly opposite the second defence line on the left bank when they encountered Captain Jean-Baptiste Brugière's company of sedentary militia posted there with some warriors by de Salaberry as a picket. A confusing fire fight broke out – Sergeant Neef of the Fourth Infantry remembered it as "a furious action" which "was supported with firmness on both sides about fifteen or twenty minutes, when we charged the enemy and drove them."[49] Actually, both sides were shaken – a Canadian eyewitness remembered the "sedentary militia and some Indians running away" with "the blue tuques of the former flying in the wind," while Purdy's advance, fearing that the woods were full of warriors, fell back on the main column.[50] Brugière managed to get control of his men long enough to form on Captain Charles Daly's company of the Select Embodied Militia which Macdonell had sent across the river. Daly and Brugière then cautiously followed Purdy's advance element as it withdrew back through the thick scrub brush.[51]

The firing now died away and there was a lull during which the remainder of Izard's brigade, the Eleventh/Twenty-Ninth and the Thirty/Thirty-First Infantry, moved forward in column along the cart track bordering the river to support the Tenth Infantry. Hampton became aware from information shouted across the river and from the location of the firing that Purdy had not "gained the ford" and his attempt to get in the rear of his enemy was lost. He decided to recall the First Brigade and sent his adjutant general, Major William King, down to the river bank to shout across an order for Purdy to pull back a few miles above and recross to the opposite bank.[52]

This being the case, it is curious that Hampton next elected to attack on the left bank, unless he meant it as a demonstration to preoccupy the enemy while Purdy withdrew. None the less, at about 2 P.M. he again ordered Izard to advance on the abatis and open fire. Izard formed his three regiments in line in the cleared area in front of the abatis and let loose a series of rolling volleys. Corporal Bishop of the Twenty-Ninth remembered that his unit first "halted under the brow of a hill and was ordered to load our muskets at which time the battle commenced on both sides of the river at a very hot note."[53]

The *Canadiens* in front of the abatis returned the American volleys with individual aimed shots, and a small boy who overheard the exchange from his family's nearby farm "was so much pleased with the rolling volleys of Hampton's men and the sputtering fire of the Canadians in reply that I regretted its cessation."[54] Much of the American fire went so high that their bullets lodged in the surrounding trees, which this same boy and his brother later cut down to get the lead. Izard's fire was also rendered less effective because his infantry were firing "buck and ball" ammunition (three buckshot pellets with each

Buck and ball, 1813
During the afternoon of 26 October 1813 an American soldier threw his .69 calibre Springfield musket into the Châteauguay River. It was retrieved more than a century and a half later and this x-ray photograph reveals it was still loaded with "buck and ball" ammunition (one ball and three buckshot). (Courtesy, Parks Canada)

musket ball) and the additional projectiles in each round diminished the velocity, range and accuracy of their fire. The *Canadiens'* fire was much more effective: they were behind cover and they took their time, making each round count. Lieutenant Charles Pinguet of the light company of the Canadian Fencibles posted in front of the abatis noted that his men fired between thirty-five and forty rounds each during this part of the action and "their aim was good," as American prisoners later told him that most of their wounded had been hit "in the head or chest."[55] Pinguet's company commander, Captain Richard Ferguson, fifty-two years old and something of a reprobate, elected to use his personal weapon instead of a musket. Described as "a great tall man," Ferguson blazed away at the Americans with the double-barrelled fowling piece he habitually carried into action.[56]

Izard's musketry may not have been accurate, but it was heavy enough to force the skirmish line of Voltigeurs and Fencibles to fall back on the abatis. The Americans, according to O'Sullivan, "mistook this for the beginning of a retreat; and much mistaken they were, for they did not occupy one inch of the abbatis."[57] Bishop of the Twenty-Ninth commented that his regiment, after having watched the Canadians retire, "gave them a cheer which was answered."[58] O'Sullivan remembered that "Huzzas re-sounded from all parts of their army; nor were we inferior in this shouting warfare" as the "companies in front cheered in their turn – their huzzas were re-echoed by those in their rear and reiterated by the troops in the front line."[59] "After these mutual cheerings," O'Sullivan continued, "volleys were for some time exchanged on both sides." De Salaberry added to this martial symphony by ordering his buglers to sound the "Advance" while Macdonell, who was now moving forward from the first defence line to de Salaberry's immediate support, recalled that by "the happiest accident possible" a party of warriors

> joined him at that moment. He [Macdonell] instantly threw them into the wood to his right, to scatter and scream their war-whoop, and by an incessant fire to threaten Hampton's left flank, sending with them a dozen of his buglers, to spread widely and keep sounding "the advance" in every direction ... and his companies in succession to cheer loudly.[60]

The cacophony and musketry on the left bank continued for a few minutes but O'Sullivan remembered that after "a short time it began to slacken, as if their [the Americans'] attention was directed to the other side of the river."

While Izard and de Salaberry's troops were exchanging fire and cheers on the left bank and King was shouting orders across the river to Purdy just after 2

P.M., the companies of Daly and Brugière made contact with the main body of the First Brigade. Purdy recorded that "the enemy made a furious attack on the column by a great discharge of musketry, accompanied by the yells of the savages."[61] "Unfortunately," he added, "the word 'retreat' was heard, which for a short time spread confusion among the corps." Alexander Neef of the Fourth Infantry remembered it somewhat differently – the problem was that the undergrowth on the right bank was

> so extremely thick that an enemy might approach us within 20 yds undiscovered (as was soon to be found the case) yet our commander did not think it proper to adopt any precautionary measures against surprise, not even so much as to post sentinels but in this careless situation our men were left to their own discretion; some were eating, others asleep, others had strayed from their posts. Thus situated the enemy … advanced undiscovered within 50 yards, …. our men not being formed for action, at first, it threw us into disorder; but the exertions of a few (not many officers at that time being at their posts), our men were soon rallied, and after a few discharges drove the enemy in every direction.[62]

Neef was being tactful – many of the officers were absent because, when the shooting had started, they abandoned their men and ran to the river bank opposite Izard's brigade. From his position, Private Charles Fairbanks saw

> on the opposite bank … about a dozen officers who had left their companies and collected at a bend in the river; as we passed they wished our Colonel to swim his horse across and bring them over; one of them was one of his own captains. He replied, "Go back to your men; if I saw Indians and knew that they would kill every one of you, I would not swim my horse across."[63]

At this point some of the miscreants plunged into the Châteauguay and Izard, who witnessed the scene, was disgusted by the sight of wet and bedraggled officers emerging from the shallow river "without their swords and hats."[64]

Enough of Purdy's men rallied to stand off Daly and Brugière and the two Canadian companies fell back. From a vantage point on a stump on the left bank, de Salaberry recognized Daly and shouted advice to him in French, "cautioning him to answer in the same language that they might not be understood by the enemy."[65] Daly and Brugière decided to mount another attack, an audacious move seeing as their combined strength was no more than seventy or eighty men while Purdy had at least 1,500 men. Using the thick under-

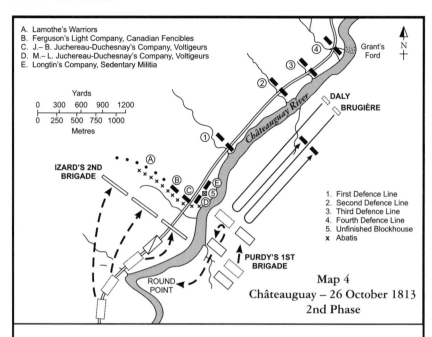

A. Lamothe's Warriors
B. Ferguson's Light Company, Canadian Fencibles
C. J.– B. Juchereau-Duchesnay's Company, Voltigeurs
D. M.– L. Juchereau-Duchesnay's Company, Voltigeurs
E. Longtin's Company, Sedentary Militia

Yards
0   300   600   900   1200

0   250   500   750   1000
Metres

IZARD'S 2ND
BRIGADE

Grant's
Ford

Châteauguay River

DALY
BRUGIÈRE

1. First Defence Line
2. Second Defence Line
3. Third Defence Line
4. Fourth Defence Line
5. Unfinished Blockhouse
x Abatis

PURDY'S 1ST
BRIGADE

ROUND
POINT

Map 4
Châteauguay – 26 October 1813
2nd Phase

1. Izard deploys his entire brigade before the abatis and a fire fight ensues between his units and the *Canadiens* defending the abatis. Macdonell moves to occupy the defence lines, throws warriors out into the woods and sounds bugles in all directions as does de Salaberry.

2. On the right bank, Daly and Brugière audaciously attack Purdy but are rebuffed. Purdy then advances, but comes under heavy fire from the two companies posted by de Salaberry on the left bank to guard his river flank. The 1st Brigade falls back in confusion.

3. Hampton orders Izard to withdraw. Purdy also retrogrades and only later learns the main part of the division has moved further back. He evacuates his wounded across the river and spends an uncomfortable night on the right bank.

growth to their advantage, however, they were able to move close to the Americans who were formed in a ragged firing line. When the First Brigade sighted them, the two companies of *Canadiens* dropped on one knee to receive the expected volley, fired a volley in reply, and then fixed bayonets and charged. It was a brave but somewhat foolhardy act. Although Neef thought there were three or four hundred "attackers," the Americans repelled the *Canadien* attack, which in some places was pushed home to the point of the bayonet. Both Brugière and Daly went down wounded, and the survivors fell back, closely pursued by the triumphant Americans.[66]

As the left flank of Purdy's line emerged from the wood onto the bank of the Châteauguay, it came in full view of the Voltigeur company commanded by Captain Michel-Louis Juchereau-Duschesnay and Longetin's sedentary militia company posted on the far shore for just such an eventuality. Neef remembered that, "as soon as the head of our column arrived at the river, a scattering fire" broke out "between our leading troops and the opposite shore."[67] O'Sullivan commented that the two *Canadien* companies "opened upon them across the river, a heavy and well-directed fire, which suddenly checked their career, and threw them back in the greatest confusion."[68] That was it for the First Brigade – Purdy's day was done, but it was not yet over.

It was now about 3 P.M., and Hampton, realizing that "the enterprize had failed in its main point," ordered a withdrawal.[69] Izard's Second Brigade pulled back "with precision and good order," he recalled, "better than they have hitherto shown since I command them."[70] Fairbanks remembered that the brigade withdrew three miles and camped for the night "in an open field, our blankets around us, our guns in our arms, and supposed we were to get a little rest after the fatigues of the day."[71] Unfortunately, "at two o'clock [in the morning] the rain fell in torrents so that we were completely drenched."

Purdy retreated down his side of the river and sent over a request to Hampton to provide a regiment to cover his crossing, only to learn that the rest of the army on the left bank had already pulled back farther, leaving his brigade isolated. Furious, he managed to float his wounded across the Châteauguay on rafts and Major Josiah Snelling of the light infantry corps constructed a floating log bridge to cross over with about a hundred men to protect them. While doing so they came under sniper fire from some of the Abenaki and Nipissing warriors who were now closing in through the woods to harass the Americans. Having got their wounded away, the remainder of the First Brigade "retired two or three miles and took up a position" in an easily defended bend in the river, where they, "exhausted by the excessive exertions of the preceding night and weary with the fatigues of the day, not having had a moment for either rest or refreshment, were compelled to endure the privation of sleep for another night." The rain, which had been intermittent through the day, came down in torrents during the hours of darkness. At about midnight there were "savage yells" in the surrounding woods" but, as Neef recalled, his comrades "fired a few rounds and the enemy withdrew."[72] Scattered firing continued through the night and Purdy became convinced he was under constant attack – he later insisted that the "enemy charged several times, and were as often put to flight." In fact, except for a few warriors who loosed off the occasional round, there were no attacks on Purdy's men during the night of 26/27 October – the First Brigade, totally undone, was fighting its own shadow and opening fire on anything that moved.[73]

On the left bank, meanwhile, Fairbanks of the New Hampshire Volunteers recalled that his regiment was ordered to move further back and had a terrible march:

> Accordingly we started on our tramp; we were not allowed to speak to each other. After groping sometime we got into our baggage wagons track; but there was mud in abundance, and the rain kept making it softer; we could see nothing, and had to almost find the way by the sense of feeling. Sometimes one would get out of the mud on to a bit of grass, and the grass being wet, his feet slippery, they would go out from under him so quickly, his gun would snap out from his hands, go ten or twelve feet, and he would land nicely in the mud.[74]

"The reader can easily imagine," Fairbanks continued, "what grotesque appearance we must have presented that morning, the mud and water dropping from our uniforms; we in fact presented an appearance unlike human beings."

De Salaberry did not pursue his enemy because he expected the Americans would return to mount a more determined assault the following day, and this time with artillery. He contented himself with pushing out his skirmish line a mile or so beyond the abatis, but other than dispatching warriors to keep contact with the enemy, he maintained his position.[75]

Shortly after the fighting had died down, Generals Prevost and de Watteville arrived at de Salaberry's position. Prevost had come to de Watteville's headquarters about noon, and about 1 P.M. the two had set out to inspect the forward position when they received a "report that our posts had been engaged with the enemy."[76] De Watteville recalled that he "immediately went ahead" but that by the time he arrived "the firing had ceased and the enemy's attack ... on the two sides of the river, had been discontinued."[77] Macdonell thought that Prevost arrived shortly after the last shots were fired, followed a bit later by de Watteville. Prevost, however, remembered it somewhat differently and reported to Lord Bathurst that, having "fortunately arrived at the scene of Action shortly after its commencement," he "witnessed the conduct of the troops on this glorious occasion; and it was a great gratification to me to render on the spot that praise which had become so justly their due."[78] The commander-in-chief paid de Salaberry an apparently genuine but somewhat reserved compliment which caused the Voltigeur officer to remark, "I hope he is satisfied, though he appeared cold."[79]

The wounded were collected and guards posted, and then de Salaberry's men, "weary with the toils of victory," slept "that night on the ground they had occupied during the day." The following morning they began to clean up the battlefield. On the right bank of the river was "found a large quantity of muskets, drums, knapsacks, provisions, etc., etc.," which "indicated the confusion into which the enemy had been thrown and with which they had retreated." The dead were buried and the casualty lists compiled.[80]

Losses were light on both sides. The official British count was two killed, sixteen wounded and four taken prisoner; however the American casualties are harder to ascertain. Hampton stated that his total losses in killed, wounded and missing did not exceed fifty men. Other American documents list total casualties of between thirty-five and eighty-two of all types, while Izard recorded that the Tenth Infantry lost one man killed and eight wounded and Sergeant Neef of the Fourth Infantry stated that Purdy's brigade lost twenty killed and forty wounded on the right bank. Perhaps the best assessment of the American losses is the statement that de Salaberry's men buried "upwards of forty" American dead.[81]

Naturally, de Salaberry's men exulted. Lieutenant Pinguet of the Canadian Fencibles was proud that his company at the abatis had fought against two thousand infantry and two hundred cavalry. There was also considerable satisfaction throughout Lower Canada that almost all the defenders were *Canadiens* and that after Châteauguay there would be no more doubts about their loyalty. "The affair," noted the *Quebec Gazette*, "is the first in which any considerable number of the natives of this Province have been engaged with the Americans since the war" and a "few experiments of this kind, will probably convince the Americans that their project of conquering this Province is premature."[82]

De Salaberry himself was less pleased. He felt that Prevost's general order announcing the victory, written the day after the battle, arrogated to others the choice of position and the deployment during the action. "The dispositions," he complained in writing, "were made by myself; no one interfered with them, and no officer of superior rank came up until after the action was over."[83] It "grieves me to the heart," he continued, "to see that I must share the merit of this action," because "if any merit is to be obtained I am entitled to the whole." This perhaps ill-judged letter resulted in strained relations between de Salaberry and his superior which ultimately caused the career of the victor of Châteauguay to be cut short.[84]

De Salaberry always acknowledged the able assistance Macdonell rendered him during the action, while for his part Macdonell stated that his *Canadien* comrade had been in command and did his best to gain his fellow officer additional recognition for his victory. In later years, after both men were gone, a dispute arose caused by claims made by English-speaking Canadian historians that Macdonell should have received the lion's share of the credit for the victory, a claim hotly disputed by French-speaking Canadian historians, and for some time a war of words was waged in the press over the matter. It was a somewhat contrived controversy whose proponents forgot that, regardless of the language spoken by the men who fought on the banks of a shallow river on 26 October 1813, they were fighting in defence of all Canada. Lieutenant Colonel Charles de Salaberry, "the man on the ground," had complete command during the action and Macdonell made absolutely no attempt to usurp or interfere with his authority, but on the contrary, acting like the professional soldier he very much was, made every effort to support him.[85]

Professionalism is the key factor here because the battle of Châteauguay is a clear demonstration of how a well-led and positioned military force can hold off an opponent vastly superior in numbers. In the final analysis, just over three hundred *Canadiens* led by de Salaberry, with the support of Macdonell, had beaten off an attack by at least three thousand American troops who came into action. It was not a question of courage, for courage was lacking on neither side; it was a question of leadership, and the fumbling and hesitant decisions and movements of Hampton and Purdy compare badly with the confident and sure decisions of the two British commanders. Châteauguay is an example of what happens when an army composed of soldiers who were regulars in name only encounters professionals.

Even worse, with the exception of Izard, who did his job (though little more), there was a complete leadership failure in Hampton's division. Hampton could not seem to decide whether or not to fight, and his performance was at best half-hearted. Purdy, a prewar regular, was not much better, and it seems clear that for most of the action he did not have his brigade under control. Purdy was annoyed with his superior, possibly because Hampton placed him under arrest shortly after the battle, and he tried to shift the blame for his troubles by penning a long letter to Wilkinson complaining about Hampton's actions throughout the autumn of 1813 which ended with a damning indictment: "Such has been the General's conduct on some occasions that I have, in common with other officers, been induced to believe that he was under the influence of a too free use of spirituous liquors."[86]

Things were no better at the lower levels. The initiative of Brugière and Daly on the right bank was in stark contrast with the behaviour of the American officers of the First Brigade who abandoned their men. This misbehaviour was an indication of the poor quality of leadership in Hampton's division, and although many of the guilty officers were disciplined, the entire episode left a bad taste in the mouths of their more competent colleagues. One of them, Major John Ellis Wool, later remarked that the battle of Châteauguay "was from its inception to its termination a disgrace to the United States army" and "no officer who had any regard for his own reputation, would voluntarily acknowledge himself as being engaged in it."[87]

V ictory or not, the next eight days were bad ones for the victors of Châteauguay, who remained in their positions under an almost continual downpour of rain. On 28 October information reached de Salaberry that the Americans were retreating and he sent out a large party of warriors to reinforce those who had been watching Hampton since the battle. Other patrols confirmed that the enemy had fallen back and returned with quantities of discarded equipment and weapons, a total of 150 muskets and six drums. On the last day of October de Salaberry learned that the enemy had withdrawn across the border to the Four Corners. The second American attempt at invading Lower Canada had failed.[88]

Hampton's nerve was shaken by his repulse. The day after the battle Purdy's brigade rejoined the main army – "in the utmost confusion," Izard remembered – and on 28 October deserters brought the information that the enemy force was about 3,000 men and that "Lieutenant General George Prevost and two other General officers, one of them De Watteville, were with them."[89] Having still received no word of Wilkinson's movement, Hampton called a council of war of his senior officers and put the question to them: "Is it advisable under existing circumstances to renew the attack on the enemy's position, and if not, what position is it advisable for the army to take until it can receive advices of the advance of the grand army down the St. Lawrence?" He later wrote Armstrong "it was the unanimous opinion" of all present that the army "immediately return by orderly marches to a position (Chateaugay [Four Corners]) as will secure our communications ... either to retire into winter quarters or to strike below."[90] There is evidence to indicate that this statement is considerably less than the truth and that the council was anything but unanimous. Lieutenant Eleazar Williams, the leader of Hampton's native scouts, who was in attendance, remembered that "astounding disclosures were made as to the tone and temper of the commanders toward each other" and that "there was great discord in their views concerning military operations, which was highly detrimental to the public service."[91] In other words, the council came close to degenerating into a shouting match.

Whether the decision was unanimous or not, once it was made, orders were issued for the army to march back to Four Corners "slowly and in good order."[92] The men in the ranks were surprised because they fully expected to renew the attack on the enemy position. "We were ordered immediately to march," remembered Bishop, "and we all supposed to attack the enemy; but I found to my astonishment that we had orders to march directly the other way, which so much disappointed me that I really would not believe it until we had our regiment paraded and marched up the river instead of down."[93] Many of the wounded, who were unable to march and for whom there was no room on the baggage wagons, were left behind and the whole business began to look suspiciously like a rout – a disgusted Sergeant Neef commented that "the affairs, from first to last, of this division of the army have appeared to me to be injudicious and, in some respects, cruel and abusive."[94]

It took the division three days of slow marches to reach the Four Corners. On 1 November, the day after his arrival, Hampton wrote a long report to Armstrong and had Major William King take it and explain the circumstances of the failure on the Châteauguay. He added a private letter in which he reminded Armstrong of his intention, expressed the previous August, to resign after operations were complete. As recent "events have had no tendency to change my opinion of the destiny intended for me," Hampton informed the secretary, it was his "determination to retire from a service where I can neither feel security nor expect honour."[95] "The campaign," he concluded, "I consider substantially at an end."[96]

CHAPTER 6

"The Yankees are coming!"

ON THE ST. LAWRENCE, 1 NOVEMBER–6 NOVEMBER 1813

Faintly as tolls the evening chime
Our voices keep tune, and our oars keep time:
Soon as the woods on shore look dim,
We'll sing at St. Ann's our parting hymn.
Row, brothers, row, the stream runs fast,
The rapids are near and the day-light's past.

Utawa's tide! this trembling moon,
Shall see us float over thy surges soon:
Saint of this green isle! hear our prayers,
Oh! grant us cool heaven and favoring airs.
Blow, breezes, blow, the stream runs fast,
The rapids are near and the day-light's past![1]

While Wade Hampton had decided to end his campaign, James Wilkinson had yet to start his. Bad weather during the first two days of November stymied all attempts to move the main part of the army from Grenadier Island to French Creek, where Brown had established an advanced position. Some units got away but a combination of snow, rain and very high wind forced them to take shelter on Gravelly Point, just at the entrance to the St. Lawrence. On 1 November, Wilkinson advised Armstrong he would "wait one day longer, and if the passage continue impracticable," the troops would cross to the mainland and march to French Creek.[2]

Wilkinson had no idea of Hampton's defeat, and he was concerned about co-ordinating his movements with those of his unruly subordinate. On 30 October, Armstrong had advised him to give Hampton "timely notice" of his

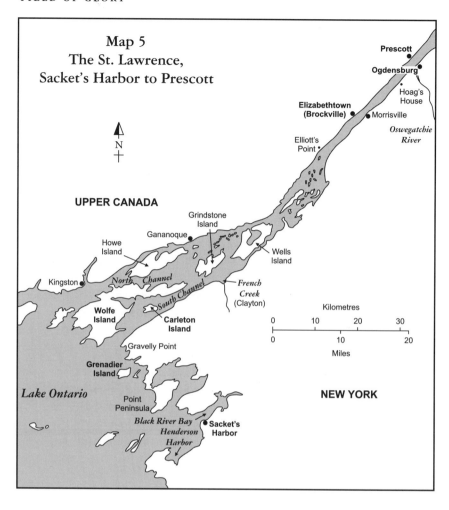

Map 5
The St. Lawrence,
Sacket's Harbor to Prescott

approach and "the place and hour of junction" but Wilkinson was reluctant to communicate directly with his hated rival lest he be disobeyed.[3] He was reduced to pleading with the secretary: "As Major General Hampton is under your orders," he wrote, Armstrong should decide whether Hampton should meet with him on the St. Lawrence or independently menace Montreal.[4] "If he is strong enough to meet Sir George [Prevost]," Wilkinson continued, "the latter will be the preferable plan, because it will have the effect to divide the enemy's force: otherwise he should adopt the first idea, hazard nothing, and strengthen my hands." Wilkinson's greatest worry was his "total ignorance of the preparations of Sir George and what we may expect to meet" on the way to Montreal. This letter, carried by Captain Charles Nourse, Wilkinson's aide, was received by the secretary at Denmark, a hamlet on the road to Utica, and

Armstrong scribbled off a brief reply that Prevost would probably be found west of Montreal and would "attempt to fight you before your junction with Hampton."[5] "Avoid this," the secretary cautioned, "and leave nothing to chance that you can settle on your own terms" as a "junction with Hampton enables you to give the law." These were the last words of advice Wilkinson was to receive from John Armstrong.

On 2 November, Commodore Isaac Chauncey brought his squadron to anchor off Gravelly Point and the next day moved to the northeast end of Wolfe Island. For nearly three weeks Chauncey's warships had been on the lake throughout a period of stormy weather, covering the army's ragged movement to Grenadier Island and making the occasional reconnaissance of Kingston to check on Yeo and his activities. They now had the task of convoying the army to French Creek and it was not a popular job because, as Captain Andrew Sinclair of the *Pike* commented, the squadron had "to descend a rappid River in the face of a superior force, at a season when we were in daily expectation of the ice setting in, strong westerly winds prevailing, every point capable of being fortified by the Enemy and our pilots ignorant of the navigation except for [small] craft."[6]

The next day, 3 November, under the bemused eyes of the sailors, Wilkinson's soldiers climbed awkwardly into a flotilla of skiffs, batteaux, Durham boats, scows and small schooners, and headed for the St. Lawrence. Despite all their recent travails, morale was high. "Our army is still a fine one," Major General Morgan Lewis wrote to his wife just before leaving, and "though it has had to encounter innumerable hardships and privations," when "united to Hampton's will be sufficient in my opinion to place our standard even on the walls of Quebec [City]." "I hope soon to write you from Montreal," was his wish.[7]

Wilkinson's vessel was one of the last to leave Grenadier and, just before embarking at 7 A.M., he wrote a brief note to Armstrong. Again, the subject on his mind was the proposed junction with Hampton and how it could be brought about without him issuing orders to that effect. "You desire me to notify Hampton of the point of Junction," he informed the secretary, but "he has treated my authority with contempt, & acted exclusively under your orders." "I wish this information could come from you," he implored, "that I may be saved the hazard of a second insult" for "what an outrage it is" for "a subordinate to resist or neglect the orders of a superior." He assured Armstrong that "in this case my feelings shall be silenced and that I will humiliate myself to make the most of this pretender."[8] This done, Wilkinson boarded his schooner and set out for French Creek.

The American commander and his army faced a voyage of about 150 miles down the St. Lawrence, one of the great waterways of North America. To get to Montreal, Wilkinson's flotilla would have to run five rapids – in descending order the Gallop, Rapide du Plat, Long Sault, Cedars and Lachine – created by the 200-foot drop in water level between Lake Ontario and Montreal. These rapids were hazardous – in 1760 a British army under Major General Jeffery Amherst making the same journey lost sixty-four boats and eighty-eight men in the Long Sault.[9]

The St. Lawrence had been the great highway of the native peoples, and Europeans had used it to penetrate the interior of the continent. France had created an empire based on the river and its adjoining lakes, and the British Crown continued the pattern, using this fine communication system to move and supply troops. The waterway also formed a useful route for white pioneers and in the two decades before the war the American and Canadian banks of the St. Lawrence had gradually been settled, but then as now, the Canadian shore was more heavily populated than the American.[10]

The impetus for settlement on the Canadian side came in the aftermath of the Revolutionary War when the Crown compensated the members of the Loyalist regiments with generous grants of land, depending on rank, along the river bank or "front" as it was called. The area around Cornwall had a distinctly Gaelic air because it had first been settled by the officers and men of the Royal Highland Emigrants, a Loyalist unit, and more Scots came with the Glengarry settlement, an attempt to provide new homes for families displaced by the clearances in the Highlands of Scotland. Further to the west in Osnaburgh, Williamsburgh and Matilda townships, there were Dutch-speaking Loyalists from Pennsylvania and Palatine Germans from the Mohawk Valley who, hardworking and thrifty, proved to be very successful homesteaders. A traveller visiting the area in 1804 noted the difference between these and the settlers from New England. He found them "more sociable than their neighbours who do nothing but for hire," he noted, while the "New Englanders sometimes give their assistance for the sake of a frolic, dinner, drink, etc., but if they can persuade a man to give the dinner early they are off presently."[11] By the time of the war, the development of the Canadian bank of the St. Lawrence was becoming advanced as the original log buildings and shanties gave way to solid two-storey wood frame houses, well-cleared and fenced fields, mills, taverns, stores and churches.[12]

Canadians used the river highway to export their products – as early as 1794 Upper Canada was self-sufficient in foodstuffs and that year 12,823 bushels of wheat were shipped to Montreal. Napoleon's closure of the Baltic ports to British vessels meant that the Royal Navy could no longer get Scandinavian timber, and the result was a demand for the Canadian product, which was cut in the interior and floated down the river to Montreal. The decade before the war proved prosperous both for those involved in this trade and those who provided services to them.[13]

When hostilities commenced in June 1812, it was vital that this communication route be safeguarded. Over the first year of the war, a protective convoy system was developed and a corps of Canadian, later Commisariat, Voyageurs drawn from skilled rivermen was created to crew the growing number of batteaux constructed to transport troops and supplies, while the defences of the military posts between Montreal and Kingston were gradually strengthened. The St. Lawrence was crucial to the defence of Upper Canada, because as one British observer noted, not only provisions but "every kind of Military and Naval Stores, every bolt of canvas, every rope yarn, as well as the heavier articles of guns, shot, cables, anchors, and all the numerous etceteras for furnishing a large squadron, arming forts, supplying arms for the militia and the line, had to be brought from Montreal to Kingston, a distance of nearly 200 miles."[14]

During the summer of 1812, war only briefly touched the communities on the St. Lawrence. The militia of both nations were early called out, and there was some excitement when they amused themselves by shouting or occasionally shooting at each other across the river but this practice gradually died out.[15] Things began to heat up that autumn. On 16 September, an American attack on a British boat convoy near Iroquois Point was beaten off by the combined efforts of British regulars and the local militia. Four days later American regulars from Sackets Harbor and New York militia mounted a raid on the little Canadian community of Gananoque on the St. Lawrence twenty-five miles below Kingston. Putting the defenders to flight, they occupied the hamlet and burned a military storehouse containing provisions.

The American commander on this raid was Major Benjamin Forsyth, who would become famous (or infamous) for his exploits as a border raider. Born in Virginia but a prewar resident of North Carolina, where he had considerable property, Forsyth had been commissioned a captain in the Rifle Regiment in 1808. At that time he would have been at least forty-five years old. In the summer of 1812 he was ordered to take his 120-strong rifle company to Sackets Harbor, where he arrived in late August. The attack on Gananoque was Forsyth's first action and his company was at Ogdensburg under the command of New York Brigadier General Jacob Brown when Brown beat off a weak British attack on that place in early October.[16]

Things were then quiet until February 1813 when Forsyth became annoyed at British and Canadian detachments that crossed the river to apprehend their deserters. He decided to retaliate by raiding Elizabethtown, ten miles above Prescott, and during the night of 6 February led a force across the frozen St. Lawrence in sleighs, which, taking the garrison of Canadian militia by surprise, occupied the village. Forsyth emptied the jail, which was full of apprehended deserters, freeing "every prisoner, with the exception of one confined for murder" who "naturally begged hard to share the fortune of the others but was left."[17] Scooping up some muskets, rifles and ammunition he found in store, he returned to Ogdensburg before dawn on 7 February with fifty-three prisoners. For this exploit Forsyth was rewarded with a promotion to lieutenant colonel.[18]

The raid on Elizabethtown was smoothly done but it caused British retaliation. Lieutenant Colonel Thomas Pearson, commanding at Prescott, asked for reinforcements and permission to raid Ogdensburg and put Forsyth out of business. Prevost refused but a few weeks later Lieutenant Colonel "Red George" Macdonell, temporarily in command at Prescott, managed to get the commander-in-chief's permission to mount a "demonstration." Assembling a force of about five hundred men from his own garrison, detachments of regular troops that had stopped at Prescott on their way to western Upper Canada, and local militia, Macdonell led them out onto the frozen, snow-covered St. Lawrence, ostensibly to drill but in reality to attack the American village opposite. Forsyth, who commanded at Ogdensburg, suspected something was up and had reinforced his own company with local volunteers and militia. He also had eight pieces of artillery in position, but since it was a common practice for the British and Canadians to drill on the ice, he held his fire until he realized that Macdonell's men were advancing straight at him. He then opened up but much of the American fire was ineffective because the untrained gunners aimed too high. Behind the British regulars was a small force of Glengarry militia acting as a reserve, and behind them marched their warrior priest, Father Alexander Macdonell, who encouraged the laggards to do their duty – when one man refused to move forward despite being twice warned, he was excommunicated on the spot.[19]

Although they took casualties, the British and Canadians closed with the defenders, who hastily abandoned the village. Forsyth and his riflemen retreated to Sackets Harbor, leaving Ogdensburg in the possession of Macdonell and his men, who removed eleven pieces of artillery and a considerable amount of ammunition and other military stores to Prescott and also burned a number of schooners and gunboats frozen in the ice. American casualties in this action were twenty killed and seventy captured while the British and Ca-

nadians lost seven killed and forty-eight wounded. Father Macdonell helped
tend the British wounded, who were returned to the Canadian shore and de-
posited in a house that doubled as a tavern. Local legend has it that this mili-
tant man of the cloth, seeing that one wounded man was as "in need of stimu-
lants as of priestly counsel," requested the wife of the tavern keeper, a known
American sympathizer, to produce some brandy but only received excuses:
"Her husband was absent and had the keys, and so on." Losing patience, the
good father "walked up to the taproom door and with one kick lifted it off its
hinges" and not only the wounded man but all present "had all the brandy
they required after their hard day's fighting."[20]

The attack on Ogdensburg began a period of relative calm along the St.
Lawrence, and for the next ten months the riverside communities existed in an
uneasy state of truce which was assisted by the fact that, after Forsyth's disappearance from the river, no American regulars were stationed on the United
States side. British boat convoys moved unmolested, and for many in both nations the war turned into a profitable business as the British army provided a
ready market for foodstuffs and wood. There were those in Upper Canada and
New York who thought that the war might be prosecuted with more vigour by
their respective governments, but they were in the minority – most people
along the St. Lawrence adopted a "live and let live" attitude.

James Wilkinson was about to change all that. Shepherded by Chauncey's
squadron, his army made steady progress down the river on 3 November.
Their voyage took them into the Thousand Islands, a picturesque region with
its multitude of small islets, some of them bare rock outcrops with one tree,
dotted across the river and a tricky place to navigate, particularly for Chauncey's larger warships, which had men heaving the lead line throughout the day
to check the depth of water. Several vessels ran aground but were got off safely

**The Stockade Barracks,
Prescott**
Originally constructed as
a military storehouse,
this stone building was
used as a hospital during
the war. It has been
restored and is today a
fine dining establish-
ment. (Photograph by
Dianne Graves)

The professional (3) – Captain William Howe Mulcaster, RN, river raider (1785-1837)
The commander of the British force that attacked French Creek and the gunboat squadron which shadowed Wilkinson's army down the St. Lawrence, William Mulcaster was determined to do damage to the enemy. (From Morgan, *Sketches of Eminent Canadians,* 1862)

– when the *Growler* struck a second time, however, she was abandoned. In some of the narrow channels traffic became congested, and the *Sylph,* having collided with the "*Fair American* and carried away her flying jib boom," was ordered to sail "to leeward" as she was "running into everything."[21] There were no major disasters and in the early afternoon the squadron came to anchor at the lower end of Wolfe Island, while the flotilla made its way into the rendezvous point at French Creek. Waiting there was Brown and he had some news – he had been attacked by a British naval force.

This attack had been made on the orders of Commodore Sir James Yeo, who had dispatched a small squadron consisting of the *Melville* (14 guns), *Moira* (14), *Sir Sidney Smith* (12) and *Beresford* (9) and four gunboats from the river flotilla. It was commanded by twenty-eight-year-old Captain William Howe Mulcaster, the officer who had saved Yeo by rescuing his commodore's flagship during the naval engagement of 28 September. William Mulcaster was a professional who had entered the Royal Navy at an early age and had served as Yeo's first officer in the sloop *Confiance* for a number of years. In 1812, he had been promoted commander and captain of the *Emulous,* based in Halifax, with which he had captured a number of American privateers before his vessel was wrecked on Sable Island off Nova Scotia. In the spring of 1813 Mulcaster accompanied Yeo to Lake Ontario and quickly proved to be one of the British naval commander's most aggressive subordinates.[22]

Early on the morning of 1 November 1813, Mulcaster raised anchor at Kingston and made his way down the northernmost of the two channels of the St. Lawrence created by Wolfe Island. As Chauncey's squadron was still out on the lake, there was no interference from the Americans and Mulcaster's biggest problem was a snowstorm that hampered visibility. By late afternoon he was approaching French Creek, a wide but shallow bay overlooked by a high wooded bluff on its western side. "The enemy," stated Mulcaster, "posted a strong detachment of infantry" on this bluff "to pour musketry on the vessels' decks." The British squadron swept by "within hail ... receiving the fire of the enemy and returning discharges of grape and canister" which caused the Americans "to abandon their post with precipitation." He moved on into the narrow bay and anchored the *Melville, Moira* and *Smith* (there not being room for the *Beresford*) and opened fire.[23]

On shore, Brown had his own brigade, the Third Artillery acting as infantry, and several companies of the Light Artillery Regiment. Brown had wisely protected his boats by drawing them up the winding creek that emptied into the bay and they were not exposed to Mulcaster's fire. Lieutenant Colonel Robert Carr of the Fifteenth Infantry remembered that the British squadron appeared just at sunset and opened a "most tremendous cannonade on us."[24] Lieutenant Colonel Abram Eustis recorded that a "heavy shot, and soon after, a second, passed directly over the tent, in which I was. On running out, I discovered two brigs, two schooners, and several gun boats, within a quarter of a mile."[25] The British fire was returned with musketry by Brown's infantry but the most effective reply was provided by three 18-pdr. guns, commanded by Captain Robert Macpherson of the Light Artillery, which were landed on the beach. Macpherson's guns were "posted on a bare rock without breastwork or defences" but his detachments,

The Royal Navy at French Creek (Clayton, New York), 1-2 November 1813
On the first two days of November 1813, Captain William Howe Mulcaster, commanding a squadron of four warships and four gunboats, attacked the American advance position at French Creek, New York. This sketch by marine artist Peter Rindlisbacher depicts the action from the northwest and shows HMS *Beresford* standing off while the three larger vessels under Mulcaster's command (HM Ships *Melville, Moira* and *Sir Sidney Smith*, in line from the viewer) anchor in the narrow mouth of the bay to bombard the shore. In the background the four smaller gunboats move around a small islet to try to get in close to the American position.

Brown later reported with admiration, acted "with cool and deliberate behavior" and scored several hits on their opponents.[26] While this exchange went on, Mulcaster sent his four gunboats up the east side of the bay to close on Brown's small craft, and Carr recorded they "nearly succeeded in getting possession of one of our schooners with our heavy artillery on board" but the British sally was beaten off.[27] After nearly an hour of firing, the light began to fail, and as his vessels had "received several shot in their hulls and a few between wind and water," Mulcaster thought "it right to haul off for the night."[28]

He was back early the next morning, just after first light. The British commander had wanted to send his four gunboats in "to annoy the enemy during the middle of the night," but the wind proved too strong so he again anchored his three largest vessels in line while trying to sneak the gunboats up the eastern side of the bay under cover of the smoke and confusion. "One merchant schooner without a soul on board was afloat," Mulcaster later reported, "but a boat came out and cut her cables as we rounded the bluff and she drifted on the rocks."[29]

Brown had a surprise waiting for him. "In the course of the night," Eustis proudly recalled, "a furnace was constructed; by morning, red-hot shot were prepared; and when the enemy again appeared, one of their vessels was set on fire, three or four times."[30] Mulcaster reported that the "enemy had mounted several guns in the night and some hot shot came on board our squadron," which is a modest way of describing a projectile that might well have been disastrous to his little squadron.[31] Assessing the situation, Mulcaster realized that the "scows and batteaux of the enemy were hauled up on the shore" and to "have brought off or destroyed them would have cost an immense number of men (considering the fine position of the enemy) which I could not afford, having to guard against the enemy's squadron in the morning." After about forty-five minutes, he decided to withdraw to Kingston, and two hours after his vessels disappeared around the bluff at the west end of the bay, the first ships of Chauncey's squadron came in view. This hard-fought little action which did credit to both sides cost Mulcaster one dead and four wounded while Brown lost ten killed and wounded.[32]

Wilkinson was not in good health when he arrived at French Creek on 3 November. He had been badly stricken with dysentery and one of his aides recalled he "had to be carried on shore" and "lodged in a tent, his malady increasing in violence."[33] The American commander was not the only sufferer. Colonel John Walbach, the adjutant general, thought "the army was sickly, principally with the dysentery; and the sickness increased daily."[34] He estimated that 80 per cent of the troops suffered to a greater or lesser extent but most "however performed duty." Wilkinson later stated that "a great portion of the troops, I commanded, were either struggling under maladies, occasioned by the poisonous provisions imposed on them, or so highly predisposed to diseases, as to have encumbered my movements."[35] This was no exaggeration – Wilkinson estimated that fourteen hundred of his men were on the sick list and unable to perform their duty during November 1813. A civilian who watched his troops march through Ogdensburg a few days later thought they resembled a "moving Hospital, much more than they did an invading army" and that "it was melancholy to see the poor sick creatures dragging on, but whose trembling limbs, refused to bear them along."[36]

Wilkinson also faced a serious shortage of provisions. Nearly half his food supplies had been lost during the passage to Grenadier Island, and by the time the army reached French Creek, it was reduced to twenty-two days rations of meat and fourteen and a half days of bread. The only thing in plenty was whisky – there were a thousand gallons or twenty-seven days rations to hand. With the supplies scattered among all the boats in the flotilla, however, no officer not from the quartermaster's department would take responsibility for them and there was continual loss from weather and theft. Abram Eustis noted that most of the boats "had no decks, and the stores in consequence, were exposed under the feet of the men," which caused more loss.[37] Macpherson of the artillery, commenting that "the army, from the inclemency of the season, with few exceptions, suffered extremely with dysentery," remembered that some of his fellow officers broke into the hospital stores, which, "used as food, proved beneficial to health."[38] His rapidly declining stockpile of provisions would limit Wilkinson's options in the near future.[39]

When he had recovered enough to transact business, the American commander completed the reorganization of the army begun at Sackets Harbor, since this was the first time his entire force of about 7,300 men had been assembled in one place. He and Morgan Lewis then devised an elaborate sailing plan for movements down the river. Each brigade and regiment was issued its own flag to be flown from the commanding officer's boat, and the army was directed to proceed in an orderly fashion with eight gunboats forming the van, followed by two infantry brigades in order of regiments, then the stores, ordnance and hospital craft; next came the last two brigades and, finally, four more gunboats bringing up the rear.[40]

Wilkinson's intention for the next day, 4 November, was to drop down to Morrisville but this movement was put off until first light on the following day, possibly because of his poor health. The weather, which had been bad or mixed for most of the last two weeks, now moderated, and a fine sunny day was spent completing preparations, including the manufacture of steering oars for the smaller boats to help them navigate the rapids downstream. The American commander also dispatched a note to Chauncey's flagship asking the commodore to detach some of his smaller warships to accompany him to Ogdensburg. Chauncey, who feared getting trapped by ice in the St. Lawrence, refused to divide his command but did promise to stay in the river until the army had passed Prescott.[41]

Wilkinson issued a number of orders at French Creek couched in the flowery prose he favoured. As the aide-de-camp once remarked, his superior "delighted in swelling sentences and round periods – most of them ending with victory or death" and he and his comrades "felt in duty bound to consider that there was no other alternative, and that we must submit to the latter if we could not compass the former."[42] Sure enough, an order was issued on 4 November that since the "enemy expects and are prepared for us, and as the thought of retreat is worse than death," Wilkinson trusted "that the minds of every man and every officer will so far accord with his own as to determine to defeat the enemy or to die gloriously on the field of battle."[43] As his troops would shortly be coming in contact with Canadian civilians, Wilkinson cautioned them about their behaviour because "nothing is so abhorrent as rapine and plunder." Should they forget that "marauding is punishable by death," he assured them he was "solemnly determined to have the first person who shall be detected in plundering an inhabitant of Canada of the smallest article of property, made an example of."[44]

Having warmed up, the American commander next drafted a proclamation addressed to Canadian civilians. "The army of the United States," he told them, "invades these provinces to conquer, and not to destroy; to subdue the forces of his Britannic majesty, not to war against his unoffending subjects." If they remained peacefully at home, the Canadians would "be protected in their persons and property" but "those who are found in arms, must necessarily be treated as avowed enemies." "To menace is unjust, to seduce dishonorable," Wilkinson concluded with a flourish, "yet it is just and humane to place these alternatives before you."[45]

Wilkinson's orders for 5 November were that the troops were to be roused at 4 A.M. and embarked an hour later, prepared to continue the voyage to Morrisville, where final preparations would be made for passing Prescott during that night. The day started well and the soldiers were ready on time – Lieutenant Joseph Dwight of the Thirteenth Infantry recorded that his brigade embarked at 5 A.M. – but then it all began to fall apart as the inexperienced soldiers tried to manoeuvre their craft into the formations specified by Wilkinson and Lewis. An hour passed in confusion, then another, and then a third, and finally Wilkinson and Lewis were rowed "about the bay to arrange the troops, in the order of progression and battle; as laid down in the diagrams furnished the officers."[46] It was fortunate the weather was good, with blue skies, because it was not until well after 10 A.M. that the vanguard of the flotilla moved out on the river, and it was early afternoon by the time the last boat had disappeared from the view of Chauncey's warships at their anchorage at the east end of Wolfe Island.[47]

Hardly had the army rowed out of sight when Chauncey's lookouts spotted British warships, moving under "fresh breezes and a westerly wind," coming down the north channel of the St Lawrence. Chauncey immediately ordered his crews beat to quarters, but the British vessels came to anchor in the north channel, about five miles distant from the American squadron, which was positioned in the gap between Wolfe and Grindstone islands. This shallow opening, where the two channels of the river join, was full of "reefs of rocks, and there" was only one passage through which "vessels can pass from one channel to the other and in this passage vessels drawing more than twelve feet water cannot pass." It was a stalemate: Chauncey could not cross into the north channel to engage Yeo while the British commander could not get past Chauncey to attack the helpless flotilla. Chauncey was determined to have a try, however, and "sent boats to sound out the best water in the channel and buoy it out," intending to lighten the *Pike*, his largest ship, so that it could cross. It proved impossible since the depth was "only six inches more water" than the *Pike* drew. The two opponents spent an uneasy night anchored so close "the bells of the ships" in one squadron could be heard in the other, and the guard-boats rowing between them occasionally exchanged musket shots.[48]

The sailors of both squadrons expected an action would take place the following day, but early on 6 November Yeo returned to Kingston. The British commander's reasons for this decision have never been properly explained, but his disappearance left Chauncey on the horns of a dilemma. He was concerned the British would occupy the strong but abandoned Revolutionary War fort on the western tip of Carleton Island, which commanded the entrance to the St. Lawrence. If this happened and Yeo moored his squadron near there, Chauncey might not be able to leave the river and could then be trapped by ice. The American commander decided to withdraw but did so in stages, first anchoring off Carleton Island, where he remained three days to prevent British occupation of that vital place, and then, on 9 November, shifting to Gravelly Point, where he remained two days before returning to Sackets Harbor.[49]

Wilkinson's flotilla, meanwhile, made muddled progress down the St. Lawrence on 5 November. The troops were passing through some of the most splendid scenery in North America but the men in the boats, many of them sick, probably did not pay much attention to the vista. The boats were dangerously overloaded – Boyd recalled that he did not have enough comfortable passage for his brigade and had to pack his men in as best he could among the casks, crates and barrels of provisions and other supplies loaded in each craft. The American commander sailed on a small schooner piloted by thirty-one-year-old William Johnston of Kingston, one of many Upper Canadians hired to serve as watermen in his armada. Johnston was later to blame the troubles with Crown authorities that made him leave his native country on a bad marriage to an American wife, but another man, Joseph Seeley, had less excuse as he was a deserter from the Incorporated Militia and faced a short and unhappy future if apprehended.[50]

To the untrained eye the flotilla was an impressive sight, but the movement from French Creek to Morrisville turned out to be a desperately muddled affair. Boyd remembered that the "flotilla was very much in disorder" while Dwight of the Thirteenth Infantry thought it was in the "utmost confusion."[51] "The commander-in-chief had arranged on paper," the aide-de-camp explained, "with the most perfect precision, the relative manner in which the flotilla … should move, and he perhaps saw no difference between a sheet of paper and a sheet of water."[52] "Every thing went on pretty orderly until we came within the varied currents which sweep" through the Thousand Islands, and the boats steered into various channels, the flotilla became disorganized and in "five minutes all was higgledy-piggledy."

By the time the sun set on 5 November, Wilkinson's army was in disarray. Only the lead boats had pulled into the proper landing place; the rest of the army, strung out for miles in the many channels of the Thousand Islands,

Scenic voyage – the American army in the Thousand Islands
In early November 1813 the American flotilla, consisting of 328 boats, batteaux, scows, skiffs, and small schooners traversed the Thousand Islands (there are actually 1868) area of the St. Lawrence, one of the most beautiful vistas in North America. (Benson Lossing, *Pictorial Field Book of the War of 1812*)

missed the designated spot in the darkness and continued down the river, passing the twinkling lights of Elizabethtown on the Canadian shore. At Wilkinson's orders, fires were built on shore near Morrisville "as signals for the boats," but as Lewis recalled "these not being perceived by those who took the north channel, part [of the army] proceeded below, and others landing at Morrisville, which produced some confusion."[53] This was a masterpiece of understatement. Lieutenant Dwight of the Thirteenth Infantry remembered the night as "so very dark and the shore so very rough" that it was "impossible to restore order" and "Brigades & regiments & even companies separated in the dark and land at different places."[54] When the last units came ashore around midnight, the army was scattered along four to five miles of the American bank of the river between Morrisville and the farm of a man named Hoag. It was not a very auspicious start for the attack on Montreal.

Wilkinson had now entered the area of the ever-watchful Pearson, the British commander at Prescott, and hard-nosed Thomas Pearson was a professional soldier to the core of his being. He joined the army as a sixteen-year-old second lieutenant in 1796, fought in Holland in 1798 and 1799, in Spain in 1800, and in Egypt in 1801, where he was wounded in the thigh at the battle of Aboukir "but did not quit the field."[55] By 1807 Pearson was a major in the 23rd Foot, and he took part with his regiment in the attack on Copenhagen before embarking the following year for Nova Scotia. He had come to Prevost's notice when he fought under that officer's command in the Martinique campaign of 1809, during which he commanded a light infantry brigade and not only "received the public thanks of the Commander of the Forces for his surprise of a French picquet under the walls of Fort Bourbon" but had also suffered a second wound.[56] Pearson remained in North America long enough to court and marry Anne Coffin, a daughter of General John Coffin, a prominent New Brunswick Loyalist, in June 1810, but four months later embarked for Portugal with his regiment. He commanded a light infantry battalion during the 1811 campaign and took part in the first siege of Badajoz. At the battle of Albuera in May 1812, which cost the 23rd Foot half the men the unit brought into action, Pearson succeeded to the command of his brigade and won both a gold medal and a brevet promotion to lieutenant colonel. A few months later his thigh bone was shattered by a round shot, which led to him being invalided into a staff job as an inspecting field officer of militia in Lower Canada, and in late 1812 Prevost appointed Pearson, "whose zeal & talents as a Soldier" he had "frequently witnessed," to the command at Prescott.[57]

The Canadian militia hated Tom Pearson. He had absolutely no patience with the martial pretensions of amateur officers and was not shy about voicing his opinions, nor was his disposition the best. Lieutenant John Le Couteur, who thought him "a regular tartar" and "singularly intemperate," was shocked to witness Pearson loudly and publicly rebuke Richard Cartwright, a militia colonel and one of the leading citizens of Kingston, "for not performing some movement which a Militia officer could not be expected to know."[58] He maintained strict discipline, which came as a rude shock to militiamen used to more easygoing officers. When he commanded briefly at Cornwall, Pearson caused such dismay among the male citizens of the village that when news spread of his being posted away, a local woman accosted him on the street with the words: "Och, Colonel dear, and are you going to lave us – sure there will be many a dry eye in the town the day you quit it."[59] But behind the stern exterior and bad temper (which was not helped by the fact that his third wound never healed properly) beat a softer heart and Pearson always respected those who stood up to him. A militia private, applying to his grumpy superior for leave to visit his family, received the usual response, "Go to Hell!" and just as quickly retorted, "Has your honour any orders for the Devil?"[60] Pearson liked that and doubled the man's leave.

Prescott, according to one British officer, was not much of a village "consisting of five houses, three of which were unfinished."[61] Located on the river at the point where the larger vessels from Lake Ontario transferred their cargoes to the boats that ran the rapids below, it was a vital link in the British logistical system. The previous winter, construction had started on a large blockhouse surrounded by an earthwork, later called Fort Wellington, but in October 1813 it was not completed, and the main defences were a series of batteries containing seventeen pieces of artillery under the command of Captain Henry George Jackson, RA, sited to command the river (which narrowed at this point to about 1,800 yards) and Ogdensburg. Pearson had taken all possible precautions – patrols were active, the local militia had been called up for duty, and the troops in garrison were ordered not "to put off their clothes at night but every person belonging to the garrison to hold himself in readiness to turn out at a moment's warning."[62] Any movement on the American side was sure to attract his eye, and when he spotted Wilkinson's chief engineer, Colonel Joseph Swift, and his assistants assessing his defences in late October Pearson dispatched militia Captain Reuben Sherwood across the river to make Swift's life miserable.[63]

On 12 October, Pearson observed American cavalry entering Ogdensburg and immediately opened fire with his two 24-pdr. guns. These troops were Lieutenant Colonel Nelson Luckett's First Light Dragoons, who had been sent

The professional (4) – Lieutenant Colonel Thomas Pearson, war horse (1780-1847)
Hawk-eyed and hard-nosed, irascible Thomas Pearson had fought in Egypt, Martinique, Holland and Spain, collecting a medal, three wounds and two brevet promotions before assuming command at Prescott, the strategic post on the St. Lawrence, in the spring of 1813. For more than six months he did not permit his garrison to undress at night in case of attack and expressed the wish that, if the Americans came down the river, he hoped "to God" to "get some account of them." He did. (Courtesy, Director of the National Army Museum, Negative 9730)

by Wilkinson to the village to rendezvous with the main army when it moved down the river. After the raid of the previous February, an uneasy truce had existed between the Canadian shore and defenceless Ogdensburg and the residents were not happy when Luckett's men drew fire. The village was crowded that day because the county court, with Judge Benjamin Raymond presiding, was in session. "The grand jury had just received their charge and retired" when the first rounds came in, "which led to much uneasiness, and after a little discussion, the session of the court was interrupted for the day" and "the room was hastily evacuated."[64] It was well that Judge Raymond adjourned because a few seconds later, "a 24 pound shot entered the room, shattering an end beam in the house, cut obliquely across the seats, but a moment before occupied by the jury, and lodged in the partition beyond." Luckett, apologizing for endangering the lives of civilians and disturbing the judicial process, rode out of town but returned the next day and his dragoons "paraded the streets, & shore, in front of the village, evidently with a design to provoke a repetition of the firing."[65] This time Pearson sent over shells from his two mortars, "the effect of which was to make them [the cavalry] leave the village hastily, when the firing ceased immediately."[66]

In the first days of November, when Pearson learned of the presence of American troops at French Creek, he dispatched a number of officers up the river to give warning of any enemy movement. One of them was twenty-eight-year-old Lieutenant Duncan Clark of the Incorporated Militia who was ordered on 1 November to proceed to Elliott's Point, five miles above Elizabethtown, to observe any enemy movement on the river. On "the appearance of an enemy," his instructions read, Clark was to "instantly take horse, and repair to

Canada's answer to Paul Revere – Lieutenant Duncan Clark, Incorporated Militia (1785-1862) Duncan Clark, shown in a photograph taken when he was in his seventies, was posted above Elizabethtown (Brockville) to warn the communities below if the Americans should come down the river. On 5 November he spotted Wilkinson's flotilla and, mounting a borrowed plough horse, rode at a furious plod along the St. Lawrence to accomplish his mission. (Archives of Ontario, S-7481)

Prescott, with all possible diligence, alarming the country as you pass down." During the evening of 5 November, Clark spotted the American armada of "some three hundred of every description of craft, including several gun-boats" coming down the St. Lawrence and immediately obeyed his orders to alert the "front" or river bank inhabitants. The problem was that Lieutenant Clark did not have a mount. Displaying commendable initiative, he commandeered the first plough horse he saw and, in a modest Canadian version of a more famous ride made by a man named Revere near Boston in April 1775, moved off at a furious plod to alert all and sundry that "the Yankees are coming!"[67]

That same evening Wilkinson was standing by a bonfire near Hoag's house on the American bank of the St. Lawrence four miles below Morrisville. His intention to pass Prescott that night had been rendered impossible by the confusion and scattering of his units during their ragged voyage from French Creek. As a result, he was forced to postpone the passage until the following night – yet more time lost.

Early the next day, Wilkinson issued orders that "the regiments and brigades which were deranged last night, must be put in strict order as speedily as possible." The flotilla was collected at Hoag's and preparations made for the coming night. Only enough men would remain on the boats to row them with muffled oars. Wilkinson's boat would lead, "followed by the whole of the ordnance boats and scows," and the brigades and other formations in order. The majority of the troops would disembark above Ogdensburg and march through it to rendezvous with the flotilla at a point below out of range of British artillery, and in order to "save all unnecessary hazard, the powder and ammunition" was to be landed and carried overland by carts and wagons. The actual water movement was to be commanded by Brown, who was familiar with the river at this point.[68]

At about noon Wilkinson was completing plans with his senior officers when a visitor arrived. Major William King, Hampton's adjutant general, had been sent with that general's report on Châteauguay to Armstrong, but unable to find the secretary at Sackets Harbor, he had returned via Ogdensburg and decided to visit Wilkinson to see if he had any communications for Hampton. Wilkinson, although suffering from dysentery, was in good humour and went on shore with King and Lewis, where they sat on a log to discuss matters. By this time Wilkinson had learned of Hampton's reverse, probably from a printed copy of the general order issued by Prevost the day after the battle, sent across the river by some friendly person. He asked King whether it was true that Hampton's division "had been defeated by a party of about three hundred men" and King replied "he could not speak with precision, of the number opposed to us, but that we certainly had to contend with a very inferior force, and that our best troops behaved in the most rascally manner."[69] According to Lewis, Wilkinson then exclaimed, "Damn such an army! a man might as well be in hell as command it," but softened these words by adding, "What is to be expected from men, who as soon as they are enlisted, are marched to the field, without having acquired the first rudiments of their profession?"[70] "However," he concluded, "my army will behave better." After some further discussion, Wilkinson asked King to take a letter to Hampton and the three returned to his schooner to have it written.

Since Armstrong was out of contact, Wilkinson was now forced to communicate directly with Hampton if the two armies were to combine against Montreal. He tried to be as tactful as possible – in the words of his aide, Captain Charles Nourse, "his motive for not couching" his letter "in more positive terms were, General Hampton's having slighted his former orders, and his not wishing, to put himself in any situation, to have his orders again disobeyed."[71] Wilkinson began by assuring Hampton that "I address you at the special instance of the Secretary of War," and that, since he was "determined" on "the attack of Montreal," Hampton had to "co-operate with the corps under my immediate orders." Wilkinson stressed the "point of rendezvous is the circumstance of greatest interest," but, since he was ignorant of "the practicability of the direct or devious roads or routes" on which Hampton had to move, he left it to the South Carolinian to determine the junction point.[72]

He would pass Prescott that night, Wilkinson continued, and would then press forward and "obtain foothold on Montreal island, at about twenty miles from the city; after which, our artillery, bayonets, and swords, must secure our triumph, or provide us with honorable graves." He appended a list of his siege artillery to indicate he had the force to accomplish this task, but on the subject of provisions stated that his "whole stock of bread may be computed at fifteen days, and our meat at twenty." As Armstrong had assured him there were ample stores on Lake Champlain, Wilkinson asked Hampton to bring two or three months of supplies "by the safest route." Finally, he returned to the matter of the junction point of the two armies, noting that his senior officers "were agreed in opinion that, if you are not in force to face the enemy, you should meet us at St. Regis or its vicinity." In conclusion, Wilkinson informed Hampton he would "expect to hear from, if not to see you, at that place [St. Regis] on the 9th or 10th instant [November]."[73]

King stayed just long enough to have a few glasses of wine and Wilkinson then reconvened the meeting with his senior officers, showed them the letter he had just sent, and the group turned to studying a map of the defences of Prescott provided by Swift. A few hours later, Wilkinson received more visitors when Colonels Edmund P. Gaines and Winfield Scott reported. Edmund Pendleton Gaines had been serving with Harrison's army in the northwest but had missed the battle of the Thames because of illness and after his recovery had been ordered to join Wilkinson. Scott had been left with his Second Artillery at Fort George when the army had withdrawn in early October. Anxious to join the operation, Scott took advantage of the discretionary orders given him by Wilkinson that permitted him to join the main army if the enemy withdrew from the Niagara – the British had done just that on 9 October so Scott turned the fort over to the New York militia and marched with his regiment along the south shore of Lake Ontario for Sackets Harbor. Their progress, delayed by shortage of transport, bad weather and bad roads, had been slow, and an impatient Scott had ridden ahead to catch up with Wilkinson, who assigned him command of the Third Artillery in Macomb's reserve brigade while Gaines received the Twenty-Fifth Infantry in Covington's brigade.[74]

In the early afternoon of 6 November, Brown assembled the senior captains of all the regiments on boats which "dropped down the river, noting the channel and the currents, until within round shot of the guns" of Prescott.[75] Wilkinson was insistent on leading, if not commanding, the water movement, but his surgeon advised that, "in consequence of his indisposition, it would be necessary for him, to stimulate against the night air" and Wilkinson accordingly dosed himself with laudanum, a mixture of opium and alcohol.[76] By late afternoon all was ready and everyone settled down to wait for darkness.

"About 8 P.M.," Major Joseph Totten recorded in the journal of the army, "we had so heavy a fog, that it was believed we could pass the British fortress unobserved, and orders were accordingly given for the army to march and the flotilla to get under way."[77] The fog was providential because it was a full moon

Night-time passage of Ogdensburg, 6 November 1813
During the night of 6 November 1813, the American flotilla ran by the British batteries at Prescott, Upper Canada, as shown in this sketch by Peter Rindlisbacher. Despite coming under heavy artillery fire for several hours, only one boat was slightly damaged and Wilkinson's army passed the first major obstacle on its way to Montreal.

that night. Rowing as quietly as possible with muffled oars, the lead boats moved down the river in front of Ogdensburg while the columns on land tramped through the village. The aide-de-camp and his jovial companions marched with the main body, but being staff officers and "fixed to no particular position of the column," they knew that "when not seen in one place" everyone would think them "properly in another."[78] This allowed them the opportunity to visit a local hostelry whose landlady "professed to have a steak or a rasher which could be made eatable in a twinkling." The young officers were anticipating this repast when "bang! bang! and bang! went the whole battery of Prescott" and "a cannon ball passed right through the upper story of the hotel, crashing and splintering its way through walls, partitions, and such articles of furniture as stood in its path." As "it was thought best to adjourn," the "stafflings" hastily paid their bill and retired out of range.[79]

Pearson and his artillery commander, Captain Henry Jackson, had been "certain of being attacked" that night; their guns were loaded and ready to fire.[80] The British were alerted to the movement of the flotilla, Totten recorded, by "a sudden change of the atmosphere" which dissipated the fog and exposed some of the boats to their view "while the column on land, discovered by the gleam of their arms, were assailed with shot and shells."[81] Brown, "on hearing the firing, judiciously halted the flotilla until the moon had set, when it got in motion, but was perceived by the enemy, who opened upon it, and continued their fire, from front to rear, for the space of three hours." Winfield Scott, in one of the boats, thought the "scene was most sublime" as "the roar of cannon was unremitting, and darkness rendered visible by the whizzing and bursting of shells."[82] Colonel Joseph Swift, taking a professional interest in the British marksmanship, recorded that little "damage was sustained by boats owing to the random fire from the fort and, as I presume, from neglect of ranging their guns by daylight."[83] Jackson excused his gunners' accuracy by noting that the St. Lawrence was 1,800 yards wide "and a boat, even in daylight, is but a small object at that distance" – and a much more difficult target at night.[84] The British fire was unrelenting but it had little effect and the flotilla passed Prescott without suffering any real harm; despite the best efforts of Jackson's sweating gunners, only one American boat was struck, one man was killed and two or three wounded.[85]

By daylight the flotilla was out of range below and Wilkinson's army had successfully passed their first major hurdle on the way to Montreal.

The news that the American army had gone down the St. Lawrence was spread, slowly by Lieutenant Duncan Clark on his plough horse, and more swiftly by better-mounted messengers. At Kingston, John Le Couteur recorded "fresh alarms" as "the American army was moving on the opposite shore."[86] Later it was learned that "the enemy who has for such a length of time been hovering about this place," as Lieutenant Edward MacMahon wrote to a correspondent, had "passed down to near Prescott with the view, we have good reason to believe, of proceeding to Montreal without delay."[87] During the morning of 7 November, reports came in from Gananoque down the river that artillery fire had been heard from the direction of Prescott during the night. When he received them, de Rottenburg began to waver in his firm belief that Kingston was the American objective and decided to put into effect Prevost's order to form a "corps of observation" to follow the enemy down the river. As his superior had requested, he gave command of this force to Lieutenant Colonel Joseph Morrison of the 89th Foot.[88]

Joseph Wanton Morrison was born in New York in 1783, the son of the deputy commissary general of British North America. Little is known about his childhood except that he was commissioned an ensign in 1793 at the tender age of eleven but this was a "paper" transaction made possible by loopholes in the system of appointing officers. Morrison's first actual service came in 1799, when he joined the 17th Foot and saw action briefly with his regiment in the Dutch campaign of that year before commencing a long spell of garrison and staff duty in Minorca, Ireland, England and Guernsey. By 1809 Morrison, described as a "most attentive, zealous and clear officer," was a major in the 89th Foot, and he was shortly promoted to lieutenant colonel and appointed to command a regiment in Trinidad. He returned to Britain in May 1812 to assume command of the 2nd Battalion of the 89th Foot and six months later was transferred with his unit to North America. Respected and liked by both superiors and subordinates, Joseph Morrison had actually seen very little action during his fourteen years in the army.[89]

The same could not be said of Lieutenant Colonel John Harvey, whom de Rottenburg attached to Morrison to act as his second-in-command and to provide "constant information of the progress and movements of the enemy."[90] The son of a clergyman, Harvey had been commissioned in 1794 at age seventeen and owed his advancement to his intelligence, industry and courage. He had seen action in almost every corner of the globe: Holland in 1794 and 1795, the Cape of Good Hope in 1796, Ceylon from 1797 to 1800, Egypt in 1801 and India from 1803 to 1807, earning a reputation for bravery. Returning to England a captain, Harvey received promotion to major in 1808 and served in a variety of staff positions until late 1812, when he was promoted lieutenant colonel and appointed deputy adjutant general in Upper Canada, where he was attached to Vincent's forces in the Niagara. It was Harvey who planned the British attack at Stoney Creek on 6 June 1813 which although it resulted in a drawn battle so shook Dearborn that he ordered his army to retreat, putting an end to the American spring offensive. When he returned to Kingston in October, Harvey had earned a reputation as an officer of "zeal, intelligence & gallantry."[91]

The professional (5) – Lieutenant Colonel Joseph Wanton Morrison, 89th Regiment of Foot, (1783-1826)
Shown as colonel of the 44th Foot in a postwar portrait c. 1822, Joseph Morrison commanded the little "corps of observation" that brought Wilkinson's army to ground at Crysler's Farm. Although he was a fourteen-year veteran of the army, the action of 11 November 1813 was his first battle. (Courtesy of the McCord Museum, M 401)

The professional (6) – Lieutenant Colonel John Harvey, the veteran (1778-1852)
Shown here in a postwar drawing, John Harvey was attached to Morrison's command as his chief of staff. Unlike his commanding officer Harvey had seen much combat during a twenty-one-year army career, fighting in Holland, South Africa, Ceylon, Egypt and India and was regarded as an officer of "zeal, intelligence & gallantry." (National Archives of Canada, C-2733)

Morrison's "corps of observation" was formed of the best units in the Kingston garrison, the 49th and his own 89th Foot. The 49th or the Hertfordshire Regiment of Foot had campaigned in Holland with the Duke of York in 1799 and served as marines during the attack on Copenhagen in 1801 before being sent to North America in 1803. Known as the "Green Tigers" from the colour of the facings or trim on their uniforms, the 49th had been the mainstay of the defence of Upper Canada in the past year, fighting at Queenston Heights and at Fort George, Stoney Creek and Black Rock before spending the long summer in the Niagara, where the unit had suffered so much from sickness that it was only a fragment of its authorized strength.[92]

The 2nd Battalion of the 89th Regiment of Foot had been raised in southern Ireland in 1804. It remained in garrison in Britain, and in 1809 with Morrison in command was described as having "a most Excellent Esprit de Corps, throughout the Battalion, which influences the Conduct of the Officers & Men."[93] Such plaudits do not come without penalty, and in May 1810 the 2/89th was posted to Gibraltar, where it lost 300 men in a very badly managed raid on the French-held town of Fuengirola on the south coast of Spain. The battalion was in poor case when Morrison rejoined it in the spring of 1812 but he rebuilt the unit and brought it to North America that same year.[94]

It took some time for the troops to be assembled and water transport collected and it was not until 10 P.M., Sunday, 7 November, that Morrison embarked about eight hundred men of the two regiments on sixty batteaux and set course for Prescott. The naval component of the force, commanded by the aggressive Mulcaster, consisted of two small schooners from Yeo's squadron, the *Beresford* and *Sir Sidney Smith*, and seven gunboats.[95]

In Montreal that same day, Prevost learned by express of the American movement past Prescott. This could only mean that the invaders were heading for that city and orders were issued for the mobilization and concentration of all regular and militia units for its defence. Assistant Surgeon William Dunlop of the 89th Foot, on his way to Upper Canada, recorded that in the immediate area around Montreal there was "not a single man fit to carry arms occupied about his farm or workshop; women, children or men disabled by age or decrepitude were all that were to be met with."[96] Now that the threat from Hampton had been stopped at Châteauguay, however, the overall mood in Lower Canada was one of optimism – the Quebec *Gazette* reminded its readers that three American generals were already prisoners of war in the province and confidently predicted Wilkinson would soon be joining them where "he may make a fourth at a whist party of Generals, and content himself for losing battles by winning rubbers."[97]

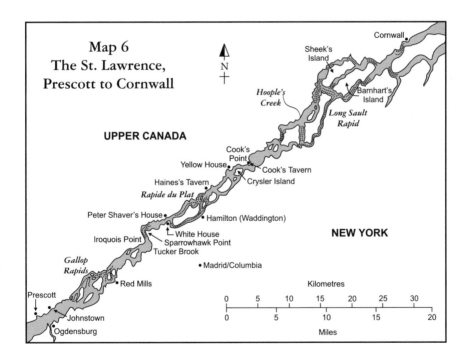

Map 6
The St. Lawrence,
Prescott to Cornwall

CHAPTER 7

"There is a spell on us"

THE PURSUIT DOWN THE RIVER, 7 NOVEMBER–10 NOVEMBER 1813

No more with your red-cross high streaming,
You'll triumphantly march o'er the plain,
But Columbia's dear eagle, bright beaming,
Shall wave where your warriors were slain.

    Long life to the true yankee army
    Success to the soldiers so brave,
    By St. Patrick old England they'll harm ye,
    And find for your veterans a grave.

Then JOHNNY BULL can't ye be easy,
For sure at the game hob-a-nob,
Our soldiers and sailors will amaze ye,
And make you give up a bad job.

    Then success, to our army and navy,
    And to generals and commodores brave,
    They'll dress you a dish without gravy,
    Which to feast on will make you look GRAVE.[1]

Pearson was furious that the enemy had managed to bypass Prescott. On the following morning of 7 November, he dispatched Jackson with two 6-pdr. guns and some militia down the King's highway, which paralleled the river on the Canadian side, to annoy the Americans. As there were still enemy troops visible in Ogdensburg, he kept his gunners busy firing at them throughout the day.[2]

These troops had been sent back by Wilkinson to recover "two of our largest vessels, loaded with provisions, artillery, and ordnance stores" which "either through cowardice or treachery" had been run into the Oswegatchie

River, which runs through Ogdensburg.[3] The job went to the Twenty-First Infantry and they spent the greater part of the day on what turned out to be a difficult task as the enemy "kept up a constant cannonade on them." As it was, two heavy mortars were left in the village for lack of transport and the small schooner *Syren,* which could not navigate the rapids below, was scuttled in the Oswegatchie with an 18-pdr. and a 24-pdr gun on board.[4]

The troops that had moved on land the previous night met the boats at the Red Mills, about eight miles below Ogdensburg. It took most of the morning for Wilkinson to assemble his army there, where the flotilla sheltered in the little bay below the long red-painted wooden building that gave the anchorage its name. That morning Wilkinson, "having been exposed to the open air all last night," according to one of his staff officers, "in consequence found himself ill."[5] To Colonel John Walbach he appeared "much fatigued, and unwell" from his travails of the previous night but the effects of the medical "fortification" taken by the American commander were also catching up with him.[6] Laudanum was a medication that had to be used carefully but Wilkinson apparently took too much and his behaviour during the passing of Prescott had been so erratic that some of his subordinates thought he was drunk. His condition the following morning was no better – his chief of staff, Colonel Joseph Swift, remembered that, "under the influence of laudanum the general became very merry, and sung and repeated stories, the only evil of which was that it was not the dignified deportment to be expected from the commander-in-chief."[7]

Wilkinson had other problems. From the American bank, his staff could see Canadian militia in arms "at Johnstown, directly opposite us, and several pieces of field artillery in motion."[8] There were concerns that the flotilla, which that day had to traverse the Gallop rapids, would come under fire and Wilkinson decided to land a force on the Canadian bank to protect this movement. He chose Colonel Alexander Macomb and his reserve brigade (now renamed "the Elite") for this task. Macomb was ordered to cross to the opposite shore and drive the enemy from his position, but if "the enemy is in considerable force, you will not risk an action, but inform me of it immediately."[9]

Macomb embarked in the early afternoon and dropped down the river. Under his command he had Forsyth's detachment of the First Rifle Regiment, Colonel Winfield Scott's Third Artillery, the Albany Volunteers and Colonel Thomas Randolph's Twentieth Infantry, a total of about eleven hundred men. It was difficult for the brigade to keep together as the boats of the Third Artillery proved swifter and forged ahead. Travelling with the artillery, Macomb was forced to pull into the American shore to wait for his slower units to catch up, and as he moved in to land, "militia, Indians and other troops came to the

The good soldier – Colonel Alexander Macomb (1782-1841)
Shown here as a brigadier general, Colonel Alexander Macomb was a graduate of West Point and a well-trained officer who commanded a brigade in Wilkinson's army throughout the 1813 campaign. This earned him a promotion to brigadier general and he was victorious at Plattsburgh in the following summer. Macomb ended his career as commanding general of the United States Army. (Benson Lossing, *Pictorial Field Book of the War of 1812*)

opposite bank, and began firing, whooping and hallooing." As his following units arrived, Macomb ordered them to divide into three groups and cross to the Canadian side; Scott was to lead the right group and Randolph the left, while Forsyth was directed to land further up the river to cut off the enemy's retreat. It was late afternoon and light was beginning to fade when these orders were carried out, but as Macomb's boats neared the Canadian shore, the enemy "fired perhaps five or six rounds and dispersed."[10]

Scott and Randolph landed just above Iroquois Point. The enemy who had faded away on their approach was a detachment of the 1st Dundas Regiment of militia under the command of Captain John Munroe. The Americans had initially been spotted by a picket of a dozen men posted at Jacob Brouse's farm near the river who, seeing "the boats and barges rapidly approaching," fired a volley "by way of welcome."[11] The shots alerted Munroe's detachment, two hundred strong, positioned in a hollow some distance away, and they advanced to the bank, fired in turn and cheered – this was the enemy whom Macomb remembered "whooping and hallooing." When the Americans pulled into the far bank, the militiamen decided they had won a victory, but when Macomb's brigade crossed the St. Lawrence in a very determined manner they took to their heels. One of the men running away was Private Jacob Brouse, who had just had the privilege of defending his own property.

Forsyth's men picked up a prisoner, a British army commissary named John Cleveland Green. Accompanied by his assistant, Thomas Gibbs Ridout, some staff and a wagon, he had been riding east on the King's highway when he saw troops wearing green uniforms landing a few hundred yards ahead. As the Glengarry Light Infantry of the British army wore uniforms of that colour, the commissary concluded they were friendly and rode ahead of his party to make contact. Unfortunately for him, Forsyth's rifleman also wore green and they promptly put him in the bag and also took a shot at Ridout, who was riding some distance behind. Ridout galloped back to his little party, assumed command and retreated to Prescott.[12]

While Macomb was busy, the main army embarked in mid-afternoon and followed him down the river. Just below Red Mills lay the Gallop rapids, the first and least dangerous of the five stretches of rough water that had to be traversed to reach Montreal. During his retreat to Prescott, Thomas Ridout watched as the American flotilla ran the Gallop. "It was a very grand sight," he thought, "to see an army of 10,000 men going down the Gallette [Gallop] rapids." "They fired at us several shots," he recalled, "taking our waggon for artillery I suppose." The young commissary was impressed with the enemy armada – "Unless this armament is destroyed, Montreal will go," was his conclusion.[13]

The American flotilla got safely through the Gallop and were reforming below when Captain Henry Jackson, RA, caught up and opened fire with his two 6-pdr. guns. Lieutenant Colonel Abram Eustis, commanding the gunboats of the flotilla, remembered that British guns "equipped as horse artillery" came "in full gallop, down the bank of the river; about ten men accompanying each gun," and fired several rounds at "General Wilkinson's schooner, and one or two at a gun-boat."[14] "To gain the advance of them, with the gun-boats under my command," Eustis "had a race with them, about a mile, and was preparing to go on shore when the enemy perceived, Major Forsyth with his corps, attempt to land, and thereupon retreated." Forsyth, whose unit formed the westernmost extension of Macomb's brigade, "advanced upon the enemy's guns" but "had his fire drawn by a couple of [cavalry] videttes, posted in his route," which permitted Jackson time to limber up his 6-pdrs. and withdraw.[15] The flotilla then continued to an anchorage at Tucker Brook on the American

Eyewitness to events – Commissary Thomas Gibbs Ridout (1792-1861)

Shown here in a drawing done when he was in his sixties, Thomas Gibbs Ridout was an officer in the commissary department during 1813. He narrowly avoided capture on the St. Lawrence in November 1813 and his letters to his father are one of the best eyewitness descriptions from the British side of the events of 1813. (Drawing by Edmund Wylie, courtesy of the Toronto Reference Library, T-14838)

bank, about six miles below Red Mills, where the troops disembarked and camped for the night.[16]

Macomb, meanwhile, moved east along the Canadian bank to Iroquois Point, which dominated a narrow stretch of the river. He encountered no enemy but discovered a half-finished semicircular defence of large, squared logs and earth which he burned. He then assembled his brigade, occupied the little hamlet of Matilda and camped for the night on the property of Peter Shaver, a miller, store owner and militia officer.[17]

It was a bad day for Peter Shaver. He had just received a boatload of luxury goods from Montreal including rum, spirits of peppermint, brandy, sugar, cloth, gloves, cravats and buttons. On 7 November Shaver was absent on militia duty, as were most of the other males in the district, and when word came that the Americans had landed, two neighbouring women, Grimma Dulmage and Nancy Brouse, did their best to hide the delicacies in the woods or various barns and sheds. Their good work was to no purpose because Macomb's troops, despite Wilkinson's orders forbidding looting, quickly uncovered the treasure, which was consumed or taken away.[18]

The culprits were likely Forsyth's riflemen, who had a reputation as the most aggressive acquisitors in the northern army. An American officer who watched them go about their business recorded that their favourite targets were British officers "and as soon as they fall do not stop to load again before they run up and plunder his Epaulets, watch – &c." Some riflemen, he commented, "had handkerchiefs full, and have made several hundred dollars in one battle" and would mash up "between two stones, some of the most elegant Silver embossed urns, tureens and plate of every description to get them in their knapsacks. The officers, generally attempt to prevent it, but Forysth is a perfect savage himself."[19] Shaver later claimed that he lost £1,177 worth of goods on the night of 7 November and to make matters worse the Americans also purloined his potatoes, apples and beehives.[20]

Monday, 8 November 1813, dawned stormy and cold. For once Wilkinson managed to get the flotilla moving at an early hour, and it dropped down to a bay in front of the "White House" (near modern Sparrowhawk Point) about three miles below Tucker Brook on the American bank. The events of the previous day, when the flotilla had been fired on by Jackson's guns and Munroe's militia, had made an impression on the American commander. He was concerned that the "active, universal hostility of the male inhabitants" of Upper Canada might be used to "great advantage" by lining the bank below "at every critical pass of the river" and decided that the Canadian

Green coats – 1st Rifle Regiment, United States Army, 1813
Lieutenant Colonel Benjamin Forsyth commanded a large detachment (about 300 men) of this regiment during the 1813 campaign. Armed with Harper's Ferry rifles as opposed to the smooth-bore muskets carried by most of the infantry in the two armies, Forsyth's green-uniformed riflemen were some of the best fighters and most dedicated looters in the northern army. (Painting H.C. McBarron, courtesy of the Company of Military Historians)

bank would have to be cleared before the flotilla passed.[21] His most effective units for this purpose were the two regiments of light dragoons who had been following the water movements of the army. The White House, situated where the river narrowed, offered an excellent place to cross over the cavalry, and indeed a man named Gray operated a ferry at that point. Soon after the flotilla arrived in the late morning, this operation commenced.[22]

It was a tedious task to transfer the 400 mounts of Lieutenant Colonel Nelson Luckett's First Dragoons and Major John T. Woodford's Second Dragoons and the 250 artillery team horses across the St. Lawrence to the landing place on the Canadian shore secured by Macomb. The most suitable craft, the eleven large, flat-bottomed, blunt-ended, artillery scows, were brought in close to the American bank and their cargo unloaded. Strong ramps were then constructed from the vessel to the shore and the horses were led on board one by one. The dragoon horses would have been no problem. Their riders stood beside them, holding the reins down just back of the bit in the horse's mouth, and if the animals started to rear, kick or pitch, the dragoon would pull their heads down to control them. The artillery horses, however, recently acquired and just driven overland from Sackets Harbor, were only half broken and would have needed more effort. No more than fifteen horses at a time could be

transported on each craft, and although the work started in the early afternoon, it was well into the night before the transfer was completed. Hour after
hour, the scows and Mr. Gray's ferry crossed and recrossed the St. Lawrence
laden with nervous, neighing and not very happy four-legged passengers.[23]

When the task was finished, the scows were cleaned and reloaded with guns
and ordnance stores. Brigadier General Moses Porter took the opportunity to
equip four 6-pdr. guns with four-horse teams for field service and shift them
to the Canada shore. These necessary but time-consuming tasks imposed yet
more delay, and many in the army were becoming concerned about its slow
progress: there "is a spell on us," thought Major William Clay Cumming of the
Sixteenth Infantry, "in two more days, we might have reached Montreal, or its
vicinity."[24]

There was also concern about the enemy. Morrison had not yet reached
Prescott, but Wilkinson's intelligence service was good, and he learned late in
the morning of 8 November that a British force was following him. This information was probably obtained from sympathizers on the Canadian side who
picked it up from members of the garrison at Prescott (where it would be
common knowledge as Pearson would have been alerted by dragoon express)
and then passed it over the river to "friends" in Ogdensburg. Lewis remembered first hearing of the British force "from a man who had called his name
Spencer" whom he conducted to Wilkinson.[25] This intelligence, coupled with
various sightings of enemy detachments on the Canadian side up-river from
the White House, caused Wilkinson to prepare against attack from the west.
Artillery pieces were offloaded and positioned on the American shore to cover
any enemy approach by boat and the Fifteenth Infantry was sent back "to annoy the enemy" should he come down-river.[26]

Sometime in the afternoon of 8 November Wilkinson called a council of
war. He first informed his senior officers of the disposition and strength of the
American forces, estimating his own at 7,000 and that of Hampton, who
would shortly be joining at St. Regis, fifty miles downstream, at 4,000 men.
According to reliable intelligence reports, the enemy's strength was 400 men at
Cornwall and 1,700 regulars and 20,000 militia in the Montreal area with another 2,500 regulars expected to arrive shortly at that city. He added, "for the
information of the council that two British armed vessels and sixty batteaux
loaded with troops" would soon reach Prescott from Kingston. The worst
news was that the supply situation was deteriorating – there were only ten days
rations of bread and twenty of meat remaining. All this being the case, Wilkinson put the question to his subordinates: "Should the army proceed with all
possible rapidity to the attack of the said city of Montreal?" After deliberation,

Lewis, Boyd, Brown and Swartout agreed that "we should proceed to attack Montreal, the object of the expedition." Covington and Porter were less certain and added the qualification that "we proceed from this place under great danger from the want of proper transport, pilots, &c., but are anxious to meet the enemy at Montreal because we know no other opinion."[27]

Word about this decision and the presence of an enemy force in their rear spread quickly through the army. Colonel Decius Wadsworth recalled that it "was well known in the camp" by the evening of 8 November, when all the troops, with the exception of Boyd's First Brigade, were shifted to the Canadian bank to reinforce Macomb.[28] As Wilkinson was now leaving friendly territory, he took the opportunity of leaving the worst of his sick in the United States and there were so many that one civilian later complained that there was "scarce a house" within thirty miles of Ogdensburg that did not have "more or less of these miserable sick soldiers in them, [with] no provisions for them, or any person left to provide and aid them on."[29] Neither illness nor starvation, however, worried the aide-de-camp and his companions. Being staff officers, they were privy to information concerning the army's food supplies but "resolved, in the lofty humour of the moment, to push ahead, even if we had only a biscuit in our pockets" as "the larders of Montreal would remunerate us for all privations which their acquisition might cost."[30]

Food stocks were also very much on the mind of Major General Wade Hampton, who that same day held his own council of war at Four Corners. Following his meeting with Wilkinson, Major William King had reached Hampton's headquarters at midnight on 7 November with Wilkinson's request for Hampton to join him at St. Regis. Brigadier General George Izard remembered being immediately summoned to discuss this communication, which "left discretionary for Genl. H[ampton]. to meet on the 9th or 10th the main army at St. Regis, or to take a position in L[ower]. Canada." Izard was "clearly of the opinion for the latter," which would be carrying out Armstrong's wish that a winter camp be constructed on Canadian soil.[31]

Wade Hampton had other ideas. The following day, 8 November, he called a council of war to deliberate on Wilkinson's letter, although, as Izard noted, the "thing is determined but *pro forma* they are asked."[32] Hampton's decision, which he communicated to his senior officers, was that his division would withdraw to Plattsburgh on Lake Champlain, and Izard "was requested to pencil" this decision which he "did as on a former occasion *Unanimously*" – a reference to the angry meeting of 28 October in which the decision to retreat to Four Corners was made after the division's repulse on the Châteauguay.

Hampton then composed a reply to Wilkinson's letter. Confessing to his rival he was "deeply impressed with the sense of responsibility" given to him "of deciding upon the means of our co-operation," he agreed St. Regis was a good junction point. But, Hampton continued, when he read Wilkinson's "disclosure of the amount of your provisions," his feelings began to change as his own logistical situation was extremely poor and it would be impossible for his division to bring more supplies to St. Regis than each of his men "carried on his back." This being the situation, if he joined with Wilkinson, he would only "be throwing myself upon your scanty means" and weakening Wilkinson "in your most vulnerable point."[33]

Hampton had a better suggestion, conceived "after consulting the general and principal officers" of his division, which was to withdraw to his "main depot" at Plattsburgh, where, by "falling back upon the enemy's flank and straining every effort to open a communication from Plattsburg to Coghnawaga or any other point you may indicate on the St. Lawrence, I should more effectually contribute to your success than by the junction at St. Regis." He proposed to do this, despite the fact that the road "between Lake Champlain and the St. Lawrence] is in many places blockaded and abbatied and the road impracticable for wheel carriages during winter." By the employment of pack horses, however, Hampton was confident that "if I am not overpowered, I hope to be able to prevent you from starving."

In plain words, far from joining the main army, Wade Hampton intended to withdraw to a position more than fifty miles from the St. Lawrence, where his division would contribute to the campaign against Montreal by attempting to supply Wilkinson with pack horses moving over bad roads in winter. This was arrant nonsense. Hampton was not only disobeying orders to join the main army, he was also refusing to comply with the secretary of war's direction to build a winter camp for both forces on Canadian territory. Wade Hampton had plainly decided the offensive was over and wanted nothing more to do with it, although he assured Wilkinson that "what can be accomplished by human exertion I will attempt, with a mind devoted to the general objects of the campaign." This communication was handed to Colonel Henry Atkinson, the divisional inspector general, to take to Wilkinson, and Atkinson was also instructed to inform Wilkinson of the poor state of Hampton's men, who were afflicted "with weakness and sickliness" because "they have endured fatigues equal to a winter campaign and are sadly dispirited and fallen off."[34]

Hampton wasted no time in getting as far away from Wilkinson as possible. Within minutes of the council of war, he issued orders for his division to march to Plattsburgh, but this movement had to be delayed until the following day as there was "much confusion."[35] The decision to withdraw was not popular and Sergeant Alan Neef of the Fourth Infantry recalled that when his comrades "were ordered to march for Lake Champlain, and not to join Wilkinson, as was Generally expected and desired," almost "every soldier denounced the bitterest curses against the author of all their unnecessary suffering and disgrace," Hampton, who "in one sad minute, deprives them of an opportunity to participate with their brethren in arms, in chastizing the opposers of American Liberty."[36]

On 9 November the division set out on the road it had cut the previous September. Corporal Bishop of the Twenty-Ninth Infantry found it "was almost impossible" to keep up with his regiment "on account of the swamps and logs that was almost continually in the way."[37] The division made thirteen miles that day but thereafter progress was slower due to snowstorms, the laborious progress of the baggage wagons and the great number of invalids in the ranks. Izard recorded, however, that Hampton was in a good mood and visited his subordinate one evening "as I am sitting down to dine and accepts my invitation to join us," and is "merry this evening."[38] On a later occasion, Izard (heeding the old British army maxim of "no names, no pack drill") recorded in his diary that "somebody was so drunk last night as to fall off his chair and remain unable to rise."[39] Hampton was less cordial to his other brigade commander, and on 15 November Izard recorded in his diary that his commander "orders Col. Atkinson to arrest Col. Purdy which is done!!!"[40] No reasons were specified, but there had been bad blood between Purdy and Hampton since the action at Châteauguay.

After eight days on the road, the division arrived at Plattsburgh only to discover that there were no quarters waiting for them and they would have to build their winter huts in the middle of a snowstorm.[41]

On the St. Lawrence, meanwhile, Lieutenant Colonel Joseph Morrison's "corps of observation" had made good progress. He landed at Prescott during the early evening of 8 November, having completed the seventy-mile journey from Kingston in about twenty-two hours. The *Beresford* and *Sidney Smith* would be unable to descend the rapids below, so the troops they carried were transferred to batteaux, available at Prescott because it was the transshipment point for convoys from Montreal, and for safety British military traffic on the river had ceased as soon as the Americans had passed Ogdensburg. Not only were boats available but also officers experienced in river transport, such as Captain Edward Davis of the New Brunswick Fencibles and Captain Robert Skinner and Lieutenant Andrew Bulger of the Royal Newfoundland Regiment, and skilled crews from the Commissariat Voyageurs.[42]

Pearson had not been idle since the enemy had passed his position. As soon as he was certain that no American troops remained in Ogdensburg, he dispatched an officer across the river to demand "an instant surrender of all public property, threatening in case of refusal to send an armed force to take both public and private property." Judge Benjamin Raymond did the negotiating and the villagers turned over, according to one report, "the property, which was trifling, consisting only of two mortars, 30 barrels of pork, 20 barrels of whisky and a few other inconsiderable items." If this commentator thought twenty barrels of whiskey were "trifling" and "inconsiderable items," it is clear he had no idea of what a welcome addition they would make to the stores at Prescott, while Wilkinson would need the two mortars, heavy brass 10-inch and 13-inch weapons, if he had to lay siege to Montreal.[43]

Because the immediate danger to his post had passed, Pearson requested permission to join the expedition and Morrison welcomed him. Pearson had already dispatched some of Captain Richard Fraser's Provincial Light Dragoons and local militia to maintain contact with the Americans – he now contributed three 6-pdr. field guns, three companies of the Canadian Voltigeurs and two companies of the Canadian Fencibles while the two flank companies of the 49th Foot, part of the Prescott garrison, rejoined their regiment. With this increase Morrison had just under twelve hundred men including a combat element the Americans could not match – thirty Mohawk warriors under Lieutenant Charles Anderson of the Indian Department. On the other hand, Wilkinson's army was estimated to be between seven and eight thousand strong.

The combined force, carried in seven gunboats and sixty batteaux, left Prescott in the early morning of 9 November and ran the Gallop in the dark. No craft were lost, and when Morrison received information that "the enemy had landed their whole force on our shore, three or four miles below, and brought over three hundred cavalry," he pulled into the Canadian bank three miles above Iroquois Point and disembarked. Captain Henry Jackson remembered that the pursuers "remained quiet until two hours before daylight," when "we moved on and at dawn came up with their pickets, which we drove in." Morrison had made contact.[44]

"This morning," Major Joseph Totten recorded on Tuesday, 9 November 1813, "the enemy menaced our rear, and a slight skirmish took place between our riflemen and a part of their militia and Indians."[45] The British did not press the attack, which was only a probe, and the shooting died down. One of Forsyth's riflemen was killed, and it was Totten's belief "the enemy were driven back," but, in reality, having made his point, Morrison withdrew.

The weather was clear this day and at 10 P.M. Brigadier General Jacob Brown marched east on the King's highway with his Second Brigade, Macomb's Reserve or "Elite" Brigade and the two dragoon regiments to clear the Canadian bank of any enemy. As they approached Nash's Creek below Matilda, seventeen-year-old John W. Loucks, one of Fraser's Provincial Light Dragoons, posted there as a scout, saw the lead American element come into view and "at once set fire to the bridge which crossed the creek and proceeded east notifying settlers on the way." Some distance down the highway, Loucks hid his horse in the woods and, climbing a large maple tree, "observed the American army march past." This done, he mounted up and, circling around the enemy, rode west and reported the American strength to Morrison, whose troops were tailing Brown at some distance.[46]

At about noon, Wilkinson's other two brigades on the Canadian bank embarked and, joined by Boyd's brigade from the American shore, moved down the St. Lawrence into the Rapid du Plat, between the White House and Hamilton, the second of the rapids that lay between them and Montreal. Again, the flotilla traversed this hazard without loss, and the army, which had been somewhat apprehensive, relaxed and "felt inclined to say," the aide-de-camp remembered, "Pugh! what a fuss has been made about trifles." But, he continued, "the pilots warned us not to be mistaken by this sample" as they "said the *Long Sault*, the *Cedars*, etc., were still ahead; that these first were only about half a mile long, while the *Long Sault* was several, and that the *Cedars* pitched and tumbled like a small Niagara." This being the case, he and his comrades "drew in our horns, and shrugged up our shoulders."[47]

The current being swift through the Rapid du Plat, the flotilla soon overtook Brown's brigades trudging along the shore and was ordered to pull in near the American bank "for several hours, to enable General Brown to make good his march in time to cover our movement."[48] At 3 P.M., it got under way again and dropped down to the Canadian bank, where it anchored just as darkness was falling above a large farmhouse called the "Yellow House" in most American accounts, having covered eleven miles during the day. A few hours later, Brown's cursing troops arrived to the taunts of their comrades who had made speedier and less tedious progress by water. Brown had encountered no enemy but it was clear that the British were following, as they "frequently threatened our rear, but never indicated an intention to make a serious attack," and he took the precaution of destroying all the bridges he crossed to impede pursuit.[49] Sentries were posted and infantry pickets and cavalry vedettes positioned and the army settled down for the night.[50]

They were camped in Williamsburgh Township, Dundas County, on the property of forty-three-year-old John Crysler. One of the prominent men in the area, Crysler had been born in New York State and had served during the Revolutionary War as a drummer boy in a Loyalist regiment. Discharged in 1784, he had received a grant of land for his services, and through energy and careful investment had become a successful businessman with interests in the lumber trade, importing and several grist and sawmills. He was elected to represent Dundas in the provincial legislature in 1804, and he also served as a justice of the peace and as a militia captain. Captain Jacques Viger, a Canadian Voltigeur officer who visited the Crysler home in the spring of 1813, thought Crysler's appearance was "not the most attractive" as he was "sombre ... seldom smiles and appears much distracted" and "his conversation is serious."[51] Crysler may have had reason to be morose, for as Viger commented, although "still a young man, he was on his third wife," his first two spouses having died in childbirth. In 1808 Crysler had married Nancy Finkle and Viger (who had a Gallic eye for a well turned ankle) commented that, if the militia officer did not enjoy luck with the ladies he "did at least have good taste" as there was "nothing more modest than this charming little companion," who was "pretty to look at." Renowned for his generosity and hospitality, John Crysler was a loyal supporter of the Crown and his unwanted visitors would have given him no pleasure.[52]

One American thought that the area around the Crysler farmstead was "pleasant, its surface level & the soil rich & apparently everything had the aspect of old settlement – that of 50 or 60 years."[53] He also noted that the "houses along the roads are numerous but we found them inhabited by women only" as "the males had fled the approach of the army or had been embodied in the militia." Other visitors were not so kind. A later British traveller described the dwellings in Williamsburgh as hovels "erected after the first trees were chopped down, and almost every second one a tavern or house of entertainment, where the opulent master, his wife, children and farm labourers and rum-imbibing customers are all mixed up higglety-pigglety in the one small room."[54] This harsh assessment had a grain of truth in it: although neat wood frame houses were replacing the original log cabins, and some structures, like John Crysler's yellow-painted residence, were nearly imposing, there were many taverns on the "front" which catered to the busy river traffic. Several such establishments thrived within comfortable distance of the Crysler house: John Haines had an inn three miles west, Michael Cook operated his log tavern two miles to the east, and a few miles further on were Michael Ault and Richard Loucks, the latter's place being described as "very indifferent."[55]

The taverns were attractive targets for the light-fingered members of

Wilkinson's army although almost every Canadian household suffered to some extent. American officers tried to keep a careful eye on their men, and personal goods were generally respected, but the "hay and grain in the barns were, however, seemingly considered lawful booty" although "much more was wasted and trodden under foot than was actually consumed." The Canadians were pleasantly surprised to find that the invaders "paid in Spanish [silver] dollars for all the provisions the farmers had to sell," currency more desirable, valuable and more easily cashed than the military scrip the British army tendered for the same purpose. As a result, for years after the war, these same farmers never spoke of their American visitors without the wistful comment, "they behaved themselves like gentlemen."[56]

Not quite everyone fell into that category, because civilian claims for losses suffered during the invasion demonstrate that some of Wilkinson's men engaged in looting. The disappearance of alcoholic beverages, livestock and other foodstuffs, warm clothing, useful items like iron pots and anything that could be burned for fuel was understandable, as was the theft of money or small, valuable and negotiable items such as silverware, but why any soldier on campaign would be interested in a sleigh as was taken from John Haines, chinaware as lost by Michael Ault or women's clothing, including gowns and stockings, stolen from Abigail Cook, is puzzling. One of the most attractive items, given its frequent appearance in many postwar loss claims, was honey, either in the pail or the hive – an indication that Wilkinson's men craved nutrition more gratifying than salt pork and hard tack.[57]

One of the honey thieves came to grief when he was caught red-handed after a Canadian farmwife complained her beehive had been stolen. The aide-de-camp remembered that "a search of the boats was at once directed, when the missing hive was found snugly rolled up, honey, bees and all, in a blanket on board one of them." The thief's commanding officer decided to restore the property and punish the offender at one and the same time. "He had the hive landed as it was discovered," the aide de camp recorded, and ordered the culprit to uncover it and take it back to where it belonged with a "few bayonets" at hand "to superintend the exact fulfilment of the sentence." The man opened up the hive "with much care" and "then whisked the hive on his back in a twinkling, and dashed like an arrow for his destination." It was a good try but it didn't work as the bees had become "very impatient of the restraint," and boiled out and, when his punishment was over, the thief was "almost blind" and "a good subject for the doctor's ointment, and the gibes of his comrades."[58]

It began to rain on the morning of Wednesday, 10 November 1813, and the downpour continued the entire day. From his boat, anchored in the river near Crysler's house, Wilkinson issued his orders. Brown was to take his Second Brigade, Macomb's brigade, two 6-pdr. guns and Luckett's First Dragoons and scour the Canadian bank to the bottom of the Long Sault, which the American commander planned to run that day. The Sault was the third of the rapids to be traversed, and as it was "long and dangerous," he directed the "officers of regiments and corps to examine the boats, and have them properly fitted to avoid accidents as much as possible."[59] To minimize loss, only the civilian boat crews, the sick and enough soldiers to man the oars would be embarked. The rest of the army would march downstream on the King's highway under the command of Boyd, who was to "prevent the enemy, who hangs on our rear, from making an advantageous attack."[60] If the British did attack, Boyd was "to turn about and beat them," but in "case of an attack in force beyond all expectation," he and Brown were "to co-operate with each other, promptly and with decision." Unfortunately, Wilkinson did not spell out just how the two widely separated generals would be able to do that.[61]

Brown got on the road at first light with about 2,600 men and two 6-pdr. field pieces but shortly discovered that all the bridges over the many creeks and streams that emptied into the river had been burned. He kept moving and sometime in the morning came across a half-completed blockhouse positioned "to assail the flotilla, in its descent of the Sau[l]t."[62] This was probably a defence work known as "Ingall's fort," after the militia officer who supervised its construction on Cook's Point a few miles east of John Crysler's abode. Brown ordered it burned and continued his march, the column convinced, as Captain Robert Macpherson remembered, that "the enemy kept in advance of us, and I likewise understood in the woods to our left."[63]

The main army waited three hours to allow Brown a good head start and then moved off at about 10 A.M., Boyd's command marching on shore and the flotilla on the river. This movement had only just begun when the rear guard came under fire, and as Brigadier General Robert Swartout recalled, there was immediate confused activity as various "accounts were brought, concerning their [the British] force; the boats which had previously sailed were remanded" and "the dragoons were detached to reconnoitre."[64] Captain Joseph Selden rode to the rear with his company of the Second Dragoons and just as quickly galloped back along the columns of the infantry stopped on the muddy highway to report that an enemy force fifteen hundred strong was closing on the army. Boyd felt his orders that "should the enemy advance," he was "to beat him back, and [then] pursue his march," left him no discretion. As both Wilkinson and Lewis were still on their boats, and as Boyd had not been "consulted as to the operations and movements of the army," and since he was an officer who carried out orders to the letter, he issued the command and the army turned in its tracks and "counter-marched in pursuit of the enemy."[65]

Lieutenant Colonel Joseph Morrison was absent from his little army when fighting broke out in the late morning of 10 November. His command had spent the night a few miles west of the Americans, probably around John Haines's tavern, and at daylight he put it in motion to follow the enemy while he took care of a chore across the river. In the last week of October, some Americans operating under a letter of marque had captured a British convoy of seven or eight boats loaded with private goods destined for merchants in Kingston and York. The captured craft were taken into the village of Hamilton (modern Waddington, New York) and their cargo stored in that place and Columbia on the Grass River (modern Madrid).[66]

Morrison's job was to get it back. After he had issued his orders for the day, he and Mulcaster took a gunboat and a detachment of fifty men and crossed over to Hamilton. Meeting no resistance, Morrison "demanded on behalf of His Majesty the surrender of all public property and prize goods."[67] His men were about to gather up these items when the British commander "heard a cannonade below, which made him impatient of delay, and he hastily spiked a 6 pound iron cannon which he found in the village, and ordered the goods and building in which they were stored to be set on fire."[68] The villagers pleaded with him not to do this as the fire would spread and destroy a good part of the 135 houses and five mills in the scenic little community. A compromise was reached and the citizens signed a "Capitulation" in which they promised to return all the merchandise at a later date plus two boats, in exchange for which "the property and persons of the inhabitants of this village" were spared.[69] Morrison and Mulcaster then departed for the Canadian bank.[70]

The fighting that started on the morning of 10 November was not intentional. Morrison's troops had set out to follow the Americans down the King's highway and, marching by John Parlow's place, a British officer asked the farmer how long it had been since the enemy had passed. Parlow told him but added that, "You needn't follow them for they are ten to your one." "Never mind that, my man," came the swift retort, "we are not asking your opinion."[71] A short while later, the lead elements came within musket shot of the enemy rear guard; Captain Henry Jackson recalled that "notwithstanding they had broken down the bridges, we came up with them" and the Americans then "showed a disposition to attack us."[72] Lieutenant Christopher Hagerman, a twenty-one-year-old former law clerk from Kingston and an officer in the Incorporated Militia who had joined Morrison as a volunteer aide at Prescott, was of the same opinion. He remembered that the British and Canadians had been "following the enemy step by step having occasional skirmishes with their rear guards and annoying them as much as possible" but, that morning, "the Enemy showed a disposition to get rid of our teazing by turning about and annihilating us."[73]

The strong American reaction occurred because Boyd interpreted his orders literally, and after having countermarched west about two miles he deployed for an attack. Major Charles Gardner of the Twenty-Fifth Infantry recalled that his regiment "commenced our march (as usual about 11)" that day when the Second Dragoons were ordered "to cut off the enemy" and Boyd "should send a brigade to support them." Gardner's brigade went to support that brigade and, finally, "the whole except Brown's, which had gone down with the light troops" moved west.[74]

What followed was, according to a British participant, "a smart little brush," but it was a most confusing day for Boyd's men. When they advanced, the British withdrew; when they pulled back, the British advanced.[75] Boyd remembered that most of that wet Wednesday was spent "marching, countermarching, and skirmishing" over wet, muddy, ploughed fields under a continual downpour of rain.[76] On the British side, Jackson brought two 6-pdr. guns into action and fired a few rounds of shrapnel "at their columns – the advances [of the two armies] exchanging compliments in the same way."[77] Gardner of the Twenty-Fifth recalled that two "little field pieces of the enemy induced our brigade to advance *to the attack*" and they "charged over fences to perhaps within 200 yards of one which directly opposite the centre, [of the] 25th" with its "balls passing over our heads." When the British gun ceased firing, the Twenty-Fifth halted and were ordered to withdraw and "it re-commenced again." "We kept on, suffering only from the effects of a *shrapnel* shell, I believe they call it, that wounded three or four men slightly and a lieutenant."[78]

Hagerman thought the American infantry "were roughly handled by our light artillery" but, "as we did not then choose to come in contact with him (our position being bad)" and the Americans choosing "not to be too eager in pursuit," it was a stand-off with the two sides snarling at each other but reluctant to close.[79] Morrison, who had resumed command by noon, did not want to bring on a major action because, thinking he was outnumbered at least five to one, he wanted to pick his ground carefully, and at this point Boyd had the best position, the cleared fields near John Crysler's farm.

Just past noon, the American situation changed for the worse when Mulcaster's seven gunboats, having run the Rapid du Plat, hove in sight and began to engage the rear element of Wilkinson's flotilla, which consisted of six gunboats under the command of Abram Eustis. Eustis had moored his vessels in a line beside a large ravine to the east of Crysler's house to protect the flotilla below. He soon realized he had a problem – his craft, basically converted civilian vessels, were more fragile than the purpose-built gunboats under Mulcaster's command. Worse, they were armed only with a 6-pdr. or 12-pdr. gun and in positive danger of being overpowered by their British opponents, which mounted weapons between 6-pdr. and 18-pdr. calibre except for the *Nelson,* which mounted a long 24-pdr. gun and a 32-pdr. carronade. Despite the odds, Eustis had to hold Mulcaster off to prevent him from descending on the American flotilla like a wolf on the fold. For its part, the flotilla could not move downstream as it faced the Long Sault rapids through which its vessels would have to move one at a time to prevent collisions, giving Mulcaster a chance to get into the congested traffic and do slaughter. Until the British threat was parried, the America flotilla was pinned in place.[80]

It was at this critical juncture, about 1 P.M., that Wilkinson finally put in an appearance. He had been inactive throughout the morning because his dysentery had been worsened by the travails of the previous three days, and his physical and mental state had not been improved by the laudanum he had been taking to ward it off. Rousing himself, he ordered two 18-pdr. guns carried in the artillery scows "to be run on shore and formed in battery" and then sent a message to Lewis that he "was too unwell to act, and directing him to assume the command."[81] Lewis, who had also remained on his boat throughout the morning, went on shore about the same time that Brigadier General Moses Porter was getting the guns into position. A few minutes later Porter opened fire and the balance now tipped against Mulcaster as artillery firing from a solid footing is much more accurate and effective than if fired from a vessel on the "watery and unstable element," to use Covington's phrase. "Old Blowhard" Porter was an expert gunner and Mulcaster, after his flotilla had been narrowly missed a few times, wisely withdrew up-river out of range.[82]

On shore, meanwhile, Lewis tried to make sense of the situation. Colonel Eleazer Ripley of the Twenty-First Infantry recalled that he "borrowed my spy glass, and viewed the enemy from different points" but Ripley "saw no general officers, advance in front of the troops with a guard of dragoons, and reconnoitre."[83] On the other hand, as Ripley noted, it "was almost impossible, to reconnoitre the enemy, as they were posted in the woods." Unable to assess the strength of his opponent with any accuracy and not really knowing what to do, Lewis did nothing and Boyd, Swartout and Covington's brigades continued to advance and fall back in the mud and the rain, in step with the enemy. They were in the middle of these evolutions at between 2.30 and 3 P.M. when artillery fire was heard from the east – Brown was in action.[84]

After having burned the unfinished blockhouse at Cook's Point, Brown had pushed down the King's highway, his progress slowed by the destruction of the bridges in his path and the terrible state of the road. The easy transportation provided by the St. Lawrence had led to the neglect of the highway on the bank. A British officer who travelled down it a short while after Brown, as "rain and sleet poured down in torrents," thought it "barely fordable, so that we found it the easiest way to let our waggon go on with our baggage, and walk through the fields," and remembered that it "was hard to say whether the peril of upsetting or drowning was the most imminent."[85]

There was no sign of the enemy and by early afternoon, when Forsyth's riflemen, who formed the advance guard, had reached Hoople's Creek, Brown had covered about eleven miles. Hoople's Creek, named after nearby farmer, flowed into the St. Lawrence about two miles above the Long Sault and the riflemen discovered that as usual the bridge had been destroyed. Forsyth and some of his men were "examining the bridge and attempting to repair it when they were fired on from behind a little rising ground" on the opposite bank of the creek. Forsyth was grazed and one of his men severely wounded, and the rest fell into confusion but quickly rallied and took cover along a split rail fence on their side of the creek, where they "kept up a scattering fire when they could see an object" or target on the east bank. The unseen enemy replied and a brisk little exchange took place.[86]

What Brown had encountered was a force of Canadian militia under Major James Dennis of the 49th Foot, the British commander at Cornwall twelve miles below. Dennis had set out that morning hoping to damage the American flotilla when it ran the Sault and also to buy time by delaying the enemy's advance long enough to permit a great quantity of military stores, mostly foodstuffs, gathered at Cornwall to be removed to safety. He had a sergeant and private of his own regiment and about three hundred sedentary militia from the 1st Stormont and 2nd Glengarry Regiments, who were, in his words, "unorganized, ill found, though high spirited and gallant." The odds of success against Brown's two brigades were not encouraging, but Dennis, a seventeen-year veteran who had fought at Queenston Heights in 1812 and Fort George and Stoney Creek in 1813, had coolly calculated the situation. His intention was to create "temporary respect from the enemy by a fallacious display of force that it induced slowness in his advance," and, as an experienced light infantry officer, he knew just what to do. Hoople's Creek, which was fairly wide, offered a good position, and after destroying the bridge (which had only been constructed the previous year at a cost of £20), he spread his militia out along the east bank. They opened fire on Forsyth "from the different parts of the bush" on their side of the creek.[87]

From the occasional glimpse they caught of their opponents and from the nature of their fire, Brown and his senior officers concluded they were facing militia in a strength of between four and eight hundred men. A swift advance with infantry, covered by skirmishers, would have been the most effective way to deal with the problem, but the creek precluded that option so Brown ordered up his artillery. Two 6-pdr. guns under the command of Captain Robert Macpherson went into action and fired canister into the bushes on the east bank, which reduced the Canadians' marksmanship and their enthusiasm. Brown next ordered Colonel Winfield Scott to take his Third Artillery up the west side of the creek "in quest of the enemy and a fording place."[88] Captain Rufus McIntire of the Third remembered that the "bushes were thick and retarded our march but we at length found a fording place and crossed."[89]

Dennis was now outflanked and it was plainly time to go. Somewhat disappointed he had been offered no chance to "effect the destruction of any of their boats which might descend the rapids," he ordered a withdrawal but his militia, though "raw and completely undisciplined," were "reluctant of retiring," although it might have been a different story if Scott's Third Artillery had got at them with the bayonet. Placing his two wounded men, Charles McKinnon and Finlay Munroe, on makeshift stretchers, he managed to pull out just before Scott's men reached his position. It "became preposterous," Dennis later reported, "for me to calculate on any movement against the enemy, and that no advantage could be derived more than might from the fire of a crowd without arrangement, and which from the general high spirits of the people themselves would bring on them an unavoidably severe destruction." He had, however, delayed the Americans for about an hour, and Brown still had to repair the bridge.[90]

This task took time as Hoople's Creek was fairly wide with soft banks and the unceasing downpour did not help. Brown was delayed more than two hours at Hoople's, and by the time he got moving again it was beginning to get dark. Having made contact with the enemy, he now put out strong advance and flank guards, which slowed his progress, and he only managed to reach the upper limit of the Long Sault by nightfall when he made camp.[91]

The time Dennis had won at Hoople's allowed him to save the contents of the depot at Cornwall. On his orders, all available wagons in the district had

Rough road – the King's Highway along the St. Lawrence
The easy transportation provided by the St. Lawrence led to the neglect of the King's highway which paralleled the river. It was cut by many streams and gulleys over which rough log bridges were constructed as shown in this late 1890s photograph taken in Edwardsburgh Township not far from the site of the battle of Crysler's Farm. Both sides burned these bridges to hinder their opponents. (National Archives of Canada, PA27310)

previously been gathered and he paused during his withdrawal from the creek to send orders ahead for the militia to load them with the supplies and transport them to a place of safety. Early in the evening of 10 November, a train of 150 wagons slowly wound its way north from Cornwall along a road that was little more than a track and made worse by the rain, to the hamlet of St. Andrew's. Here it paused for an hour's rest before continuing to McMartin's Mills, where Dennis and his men joined and the convoy stopped for the night. At this point, many of the militia, considering they had done their little bit for King and country, departed for home, and Dennis reported "many desertions" as a result of the "dreadful state of the roads and the severe rainy weather" which "has tended much to excite a disposition to this criminal conduct." Dennis should not have complained too much as his raw levies had performed well at Hoople's, and more importantly, although they could not know it at the time, the Stormont and Glengarry militia had just removed from James Wilkinson's reach the very provisions he so desperately needed to attack Montreal.[92]

While Brown and Dennis had been squabbling to the east, Lewis and Morrison had been scratching at each other near Crysler's farm. Morrison refused to be drawn into a serious engagement, since he was not willing to give battle on ground not of his own choosing, and he contented himself with annoying the Americans, while the artillery of both sides engaged at such long range that neither side suffered much injury. Morgan Lewis was unsure what to do. As best he, Boyd, Swartout and Covington could judge, their opponents "amounted to about five hundred" men, which in Lewis's opinion "was not sufficient to prevent the advance of the troops" east toward the Sault.[93] But no one seemed willing to give the necessary orders to break off, and so the officers and men of the three American brigades had a wet and wretched time dragging themselves through fields turned into soft, glutinous, black muck by the rain. By late afternoon, having suffered about five hours of this seemingly mindless activity, they were exasperated, a feeling succinctly captured by Major William Clay Cumming of the Sixteenth Infantry in his description of that miserable afternoon (although he was mistaken about the identity of the general in command). Cumming was "perfectly convinced we had no general," as

> Wilkinson was sick. Lewis was also & what if he had not been? But Boyd, Tippecanoe Boyd was well; oh very well! To him, and to Col. Walbach, by the graces of the President, an Adjutant General, we were delivered over to be tormented. We were marched now here, now there, without any system, or any apparent design, but to learn whether the army liked cannon shot as little as certain generals. For during the greater part of those profound evolutions, the enemy were amusing us with roundshot & shrapnel shells.[94]

The light began to fail in the late afternoon, and the demonstrations ordered by Lewis and Boyd had, in Totten's words, "so far wasted the day" that the pilots of the flotilla were afraid to enter the Sau[l]t (a continued rapid of eight miles)" in the dark.[95] It was decided (by whom is not clear) that both the flotilla and the troops on shore would move down-river two miles and take a position below Cook's Point, the next headland on the Canadian side, for the night. As the boats were put in motion, Lewis's troops broke off and tramped east along the muddy highway past Crysler's yellow house to the fields surrounding Michael Cook's tavern, where, "as a measure of precaution," they were ordered to "lay on their arms, which they did, though it rained hard all night."[96] Brigadier General Robert Swartout was disgusted when "after spending the whole day in marches and countermarches," the army "halted for the night within a trifling distance of the place of their last encampment."[97]

Lieutenant Colonel Joseph Morrison, on the other hand, had reason to be pleased as darkness fell on the evening of Wednesday, 10 November 1813. He had prevented his enemy from descending the Long Sault, which if they had done and left a strong rearguard, might have prevented his pursuit and allowed the greater part of Wilkinson's army to get far enough ahead that he would have had difficulty catching it before Montreal. Better still, the Americans had given Morrison the ground he wanted, and if they tried to attack him in the morning, he would be able to give battle on the position of his choice. He moved his troops forward to John Crysler's farm, established his headquarters in that gentleman's house, and pushed out pickets and vedettes a mile to the east to prevent surprises in the night.

Morrison did have one problem. That day he had received a communication from de Rottenburg ordering him to break off the pursuit and return to Kingston. This directive resulted from information that a "very considerable force [of Americans] still remains at and in the vicinity of Gravelly Point (some say 5,000 men)" near Kingston.[98] This intelligence was false but de Rottenburg, concerned for the safety of the naval base on Lake Ontario, ordered Morrison to return to that place "with all possible dispatch," while Yeo sent a similar order to Mulcaster. This neither officer wanted to do – Morrison because he was in contact with the enemy and in a good defensive position, and Mulcaster because the enemy flotilla would be an attractive target when it ran the Sault – but orders were orders and could only be disobeyed with very good reason. Morrison therefore called a council of his senior subordinates to be held that evening in John and Nancy Crysler's home.[99]

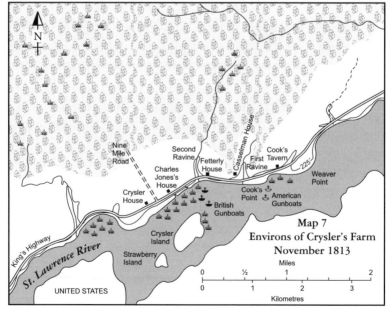

Map 7
Environs of Crysler's Farm
November 1813

Crysler's Farm, 1857
This crude drawing may be the only extant illustration of John Crysler's farmstead in
Lot 13 west of Williamsburgh Township, Dundas County. The smaller structure on the
right was probably the first residence of the Crysler family; the larger two-storey residence in the centre is the famous "Yellow House" of the time of the battle. To the left
are outbuildings. (W.S. Hunter, *Hunter's Panoramic Guide from Niagara to Quebec*)

It had been a long day for everyone in Wilkinson's army, but particularly for
Major General Morgan Lewis. Toward evening he felt unwell and, turning over
command to Boyd, retired to his boat. Boyd was busy for several hours arrang-
ing the encampment and it was not until about 9 P.M. that he had time to think
about the morning and repaired on board Wilkinson's boat to "report the affair of the day, and to ascertain who was commanding officer."[100] By this time
Wilkinson was "so extremely ill as to be unable to sit up, and was confined to
his bed in a small berth under the quarter deck of his passage boat."[101] Major
Ninian Pinckney, his chief aide, informed Boyd that the commanding general
was unable to receive him and referred him to Lewis for orders and Walbach,
who made a similar request, was also turned away. Boyd accordingly went to
Lewis's boat and took that officer's instruction "to return on shore, and defend
his position, and the flotilla for the night."[102]

Command and control was much less confusing in Morrison's little army.
That evening his officers assembled in the Crysler home and Morrison made
the decision not to break off contact. A letter to this effect was dispatched to de
Rottenburg and Yeo, and as disobedience of a direct order was a serious matter,
Morrison and Mulcaster took out the insurance of sending copies of all their
communications to Prevost with an explanation of their reasons. These messages were handed to dragoons who were to pass them along the express service
established between Kingston and Montreal. As the American troops were bed-
ded down close to the river bank, it was little problem for the riders to circle
around the enemy camp. The dragoon express system was efficient – Prevost at
Montreal had Morrison and Mulcaster's letter in his hands the next day.

CHAPTER 8

"Take the King's shilling!"

SOLDIERS AND SOLDIERING IN 1813

A bold fusilier came marching back through Rochester
Off for the wars in the far country,
And he sang as he marched
Through the crowded streets of Rochester,
"Who'll be a soldier with Wellington and me?"

> *Who'll be a soldier? Who'll be a soldier?*
> *Who'll be a soldier with Wellington and me?*
> *And he sang as he marched,*
> *Through the crowded streets of Rochester,*
> *"Who'll be a soldier with Wellington and me?"*

The King he has ordered new troops onto the continent,
To strike a last blow at the enemy.
And if you would be a soldier,
All in a scarlet uniform,
Take the King's shilling for Wellington and me.

> *Take the King's shilling! Take the King's shilling!*
> *Take the King's shilling for Wellington and me.*
> *And he sang as he marched,*
> *Through the crowded streets of Rochester,*
> *"Take the King's shilling for Wellington and me!"*[1]

While their senior commanders planned for the morning, the officers and soldiers of both armies made ready to pass an uncomfortable night – "very cold, raining and sleeting" one remembered in later years.[2] Under the downpour, the standard precautions for spending the hours of darkness in close proximity to the enemy were put in place – sentries were posted and outlying pickets of infantry and vedettes of cavalry positioned. These essential chores taken care of, rations were distributed as was the daily tot provided by

**Keeping warm and keeping dry –
Canadian Fencible in greatcoat**
Most of the British and Canadian troops
camped on John Crysler's fields during the
night of 10 November had been issued with
warm greatcoats as shown in this modern
reproduction worn by a member of the
Canadian Fencibles re-enactment unit.
(Photograph courtesy of Janice Lang)

both armies: rum for the British and Canadians, rye whisky for the Americans. The men then settled down, huddling around bonfires fuelled by fence rails and trying to dry their thick woollen coatees, which, thoroughly soaked during the day, had become uncomfortable sponges. Most of the British and Canadian troops had thick, grey greatcoats to protect them from the weather; the Americans were less fortunate, most possessing only thin, miserable government-issue blankets, unless they had been lucky enough to acquire more useful gear such as the "sailor's jackett" one had borrowed from Jacob Shaver up river.[3]

Most of the soldiers trying to stay dry and comfortable that miserable night were infantrymen. Infantry were the backbone of the armies of the War of 1812 (if not the backbone of all armies) and the tactics employed in battle were based on the capabilities of the infantryman's weapon: the smooth-bore, flintlock musket. In the case of Morrison's troops, this musket was the .75 calibre (.75 inch) India Pattern; in the case of Wilkinson's soldiers, the .69 calibre 1795 (or later variant) Springfield. There was not much to choose between them: both were highly inaccurate, had limited range – about 150 yards – and were difficult to load and fire. The musket was only effective if used *en masse,* and the basis of land combat in 1813 was the deployment of large numbers of musket-armed troops against similar opposing formations. It took well-trained soldiers to manoeuvre under fire in such formations, and armies of the time put much energy into training their infantry to perform properly on the battlefield.

Reducing the subject of Napoleonic infantry tactics to its utmost simplicity, there were two basic formations, the line and the column. A unit deployed in line formed in two or three ranks (a rank is a series of soldiers standing beside each other). The advantage of the line was that it covered the greatest extent of ground and brought the maximum number of muskets to bear; its corresponding disadvantage was that troops so formed could only move slowly because they had to pay attention to their dressing, or alignment. The column (actually a thickened line) was formed in various ways – the most popular version was two companies wide and between ten and thirty ranks deep depending on the strength of the regiment. The column could move more quickly than the line, particularly over rough ground, and it was favoured by most armies as their attack formation (the British army being a notable exception) but its drawback was that only a fraction of its men could effectively fire their weapons.[4]

Manoeuvring in either formation required lengthy training. The British army believed it took three years before an infantryman was fully trained and dependable in battle, as opposed to merely knowing the rudiments of his drill. British training was based on the 1792 *Rules and Regulations for the Movements of His Majesty's Infantry* written by Major General Sir David Dundas, who stressed the line formation, which he felt was the paramount one for both fire and movement. British doctrine held that a two-rank line of infantry, posted on good ground, screened in front by skirmishers and supported by artillery, was nearly unbreakable, and experience in Egypt, Italy, Portugal and Spain, where British infantry in line, using disciplined musketry, had defeated superior numbers of French infantry, had proved the validity of the concept. Dundas's *Regulations* was used for the instruction of battalions and brigades but, for training at the company level and below, it was supplemented by the *Manual and Platoon Exercises* of 1804 (and several subsequent editions).[5]

One of the criticisms levelled at Dundas was that he did not pay enough attention to those soldiers who did not fight in close-ordered formations – the light infantry. He was certainly aware of the importance of these specialists used for skirmishing, advance and rear guards, reconnaissance, outpost work and, in battle, protecting the main infantry line from enemy skirmishers. But although each British battalion possessed a company of light infantry, Dundas devoted just nine pages to their instruction and his neglect became apparent in the 1790s when British armies encountered the numerous and well-trained French light infantry. This lack was remedied by the appearance of additional manuals, including one written by Francis de Rottenburg, now commanding in Upper Canada. Morrison was fortunate that he had with him not only the light company of the 49th but three companies of the Canadian Voltigeurs, a specialized light infantry unit.[6]

All these manuals formed the theoretical foundation for British infantry training, which at the battalion level was unceasing. In a well-run unit, new officers and men were immediately placed in an "awkward" squad to learn their drill under the eye of an NCO. This was the case in the 89th Foot and, in a letter to his parents, Lieutenant William Bell, who joined that regiment in 1808, described his basic training:

Red coats – officers and soldier of the 100th Foot, 1813
Private, captain and major (right) of the 100th Regiment of Foot, which played a prominent role in the attack on Fort Niagara in December 1813, the final act of the campaign. The soldier wears a coatee of brick-red wool and his unit is distinguished by the colour of the facings or trim on his collar and cuffs and the shape of the embroidery around his button holes. (Painting by Donna Neary, courtesy of the Company of Military Historians)

I have been out at six o'clock in the morning at drill for some time past …… We are drilled among the men exactly the same as a private soldier [and] Officers who had been a number of years in the service were receiving their instruction at the same time and in the same manner. We began with the facings and went through all the different steps and evolutions of marching squads. We were then exercised with the firelock [musket] and I am the only one dismissed as being complete – which is owing to my constant and un-wearied attention at the drill rather than to any peculiar aptness in myself to learn.[7]

Drill did not cease when a unit went into the field, although the more elaborate evolutions in Dundas's *Regulations* were usually dropped in favour of the bare tactical essentials, which were defined by an officer of the 88th Foot (a regiment that, when not marching or fighting, drilled four hours daily on campaign) as "line marching, echelon movements, and formations of the square in every possible way."[8] Drill was serious business and any deficiencies were sure to be noted by the general officers who twice a year examined each unit. In 1815 the general who inspected Morrison's 89th Foot noted its evolutions were "according to established Regulation, the Order of Review and Field Exercise is adhered to; the latter, and Movements are performed with precision, the formations are correct and [carried out] with a proper degree of celerity."[9] The purpose of this never-ending labour was to ensure that every officer and man could function with automatic precision in the heat of battle.

In 1813 the United States Army was much less successful in preparing its troops for action because it had a major problem – it had no single authorized infantry manual. From 1779 to 1812 American soldiers trained according to Steuben's famous "Blue Book" first introduced to Washington's Continental Army at Valley Forge. Drawn primarily from the British *Manual Exercise* of 1764, this little primer admirably suited the limited needs of the American military establishment for more than three decades. In the period immediately preceding the war, knowledgeable commentators, aware of new tactical developments in Europe, agitated for its replacement by the French 1791 *Règlement*, which later became the manual of Napoleon's army. Foremost among these critics was William Duane, publisher of the Philadelphia *Aurora* and an influential Republican, who brought out a radically abridged translation of the *Règlement* in 1812 which he called *A Hand Book for Infantry*. Duane was unable to sell his work to the regular army because then Secretary of War William Eustis had previously authorized Brigadier General Alexander Smyth to prepare an official condensation of the French work which appeared in the spring of 1812 as *Regulations for the Field Exercises, Manoeuvres and Conduct of the Infantry of the United States Army*. A functional abridgement of the original French manual that also contained much useful matter from Steuben, Smyth's *Regulations* formed the basis for infantry training in the northern army until early 1813.[10]

At this point, things became confused. Armstrong was a friend of Duane and believed, as he told a Senate committee shortly before he took over the War Department, that Duane's *Hand Book* was the "best preliminary instruction" for infantry.[11] After becoming secretary of war, Armstrong put this belief into practice – on 19 March 1813, one day after he commissioned Duane a colonel and appointed him an adjutant general, Armstrong ordered the *Hand Book* to "be received and observed as the system of Infantry Discipline for the Army of the United States."[12] This flagrant act of patronage annoyed many officers, who regarded Duane's work as vastly inferior to Smyth's, and when Armstrong arrived at Sackets Harbor in September 1813 he was bluntly told the *Hand Book* was not being used because "it was objectionable & that the order establishing it required re-consideration."[13] In any case, most officers in the northern army had chosen to interpret that order with great latitude, pretending that the *Hand Book* only supplemented *not* replaced Smyth's *Regulations*, and regimental commanders had gone their own merry way, most continuing with Smyth, some using Duane and others reverting to Steuben. One unit commander displayed initiative if not common sense and compiled his own manual, while Colonel Eleazer Ripley used the British manual to train his Twenty-First Infantry.[14]

Although many of the American regiments camped around Michael Cook's tavern had drilled constantly at Fort George or Sackets Harbor in the previous six months, much of this work was to little avail because they had trained according to different manuals. When he arrived on the frontier, Wilkinson had ordered that the *Hand Book* to be used as the manual for his command and had increased the amount of drill but this step had been disrupted by the recent movement of the army and its reorganization. The result was that a unit could not manoeuvre with any degree of ease or speed when brigaded with another unit instructed according to a different text. It was also significant that neither Smyth nor Duane made any mention of light infantry, but then neither did the French original from which they were derived. One company in each American regiment could supposedly be designated a light infantry company but the United States Army in 1813 had no formal established doctrine or organization for these very necessary specialists.[15]

The purpose of all infantry training was to bring the largest number of troops within range of the enemy, at which point it came down to musketry, and both armies emphasized musketry instruction. By regulation every British soldier received thirty live and sixty blank rounds for practice each year, although this was not always possible – the same officer who inspected the 89th Foot in 1815 noted that the battalion had "no opportunity" for "ball practice" in the previous year.[16] British doctrine (and that of most armies) emphasized rate of fire, not individual accuracy, because the entire company or battalion was the weapon, not the single soldier. British infantry were not taught to individually aim their weapons but to simply present them in the general direction of the enemy and on command fire as fast as possible. The theoretical maximum was four to five rounds per minute but in combat few soldiers were able to sustain that rate, and well-trained infantry might get off two to three rounds per minute, but not for long periods for their weapons soon became plugged with powder residue and the barrels became too hot to hold.[17]

Individual target practice was regarded as less important than volley firing and most practice consisted of an entire company firing at a target representing the front of an opposing company. One such exercise, held at Quebec in November 1812, provides an interesting comment on the accuracy of the musket. Fifty-five men of the Quebec militia and a similar number from the regular 103rd Foot fired six volleys at a target 150 yards away which represented the front of an infantry company. The regulars "carried the palm," placing "93 balls in their target, whilst [the militia] company only placed 67 in theirs."[18] In other words, under optimum conditions, two infantry companies each fired 330 rounds at a target 150 yards distant with one company registering 93 hits and the other 67 hits. With results like these, it is small wonder that volume of fire was emphasized over accuracy.[19]

The American army, while also stressing rate of fire, appears to have laid some emphasis on individual marksmanship, a difficult thing with the musket, which had a propensity to fire high. Period armies were aware of this weakness of the weapon and had developed "levelling" techniques to compensate for it, but in the heat of action the number of rounds fired counted for more, and since both firing soldier and target were usually obscured by the smoke of their discharges, levelling was not popularly used. It was known and practised in the American army: Captain Mordecai Myers of the Thirteenth Infantry trained his company to fire at the top rail of a split-rail fence as a means of teaching them the correct angle at which to hold their weapons.[20] It also appears that American regulars, many used to handling firearms since childhood (which was not always the case with Europeans), were capable of aimed fire, even in the heat of a stand-up infantry firefight. The figures for officer casualties suffered in major War of 1812 engagements demonstrate that British officers usually suffered higher losses than their American counterparts, which might lead to the conclusion that American infantrymen deliberately picked their targets.[21]

The infantryman's second weapon was his sixteen- or seventeen-inch-long bayonet, which he could attach to the muzzle of his musket, so converting it into a spear. The bayonet was a weapon more talked about than used and its primary function was psychological – to inspire fear in a shaken enemy *that it actually would be used* and assist in breaking their nerve, and sending them off the field. Although bayonet charges were a common feature of combat during the Napoleonic wars, they rarely resulted in hand-to-hand fighting because almost always one side or the other gave way. Hand-to-hand fighting with the bayonet, or anything handy that could be used as a weapon, did, however, take place in woods, villages and fortifications where the fighting was more desperate and it was harder for the troops engaged to run away.[22]

If the musket had many disadvantages, the same could not be said of artillery, the other combat arm of the two forces camped by the St. Lawrence that rainy night. The main artillery weapon was the smooth-bore gun, often improperly termed a "cannon," an extended, hollow iron or brass cylinder, open at the muzzle end, and mounted on a sturdy two-wheeled wooden carriage.[23] Guns fired two types of projectiles, roundshot and canister. Roundshot, often incorrectly called a "cannon ball," was a solid iron sphere used at medium and long ranges (about 350 to 800 yards for the 6-pdr. field guns of both Wilkinson's and Morrison's gunners) to destroy men, horses and structures. Guns were designated by the weight of shot they fired: thus, a 6-pdr. gun fired a shot of the same weight and roundshot could be devastating – under optimum conditions, a 6-pdr. shot would penetrate nineteen human beings or seven feet of compacted earth. The second projectile, case shot (canister in the United States artillery) was a tin container filled with lead bullets that sprayed a lethal shower in front of the gun like a large shotgun shell. Canister or case was used to kill men at close range (up to 350 yards for the Royal Artillery and up to 500 yards for the United States artillery). Under best conditions, six rounds of canister could inflict the same number of casualties as a single volley of musketry by a battalion of five or six hundred infantry. Morrison's artillery commander, Captain Henry Jackson, had a third projectile used only by the Royal Artillery in 1813. This was spherical case shot, commonly called shrapnel after its inventor, Lieutenant Colonel Henry Shrapnel, RA, and was an explosive shell filled with musket balls that extended the antipersonnel effectiveness of case shot out to the range of roundshot.[24]

It has been calculated by one modern commentator that a well-served artillery piece of the Napoleonic period firing at close or medium range could expect to inflict one or two fatal casualties for every round fired, or between sixty and 120 fatal casualties for every hour it was in action. Another historian has questioned this statistic but has concluded that artillery inflicted between 20 and 25 per cent of all the casualties in any major battle during this period. This same author emphasizes, however, that, besides inflicting casualties, artillery had a secondary role: it "frightened and disturbed soldiers, wearing down their courage, sapping their morale and disrupting the cohesion of their units."[25] A combat veteran of Wellington's army agrees, noting that although artillery pieces "make more noise and alarm than they do mischief," a soldier was "much more alarmed at a nine pounder shot passing within 4 yds of his head than he is of a bullet at a distance of as many inches, although one would settle him effectively as the other."[26] The reason soldiers feared artillery was simple – artillery projectiles, particularly roundshot, caused horrific wounds. Men were disembowelled, or their heads or limbs were blown off or they were cut in half, while their comrades standing beside them not only witnessed such terrible sights but were often splashed with the residue. Nothing so disheartens a soldier as to be forced to take punishment from a weapon against which he has no chance to hit back.[27]

The object of combat in 1813, as it is in all wars, was to destroy an enemy's will to fight, to inflict such heavy losses upon him that he would voluntarily or involuntarily quit the field. How much punishment an army could deal out or withstand depended on the quality of its infantry, and during the Napoleonic period the infantryman's battlefield was a terrifying place. He fought in plain view of the enemy, in tightly-packed formations; he was unable to leave the ranks to obey his natural urge to take cover, his vision was usually obscured by smoke, and nearby comrades were destroyed by artillery fire, not to mention the noise, confusion, tension, fatigue and stench. A soldier could not obey his instinct to get as far away from such a place as fast as possible because men who ran suffered severe penalties, either from the enemy or from their own army, and once in combat they had no real choice but to stand and fight. How well they performed depended on their morale and the quality of their morale was a direct outcome of their training, experience and – above all – their leadership.

In terms of leadership, Morrison had a clear advantage over his opponents as he could draw on the knowledge of seasoned officers and NCOs who were members of an army with recent experience of victory.

It had not always been that way. The British army had emerged defeated from the American Revolutionary War in 1783 to enter a demoralizing period of decline that lasted more than a decade, and at the outbreak of the great war with France in 1793 it was, as one of its officer remarked, "lax in its discipline, entirely without system, and very weak in numbers."[28] The army's initial encounters with the French confirmed this assessment and it was not until the appointment of the Duke of York, a son of George III, as commander-in-chief in 1796, that a turnaround began. The duke had the authority and the power to make the necessary changes and he initiated a period of reform that saw updated manuals adopted, training improved, the creation of both a Royal Military College for new officers and a staff college, and important modifications to the system for promoting officers. After a bumbling operation in Holland in 1799, the new army's first real test came in Egypt in 1800-1801, where under Lieutenant General Sir Ralph Abercromby, it was victorious in a gruelling six-month campaign. Following the Peace of Amiens in 1802, much of the army returned home, and when war resumed in 1803, it received two years of intensive training while defending Britain against Napoleon's threatened invasion. It gained a signal victory over the French in its next major test, which came at Maida in Italy in 1806, and although there were defeats at Buenos Aires in 1807 and Walcheren in 1809, these resulted from poor leaders, not poor troops. When it arrived in Spain in 1809 to commence the five-year campaign to free the Iberian Peninsula of French domination, the British army was the only force in Europe capable of beating Napoleon's legions in open battle and by 1812, under the Duke of Wellington, it won an impressive string of victories in Portugal and Spain.[29]

It was able to do so because of the high quality of its officers. It is a common misconception that British officers of this period were genteel dandies who bought their promotions through the purchase system. An officer could still purchase his first commission but, with the massive expansion of the army caused by the Napoleonic wars, most new entrants were appointed directly from civilian life, provided they met the modest minimum requirements. The candidate had to be "a gentleman" (basically meaning he could read and write), a minimum of sixteen years of age (although many were younger) and be vouched for by a serving senior officer. Beginning in 1796, reforms required an officer to serve a minimum time in each rank, and vacancies from combat or death on active service were filled first by regimental seniority and next by merit, which by 1813 meant that few promotions were filled by purchase. Officers, particularly junior ones, tended to spend long periods with their regiments – the captains of the 49th and 89th Foot camping on John Crysler's fields had an average of twelve years of service with their units, while the lieutenants and ensigns had an average of four and a half. Typical of the serving British officer was Captain Henry Ross Gore, a company commander in the 89th Foot. He had joined the army as a fifteen-year-old ensign in 1800, obtained a lieutenancy by purchase in 1803 and a merit promotion to captain in 1807 but six years later he was still a captain, and it would take him another six to make major – and this in a time of ceaseless warfare.[30]

One of Gore's brother officers in the 89th, the unlucky Captain George West Barnes, had risen to captain by purchase, but in the rather unfashionable Cape Regiment in South Africa. Barnes then exchanged into the 89th, but his

The serving British officer – Captain Henry Ross Gore, 89th Foot (1785-1853)
Typical of the regular officer, twenty-eight-year-old Henry Ross Gore joined the army as an ensign in 1800; thirteen years later he was a captain and it would take him another six to make major. Even during wartime, promotion was slow in the British officer corps, which, contrary to legend, was not composed of aristocrats who purchased their advancement but of long-service professionals. (Miniature courtesy of Mrs. Piers Mackesy)

career was blighted at the ill-fated attack on Fuengirola in October 1810 when he became separated from his company during the withdrawal and was court-martialled for "misbehaviour before the enemy." The court found Barnes guilty but "in Consequence of the good conduct of the Prisoner," did not confirm a charge of "Personal Cowardice" but did dismiss him with ignominy from the service. Fortunately for Barnes, extenuating circumstances were brought to light, and a successful appeal brought his reinstatement in rank and regiment in late 1812.[31]

The 49th Foot, having served in North America for more than a decade, had a number of officers of Canadian birth. One was twenty-nine-year-old Captain Harry Smith Ormond, the son of a Loyalist from New Brunswick, who had been with the regiment since 1799. A fellow company commander, twenty-nine-year-old Captain Thomas Nairne, was the son of a wealthy retired officer who had settled on a large seigneury at Murray Bay (modern La Malbaie, Quebec) in 1763. His father's connections secured an ensign's commission for Nairne in the 18th Foot in 1804, but like so many young officers he fell into debt through gambling and, becoming disenchanted with the army and wishing to return to North America, exchanged into the Newfoundland Regiment in 1810 preparatory to retiring on half pay. The approach of war changed his mind and in December 1812 Nairne transferred to the 49th Foot. Nairne's senior lieutenant, twenty-year-old Lieutenant Daniel Claus, the son of William Claus, the deputy superintendent of the Indian Department in Upper Canada, had joined the regiment in 1811 through the good offices of Major General Isaac Brock. Claus had not yet recovered from sickness contracted in the Niagara the previous summer and was in such a bad way during the night of 10 November that his commanding officer, Lieutenant Colonel Charles Plenderleath, invited him to share the shed Plenderleath had managed to procure for his quarters. Nairne's other lieutenant, John Sewell, aged nine-

**Canadian officer in the British Army –
Lieutenant Daniel Claus, 49th Foot
(1793-1813)**
In 1813, twenty-year-old Daniel Claus, the son of an official in the Indian Department, had been with the 49th about two years and had seen much hard service in the Niagara. He was so sick the night before the battle that his commanding officer invited him to share his own quarters, one of John Crysler's sheds. (National Archives of Canada C95817)

The professional (7) – Major Frederick George Heriot, light infantryman (1786-1843)

Frederick George Heriot, shown here in a postwar portrait, commanded the light troops in Morrison's little "corps of observation," which consisted of his own Canadian Voltigeurs, thirty Mohawk warriors and a dozen Canadian dragoons. The veteran Heriot, a Scot from Berwickshire, had twelve years of service at the time of the battle. (From *Canadian Antiquarian and Numismatic Journal*, 1911)

teen, from Quebec City, was the illegitimate son of Jonathan Sewell, the chief justice of Lower Canada, but the judge had done his best for his natural offspring by securing him a commission in the 49th in 1811. Also serving in the unit was nineteen-year-old Lieutenant Samuel Holland, commanding the grenadier company of the regiment in the absence of its captain, and the son of a barrack master in Prince Edward Island. All five of these officers had seen action: Ormond had been prominent at the battle of Queenston Heights in 1812 and had fought alongside Holland, Nairne, Sewell and Claus at Fort George and Stoney Creek during the following summer.[32]

The officers of the Canadian Fencibles and Canadian Voltigeurs, members of recently-raised units, had less time in service – between eighteen months and two years on average for the Fencibles and about a year for the Voltigeurs. About half the enlisted men in the Fencibles were *Canadiens* and their officers were either from the same background or could speak French. The Voltigeurs were almost all *Canadiens*, and although their senior officer, Major George Heriot, was a Scotsman from Berwickshire, he spoke fluent French. One of his company commanders, Captain William Johnson, was, like Sewell of the 49th, born on the wrong side of the blanket, being the result of a liaison between Sir John Johnson, the superintendent of the Indian Department, and an American woman that predated the Revolutionary War. Heriot himself was romantically linked with Johnson's half-sister, the lovely Clarissa Johnson Bowes, recently widowed after her husband, Major General Barnard Bowes, had been killed in Spain at the battle of Salamanca in June 1812.[33]

With shorter periods of service, the officers of these two Canadian units were similar to their American counterparts a few miles away. Not one of the commissioned personnel in Captain Mordecai Myers's Thirteenth Infantry, from the lieutenant colonel commanding down to the most junior third lieutenant, had been in service prior to March 1812, just nineteen months past, and most of the other regiments in Wilkinson's army were the same. Of the senior officers, Wilkinson, Boyd, Porter, Macomb and Covington were prewar regulars – and Macomb was at least a graduate of and former instructor at the military academy – but Lewis, Swartout and Brown had been appointed directly from civilian life. Things did not improve at the middle level. Of the sixteen infantry regimental commanders with Wilkinson, nine had joined from civilian life in 1812 while seven had seen some service in the peacetime regular army, of which four had been appointed in 1808 while two had served briefly in the 1790s. The only Americans whose background could compare with men like Pearson and Harvey were Colonel Daniel Bissell of the Fifth Infantry, who had been serving continuously since 1792, and Colonel John Walbach, a German with two decades of service in four different armies.[34]

Wilkinson was fortunate in one thing: compared to Hampton's rather brittle division, few of his units were composed of raw recruits. Only two of Hampton's nine regiments had served before the spring of 1813; the remainder were newly raised from men who had enlisted for twelve- or eighteen-month periods. In contrast, most of Wilkinson's units had been raised in 1812 and had seen action, while approximately three-quarters of his 7,300 men had enlisted for periods of five years or the duration of the war.[35]

The question is why they would have enlisted in the first place as, despite the fact that the United States was at war, service in the regular army was not at all popular. "Americans," an observant but somewhat supercilious British commentator wrote, disliked being soldiers as:

> The business does not at all suit their dispositions, for they are never happy unless they are trading and scheming in some way or other, and they consider it almost a disgrace to be a soldier, as they conceive a man must be a *poor, dispirited* creature who demeans himself to be under the control of others, as a soldier must be, and that no genuine American, having the true *spirit of liberty*, would ever degrade himself so far as to be a *rigular*.[36]

Probably most American enlisted men, aside from the very few who joined out of patriotism, were forced into the army by sheer economic necessity. Recent studies have demonstrated that many of the recruits for the wartime army were "men of respectable social status" but "close to the margins of that respectability."[37] More than half were landless agricultural labourers or unemployed tradesmen who "had felt the impact of economic dislocations brought about by the Embargo Acts, the pressure of population growth [on the eastern seaboard] and the restructuring of traditional artisan craft activities into early industrial manufactories."[38] They were mainly young men, with an average age of about twenty-five, who chose the army as the best of a bad lot, but other than two meals a day the compensations were pretty slim as a private earned eight dollars (later ten) a month in a time when agricultural labourers earned between fifty cents and a dollar a day. The greatest incentive was the grant of 160 (later 320) acres of land at the end of service, which, if the soldier did not settle on it, would at least provide a negotiable asset. But first he had to survive the discipline, the perils of combat and, worse still, illness – for every American soldier killed in action during the War of 1812, at least two died from disease.[39]

Throughout that war the United States Army experienced difficulty in finding men. Recruiting parties commanded by an officer or sergeant and usually including a drummer and other musicians plus "a few handsome, well-dressed men, who, from their appearance and activity, may be enabled to give a spirit" to the "business" made their way from place to place across the republic looking for trade.[40] It was just such a colourful group entering his sleepy little Vermont village that had snared Jarvis Hanks the previous spring and, with his parents' consent, Jarvis had enlisted as a drummer at the age of thirteen. Recruiters quickly learned the best fishing method was to haul up in front of the local tavern, have the musicians play "Yankee Doodle" or "Hail Columbia," and then buy everyone a free drink while extolling the virtues of the national cause, military life and the size of the recruiting bounty. Things sometimes got out of hand, though, and one citizen complained to the secretary of war about a "dissipated capt. H. walking from Tavern to Tavern and from shop to shop, drinking, singing, etc., soldiers about him following his example – capt. grosly rude and insulting in his deportment – soldiers equally so."[41]

American recruiters were not discriminating, nor could they afford to be. Very early on, the minimal standards of the prewar service – that a man had to be less than thirty-five years of age and at least five feet six inches in height – were dropped, and by 1813 the only restrictions were that no man was to be taken who had "ulcerated legs, scalded head, rupture, or scurvy" or was "an habitual drunkard, or known to have epileptic fits."[42] Recruits had to pass a medical examination but it must have been most perfunctory, because the War Department felt constrained to insist that medical examiners not pass any man "who has not stripped all his clothes, to the end that it be ascertained as far as possible, that he has the perfect use of every joint and limb."[43] Basically, recruiters took who they could get and the result was that many new entrants were "habitually intemperate, with constitutions broken down by inebriation and its consequent diseases; whose bloated countenance exhibited false and insidious marks of health."[44]

The British army used similar methods of personnel acquisition. Although the Royal Navy obtained much of its manpower by impressment or conscription, enlistment in the regular army for "universal" or overseas service as opposed to home defence was always voluntary. Magistrates sometimes assisted the process by offering convicted felons the choice of a red coat or transportation to Australia, but men obtained this way were usually more trouble than they were worth. Most were brought in by recruiting parties which, like their American counterparts, roamed through the countryside drumming up trade. John Shipp, an eleven-year-old orphan and recent graduate of his parish poorhouse, never forgot the day in 1794 when "the shrill notes of the fife, and the hollow sound of a distant drum, struck on my active ear" and he "scampered off" to watch a recruiting party set up shop in the local market place. Spellbound, Shipp listened as a sergeant, addressing himself to the rustics gathered round, began "a right speech" about "Gentlemen soldiers, merry life, muskets rattling, cannon roaring, drums beating, colours flying, regiments charging and shouts of victory! victory!"[45] "At these last words," Shipp remembered, "the bumpkins who had just enlisted let their flowing locks go free, and waving their tattered hats, give three cheers for 'The King, God Bless Him,' in which I joined most heartily." John Shipp enlisted as a drummer and spent twenty-nine years in the army, rising to the rank of lieutenant.[46]

Snagging dewey-eyed innocents like Shipp was no great feat but most men took more persuasion. It usually came in the form of free drinks all round and a generous bounty, varying from two to twenty-seven guineas, a considerable sum at that time. If the recruiter found a likely prospect, he had to get him before a magistrate to swear his age and place of birth and that he was not a deserter from the army or navy, nor an apprentice, but had voluntarily enlisted. The magistrate then read the articles of war which informed the new man he would be subject to the death penalty for mutiny, attempted mutiny or desertion, and the recruit swore an oath of loyalty to the Crown, signed his name or mark on the attestation form and was dispatched to a surgeon for a medical examination as perfunctory as its American equivalent. British infantry recruits had to be between sixteen and thirty-five years of age and have a minimum height of five feet two inches but older and smaller men were often taken into service.[47]

After taking the "King's shilling," the new recruit joined his fellow unfortunates, who, assisted by the veterans, proceeded to dispose of their bounty as quickly as possible. It was usually drunk before arrival at the regimental depot, where as the old soldiers' song put it, "your money being gone, your duty comes double."[48] John Harris, who enlisted in Ireland in 1804, remembered that when time came for his party to proceed to the depot, the "whole lot" were "three sheets to the wind," and when they paraded before the door of the Royal Oak, the landlord and landlady of the inn, who were quite as lively, came reeling forth, with two decanters of whisky, which they thrust into the fists of the sergeants, making them a present ... to carry along with them, and refresh themselves on the march. The piper then struck up, the sergeants flourished their decanters, and the whole route commenced a terrific yell. We then all began to dance, and danced through the town, every now and then stopping for another pull at the whisky decanters. Thus we kept it up till we had danced, drank, shouted, and piped thirteen Irish miles, from Cashel to Clonmel.[49]

The Emerald Isle, with its poverty and ever-expanding population, was a prime source of manpower. More than 90 per cent of the enlisted men of the 89th Foot, a unit raised in southeast Ireland, were Irish, but it is noteworthy that nearly half the nominally English 49th Foot were from the same place. In both these units, men who enlisted out of patriotism were far fewer than those forced into service by economic necessity. The most common occupation listed by the men of the 49th and 89th Foot was "labourer," about 90 per cent in the case of the 89th and 75 per cent in the 49th, while the balance described themselves as tradesmen – mainly weavers, carpenters, gardeners and cobblers, occupations susceptible to economic downturns. They averaged just under thirty years of age and many had been with their regiments for long periods – about ten years and seven months in the 49th and seven and a half years in the 89th Foot.[50]

These men were the "redcoats" of legend. They received a shilling a day, but "stoppages" or deductions from their pay for rations and "necessaries" (articles of clothing and equipment provided by the Crown) ate up much of it, although they had a chance of a small pension if they were disabled or survived twenty-one years in the service. They included men like Private George Braithewaite of the 49th Foot, a thirty-one-year-old former shoemaker from Durham – six feet one inch tall with brown hair and hazel eyes according to his documents – while some were old soldiers, such as Private James Flynn of the 49th from Kildare, completing his seventeenth year with the colours, or Alexander Lang of the 89th, who had enlisted at Fermanagh in Ireland and was on his thirteenth. A fourteen-year-old boy soldier, Private James Campbell of the 49th from Antrim, had only been with his unit a few months and NCOs like Sergeant Thomas Buckeley of the 49th, a five-year veteran, or Sergeant Dean William of the 89th, a Dubliner, kept a careful eye on such green men.

These sergeants would also have liked to have kept a careful eye on the drummers such as Charles Hawker and John Coppin of the 49th and William Mudridge of the 89th because drummers had a reputation for getting into mischief. Their discipline, however, was the province of the regimental drum-major, an august personage who was sure to resent any intrusion into his sphere of authority, but such was the character of his subordinates that one military author only half-jokingly advised drum-majors that, if they had any spare time, to flog their "drummers round" because, if "they do not then deserve it, it is pretty certain they lately have, or shortly will; besides correction tends to keep them good, when they are so."[51]

Compared to their British comrades, the men of the Canadian Fencibles and Voltigeurs were younger but came from similar backgrounds. The average age of an enlisted man in the Voltigeurs was twenty-four years, nine and a half months, and just under half were former tradesmen while about 40 per cent were labourers or farmers (probably hired hands). The Fencibles were supposedly recruited from none but Canadians but nearly a quarter were from the British Isles and about a fifth were "foreign," including many Americans, while, of those born in North America, about half were *Canadiens*. The average age of the men in the one company of the Fencibles for which there exist detailed records was twenty-three and about six in ten listed their civilian occupation as "labourer."[52]

Whatever his age and origins, the soldier of 1813 led a hard life that was strictly regulated with drill, fatigues and duty occupying almost every waking hour. His colourful uniform looked splendid but it was hard to keep clean, highly uncomfortable and included a tight leather collar, or stock, that forced him to hold his head rigid and upright. Rations were no compensation, being scanty and sometimes inedible, while the pay was miserably low and usually in arrears. For many, the only relief from the grind came through alcohol, and intoxication was the curse of all armies in 1813.

Discipline was ferocious. Minor punishments in British and Canadian units included extra drill, confinement to barracks and loss of liquor ration, but more serious offences usually resulted in flogging. Many in the British army regarded flogging as necessary to keep the hard core element in the ranks under control, among them Private William Lawrence, who received four hundred lashes for absenting himself from guard duty but still thought the punishment "as good a thing for me as could then have happened, as it prevented me from committing greater crimes, which might at last have brought me to my ruin."[53] Others, such as Lieutenant George Bell of the 34th Foot, while agreeing there were many "bad characters sent out to fill the gaps in our ranks, sweepings of prisons in England and Ireland," regarded flogging as "inhuman" and decided that, "if ever I had the chance of commanding a regiment, I would act on another principle."[54] Flogging had been used in the

British military discipline – flogging

Flogging with the cat of nine tails was the most common form of punishment in the British army in 1813. By regulation, regimental courts martial were prohibited from awarding more than 999 lashes; punishments of a greater number were the province of general courts martial. (Watercolour by Eugene Leliepvre, courtesy Parks Canada)

British military discipline – execution by firing squad at La Prairie, Lower Canada, 1813

This drawing of a military execution is morbidly interesting because of the amount of detail it contains. Note the condemned man's hair standing on end and the expressions on the faces of his fellow unfortunates who await their turn. (National Archives of Canada) peacetime American regular army but had been abolished by the War Department at the beginning of the war as an inducement to recruiting, although officers like Wade Hampton devised substitute punishments that were just as painful and often more injurious.[55]

Given these conditions, it is not surprising men fled the service in large numbers. During the War of 1812, 1,570 enlisted men deserted from British regular units stationed in the two Canadas compared with 2,733 lost from combat and sickness. It was just as bad, if not worse, in the United States Army, which, it has been estimated, lost just over 10 per cent of its total wartime strength, between 5,000 and 5,700 men, through desertion. To stop this exodus, American commanders made increasing use of the death penalty, only three soldiers were executed in 1812, but 146 were shot or hanged in 1814, and during the thirty months the conflict lasted 205 American soldiers were executed. In contrast, the Duke of Wellington, commanding a force of similar size, condemned only 118 men during five years of campaigning in the Peninsula, but Wellington of course also punished deserters by flogging, 1,000 lashes being the standard penalty for men apprehended trying to desert to the enemy.[56]

One group of fighting men camped near the St. Lawrence that night could not have cared less about discipline or the wishes of regular officers and these were Lieutenant Charles Anderson's thirty Mohawk warriors. They came from Tyendinaga, the settlement at the Bay of Quinte on Lake Ontario established in the 1780s by their chief, "Captain John" Deserontyon, after his people lost their ancestral lands in New York at the close of the Revolutionary War. Deserontyon and his people had been among the Crown's staunchest allies in that conflict, spreading terror throughout the frontier in a series of devastating raids, and they had come out again for the Crown in 1812, fighting at Sack-

Loyal ally of the Crown – Mohawk warrior
This watercolour from 1804 shows a Mohawk warrior as he might have appeared in November 1813 although he would have been likely to have had warmer clothing. This man has painted his face red and black, the favoured colours for battle. The thirty warriors who fought at Crysler's Farm had an effect out of all proportion to their numbers. (Watercolour by Sempronious Stretton, National Archives of Canada, C-14827)

ets Harbor in May 1813 and in the Niagara peninsula during the summer. These warriors were devout Christians – their chapel at Tyendinaga was one of the oldest churches in Upper Canada – but utterly terrifying in battle. Lieutenant John Le Couteur, who attended service in their church, thought that after "having witnessed these men scalping, looting, Yelling and carousing" in the Niagara "it was very striking and imposing to behold them listening to the Divine truths of Christianity" from "a translation of St. John's Gospel into the Mohawk language."[57]

Tyendinaga was not a populous settlement. The Indian Department calculated its military strength at only fifty warriors, and a good part of the male population was thus serving with Morrison. The warriors commonly went by two names – their "jaw breaking" (as John Le Couteur termed them) Mohawk names and their white names. Understandably, Shagaunnahquodway was often called Captain Jim, Naliwhaquask was King James and Pahgushjeneny, Pahahiwickjecomwaby and Patitickowa usually went by the simpler handles respectively of Old Peter, Big Jacob and John Pigeon. Inured to bad weather and adept at living in all conditions, the Mohawks were the most comfortable men in either army and their presence guaranteed the security of the British and Canadians camped on John Crysler's muddy fields.[58]

The rain continued to fall throughout the night. At about 10 P.M., Lieutenant Colonel Robert Carr of the Fifteenth Infantry, part of Brown's force down river, recorded in his diary that it was "raining now and has rained considerably during the day – we are wet to the skin and having no tents or shelters but bushes, must pass a very uncomfortable night."[59] Near the scene of Brown's action that afternoon, Mary Whitmore Hoople, the wife of the man after whom Hoople's Creek was named, tended to the wounded American rifleman who had been left in her care. It was fortunate for this man that he had been carried to her house as Mary Hoople, known to her neighbours as "Granny Hoople," was the local midwife and medicine lady and had learned her skills during a seven-year period of captivity with the Delaware nation. She now put that knowledge to work to ease the suffering of the American, who was in a bad way.[60]

By now, Abigail Cook had put her brood to bed while her husband, Michael, toted up his losses in livestock and foodstuffs and cursed James Madison and all his works. A few hundred yards to the west at the Casselman place, the family's horses, cows and chickens had long disappeared to assist the republic's war effort but they had managed to save their sheep by hiding them in the cellar of their farmhouse. Their neighbour Peter Fetterly lost his potatoes, oats and barnyard fowls, and his sheep. If John Crysler was not still required for military duties, he and Nancy were trying to get to sleep as best they could, in the middle of twelve hundred guests with a sentry outside the door.[61]

Aboard the gunboats moored on the river, the watches had been set for the night and the weapons protected from the rain with sailcloth, while the crews tried to keep dry below decks. Young officers like twenty-one-year-old Canadian Lieutenant Christopher Hagerman and seventeen-year-old American Lieutenant William Smith, probably too excited to sleep, dreamed of future fame while newlyweds such as Lieutenant Guillaume-Verneuil de Lorimier of the Canadian Fencibles, whose wife of ten months was expecting their first child any day, and Lieutenant Henry Kersteman of the Royal Artillery, who had married a Kingston girl a few months before, dreamed of the blissful past. Surgeons John Korb and William Woodforde of the British army and James Ross and Amasa Trowbridge of the American army checked the sharpness of their "capital instruments" and wondered whether they had enough tourniquets, bandages, splints, and other such items should there be a major action in the morning. For Drummer Jarvis Hanks of the Eleventh Infantry, fourteen years old and eight months a soldier, it had been a long and tiring day so, jamming his leather shako firmly on his head, he curled up in a ball beside his company's fire, trying to stay as close to the blaze and the warmth as possible.[62]

Camp fire, Canadian Voltigeurs, 1813
The night of 10 November 1813 was wet and miserable and the men of both armies were hard put to keep warm and dry. (Watercolour by Eugene Leliepvre, courtesy Parks Canada)

PART III

The Battle of Crysler's Farm

11 NOVEMBER 1813

The pride of Mulcaster's Mosquito Fleet

His Majesty's Gunboat *Nelson* in action on the St. Lawrence in November 1813. The largest vessel in Mulcaster's squadron, she carried a 24-pdr. gun and 32-pdr. carronade and was greatly respected by her American opponents, who were much smaller and not nearly as well armed. Sketch by marine artist Peter Rindlisbacher.

CHAPTER 9

"Jack, drop cooking, the enemy is advancing!"

11 NOVEMBER 1813, 6 A.M – 2 P.M.

Hark! I hear the Colonel crying,
"March, brave boys, there's no denying,
Colours flying, drums are bayting,
March, brave boys, there's no retrayting!"
Love, farewell!

The Major cries, "Boys, are yez ready?"
"Yes, yer honour, firm and steady;
Give every man his flask of powdher,
And his firelock on his shouldher!"
Love, farewell!

Oh, Molly, darling, grieve no more,
I'm going to fight for Ireland's glory;
If I come back, I'll come victorious;
If I die, my sowl in glory is!
Love, farewell![1]

The rain stopped falling during the night but the dawn of Thursday, 11 November 1813, was grey and overcast with a strong wind from the west. In the camps of both armies, NCOs woke the drummers whose task it was, in Brigadier General John Boyd's words, to rouse the "fatigued soldier from his wet and unsheltered bed."[2] Drummer Hanks presented a comical sight that morning. While trying to stay warm during the night, he had placed his head and feet too close to his company's fire and his "cap and shoes were burnt so badly as to be nearly valueless."[3]

Limping along, Jarvis joined his fellow drummers, who, blowing on fingers numbed by cold, stripped the painted linen covers from their instruments and tightened the calf skins of the heads, which had been slackened by the humidity. Drums were the heart of Napoleonic armies and they were colourfully decorated – those of the 49th Foot were painted the green of that regiment's facings while those of the 89th were black, but all British and Canadian drums boasted the royal cypher of His Britannic Majesty, King George III of the United Kingdom. The drums of their American counterparts were no less decorative, being dark blue trimmed with red and embellished with the patriotic eagle emblem of the republic.

That morning the bleary-eyed, cold and wet drummers would probably not have cared much about the heraldry of their respective nations. No doubt complaining, they took post in their regimental areas and made ready, elbows high and sticks above their eyes, waiting for the duty drummer in each camp to begin. As soon as he commenced to rattle away, the signal was picked up by each drummer, from right to left in turn, until all were beating in unison, bringing their sticks down hard to make the noise carry.

The two armies started the day with different calls. British and Canadian drummers, such as Charles Hawker of the 49th Foot and William Mudridge of the 89th, beat the traditional "Reveillee," a series of fast rolls that in the previous half-century had acquired lyrics, which ironically commemorated the defeat of a British army under Major General John Cope by the highlanders of "Bonnie Prince Charlie" in 1745. "Hey Johnnie Cope, are ye waking yet, or are ye sleeping, I would wit? Oh, haste ye, get up, for the drums do beat, and its fie Cope, rise in the morning." Normally, Jarvis and the other American drummers would have pounded the same call but, a week before, Wilkinson had ordered that his first signal of the day was to be the "General," commonly used when an army was ready to march. Jarvis and his comrades therefore played that call, possibly reciting the little ditty that went with it to mark time: "Don't you hear your General say, Strike your tents and march away, way, way! Way, boys, Way! Strike your tents, and march away!"[4]

Given the miserable conditions of the previous night, it is likely this effort was wasted, as most of the drummers' comrades were probably long awake before this cacophony reverberated along the banks of the St. Lawrence. For those who had spent the night on duty with the guards or pickets, the sound of the drums would have been welcome as it marked the moment when the safety of their comrades was no longer solely their concern and they could leave off challenging, look forward to being relieved, and get something to eat. The muddy fields around Michael Cook's tavern and John Crysler's yellow-painted residence gradually came alive with movement as, willing life into limbs made stiff by cold, men threw off sodden blankets or coats and struggled to their feet.

The routines of the military day now commenced. Their movements hastened by the curses of sergeants and corporals, the infantry formed in their companies, ready for roll-call and inspection by their officers, who because of the rain would pay particular attention this morning to the condition of their men's muskets and the state of their ammunition. The dragoons looked to their mounts, brushing and feeding them before saddling them in preparation for movement, while the gunners carefully inspected their ammunition, gently rolling the cartridges between their hands to loosen any powder that might have caked or solidified from humidity during the night. These chores taken care of, the men drew their rations if they had not been previously issued and cooked their breakfasts.

Near the woods that separated the two armies, the outlying pickets were relieved. The rain of the last few weeks had stripped the leaves from the trees, and the grey light of dawn revealed to both armies just how close their outposts had been during the night. Inevitably, some American, British or Canadian soldier – or Mohawk warrior – got a little excited and fired a shot at a shape flitting through the brush. This drew return fire, and once started, the squabbling continued for some time. Brigadier General Robert Swartout remembered that at reveillee or shortly after, there "was an affair of pickets."[5] Colonel John Walbach agreed that such an "affair" took place but did not think much of it, noting only that "a pistol shot or two was fired" and the American troops "made no movements, in consequence of it."[6] The exchange of fire between the pickets was heavy enough, however, for Morrison to order his army to "stand to," or form ready to meet an attack, an order that caught Lieutenant John Sewell of the 49th Foot by surprise. Like many a young officer before and since, Sewell dreamed of cutting his way to fame by means of his sword, but that drab morning he had found a more prosaic use for the weapon. He was "toasting a piece of pork" on its point when his breakfast was interrupted by a shout from his company commander, Captain Thomas Nairne: "Jack, drop cooking, the enemy is advancing!"[7]

The shooting gradually died away but, taking no chances, Morrison kept his troops formed in their units. The previous night the British commander had finalized his dispositions in the event of an attack, but as there was no sign of that, he judged it enough to keep his little army ready for any eventuality. Morrison had just under 1,200 men under command that morning (see Appendix F). His main strength lay in his two regular battalions. Lieutenant Colonel Charles Plenderleath's 49th Foot had been reduced by disease and casualties, and although all ten companies were present, the battalion mustered just under 400 men, less than half its authorized strength. Morrison's

Second ravine

Battlefield memorial
obelisk erected 1895

First ravine

Prunner Shoal

Cook's Point

The vanished battlefield – the area east of John Crysler's farm
This aerial photograph of battlefield looking north, taken before it was flooded in
1958, shows the original location of the memorial, the first and second ravines and
Cook's Point. John Crysler's and Charles Jones's farmhouses were to the west of this
scene and Michael Cook's tavern would have been somewhere in the lower right corner
of the photograph. The beach or shoal at the bottom right of the picture is where
Wilkinson's flotilla was anchored on the morning of the battle. The first and second
gullies to the west of the second ravine appear on 1913 ordnance maps but had been
filled in by the time this photograph was taken forty-five years later. The two larger
ravines, flooded by autumn rains, with muddly and slippery sides, posed a very real
problem to the movement of artillery and formed troops. In November 1813, the area
from Cook's Tavern west to nearly the second ravine was a mixture of woods with some
cleared fields. The main scene of the action was between the second ravine and the
location of the battlefield memorial. (Photograph, courtesy of William Patterson)

own 89th Foot, this day under the command of Major Miller Clifford, was in
better case – the eight companies present numbered 480 men. Being old
Canada hands, the 49th were wearing their warm grey greatcoats, but Clifford,
new to the country, had ordered the 89th to put theirs aside, and they were
turned out in their brick-red coatees. The grenadier and light companies of
the 49th, which had formed part of the garrison at Prescott, remained with
Pearson as did a detachment of two companies of Canadian Fencibles, numbering about 100 men. Major Frederick Heriot commanded the light troops,
consisting of three companies of his own Canadian Voltigeurs, numbering
about 150, Anderson's thirty Tyendinaga Mohawks and about a dozen of Cap-

tain Richard Fraser's Provincial Light Dragoons, which formed the skirmish line to the east, while the artillery was provided by Captain Henry Jackson's three light brass 6-pdr. field guns. Finally, there were about sixty Dundas militia present but nobody was counting on them to stick around if things got hot.[8]

Morrison knew that Wilkinson's strength was between seven and eight thousand men, but he was also aware from information brought in by express riders that at least two thousand were down river. That still left him facing odds of between four and five to one. On the other hand, he had reason to be confident as he occupied a very strong position – in the words of a later commentator, the British commander had "a fair field" and need ask "no favour."[9]

It was indeed ideal ground. John Crysler's yellow house was located west of the junction of the King's highway, which paralleled the river, and the Nine-Mile Road, which ran north at right angles from it. Looking east from this intersection was a fairly flat expanse of ploughed farm fields covered with a sparse crop of fall wheat and cut across by split rail fences, which stretched nearly a mile to the wood that lay between the two armies. This cleared area, about a half mile wide, was bounded on the north, or Morrison's left, by a swampy pine wood, obstructed by fallen timber, and on the south by the St. Lawrence. The river was guarded by Mulcaster's gunboats, and with both flanks secure Morrison had only to worry about a frontal attack directly from the east.

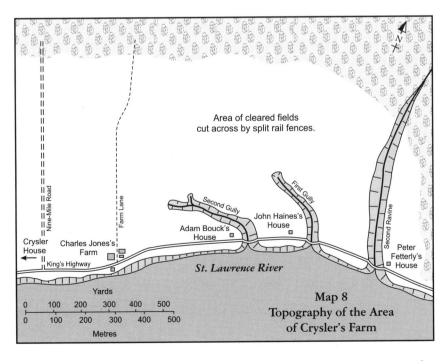

Map 8
Topography of the Area
of Crysler's Farm

The battlefield as it appeared in 1913
This interesting 1913 photo taken during the battle centennial from atop a barn along the Jones farm lane illustrated in the tactical maps shows the river bank to the east. In the background is Cook's Point, where the American gunboats took station and betweeen the point and the position of the photographer is the vanished battlefield. (Photo by George Harold Van Allen, courtesy of Dr. Traer Van Allen)

Between John Crysler's yellow house and the American camp at Michael Cook's tavern were two large ravines and two smaller gullies. For ease of reference these terrain features will be referred to by number from east to west (see Maps 7 and 8) as the first and second ravines and the first and second gullies. The first ravine was in the woods that separated the two armies, about 800 yards west of Cook's tavern, while the second ravine was about 1,000 yards to the west of the first, in the area of cleared fields and about 200 yards from the tree line of that woods. The first gully lay 250 yards and the second gully 500 yards west, respectively, of the second ravine. These depressions would make it difficult for large, formed bodies of troops to close with Morrison's main line positioned behind them.

The roads also favoured the British commander, providing forward and lateral communication that would allow him to deploy swiftly to counter any threat. It was good ground, it was fine ground, and Morrison knew it, but as he was badly outnumbered, he kept his troops formed along the Nine-Mile Road and contented himself with pushing Heriot's skirmish line out to the east side of the first ravine. He then waited for developments.[10]

In the American camp matters were confused that morning. Wilkinson's intention for 11 November was to run the Long Sault rapids and link up with Brown's force downstream. Toward this end, the greater part of his troops remained on shore under Boyd, and only the sick and a "boat guard" of about six hundred men under Lieutenant Colonel Timothy Upham of the Eleventh Infantry were permitted to embark on the flotilla. Wilkinson had communicated this intention to Morgan Lewis the previous night when he turned over command to that officer, and early in the morning of 11 November Lewis ordered Boyd to march down the river on the highway while the flotilla proceeded by water. What Wilkinson apparently did not tell either Lewis or Boyd was his concern that the Canadian bank below be cleared of enemy troops before the flotilla was "committed" to the Sault, "which allows no retreat, no landing, no turning to the right or left but where the impetuosity of the current impels."[11] He was therefore determined to wait for word from Brown that the bank below was open before moving and, with this in view, ordered Colonel Daniel Bissell to take his Fifth Infantry by boat ahead of the flotilla and secure Barnhart's Island, just above Cornwall, as there had been reports that it was garrisoned by the enemy.[12]

Boyd, under the impression that Lewis was in command, obeyed that officer's orders and the troops on land got under way about 8.30 A.M. Marching with the Eleventh Infantry was a proud Jarvis Hanks, whose scorched apparel had been replaced by new items from the clothing stocks carried on the boats, but the column had only moved about a half mile when one of Wilkinson's aides galloped up with an order to return. No reason was given for this change in plan but, in response, Boyd turned about and the army was soon back at Cook's Tavern (see Map 7), occupying "the ground, it did on the previous evening."[13] When Lewis, who had remained sick on his boat, heard of this from Surgeon Ezekiel Bull, Wilkinson's doctor, he sent an aide to his superior "to enquire the reason" and for the first time learned that Wilkinson had decided to wait until "information had been received from General Brown"[14] The commanding general also informed Lewis that Bissell's planned movement had been delayed because his pilot had deserted during the night.[15]

None of this was communicated to Boyd, who became confused as to who was in charge – Wilkinson had supposedly turned over to Lewis the previous evening but was still issuing orders, and as Boyd later dryly remarked, "ambitious to be first in service of his country, he tenaciously held command."[16] For his part, Lewis also issued orders, some of which countermanded those issued by Wilkinson. As if this was not bad enough for Boyd and his infantry waiting patiently on the highway, it began to rain about 10 A.M. and at almost the same moment British gunboats were sighted coming down the river.

Captain William Howe Mulcaster, RN, had been unable to resist the lovely target presented by the hundreds of boats beached near Michael Cook's tavern and decided to make another attempt to get at the flotilla before it descended the Sault. Between 9 and 10 A.M. he led his seven gunboats, the large and powerful *Nelson* in the van, down-river. They took station at the foot of Crysler's Island, in mid-river below that man's residence, and opened fire, but it quickly became apparent to Mulcaster that he could not do much harm to the enemy. The current was very strong, about four or five knots at this point, and it was difficult for the gunboats to maintain a midstream position which offered the best opportunity to hit the enemy, while the fire of those vessels stationed in the quieter water near the bank was less effective because the headland of Cook's Point partially sheltered their targets. To make matters worse, the British vessels were firing at extreme range and only the 24-pdr. gun on the *Nelson* had any real chance of hitting the Americans; the 6-pdr. and 12-pdr. guns on the smaller vessels could barely reach their target.[17]

As was the case the previous day, Mulcaster's fire was returned by Eustis's gunboats, which took station off Cook's Point between the British and the flotilla. Eustis was not only outgunned, he was also outnumbered, as four of his craft had just been detached to escort Bissell when that officer finally got under way at almost the same time Mulcaster appeared. The exchange of fire went on for some time but, watching from a position near Crysler's house, Captain Henry Jackson, RA, taking a professional interest in this action conducted at "long shot," commented that there "was little injury to either side."[18] Elias, the young son of Michael and Abigail Cook, would have disagreed with that assessment – in later years he remembered that as 24-pdr. roundshot from the *Nelson* came crashing through the trees around his father's tavern, his mother hustled her brood "into the cellar for protection."[19] Morgan Lewis, noting that Mulcaster's fire "did us no injury," thought the enemy "merely intended to retard our movements and we paid no attention to him."[20]

In fact, the British attack elicited a strong but unplanned American response. Many of the boats in the flotilla hastily moved as far down the Canadian bank as possible while other craft struck out for the safety of the American shore. Resorting to a tactic that had worked the day before, Wilkinson ordered an 18-pdr. gun disembarked from the artillery scows and positioned to drive off the attackers. This order was apparently given to Brigadier General Moses Porter but there is no evidence that it was carried out as Porter's movements on 11 November 1813 are a matter of mystery. The next senior artillery officer, Colonel Decius Wadsworth, proved no more helpful. He was on his vessel when the British gunboats appeared, and presuming "it would be necessary, to land some artillery; there was only one practicable place of landing; the passage to which, was rather obstructed by boats of the flotilla, and mine among others," he "crossed over to the American side [of the St. Lawrence], to get out of the way, and prevent confusion."[21] Instead of returning to the Canadian shore when the anchorage was clear, however, Wadsworth then "followed the boats, collected on this side, and entered the Saut." Taken at face value, this statement indicates that part of the flotilla, including some of the artillery scows and the second-ranking officer of that branch in the army, departed without orders for places unknown.[22]

Roundshot were still landing near Cook's tavern or splashing along the surface of the river like skipped stones at 10.30 A.M. when Cornet Thomas Robinson of the First Dragoons arrived with a message from Jacob Brown.[23]

For Brown, 11 November 1813 turned out to be a good day. He was on the move early, breaking camp at the head of the Sault at first light in preparation for clearing the Canadian bank of the rapid. Lieutenant Colonel Robert Carr of the Fifteenth Infantry remembered it as a miserable morning, "rainy with squalls of snow," but the weather did not prevent Brown from carrying out his tasks.[24] Luckett's First Dragoons were sent ahead to reconnoitre, and when they reported no opposition he advanced rapidly down the three-mile length of the rapids and by about 8.30 A.M. had reached Sheek's Island at the foot. Sending a message to the main army that the Sault was clear of the enemy, Brown then pushed on for Cornwall.[25]

The village was not defended. Major James Dennis and most of the local militia were with the wagon train of supplies, preparing to pull back by a roundabout route to Coteau du Lac, the next defended position west of Montreal. Dennis had also ordered all the military water transport in Cornwall to move down river for safety, but in order to keep an eye on developments he had posted three militia officers at various points "so that the enemy cannot move without being observed by one of them."[26] One of these officers recalled that most of the male inhabitants of the area of Cornwall were either with Dennis or had melted into the woods and there was "no[t] a Soul" to be seen "but a few Women Lamenting the absence of their husbands."[27] The only British or Canadian forces in the area of the village were a small scouting party of the 1st Stormont Regiment of militia commanded by Captain David Sheek and a force of native warriors from St. Regis led by Lieutenant Isaac Le Clair of the Indian Department.[28]

Sheek and Le Clair could offer no resistance to Brown's two brigades, which occupied Cornwall around midday after a gruelling eleven-mile march along muddy roads under intermittent rain and snow squalls. At about the same time, Bissell's Fifth Infantry, having made good progress down the river, landed unhindered on Barnhart's Island, where "from fires, breast works of logs, abbatis, blinds and trails," Bissell concluded "that an enemy had been posted there" but were now gone.[29] The boats of Brown's brigades, which had waited above the Sault, now came down and anchored with Bissell's craft at the foot of the island, and Brown, Bissell and their troops settled down to await the arrival of the main army, which they shortly expected to appear.[30]

Brown's camp was at the western edge of Cornwall, but to safeguard against surprises he placed a strong picket at Cahone's house, three miles east of the village. Le Clair and his warriors attacked it during the early afternoon – one of the militia scouts, Lieutenant Colonel Joseph Bouchette, got within a mile of Cahone's but "was prevented from going further – by the Noise of firing of the advanced Picquet of the Enemy or scouting parties which were quite near us." The attack was rebuffed and a few minutes later Bouchette encountered warriors "running to the Interior" who told him that the enemy were in strength at Cahone's place and not to be shifted.[31]

In Cornwall itself, Brown's "officers took possession of the farm houses, the men bivouacked in the field." None "but women and children" remained in the village, and they were naturally enough concerned about the treatment they could expect from the invaders. Brown's troops, however, proved to be "civil and quiet, and no insult either by word or act was offered any of the inmates of the houses though the intention to destroy the town as well as the farmhouses before the advance on Montreal was continued, was freely expressed by both officers and men." The locals, however could not help but compare the appearance of the invaders, dirty and dishevelled after weeks in open boats, with the British and Canadian regulars who frequently passed through the village. The Americans "looked very little like soldiers – there was neither drill nor discipline among them," they recalled, and their officers "seemed to command neither respect nor obedience from the men, most of whom appeared more anxious to get home than to fight."[32]

Although Brown's troops behaved well at Cornwall, they did help themselves to "the contents of the barns and granaries, and to all the provisions they could lay their hands on" while "every stick of fence on the farms was burned, and diligent search was made for any valuables that might have been concealed in cellars and gardens." One of the farms serving as a bivouac belonged to Captain Thomas Anderson, a former Loyalist officer, and Mrs. Anderson's "winter stock of preserves" which "had been carefully hidden in one of the garden beds" was "discovered by some of the enemy, who prodded the ground with their iron ram rods." These treasure hunters (probably Forsyth's riflemen) missed a better prize because "the good lady's small stock of plate and jewelry was more successfully concealed." On the other hand, several village stores "were patronized in a way that did not add much to the profits of the owners."[33]

Whether soldier or civilian, everyone in Cornwall stopped what they were doing in early afternoon when the noise of artillery fire was heard from up the river. Once started, it did not let up, and as the distant booming continued, Brown's men confidently assured the Canadians that now "the Britishers are catching it."[34]

After a frustrating hour, Mulcaster broke off his attack at about 11 A.M. and withdrew most of his vessels up river but left three gunboats in positions where they could support Morrison. The *Nelson,* his largest and most heavily-armed craft, took station near the foot of Crysler's Island, while a smaller vessel was anchored near the Canadian bank and another at the head of the island.[35]

Throughout the naval duel, Morrison's troops had remained formed along the Nine-Mile Road under a gentle fall of rain. The quarrelling along the picket line had long since died away and both they and their commander were beginning to grow impatient. Jackson of the RA remembered that late in the morning the enemy "appeared to be moving off" and "we were all expecting the word to march," but the report turned out to be false.[36] Morrison, Harvey and Pearson began to wonder what Wilkinson was up to as the Americans appeared frozen in place.

While waiting, some comic relief was provided by Samuel Adams from Edwardsburgh, a private in the Dundas militia who had volunteered to serve that day with Fraser's dragoons. Described as a "tall, handsome, active, and very powerful young man," Adams had no particular duty assigned to him and therefore "resolved to have a foray on his *own hook.*" Early that morning, he left the British lines and rode around the American position, emerging on the river bank in the rear of the enemy camp, where he tethered his horse in the wood and then moved close to the highway. A passing troop of American dragoons forced him to seek cover "behind an old log, which barely served to conceal him from the horsemen, who, in their hurry, passed within a few feet without observing him." A few minutes later, Adams spotted two enemy officers, "in dashing uniform," walking up the highway and, jumping from cover with raised musket, took them prisoner. He marched these two Americans, Captain White Jones and Charles Bruce, "back through to the woods, and reached head-quarters by the same route he had left, with his prize" – a feat that was all the more impressive because Adams's musket was not loaded. The two prisoners were interrogated by Morrison and Harvey, and after they had signed a parole not to attempt to escape until formally exchanged, were dispatched on foot to Prescott under guard. As Adams told the story, his "exploit was rewarded with a pair of cavalry horses branded U.S. which he retained for many years afterwards."[37]

If Sam Adams had been in the vicinity a few hours later, he might well have scooped up another American. Lieutenant Reynold M. Kirby of the Third Artillery, a twenty-three-year-old former lawyer from Pittsfield, Massachusetts, who had received his commission only a few months before, had been trying to catch up with his unit for weeks. The previous day, Kirby had crossed over the St. Lawrence with a party of officers and civilians (including ladies) also trying to find the army, and they had spent the night in Loucks's tavern, a few miles to the east of the main camp. Kirby noted there were no Canadian men of military age to be seen as all "the males had fled the approach of the army or had been embodied in the militia, which we understand was assembled at Cornwall."[38]

On the morning of 11 November, which he remembered as "cold & wet," Kirby and his fellow travellers waited in vain for the appearance of the flotilla, and when the young artillery officer saw Brown's messenger, Cornet Thomas Robinson, and his escort riding up the highway, he hailed the cavalry officer to find that Brown had "succeeded in dispersing the militia at Cornwall without opposition." As the morning wore on and nothing happened except "a slight & interrupted fire of musketry" from "the army above," Kirby "became convinced that the enemy were attempting to delay" the flotilla's movement "by threatening an attack." Anxious to see his first battle, he therefore "set out on foot for the scene of the action."[39]

By noon Morrison was becoming impatient as his enemy had been in a state of suspended animation for hours. He decided to get something going and ordered Heriot to push his light troops closer to the enemy camp. Between 12 and 1 P.M. Heriot's three companies of Voltigeurs, Anderson's Mohawks scouting ahead, moved east through the woods. As they advanced, they passed near the Fetterly house, located between the two armies, and a friendly soldier, seeing Mrs. Fetterly and her eleven-year-old daughter, Agnes, in the yard, warned her to take the child and go into the cellar "as there was going to be a battle."[40]

Things got steadily worse for John Boyd throughout the morning. By noon his troops had been standing for two hours in a "drisling rain" and were still waiting for their generals to make up their minds.[41] Boyd had received a "variety of verbal orders" which were "generally countermanded, before they were executed."[42] He was growing doubtful of Wilkinson's resolve as it appeared it "was not the object of the Commander in Chief" to fight a battle because he had detached Brown "with the elite of the army," had not reinforced Boyd with the six hundred men of the boat guard but instead had sent "away a valuable part of the flotilla, with the two principal [artillery] officers."[43] Despite their seeming reluctance to fight, however, Boyd noted that "the two Major Generals, although confined by indisposition, still continued to command."[44]

Wilkinson refused to either give up or take up control of his army. He sent a note to Brown with the interesting but not very serviceable information that he was feeling "the heavy hand of disease" and was "confined to my bed while the safety of the army intrusted to my command, the honor of our armies, and the greatest interests of our country are at hazard."[45] Even his surgeon, Ezekiel Bull, was confused about who controlled the army – it was later his opinion that Wilkinson did not "resume the *formal* command" on 11 November.[46] But Wilkinson persisted in issuing orders and then reversing them and his indecision may have been due to the "variety of reports respecting their [the British] movements and counter-movements" which were "successively brought to the General, which impressed him with the conviction that the enemy had determined to attack his rear as soon as the flotilla should put off and the troops to commence their march."[47]

Meanwhile, Boyd and his men continued to wait. Wilkinson had not bothered to tell Boyd he had received information from below; Boyd attributed the confusing orders which were countermanded before executed to the "want of information from General Brown," not knowing that such information had already been received.[48] Just past midday, a "violent storm" of rain began, drenching the three brigades of infantry formed on the highway. This was the last straw for Boyd, who rode to the river and shouted across to Wilkinson's boat demanding "some decisive or discretionary orders."[49] Half an hour later, a response came in the form of Colonel Joseph Swift, who landed with a "specific order" that "the flotilla would be put off in 20 minutes" after "4 pieces of artillery would be landed to reinforce the rear guard which would follow the boats" but "should the enemy harass the rear," Boyd was to "turn and beat him back."[50] It was now about 1.30 P.M.

It took time to land the guns. The arrangement of the flotilla had been disrupted by Mulcaster, both Porter and Wadsworth were absent, and because the next senior artillery officer, Abram Eustis, had to remain with the gunboats, command of the artillery devolved on a relatively junior officer, Lieutenant Henry Knox Craig of the Second Artillery Regiment. Craig shortly discovered he had a major problem: there were no horses to draw the four 6-pdr. field pieces he had been ordered to bring ashore. Someone – the culprit was never identified – had sent the 250 artillery team horses, which had been crossed over at the White House three days before, down the river with Brown and they were now happily grazing somewhere near Cornwall. Fortunately, proper harness was available and luckless members of Major John Woodford's Second Dragoons were ordered to surrender their mounts to Craig, but there was a further delay as his cursing gunners struggled to convert independent-minded cavalry horses into more docile draft animals. This task had only begun when Boyd received word from Captain John Selden's dragoon vedettes that a "body of two hundred British and Indians had advanced into the woods that skirted our rear."[51]

John Parker Boyd was a simple man who liked to keep things simple. He had a positive order to assail the British if they harassed the army and, as that condition had apparently come to pass, he decided to obey it. He directed Brigadier General Robert Swartout, whose Fourth Brigade was at the rear of the column on the highway, to seek the enemy and attack. Covington's Third Brigade and Boyd's own First Brigade, under the command of Colonel Isaac Coles, were ordered to support Swartout and all three formations were immediately put in motion toward the west. As Ripley of the Twenty-First Infantry later recalled, this advance was not a "simultaneous movement of corps and brigades in order of battle but one of the whole column towards the enemy."[52]

Deducting Upham's 600-strong boat guard and the sick (about one man in five) who remained with the flotilla, Boyd had between 2,200 and 2,400 infantry under command, while Woodford's Second Dragoons, although weakened by the need to contribute horses to the gun teams, still mustered between 120 and 150 sabres (see Appendix E). Trailing along considerably in the rear of the infantry were Lieutenant Armstrong Irvine's two 6-pdr. guns, which had been landed a few days before, and as soon as he got his balky prime movers sorted out, Craig would eventually bring up four more pieces of the same calibre in support. Although Boyd only had just over a third of Wilkinson's total strength, it was about half the healthy men in the army and he was confident it was force enough to handle an enemy of the strength he had fought the previous day.[53]

It was just past 2 P.M. and the rain had stopped falling when Swartout's lead element, the Twenty-First Infantry Regiment, entered the woods. They immediately came under fire. Legend has it that the opening shot of what was to become the battle of Crysler's Farm was discharged by a Mohawk warrior from behind the cover of the Fetterly family's bake oven. Whoever was responsible, this time the firing, once started, did not stop.[54]

Swartout's Fourth brigade, between eight and nine hundred men formed in column of march, angled to the north end of the wood, where Heriot's skirmishers were pressing most heavily on the American pickets. The orders to advance and the brigade's subsequent movement came so quickly that Colonel Eleazer Ripley, the commanding officer of the lead Twenty-First Infantry, was absent from his unit when it moved off, and it was led by Major Joseph Grafton. Behind Grafton came the other two units of the brigade, the Fourteenth and Eleventh Infantry in that order. Badly outnumbered and possibly somewhat shaken by the ferocity of the American reaction, Heriot's Voltigeurs and Anderson's Mohawks fired and pulled back, taking care to keep in the cover of the trees. Surgeon Amasa Trowbridge of the Twenty-First Infantry, a thirty-four-year-old resident of Jefferson County, New York, who had volunteered to serve in the army, remembered that his comrades drove their enemy back "after a short skirmish" but "they kept up a sharp fire upon our advancing columns."[55]

Swartout's brigade had been the last one formed in the army and his three regiments varied in quality. The Twenty-First Infantry, recruited in Massachusetts and New Hampshire, had fought at York and Sackets Harbor the previous spring and its reputation as a well trained and disciplined regiment was mainly due to the efforts of its commanding officer, thirty-one-year-old Eleazer Wheelock Ripley, a Boston lawyer and former Speaker of the Massachusetts House of Representatives and one of the few New Englanders to hold a senior position in the army. Lieutenant Colonel Timothy Upham's first battalion of the Eleventh Infantry (the second battalion was with Hampton) was also a solid unit but had not seen any action for a year, and that was during the confusing affair at Lacolle Mill in November 1812. At this moment, however, Upham was absent commanding the boat guard. Lieutenant Colonel Timothy Dix's Fourteenth Infantry from Maryland and Virginia was the hard-luck outfit of the brigade. It had arrived on the Niagara frontier the previous autumn and had spent a rough winter but, thereafter, things went downhill for the Fourteenth: it was decimated at Beaver Dams in June, losing 332 officers and men taken prisoner, and the remnants of the unit had been sent to Sackets Harbor, where it was reinforced by a strong detachment from its home states. Unfortunately, the Fourteenth had suffered so badly from illness that when it embarked for Grenadier Island in late October, it mustered only 267 men fit for duty. Dix, a native of New Hampshire who had been commissioned directly from civil life in the spring of 1812, had served with the unit since the beginning.[56]

Entering the trees behind Swartout, Brigadier General Leonard Covington opted to move his Third Brigade, which had a strength of between nine hundred and a thousand men, in a more deliberate fashion. He formed his regiments, the Ninth, Sixteenth and Twenty-Fifth Infantry, in close column and advanced carefully through the main part of the woods near the river, but as Major Charles Gardner of the Twenty-Fifth recalled, this movement soon became disordered as the leading elements "heard the 4th brig[ade]. engaging the enemy" and becoming excited, started to run over "ground to derange the best troops."[57] The brigade began to lose cohesion and it was further disordered by the necessity of climbing over or kicking down a series of split rail fences. Coming to the western skirt of the woods, "a huzza was given," complained Gardner, apparently on Boyd's orders, which rendered the brigade officers' attempts to control their men ineffectual as their orders could not be heard above the cheering.[58]

Some distance to the rear, Isaac Coles's First Brigade moved on Covington's right but behind Swartout. Because Bissell's Fifth Infantry, his strongest regiment, had been detached that morning, Coles's formation was the weakest brigade, numbering only 450-550 men. It also moved in column of march with the Thirteenth in the lead, followed by Coles's own Twelfth Infantry, commanded this day by Major Robert C. Nicholas. Recruited in Virginia and Maryland, the Twelfth had not seen much fighting although it had been on the northern frontier for more than a year. It had arrived at Niagara in the autumn of 1812 and had participated in a few skirmishes but had suffered much from disease the following winter. The unit spent the long summer at Fort George, seeing little real action before moving down the St. Lawrence. Colonel James P. Preston's Thirteenth Infantry from New York had a reputation as a well disciplined unit that performed well in battle. The Thirteenth had fought at Queenston Heights in October 1812, where it lost half its strength and it was consolidated with the Fifth Infantry during the winter of 1812-1813 before playing a major role in the attack on Fort George in May 1813. In the northern army the regiment's nickname was "the snorters" because a previous commanding officer had ordered its officers and men to grow moustaches.[59]

Isaac Coles was a Virginian who had briefly served as a captain in the prewar army. He had been appointed a major in the Twelfth Infantry at the outbreak of war and had risen to the rank of colonel by the autumn of 1813. This was his first experience as a brigade commander and it showed in the orders he issued, orders that confused his units. With only a very basic level of training, American infantry regiments usually tried to march in the same sequence of companies to simplify deployment from column into line. If a unit had to reverse direction, it was common practice to countermarch, or wheel the entire column around to take up the new direction, retaining the same company in the lead. Unfortunately, as Lieutenant Joseph Dwight of the Thirteenth remembered, Coles, "instead of ordering [us] to countermarch, ordered the right about face," which meant that the Thirteenth simply turned in its tracks and moved west.[60] Its companies and those of the Twelfth were now in inverted order, and matters got worse when the brigade approached the wood, where Coles ordered it to advance through the trees "from the left" or the rear of the column – possibly an attempt on his part to re-invert his formation to restore the normal sequence of companies. The result was that the First Brigade degenerated into a confused mob.[61]

As Swartout and Covington's brigades advanced, they came under fire from Heriot's light troops, experienced skirmishers. The three companies of Canadian Voltigeurs, each about fifty men strong, commanded by Captains Jacques Adhémar, William Johnson and Jacques-Clément Herse, had fought at Sackets Harbor the previous May and spent the summer skirmishing around Fort George, while their native comrades had been trained in bush warfare since childhood since it was not all that different from their normal occupation of hunting.[62]

Light infantry like the Voltigeurs worked in loose, but still controlled, formations based on pairs of soldiers. One man would fire while his partner covered him with a loaded musket, and after the first man had discharged his weapon, he would "slip around the left" of the second soldier who would "make a short pace forward, and put himself in the other's place, whom he is to protect while loading."[63] British light infantry were trained to always fire from the right side "of the object which covers them so that the second man "may step forward without being exposed." When the first man had loaded, he would "give his comrade the word *ready*, after which, and not before," the second man would "fire and immediately change places as before."[64] The Voltigeurs picked their shots carefully, trying to make each round count. Spread out among the scrub pine and underbrush in their drab grey uniforms, they were difficult to spot as, obeying commands communicated by shouts or whistles, they fired and moved back from tree to tree, buying time and slowing the American advance.[65]

Their native comrades also liked to fight in pairs, but to minimize casualties usually changed position after every shot, employing the smoke discharged by each round to cover the movement. Just as white troops had their flags, uniforms, rank insignia and medals to "heighten self-esteem and group identity," so too did Old Peter, Captain Jim, Joseph Skunk, Big Jacob and their fellows have their own version of military panoply.[66] Before entering battle, they adorned themselves with feathers and other ornamentation believed to have spiritual powers and usually painted their faces and sometimes their bodies – the favoured colours being red, associated with life, and black, identified with danger and death. The warriors also engaged in psychological warfare. If fighting their own people they might sing songs about what would happen if they got hold of their enemies but since white soldiers would not understand and therefore not be affected by these blood-curdling threats, Anderson's Mohawks contented themselves with shouting "like demons."[67] It worked just as well – a British officer who watched some warriors happy in action during the war commented that it was a "point with them at every discharge of the rifle to shift their position, and whenever they knocked a fellow over, their yelling was horrible."[68]

So it was in the woods between the two armies on 11 November 1813 – shots, shouts, howls and whistles – as the *Canadiens* and Mohawks fired and fell back. Weight of numbers quickly began to tell, as Swartout and Covington, despite the confusion in their ranks, were moving with nearly two thousand men on Heriot, who had less than two hundred. In any case, Heriot's job was not to stop the enemy advance but to delay it long enough to give his commanding officer time to make his own preparations.

As the three American brigades moved through woods, Boyd and Colonels Joseph Swift and John Walbach, who would serve as his principal subordinates in the coming hours, kept pace, riding on borrowed dragoon horses behind Woodford's dragoons along the highway. It seems likely that John Boyd, if he had even thought about what he was going to do that afternoon, counted on fighting the same type of scrap as had occurred the day before – a short, sharp action to drive the British back, followed by deployment into a defensive position which, supported by his field artillery, would prevent interference with the flotilla's movements.

In any case, the thing looked to be starting well. The sheer vigour of the American advance pushed Heriot's skirmishers west from the first ravine to the second, a distance of nearly a mile. In Boyd's words, the enemy "first attacked us in the woods; we drove them from thence."[69] The lead regiment, the Twenty-First Infantry, was approaching the western skirt of the woods when its "scouts suddenly reported that the enemy was formed" beyond the trees.[70] Grafton was unable to check his troops' eagerness and the Twenty-First "pushed from the woods" to discover themselves in full view of a strong British force deployed at the opposite end of an expanse of open fields. A few hundred yards away was a line of a half dozen mounted men, and Grafton's men immediately opened up at them.[71]

Trooper John Loucks and his comrades of the Provincial Light Dragoons watched as blue uniforms came into sight at the tree line. Loucks later recalled that an "enemy platoon halted and fired a volley" at the little group but, due to the range, it only "ploughed up the sand about the horses' feet." The dragoons had been posted as a vedette to warn of an enemy advance, and as that was obviously taking place, Loucks wheeled his horse and galloped with more haste than decorum back to the nearest regular unit to report. His information was somewhat redundant as by now almost everyone in Morrison's command had been alerted by the firing in the woods. A British officer (it may have been Pearson) thanked the excited teenager for his information but quietly advised him that while it "was all right to fall back," it "was not good form to ride so fast in the face of the enemy."[72]

Morrison was prepared to meet the American onslaught. As the sound of musketry came closer, he moved his units from the Nine-Mile Road into the "position selected for the detachment to occupy."[73] It was a position, John Harvey noted, that "fortunately was not more extensive than our little band" could hold, and the "dispositions were therefore easily made."[74] On his right flank, advanced on the King's highway behind the first gully, was Pearson with the flank companies of the 49th Foot and the detachment of Canadian Fencibles. Supporting Pearson and somewhat to his left rear was Captain George West Barnes and three companies of the 89th in a position to keep contact with the main body of the army, which consisted of the remaining eight companies of the 49th and the five of the 89th deployed in open columns on a farm lane that ran directly north from the farmstead of Charles Jones. Morrison and Harvey, their aides and staff, which included militia Captains John Crysler and Reuben Sherwood, took position nearby, and as the firing in front drew nearer, Morrison gave the order and Plenderleath of the 49th and Clifford of the 89th deployed from column into line.[75]

The two battalion commanders first shouted the cautionary order, "Wheel up into Line!" which was repeated by the individual company commanders. Next came "March!" and as the lead companies in each regimental column remained stationary, those behind deployed at the quick step into line abreast of them, the 89th to the left, and the 49th to the right of their respective lead companies. When this movement was complete, the command "Halt, Dress!" was issued and the two battalions "dressed" or aligned their ranks and adjusted any gaps that had opened in the intervals between the companies during the wheeling. The 49th and 89th Foot were now deployed in a line of two ranks separated by a distance of one pace (two and a half feet) with the men in each rank occupying, by regulation, twenty-two inches of space and standing

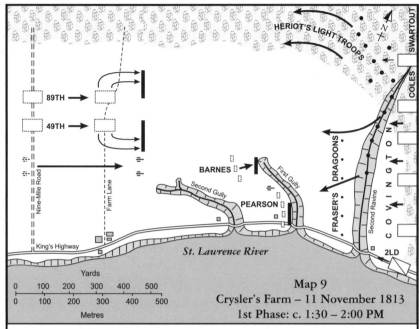

Map 9
Crysler's Farm – 11 November 1813
1st Phase: c. 1:30 – 2:00 PM

1. As Heriot's skirmishers delay the American advance, Morrison positions his troops. The main part of the 49th and 89th move forward from the Nine-Mile Road to Jones's farm lane and then deploy into line, as do Barnes's three companies of the 89th and Pearson's advance posted behind the first gully. Jackson positions two 6-pdr. guns on the right of the main line and one gun under Kersteman to support Pearson.

2. As Boyd's three brigades push through the woods, Heriot's skirmishers withdraw to the woods in the north or to the cover of the second ravine. Fraser's vedette of Canadian dragoons also withdraws when the Americans appear in the tree line.

so close to their neighbours that they could feel their sleeves. The company commander, usually a captain, took post at the right of the front rank of his company and the senior lieutenant stationed himself at the left of the same rank, while the other officers and sergeants took post in the rank of file closers (a file is a group of men ranged one behind each other) three paces (seven and a half feet) behind the rear rank. The task of the file closers was to fill in gaps in the two fighting ranks caused by casualties, "to keep the others closed up to the front during the attack, and to prevent any break beginning in the rear" or, more simply said, to prevent men running away – on "this important service," the British manual noted, "too many officers and non-commissioned officers cannot be employed." The drummers of each battalion took post in two groups six paces (fifteen feet) behind the last infantry rank. As Plenderleath and Clifford's men deployed, Pearson's detachment near the river bank and Barnes's three companies of the 89th went through a similar evolution as they made ready to meet the American attack.[76]

In the centre of each battalion the colour parties now removed the black oilskins which covered their colours and shook them out into the wind. If the drums were the heart of a British infantry battalion, its two colours were its soul. The King's Colour was the Union Standard with the regimental number painted or embroidered in gold Roman numerals and encircled with a wreath of roses and thistles, the whole surmounted by a Crown. Both the 49th and 89th had similar King's Colours but their Regimental Colours differed – the Regimental Colour of the 49th Foot was the green of its facings except the upper canton, which was the Union standard, while that of the 89th consisted of a red St. George's Cross, the upper canton of which was the Union standard and the remaining cantons the black of its facings. Colours were the visible symbol of a unit's history and its triumphs, its battle honours were painted or embroidered on them. The 49th Foot had two: "Egmont-op-Zee" commemorated the Duke of York's victory over a French army in Holland in 1799 while "Copenhagen" recorded a naval action fought in 1801 during which the 49th served as marines on board the fleet. However, the colours of the 2nd Battalion of the 89th Foot, a relatively new unit, carried no honours and its one previous action, in Spain in 1810, had been an utter disaster.[77]

Colours were more than ceremonial trappings. They served a practical function as a guide for alignment in the smoke and confusion of battle and as a rallying point for a sorely pressed regiment, and they also marked the position of the battalion commanding officer, who took post immediately in front of them so that he could easily be found in battle. That day the two colours were carried by the two most junior officers in each battalion and they had a job to hold them steady in the face of the stiff breeze from the west. It was also an extremely hazardous duty as these devices, six feet on the hoist and six and a half feet in the fly, mounted on a pike nine feet, ten inches in length, were attractive aiming-points. Since victories in this period were often judged by the number of colours captured, they were also prime objectives and vicious hand-to-hand fighting often took place over possession of these visible marks of an army's pride. At the battle of Albuera in 1811, sixteen-year-old Ensign Edward Thomas, carrying the Regimental Colour of the 3rd Foot, was surrounded by French lancers, who demanded he surrender his charge. "Only with my life," Thomas replied, and the French took both that and his colour.[78] Lieutenant Matthew Latham, carrying the King's Colour of the same unit, refused to give it up to the lancers who encircled him so they severed his left arm

and cut him across the face with their sabres, pierced him with a dozen lance-thrusts and, just for good measure, trampled him with their horses. As he fell, Latham managed to tear the colour from its pike and conceal it beneath his body where it was later recovered – incredibly, he survived his wounds. Lieutenant John Sewell recorded that the 49th Foot had a grim tradition that the bearer of its Regimental Colour "was always hit in action."[79] Such had been the case at Egmont-op-Zee in 1799 and, Sewell believed, at Stoney Creek the previous June.[80]

Their colours were visible to the "rank and file" of the two battalions, the privates and corporals who did much of the fighting and suffered most of the casualties. The soldiers of Plenderleath's eight companies of the 49th in their grey greatcoats and Clifford's five companies of the 89th in their dull, brick-red coatees were standing with shouldered arms, their 9½ lb. India Pattern muskets (the "Brown Bess" of legend) resting on their left shoulders, the butts held by the left hand and the lock facing to the right. Crossing on their chests were two-inch-wide buff shoulder belts from which were suspended the black leather cartridge box on their right hip and a scabbard carrying the bayonet on the left. They may have had their canteens that afternoon but it is likely that they had left the haversacks, in which they carried their rations, and the heavy square knapsacks, in which they carried all their other worldly possessions, in some safe place under the guard of a trusted man. The regulars waiting on the muddy fields that dull day in November were stripped for action in what modern soldiers call "fighting order."[81]

As the sound of the firing came closer, Clifford, Plenderleath, Pearson and Barnes ordered their men to load. Normally this would be done some time before action was imminent, but as it had already rained that morning and the skies were threatening, they probably held off as long as possible because, once loaded and primed, muskets were susceptible to dampness, and both battalion commanders would want to ensure that their first volley, properly and carefully loaded, would be as effective as possible.

At the command "Load!" Privates George Braithewaite of the 49th and Gideon Gibson of the 89th – and each of their comrades in the rank and file – brought his weapon down off his left shoulder and held it suspended across his chest with his left hand while with his right forefinger and thumb he pulled the lock back to the half-cock position. Reaching into his cartridge box, he pulled out a cartridge, a twist of stiff paper containing a .71 calibre lead ball weighing just over an ounce and seven drams of black powder. Biting off the end without the ball and tasting the bitter charcoal, he shook some of the powder into the pan of his musket, closed the pan and dropped the musket butt to the ground. He then poured the remainder of the powder down the bore, followed it with the ball and the paper in that order and, pulling his iron ramrod from the brass "flutes" that held it below the barrel with his right hand, inserted it into the muzzle and rammed home the ball and the wad formed by the cartridge paper, giving the whole two quick strokes at the bottom to seat it securely. Returning his ramrod, the soldier completed the procedure by shouldering his weapon again. Done in slow time without hurry, this entire sequence might take up to thirty seconds – in action, a trained man was expected to load and fire between two and three rounds per minute.[82]

The fighting in front was now close enough for Morrison's troops to see the occasional glimpse of Heriot's Voltigeurs and Anderson's warriors slipping through the trees. Some of the skirmishers ran out of the woods and took cover in the second ravine but most withdrew through the shelter of the pine woods to the north.

A few minutes later, in John Harvey's words, "the enemy shewed his columns in the woods in our front, consisting of three heavy ones (apparently brigades) of Infantry" and "a considerable body of Cavalry on the Road [the King's highway] on his left."[83] As the Americans debouched from the trees,

Morrison calculated their strength at between 3,000 and 4,000 men but Harvey was convinced it was "not less than 4,000 and strong in an Arm of which we were wholly destitute" – cavalry (apparently Fraser's dozen dragoons did not qualify as the real thing in his eyes). Lieutenant Christopher Hagerman thought "the American approach in close column, divided into three divisions" was "very imposing," and there were some in the British ranks whose courage began to ebb as they watched more and more blue coats come into view.[84] Sewell of the 49th overheard a nearby sergeant remark that "there are too many, we shall all be slaughtered" and moved quickly to nip that attitude in the bud by coldly telling the man that "it will be better for you to die doing your duty, than to be shot for mutiny."[85] Even that old hand John Harvey, a veteran of a dozen actions on three continents, was impressed. "As the Enemy advanced out of the Woods," he later commented, "I plainly saw we had nothing to trust to but *every Man doing his duty*."[86]

When they arrived at the edge of the cleared area of fields, the American commanders were no less impressed by the sight of their enemy drawn up in front of them. Boyd and Swartout estimated the British strength to be 2,500 men, about twice the actual number, while Swift thought it at least 1,600. Only the more experienced Walbach calculated it accurately – between 1,100 and 1,200 men. The problem was not British numbers; it was their position. In Boyd's opinion, the enemy "had judiciously chosen his ground among the deep ravines which everywhere intersected the extensive plain" that lay in his front.[87] If he had planned on fighting a long-distance rearguard action, Boyd now realized he might have something quite different on his hands.[88]

Although it was not in his character, Boyd may have hesitated at this moment. The enthusiasm of his infantry, however, rendered impossible any thought of caution for such was their eagerness to get to grips with the enemy that it proved difficult for the brigade and regimental commanders to check their forward movement. Major William Clay Cumming of the Sixteenth Infantry, having suffered from his generals' leadership on 10 November, later commented that "our sage leaders" were probably planning to demonstrate their "passion for manoeuvring" as they had the previous day but "were carried into battle by the sheer blind ardor of our army; for I very much doubt whether Boyd & Walbach had formed any serious design, either of fighting or not fighting."[89] As the three American brigades left the shelter of the woods and their officers struggled to get them deployed, they immediately came under a "heavy and galling" fire from the British artillery.[90]

CHAPTER 10

"They came on in a very gallant style"

11 NOVEMBER 1813, 2.00–3.30 P.M.

To meet Britannia's hostile bands
We'll march, our heroes say, sir,
We'll join all hearts; we'll join all hands;
Brave boys we'll win the day, sir.
   Yankee doodle, strike your tents, yankee doodle dandy,
   Yankee doodle, march away, and do your parts right handy.

Full long we've borne with British pride,
And sue'd to gain our rights, sir;
All other methods have been tried;
There nought remains but fight, sir.
   Yankee doodle, march away, yankee doodle dandy,
   Yankee doodle, fight brave boys, the thing will work right handy.[1]

As soon as the American columns appeared in the tree line, Captain Henry George Jackson, who had already calculated the distance from his guns to the edge of the woods, opened fire. A ten-year veteran of the Royal Artillery, Jackson had been commissioned as a second lieutenant in 1803 directly on graduation from the Royal Military Academy at Woolwich, the training school for British artillery and engineer officers. He had arrived in North America in the spring of 1813 as the second-in-command of Captain James P. St. Clair's company, which seems to have been a very good unit as an inspecting officer commented that, in the matter of "either officers or men," no "finer [artillery] Company ever set foot in the Canadas."[2] When St. Clair brought his men to Kingston during the summer, Jackson had been detached to Prescott to command the artillery there. Most of his duties were concerned with ensuring that the defensive batteries were properly manned and equipped but there was also a number of field pieces in the garrison and since Pearson's standing orders directed that in the case of an alarm Jackson was to turn out two 6-pdr. field pieces fully manned "ready to move wherever Circumstances might require them," he had taken care to keep up his gunners' skills with these weapons.[3] When he joined Morrison, Jackson brought along three guns of this calibre with full teams for the weapons and their attendant vehicles.[4]

Jackson had positioned his artillery to cover Morrison's entire front. One gun under his subordinate officer, Lieutenant Henry Kersteman, was stationed with Pearson's advance in the forward position on the highway while the other two were at the right flank of the main British line at an elevation high enough, in Sewell's words, to "fire over our bayonets" without hitting friendly infantry.[5] Fifteen to twenty yards behind each gun, squat on its grey-painted carriage with its dull green brass (actually bronze) barrel pointed east, was its limber, and at a safer distance back a wagon with its reserve ammunition. Each 6-pdr. was manned by a gun detachment, nine men at full strength for a field piece of this calibre, commanded by an experienced NCO, almost always a sergeant. The men in these detachments were regulars wearing the blue uniforms of the Royal Artillery. Militia gunners were available but they would not be much help in a hot action in the open – in the opinion of Major General George Glasgow, the senior British artillery officer in North America, militiamen usually proved "of no use" in battle as "they expend a great deal of ammunition while the Enemy are at a distance and as soon as he approaches they spike the guns and run away."[6] If any of these amateurs were with Jackson's gun detachments, he probably consigned them to duties in the rear to keep them out of the way.[7]

Morrison did not have to tell an officer of Jackson's experience that the performance of his artillery would be crucial to the outcome of the battle. His guns were the only weapons that could hit the enemy at long range, and as the odds in these opening minutes of the action appeared to be at least three or four to one in favour of the Americans, the more casualties Jackson inflicted on the enemy, the less pressure they would be able to exert on Morrison's outnumbered infantry. The gunner officer's task was simple – he had to kill as many Americans as he could as fast as he could.

To do so, he had three different projectiles to choose from: case shot, roundshot and spherical case shot. The most useful against closely-packed infantry formations was case shot, or canister, but it was only effective at short ranges, between 100 and 350 yards, and the American infantry spilling out of the trees between 600 and 1,000 yards from his guns, were too distant. Some of the enemy units were within the maximum effective range of roundshot but the conditions were not the best as the ground around Crysler's farm was wet

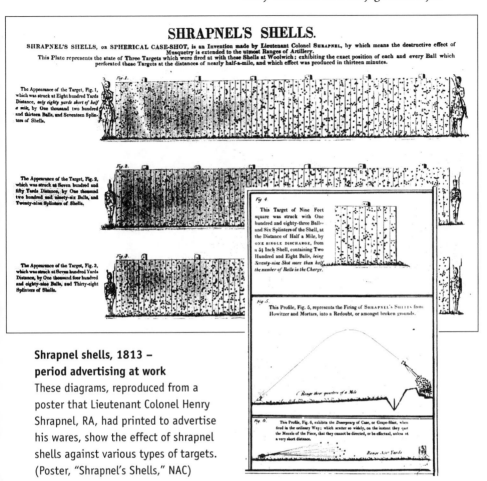

Shrapnel shells, 1813 – period advertising at work

These diagrams, reproduced from a poster that Lieutenant Colonel Henry Shrapnel, RA, had printed to advertise his wares, show the effect of shrapnel shells against various types of targets. (Poster, "Shrapnel's Shells," NAC)

and muddy. Gunners liked to land roundshot in front of an infantry target and bounce it through the ranks in a series of "grazes" or ricochets that doubled and redoubled its effect, but wet ground acted as a cushion, slowing it down and reducing its range and effectiveness. Jackson, therefore, turned to his third projectile, spherical case shot.[8]

Commonly called shrapnel, spherical case was a hollow, thin-walled iron sphere filled with a bursting charge of powder and twenty-seven musket balls (in the 6-pdr. variety) exploded above the target by a fuze. Spherical case provided Jackson his best chance to do harm to the Americans, and not only was he fortunate to have this projectile; he was fortunate to have enough of it, for it was often in short supply in North America. There had been sufficient 6-pdr. spherical case at Prescott for him to provide his weapons with the minimum scale of twenty rounds per gun and he probably brought more.[9]

British field artillery, 1813
Captain Henry Jackson, RA, had three brass (actually bronze) 6-pdr. field guns similar to this weapon at the battle. The workhorse fieldpiece of both armies during the war, the 6-pdr. gun was a good balance between mobility and firepower. (Reproduction period artillery at Fort George NHS, courtesy of the Friends of Fort George)

The British artillery commander transmitted his firing order to his gun commanders in the formula of target, type of projectile and number of rounds, as in, "Infantry column in front; two rounds spherical case, fire when ready." He did not concern himself with the loading, aiming and firing of the weapons. That was the province of the NCO commanding each gun detachment – his job and that of Kersteman, was to position their weapons properly, ensure they were supplied with ammunition, observe and correct the fall of shot and identify targets.

At each field piece, the experienced gun commander would probably have anticipated the choice of spherical case and had a round ready for loading. On receiving the firing order, the detachment swung into action. Spherical case was a tricky projectile that required experience and nice judgement to use properly – if the shell exploded too soon or too low in its trajectory, its bullets ploughed harmlessly into the earth in front of the target; if too high, they fell behind it. The ideal was to achieve what modern gunners call an "air burst" above and just in front of an enemy infantry formation, sending a lethal spray into the crowded ranks. To do that required the right choice of fuze. In 1813 artillery fuzes were tapered hollow beechwood tubes, about six inches long, tightly packed with a combustible mixture that burned at a predictable rate. The outer surface was ribbed, each rib representing a half second's burning time. The correct time of flight having been estimated, the gunner cut the fuze at the rib that most closely corresponded, and inserted it into the aperture at the top of the shell using a wooden setter and mallet to make sure it was tight.[10]

While the shell was being fuzed, another gunner brought the propellant charge, three-quarters of a pound of black powder in a stiff flannel bag, to the front of the gun, inserted it in the muzzle and stepped back to let his opposite number shove it home to the bottom of the bore with the rammer. The shell, now fuzed, was next loaded and pushed firmly home by the rammer. When both were seated securely, a gunner at the rear of the piece reached over and shoved a brass priming wire down the vent (the aperture on top of the breech of the gun by which the charge was ignited) to "prick" or break open the flannel bag of the propellant charge in the bore. He then inserted a tube, a three-inch, hollow length of tin or goose quill packed with mealed powder, into the vent. At the end of this procedure, which took less than a minute from the setting of the fuze to the insertion of the tube, the gun was ready to be aimed and fired.[11]

"Laying" or aiming an artillery piece required experience, knowledge of the weapon and projectile, and an appreciation of the rudiments of ballistics. This being the case, it is likely that Jackson's gun commanders laid their own weapons as they were the most experienced men in the three detachments. Since their targets were brigades of infantry in column or starting to deploy into line, the gunlayers would not have worried too much about traversing, or aligning their weapon in the horizontal plane – the 6-pdrs. would have simply been pointed at the approximate centre of the target, marked by the blue and buff colours of each American infantry regiment, using a handspike inserted in the end of the trail of the gun carriage. Satisfied, the layer would then step

National Standard, Eleventh Regiment of United States Infantry, 1813
This colour, six feet in the hoist by seven and a half feet in the fly, was carried at Crysler's Farm. It is dark blue silk with a light blue scroll edged with gold bearing the unit designation in gold letters. The galaxy of seventeen stars above the eagle represent the states of the union in 1812. (Courtesy, U.S. Military Academy Museum, West Point)

close to the breech and elevate, or align his weapon in the vertical plane. Now, he would take more care, because judging elevation correctly was essential to firing spherical case with effect. With one hand on the screw beneath the breech that raised or lowered it, he would look down the length of the barrel, and using the computer that is the human brain take into account all the variables that might affect his trajectory, compensate for them and arrive at a correct solution for the elevation.

There were many variables to be considered. Because the day was damp, the powder in the propellant charge would probably burn less evenly and its force would be weaker, so the gunlayer would increase the elevation to compensate, sending the shell on a higher and hopefully longer journey. On the other hand, there was a stiff wind blowing towards the target and, if the elevation was too high, it might carry the shell over it, so perhaps the variables of damp powder and wind cancelled each other out. Then again, the moisture in the air on this grey, wet day would act as a "drag" on the shell in flight, affecting its range, so maybe it was better to add that extra twist of elevation. But the layer also had to consider that, since the position of his gun was just slightly higher than the target, he needed less elevation. On the other hand, the weapon he was firing might be an older piece, coming to the end of its useful service life of five to six hundred rounds at full charge, with a bore so worn it needed an extra bit of elevation to compensate for the fact that more of the explosive gases of the propellant charge escaped around the projectile and reduced its velocity. All this, and more, went through the gun commander's head in a split-second as he made his adjustments until he was satisfied and stepped back. After making sure his men were clear of the wheels, the gun commander gave the command, "Fire!"

At this, a gunner at the left rear of the piece reached over the gun wheel and ignited the tube in the vent in the top of the breech by means of a portfire, a tightly rolled stiff paper tube filled with a flammable composition that burned slowly and steadily. The tube in turn set off the propellant charge and the 6-pdr. discharged with a loud, deep bang that pushed on the eardrums; a shower of sparks and flaming matter was ejected from its muzzle; and weapon and gunners were surrounded by a cloud of dense, acrid powder smoke as the weapon recoiled several feet. It was immediately run back up to its firing position as the shell flew toward its target, a faint trail of wisping smoke from the burning fuze (which had been ignited by the explosion of the propellant charge) marking its progress. When the fuze burned down, the shell exploded in a flash of white smoke sending twenty-seven musket balls with enough velocity, as its inventor proudly asserted, to penetrate a wooden board two inches thick, slicing through leather and wool, skin, muscle, bone and tissue.[12]

Jackson's gunners were right on target. In his promotional literature, Henry Shrapnel claimed that under optimum conditions forty rounds of his product (albeit from calibres larger than 6-pdr.) fired at a range of 800 yards had hit a target representing the frontage of an average infantry company with 1,213 balls and seventeen shell splinters. Some allowance must be made for exaggeration in advertising and conditions at Crysler's Farm were not optimum, but on the other hand Jackson's gunners had a much larger target. The British artillery commander recorded with satisfaction that his detachments' shooting was good and that the American columns "suffered dreadfully from our firing Shrapnell shells."[13]

Boyd confirmed this assertion, later reporting (with considerable understatement) that his troops "were annoyed by the shot and shrapnell shells," but attributing the fire to Mulcaster's three gunboats, which had chimed in when Jackson opened fire.[14] Claiming there were nine of these vessels in action, Boyd complained that the "field of battle was so situated, as to allow considerable execution from the boats, and our army felt the effect."[15] Opinions differ on the effectiveness of the gunboats' fire. The historian James Croil, who later lived near the battlefield and was familiar with its topography, learned from veterans of the action that because the fields on which the armies were positioned were some twenty-five feet above the river, the gunboats' fire was not that destructive to the Americans. He commented that Mulcaster's craft "should have anchored in mid-channel; but as the current here is very rapid, and of great depth, this arrangement could not be carried out."[16] The vessels therefore could not completely enfilade or fire across the width of the battlefield, "so that they proved of less service in the action than they otherwise might have done." There is no doubt that the sailors landed some rounds because in recent years a 24-pdr. roundshot was dug up on the scene of the action, almost certainly fired from the gun of that calibre mounted on the *Nelson*. But Mulcaster's naval gunners did not have spherical case and Boyd's reference to being "annoyed" by "shrapnell shells" indicates that the weapons doing harm to his troops were Jackson's well-served field pieces.[17]

The three gun detachments continued to fire at a steady rate, probably about one round every minute or minute and a half. The gunners could be cool and collected in their work for they were beyond the range of enemy musketry and as the American artillery had yet to appear they did not have to fear counter-battery fire. They tried to make every round count as their supply of spherical case was limited and Jackson had already used some during the fighting of the previous day.

The intelligent officer – Colonel Joseph Swift, United States Army (1783-1865)
The first graduate of the military academy at West Point, Joseph Swift served as Wilkinson's chief engineer and chief of staff during the St. Lawrence campaign. An intelligent and highly effective officer, he laboured hard during the battle to make up for the deficiencies of his superiors. (Courtesy, U.S. Corps of Engineers Museum)

The noise of musketry and artillery fire alerted Wilkinson and Lewis, in their respective sickbeds on their boats off Cook's tavern, that Boyd had got himself into a major fight. Lewis was amazed – some time before he had been told that Wilkinson had issued an order that the flotilla was to move down the river and Boyd was to march on land. Before that time was up, he recalled, "we were surprised by a smart firing of musketry" as Boyd, "instead of embarking, had sent out Swartout's brigade to give them battle."[18] Wilkinson, who was better informed, knew Boyd had orders to attack the enemy should they harass the army, but when the shooting started, he was unable to rise to assist his subordinate. As the firing continued without pause, he complained to Surgeon Ezekiel Bull that he "regretted his inglorious, and almost helpless, situation" and "only begged for health sufficient to mount his horse and die at the head of his comrades."[19] By this time in the campaign, many of his officers and men would have dearly loved to have seen that wish granted.

The six hundred men of Lieutenant Colonel Timothy Upham's boat guard – "the ablest men" in the army according to Major Charles Gardner of the Twenty-Fifth and drawn from every regiment in Boyd's three brigades – were not only capable of aiding their comrades but anxious to do so.[20] Captain John W. Weeks of the Eleventh Infantry recalled that half his company was fighting with the regiment while he "with the residue" and "some hundreds of others, was by order of Maj. [sic] Upham paraded on the bank of the river, where they remained for some time after the firing commenced."[21] When the "action became warm and general," Upham sent Captain Mordecai Myers of the Thirteenth Infantry to Boyd on the field for orders to get into the action, but Boyd's response was that Upham's command should "remain and protect the boats, baggage, women, etc."[22] and Myers returned with this order. Upham, thinking that Boyd had the situation well in hand, then dismissed the guards to the boats of their various units.

Shortly after the action commenced, Colonel Joseph Swift rode back to the flotilla to hasten Irvine and Craig's artillery to the scene of the action. He later recalled that during the engagement his "duties were two-fold, that of engineer and aide to the commander-in-chief" and he "therefore, being at various points in the field with orders, saw every movement and every neglect of movement."[23] Twenty-nine years old and the first graduate of the military academy at West Point, Swift had been in service thirteen years and was one of the most technically proficient officers in the United States Army. His professional knowledge and common sense had gone a long way to balance Wilkinson's inadequacies and this day he would prove an asset.[24]

Swift knew Boyd would need artillery support, and as it happened, the American gunners were doing their best. Irvine's two properly equipped 6-pdrs. had got away first, moving behind Woodford's dragoons on the King's highway until they encountered the slippery, muddy banks of the first ravine nearly bisecting the woods between the armies. Realizing it would be difficult to get his equipment across this obstacle, Irvine took a long detour to the north, his progress hampered by the underbrush, the mud and the many rail fences in his path. For his part, Craig had first to land the four 6-pdr. guns from the ordnance scows, but the flotilla had become badly scattered during Mulcaster's attack and this imposed delay. When he finally got the four weapons and their limbers and ammunition wagons ashore, more time was required to harness them to the horses taken from Woodford's dragoons. It was an hour at least after the first shots were fired before Craig was ready to move out, following Irvine's clearly visible tracks on the long detour through the woods.[25]

As he watched from near the centre of the 49th Foot, Lieutenant John Sewell thought that the fire of Jackson's "field pieces with shrapnels hastened the enemy in the forming of his line, and returning our fire."[26] Easier said than done. Major Charles Gardner of the Twenty-Fifth Infantry of Covington's brigade recalled that his men began to open fire without orders as soon as they cleared the woods, and Gardner and his fellow officers had difficulty in deploying them into line. "I had not conceived that men would have been so difficult to form in any situation," he later commented, "we could not recover any order."[27] All three brigades probably experienced similar problems as there had been no opportunity to train in brigade-size formations since the army had been reorganized just a few weeks before, and still worse, some of the regiments had been trained on different manuals with different words of

Unit commander – Colonel Eleazer Wheelock Ripley, Twenty-First Infantry (1782-1839)
Eleazer Ripley, shown here in brigadier general's uniform, was one of the better regimental commanders in Wilkinson's army. His leadership qualities were of little avail, however, in the situation in which he found himself on 11 November 1813. (Courtesy, Hood Museum of Art, Dartmouth College)

command. In the end, the confusion at the unit level was probably resolved by officers and NCOs simply pushing the men into their correct places.

On Gardner's right, Colonel Eleazer Ripley caught up with his Twenty-First Infantry. It was Ripley's later impression that "there was an error somewhere" because he "had no idea of encountering any enemy, but the militia, and a few regulars, who had been hovering about them, the previous day." He first became aware that things were different when, he met "within half musket shot," or 75 feet, "a body of regular troops, who rose from a ravine."[28] These men were probably some of Heriot's Voltigeurs who had been sheltering in the second ravine. They fell back and Ripley "commenced the action by a sharp fire of musketry" on the main British line.[29] These were brave words but, given the range, between 500 and 600 yards, this fire had almost no effect.

Pushing forward, still in column, the Twenty-First encountered the first of the many split rail fences that cut across the battlefield and Ripley jumped over it "alone, and from the side nearest to the enemy called to his men, who rarely needed an encouragement so hazardous to their commander."[30] Lieutenant Joseph Dwight of the Thirteenth Infantry of Coles's First Brigade, which moved behind and somewhat between Swartout and Covington, remembered that his unit was still so disarranged from marching in inverted order that, when the "men were ordered to form platoons" in line, "the previous *errors* had so entirely disarrayed them that they could not do it, but retreated in great disorder."[31] Shouting officers regained control and the Thirteenth "again advanced."

Gradually, as the regimental officers got their units sorted out, Boyd's troops deployed for battle. Woodford's dragoons took post on the highway near the river, while to their right Covington formed the three regiments of his brigade in line on the east side of the second ravine, with the Sixteenth Infantry on the left, the Twenty-Fifth in the centre and the Ninth on the right. Coles's two regiments, the Twelfth and Thirteenth Infantry, took position on Covington's right somewhat distant from it in a position to support Swartout, whose three regiments, the Twenty-First, Fourteenth and Eleventh, remained in column at the edge of the woods bordering the battlefield on the north. At that moment, Reynold Kirby, anxious to see his first battle, arrived to find the American line "formed with its left upon the river & extended for near three fourths of a mile across cleared fields & its right protected by a wood" while the "enemy was formed opposite to it & seemed to occupy the same front." Fascinated, Kirby traversed the ground "from the left to center as a mere spectator" but decided to return to the flotilla for orders as it occurred to him that he "could give no good account of myself should I be wounded" as he had "no business there."[32]

Nothing in John Boyd's previous military experience had prepared him for the situation he now faced. Nearly twenty years before, Boyd had commanded a force of native levies for the Nizam of Hyderabad in India, one of a number of such mercenary corps in that potentate's army, but the Hyderabad army's one major battle while Boyd was in its service, against the Mahrattas at Kharda in 1795, had been a disastrous defeat. In 1811 he had led the Fourth Infantry at the battle of Tippecanoe, but that action had been fought from a good defensive position against warriors of the Northwestern nations who had no artillery. His brigade had made an assault landing at Fort George in May 1813 in the face of stiff resistance from British regulars, but there he had been backed up by well positioned warships that laid down a heavy covering bombardment. John Boyd was now facing a force of regular infantry, supported by artillery and positioned on good ground of their choosing.[33]

He had the three basic choices all generals have in such a situation – he could attack, maintain his position, or withdraw. Given his nature, Boyd probably did not contemplate withdrawal as, despite widespread doubts in the northern army about his intelligence, no-one ever questioned Boyd's courage. He could maintain his position until his artillery arrived to give him the long-range support he needed, but by the time his guns got up, his infantry would have suffered such heavy losses from the British artillery that they might not be fit to fight. The third and best alternative, as Boyd must have seen it, was to attack – to move his superior numbers of infantry within musket range of the British and overwhelm them by fire. The best place to do that would be on his right, for on his left the second ravine and the two gullies running inland from

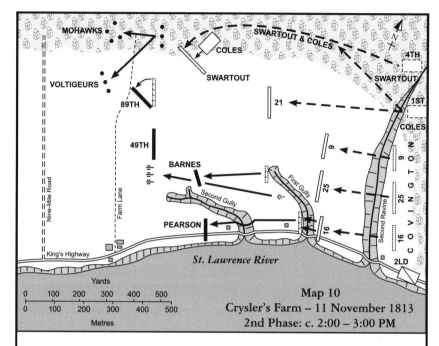

Map 10
Crysler's Farm – 11 November 1813
2nd Phase: c. 2:00 – 3:00 PM

1. Boyd orders Swartout and Coles to attack the British left flank. Heriot's skirmishers stage a fighting withdrawal as the two American brigades move through the woods parallelled in the open by the 21st Infantry. As Swartout's brigade emerges from the woods it begins to deploy into line.

2. Morrison wheels the 89th back, refusing his left flank. The 89th fires several disciplined volleys into Swartout's brigade.

3. While Morrison is preoccupied with his left, Covington opts to attack the British right. His three regiments move forward in line to the first gully and their weight of fire hits Barnes and Pearson. Pearce orders the 16th Infantry to charge across the first gulley, forcing Pearson, Barnes and Kersteman back.

the river created obstacles difficult for formed bodies of troops to cross. On the right, the pine woods were no easier for movement, but there his infantry could take advantage of the cover they provided to hit the vulnerable flank of the main British line, which was not as wide as his own line. His decision made, Boyd rode over to Swartout and ordered him to "turn the enemy's left flank," directing Coles's First Brigade to support the Fourth Brigade's attack.[34]

The evidence as to how Swartout and Coles deployed for this attack is imprecise. It would seem from Ripley's later recollections, and from Harvey's comment that the American general had "riflemen on his right" flank, that the

Twenty-First Infantry deployed into line near the skirt of the northern wood and advanced in the open. The other two regiments of Swartout's brigade, the Fourteenth and Eleventh, advanced in close column (a compact formation with a single-company front and all companies of a regiment closed up tight behind each other) through the wood itself. Coles seems to have adopted a similar formation, which made sense as the swampy pine thicket, strewn with fallen timber, rendered an attempt to move in line impossible, while even a regiment formed in the more normal "attack column" with a two-company front would find it difficult to retain even the sketchiest alignment while advancing at any speed through the undergrowth. Short of going in single file, which was ludicrous as there were enemy skirmishers in the woods, regimental columns with a one-company front offered the best method of moving relatively quickly while still keeping a semblance of formation. When the two brigades reached the edge of the woods near the enemy left flank, they could deploy into either line or an attack column.[35]

With much shouting, the two regiments of Swartout's brigade (the Fourteenth and the Eleventh) formed their companies, one behind the other, closing up the distances between the companies until each regiment, depending on its numbers, formed a solid mass about thirty soldiers wide and as many as twenty ranks deep. Next came a gap and then the two regiments of Coles's First Brigade, the Twelfth and Thirteenth Infantry, followed in a similar formation. By this time Coles had probably taken the opportunity to correct his initial mistakes in deployment and it is likely the senior regiment, the Twelfth, now properly led the brigade column. The two brigades then plunged through the pine forest making for a point north of Morrison's left flank.[36]

On their left, Ripley's Twenty-First paralleled their progress by advancing in a line of two ranks across the open fields. In the centre of the regiment were its two colours, carried by junior officers and escorted by a "guard of the colours" consisting of eight senior corporals. As in the British army, each American regiment had two of these devices. The dark blue National Standard, six feet in the hoist by seven and a half in the fly, was adorned with the eagle of the republic surrounded by a galaxy of seventeen stars representing the states of the union and a scroll with the regimental identification, while the smaller buff or yellow Regimental Colour, five feet on the hoist by six on the fly, was similarly decorated. A unit took its pace and alignment from its colours; one American manual stressed it was "of the utmost importance while marching in line" that the colour bearers "should be thoroughly instructed to observe the precise length and exact cadence of step, and be able to follow a given direction without deviation."[37] What sounded good in theory was not easy in practice, however, as the two junior officers trying to hold these heavy, flapping articles upright on their nine-foot pikes in a stiff breeze also had to watch their step among the wet, muddy plough furrows, not to mention the rail fences that had to be pulled down or crossed as the regiment advanced. The result was that the Twenty-First had to halt at frequent intervals to dress its ranks, and its rate of advance was not much faster than the units in the woods on its right.[38]

The progress of the main body through the tangled undergrowth of pine forest was difficult. The men in the densely packed columns stumbled into pools of water and stepped over or around fallen timber which disrupted their formation. They were harried by Heriot's Voltigeurs and Anderson's Mohawks, who met the appearance of the blue-uniformed columns with aimed fire. Again, the skirmishers' task was not to halt the American advance but to delay it and this they did, firing and falling back. Big Jacob, Shawindas, John Sunday and their comrades engaged in their favourite psychological warfare and the woods rang with shots, shouts and howls. Lieutenant Joseph Dwight of the Thirteenth Infantry remembered that the column "was fired upon by the enemy," which caused confusion in the ranks, but the officers and NCOs restored order and the unit advanced again with its "men well closed up in order to form the line with quickness and precision."[39]

The American advance was stung but not stopped by the fire of the British skirmishers. As Heriot's men fell back parallel with the left flank of Morrison's line, they gradually ceased firing and broke contact, the Voltigeurs running to the 89th Foot and the Mohawks further into the woods. From his post near the centre of the 49th, Sewell suddenly saw Heriot, who was mounted, exit the woods at speed, "riding between the two lines of fire, i.e., of his friends and foes," and remembered the Voltigeur officer "was near being made prisoner." Close behind Heriot were his *Canadiens*, Sewell next "observed the Voltigeurs bolting out of the woods on the left of our line, like greyhounds and simultaneously I saw a column of the enemy debouch from the same wood, threatening the left of the 89th Reg[t] at about 50 yards." This was an exaggeration: the head of the American column, the Eleventh Infantry, was probably within 100 or 150 yards of the British left flank.[40]

Their appearance was no surprise. The noise of the firing in the woods and the advance of Ripley's Twenty-First Infantry in line had marked the progress of the American advance, and when the Eleventh Infantry emerged from the trees in a somewhat ragged close column, Morrison had already decided on the appropriate countermeasure. He would "refuse" or protect the vulnerable flank of his main line by swinging the 89th Foot backward so that it faced the oncoming enemy. At the command, the right-flank company of the five under

Clifford's command wheeled back to the left until it was at the correct angle and the remaining four companies then about-faced and marched until they were abreast of the right-flank company on its new facing. They then halted, made another about face, and dressed their ranks. The 89th Foot was now formed at a rough 45-degree angle to the line of the 49th and facing directly at the Americans pouring out of the woods.[41]

At this point, Plenderleath and Clifford probably ordered their men to fix bayonets, since the enemy were now within a distance that might require this safeguard. Loading a musket with a bayonet attached to the muzzle was a cumbersome business at best, and its one pound of extra weight made the weapon, already difficult enough, even harder to handle and fire, but as the enemy were close, the two battalion commanders would have taken this sensible precaution. On the command, "Fix Bayonets!" Private Hugh Roberts from Caernarvon, Wales, just sixteen years old, in the ranks of the 49th and twenty-eight-year-old Private Thomas Fallon from Galway, Ireland, with the 89th drew their 17-inch-long triangular blades "with the utmost celerity" from the scabbards on their left hips and then, with a metallic clatter, fastened them securely on the muzzles of their muskets before returning to the shoulder arms position.[42]

As the Eleventh and then the Fourteenth Infantry cleared the trees, one British observer thought the Americans "came on in a very gallant style."[43] Swartout began to deploy into line to bring the maximum number of muskets to bear, but his men, unable to control their enthusiasm at being within decent range of the enemy, opened a ragged individual fire that hampered this evolution, as once soldiers stop and start firing it is hard to get them moving again. The men of Ripley's Twenty-First Infantry, coming up on the left flank of the brigade, joined in, and although Ripley and his officers tried to prevent this waste of ammunition, it continued. John Harvey recalled that, "on arriving within musket distance the enemys columns halted and commenced a heavy but irregular fire."[44] The Americans cheered, jeered and shouted, but young John Loucks, watching from Pearson's advance position near the river bank, noted that the British line "stood silent and stock still firing not a shot."[45]

This silence was no accident. Nearly two decades of almost incessant warfare had taught the British army that to be effective musketry had to be concentrated and delivered at short range. To do so, infantry officers had to maintain control of their men lest the nervous tension each soldier suffered on watching the advance of the enemy betrayed him into letting off a round that would result in ragged individual fire which, once started, was very difficult to stop – as their American opponents were demonstrating. British infantry officers therefore did not exhort their men with shouts or slogans as it had been proven many times that the best approach was to keep them as calm as possible. To reduce tension, a wise officer might make an attempt at humour, probably rather weak under the circumstances, but still appreciated. A quiet word or two, with frequent use of "steady," was the most common approach to relieving tension in the ranks and getting the men to hold their fire. "Be steady, my boys," a British colonel told his regiment during an action in Spain as they watched a superior enemy force march closer, "reserve your fire till they are within ten paces, and they will never penetrate you."[46] Major Miller Clifford and his company commanders used a variation on this theme as they watched the Americans pour out of the woods.

When Morrison judged the time and the distance to be right, he gave Clifford the order to fire. The commander of the 89th opted to deliver his crucial, well-loaded, first volley by "wings"; that is to say, the right three companies of the 89th fired first, followed after a few seconds pause to permit these companies to start their loading procedure, by the left wing of two companies. The order to fire by wings was first issued to warn the company commanders of what was to come and it was shortly followed by "Make Ready!" At this, the rank and file brought their muskets down off their left shoulders, positioning them upright with the left hand holding the stock above the lock and the right hand securing it below while at the same time thumbing back the lock to full cock with the right thumb. After a three-second pause came "Present!" and the two ranks aimed their weapons at the Americans between 100 and 150 yards distant. Another three-second pause, then "Fire!", and the three companies on the right were immediately covered in smoke as they discharged their weapons, followed shortly by the two companies on the left.[47]

As it was intended to, this first concentrated volley – between 250 and 280 rounds at short range – caught the Eleventh and Fourteenth Infantry attempting to deploy from column into line. Sewell remembered that the 89th's volley hit Swartout's brigade when it was "still in close column."[48] The cohesion of both American regiments, already shaken by the inability of their officers to stop their men's individual shooting, was ruined. Before they could recover, the 89th let loose a disciplined series of smaller volleys fired from right to left along its front.[49]

This time Clifford had chosen to fire by platoons, the small fire-and-manoeuvre units organized in each company before battle. In the British army platoons were to be a minimum of twenty-five men in two ranks, and two would normally be formed in each company. Care was always taken to keep these tactical sub-units up to strength during a battle; if casualties were taken, a company might reform into a single platoon, and if things became worse, two companies might combine into a single platoon. With an average strength of fifty-five rank and file per company, Clifford's five companies would have formed ten platoons, and in succession, the orders "Ready! Present! Fire!" were issued as the 89th sent a series of "rolling" volleys into the Eleventh and Fourteenth Infantry. These volleys were continuous, as by the time the last platoon on the left had fired, the first on the right had reloaded and was ready to fire again. To make things worse for the Americans, Jackson contributed some spherical case from his two guns that would bear.[50]

The effect was devastating. From his vantage point, John Loucks watched the head of Swartout's column disintegrate. "As the enemy advanced," he remembered, "the 89th poured into their line a steady fire and the cannon raked them" producing a "withering shower of bullets."[51] Major Charles Gardner, observing from the position of the Twenty-Fifth Infantry opposite the 49th, was impressed by the professionalism of his enemy, whose "line was the most admirable I have ever seen and its fire was in regular vollies."[52] Lieutenant Colonel Timothy Dix, commanding the Fourteenth Infantry, was cut down, and Swartout's brigade, already staggering, broke just as Coles's two regiments, the Twelfth and Thirteenth, emerged from the trees behind. There was immediate confusion and mixing of units as Swartout's officers tried to regain control of their men while Coles's officers tried to maintain control of theirs. Only Ripley's Twenty-First was still in good order as, being some distance from the British fire and not its major target, it was less affected. Ripley tried to advance and cover the other two brigades until they could sort themselves out but found that it was no use as his men, instead of going forward, broke from the ranks, "dodged behind stumps and opened individual fire."[53]

Seeing the enemy was reeling, Harvey suggested to Morrison it might be a good idea to send them home by advancing both the 49th and 89th to close range. The British commander agreed and orders were given to "advance the line in Eschellon [sic] of Battalions."[54] The five companies of the 89th now pivoted independently 45 degrees to the right, changing that unit's solid line into a staggered formation of companies. For his part, Plenderleath's right-flank company moved forward on its own, until it had reached the prescribed interval, followed by the next company and then the third until all his companies were in a staggered formation similar to that of the 89th. Both battalions then advanced directly to their front. While doing so they were no doubt aware, as their manual stressed, that

> Could the march in Echellon be always executed with the greatest accuracy, each flank leader covering a certain file of his preceding division, at a cer-

tain distance, would ensure exactness: but this alone is not be trusted to, and is rather to be considered as an aid than as an invariable rule; for the unsteady or open march of one or more divisions, if productive of a waving or shifting of the following ones, would in a sensible manner influence the whole. ...... In this, as in every other case, the perfect perpendicular march of the first leader, in consequence of his body being truly placed, and his attention solely given to this object, is what will much determine the precision and justness of the whole.[55]

All sound advice, to be sure, but authors of drill manuals (in this case General Sir David Dundas) never seem to have contemplated that the elaborate and complicated evolutions they so enthusiastically prescribed might have to be performed on some surface other than the smooth expanse of blond gravel that constituted the Horse Guards Parade in London. It was a different matter for infantry to perform the "march in Echellon of the Battalion" in a wet farm field in Upper Canada, "knee deep in mud," with slippery furrows ready to trip the unwary if they kept their eyes on their alignment and not on the ground in front of them – not to mention the enemy waiting for them.[56] The advance of the 49th and 89th Foot on 11 November 1813 was nothing as smooth as their manual would have had it and would probably have brought tears to the eyes of any self-respecting drill sergeant. It did, however, get the job done.

The two units moved forward, "occasionally firing by platoons."[57] The sight of that red and grey line advancing steadily towards them, pausing to fire from time to time, was too much for the First and Fourth Brigades, and they broke for the cover of the pine woods. Plenderleath remembered that the 49th "commenced firing regularly by platoons, which soon threw the advancing Americans into confusion and drove them back beyond the range of fire."[58] It was Harvey's feeling that the "superiority of [the British] fire aided by that of our three Field pieces which were admirably served, gave after a severe contest the first check and repulse to the enemy and his columns fell back."[59] Sewell agreed that his comrades' fire "was too much" for the Americans, who ran to the "cover of the wood."[60] The 49th and 89th now halted but continued to fire at the retreating Americans.

Swartout's and Coles's officers were not able to check the flight, and the four regiments – the Eleventh, Twelfth, Thirteenth and Fourteenth Infantry – retreated east in great confusion through the swampy thickets. Dwight of the Thirteenth remembered that orders were heard (as they often are on such occasions) for his unit to break off the battle and withdraw to the flotilla. We "were ordered to return and embark on the boats," he remembered, and the

Thirteenth kept moving.[61] Heriot's Voltigeurs now moved back into the pine woods and were joined by Anderson's Mohawks, who reappeared to snipe at the two retreating brigades. The warriors' howls and shrieks unnerved some of the Americans, who being unfamiliar with Indian fighting "were terrified beyond measure," and "not knowing wither they went, plunged into the woods, to escape the dreaded horrors of the scalping-knife."[62] The repulse came perilously close to being a rout, but after a considerable distance Swartout and Coles were able to stop most of their men and start reforming.[63]

Ripley attempted to cover the retreat with his regiment, but now a problem became apparent. Boyd had gone into action with making arrangements for a reserve supply of ammunition to be brought forward, and the First and Fourth Brigades had wasted much of their ammunition by undisciplined musketry at long range. Ripley was the first to feel the effect – all his attempts to get his men to conserve fire were useless and they persisted in "shooting until their ammunition was exhausted, whereupon they could not be prevented from retiring."[64] At first singly, but then in larger numbers, men began to leave the firing line of the Twenty-First and make for the rear. Since his regiment was disintegrating around him, Ripley ordered a withdrawal, and the Twenty-First pulled back to the skirts of the woods between the two armies and formed on the right flank of Covington's Brigade.

Trying later to find an excuse for the repulse, Boyd seized on the shortage of ammunition. Swartout's brigade, he reported, was first engaged and "having expended all their ammunition, were directed to retire to a more defensible position to wait for re-supply."[65] Unfortunately, he continued, this "movement so disconnected the line as to render it expedient for the 1st [Coles's] Brigade likewise to retire." This statement ignores the considerable contribution made by the 49th and 89th Foot to his retrograde movement and also overlooks the fact that it was Boyd's own responsibility to ensure that his troops were properly supplied with ammunition before going into action and resupplied once there.[66]

The threat to Morrison's left was over. In a brief but intense action, which a British participant recalled being "as sharp as any I have ever witnessed," two American brigades with a total strength of between twelve and thirteen hundred men had been completely repulsed by the disciplined firepower of half their number.[67] As Heriot and Anderson's skirmishers pushed through the pine woods to keep pressure on the fleeing Americans, Morrison might have breathed a sigh of relief. Most likely he did not have time, as almost simultaneously with the disappearance of the danger to his left, a new and more serious peril arose on his right.

While Boyd concentrated on the left flank of the British line, Brigadier General Leonard Covington had been eyeing the right near the river. After emerging from the woods, his Third Brigade had deployed into line immediately east of the second ravine. Some of Heriot's Voltigeurs, who had taken shelter in the ravine, were evicted "by the well-directed fire of the brigade" and hastily retired to Pearson's advance, posted behind the first gully some 250 yards to the west.[68]

Covington now assessed the situation. The main British line appeared to be preoccupied with the fighting on the opposite flank, and because it was posted some distance to the rear of the enemy advance, which was apparently only a few hundred men strong, he saw an opportunity and on foot led his Third Brigade, about 1,100 men, forward in line across the second ravine. It was no mean obstacle. Autumn rain had flooded the small creek which had cut this terrain feature; its twenty-foot-high banks were muddy and slippery, and the lowest part was under several feet of water. Colonel Cromwell Pearce of the Sixteenth Infantry remembered that his unit moved down into the depression which instantly destroyed their alignment, and then began to climb its western side, some men losing their balance and sliding to the bottom in the treacherous and slippery footing. "On ascending," he recalled, "our troops were brought within pistol shot of the enemy, in the rear of the village of Williamsburgh" – in fact these were probably the buildings and barns of one of John Crysler's neighbours.[69]

The Third Brigade was now within decent musket range of Pearson's command, two companies of the 49th Foot and two of the Canadian Fencibles formed in line behind the first gully. A tested veteran like Thomas Pearson was not overawed by the odds: thirty months before he had marched up the heights of Albuera with the 2,000 officers and men of the Fusilier Brigade to attack 5,600 French on the high ground; when that action was over, the enemy was broken but less than half the fusiliers remained on their feet. As the Sixteenth appeared at the top of the west side of the ravine, Pearson ordered his four companies to fire their first, properly-loaded and most effective volley at it, while at the same time Lieutenant Henry Kersteman, RA, opened up with canister from his 6-pdr. gun.

Pearce and his officers were trying to reform the Sixteenth when the British volley caught it – in Pearce's words, the enemy "poured in a destructive fire" which caused many casualties.[70] Major William Cumming of the Sixteenth remembered that the unit was "scarcely formed on the other side" when they were struck and the brigade commander, who was on foot with his men, took a musket ball or canister bullet in the stomach.[71] Displaying remarkable *sangfroid*, Covington told Pearce "he was mortally wounded; and that command of the brigade devolved upon him" and was then carried with the other wounded back to the shelter of the ravine.[72] Moments later Cumming was wounded: "I received a musket shot in the thigh, which passed thro' under the bone without injury to it. I was still able to walk & advanced with the regiment."[73]

At this point, a lesser officer might have pulled back, but Cromwell Pearce was a cut above average. Forty-one-years-old and from a farm background in Chester County, Pennsylvania, he had always displayed an aptitude for soldiering, and after a brief stint in the regular army in 1799-1800, progressed through the ranks of the state militia until by 1812 he was a major general. When war broke out, Pearce was a natural choice for the command of the Sixteenth Infantry, a unit raised in the Keystone state, and he cheerfully dropped in rank to command it. He had marched his unit to Plattsburgh in the autumn of 1812 and it had fought at Lacolle Mill, before moving to Lake Ontario where the Sixteenth had seen heavy fighting the following year in the attacks on York and Fort George in April and May and the confusing night action at Stoney Creek. Pearce's Sixteenth Infantry was a solid, steady and well commanded unit.[74]

Despite the weight of the British fire, Pearce managed to reform in line at the western edge of the second ravine. He opened up at close range on Pearson's four companies and Kersteman's gun and also seems to have thrown out at least one company as skirmishers which took cover in the first gully immediately in front of the British position and contributed aimed fire at Pearson's line. On Cromwell Pearce's right, Colonel Edmund P. Gaines's Twenty-Fifth Infantry, which also moved forward, joined in with musketry and this concentration of fire soon began to take effect. Pearson's horse was shot from under him and a number of officers of the 49th and Fencibles were hit, including that expectant father, Lieutenant Guillaume de Lorimier of the Canadian Fencibles, as were some of Kersteman's gunners. Jackson later remarked that the enemy was "at one time not more than two hundred yards" distant from his two guns and "their light troops much nearer, as my men were wounded by musket balls."[75] At this point, confusion broke out, possibly because Pearson was momentarily out of action, struggling to get from under his dead horse or attempting to recover his senses from the fall. After giving the British "a number of deadly fires," Cromwell Pearce saw them wavering and ordered an immediate charge with the bayonet.[76]

As the Americans moved forward, Pearson decided to pull back behind the second gully. This withdrawal was not orderly as both the flank companies of the 49th and the Canadian Fencibles had men taken by the oncoming Americans. It also caused problems for Jackson, who remembered that, "as our advance fell back," it was "so close to me that I could only keep but one gun in line."[77] What he meant was that Kersteman's gun had to limber up quickly to avoid capture while Pearson's new position blocked the fire of Jackson's second gun behind so that he had only one piece in a clear firing position.[78]

The Sixteenth now moved down and then clawed its way back up the other side of the first gully and reformed in line on its western side. Cumming was proud that his regiment "approached nearer the enemy's [main] position than any other, driving in their light troops & taking several prisoners."[79] Their advance was paralleled on the right by the Twenty-Fifth Infantry – Gardner of that regiment remembered that the unit charged "over two deep ravines" (actually the second ravine and first gully) and drove "the enemy beyond the ground they occupied."[80] On Gaines's right, Lieutenant Colonel Thomas Aspinwall's Ninth Infantry also moved forward.[81]

It was at this moment that Reynold Kirby rejoined the action. When he had gone back to the flotilla, Kirby had reported to the first senior officer he encountered. This was Swift, who gave him command of "40 or 50 men whom were collected, having left the field for the purpose of bringing off the wounded" and he ordered the young artillery officer "to attach myself with them, to the first regiment which I could join." Happy to have a job to do, Kirby marched his little force west along the King's highway and found that the Americans "now had evidently the advantage as the enemy retired fast & we followed up our success." He formed on Pearce's left flank.[82]

Morrison had been preoccupied with the threat to his left when Covington's infantry had pushed back his right, but he quickly became aware of the new danger, later recalling the enemy's "efforts were next directed against our right." To meet it, he chose to employ the same tactic that had just been successful against Swartout and Coles – to advance his main line within close range and employ its disciplined firepower to repel the Third Brigade. To be prepared for a renewed threat to his left, however, the British commander decided that he would carry on moving in echelon. By using this formation, he would continue to keep his left flank refused and, if it was again threatened he could quickly swing the 89th back into line to meet it.[83]

The battalion commanders put the order into action and the two battalions began a measured but steady advance against the enemy. To an admiring John Loucks, watching from the river bank, it appeared Morrison's intention was to "hasten down across the field to meet the new assaults" by the river and the two battalions may have moved obliquely to the right to bring them into better range of the Third Brigade.[84]

When the 49th and 89th Foot were at extreme musket range, the Americans opened up. Under a "heavy but irregular fire" the two British units were ordered back into line, to reply and, having deployed in that formation, they commenced a "regular firing of Platoons and Wings."[85] The Third Brigade returned fire and the opposing lines blazed away at each other.

It was hard and brutal work. When a man fired, he was showered with a spray of sparks and burning powder grains from the pan of his musket which might scar his face or even set fire to his clothing, and he was nearly blinded by smoke – to prevent injury to their eyes, many men closed them when firing. Soldiers in the front rank were deafened by the discharge of the weapons of the rear rank a few inches from their ears, and not a few front rank men were killed or wounded by clumsy rear-rank comrades. A man's right cheek and shoulder, pounded by the recoil of the butt, were usually bruised black after a few rounds, and his mouth was stained from biting off the end of his cartridges, which also left him with a raging thirst caused by the acrid taste of powder. Things got no better as firing continued. His musket became too hot to handle; its vent might become plugged from powder residue, forcing him to use of the little pricker and brush attached to each infantryman's shoulder belt or coatee; his flint might be knocked out, and in any case had to be replaced at frequent intervals when it became dull and would not strike sparks. Some men fired off their ramrods, while others failed to realize their vents were blocked, and when they pulled the trigger only got a "flash in the pan" because the main charge in the bore had failed to ignite – they would load round after round with dire results when the whole finally did take fire.

Occasionally there would be an ominous "thump" or "whack" as a musket ball hit home. When men like Private James Flynn, aged thirty-eight, from Kildare or Corporal Richard Curley, aged nineteen, from Killarney (both wounded during the action), or their American counterparts, tumbled to the ground, they were dragged out of the ranks and the gaps were plugged by the file closers, who would move men in to fill them. In 1813, armies possessed only rudimentary casualty evacuation systems. If there was time and manpower available, the wounded were removed from the firing line; if not, they were simply pulled clear and left, their comrades forced to ignore their moans and entreaties. British practice was for a regimental surgeon and one or two of his assistants to be stationed some distance behind the colours of a unit to provide first aid, but since Morrison had only two surgeons in his little army, William Woodforde and John Korb, it is likely they remained in the dressing station established in John Crysler's house and the casualties were brought there. The American wounded were taken first to the shelter of the second ravine behind their line for immediate attention and later to the flotilla. Men who could not walk were carried on stretchers improvised from fence rails, mus-

The subaltern in old age, Colonel John Sewell, (1794-1875)
In this photograph taken late in his life, John Sewell is wearing the General Service Medal, 1793-1814, with the Crysler's Farm clasp. The illegitimate son of the chief justice of Lower Canada, he fought as a nineteen-year-old lieutenant in the 49th Foot at the battle and left an eyewitness account of the action. (Courtesy, William Patterson)

kets and blankets. The stretcher-bearers (a good job for the militia) were sometimes drummers, who in battle were given all necessary non-combat duties but men from the ranks would often try to assist wounded comrades, although this was frowned upon as these men often did not return to the fight. To offset this, Joseph Swift had collected a detachment of these Good Samaritans when they arrived at the flotilla and returned them to action under Kirby's command.[86]

In both lines the officers were visible to their subordinates and they were expected to set an example of aplomb and coolness. It was a point of honour for officers not to leave the fight unless they were seriously wounded. Sewell recalled that a captain of the 49th Foot was knocked over and believing himself injured

> went to the rear, and reported himself to our Surgeon. On being examined no wound could be found. The medical man advised his immediate return to the Field. He resumed the command of his company and saw the end of the action. In the evening on taking off his black silk neckcloth, he found a rifle [actually musket] ball that had perforated many folds of the silk, but not far enough to draw blood. The blow of the ball staggered him and produced nausea; this naturally induced the belief of a serious wound.[87]

An activity that was constant during the fight was ammunition resupply. Since the emphasis was on rate of fire and not accuracy and so many rounds were wasted, infantry quickly exhausted the limited supply in their cartridge boxes – thirty-eight rounds in the case of Boyd's infantry and sixty in the case of Morrison's troops. Boyd had been remiss in this aspect, but his neglect had been remedied by Swift, who, in response to urgent requests, had organized

232

work parties, including Canadian William Johnston, who brought ashore the small casks of musket cartridges carried on the boats. They were lifted to waiting dragoons, who balanced them on their saddles and rode west to the infantry units, where the cartridges, tied in packages of fifteen rounds, were distributed to the rank and file by officers and drummers like Jarvis Hanks of the Eleventh Infantry.[88]

Morrison's supply system was more orderly. British musket cartridges came in half barrels weighing 108 lb. which were normally transported in small two-wheeled carts accompanying each battalion. Since Morrison's two regular regiments had moved by water from Kingston, they may not have taken their carts with them but may instead have impressed ordinary farm wagons into service. Whatever type of vehicle was used, it was stationed a safe distance behind the firing line, probably in the Jones farm lane, where selected men (another good job for the Dundas militia) opened the barrels and distributed the ten-round packages of cartridges to the drummers of each unit, who would fill their shakos or haversacks and take them to their comrades. During lulls in the fighting they would move down the ranks with these containers held out in front of them, and each man who needed cartridges would take some.[89]

On and on it went – "ready … present … fire!" The officers in both lines tried to control their men so that they delivered regular, concentrated volleys, which had more effect than ragged, individual fire. For this reason, both sides probably used platoon volleys, as it was easier for the officers to manage these smaller fire units. This firefight of opposing lines was a situation in which training and discipline counted for much, and it was clear which army was superior in these aspects – sheltering in the cellars of their houses, the local civilians could easily distinguish between the musketry of the two opponents, since the American firing was "irregular, a pop, pop, popping all the time" while the British volleys were "all together and at regular intervals like tremendous rolls of thunder."[90]

The exchange probably continued for no more than ten to fifteen minutes although it would have seemed like an eternity to the hardworking infantry in the opposing lines. Jackson's three gun detachments also made a contribution, and the weight of the British fire fell on Gaines's Twenty-Fifth Infantry. This regiment was one of the strongest units in Wilkinson's army, bringing about 450 men into action, but it was a relatively green unit that had only participated in one action, at Stoney Creek the previous June, and Gardner later claimed that half the men in the regiment were raw recruits. Neither Gaines nor his second-in-command, Lieutenant Colonel Jonas Cutting, could prevent the unit from breaking from the concentrated British fire and, in short order, the Twenty-Fifth disintegrated into a mob running for shelter in the second ravine or beyond.[91]

Cromwell Pearce managed to hold the Sixteenth steady in the face of heavy fire not only from Pearson, who had managed to reform, but also from Barnes's three companies of the 89th to his right front. He returned fire but after a short time his cartridges began to run low, and after consultation with his officers, Pearce "deemed it proper to return to the [second] ravine, and wait a supply of ammunition."[92] When Cumming, who was "determined to hobble on to victory" despite his wound, realized that because of "the failure of our ammunition, that we must retire," he decided his day was done and managed "to limp off with the assistance of a couple of soldiers till I borrowed a dragoon's horse."[93] As Lieutenant Reynold Kirby, on the Sixteenth's left flank, remembered it, the Third Brigade's fire gradually "slackened, many of the Regts. having exhausted their ammunition & no provision having been made to renew the supply, we were compelled to fall back."[94] In good order, the Sixteenth Infantry withdrew to the shelter of the second ravine and Pearson promptly reoccupied his original position behind the first gully. He had only been forced back briefly – "for a very short time" in Jackson's words – and Kersteman moved forward again with his 6-pdr. to support him.[95] Morrison's right flank was now restored.

After the Sixteenth and Twenty-Fifth Infantry broke off, it fell to Aspinwall's Ninth Infantry to continue the battle. Only twenty-seven years of age, Thomas Aspinwall was a Bostonian whose grandfather had been killed at Concord in 1775 in the opening minutes of the Revolutionary War. He had commanded the Ninth for just six weeks, but it was a sound regiment that had been prominent in the defence of Sackets Harbor in May. Just as the "centre and left" of the Third Brigade "were compelled to fall back," Aspinwall remembered, the Ninth "was advancing to attack the enemy's artillery in flank."[96] This would seem to indicate that his objective was Jackson's two guns at the right of the British main line but the Ninth found itself "unsupported and exposed to the fire of their artillery and of a superior force of infantry" and received "showers of grape" (actually spherical case shot or canister). The British artillery fire was "followed by that of their infantry," and realizing the Ninth was the only unit of the Third Brigade still actively engaged, Aspinwall ordered it back to its original position on the east side of the second ravine.[97]

It was at this time, about 3.30 P.M., nearly ninety minutes after the fighting had commenced, that the American artillery finally came into action.

CHAPTER 11

"Charge mit de dragoons!"

11 NOVEMBER 1813, 3.30–4.00 P.M

Let Bacchus's sons be not dismayed,
But join with me each jovial blade,
Come, booze and sing and lend me aid,
To help me with the chorus.

> *Instead of spa we'll drink brown ale,*
> *And pay the reckoning on the nail,*
> *From debt no man shall go to jail,*
> *From Garryowen in glory.*

Our hearts so stout have got us fame,
For soon 'tis known from whence we came,
Where'er we go they dread the name,
Of Garryowen in glory.

> *Intead of spa we'll drink brown ale ...*[1]

The artillery was the most effective component of the American regular army during the War of 1812. It had benefited greatly from the establishment of West Point in 1802 to educate gunner and engineer officers in the technical aspects of their profession and there was a higher proportion of academy graduates in the artillery units of the wartime army than in the infantry or cavalry. These units also enjoyed the presence of some of the most capable officers in the army, including George Izard, Alexander Macomb and Winfield Scott, with the result that they were better led and better disciplined than their infantry and cavalry counterparts and usually suffered from a lower rate of sickness, an additional indication of the quality of their leadership. The Second and Third Artillery Regiments were the elite of the northern army and had performed well as infantry on a number of occasions, notably at Queenston Heights in 1812 and Fort George in 1813.[2]

Unfortunately, 11 November 1813 was a not a good day for American gunners. The senior officers of that arm being either absent or preoccupied with other duties, command of the artillery had devolved on Pennsylvanian Lieutenant Henry Knox Craig of the Second Artillery. Craig had sent Lieutenant Armstrong Irvine with two 6-pdr. guns ahead while he landed four other weapons of the same calibre from the boats and harnessed them to horses borrowed from the dragoons. Forced to take a long and winding detour to avoid the impediment of the first ravine, Irvine had taken some time to reach the scene of the fighting, but some time after 3.00 P.M. he emerged from the woods between the two armies and moved west along the highway to a position in front of Woodford's Second Dragoons. He was now on the east side of the second ravine and about 800 yards distant from the closest British units. This was extreme effective range for roundshot but Irvine, an 1811 West Point graduate, could see Boyd's infantry needed support, so he made ready for action.[3]

His gun detachments unhooked their black iron 6-pdrs. from their limbers and removed the ready-use ammunition chests from the trails of the two carriages. For safety, the limbers and ammunition chests were then positioned 25, and the ammunition wagon, 50 yards to the rear of the gun. The gunners next went through a loading procedure similar to that of Jackson's Royal Artillery but using 6-pdr. fixed ammunition – the iron roundshot and its attendant flannel cartridge containing one and a half pounds of black powder being fastened as one unit to a wooden base – which facilitated ease and speed of loading. When the projectile was securely seated at the base of the bore, the cartridge pricked and a tin firing tube inserted in the vent, the gunlayer stepped up and, using his two thumbnails as a guide, sighted down the top of the barrel, traversing the piece by means of orders to the gunner manning the handspikes at the end of the trail and elevating it by means of the elevating screw beneath the breech. Irvine's gunners had a somewhat easier task than Jackson's men – they were not firing shell so did not have to be concerned about judging trajectory as accurately although they were firing into the wind and this had to be taken into account. Their aiming marks were the most visible points of the British line, the colours of the 49th and 89th Foot.[4]

All being ready, Irvine gave the order, and both guns were enveloped in smoke as they recoiled five to six feet. The detachments then reloaded, the gunner at the breech taking care to "seal" the vent with a leather thumb stall to prevent smouldering fragments from the previous discharge flaring up when a fresh round was rammed down the bore, which might ignite the cartridge and

The most effective arm – gun detachment of the 2nd United States Artillery Regiment, 1813
The best led and best trained branch of the northern army in 1813, the American artillery had a very bad day on 11 November 1813, being unable to render their infantry comrades proper support until late in the action. Note the gunner thumbing or blocking the vent at the breech of the gun to prevent remnants from the previous discharge flaring up when the next round was loaded. (Painting by H.C. McBarron, courtesy Company of Military Historians)

fire the gun prematurely. If this took place and the man wielding the rammer was still alive and had both his hands, tradition held he was entitled to a free swipe with the rammer staff at the ventsman's head to express his extreme displeasure. This was only one of a number of dangerous mishaps that could occur when serving a smooth-bore artillery piece, and Irvine's gunners, despite the tension of combat, moved as deliberately as possible to avoid accidents. The American artillery manual stressed that when going into action officers should take care their guns were "fired slowly at first, and the conduct of the men so regulated, as to restore to them their presence of mind" so that they would eventually "assume a tranquil and intrepid countenance in the heat of an engagement and perform their duty with alacrity."[5]

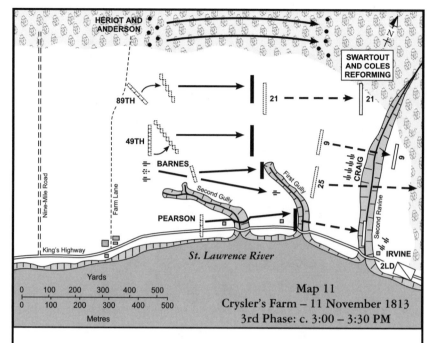

Map 11
Crysler's Farm – 11 November 1813
3rd Phase: c. 3:00 – 3:30 PM

1. After Swartout and Coles retire in confusion, Morrison orders the 49th and 89th to advance in echelon, thus keeping his left refused. The two units move forward, pausing frequently to fire and then deploy into line to take Covington's units under fire. A firefight ensues.

2. The disciplined British musketry, aided by Jackson's artillery, is too much for the 25th Infantry and it breaks. The 9th and 16th Infantry keep firing but begin to run out of ammunition. They withdraw to the shelter of the second ravine and Barnes, Pearson and Kersteman reoccupy their former positions.

3. American artillery arrives and Irvine opens fire with two 6-pdr. guns. Craig comes up with four more guns and Swift positions them on the west side of the second ravine where they bring heavy fire against the 49th.

Irvine watched the fall of shot carefully. Gunners of this period tried to hit their mark with no more than three rounds – if the first was over and the second under, the third should be on target, or, as the old German expression put it: "The first round is for the devil, the second for God, and the third for the King." Given the range and the wet, muddy ground, Irvine found it difficult to observe and correct his fire as there was no cloud of dust to show the location of the first graze or landing of the shot. Although Surgeon Trowbridge of the Twenty-First Infantry thought the fire of Irvine's two guns was very "destructive to the enemy," it is likely it did little harm.[6] It did, however, assure Boyd's infantry that their own gunners were now in action to match the fire of the British artillery, which had been unceasing since the action had commenced.

On his boat the American commander and his chief aide, Major Ninian Pinckney, listened to the guns. Pinckney ventured the opinion that the intensity and duration of the discharges indicated "the enemy were retiring" but Wilkinson "considered the firing too long, and too hot."[7] He decided to commit his reserve and ordered another aide, Major Robert Hite, to find Upham and tell him "to take every man that could be spared, to reinforce General Boyd." Hite went ashore only to find that Upham had reformed the boat guard on the highway, prepared to march.[8]

They were ready because Swift had come to the same conclusion as Wilkinson at almost the same time. The engineer officer had remained at the flotilla to organize casualty evacuation and ammunition supply, and thanks to his efforts a steady flow of cartridges had been landed from the boats and transported by Woodford's dragoons to the infantry. As the firing continued, Swift realized Boyd was hard pressed and decided that the reserve should move to the scene of the action. Mordecai Myers of the Thirteenth Infantry remembered the engineer told him "to form my guard, and march to the field" and in response Myers moved west with eighty-six men, "including one of my pilots who volunteered (a fine fellow he was)."[9] Hard on his heels came Upham with the main body. Having done what he could to ensure all available reserves were in motion and ammunition was on its way to the firing line, Swift then rode ahead.[10]

He arrived on the battlefield at about the same time Lieutenant Henry Craig's four guns emerged on the King's highway after completing their long detour around the first ravine. By this time, all three brigades had pulled back behind the second ravine to reform and resupply with ammunition and, on the American side, the battle was largely being carried on by Irvine's two 6-pdrs., which continued to hammer away at the British line. Swift could see that Irvine's fire was not having effect, and when Boyd rode over to consult with him, he suggested that Craig's guns be placed in the centre of the American position, on the west side of the second ravine, where they would be in a good position to support the infantry when they returned to the battle. Boyd concurred and Swift undertook to guide Craig to the correct position. The four gun detachments followed the engineer north along the east bank of the second ravine until they reached a point about 300 to 400 yards from the highway, where he directed them to cross over and take up a position on the far side.[11]

One by one, the four 6-pdr. guns were slowly and carefully driven down the slope of the ravine, the gunners, assisted by extra men from the other detachments, using bricoles or shoulder harnesses hooked on to the carriage to brake the heavy and bulky vehicles lest they turn sideways in the mud and tip over or run down the team in front. Other men tried to control and soothe the horses, who, already disgruntled at being demoted from cavalry chargers to mere draught animals, were made even more unhappy by the continuous loud bangs of shrapnel shells, the rattle of musketry and the general terror and confusion. Having arrived at the bottom, each 6 pdr. (which weighed about a ton with its carriage) was in turn dragged to the opposite slope through the flooded creek at the bottom, which came up to the axles of the gun carriages. Now the gunners helped push and pull the carriage up the far slope, cursing when they lost their footing in the slick, wet ground until the weapon finally reached the top. When the first gun was in place, the same process was repeated for the other three. It was a tiresome business to get the four 6-pdrs. across the ravine, and before it was finished gunners, horses and carriages were plastered with a thick coating of Upper Canadian mud.

Craig was now directly opposite the 49th Foot. He was also somewhat exposed, since the collapse of the Twenty-Fifth Infantry, which had taken place while he was moving up from the highway, had removed the nearest infantry support and the main British line, which by now had ceased fire to conserve ammunition, was 300 to 400 yards away. This was good range for roundshot and long range for canister but, as the latter projectile was more destructive, Craig opted to use it. He opened fire at the 49th Foot, each of his guns firing in turn to reduce the smoke and confusion in the gun position.

Craig's aiming-point was the colour party of the 49th Foot and his fire soon had effect. Ensign Sylvester Richmond, carrying the Regimental Colour, was hit, as was the officer carrying the King's Colour, but their duties were taken over by other officers or sergeants. Gaps appeared in the ranks as Craig's canister rounds, containing between forty-three and sixty-three musket balls depending on type, hit the unit. They were immediately filled by the file closers. By now, after more than an hour of fighting and the loss of many men, the companies had shrunk so much that during pauses in the firing they were moved closer to each other. The rank and file were not the only ones to get hit: Captain Edward Davis of the New Brunswick Fencibles, serving on Morrison's staff, had his horse shot from under him and Plenderleath took a canister bullet in the thigh but, ignoring it, continued in action.[12]

From their position behind the two battalions, Harvey and Morrison watched the 49th shudder from the effect of Craig's fire, then recover and steady itself. The two officers had observed the approach of the American artillery, but since the enemy brigades appeared to have reformed they thought that they were about to receive a major infantry attack supported by artillery. As Harvey later commented, the enemy began "to advance again in a more determined manner supported by three or four Field pieces."[13] As soon as Craig opened up, the two British officers realized they had a problem – his guns were outside good musket range, while their line was within canister range. They would either have to pull back or advance to remove the threat.

Suggesting to Morrison "it would be impossible in our advanced position to stand long against the Grape from his Field pieces," Harvey advised him to move the 49th against the enemy artillery in line with "the 89th in Eschellon [sic] supporting" – in plain words, Plenderleath's unit would charge the American guns.[14] This was a somewhat risky proposition, for the 49th would be advancing directly at Craig without benefit of direct support since the 89th, in echelon to its left rear, could not bring musketry to bear on the American gunners to keep their heads down. It was a difficult situation but Joseph Morrison not only had to accept it, he had to deal with it – he ordered Plenderleath to advance.

The 49th marched straight into disaster. As its grey line approached, Craig and his subordinate, Lieutenant William Smith, doubled their rate of fire, while Pearce's Sixteenth Infantry to the left and Aspinwall's Ninth Infantry to the right, their ammunition having been replenished by the hardworking dragoons, opened a heavy long-distance fire of musketry.

Plenderleath soon realized it would not work. It was impossible to move faster to close with the American guns because, as Sewell commented, the 49th had to cross "ploughed, heavy, wet ground intersected by two parallel snake fences, that we had to pull down" and which "much retarded" the regiment's progress because once over or through these obstacles it had to pause to dress its ranks.[15] On the other hand, if Plenderleath halted to deliver fire against his target, the 49th would continue to take heavy losses from the American artillery. Sewell later claimed that not "a shot was fired to cover our advance," and "consequently there being nothing to disconcert the enemies' fire it was well directed on us from riflemen and artillery and in the short space of ten or less minutes we lost 11 officers out of 18 killed and wounded and men in proportion."[16] Among the casualties was Sewell's company commander, Captain Thomas Nairne, killed when a "Ball entered his head above the left Ear & passed thro' on the other Side, he fell lifeless in the same Instant."[17] Lieutenant Daniel Claus immediately moved over from the left of the front rank to the right to assume command – within minutes he was hit in the ankle by a canister bullet, and Lieutenant John Sewell took over the company.[18]

Shaken, the 49th Foot came to a halt as officers and sergeants struggled to keep the ranks aligned and close the gaps which opened when men fell. The 89th, in echelon to their left rear, could not render their fellow regiment much assistance and Sewell decided the business could only "end in disaster" as, with their "ranks broken, the old and bold 'Green Tigers' were helpless under a deadly and unreturned fire."[19]

It was a tense moment but Plenderleath kept his head and issued a series of orders not contained in the official manual "with the sang-froid of an ordinary parade" that pulled the 49th back a safe distance, a manoeuvre "executed with the coolness of a review," Sewell proudly recorded, "notwithstanding being made under grape and canister from the enemies' guns to which we were in close proximity."[20] Reforming in line, Plenderleath then opened a "fire by platoons from centre to flanks" on the American guns at long range.[21] Having witnessed his dilemma, Barnes of the 89th Foot moved his three companies closer to the American guns to take the gunners under fire. To thirty-three-year-old Captain Samuel Devins Harris of the Second Dragoons, a Bostonian from a wealthy background (his father had owned the wharf that had been the scene of the Boston tea party), it appeared as if the separate components of the British line (Clifford's 89th, Plenderleath's 49th and Barnes's companies of the 89th) were advancing in echelon on Craig's guns "with their whole force in three columns."[22]

The repulse of the 49th Foot was Morrison's first check. Writing years later from the point of view of a junior officer, John Sewell was critical about what he considered the unnecessary losses caused by an advance without any support. In his opinion, "any regimental officer of the most humble attainments would have closed with the enemy by wings or alternate companies supporting one another as they advanced."[23] Although resentful about the cost, Sewell was proud of his regiment's behaviour:

> The Reader will perceive that the charge of the 49th was not persevered in. Let us inquire why the line, broken as it was, by distance, and impediments, could not have been re-formed under the enemy's fire? Had there been want of courage on the part of the men, or any deficiency on the part of the officers or their leader? On the contrary – the circumstances under which the line was formed were more creditable, though not so advantageous as a successful charge.[24]

Morrison later reported that the 49th was "directed to charge the gun[s] posted opposite to ours, but it became necessary within a short distance … to check the forward movement in consequence" of a new threat.[25] Sewell, who had moved to the company commander's position at the right of the first rank after Nairne and Claus had been knocked down, identified this danger. He could now see more of "the enemy and more of the field" and, to his "no small anxiety," the young officer observed a squadron of American cavalry "galloping up the high road" directly at his regiment's right flank.[26]

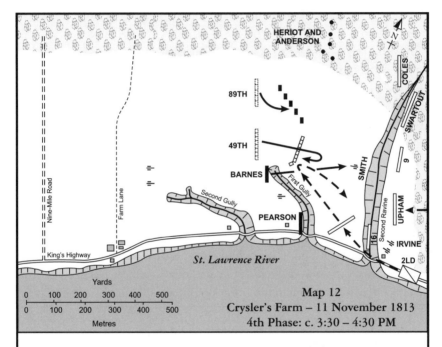

Map 12
Crysler's Farm – 11 November 1813
4th Phase: c. 3:30 – 4:30 PM

1. The 49th, with the 89th on their left, advance against Craig's guns but are repulsed. By this time Boyd has reformed his brigades in line at the edge of the woods, preparatory to returning to the battle.

2. Barnes begins to move on Craig's guns. Craig withdraws three of his weapons across the second ravine but leaves one gun under Smith in action. Walbach orders Woodford's dragoons to charge and save the guns and they do so, but are repulsed by the heavy fire of the British advance and Ellis commanding the right flank company of the 49th. Barnes then advances and captures Smith's gun.

3. Around this time Boyd orders a withdrawal and his brigades move back through the woods to Cook's Tavern just as Upham's boat guard arrives. The British now move forward and Upham, badly outnumbered, is forced to retreat.

While Craig and Smith were decimating the 49th Foot with canister, Brigadier General John Boyd had reason to be more satisfied with his situation. As the British line pulled back from its abortive attack on Craig's guns, his three brigades (less the Twenty-Fifth Infantry, which had melted away) were formed on the east side of the second ravine, ready to renew the action. Cromwell Pearce, now commanding the Third Brigade, remembered that at this point it was something of a stalemate: the American infantry had "formed line on the brink of the [second] ravine opposite the enemy" and "both lines opened a fire on each other," which given the distance of between 400 and 500 yards, well beyond the effective range of musketry, did little harm to either party.[27]

It is unlikely Boyd had even contemplated his next move. He had pitch-forked his command into this action without any thought – in Cromwell Pearce's words, there "had been no preparation for an engagement" and there is some evidence that during the afternoon of 11 November 1813 Boyd did not exercise direct command of his force but simply let his brigade commanders fight their own separate battles.[28] Such was the opinion of Gardner of the Twenty-Fifth, who remained on the field after the greater part of his unit had disappeared into the woods and also later wrote that the army "fought as it was in detachments" with "no benefit of a commanding general" as "No Gen. appeared "to be responsible" on the field.[29] In Boyd's mind, he was simply executing Wilkinson's orders that, if the army's rear was threatened, he was to beat the enemy back, and in his opinion, having pushed the British back, the flotilla was no longer in danger, and he had done his duty. His problem was that, having got his command into this hot little action, how was he to get it out?

While Boyd cogitated, Craig's gunners fired at Morrison's infantry, but Barnes's three companies of the 89th were now close enough to take the Americans under fire. Since Boyd gave no orders for his infantry to cross the second ravine and support Craig, his four guns were becoming increasingly vulnerable as Barnes edged closer. It was probably Swift who realized the plight of the artillery and suggested to Boyd they be withdrawn across the ravine for safety. The order was given, Craig ceased fire and his men began the onerous job of traversing the depression a second time, but this made his situation even more precarious, for if the British line to his front renewed its advance he would not be able to place the same volume of fire against it and might be overrun. For this reason, Lieutenant William Smith kept one gun in action to cover the withdrawal. The gunners' predicament attracted the attention of several officers, including Ripley of the Twenty-First and John Walbach, who was stationed near Woodford's dragoons on the highway. Walbach decided to do something about it.[30]

Jean-Baptiste de Barth Walbach, to give the man his full name, was one of the more interesting officers in Wilkinson's army. The son of a noble German family, Walbach had graduated from the French artillery school at Strasbourg and then served as a lieutenant of hussars in the French army. In 1792 he joined the royalist forces fighting the new revolutionary regime before taking service with one of the many small German states. Six years later, Walbach travelled to the United States to visit his father, who had emigrated to Pennsylvania, and he arrived just as the American army was being expanded because of a threatened war with France. Walbach, by now thirty-two years old, received a commission as a lieutenant of light dragoons but was discharged when his unit was reduced in 1800. However, an officer with his professional background had much to offer and in 1801 he received a commission in the artillery and by the outbreak of war had reached the rank of captain. Thereafter promotion came more swiftly, as Walbach moved through a series of staff appointments, serving as a deputy quartermaster general and assistant adjutant general before becoming an adjutant general with the rank of colonel in the summer of 1813.[31]

According to men who served with him, Walbach never quite mastered the English language, which he always spoke with a heavy German accent. He did, however, have sufficient grasp of English metaphor to make frequent resort to his favourite oath, "By Jove!" (maybe "By Yove"), which he probably exclaimed as he watched Craig's gunners struggling to get their bulky weapons back across the second ravine.[32] Approaching Woodford of the dragoons, Walbach asked him "if a charge of cavalry were practicable" and the Virginian in turn consulted his senior captain, Samuel Harris, who replied that not only was a charge practicable but "not a moment should be lost" if Craig's guns were to be saved.[33] "At this critical moment," Harris commented, the cavalry "alone were left to save the Cannon & the Honor of the Army" because the enemy "had reached almost within grasp of the pieces." On hearing this, Walbach gave the order to Woodford: "Charge mit de dragoons!"[34]

Up to this time the Second Dragoons had not had a very good war. The unit had been established in January 1812, but not until the autumn had enough men been recruited for it to concentrate at Greenbush, New York, where it commenced training. There was no authorized cavalry manual so instruction was provided by one J.A.P. Poutingon, an expatriate of the French army, who found the work arduous and complained to Secretary of War Eustis that he was forced to spend his days in the saddle "hallooing from right and left" and shouting "such one your fist – such one your toes in – second rank such

Garryowen and Glory – United States Light Dragoon, 1813
On 11 November 1813, Major John T. Woodford's squadron of the Second Regiment of United States Light Dragoons mounted the only charge made by American regular cavalry during the War of 1812. It was unsuccessful but their sacrifice saved most of their artillery. (Painting by H.C. McBarron, courtesy Parks Canada).

thing."[35] "Is it any profession," he whined, "who can destroy the constitution health of a man, as that of hallooing all day, and every day in the year," and respectfully requested a massive pay raise for spending eight hours each day "on the field hallooing and galloping and spitting the blood."[36]

The excitable Frenchman was not with the Second Dragoons when they moved north to the Niagara in the spring of 1813. The unit participated in the attack on Fort George in May, landing on the other side of the fort to cut off the British retreat, but the dilatory movements of the main force under Morgan Lewis allowed the enemy to escape. One squadron was at Stoney Creek, where it charged not only the British 49th Foot but also for good measure Pearce's Sixteenth Infantry. A similar problem occurred during the action at Beaver Dams a few weeks later when a troop of the Second came under fire and swiftly galloped out of harm's way, unfortunately in doing so "plunging thro'" friendly infantry and "knocking down and breaking" them.[37] Incidents like these highlighted both a lack of training and the difficulty of employing mounted troops on the northern frontier, where, in Pearce's opinion, the heavily wooded terrain "rendered successful operations of cavalry nearly impracticable."[38] The regiment experienced continual problems finding enough mounts and forage to feed them, and in June 1813 the greater part was withdrawn from the frontier to Utica, New York, to fatten their horses and train. From there it had moved overland to the St. Lawrence to participate in the offensive against Montreal.[39]

Woodford's squadron had numbered some 200 sabres that morning, but in Harris's words had been "so reduced thro' the day by repeated details" for dispatch riders, staff officers' mounts and guards, ammunition carriers and the loss of some horses to pull the artillery, that he was unable to bring more than 150 men onto the battlefield in their proper role.[40] They had been spectators for much of the action and Jackson had occasionally spared a round for them but, although Harris complained they were "exposed to the enemy's fire," it could have been much worse.

Given the ground and the disposition of the British forces, the attack would not be easy for Woodford to make. To have any chance of success, attacking cavalry had to hit its target with both mass and velocity; if the troops broke formation or if their movement was slowed, the effect would correspondingly be reduced. Woodford had to charge the enemy troops nearest to Craig's guns – Plenderleath's 49th Foot or Barnes's three companies of 89th. Because Barnes was covered by the first gully, the target would have to be the 49th, and although there was open ground all the way, it was cut across by the ubiquitous rail fences. If Woodford was successful, there was a chance that his dragoons could cave in the right flank of the 49th Foot and save Craig's guns, but he had only one chance to make the thing work because cavalry was often "incapable of making a second charge if once repulsed; it cannot rally again."[41]

Woodford led his squadron in column of fours over the second ravine and reformed them on the western side, where they immediately attracted fire from Jackson's gunners and musketry from Pearson and Barnes. This rendered the task of forming a two-rank line for the charge difficult as the horses, whose afternoon had been no better than that of the dragoons, were unsettled by the bangs of shrapnel shells above their heads and the occasional disarray caused by the fall of a man or horse that had been hit. Woodford, therefore, did not delay the process, and as soon as the squadron was in approximate order, took position in the centre of the front rank and gave the command "Draw swords!"[42]

His men used their right hands to pull their 34-inch-long Starr sabres with a rasp from the iron scabbards suspended on their left hips, taking care at the same time to slip their hands through the sword-knot attached to the hilt, a somewhat tricky business as they were wearing heavy buff leather gauntlets. The sabre drawn and the knot secured around the dragoon's wrist, he rested it on the cap of his right-hand pistol holster, one of two fastened in front of his saddle. As there was a shortage of cavalry sabres, some of Woodford's men had only their .54 Harper's Ferry or .69 calibre North flintlock pistols. Where this was the case, they now drew one of these weapons, which had been loaded on coming into action, and holding it in their right hand, checked the priming. Firing flintlock pistols while riding a horse could be a dodgy thing – if the weapon was discharged too close to the mount's ear and pricked the sensitive inner tissue with flaming grains of black powder, Dobbin was understandably inclined to buck his troublesome passenger off and go in search of quieter pastures to ruminate on the matter.[43]

These preparations, which took less time to complete than to describe, being made, and satisfied that his men were as ready as they could be, Woodford gave the command "Walk!" It was repeated up and down the ranks by the officers and the two ranks moved forward, officers and NCOs trying to preserve the alignment of the ranks, shouting at men who surged forward or dropped back. Selecting the right flank of the 49th as his objective, Woodford moved directly at it, and his men took their direction from him. When he had covered about one hundred feet, the Virginian gave the order "Trot!" and the pace accelerated, the horses' hooves throwing up clods of mud, and the alignment of the ranks became more ragged despite all efforts. Woodford, calculating the distance covered, waited until about two hundred and fifty feet had passed and then ordered "Gallop!" and the squadron now accelerated again – the alignment grew even more ragged, the drumming of the hooves became very audible and the white falls or tresses attached to the dragoons' leather helmets streamed out behind. When he judged his men were at the proper speed, Woodford shouted "Charge!", and if the Second Dragoons had a trumpeter or bugler with them that day, he sounded the call as the men spurred their horses to a dead run and "gave point" with their sabres, raising them off their holsters and extending them straight out above their horses' right ears, blade upwards.[44]

This was how it worked in theory, but this is not quite what happened on 11 November 1813. In order to reach Plenderleath's right flank, the Second Dragoons had to ride across the front of Pearson and Barnes, who took full advantage to pour a hot flank fire into the blue-uniformed ranks. Pearson's four companies, some firing from behind the buildings of one of Crysler's neighbours, were more distant, and their angle was poor, but they got off a scattered volley which probably did not do much damage. As the dragoons moved towards the 49th, however, their direction brought them closer to Captain George West Barnes's companies and, this day, Barnes was determined to salvage a rather shaky career. He waited until the Americans were near and then poured in a concentrated volley before wheeling his left-flank company back to the left and firing another heavy volley into their rear as they rode by. Finally, Lieutenant Henry Kersteman, RA, commanding the 6-pdr. gun positioned to support Pearson, saw a chance to do good work and got away at least one round of canister from his 6-pdr. which brought horses and riders tumbling to the ground. At this, Jackson noted with satisfaction, some of the American cavalry went "to the right about" and rode "back more rapidly than they advanced, leaving some men and horses on the field behind them."[45] Morrison later praised both Barnes and Kersteman, reporting that the enemy cavalry was received in a "gallant" manner "by the companies of the 89th under Captain Barnes and the well directed fire of the artillery."[46]

This heavy, close and accurate fire shook Woodford's squadron. His two ranks, their alignment already awry as faster horses pulled ahead of their comrades despite the best efforts of their riders, lost all cohesion. As men and their mounts tumbled to the ground, those horses coming behind swerved to avoid them because horses dislike treading on living creatures. Other dragoons (or their horses), unwilling to face this fire, wheeled and rode away. The result was that the squadron deteriorated from a military formation to a fast-moving clump, but despite their losses, the Second Dragoons had got past the gauntlet of Pearson, Barnes and Kersteman and were now racing at full speed toward the open right flank of the 49th Foot.

That flank was formed by a company commanded by Lieutenant Dixie Ellis. A thirty-five-year-old native of Ireland who had served nine years in the ranks before being commissioned, Ellis had been with the 49th since 1803 and had fought in every engagement since the war had begun. He watched as the blue-uniformed dragoons thundered closer and, judging the time nicely, waited until the last possible moment and then, as an admiring John Sewell looked on from the centre of the battalion, wheeled his company "four paces" back to the right to face the oncoming dragoons and "poured in [a] volley" at them at the same time as Barnes's companies, having reloaded, sent another volley into their rear.[47]

Woodford's squadron fell apart. Some men rode for shelter in the second ravine, while others stopped and fired at the British ranks with their pistols, which, given the accuracy of these wretched articles, would probably have been more effective if they had thrown them. John Woodford, a brave Virginian, continued to ride forward. Sewell thought the American cavalry commander "a gallant one; he leapt over the fence and was riding toward our right, but alone; some of the men rushed out to attack him with their bayonets fixed, but observing that he was unassisted he took the fence again in good hunting style and followed his men who were in good retreat."[48]

It was over. Pearce recalled that the dragoons rode back "in disorder."[49] Their effort had been costly – Samuel Harris, whose coat was "twice pierced by musquet balls," was one of the survivors, but on the ground over which the squadron had ridden lay the bodies of eighteen men killed and twelve wounded along with between twenty-five and thirty dead and injured horses, some shrieking in pain.[50] This sacrifice had not been in vain because their charge had momentarily halted Barnes's advance and distracted British attention long enough for Craig to get three of his guns to safety. Only the fourth weapon, under Lieutenant William Smith, now remained on the west side of the ravine.

A native of Morristown, New Jersey, seventeen-year-old William Smith had graduated from West Point in 1811 and was now, on the eve of his birthday, taking part in his first battle. Some months before, when his sister had expressed concern for his safety, the teenager had chided her for wishing "to see me removed from the scene of danger; for although you are a female, it ought to be your pride to see me risk (and even sacrifice) my life for my country." Admitting that he was "ambitious of fame," William Smith had "no desire to seek death," but if it was his fate "to fall in battle, such a death will perhaps rescue my humble name from oblivion." Given Smith's attitude it is not surprising that when most of his gun detachment was killed or wounded the young officer refused to leave his gun "as long as he was able to discharge it," and "actually fired it off himself (after losing nearly all his men)."[51]

It would be nice to record that such courage was rewarded, but as soon as Woodford's cavalry had ridden off, Barnes pushed his three companies closer and they fired a volley that cut Smith down. Giving a cheer, the 89th then "spiritedly charged" the American position and captured both the badly wounded Smith and his gun. In John Harvey's opinion, this was the feat that "decided the fate of the day."[52]

CHAPTER 12

"Field of Glory"

11 NOVEMBER 1813, 4.00–8.00 P.M.

Great guns have shot and shell, boys,
Dragoons have sabres bright.
The artillery fire's like hell, boys,
And the horse like devils fight.
But neither light nor heavy horse
Nor thundering cannoneers,
Can stem the tide of the foeman's pride,
Like the British bayoneteers!

The English arm is strong, boys,
The Irish arm is tough.
The Scotsman's blow the French well know,
Is struck by sterling stuff.
And when before the enemy
Their shining steel appears,
Goodbye! goodbye! how they run, how they run!
From the British bayoneteers![1]

For a few minutes after the loss of Smith's artillery piece, there was a pause. "Both sides ceased firing at the same moment," Swift recalled, "for no apparent cause, as neither side made any forward movement to charge further."[2] The Royal Artillery, however, soon returned to work, keeping up, as Trowbridge of the Twenty-First commented, "a steady fire" on "everything that appeared on the field to annoy them." Irvine's two guns, which had fired on and off during the recent fighting, replied and a long-range artillery duel commenced.

Morrison took advantage of this lull to push his entire force forward to the west side of the second ravine, to within good musket range of Boyd's line. First came the cautionary order, "The Battalion will Advance!" and next,

The Battle of Crysler's Farm, 11 November 1813
This panoramic oil painting by Adam Sherriff Scott, which dates from the early 1960s, depicts the high point of the action and is on display in the battlefield memorial building at Upper Canada Village. In the left middle ground, Lieutenant Henry Craig and Armstrong Irvine's 6-pdr. guns are withdrawing while, in the centre middle ground, Lieutenant William Smith keeps one gun in action. Behind Smith, Major John Woodford's Second Dragoons charge the right flank of the 49th Foot, whose line is

"March!" At this word, the 49th and 89th moved forward, marching at a sedate seventy-three paces (a pace is two and a half feet) to the minute in order to preserve their alignment, each man in the rank and file supposedly careful to hold "his body perfectly square" so that he could "just feel the touch of his neighbour."[3]

As he watched that steel-tipped British line coming closer, unshaken after more than two hours of fighting, Boyd began to have serious doubts about how this thing was going to end. As he later wrote:

My orders from General Wilkinson were, should the enemy advance upon us, to beat them back. They first attacked us in the woods; we drove them from thence, into a plain; from the plain to a ravine, where their main body was posted, from thence into an open space interspersed with smaller ra-

marked by their two colours and the regularly spaced puffs of smoke from firing platoons. In the background the three rather too large British gunboats contribute their efforts to the battle. Although incorrect in some details concerning unit positions and uniforms (and the number of mounted American officers, most of whom had no horses), this dramatic rendering gives a good general impression of the last phase of the action. (Courtesy, Upper Canada Village)

vines, enfiladed, and raked by their gunboats. We then drove them, to where their right was under protection of their gunboats; and their left on a wood, lined with incorporated militia and Indians.[4]

"Considering my orders to have been executed," he concluded, "and some of our troops giving way, I ordered the main body to fall back, and re-form where the action first commenced" – in other words, at the edge of the woods.

The three infantry brigades accordingly drew back to the skirt of the trees: Coles's First on the right, Swartout's Fourth in the centre and Pearce's Third (less most of the Twenty-Fifth Infantry) on the left flank. This movement made no sense to Pearce as all three brigades had been "furnished with a supply of ammunition" and were "ready to renew the conflict," but instead they were now "ordered by General Boyd, to take post on the east [actually west] of the strip of woods, where they first formed."[5] Reynold Kirby, whose little detachment was formed with the Sixteenth Infantry, remembered that after having reached the new position it "reformed the line" and "expected a renewal of the combat."[6] This was also the opinion of Walbach, who also "expected the attack would have been renewed, after reorganizing the brigades; and was fully convinced, if it had been, the enemy would have been beaten."[7]

But it was not to be. Boyd now received an order "brought (I presume) by one of the field aides [to General Wilkinson], to fall back to the boats, perhaps half a mile distant."[8] The confusion in the American chain of command, evident the entire day, was still going on – neither Wilkinson nor Lewis ever admitted ordering a withdrawal and Boyd could not remember who transmitted the order. Nonetheless, he obeyed it, and his three brigades formed in column of march and prepared to move back to Cook's tavern just as Upham's boat guard emerged from the trees.[9]

In the lead was Mordecai Myers's company of the Thirteenth Infantry. On his way forward Myers had encountered the remnants of the Twenty-Fifth Infantry running "helter skelter" through the woods and then he came upon Lieutenant Colonel Jonas Cutting, the unit's second-in-command. "Colonel," said Myers, "where are you going?" Cutting replied, "My men will not stand." "But," responded the young officer from New York City, "you are leading them." The first person Myers met when he reached the battlefield was Boyd, who rode up and shouted, "Rush on my 'jolly snorters', you are wanted." Myers accepted the compliment but wisely "halted a moment to let my men go into action cooly," and then marched onto the field.[10]

The main body of the boat guard, moving "at a quick step," was hard on his heels, having passed on their way a stretcher party carrying back the wounded Covington. On seeing them arrive, Boyd "galloped up" but proved no more helpful to Upham than he had to Myers. When Upham asked "what position he should take," Boyd "made no answer." "What orders, Genl.?" persisted Upham, to which Boyd replied "give three Cheers and rush on!" This was encouraging but not very helpful, and Upham got no further direction for, having delivered himself of that sentiment, Boyd wheeled his horse and rode off the field.[11]

Upham, a thirty-year-old minister's son from Charleston, Massachusetts, who had always displayed a "strong passion for a military life," decided to fight.[12] He moved his force, six hundred strong, out from the tree-line and onto "the Wheat stubble" of the open fields where they immediately came under fire from Jackson's guns. Captain John Weeks of the Eleventh Infantry remembered that "the enemy directed his grape shot [actually shrapnel] towards the front of the little Column" and hit his boot with a bullet. The boat guard was now in action and "the March was Continued over this field" onto "the plain where the Enemy was in line & very near his centre, at the distance of easy musket shot." Here, Weeks remembered, their "line was formed and a very brisk fire opened." The British returned it with musketry and artillery but it was a very unequal contest.[13]

As Upham was coming onto the field, Boyd's three brigades were departing it in column of march. Jackson took full advantage of the good targets these closely-packed columns presented, and he had preserved some of his spherical case for just such an opportunity. Kirby remembered that toward "the close of the action we suffered much from grape shot & shrapnel shells which were dealt out by the enemy in abundance & with much skill."[14] To the British artillery commander, whose gunners had opened the battle, it appeared they were now about to close it and his fire alone was forcing the enemy to retire – the "American columns soon began to waver," he recalled, "and one after the other broke and ran."[15] Once Boyd's infantry, followed by Craig and Irvine's artillery, disappeared into the trees, Upham's little force was left to carry on alone.

As a result, they suffered heavy casualties. John Weeks remembered that as the boat guard took up its positions

the last of the troops who had been engaged were seen filing off by the right, leaving the whole extent of the enemy's line unoccupied – as soon therefore as Maj. Upham's fire commenced, it drew a very destructive one from the enemy line being a cross fire from their wings (owing to their vastly greater length of line) & very sharp in front. You may judge something of the position by the fact, that out of thirty-three men [under his command] ... fourteen were killed or wounded in very few minutes.[16]

Things were no better with Myers's company, which had formed into line "on the enemy's right flank, where my 'buck and ball' told well."[17] The position was a good one, "within 200 yards of the [British] right flank" and his men "kneeled on the left knee behind a stone wall about two feet high." Myers had been wounded while moving to this wall by a musket ball that passed through his left arm "two inches below the socket" but he had ignored it and continued in action. He now was hit again. For his part, Weeks realized the situation was hopeless and asked Upham if perhaps they should not fall back. Upham made no reply, but Weeks insisted that "a few Minutes more would bring every man to the ground," and Upham, reluctantly, gave the order to withdraw.[18]

It was about 4.30 P.M., and the light was beginning to fade. The skies, which had been threatening all afternoon, now opened up and a "most violent fall of rain commenced."[19] To Morrison, this final stage of the battle appeared to be an attempt by an American rearguard "to check our advance."[20] Harvey noted that "efforts were still kept up but the fire of our Platoons and Guns and above all the steady countenance of the troops finally drove the enemy out of the field and about half past four o'Clock he gave up the contest and retreated rapidly through the woods covered by his Light Troops."[21] Morrison ordered Pearson to keep the pressure on and that crusty veteran, using the flank companies of the 49th and Heriot's Voltigeurs, moved forward to screen the advance in a fashion that Morrison thought most "judicious."[22] As the British skirmishers disappeared into the trees at the eastern edge of the fields, the firing gradually died away. The battle, which by Jackson's calculation had lasted two hours and twenty minutes, was over.[23]

The British and Canadians, physically and emotionally spent, gave three weak cheers and moved forward to the positions formerly held by the Americans. The dead lay where they had fallen – Trooper John Loucks "saw an enemy soldier that had been hit in the head by a cannon ball, and all that was left of his head was his lower jaw."[24] A British soldier, "badly wounded in the groin," asked Loucks "if he could take him where he would receive proper attention," and the teenager placed the man on his horse and took him to one of the nearby farmhouses from which the civilians, somewhat dazed by the long afternoon, were beginning to emerge. The soldier who had warned Mrs. Fetterly to take shelter at the beginning of the action returned to tell her "that the danger was over."[25] In front of the house were a number of dead and wounded – "a gruesome sight" for little Agnes Fetterly.[26]

Although the fighting had stopped there were men, maddened by the fear and tension of the past few hours, who did not understand that the battle was over and the enemy no longer represented a threat. As his company advanced, John Sewell of the 49th Foot witnessed an incident that haunted him for decades. His company was moving through an area scattered with dead and wounded when a "wretch, I can't call him a soldier, left his ranks and went some three or four paces to his left, and literally pinned a wounded and unresisting American soldier to the earth, with his bayonet."[27] "Ruffians of this caste are few happily," recorded the young officer, "but they awfully augment the horrors of war." When he was certain that it was all over, Sewell returned in the growing dark to the body of Captain Thomas Nairne, in order to retrieve his personal possessions and make arrangements for his burial. He was shocked to discover that in the few minutes that had passed someone (Sewell always suspected one of the Canadian Fencibles) had stolen poor Nairne's watch.[28]

There were others collecting mementoes of the battle. As the shooting ended, Shawindas, John Snake, John Pigeon, Patickewa and their fellow Mohawks materialized from the pine woods to the north, and pulling their small, sharp scalping knives from their sheaths, walked purposefully toward the American dead. The warriors had fought the white man's battle for the white man's cause, but now they intended to take the traditional trophies of their people as a mark of their prowess. Their ferocity during the action had been terrifying – that night, fourteen American soldiers, "more dead than alive with fright, were captured in *a pile*" by a detachment of the Dundas militia in the "Nudel Bush," a swamp north of the battlefield.[29]

As Upham withdrew through the woods, Pearson's skirmishers followed, but they did not press too closely, for their task was not to fight but observe the Americans and screen the main force from any enemy attempt to renew the fighting. In the words of Lieutenant Christopher Hagerman, Morrison's troops "had suffered too severely and they were too near their reinforcements to follow them with any other than our light troops." [30]

Not all the Americans left when Upham withdrew. Mordecai Myers, whose wounds were beginning to cause him pain, had to give up command of his company to his lieutenant. Noticing an artillery piece nearby in the dark and rain, he decided to walk toward it, hoping to catch a ride on its carriage back to the flotilla. "I was very near," Myers recorded, "when I discovered the British uniforms" – the gun was Smith's 6-pdr. captured earlier in the action.[31] Myers "immediately turned and walked leisurely towards the retiring troops," but the British

did not fire at me or pursue me until I rose from a ravine; they then fired … it was with great difficulty, with the use of only one hand, that I got out of the ravine. I fell in with a man who had a horse and a keg of ammunition; I took the horse and finally reached the boats. The horse was led part of the way by a camp woman.

Many of the American wounded were left on the field. Surgeon Trowbridge recorded that forty casualties, carried to the shelter of the second ravine during the fighting, were placed in the care of Surgeon Fenn Denning, who volunteered to stay behind and look after them.[32] As soon as his regiment withdrew, Lieutenant Colonel Thomas Aspinwall of the Ninth Infantry handed over to his second-in-command and went to where one of his junior officers, Lieuten-

They weren't so pretty in the field – American army surgeon and sergeant of the Regiment of Light Artillery, 1813
Unfortunately, there were few horses to spare in Wilkinson's army and most officers moved on foot. The Regiment of Light Artillery (or horse artillery) provided most of the artillery detachments for Wilkinson's army. (Painting by H.C. McBarron, courtesy United States Army)

ant David Townsend, had fallen to see if he could get him removed to the flotilla. As he later wrote the young man's father, Townsend was "reclining and supporting himself on his arm and, although the ground [had been] continually torn up all around him by grape, canister and musket balls and he was in extreme pain," Townsend displayed "not the least symptom of concern, or complaint."[33] Aspinwall "procured four men to carry him from the field and left him in their hands under the charge of Lt. [Loring] Palmer" but

> was afterwards informed by Lieut. Palmer, that, to avoid the dangers of the open field, he was induced to pass through a woods, somewhat in rear of the right of Our army, where, some of the enemy's sharpshooters were discovered coming out of the thicker part of the woods in pursuit of the party which obliged them to hasten so fast that it occasioned the most excruciating pain to the Capt, who found it at last so entirely unsupportable, that he requested them to leave him, as it was impossible for him to proceed any further. Lt. Palmer took off his own coat and covering him up left him and much to his satisfaction observed that the enemy did not notice the spot

where he lay. He then proceeded to a neighbouring house and informed the owner, where your son was, of his name, rank and that any care, or expense he might bestow on him would be amply and gratefully remunerated.

Arriving back at Michael Cook's tavern, Boyd was disgusted to find that many boats in the flotilla "had already put off, some of which, in the early part of the action, had descended the river, near General Brown's position" at Cornwall.[34] Because he felt he had done his duty, Boyd formed his command to wait in the dark and the rain for further orders from Wilkinson. Major Ninian Pinckney landed shortly thereafter with a message from the latter asking Boyd "whether he could maintain himself, on the bank that night." Boyd replied "that he could not; that it was necessary the men should embark, to have an opportunity of cooking, and obtaining a peaceable night's rest."[35]

While this exchange was going on, more of the boat crews took matters into their own hands and pushed off without orders, inciting a near panic, and they were shortly followed by others. Pinckney remembered that Wilkinson "exclaimed against" this flight as it "was contrary to his wish" and the aide tried "to stop the movement, but was not able."[36] Kirby recalled that the panic induced by this movement caused Boyd "to order all to the boats, on gaining which we put off from the shore in the utmost confusion."[37] Not only was the embarkation confused, there was trouble getting many of the boats into the water as the strong wind from the west that had been blowing throughout the day had left many high and dry. The artillery was not re-embarked; Wilkinson instead ordered Walbach to take charge of the five remaining field pieces and, with the Second Dragoons acting as an escort, deliver them, "*at the peril of my life,*" Walbach recalled, to Brown at Cornwall.[38] As he prepared to carry out this order, Walbach was furious that Boyd "gave the orders, for the embarkation of the troops after the battle" without his knowledge, leaving him on the shore with only Woodford's dragoons and Craig's gunners and the enemy less than a mile away.[39] He started down the highway and arrived at Cornwall at about 2 A.M. the following morning. Major William Cumming of the Sixteenth Infantry was thoroughly disgusted by the army's withdrawal. Cumming, who had been forced to leave his unit to seek medical attention, had "seen enough during the day to wound my feeling as a man, a soldier & an American":

But most humbling of all to my pride was the precipitation of our retreat. It was scandalous. The Surgeon had scarcely time to bind my wound after I had returned to the boats before an instant embarkation was ordered. We ought to have retained our position for our reputation's sake.[40]

Not more than ninety minutes after the last shot had been fired, Wilkinson's army had departed from Cook's tavern, to return no more – much to the great joy of Michael and Abigail and their neighbours.[41]

The flotilla, Reynold Kirby recorded, "fell down the river four miles" and "landed on the American side in a large meadow surrounded by woods." Wilkinson had put distance and the St. Lawrence between his army and Morrison but he was still above the Long Sault rapids, an obstacle that would have to be traversed in the morning. "It had become cold," Kirby recalled, and "we made our fires & pulling the haystacks to pieces lay down for the night, which by the disaster of the day was a gloomy one." Many of Boyd's officers and men felt they had beaten off a British attack, but they were confused about the outcome of the fight. Although they "had repulsed the enemy," puzzled Kirby, "still everything was the appearance of a defeat," for "we had left our killed & many of our wounded on the field of battle together with a piece of artillery which had been disabled & its commander Lieut. Smith, mortally wounded." Kirby concluded that the outcome "would have been far different & Genl. B[oyd]. would have acquired much honor had not some mistakes been committed." In his opinion, the army had been

> too much hurried on coming into action, which caused ... considerable confusion. No ammunition waggons followed the regiments into the field. There were but 4 [sic] pieces of artillery when we might from the boats have taken 10 or 12. (Note. The enemy had seven) And if 400 or 600 men which might have been unduly spared from the boats had been thrown into the wood upon our right & while the enemy were amused in front by our artillery & musketry, their left might by such a force have been turned – their rear gained – the consequences of which would have been their total defeat & with proper management their whole force captured.[42]

Drummer Jarvis Hanks, who had just seen his first action despite a recruiting officer's promise to his parents he would never be exposed to combat, was undecided – to him it was "difficult to say which [side] had the advantage, on the whole."[43] Lieutenant Joseph Dwight of the Thirteenth Infantry had no doubt whatsoever that the northern army had just been "most shamefully beaten" in an engagement in which there "was no order or system displayed on our part," although his comrades had "fought well when not disheartened by conflicting orders."[44] Captain John Weeks of the Eleventh Infantry agreed about the performance of his superiors: "I never was advised of the particular plan of our Generals for fighting that battle, if plan there was."[45] To "sum up all the calamities that had befallen us," stated Lieutenant John O'Connor, "the commander in chief was confined to his bed, the second in command was unequal to the task, while the Brigadiers were worse."[46]

The generals themselves were no more happy. Wilkinson was angered by the unauthorized flight of the flotilla because his "enemy would say we had run away and claim a victory."[47] Morgan Lewis, who had done nothing during the day, was critical of Boyd. Writing his wife a few days after the engagement, he commented that although "our troops maintained their order" and "three times charged and drove the enemy from their position behind fences," the "impetuosity of Boyd, it is said, (but you must not say it) threw our lines into disorder, broke their ranks, and the enemy drove us in turn."[48]

Responsibility for the defeat must be charged to Boyd, Lewis and, most of all, James Wilkinson. Despite his lengthy military career, Wilkinson had never commanded even a regiment in combat, let alone an army of more than 7,000 men, and his actions and those of Morgan Lewis on 11 November 1813 were irresponsible. Wilkinson's one positive step that day had been to order Upham to reinforce Boyd, but this order had been anticipated and issued by Swift. Other than that, neither general had done a single thing to assist their subordinates, yet although they refused to exercise command, they refused to give it up, and the result was disastrous. It therefore fell on John Boyd, an officer clearly promoted well beyond his level, to fight the battle – and a very bad job he made of it.

Boyd committed his infantry before his artillery could properly support them and did not use his superior strength to advantage but instead wasted the lives of his troops in separate and uncoordinated attacks which were defeated in detail by a well positioned opponent. Both he and his brigade commanders encountered problems deploying and manoeuvring their formations, problems resulting from their own inexperience and the poor and confused state of training in their commands. It was also Boyd's responsibility to ensure that his troops were supplied with ammunition before and during the action, and in this he was totally remiss. For most of the engagement, John Boyd seems to have wandered aimlessly about wondering what to do next, and without the efforts of Swift and Walbach the day might have been worse than it was, because, in effect, no American officer was in overall command during the battle.

Boyd was not responsible for the particular problems the artillery encountered – this was the province of Brigadier General Moses Porter. Porter may not even have been present with the army on 11 November, although it appears that the order issued in mid-morning to land and position an 18-pdr. gun to drive off Mulcaster was received by him. Thereafter, he took no part in the action, nor did his two senior subordinates, Wadsworth and Eustis; however,

Eustis had the important duty of commanding the gunboats protecting the flotilla and could not be spared for service on land. The result of this vacuum was that a young lieutenant was left to sort out the mess caused by the absence of the horses, and although Henry Craig did his best, the artillery, the only arm with the training and the weapons to do serious harm to their enemy, arrived too late to change the course of events.

The few positive events of the afternoon had been brought about by such senior officers as Covington (who paid the penalty), Swift and Walbach, and unit commanders like Cromwell Pearce of the Sixteenth Infantry, Eleazer Ripley of the Twenty-First, Timothy Upham of the Eleventh and John Woodford of the dragoons. Their successes, however, were local and short-lived, and at best they only managed to stave off a worse defeat. These officers accomplished what they did because of the courage of their men, but the sad fact is that in war fortune more often favours the competent than it does the brave.

I n contrast, Lieutenant Colonel Joseph Morrison's officers and men had no doubt about the outcome of the action. The events of the day, incidents of the fighting, the loss of friends, were endlessly discussed around the camp fires lit that night on John Crysler's fields. The predominant feelings were relief that it was over and pride in beating off a superior enemy force. Some were even inclined to be cocky, "This was *Jonathan's* debut on the open plain," one officer commented ("Cousin Jonathan" being the popular British and Canadian term of derision for Americans), "and I think for the future, he will prefer his old mode of acting in the bush."[49] Lieutenant Colonel John Harvey was just a tad arrogant – he later quipped that the enemy advanced "at the *pas de charge à la française* which was quickly changed by a well directed fire from our Field Pieces into one more comporting with the dignity of the American Nation."[50]

Morrison's troops were also conscious that this engagement, unlike so many previous actions of the war, had been fought in the open between large numbers of regular troops and that superior training and discipline had prevailed. As Sewell put it, courage, "the essential element to the obtaining of victory, will not suffice without the knowledge of Field Duty."[51]

Joseph Morrison had good reason to feel satisfied during the evening of 11 November 1813 because he had done what every soldier dreams of doing, fighting the perfect battle. He had picked an excellent position and used the superior discipline and firepower of his troops to repulse an enemy he believed to be more than three times his number. He had experienced two problems during the action: the advance under Pearson had been pushed back and the attack of the 49th Foot on the American artillery had been repulsed. Pearson, however, had quickly restored the situation on the right, and the rebuff of the 49th, due more perhaps to an overly optimistic assessment of the situation than to any shortcomings on Morrison or Harvey's part, had not adversely affected the outcome. The British commander's success was all the more amazing because this was his first action, but then he possessed the assets of a well-trained force of regulars and the advice and support of very experienced senior subordinates.

In the end what it had come down to was that a small but professional army had defeated an opponent superior only in numbers. The credit for the victory went to Morrison because he had command, but as Lieutenant Christopher Hagerman of his staff emphasized, it was a success won by his little army as a whole:

It would be impossible to speak in too high terms of the conduct of our officers and men. Col. Morrison though not over 30 years of age, showed a coolness and judgement which must ever render to him the greatest honor. Col. Pearson is well known for his intrepidity and intelligence, and on this occasion he very considerably increased his character for both. Lt. Col. Harvey Dy. Adjt. Genl. who accompanied Col. Morrison from Kingston, proved an able assistant and to him a great share of the praise is due for the result of the day. Lt. Col. Plenderleath of the 49th & Major Clifford of the 89th at the head of their respective corps, ably managed each battalion – who bore the brunt of the action. Cap. Jackson had charge of the Field Pieces, and did great execution. The Troops that were drawn up fired at the word of Command, and with the utmost regularity. No particular instance occurred where individual valor was shown, nor do I believe that any opportunity offered, although it may sometimes be convenient to magnify trifles. The field piece was abandoned and required no extraordinary exertion to be borne away. Major Heriot very usefully managed the light troops, and equal benefit was experienced from the Indians under Lieut. Anderson.[52]

When it was all over, Morrison scribbled a note to his superiors. Dated "Christler's, 11 November," it was brief and to the point:

The enemy attacked us this morning, supposed from 3 to 4,000 men in number, and has been completely repulsed and defeated with a very considerable loss, a number of prisoners and one gun taken by us; the loss of the enemy cannot be less than 4 or 500; ours has been severe. The Americans were commanded by Generals Lewis and Boyd.[53]

The copy for de Rottenburg was handed to one of Fraser's dragoons, who galloped west for Kingston, while John Crysler volunteered to take the copy east to Montreal and rode out a few hours after the shooting stopped. On his way he encountered Major Richard Dennis's militia with their wagon train of supplies. Having heard the noise of the firing up the river, they had been "indulging in all kind of surmises as to the result of the engagement," but the militia's anxiety was relieved when Crysler rode up, "direct from the battle-field with news of the enemy's defeat," on which the citizen soldiers tossed their hats in the air "and made the neighbouring forest to resound with their vociferous cheering."[54]

At Montreal that day, Lieutenant General Sir George Prevost signed a letter to Morrison that the victor of Crysler's Farm would not read for some time but which would give him great satisfaction when he did. Prevost completely supported Morrison and Mulcaster's decision to disobey the order to break off the pursuit. "I entirely approve," he advised Morrison, "of your having decided in persevering in following the enemy's army moving toward Lower Canada" notwithstanding "the order you received from Major General De Rottenburg to retire to Kingston."[55] The British commander-in-chief was confident in the outcome of any encounter with the enemy because he "placed great reliance" on his subordinate's

> intelligence, activity and enterprise and that of the field officers under your immediate command and trust that my expectation will not be disappointed but that by an unwearied and daring system of attack upon the rear and flank of the American army, ably supported by the gunboats, you will be enabled to cripple their expedition as to the principal cause of its object being frustrated.

If Morrison was "to press boldly," Prevost continued, his little army would earn themselves "a field of glory" and he was certain the younger officer appreciated the opportunity he had been given to display his "talents in the honorable support of the fame of the British Army and best interests of your country."

As the events of that long afternoon had shown, there was never any need for the commander-in-chief to have had doubts on that score.

PART IV

The Aftermath

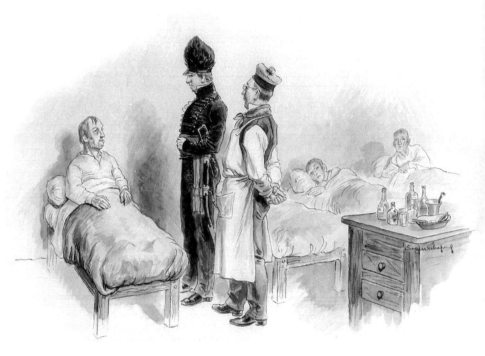

The aftermath – a military hospital, 1813
The rather well appointed military hospital illustrated here was unusual. Most of the wounded men from the battle were treated in much more primitive facilities.
(Watercolour by Eugene Leliepvre, courtesy Parks Canada)

CHAPTER 13

"Beat the drums slowly and play the fifes lowly"

THE RESIDUE OF GLORY

As I was a-walking down by the Lock Hospital
Dark was the morning and cold was the day,
When who should I spy but one of my comrades,
Draped in a blanket and cold as the clay.

Then beat the drums slowly and play the fifes lowly,
Sound the "Dead March" as you carry me along,
And fire your muskets right over my coffin,
For I'm a young soldier cut down in his prime.

Got six of my comrades to carry my coffin,
Six of my comrades to carry me on high,
And each of them carry a bunch of white roses,
So no-one may smell me as we pass them by.[1]

On the day after the battle, Lieutenant Colonel Joseph Morrison seated himself at a table in John Crysler's home and took pen in hand to write his official account of the battle. "I have the heartfelt gratification," he began, "to report the brilliant and gallant conduct" of his army "as yesterday displayed in repulsing and defeating" an American force consisting of "between 3,000 and 4,000 men." Morrison's account of the action was a concise document that opened with a brief description of the ground, and then went on to the initial British dispositions, the American movements and his counter-movements until the late afternoon, when the enemy "gave away at all points from an exceeding strong position." He acknowledged the efforts of individual officers: Harvey, Pearson, Plenderleath, Heriot, Clifford, Jackson, Barnes, Anderson of the Indian Department and Christopher Hagerman received mention in the dispatch – while, as for rest of his officers and men, they "did their duty." Knowing how much he owed to John Harvey, Morrison later wrote a separate letter to Prevost explaining he would "be wanting to those feelings of rectitude" if he did not state that Harvey's "ability and judgement greatly contributed to the success of the day."[2]

The British commander provided no estimate of the American casualties in the action but Harvey, writing the same day, thought that the total enemy loss in killed, wounded and prisoners "may be safely estimated at 600 or 700 men."[3] Both men recorded that "upwards" of 100 prisoners had been taken but Morrison noted that as prisoners were still being collected he could not furnish "a correct return of them."[4] The number of Americans captured at Crysler's Farm is difficult to establish because the register of the prisoner-of-war facility at Quebec City, normally very carefully kept, is somewhat confused for November and December 1813. The best estimate, based on Morrison and Harvey's figure of "upwards of 100" and the register, would be that at least seventy-five of Wilkinson's men were captured. The victors also found between three and four hundred American muskets abandoned on the battlefield.[5]

The victory had not come cheap. "I regret," Morrison wrote, "to find our loss in killed and wounded has been so considerable" and he listed his overall casualties as 22 dead, 148 wounded and 9 missing for a total of 179 or about 15 per cent of his force engaged. Not surprisingly, the heaviest losses were suffered by the units under Pearson: the 49th flank companies lost 20 of the 76 men they brought into the action, nearly a third, while the Canadian Fencibles' loss, 20 of 108 men, was about a fifth. The casualties of the two regular battalions were not as severe. Plenderleath's eight companies of the 49th reported 7 killed and 43 wounded, nearly 17 per cent of their strength, while Clifford's 89th Foot, including Barnes's three detached companies, had 5 killed and 62 wounded, almost exactly 14 per cent of the men brought into action. Heriot's Voltigeurs and Anderson's Mohawks, fighting from behind cover, got off more lightly despite the fact they had been closely engaged throughout the action, the *Canadiens* losing 4 killed and 9 wounded of a total of about 150, and the warriors reporting 1 wounded and 3 missing. Jackson's losses were light, 2 gunners and 1 driver wounded while Fraser's dragoons had 1 wounded, as did the Dundas militia.[6]

These were the official figures but other evidence suggests that Morrison's losses may have been somewhat higher. A separate return exists for the Canadian Fencibles which states they lost 9 killed (one man having died of wounds), 1 officer and 3 men missing and presumed prisoners, and 14 wounded. If de Lorimier and Ensign Henry Armstrong (who were still alive when Morrison compiled his return) are added, the Fencibles figure totals 29 as opposed to the 20 in the official casualty list, or just under a third of the men of the unit that participated. A similar document for the 49th Foot reports 15 enlisted men killed and 33 wounded, which if the 2 officers killed and 6 officers wounded are added, gives a total of 56 compared with the 50 of the official report. If this trend to slightly higher casualties is constant among all the British and Canadian units that participated, Morrison's losses at Crysler's Farm were probably over 200 or nearly a sixth of his command.[7]

Having completed his report, Morrison sent it to Kingston by dragoon messenger but selected Captain George Barnes of the 89th Foot to take a duplicate to Prevost at Montreal, an indication of his approval of that officer's performance during the action.[8]

On the other side of the St. Lawrence, Brigadier General John Boyd of the United States Army faced a more difficult task when reporting on the battle. His official account, also written on 12 November, was nearly twice the length of the British commander's effort and was fairly accurate until it reached the end of the action. The retirement of Swartout and Covington's brigades, Boyd explained, occurred because "having expended all their ammunition" they had "fallen back to a more defensible position to wait for a re-supply." This was true, but he did not say why, after having been resupplied, they had not gone back into action, only that he had been ordered to withdraw to the flotilla. The artillery, he regretted, "did not reach the ground until the line [of infantry], for want of ammunition, had already begun to fall back" and the loss of one gun was due to the death of its officer and most of the gun detachment. As for the light dragoons and Upham's boat guard, or "reserve" as Boyd termed it, it was his feeling that if things had been different, they would have been more effective. Upham's force did not arrive in time "to participate in more than a small part of the action," but "the activity and zeal they displayed while engaged evinced the benefit that might have been derived from their earlier assistance." Woodford's squadron "was early on the ground," he wrote, but "the nature of the ground and the disposition of his [Morrison's] line did not admit of those successful charges which their discipline and ardor, under more favorable circumstances, are calculated to make." This statement ignores the fact that Woodford's dragoons did charge but were sent reeling back by the musketry of Morrison's infantry and the canister of Jackson's artillery.[9]

Boyd mentioned the names of most of the senior officers who had participated, particularly Covington "whose readiness to enter the field was an earnest of his subsequent activity." "Allow me to express my regret," he assured

Wilkinson, "which is felt in common with the army, that the severity of your indisposition deprived us of your presence in the action." And then it came – one long and breathless sentence in which Boyd attempted to rationalize his defeat:

> Permit me now to add, Sir, though the result of this action was not so brilliant and decisive as I could have wished and the first stages of it seemed to promise, yet, when it is recollected that the troops had been long exposed to privations and fatigues, in inclement storms from which they could find no shelter, that the enemy were superior to us in numbers and greatly superior to us in position, supported by 7 or 8 gunboats, that the action being unexpected was necessarily commenced without much concert, that we were by unavoidable circumstances deprived of our artillery, and that the action was obstinately and warmly contested for more than three hours, during which there were but a few short cessations of musketry and cannon – when all these circumstances are recollected perhaps this day may be thought to have added some reputation to the American arms.

It was a good try but wishing it so does not make it so.

The bill for this action, "not so brilliant and decisive" as wished, came to 102 killed and 237 wounded, but Boyd provided no figure for his missing.[10] Assuming that the best estimate for American prisoners was 75, the total American loss at Crysler's Farm, basing the figures for killed and wounded on Boyd's official return, was over 400 men, or about 13 per cent of the force engaged. Other officers estimated the casualties as much higher. Swift thought the three infantry brigades lost "every fifth man killed or wounded."[11] Reynold Kirby, who had a chance to view the entire field, estimated that "one fourth of the whole force in the action were either killed, wounded, or missing."[12] Gardner of the Twenty-Fifth, perhaps influenced by having been exposed to Jackson's artillery most of the afternoon, estimated the American losses as being as much as 40 per cent of the troops in action.[13]

The American casualty return did not break the losses down by unit, which might be an indication of the confusion in Wilkinson's army after the battle. The names and units of 18 officers killed or wounded at Crysler's Farm are known, however, and their losses were distributed as follows: 6 from Covington's Third Brigade, 5 from Swartout's Fourth Brigade, 4 from Coles's First Brigade and 3 from the artillery, dragoons and staff. Assuming that the overall distribution of casualties was in the same proportion, a possible breakdown of the killed and wounded by brigade would be as follows: Coles's First Brigade, 22 killed and 53 wounded; Covington's Third Brigade, 34 killed and 79 wounded; Swartout's Fourth Brigade, 28 killed and 66 wounded; staff, artillery and light dragoons, 17 killed and 40 wounded.[14]

Wilkinson sent Boyd's report to Armstrong and added some padding of his own. In fact, he contributed no less than three communications on the action. His official report was dated 16 November and attached was the daily journal of his army kept by Major Joseph Totten, but given the flowery wording, the entry for 11 November was probably written or embroidered by Wilkinson himself. On 18 November, Wilkinson wrote a second letter to Armstrong which he asked to be considered as "an appendage to my official communication respecting the action of the 11th instant."[15]

Wilkinson regretted he was too ill to command at the battle. Though "enabled to order the attack," he confessed, "it was my hard fortune not to be able to lead the troops," as "I was confined to my bed and emaciated almost to a skeleton, unable to sit on my horse or to move ten paces without assistance." Never a man to let facts get in the way, James Wilkinson then did his level best to make out that Crysler's Farm had been an American victory.[16]

It took some work and he began with the opposing strengths. It was difficult, Wilkinson wrote, "to say with accuracy what was our number in the field, because it consisted of indefinite detachments," but he thought that between 1,500 and 1,700 of his men had gone into action. As for the British, he at first estimated that they numbered between 1,000 and 2,000, but in his letter of 18 November Wilkinson was more specific and provided a detailed breakdown, based on information from prisoners and deserters, of the composition of Morrison's force, which he claimed numbered 2,170 men. This information was inaccurate since it included 420 men from three units, the Glengarry Light Infantry, the 100th Foot and Incorporated Militia, not at the battle, and nearly doubled the strength of those units that were present.[17]

Not only did the American commander consider his strength to be inferior, he also complained his troops were untrained. Despite these disadvantages, he felt the fight "reflects high honor on the valor of the American soldier, as no example can be produced of undisciplined men with inexperienced officers braving a fire of two hours and-a-half without quitting the field or yielding to their antagonists." Boyd had also stressed the poor state of training of the men under his command, but neither officer seemed to feel any great responsibility for this shortcoming.[18]

It was Wilkinson's belief that success or failure in an action had to be based on what the opposing commanders wanted to achieve. As he put it, "he is to be accounted victorious who effected his purpose," and Wilkinson was "bound by the instructions of his Government and the most solemn obligations of duty to precipitate his descent of the St. Lawrence by every practicable means," while Morrison was required "by duties equally imperious to retard and if possible prevent such descent." "The British commander," Wilkinson wrote, "having failed to gain either of his objects can lay no claim to the honours of the day." He argued this opinion more strongly in the army journal, noting that, as Morrison had not prevented him from descending the river, "it follows incontestably that he had no fair ground on which to claim a victory."[19] If Morrison was not victorious, then Wilkinson must be victorious.[20]

The American commander skipped blithely over "the accidental loss of one field piece, notwithstanding it had been discharged fifteen or twenty times" before it was captured. He attributed the successful conclusion to the battle to what he thought was a masterful rearguard action by Upham's detachment, noting that the action "terminated a few minutes after their arrival on the ground" but not referring to the fact that by the time Upham showed up the rest of Boyd's force was withdrawing. No mention was made of the army's embarkation and near-panic-stricken crossing to the American shore – only that the "troops being much exhausted it was considered most convenient that they should embark, and that the dragoons with the artillery, should proceed by land" and the "embarkation took place without the smallest molestation from the enemy." All in all, if one is to believe James Wilkinson, it had been a good day's work, and although "the imperious obligations of duty did not allow me sufficient time to rout the enemy," he assured Secretary of War Armstrong that "they were beaten."[21]

When the shooting stopped in the late afternoon of 11 November, the scene of the action was covered with the casualties of both armies. Most of the lightly and ambulatory wounded were taken to nearby farms during the action or immediately afterward – John Crysler's house, barns and sheds became makeshift hospitals as did the residences of the Fetterlys, Joneses, Haineses, Casselmans, Cooks and others. Some of the American wounded remained on the ground through the night that followed – Thomas Ridout rode across the "field of glory" on the morning of 12 November and remembered it being "covered with Americans killed and wounded," with "some scalped," and dead "horses intermingled among them."[22]

That day, work detachments began to deal with the residue of glory. In later years James Croil learned from local civilians that most of the corpses were placed in shallow trenches, with fifty "buried in one huge grave, on a sand knoll close by the nine-mile road, fifteen in another grave in an orchard by the river side, thirty on Soprenus Casselman's farm, and the rest chiefly where they fell."[23] Into these pits went the bodies of Sergeant William Bell, Drummer John Coppin and others of the 49th Foot, including Private John Torrance, who would never see Kerry again, Corporal John Murphy and Private Michel Janvin of the Canadian Fencibles, Corporal James Kain from Morton Salop in England and Private George Rose from Cork in Ireland, who were laid with their comrades of the 89th Foot, while Lieutenant David Hunter of the Twelfth Infantry was buried in one of the trenches excavated for the blue-uniformed American corpses, far from his home in Virginia. Nairne of the 49th was buried in a wooden coffin hastily knocked together but before it was closed Plenderleath cut off a lock of his hair to send to his family at Murray Bay. These mass burials were hasty affairs and Croil notes that the "hurried sepulture is attested" by many "skeletons having been turned up by the plough" in the years following the battle.[24]

The Crysler property, with its large house and numerous outbuildings, became the primary hospital, and Surgeons William Woodforde and John W. Korb set up shop there on the day of the action. They would have chosen the largest and brightest rooms for operating theatres, and almost certainly Nancy Crysler's spotless parlour was defiled as the medical men prepared, following advice in one of their standard texts, to "lay all your apparatus, such as your capital instruments, needles, ligatures, lint, flour in a bowl, styptic, bandages, splints, compresses, pledgets [small wads] spread with yellow basilicon [ointment], or some other proper digestive; thread, tape, tow, pins, new and old linen cloth, a bucket of water to put your spunges in, another empty to receive the blood in your operations; a dry swab or two to dry the platform when necessary."[25] The "platform" was the operating table, likely a door removed from its hinges and placed across two casks or chests. The "capital instruments" which British regulations required every military surgeon to possess were an amputating saw with a spare blade or two, two trephines, trephine forceps, one "elevator," two or three amputating knives with well-honed blades six to eight inches in length, bone "nippers," long forceps, tourniquets of various sizes, a variety of scalpels (also well-honed), various probes and more esoteric implements such as a probang, a trocar and a canula. Woodforde and Korb had no concept of antisepsis but did know that vinegar was useful for cleaning wounds and requisitioned several barrels from Crysler's cold store.[26]

Carried on makeshift stretchers, the wounded started to arrive shortly after the fighting began. Following the counsel to "always take care of him who is in the most immediate danger," the lightly wounded were laid on pallets or on the floor while Korb and Woodforde tended to those with serious injuries. There was not much they could do for abdominal and head wounds – the ba-

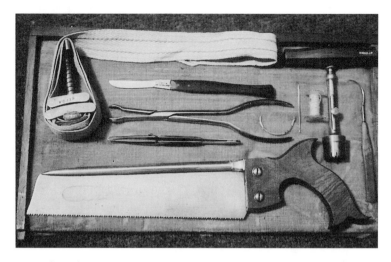

The surgeon's tools
This amputating kit belonged to Surgeon Henry Grasset of the British army in the War
of 1812. It includes amputation saw, knife, scalpel, forceps and tourniquet. (Courtesy
of the Canadian Museum of Health and Medicine at The Toronto Hospital)

sic treatment was to clean and stitch these injuries, cover them with a plaster
or an oiled linen or poultice bandage containing bread soaked in milk and put
the unfortunates aside until they got better or, more likely, died. Wounds of
the limbs were easier to treat, particularly those inflicted by musket balls that
did not shatter bones or destroy joints. These were cleaned and the ball was
removed by forceps, although one period authority suggested that "probing or
poking" be "used as sparingly as possible" as "such a method is highly detrimental to the patient." If the surgeon had to probe for an embedded ball, this
same writer advised using the fingers as he "could never bring myself to thrust
those long forceps the Lord knows where, with scarce any probability of success." The ball and any extraneous material (many wounds contained bits of
wad or clothing) being removed, the wound was stitched, plastered and covered
with a bandage, and the sufferer removed to make room for the next man.[27]

Amputation was the most common surgical procedure for wounds of the
limbs where joints were destroyed or where there was considerable damage to
the surrounding tissue, and most wounds caused by artillery projectiles fell
into this category. Period medical thought was divided on just when to amputate – whether as soon as possible or after waiting some time. Surgeon James
Mann of the American army admitted it was "difficult to determine, most correctly, whether it is best to amputate immediately, or defer it," but on balance
felt the risk of infection from a lengthy stay in the hospitals of the period was

diminished by amputation as "it converts a gun-shot wound into one which is capable of being speedily healed, and obviates the causes that produce hospital fever and gangrene."[28] Medical professionals were starting to become aware of the existence of shock – Surgeon George Guthrie of Wellington's army, perhaps the foremost British authority on battlefield surgery of that time, noted that if "a soldier at the end of two, four, or six hours after the injury has recovered from the general constitutional alarm occasioned by the blow, his pulse becomes regular and good, his stomach easy, he is less agitated, his countenance revives, and he begins to feel pain, stiffness and uneasiness in the part: he will now undergo the operation [amputation] with greatest advantage."[29] Most surgeons preferred to amputate as soon as possible as the "neglecting at this critical juncture of taking off a limb frequently reduces the patient to so low a state, and subjects the blood and juices to such an alteration, as must unavoidably render the subsequent operations, if not entirely unsuccessful, at least exceedingly dubious."

Surgeons were cautioned to "use expedition but not hurry" during this procedure and they were experienced and skilled at carrying it out. If there was time – and there probably was not – they were also advised before "entering on any capital operation" to "encourage the patient (if he is sensible) by promising him, in the softest terms, to treat him tenderly and to finish with the utmost expedition." "Sensible" is the important word, because although medical men knew that the body of a patient about to undergo amputation should be "in a laxative state; and when pain puts it on the rack, immediate recourse must be had to the sovereign and almost divine powers of opium," it is unlikely Woodforde and Korb had enough opiates to fully anaesthetize their patients. British regulations provided four ounces of pure and sixteen ounces of diluted opium (either with alcohol or in paste) for every 250 men, but since the drug was in demand to treat the dysentery that was the bane of the army, it was in short supply and surgeons probably would have made use of the less palatable but necessary alternatives of alcohol, strong assistants, straps or ropes. Whichever method was used to keep the wounded man still, the tourniquets, knives, retractors, saws and needles in the surgeon's kit came into play as the procedure was carried out. Among the men who underwent amputation was Lieutenant Daniel Claus of the 49th Foot. The surgeons took his took leg off below the knee during the night of 11 November and afterward he was laid in a small room with nine wounded men of the 89th Foot.[30]

During the Napoleonic Wars, operating theatres after a battle resembled nothing so much as a busy butcher shop. When an operation was finished, the amputated limb was taken away, the table or "platform" was sluiced with water

Right
Facial wounds
The man on the left received a gunshot wound through both eyes and the one on the right through the cheek. Both lost their sight and sense of smell. (Watercolour by Surgeon Charles Bell, courtesy Parks Canada)

Left
Round shot wound
This man's left arm was carried away by round shot. Eleven days later there was no bleeding and the wound was healing well. (Watercolour by Surgeon Charles Bell, courtesy Parks Canada)

and a sponge and the next unfortunate was lifted onto it amid the sobs, entreaties and screams of his fellow sufferers. "In regard to the wounded," surgeons were counselled to "act in all respects as if you were entirely unaffected by their groans and complaints, but at the same time" to "behave with such caution, as not to proceed rashly or cruelly, and be careful to avoid unnecessary pain." Given the sheer numbers of wounded, the absence of effective anaesthesia, and the primitive state of their procedures, the surgeons must have caused a great deal of pain and must have known they did.

Once the wounded man had received his initial examination and treatment and his wounds were dressed, period medical thought insisted he be bled: "It will be advisable to open a vein immediately, and take from the arm a very large quantity, and to repeat bleeding, as circumstances may require, the second, and even the third day." Barbaric as this may sound, bleeding was a widespread practice in the early 19th century, for "repeated bleedings in the beginning draw after them many advantages; they generally prevent, and always lessen, any feverish attacks." If the patient was still alive the day after initial treatment, the second great tenet of medical thought was put into practice – "purging" by means of emetics or laxatives, as it was regarded as necessary "that the body should by all means be open." Between repeated bleedings and purgings, the convalescent's dressings would be changed (as the milk and bread poultices quickly became foul) and his wounds washed with vitriol, a well-diluted sulphate mixture, which though it caused blistering and pain, kept the wounds clean.

The British and Canadian wounded, and those Americans who were captured, received treatment but some wounded Americans received no care at all. One of the most outrageous results of the battle of Crysler's Farm was the fate of forty-six American soldiers, possibly the most seriously wounded of those evacuated from the battlefield, who were rowed across the St. Lawrence to the United States on 11 November and simply "thrown into a house and there left without further care" and not "even a blanket to cover them" when the army retreated down the river. Appalled local civilians did what they could and were overjoyed when three army surgeons, travelling overland to join their units, unexpectedly arrived on the scene. Unfortunately, these officers "swore they would not trouble themselves with them, because they did not belong to their Regiments, and left them without so much as looking at their wounds." "In the situation," a witness reported, the abandoned casualties "were left to welter in their own blood for 8 days, with no other assistance than could be given by a very few poor inhabitants" with very limited resources. More than a week after the battle two civilian doctors finally arrived "and spent three days in dressing their wounds," but "mortification [gangrene], in a number of instances, had extended to a dangerous point, and in others to be fatal, and vermin at pleasure ravaged their ghastly wounds."[31]

The wounded in British hands received better care. The great danger was gangrene, and although the incidence of classic gangrene was lower in North America than it was in Europe (possibly because many European farm fields were heavily manured with animal ordure) it was not unknown. When the surgeons amputated young Daniel Claus's leg above the knee in the week following the action, it was almost certainly an attempt to save him from gangrene. Some of the wounded died quickly, and this was probably merciful. Granny Hoople's rifleman lasted only twenty-four hours and was buried on her property – the American government later compensated her for her efforts. Lieutenant Guillaume de Lorimier of the Canadian Fencibles died on 12 November – his son, Guillaume-Henri, was born twenty-seven days later. Ensign Henry Armstrong of the same unit died the following day. Others lingered for weeks, including young Lieutenant William Smith, who lasted until 2 Decem-

Good Samaritan – Mary Whitmore Hoople (1787-1858)
Mary Whitmore Hoople learned her medical skills during a seven-year period with the Delaware nation and tried hard to save the life of an American rifleman badly wounded at Hoople's Creek on 10 November 1813. She was unsuccessful but the United States later compensated her for her efforts. (Courtesy Stormont, Dundas and Glengarry Historical Society)

ber. Daniel Claus lived for nearly a month after the battle, but expired after suffering his second amputation. His parents and sister, who came from the Niagara to nurse him, arrived too late to see him alive. Some indication of the mortality rate of the wounded is revealed by a return of the 89th Foot dated 24 December 1813, which divulges that of fifty-seven enlisted men of the unit wounded at the battle, eighteen or nearly one-third died in the six weeks following the action. The mortality rate for the other units of both armies would have been similar, if not worse in the case of the American army.[32]

Those still alive and able to be moved in the third week after the battle, were taken from the makeshift farmhouse hospitals to better locations at Prescott or Cornwall. Surgeon William Dunlop was in charge of the convalescents at Prescott and found one of his biggest problems was preventing the local Dutch and German civilians from spoiling his British and Canadian patients. Dunlop never "trusted them near the American wounded" because, having suffered grievously for supporting the Crown during the Revolutionary War, their "hatred of the Americans was deep rooted and hearty."[33] As directed by regulations, Dunlop placed his patients on the "low hospital diet" which consisted of a pint of "Milk-Porridge or Rice-Gruel" in the morning and evening, and weak meat broth with milk and bread pudding at midday. The theory was that such a regimen would discourage fevers but if surgery, bleeding, emetics, laxatives and infection had not already carried a man off, this diet would greatly assist him on his way. The civilians were quite rightly horrified and Dunlop had the greatest difficulty preventing "them cramming my patients with all manner of Dutch delicacies" as they were convinced that "unless you give de wounded man plenty to eat and drink it is quite certain he can never

Honest doctor – Surgeon William "Tiger" Dunlop, 89th Foot (1792-1848)
Dunlop cared for the convalescent wounded from the battle and was honest enough to admit that some recovered because of the remedies he employed or in spite of them. Dunlop settled in Canada after the war and wrote an intelligent and humorous account of his military experiences. (Archives of Ontario, S-17142)

get through."[34] Being a doctor, Dunlop knew better of course but he was at least an honest member of his profession. As he later admitted, "my patients gradually began to diminish – some died, and these I buried," while "some recovered by the remedies employed, or [in] spite of them."[35]

Most of Wilkinson's wounded, including Covington, Cumming and Myers, were on board the flotilla when the army ran the Long Sault in the morning of Friday, 12 November, after a cold night camped in a meadow on the American side of the river. In the late morning the flotilla rendezvoused at Barnhart's Island above Cornwall where, in Wilkinson's words, they joined "that excellent officer," Brigadier General Jacob Brown, who had crossed his two brigades from Cornwall earlier in the day.[36] There was no sign of the enemy and Wilkinson, determined to convert defeat into victory, issued a general order that the enemy had been "repulsed in the affair of yesterday." However, his troops were to hold themselves "ready for action at moment's notice – our safety, the honor of our arms, and the interest of the nation depend on the strict observance of this order." If flowery words had been bullets, James Wilkinson might well have conquered the world.[37]

Brown was not the only officer waiting on the island. Colonel Henry Atkinson had arrived from the Four Corners with Hampton's letter of 8 November telling Wilkinson of his decision to withdraw to Plattsburgh. Atkinson had first gone to St. Regis and was waiting there on the afternoon of 11 November when he heard the sound of artillery. Concluding that the British had caught up with the main army, he scribbled a note to this effect and sent it to Hampton. The next day, when he saw the flotilla descending the river, Atkinson

279

crossed to deliver his message. Wilkinson took it very badly. One of his aides remembered that he talked about immediately resigning his command, but bearing up, convened a council of war of his senior officers – Lewis, Boyd, Brown, Swartout, Porter, Macomb, Walbach and Swift – to decide whether, given Hampton's decision and the state of the provisions, the campaign should continue. An inventory revealed that only nine days' rations of bread and six of meat remained, and the decision was made that "the attack on Montreal should be abandoned for the present season and the army, then near Cornwall, should be immediately crossed to the American shore for taking up winter quarters."[38] This decision, Swift later wrote, was made because of "want of bread, want of meat, want of Hampton's division, and the belief that the enemy force was equal, if not greater than our own."[39] It was not a popular decision with the more junior members of the council, who, Swift commented, discussed the matter among themselves and felt that "with Brown as leader, no character would be lost in going on to Montreal."[40]

The American commander drafted a letter for Atkinson to take to Hampton in which he made it clear where the blame was going to fall. Wilkinson had always been a reluctant warrior, and Hampton's withdrawal gave him the perfect pretext to call the whole thing off while at the same time shifting responsibility. He told the South Carolinian that he lacked "*language to express my sorrow for your determination not to join the division under your command with the troops under my immediate orders.*"[41] Hampton's decision to withdraw to Lake Champlain defeated "the grand objects of the campaign in this quarter, which, before the receipt of your letter, were thought to be completely within our power, no suspicion being entertained that you would decline the junction directed."

Wilkinson's options for winter quarters were limited – he could not return to Sackets Harbor, and the only other choice was the nearby settlement of French Mills, New York. Preparations now began for the move to that place. The big problem was transporting the army's horses across the St. Lawrence, which if the scows were used as they had been at the White House four days previously, would take a long time. Against the advice of the cavalry officers, an attempt was made to swim the horses over, but it failed because of the current and the distance. The animals were therefore returned to the United States in forty batteaux, two or three in each craft, and that laborious task occupied the rest of the day and much of the following night.[42]

On the morning of Saturday, 13 November, Wilkinson informed his army in a general order that the campaign was at an end. They were "to embark without loss of time, yet are not to be hurried in leaving the Canadian shore," from which they had been "compelled to retire by the extraordinary, unexampled, and it appears unwarranted conduct" of Hampton in refusing to join the main army "agreeably to positive orders." Deprived of this reinforcement, Wilkinson felt "himself bound by a sense of regard to this meritorious corps, and of sacred duty to the United States, to spare the lives of brave men, and not to hazard the character or interest of the nation by an unequal conflict." With regret "and the deepest mortification," he therefore suspended "the attack on Montreal; but he assures the army that it is not abandoned."[43]

That morning, Leonard Covington died after more than thirty-six hours of agony from his stomach wound. In his lucid moments he took care to dispose of his possessions: his riding boots and best horse to his aide, Lieutenant Joseph Kean of the First Dragoons; his dirk to his son; his regulation sword and "his riding Horse, his dress sword, his mules, his watch & his purse" to his brother in Washington. Covington had earned the respect of the army and his was a death much regretted.[44]

Covington's body was on board the flotilla when it sailed late in the morning. The last boats had just left Barnhart's when Carr of the Fifteenth Infantry recorded that Canadian militia "appeared immediately." The flotilla crossed to the American bank and made a long and tedious passage eight miles down the St. Lawrence before entering the winding Salmon River and ascending it six miles to French Mills. It arrived in darkness and disembarked, and a somewhat exasperated Robert Carr of the Fifteenth Infantry recorded that orders were given for flotilla to "be scuttled and sunk and the troops build huts for the winter!!!"[45]

M orrison received reports of Wilkinson's movements from the militia at Cornwall. He was not able to further harass his opponents, since Wilkinson's hasty withdrawal to the United States the day of the battle had broken contact between the two forces and Morrison did not have strength enough to cross the river and attack. As he explained to Prevost, "the enemy's movements have been so rapid that, acting with the caution the disparity of the respective forces rendered necessary, has prevented our again engaging him."[46] On 13 November, his troops having taken care of the wounded and the dead, he continued down river. Jackson's three 6-pdr. guns were embarked on batteaux, as were some of the infantry, but the greater part of the little army set out on the King's highway for Cornwall. Lieutenant Henry Kersteman was supervising the embarkation of the artillery when he was killed by a careless private of the 89th Foot who accidentally fired his loaded musket while trying to use it to light his pipe. Jackson was appalled by this tragedy as was the senior

Bottled up – the Salmon River at Fort Covington, New York (French Mills)
On 13 November 1813, Wilkinson took his army six miles up the Salmon River to winter at the isolated settlement of French Mills. British officers rejoiced because he had now nicely bottled himself up in this narrow river and they would have no problem stopping him from trying to renew the offensive against Montreal. (Photograph by Dianne Graves)

artillery officer in North America, Major General George Glasgow, who noted that Kersteman "left a young widow in great distress in Kingston where he was lately married."[47]

On 14 November Morrison sent militia Captain William Gilkison under a flag of truce to French Mills. The two American officers, Captain White Young and Charles Bruce, whom young Sam Adams had bagged on the morning of the battle, had violated their parole and escaped to the United States while being escorted to Prescott. Morrison wanted them back and took the opportunity in the letter to broach the subject of the looting of "the property of the peaceful and unoffending Inhabitants" of Upper Canada "which had marked the progress of the American army during [and here was a nice turn of phrase] its *short continuance* in this Province."[48] Wilkinson replied he would investigate the circumstances of Young and Bruce, and assuring the British officers that looting was abhorrent to both the United States and its army, he enclosed a copy of his general order of 4 November in which he had warned his troops that "marauding is punishable by death" and threatening heavy punishment for "the first person who shall be detected in plundering an inhabitant of

Canada of the smallest article of property."[49] Harvey informed Prevost that he considered this a pledge by the American government to "make good" the property losses of Canadian civilians, but in this he was wrong, as it would be the Crown who would provide compensation and it would not be paid until more than a decade after the war.[50]

Mulcaster's gunboats and the batteaux ran the Sault on 15 November and joined the infantry at Cornwall. Jackson immediately undertook a reconnaissance by boat and found the Americans had nicely bottled themselves up, since the mouth of the Salmon River was "little more than twenty yards wide, so that their boats must come down singly" and well-positioned artillery would be "able to prevent their coming out."[51] As Harvey reported to Prevost, although the Americans were spreading the rumour they were going to renew the offensive, it was his belief that "whatever desire the Generals of the American armies may feel to persevere" in an attack on Montreal, "so little disposed will they find their troops to second their and Mr. Madison's grand views, that they will find themselves deserted by the army, which will disperse if not suffered to *go home*."[52]

Morrison, Harvey, Jackson and other senior British officers fully expected Prevost to launch an attack to drive the enemy from French Mills since the American presence there in close proximity to the St. Lawrence might cause future problems. Harvey suggested to the British commander-in-chief that an attack with the large force gathered for the defence of Montreal "from your side" would permanently end American aspirations against that city.[53] For his part, Mulcaster was confident that a force of only eight hundred men could destroy the American camp and scatter Wilkinson's army. However, the cautious Prevost did not issue the order and, in Jackson's opinion, thus lost "the most favourable opportunity of destroying that [Wilkinson's] army he is ever likely to have."[54] This failure to follow up success was disappointing to Jackson and other officers who were "much annoyed that Sir George Prevost did not reinforce us and let us immediately attack the Americans, and at the same time push on from the Chateguay [sic] frontier, by which we should have had them between two fires."[55] Even Lord Bathurst could see the danger on the inaccurate maps he used to follow the course of operations in North America and warned Prevost that it would "be prejudicial to your future operations, if Genl. Wilkinson has been allowed to establish himself" near the St. Lawrence.[56] But Prevost was content with having repelled the invasion and could not bring himself to order an attack which might result in heavy casualties although the potential result justified the risk.[57]

Throughout the Canadas there was universal rejoicing when news was received of the victory at Crysler's Farm. In Kingston, the *Gazette* went to press on 12 November with the comment that "we have heard nothing of the progress of the American army since its departure from Johnstown," but early the next day Morrison's hastily-scribbled note written at the close of the action arrived and was set in print with the banner: "POSTSCRIPT HIGHLY IMPORTANT."[58] The following day, de Rottenburg issued a general order containing the full contents of Morrison's official dispatch, expressing the "highest satisfaction in announcing this glorious event" and praising Morrison's troops who had "displayed the true spirit of British soldiers, which can never fail of asserting its superiority over the enemy whenever he has the temerity to risque a trial."[59] At Prescott, Pearson finally relaxed the standing order issued nearly eight months before requiring the soldiers of the garrison to sleep in their clothes ready to repel an attack – they were now "permitted to undress themselves and go to bed except one third of each Regiment or detachment who are to lie down with their accoutrements."[60]

Word of the triumph reached Montreal late on 13 November, and the city, noted Lieutenant Christopher Hagerman, was greatly "relieved from much anxiety occasioned by the *imposing puffs* of the enemy which *appeared* to *threaten* their existence."[61] Prevost issued a general order "to be publicly read at the head of every regiment of regular troops and battalion of militia" in both provinces celebrating Morrison's "daring little band" but giving few details of the action.[62] At Quebec City, his eighteen-year-old daughter, Anne Elinor, recorded that "sad and most anxious" were the days between 9 November when she and her mother learned that the Americans had passed Prescott, and 15 November, when they "had the happiness of hearing that the Enemy had been defeated by Colonel Morrison!" It was an exciting moment:

> Well do I remember that day. Mrs. Brenton and her daughter dined with us. Just after the cloth was removed an unusually loud ringing of the door bell startled us all – I ran into the passage and met Mr. Molson, the proprietor of the Steamboat with a packet of letters in his hand, and heard the joyful news "Colonel Morrison has beaten the Americans and taken 400 prisoners!" This brilliant affair put us in high spirits and seemed almost to put an end to anxiety.[63]

The threat of invasion having ended, Prevost released the militia of Lower Canada to their homes on 17 November. He praised them for "the loyalty and zeal they have manifested at the prospect of encountering the Enemy." Although the American offensive had been checked by "the bravery and discipline of His Majesty's Troops in the Upper Province" and the United States had been frustrated in its intention of taking Montreal, the British commander-in-chief expressed his confidence that, had the enemy "been able to reach it, whatever might have been his force, he would have met with that steady and determined resistance from the Militia" of Lower Canada "which would have terminated this third attempt for its Invasion like those which preceded it, in defeat and disgrace."[64]

This was intended to bolster the spirits of the militia, but if Wilkinson had managed to get as far as Montreal in November 1813, he would have encountered a sizeable force of regular troops. By this time, not counting the 1,000 men under Morrison's command at Cornwall, Prevost had amassed near the city five battalions of Royal Marines and British and Canadian regulars, five battalions of Select Embodied Militia and nearly a full regiment of British and Canadian dragoons, a total of about 6,000 men, plentifully supported by field artillery manned by a company of Royal Artillery and two of Royal Marine Artillery. This was more than enough to ward off the less than 6,000 healthy with Wilkinson when he went into winter quarters at French Mills.[65]

Prevost could now relax, but he had some unfinished business. He was displeased with de Rottenburg and Yeo for ordering Morrison and Mulcaster to withdraw to Kingston. Not only did he inform them that he fully approved of Morrison and Mulcaster "not complying with the orders sent by the Commodore & yourself," but he tore a strip off both officers, who had in his opinion done "so little" to impede the American movements down the St. Lawrence.[66] This was bad enough, but when the British commander-in-chief learned de Rottenburg had published the full contents of Morrison's official report of the battle with details of troop strengths and movements, he erupted and issued a strongly-worded general order to the army in North America that publicly rebuked de Rottenburg because Morrison's report "could not be held by Major General de Rottenburg as a document at his disposal, but merely as a Report passing through his hands, in conformity with the usage of the Service."[67] De Rottenburg's days as the commander in Upper Canada and those of his subordinate, Major General John Vincent, were now cut short and early in December they were replaced by Lieutenant General Gordon Drummond and Major General Phineas Riall respectively, younger and more aggressive officers. The German veteran had done his best but he was just too old for active service, and he received a subordinate command in the lower province, where he remained for the duration of the war. De Rottenburg at least had the consolation of his pretty Swiss wife, Julia, thirty years his junior and regarded by many as the most beautiful woman in Montreal.[68]

Lieutenant Colonel Joseph Morrison, on the other hand, garnered the victor's laurels. Prevost selected him to carry the official dispatches of his own triumph to the Prince Regent in London, which would not only reunite the young colonel with his family but guarantee him promotion. Unfortunately, Morrison arrived at Quebec City too late to embark but the commander-in-chief attached him to his own staff for several weeks to give him a rest.[69]

As Prevost's daughter, Anne Elinor, remembered, the social season in the capital of British North America was in full swirl, and Morrison was lionized:

On the 7th January [1814] a grand Ball and Supper were given by the Officers of the Garrison to my Father. I never thought so much of any ball in my life. I had been engaged to W.R. for the second set for a fortnight, and it had been arranged that I was to open the Ball with Colonel Morrison. Dear Colonel Morrison! – more interesting and agreeable than ever – our Victorious Hero! My third partner was to be the Hon. Major de Courcey – a rattling, amusing pleasant person – also married. They were just the trio I liked to dance with.[70]

The beautiful Christine "Rusty" Nairne, the reigning belle of society at Quebec City, did not appear at this affair, for she was in mourning for her brother, Thomas, killed at Crysler's Farm. Nairne's body was disinterred and John Sewell brought it to Quebec by sleigh. On a cold day in January 1814, Nairne was laid to his final rest in a funeral service attended by the officers of the garrison and many civilians.[71]

If the northern army thought its travails were over now that the campaign had ended, it soon learned otherwise. The little hamlet of French Mills, which derived its name from the *Canadiens* who had established a logging camp there in the 1790s to cut timber for the nearby Montreal market, was one of the most isolated settlements in the United States. A desolate place a scant two miles from the border, the Mills boasted an unfinished blockhouse, two sawmills, a tavern and a dozen or so houses. Lieutenant Reynold Kirby was not impressed – the "face of the country where we are now located with a prospect of remaining a long time is wild and uninhabited," he complained, and "situated directly upon the northern line of the U.S. & of course in the 45 degrees in north latitude."[72] Carr of the Fifteenth Infantry was no happier, since there was "no forage or provisions except the army supplies" and his regiment had only four days' supply of foodstuffs when it disembarked.[73] The two dragoon regiments and most of the artillery horses were sent to Malone, about ten miles

Regimental officer – Lieutenant Colonel Robert Carr, 15th Infantry
Shown here in old age, Robert Carr participated with his unit, part of Jacob Brown's 2nd Brigade, in the St. Lawrence campaign and recorded his experiences in a useful diary. (Benson Lossing, *Pictorial Field Book of the War of 1812*)

southeast, where there was forage available, but the many sick and wounded of the army remained at the Mills. Covington's body lay in state in the village tavern until it was buried with full military honours on 16 November and in his memory French Mills was renamed Fort Covington after the war.[74]

The troops were "ordered to make the utmost exertions to get under cover" with unit commanders "to superintend the erection of huts for their respective regiments."[75] Owing to the poor physical state of many of the men and the shortage of tools, it was a slow and tiring process. Carr's regiment was "destitute of tools," possessing only "axes like lead or pewter" and, as there were few horses and no oxen available, his men had to drag the trees they cut with such poor implements back to the campsite.[76] Moreover, the winter of 1813 came early and Kirby recorded on 16 November that the "weather is cold & the ice is forming in the [Salmon] river."[77] Jarvis Hanks remembered that "snow was soon four feet deep and the cold excessive," but his comrades of the Eleventh Infantry erected their tents, "built temporary fire-places of stones and clay mortar and made ourselves as comfortable as the case would admit."[78]

There were many officers at French Mills who did not want to experience the arctic pleasures of a Canadian winter. "Generals and subalterns wished to be excused," a disgusted Colonel Cromwell Pearce recalled, "before a log was cut, or a hut erected."[79] This was no idle complaint. Wilkinson put himself on the sick list four days after his arrival and moved to more comfortable quarters in Malone, but that was not far enough and, three weeks later, complaining to Armstrong that "repose and retirement from incessant avocations of duty, have become absolutely necessary to the restoration of my health, and the re-establishment of my constitution," asked permission to spend the winter in Albany, 150 miles to the south. As Wilkinson put it, "I am willing to die at my post but not when unable to draw my sword."[80] Permission was refused in Wilkinson's case but an ailing Morgan Lewis was allowed to withdraw to New York City. Boyd was the next senior general and Wilkinson planned for him to assume command at the Mills until he "discovered in the army, an insuperable

Regimental officer – Major Charles K. Gardner, 25th Infantry (1787-1869)
A highly intelligent and perceptive officer, Gardner raged about the inadequacies of his generals during the campaign in letters to his friends. He went on to better things, serving as Brown's chief of staff during the Niagara campaign of the following summer. (Benson Lossing, *Pictorial Field Book of the War of 1812*)

repugnance" to that officer, particularly on the part of Brown, who "swore to me," Wilkinson later commented, "that sooner than serve under General Boyd, he would resign."[81] Boyd was granted leave to get him out of the way and Brown assumed command at the Mills, which caused rejoicing because, as Gardner of the Twenty-Fifth Infantry commented, Brown's "acquaintance with this frontier rendered him peculiarly adequate to this command."[82] Gardner and many others in the northern army regarded the New York general as "more efficient than most of our generals in any situation," and had "the fullest confidence in his vigilance – and do not fear a surprize."

Boyd was followed on the road south by Robert Swartout and many field officers. "Every morning's [daily] order added to the list," remembered Pearce, who was one of the few regimental commanders to stay with his unit. The Pennsylvanian was particularly offended by the officers of one unit which "was left without even a Captain in aid in preparing quarters for the men." This unsubtle reference was to the Twentieth Infantry, commanded by Colonel Thomas Mann Randolph, which had only arrived on the frontier in early November. Randolph "obtained leave of absence on 'urgent business,'" Pearce commented, "having an eye, it was surmised, to promotion; but he was disappointed and soon resigned on account of the great exposure [he had] suffered] in the campaign."[83]

There was more to it than Pearce knew. The forty-two-year-old Randolph was the son-in-law of ex-president Thomas Jefferson and resided at Monticello, Jefferson's estate in Virginia. He had been commissioned a colonel directly from civilian life because, as Madison informed Jefferson, he "could do no less than give the public a chance of having the benefit" of his talents.[84] Thomas Randolph displayed few talents as a soldier. He set out with the Twentieth Infantry, 600 strong, from Fredericksburg, Virginia, in early August 1813, but by the time he reached Grenadier Island on 3 November, his unit was down to 230 men. After just fifteen days of active service, during which he participated in two minor actions on 7 and 10 November, Randolph applied for leave; his health was suffering and, because of his "restless, unquiet, and impatient nature," he abhorred the thought of inactivity.[85] Wilkinson furloughed Randolph on the condition that he, as the commanding general wrote to Armstrong, "having been a Spectator of my conduct" during the campaign would give a favourable account of it to the secretary of war.[86] When Randolph arrived in Washington in mid-December, Madison offered him the post of federal collector of revenue in his own congressional district and, although he assured the president that "the conquest of Canada" was still his "favourite object," Randolph accepted the position, which came with an annual salary of $4,000 – nearly twice that of a major general.[87]

Another scion of a prominent family who received permission to depart was Major Henry Lee, one of Wilkinson's aides. The son of General Henry ("Light Horse Harry") Lee of Revolutionary War fame, this officer had also been commissioned a major from civilian life in April 1813, and his only military experience had come during the recent campaign. Wilkinson directed Lee to visit the secretary of war on his way south to plead the case he was starting to build against Hampton – a task that Lee faithfully performed before continuing on to his estate, "Stratford," near Fredericksburg.

The northern army was better off without such well-connected dilettantes because it had problems enough – it was half-starved and disintegrating from sickness. On 17 November Carr recorded that the provisions "will only hold out a few days more," and although Wilkinson ordered ninety days rations to be forwarded as soon as possible, the condition of the roads, the distances to be covered and the rotten weather ensured that it would be some time before they arrived.[88] Starvation was avoided by putting the troops on half rations, small comfort for men forced to do hard physical labour in temperatures that, by mid-December, were well below zero Fahrenheit.[89]

The plight of the sick and wounded was terrible. Wilkinson estimated that he had 1,400 invalids, just under 20 per cent of his strength, when he arrived at French Mills and within a few weeks this number had increased to 2,000. For nearly six weeks, 450 of the worst cases were sheltered in tents in freezing temperatures that, one awful day, dropped to minus thirty degrees Fahrenheit. "Our sick are destitute of almost every necessity and are daily increasing," wrote Lieutenant Colonel James Miller of the Sixth Infantry to his wife in early December, "and I very much fear we shall have a distressed and destructive winter, but hope for better times."[90] Gardner of the Twenty-Fifth was convinced that the northern army was being "permitted to die a natural death" and "will I fear hardly survive the commencement of another campaign."[91]

Catastrophe was only averted when the very competent Surgeon James Mann arrived on 15 December to supervise Wilkinson's medical services. Mann immediately requisitioned "an academy, the arsenal and two private houses, to hospital purposes" in Malone and within ten days "these buildings, sufficiently capacious to accommodate 250 men, were made comfortable; in which each patient had a separate bed."[92] The wards "were warm, even during the utmost severity of cold" and the "sick admitted here, except such as were quite exhausted by disease, daily improved in their health, by the change from cold lodgings in tents, to more temperate houses." It was Mann's belief that the "health of men depends much on the officers immediately commanding companies." Brown took this advice to heart and shortly issued an order at French Mills directed at his company officers, who were to pay "more attention to the health and comfort of the soldier" as their "ranks must not be thinned in camps & quarters."[93] "The gallant soldier," Brown informed them, "must not perish ingloriously in filth and wretchedness, but the officer whose duty it is, will if possible, preserve him for his country and let him fall himself if necessary, as becomes a soldier, on the bed of *honour*."

The health of the army improved as, working in conjunction, Brown and Mann spared no effort to improve conditions. The winter huts were completed by the end of December, and the sick either returned to health or were removed to the hospital at Malone, while rations arrived in time to ward off starvation. Clothing was scarce, particularly warm clothing, and young Drummer Hanks, whose pants had been reduced to an immodest state, sacrificed one of his two blankets to make "a pair of pantaloons" as he "needed the latter article more than the former. Oh! what a pair of breeches!"[94]

By New Year's Eve, Brown felt secure enough to celebrate. Lieutenant Reynold Kirby (who was not invited) recorded on the first day of 1814 that "Genl. Brown had a *ball* last night at his quarters" and the "ladies were from the distance of 20 miles & might have amounted, I am told, to twenty." All went well until 3 A.M. on 1 January 1814, when the camp "was awakened by an alarm gun & the beat of the long roll" and "firing commenced on picket No. 1." The whole army "was under arms until morning" when it was discovered that the "alarm was occasioned by some citizens of the vicinity *firing in the New Year*."[95]

If Colonel Hercules Scott of the 103rd Regiment of Foot had had his way, Brown's men would have been suffering worse things than a few rounds loosed off by celebrating civilians. Scott had assumed command at Cornwall after Morrison was ordered to Quebec City, and his first step was to send the intrepid Reuben Sherwood across the St. Lawrence to examine the American camp at the Mills. Sherwood returned with a detailed map of the enemy's position and the information that the troops appeared to be sickly and half-starved. Forbidden by Prevost to mount an attack, Scott decided to engage in a little psychological warfare and had a small handbill printed which was dropped or posted in the vicinity of the Mills. This propaganda leaflet promised that "all American Soldiers who may wish to quit the unnatural war in which they are at present engaged will receive the arrears due to them by the American Government to the extent of five month's pay" and "no man shall be required to serve against his own country."[96] Although American historians have denied it had any effect, a fairly steady stream of deserters, exasperated with the conditions at French Mills, made their way to Cornwall and provided much useful information.[97]

Captain William Mulcaster of the Royal Navy decided to do more. His small flotilla of gunboats remained at Coteau du Lac farther down the St. Lawrence over the winter to counter the threat posed by the encampment at the Mills. The aggressive naval officer wanted to get at the 300 or so boats of Wilkinson's flotilla, which in fact had not been scuttled but were now frozen in the ice-bound Salmon River. Their distance from the St. Lawrence and the strength of the enemy position prevented Mulcaster from going up the Salmon with his vessels, so he decided "to have their destruction attempted by means of carcasses [incendiary devices] conveyed in a canoe." Midshipman John Harvey and Seaman George Burnet volunteered to make the attempt.[98]

A sudden thaw made the scheme feasible. Under cover of darkness, Harvey and Burnet paddled a canoe loaded with the deadly articles along the Salmon, gliding silently past unwatchful American pickets on the river banks and got in close to the Mills. Disembarking, they made their way to the flotilla frozen in the river banks, "placed a carcass in one of the gunboats" and were "on the point of firing it when the ice breaking about the boat unfortunately discovered them" to an American sentry. The alarm "being given they were compelled to relinquish the attempt" but were able to paddle safely back.[99]

The sequel to this exploit was even more amazing. Mulcaster learned from American deserters that "the enemy's magazine, situated in the middle of their encampment, might be blown up." Harvey and Burnet volunteered to make the attempt and, joined by Midshipman George Hawkesworth, set out "on this desperate service" being "supplied with combustible material." The trio had no problem in landing on the American bank and hid in the woods around French Mills, waiting for an opportunity "to effect their purpose [but] they found the magazine more strongly guarded than had been supposed." Harvey, "unwilling to relinquish the enterprise, went into the American camp in disguise, where he remained two days undiscovered" and "obtained correct information." Unfortunately the midshipman was betrayed to "General Brown, who would certainly have executed him but for the adroit manner in which he effected his escape, which can only be equalled by his previous determined resolution." The Americans, by now thoroughly alerted, tightened their security, discouraging future attempts, but Commodore Sir James Yeo was impressed by Midshipman Harvey's conduct and promptly promoted him lieutenant.[100]

The presence of a large camp at French Mills did not hinder the busy cross-border trade carried on by American civilians catering to the needs of the British forces in the Canadas. Thomas Gibbs Ridout, a military commissary at Cornwall during the winter of 1813-1814, remembered that the country around the village was "so excessively poor that our supplies are all drawn from the American side of the river."[101] But it was not a problem, Ridout remembered, since the Americans brought "droves of cattle from the interior under pretence of supplying the army at Salmon river [French Mills], and so are allowed to pass the guards, and at night cross them over to our side." In January 1814, Forsyth scoured the American shore of the river with his riflemen and burned all boats not under military guard but this did not put a stop to international commerce. A few months later, Surgeon William Dunlop witnessed a transaction between "Red George" Macdonell, then commanding at Cornwall, and a major of the Vermont militia, who sold the Scot some "fine critters" as "ever had hair on 'em." Money changed hands, wine was drunk and the American toasted Macdonell, whom he thought "a leetle the genteelest man to deal with ever I met with, and I'll tell all my friends how handsome you behaved to me." "They do say," the Vermonter concluded, "that it is wrong to supply an innimy and I think so too; but I don't call that man my innimy who buys what I have to sell, and gives a genteel price for it." And off he went.[102]

CHAPTER 14

"The fault is with the generals, not the men"

THE WINTER OF DISCONTENT, NOVEMBER 1813–FEBRUARY 1814

Why, soldiers, why,
Should we be melancholy, boys?
Why, soldiers, why?
Whose business 'tis to die!
What, sighing? Fie!
Damn fear, drink on, be jolly, boys!
'Tis he, you or I,
Cold, hot, wet or dry,
We're always bound to follow, boys,
And scorn to fly.

'Tis but in vain,
(I mean not to upbraid you, boys),
'Tis but in vain
For soldiers to complain.
Should next campaign
Send us to Him who made us, boys,
We're free from pain.
But should we remain,
A bottle and kind landlady
Cures all again.[1]

Major General James Wilkinson was not only concerned about the state of his army; he also had other, more pressing, problems. There was the question of responsibility for the failure of the campaign, and from the time he landed at French Mills to the following spring he jockeyed with Armstrong and Hampton to elude it. Armstrong, however, was no slouch at this game, and he was early in play. In the first week of November he reached Albany and wrote Wilkinson on the 15th that he would "at this place await the result of your pending movements, and hope soon to hear from you."[2] Three days later, Armstrong communicated that he had learned the garrisons of Kingston and Prescott had overtaken Wilkinson on the St. Lawrence and had handled him "roughly." The secretary placed no credence in such an obvious falsehood, for Wilkinson must have moved too swiftly for such a thing to have happened and even if it had the secretary knew if Wilkinson found a "corps capable of disturbing the main action of the campaign," he would "have taken effectual measures to beat and destroy it."[3] This being the case, "the garrisons of Kingston and Prescott destroyed" meant that Upper Canada "was won," even if Montreal was lost. Sometimes in John Armstrong's fertile but feverish mind, wish, intent and event got tangled up.

During November, the secretary had corresponded more frequently with Hampton, who as soon as he arrived at Plattsburgh got busy justifying his withdrawal to Lake Champlain. He sent Armstrong copies of Wilkinson's letter of 6 November and his response of 8 November and telling him that his division was "dropping off by fatigue and sickness to a most alarming rate" and "assuming their *native rawness.*"[4] Hampton followed this up with a vindication of his refusal to join the main army, a decision only made "under the *impression of absolute necessity,*" because "General Wilkinson had no spare transportation for us and the junction would have reduced the stock of provisions to eight or ten days for the whole." Although Hampton promised "all that is possible" would be attempted, he believed the "disposition of the enemy's force must determine our success."[5]

On the day of the battle of Crysler's Farm, Colonel Henry Atkinson had scribbled a hasty note from St. Regis to Hampton stating that the main army had been overtaken by the British and that a heavy action was being fought. "I beg you to receive this as news and not to be relied on," Atkinson added, but Hampton passed it on to Armstrong with a query as to his next step.[6] The secretary had this note in his hands on 15 November when he wrote Hampton that he was concerned about the "interruption any partial engagement may give to the main action of the campaign" and advised the general that the outcome of Atkinson's meeting with Wilkinson would "decide the character and extent of your operations."[7] If Wilkinson had been defeated, the secretary added, it was clear "that any movement below," that is, any movement on Hampton's part, "cannot safely be more than a feint." Hampton took these words as an approval for his withdrawal and was in a cocky mood when Atkinson arrived at Plattsburgh with Wilkinson's note of 12 November accusing him of defeating the "grand objects of the campaign." He passed it to Armstrong with the comment that "of the insinuations it contains, I shall say nothing," but on "so plain a case, and an attempt unworthy of the occasion, common sense will afford every explanation I could wish."[8] Hampton also informed the secretary that after making arrangements for placing his troops in winter quarters he would travel to Washington to offer his resignation personally to the president.[9]

A few days after he arrived at French Mills, Wilkinson moved to the attack. On 17 November he wrote Armstrong expressing "amazement and chagrin at the conduct" of Hampton as the "game was in view, and had he performed the junction directed, would have been ours in eight or ten days." Hampton's withdrawal had resulted in the "hopes and honour of the army" being "blasted." Wilkinson was also in a confident mood and advised Armstrong that "your military system requires thorough revision, and your military establishment great reform, before we can put to best advantage the natural force and courage of our countrymen." The commanding general did finally admit defeat at Crysler's Farm though when he added that "British officers have acknowledged our dauntless courage, but observed we were undisciplined and fought without order, and indeed the scenes of that day justify these observations."[10]

This letter was handed to Swift for delivery. Swift was also given an order for Hampton to immediately march his division back to the Four Corners and it was to be obeyed for, as Wilkinson assured Hampton, "the safety of this corps, the honor of our arms and the important interests of the nation depend on the prompt and punctual exhibition of this order, no doubt can be entertained that it will be strictly charged."[11] Having delivered the order, Swift was to "communicate directly" with Wilkinson "the result, to which you will be pleased to add freely and confidentially every observation material to the service which you may have made."[12] That being done, the engineer was to continue to Albany to deliver the letter to the secretary and explain certain things which Wilkinson deemed "improper to commit to paper." Finally, Swift was to proceed to Washington "to learn what may be my destiny."

Riding hard, Swift reached Plattsburgh late in the evening of 19 November, got Hampton out of bed and handed him Wilkinson's order to march. Although Swift said nothing about the condition in which he found Hampton, word spread rapidly through the northern army that Hampton was drunk. However, if so, he sobered up quickly enough when he read the order and heard what Swift had to say, for as the engineer reported to Wilkinson, Hampton was ready to obey "with an army out of spirits, not more than one thousand six hundred effectives." It was never Hampton's intention, Swift told Wilkinson, to disobey any order of yours, and that his non-junction was in consequence of the opinion that he was required to act upon your letter of 6th; and from General Armstrong's letter to him [of 15 November], which he showed me, there was no intimation of joining you above Chateaugay. General Hampton pledges his sacred honor to me that it was his desire to have formed a junction with you. The last letter of General Armstrong to General Hampton has this expression in it: "The enemy have been able to overtake General Wilkinson and detain him as high up the river as Cornwall; it is evident that the movement below cannot safely be more than a feint.[13]

Having seen the conditions of the roads between French Mills and Plattsburgh, Swift did not favour moving Hampton's division from Plattsburgh since a force should "be left here to guard this pass and depot." It would be better to move the main army to Plattsburgh, "making General Hampton to build huts for your troops." A new offensive could be launched against Montreal in the spring, but for the time being Swift advised holding Plattsburgh, Fort George and Sackets Harbor "with strong garrisons till our army has time to be reformed." The engineer then left for Albany to carry out the second part of his mission.[14]

Hampton was shaken by this visit, as well he should have been. Suspecting rightly that Wilkinson had worse things in store, he opted to leave for the south before his troops had completed their winter quarters, and on 24 November crossed Lake Champlain to Burlington, pausing just long enough to write a note to turn over command to Izard. "Before going away," Izard recorded, Hampton also "granted leave of absence to almost every efficient officer of the division."[15] Since Izard was too ill to assume his duties, he released Colonel Robert Purdy from arrest and gave the division over to him. Purdy, sensing a favourable shift of the wind, immediately wrote a long letter to Wilkinson complaining about Hampton which ended with the accusation that the general was a heavy drinker. Be that as it may, there were no tears in his soldiers' eyes the day Wade Hampton left them – Private Charles Fairbanks of the New Hampshire Volunteers, alluding to both his general's business concerns and his private pleasures, recorded that "General Hampton left us with no barracks and nothing but tents to keep us from freezing" and "went to Washington, gave up his commission, then went home and commenced making whiskey." "I think he would be apt to do better at that," Fairbanks concluded, "than commanding an army, and that it were much better for the government and soldiers that he should."[16]

But Wilkinson was not yet finished with the South Carolinian. On 24 November, having received Swift's report, he wrote Armstrong that, with "respect to the unfortunate issue of the campaign, I disclaim the shadow of blame because I know I have done my duty and more than my duty and so do those with whom I have acted." It was to "*General Hampton's outrage of every principle of subordination and discipline may be ascribed the failure of the expedition*" and Wilkinson had only refrained from arresting that officer because he desired that the order for the arrest "should proceed from the highest authority" – from Armstrong himself.[17]

Wilkinson did not wait for a reply, but two days later he sent Major Ninian Pinckney to Plattsburgh with an order for Hampton to consider himself under arrest for disobedience of orders in "declining to join the corps under my immediate direction" whereby Wilkinson "was compelled ... to abandon the enterprize destined against Montreal."[18] Fearing that Hampton might have left for the south, Wilkinson added, "Should this find you elsewhere than at Plattsburgh, you are to return to that place forthwith and abide your trial, under the penalty of a breach of arrest; and should you have left the district of my command, it will make an additional charge against you." It was too late. When Pinckney rode into Plattsburgh, the prey was gone and the aide "despaired of accosting him & therefore forwarded the arrest" order to Washington.[19]

Hampton's escape infuriated Wilkinson. When he learned his archenemy had granted wholesale leave at Plattsburgh, leaving "barely enough" officers to perform routine duty, that the division's winter quarters had not been prepared and that its logistical arrangements were in such a mess that piles of public stores were scattered along the streets of Plattsburgh, he went for the jugular.[20] Complaining to Armstrong about such "pernicious and unwarrantable conduct," he refrained from charging Hampton "with traitorous designs" but acidly commented that "in any other government, a military officer who first defeated the object of a campaign by disobedience of orders," and then "furloughed all the efficient officers of the division he commanded on a national frontier, in the vicinity of an enemy, would incur heavy penalties."[21]

Having disposed of his rival, things were looking good for Wilkinson, and it now only remained to see where he stood with Armstrong. Joseph Swift, who reached Albany on 25 November, was the first of at least four emissaries Wilkinson sent to the secretary to report back. Swift found the secretary the guest of Governor Daniel D. Tompkins, along with Major General William H. Harrison, the commander of the northwestern army. As Swift recalled, Armstrong read the despatches and then enquired into the condition of the army and Swift "gave him in detail the condition in which I had left them, and of the movements on the St. Lawrence." Armstrong "attributed the result [of the campaign] to the negligence of both generals," but the tactful engineer felt he "could not with propriety" disclose this to Wilkinson and simply informed his superior that Armstrong was "dissatisfied" with both men.[22]

Another emissary, Major Henry Lee, had a long interview with the secretary at New York on 13 December. According to Lee, Armstrong did not expect Wilkinson "to prosecute the expedition against Montreal, without the junction or real co-operation of General Hampton" but that Wilkinson's order to Hampton dated 6 November could "be interpreted as intending to give General Hampton discretion, both as to the point of junction and the mode of co-operation." Be that as it may, Lee continued, when Hampton withdrew "from the sphere of hostility, abandoned his own provisions, and when his men were described by himself, as worn out by toilsome and comfortless marches, retired by a route less practicable and more extended than the one which led to St. Regis; and occupied such a position as rendered the co-operation impossible," it was the secretary's opinion that the South Carolinian "had behaved with absurdity and disobedience, ignorance and obstinacy."[23]

Armstrong assured Lee he had never given Hampton an independent command but had only "observed" to the South Carolinian "by way of removing his uneasiness on the subject," that Wilkinson "would not interfere with the interior arrangement or organization of his corps." Lee also reported that the secretary "remarked that the heavens, rather than the strong holds and prowess of the enemy, had, before the defection of Hampton, foiled or defeated our enterprise; that the storms of October were our conquerors; and that to them it was not disgraceful to yield." All in all, Lee continued, Armstrong left him with the feeling that the secretary "was satisfied with your conduct, and friendly to your person."

After reading Lee's letter, Wilkinson must have felt relieved. He had failed to take Montreal, but his career, which had come perilously close to foundering over the last four months, looked to be safe. What he did not realize was that Armstrong was saying different things to different people – two weeks before Lee talked to the secretary, Armstrong had told Colonel Henry Atkinson of Hampton's staff that he "attached blame to General Wilkinson" and was "perfectly satisfied with the conduct of General Hampton."[24]

While Armstrong, Wilkinson and Hampton tried to shift or evade responsibility for the failure, the morale of the northern army hit rock bottom. It was both ashamed and angered by the results of an operation that one American historian has called "an outrage upon reason and common sense, and justly entitled to the odium which has been attached to it and its imbecile commander" because "it forms one of the darkest pages of American history."[25] Those words were written forty years after the event – in the winter of 1813-1814 feelings were much stronger, and they were well expressed by Brigadier General Jacob Brown, who was "somewhat ashamed to be even heard from – not that I am conscious of having disgraced myself but from a conviction that the events of this Campaign are most disgraceful to the Army and Country." Brown would have much preferred "the Glory which Col. Morrison and his gallant *little Band* so fairly earned on Christlers [sic] Field to all the honor that could be obtained by the conquest of a kingdom in the bungling and indecisive manner in which we moved."[26]

There was widespread anger at those responsible for the defeat. "The St. Lawrence campaign is at an end," one American remarked, "and this is their 'Grand Plans' that would confound every European. What stupid asses they are."[27] In a letter to his wife Lieutenant Colonel James Miller echoed this blunt sentiment: "Never was there an army so completely cursed and damned with the miserable arrangements of stupid asses of Generals as ours."[28] Feelings in the republic ran so high over the winter, Surgeon Amasa Trowbridge of the Twenty-First Infantry recalled, that there was "constant bickering" between soldiers and civilians, and officers "met in the streets and cities" so much ridicule that they "travelled without uniform or epaulettes, ashamed of [their] profession."[29]

Because it was the custom of American newspapers to print official documents, the correspondence of Armstrong, Wilkinson and Hampton, planted by friends or enemies of the triumvirate, added fuel to the fires of discontent. "Wilkinson has been most assiduous in his exertions to forestall public opinion *versus* Hampton," a livid Major Charles Gardner complained in January 1814, "but the publication of the letters themselves, has completely knocked from under him the seed of his defense," and "he is boldly placed on a false ground, as he put up a false pretense to justify an act of open corruption – which is saying a great deal."[30] Like many in the northern army, Gardner believed Wilkinson had been drunk "during his descent of the St. Lawrence" and refused to accept his "excuse for intoxication" – that it was brought on "by tonic and mixtures." The behaviour of generals "unqualified even to command a company!" exasperated Colonel Edmund Gaines, who demanded changes: "Give us generals who will deign to be civil to each other & subordinate to the proper heads and act with a single view to the public weal."[31] Reflecting on the matter in later years, Colonel Winfield Scott rhetorically asked whether "a coxcomb" who "merely wants a splendid uniform to gratify his peacock vanity – be allowed unnecessarily to lose his men by hundreds, or by thousands, to surrender them in mass, or cause them to be beaten by inferior numbers; shall such imbeciles escape ignominious punishment?"[32] "In every such case," Scott concluded, "Humanity – as loudly as Justice – calls for death."

Junior officers were no less outraged. Lieutenant Joseph Hawley Dwight of the Thirteenth Infantry, commenting on the generals he had served under in 1813, acidly recorded "the blessed effects of having plow joggers for generals whose greatest merits consist in being warm partisans and supporting the administration right or wrong."[33] Lieutenant John M. O'Connor of the Third Artillery tried to explain the feelings of the army:

> To picture to you our grief and chagrin is impossible; we remember our bleeding Country, our unfortunate Army & the expectations of our friends; there were many eyes that wept over our misfortunes on that day. But it is weakness to despair and folly to aspire?; the Army had not disgraced itself by either Cowardice or any act unworthy of the brave. The fault is with the Generals not the men.[34]

The refrain that the problem lay with the senior officers and not their subordinates was common, but the professionals (and after eighteen months of war there was a growing number of officers in the northern army who had become exactly that) knew that what was required was not only better leaders but also better training. "Our arms," wrote Major Eleazer Wood of the engineers, "I consider to be at the lowest possible state of degradation."[35] Brown agreed: "Our troops are as yet very imperfectly trained," he observed, and are "better fitted for the defence of positions than for Field engagements."[36] He was confident, however, that a "few years of war" will "place us on high ground as a military people," but first there was much work to be done, as the American soldier would "continue to be disgraced until we have an Army moulded and formed upon some settled principals of Tactics and subjected to the severest discipline and this Army is blest with a sound and efficient Head."[37]

Many analyzed the campaign, among them Surgeon James Mann, who thought that it belonged "to officers versed in high military tacticks" to approve of a plan "of invading an enemy country, and entering it at its centre of population, during an inclement season of the year, and when its severity was rapidly progressing, with an army feeble, destitute of clothing and provisions."[38] Even if Wilkinson had reached Montreal, Mann noted, he would have faced a "far superior force" at a point "where resources could not be obtained."

One of the more balanced assessments came from the pen of Swift, a witness to many of the command decisions that had led to defeat. It was his opinion that

> the sojourn of General Armstrong on the frontier in the autumn had excited the jealousy of General Wilkinson. As the event is, both of the generals and Secretary would gladly attribute the failure to any cause than their respective errors. The immediate cause of the failure is the delay on the river; overtaking our army by the British on 11th November ended the campaign. My impression is that a junction of Wilkinson and Hampton was not intended, and by consequence an assault on Montreal was not purposed after October, if previously. One of the main causes of delay is bad bread, and its consequent bad health. Our chiefs were old, and from the date of the movement from Sackett's Harbor the two oldest, Wilkinson and Lewis, had not a day of sound health until winter.[39]

"If the army had been led by Brown," Swift concluded, "the end had been better than it was."

Ironically, their enemy was less critical. Canadian Robert Christie, who had an opportunity to talk to British veterans of Crysler's Farm, wrote in 1818 that the action was "in the estimates of military men, considered to be the handsomest affair during the late war, from the professional science displayed in the course of the action, by the adverse commanders."[40] During a postwar visit to Washington, Major John Baskerville Glegg of the 49th Foot was surprised to learn that Crysler's Farm was considered "disgraceful to the name and military reputation of America" – the officers of his own regiment regarded it as "a well contested day, and the fortunate result attributable solely to a very decided superiority of discipline and experience."[41] The entire autumn 1813 operation, Glegg continued, "derived much additional interest from having surmounted obstacles which had not been previously encountered" meaning "those arising from the good military disposition and gallantry, which were equally conspicuous on the part of the enemy."

Surgeon William Dunlop of the 89th Foot felt that the American army had been defeated because its troops were inferior "in drill and discipline, the great majority of them having been enlisted for a period too short to form a soldier." They had been forced to undertake "long and harassing marches through an unsettled country," were "exposed to fatigue and privation that was rapidly spreading disease among them" and "dispirited by defeat." Finally, there was a constantly increasing enemy hanging on their rear while in their front, was an opponent of equal strength." Even if the Americans had taken Montreal, it was his opinion that they could not have held it. "On the whole," Dunlop concluded, "any reflection on the conduct of General Wilkinson by those great military critics, the editors of American newspapers, to the contrary," that "in withdrawing with a comparatively unbroken army to his intrenchment on Salmon River, the American commander did the very wisest thing that under all the circumstances he could have done."[42]

Even that hardened warhorse, Lieutenant Colonel Thomas Pearson, rendered a compliment to his enemy during one of his rare gracious moments. "Ah!, Sir," he told an American officer who visited him under a flag of truce after the campaign ended, "your troops are the bravest men I have ever seen, but your officers know little of service."[43]

Secretary of War John Armstrong fancied he knew a lot about service – his problem was politics. His arrogant and abrupt manner had made him powerful enemies, particularly among the more genteel Virginians who composed most of Madison's cabinet and who knew the secretary of war despised them. Armstrong's most implacable enemy was Secretary of State James Monroe, who had refused the War Department the previous year in the expectation he would be appointed general-in-chief, which would have given him a springboard for the presidency. When Armstrong took over in February 1813, he put an end to Monroe's martial ambitions, and Monroe never forgave him. While the secretary was absent on the frontier in the autumn of 1813 and Madison was lying ill at his estate, Monroe assumed a watching brief over the War Department and took the opportunity to have all official correspondence rerouted through his office, an action that infuriated the president when he returned to Washington in early October. An unabashed Monroe told Madison he should get rid of Armstrong but the president, knowing Monroe had his own agenda, kept the secretary despite serious political problems caused by the failure of the recent campaign.[44]

For Madison, that failure could not have come at a worse time. Wellington and the armies of Russia, Austria and Prussia were poised on the borders of France and it appeared that the great war in Europe would shortly be over and Britain would be able to send major reinforcements to North America. Throughout 1813, the Royal Navy had gradually exerted its strength and by November the American coastline from New London, Connecticut, southward was under blockade. The British decision not to blockade the New England ports was a calculated move because New England was openly against the war and quite happy to trade with the enemy, completely ignoring a renewed embargo act passed by Congress. In November 1813 alone, one government report estimated that a group of Boston businessmen had exported thirty thousand barrels of flour to Halifax. As a result of the partial blockade, domestic prices drastically increased while customs revenue, the prime source of government income, declined to about a tenth of prewar levels. Having had difficulty obtaining a $16 million dollar loan to finance the war at the beginning of 1813, Madison now had to raise $45 million to keep the nation afloat in 1814. Some regions of the United States, which had never favoured the war, were openly antagonistic to the central government; on 10 November the governor of Vermont withdrew the state militia from federal service, asserting that in future it would only be used to defend Vermont and for no other purpose. Madison had placed great hopes on the Russian offer to mediate an end to hostilities but these were dashed when Britain flatly refused the Czar's initiative. As 1813 drew to a close, the United States was bordering on bankruptcy and dissolution.[45]

When Swift arrived in Washington in early December he found the president "much grieved by the failure of the campaign."[46] Swift remembered the main topic of conversation in the capital was "the selection of officers for the army as leaders," for "it was generally believed that had younger officers been placed in command of the armies of Wilkinson and Hampton, Montreal would have been taken." The other question of the hour was John Armstrong's continued absence from Washington, which one congressman noted was "all things considered a little singular."[47]

Armstrong was aware the knives were being honed for him and was in no rush to return to the capital. He lingered in New York until Christmas Eve, and during this time his major contribution to the war effort was to suggest that a modified form of conscription be introduced – a measure that found no favour in Congress and was changed to a paper augmentation in the size of the army, an increase in the pay of privates to ten from eight dollars a month and a doubling of the land bounty. Armstrong also worried about the repercussions from the recent campaign and managed to inveigle a New York congressman into demanding a government inquiry, which he hoped to be able to control because he held the documents.[48]

On 25 November 1813, the secretary sat down to summarize the year's accomplishments in a report for Congress. As might be expected, his arguments that the war was progressing well were somewhat hollow but Armstrong stressed that successful attacks had been made on York, and Forts Erie and George, and that the power of the Indian nations in the Northwest had been broken by Harrison, Detroit had been retaken and the United States controlled Lake Erie. As for the two major offensives against Kingston and Montreal, the secretary admitted failure but brightly assured his readers that even if the "special objects" had not been taken, these operations reflected "the highest honor on the discipline and prowess of our soldiery" and offer the "best assurance of eventual victory."[49]

Unfortunately for Armstrong, a few weeks after he penned this inflated document, word came of a new disaster in the north, this time on the Niagara frontier.

Before departing with his regiment to join Wilkinson, Winfield Scott had turned over Fort George to New York Brigadier General George McClure, who commanded a 1,500-strong brigade of militia. At first, things went well for McClure since the closest British troops were at Burlington Heights, forty miles to the west, but he began to experience problems with the civilians in his area when his poorly-disciplined militia engaged in wholesale looting. Although he assured the Canadians their lives and property would be protected if they remained "perfectly neutral," McClure publicly admitted some of his men had committed "illegal and unauthorized and forbidden pillage."[50] He was concerned, as he confessed to Armstrong, that unless he could get his levies under control their excesses might provoke British retaliation.[51]

The situation in the Niagara was made worse by the presence of Joseph Willcocks. An Anglo-Irishman, the forty-year-old Willcocks had arrived in Upper Canada in 1798 to begin a controversial career as a government official, member of the provincial Legislative Assembly and newspaper publisher. In early July 1813, Willcocks had offered to raise a force of Canadians to fight for the United States. The offer was accepted and Willcocks formed the "Canadian Volunteers," a unit of mounted men who served as guides, scouts and spies gathering intelligence about British troop dispositions from a network the newly minted Lieutenant Colonel Joseph Willcocks, United States Volunteers, organized among sympathizers in the civilian population.[52]

The situation continued to deteriorate in October. McClure's militia's three-month term of service would expire on 9 December, and all attempts to get them to re-enlist met with failure, while the local people, suffering from both his men and the Volunteers, were becoming restive. Things changed for the better at the end of the month when Major General William Henry Harrison arrived at Fort George from the west with 1,100 regulars. Harrison and McClure made plans to attack Burlington Heights, but before they could put them into effect Armstrong ordered Harrison to Sackets Harbor and on 15 November Harrison embarked his troops on Chauncey's squadron. Before leaving he advised McClure to "make use of the zeal, activity and local knowledge which Col. Wilcox" possessed to "counteract the machination of the enemy and ensure the confidence of our friends amongst the inhabitants."[53] In response, McClure appointed Joseph Willcocks "Police Officer" for the American-controlled part of the Niagara. "King Joe," as he was called, promptly unleashed a three-week reign of terror as his men arrested prominent local Canadians without cause.[54]

Despite appeals to Armstrong and New York Governor Daniel Tompkins, McClure had still received no reinforcements by the end of November. An anxious Willcocks also appealed to Armstrong for more troops, otherwise "the British will not only repossess it [Fort George] but will completely lay waste the opposite frontier as soon as slaying [sic] commences."[55] Guided by the Volunteers, McClure made a reconnaissance in force of Burlington Heights on 26 November and found the enemy to be in greater force than suspected. Meanwhile, his own strength steadily dwindled as his men finished their terms and departed; by 10 December, he had just two hundred men under command.[56]

McClure was in possession of a standing order from Armstrong that if the defence of Fort George rendered it necessary to destroy the neighbouring village of Newark, he was authorized "to apprise its inhabitants of this circumstance and invite them to remove themselves and their effects to some place of safety."[57] On 10 December he called a council of war of his senior officers, which took the somewhat surprising decision to abandon Fort George *but to burn* Newark. The residents were given a few hours' notice to leave their homes and then Willcocks (who had lived in Newark prior to the war) and his Volunteers put it to the torch. The burning houses provided a backdrop that night as McClure and Willcocks withdrew across the river to the United States.[58]

Lieutenant General Gordon Drummond, now commanding in Upper Canada, was coldly furious when he learned of the "disgraceful and inhuman act of burning the beautiful and flourishing village of Newark, by which upwards of an hundred families were left without a roof or fireside to shelter themselves from the most inclement weather, at the coldest season of the year."[59] He decided to retaliate and ordered his principal subordinate, Major General Phineas Riall, to initiate a campaign of fire and sword against the American side of the Niagara River.[60]

The first task was to take Fort Niagara and it would not be an easy one. This stronghold, well-sited on the American bank at the mouth of the river, was protected on two sides by water and defended on its landward side by a ditch and a rampart. The interior was dominated by a brace of two-storey redoubts and the thickly-walled mess building, miniature fortresses in their own right, and there were twenty-seven artillery pieces in position and a garrison of about four hundred men. Neither McClure nor Willcocks was at the post, which was under the charge of Captain Nathaniel Leonard, an officer with a very dubious reputation who had been left in command by Wilkinson despite a direct order from Armstrong to replace him with a more competent man. Nonetheless, Leonard and his officers had prepared a sound defensive plan and the garrison was in a constant state of alert in the days following McClure's withdrawal from Upper Canada.[61]

The job of taking Fort Niagara went to Colonel John Murray. A professional officer with twenty-two years of service, he was a good choice, and he assembled a force composed of 562 men from the 100th Foot and picked detachments from the 1st and 41st Foot plus a handful of gunners. Murray planned a surprise attack – his assault force, equipped with scaling ladders, would cross the Niagara River under cover of darkness, seal off and neutralize the outlying pickets, and then attack the fort at three separate points. Murray ordered his men not to load their muskets without orders and emphasized that "the bayonet is the weapon on which the success of the attack must depend."[62] It took some time to assemble the necessary boats, but by the late afternoon of 18 December all was ready at the staging-point, two miles up river from the fort.[63]

Every soldier waiting for darkness to fall that winter day knew he was about to undertake a very risky operation. Lieutenant Maurice Nowlan of the grenadier company of 100th Foot had more reason than most to be concerned, for he was deeply in love with Agathe, his young bride of eighteen months. On the day he was to cross the river, Nowlan wrote her he was about to storm the Fort Niagara and confessed it broke his "heart to write you now until the business is over, for I have great hopes to survive, tho' it will be [a] wicked business." Before he sealed the letter young officer added a brief, emotional postscript: "My Dearest jewel dont torture yourself with grief if you should chance to get this before I have time to write you again ... hope for the best, my only Heart."[64]

About midnight on a frosty winter evening, Murray's lead elements crossed the Niagara. We "were as silent as possible," remembered Private George Ferguson of the 100th Foot, "the oars were muffled – not a word uttered above a whisper, and that only in command."[65] They landed unobserved and moved north along the river road to the hamlet of Youngstown, where to their delight they discovered that because of the cold the American sentries had withdrawn into nearby houses. The assault force used their bayonets to make quick and quiet work of the Youngstown picket and then moved towards the fort.[66]

It was nearly 5 A.M., and they split into three groups that had no difficulty gaining entry into the fort. Elated by this success, the attackers made the bad

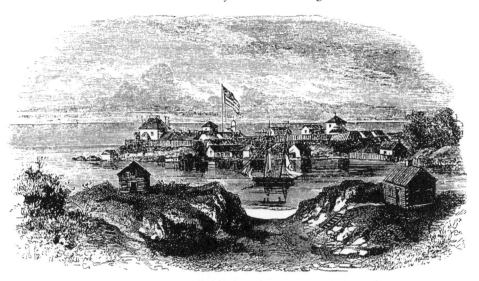

Little Gibraltar – Fort Niagara as seen from Fort George, c. 1860
Strategically located at the mouth of the Niagara River, Fort Niagara was a strong position and its loss to the British in December 1813 was the final event of the autumn campaign of 1813. (Benson Lossing, *Pictorial Field Book of the War of 1812*)

mistake of cheering. This roused the defenders, who were, Private Ferguson remembered, "confused and frightened, and commenced firing" from the interior buildings while their women "supposing we had Indians with us, were greatly frightened, and ran around shrieking most piteously."[67] The American fire "exasperated our men," Lieutenant Henry Driscoll of the 100th Foot recalled, and they "rushed wildly into every building, bayonetting every American they met," although many were "crying out for quarter."[68] When the officers realized what was happening, they tried to get their enraged troops under control.[69] In the middle of this bloodbath, Captain Nathaniel Leonard, the American commandant of the fort, rode up to the gate and was promptly put in the bag by the British sentry at the gate. Incredibly, despite the fact his post was on alert, he had elected to sleep at his house four miles away. By this time, Murray's officers had managed to check the rage of their men, and as first light appeared, the fighting ended.[70]

Fort Niagara now belonged to the Crown. Between sixty-five and eighty Americans, most killed with the bayonet, lay sprawled in the courtyard and in the blood-drenched rooms of the interior buildings; fourteen had been wounded and 354 taken prisoner. British losses were surprisingly light, six killed and five wounded, but among the dead was Lieutenant Maurice Nowlan of the 100th Foot, whose "body was found, the breast pierced by a deep bayonet wound, at the bottom of which were a musket ball and three buckshot."[71] Around him were the bodies of three Americans he had killed with either his pistol or his sword. The large American garrison flag, with its fifteen stars and fifteen stripes, was carefully folded and presented to Lieutenant General Drummond as a souvenir of the victory, and the Union Jack was run up over Fort Niagara. It would fly there until the end of the war.[72]

In the days and weeks that followed, Major General Phineas Riall exacted a massive retribution for the destruction of Newark. There were no enemy regulars to oppose him, and sweeping aside hastily-assembled forces of militia, he moved steadily south along the American side of the Niagara River destroying every village, hamlet and habitation in his path. On 29 December the British general took the villages of Black Rock and Buffalo and burned them to the ground except for one house in the latter place which was "left standing because there was a female in it badly wounded, who must have perished if she had been removed out into the snow."[73] By the first week of January 1814, the American side of the Niagara River, like Newark, was a collection of smoking ruins.[74]

This catastrophe, for which he bore no little responsibility, added to John Armstrong's problems. He was forced to order Wilkinson, as the senior general on the frontier, to formally disavow McClure's destruction of Newark to Prevost, which he did, stating that the "deed was abhorrent to every American feeling."[75] For his part, Prevost issued a lengthy proclamation two weeks after the razing of the Niagara stating that it was in retaliation for the "miseries which the unfortunate inhabitants of Newark had been made to suffer" but that his forces would refrain from such acts in the future unless further provoked by the United States.[76] In Washington, spirits lifted in late December when Madison received a letter from the British foreign secretary, Lord Castlereagh, offering direct negotiations to end the war. The offer was quickly accepted, and plans were made to send an American diplomatic team to meet with a British mission.[77]

In the meantime, Armstrong had to think about plans for the spring and he was determined that future operations would be carried out by younger and more aggressive generals. In January 1814 the secretary was able to gain promotion for eight officers who had performed well the previous autumn: Brigadier Generals Jacob Brown and George Izard were made major generals while Colonels Daniel Bissell, Edmund Gaines, Alexander Macomb, Eleazer Ripley, Winfield Scott and Joseph Swift became brigadier generals. At the same time Major Generals Henry Dearborn and Morgan Lewis and Brigadier Gen-

War fighter (1) – Major General Jacob Brown (1774-1828)
For the United States, one of the few positive results of the disastrous 1813 campaign was that it led to the promotion of a new generation of younger, more aggressive officers who had acquired their trade the hard way – in the field. Foremost among them was Jacob Brown, who had learned what not do in 1813 and put this knowledge to good use the following summer. He would end up as the most successful American general of the War of 1812. (Benson Lossing, *Pictorial Field Book of the War of 1812*)

eral John Boyd were shunted to posts where they could do limited damage while Robert Swartout was restricted to the quartermaster's department. These were positive steps, but Armstrong still had to deal with the leading players of the 1813 fiasco, Wilkinson and Hampton.

In January 1814 Congress investigated the conduct of the war on the northern frontier, but since the War Department provided most of the documentation, Armstrong was able to control the evidence and submitted edited versions of the relevant documents, and in at least one case, a document purporting to be an extract from his daily journal concerning the discussions held at Sackets Harbor on 4 October 1813, he may have totally fabricated evidence. As Wilkinson acidly remarked, "Whoever is well acquainted with General Armstrong's mental organization, will scarcely believe, that he ever descended to keep, a diary of diminutive incidents; yet no one can doubt *his capacity*, to form a *journal* to meet any occasion."[78] The final report, titled "Causes of the Failure of the Army on the Northern Frontier," was tabled on 2 February and although Armstrong hoped it would shift the blame onto Hampton and Wilkinson he did not emerge unscathed. Responsibility for the failure of the campaign, as one senator remarked, could not be determined, but what was clear was "how badly every operation was contrived, how wretchedly executed, and the jealousies, and insubordination of the officers."[79] Despite increasing pressure to get rid of Armstrong, Madison continued to support him, although by now even the president entertained serious doubts about the man's competence.[80]

Having survived Congressional scrutiny, Armstrong turned to the problem of the two generals. Hampton was disposed of quickly and quietly. The order

War fighter (2) – Colonel Winfield Scott (1786-1866)
A rising star in the northern army, Scott commanded the Second and Third Artillery Regiments during 1813. Promoted to brigadier general at the age of twenty-seven in early 1814, he was responsible for training Brown's Left Division which, during four months of bloody fighting in the Niagara, restored the reputation of the American soldier. (*Portfolio Magazine*, 1816)

for his arrest had been forwarded to Washington, but Armstrong did not act on it because on 31 December 1813 Hampton sent copies of all his official correspondence relating to the campaign to the War Department and requested the secretary add copies of his own letters and lay the whole before Madison. If the president thought there were grounds for a court martial, Hampton was prepared to undergo the process. If not, he requested an expression of confidence in writing from Madison and the withdrawal of Wilkinson's arrest order. Armstrong was reluctant to court martial Hampton because it might prove embarrassing to himself, and so the arrest order was simply invalidated and the South Carolinian allowed to retire without penalty.[81]

Wilkinson was a more troublesome case and the secretary left him in command on the northern frontier while he prepared the groundwork for his removal. Wilkinson spent much of December 1813 and January 1814 bombarding Armstrong with lengthy letters containing half-baked plans for offensives on Lake Champlain, Lake Ontario, the St. Lawrence or in the Niagara that were an embarrassment to read. While Wilkinson engaged in fantasy, Armstrong decided to break up the camp at French Mills and shift the troops there to Lake Champlain or Lake Ontario. At the end of January 1814, Brown was ordered to march two thousand men to Sackets Harbor, while Wilkinson took the rest east to Plattsburgh, and on 3 February the army at the Mills began preparing for the move, burning the boats of the flotilla and the recently completed winter huts. Those stores and provisions that could not be carried were either burned or dumped in the Salmon River although vast amounts seem to have been simply abandoned or half hidden in the surrounding forest. The sick, who still numbered over four hundred even at this late date, were loaded onto sleighs and sent to Burlington, where they were placed in hospitals organized

War fighter (3) – Lieutenant Colonel James Miller (1776-1851)
James Miller, shown here in the uniform of a brigadier general, commanded the Sixth Infantry during the St. Lawrence campaign – he thought most of his generals were "stupid asses" and he was right. On 25 July 1814, Miller commanded the Twenty-First Infantry when it met the British 89th Foot again at the battle of Lundy's Lane. This time the result was different. (Courtesy, Essex Institute, Salem, Neg. 150222)

by Surgeon Mann. On 9 February the northern army marched out of French Mills.[82]

Spies reported the activity to the British at Cornwall. Hercules Scott and Joseph Morrison (just returned from a pleasant spell of duty in Quebec City) sent the ubiquitous Sherwood across the river, and Sherwood confirmed the Americans were packing up. He had also picked up some more interesting news – the goods captured on the St. Lawrence in October, which had been taken to Madrid, New York, for safety were not going to be returned as stipulated in the agreement Morrison and Mulcaster had signed at Hamilton the day before Crysler's Farm. Instead the authorities were about to offer them for sale by auction at Madrid "for the benefit of the American government."[83]

Morrison decided to put in a pre-emptive bid. Acting on his orders, Sherwood crossed to Hamilton on the night of 6 February with a small detachment of thirty-three Royal Marines and Incorporated Militia. They surrounded the village, impressed all the sleighs and drivers they could find, and moved to Madrid, fourteen miles away. Sherwood took possession of the disputed goods, turned over to the locals what he could not transport and set out on the return trip. The Madrid militia, which gathered too late to apprehend his party, "rallied to pursue" until they came across "a quantity of shrub, a very agreeable mixed liquor" which the wily Canadian had left in a conspicuous place.[84] This had the "designed effect" because the pursuers lost cohesion and returned home in the best of moods. Sherwood reached the St. Lawrence early in the afternoon of 7 February, his detachment "decked out with ribbons and streamers of brilliant colours, which formed part of their capture." He rendezvoused with his boats waiting under the command of Lieutenant Peter Shaver of the Dundas militia and returned to Upper Canada, not having lost a man.[85]

This was only the beginning. Scott and Morrison waited until Wilkinson's troops had left French Mills, and then took a strong detachment of the Canadian Fencibles and 103rd Foot to the abandoned camp, recovered a great stock of usable provisions and completed the destruction of the flotilla. Each private in this expedition received thirteen shillings prize money, about two weeks' pay, when the materiel was bought by the Crown. Scott was back on 19 February to mount a major undertaking in conjunction with Pearson from Prescott. They set up a base camp at the Mills and raided Malone, Wilkinson's former headquarters, and Four Corners, and again large amounts of abandoned stores were loaded onto hastily impressed wagons and headed for the Mills and eventually British territory. The detachment from Prescott was furnished with sleighs and teams impressed on the Canadian side, and there was much jolliment on the return trip when the men following one vehicle burdened with a hogshead of whisky ran up behind it at frequent intervals and drew off some using their bayonets as drills. Hopefully, this was not the same sleigh that broke through the ice of the St. Lawrence during the return crossing – the men jumped to safety but the horses and vehicle disappeared into the dark water without a trace. On 24 February 1814 Scott made his last raid on Salmon River but the pickings by now were slim and this time the privates only received five shillings prize money.[86]

Colonels Joseph Morrison, Thomas Pearson and Hercules Scott were able to roam at will on the south bank of the St. Lawrence because the United States Army had withdrawn from the area. Their raids "created a general feeling of insecurity" on the American shore of the river since the citizens knew that "their lives and property were alike at the mercy of the British" and from this time until the end of the war they were careful to do nothing that "might provoke retaliation, or invite an unceremonious visit" from their northern neighbours. The autumn campaign of 1813, intended to cut the lifeline of Upper Canada and seize Montreal, had not only been a total and costly failure – it left the strategically important St. Lawrence valley under complete British domination.[87]

CHAPTER 15

"And gentle peace returning"

THE FATE OF GENERALS AND OF MEN

When wild war's deadly blast was blawn,
And gentle peace returning,
Wi' many a sweet babe fatherless,
And many a widow mourning, –
I left the lines and tented field,
Where long I'd been a lodger,
My humble knapsack all my wealth,
A poor but honest sodger.

For gold the merchant ploughs the main,
The farmer ploughs the manor;
But glory is the sodger's prize;
The sodger's wealth is honour;
The poor brave sodger ne'er despise
Nor count him as a stranger;
Remember he's his country's stay
In day and hour of danger.[1]

Major General James Wilkinson remained in command on the northern frontier until the spring of 1814. Through January and February, Armstrong collected evidence to be used against him and ordered Wilkinson to send copies of "all Councils of War which may have been held under your order or request during the late Campaign, noting particularly the question proposed, the numbers present, & the votes given by them respectively."[2] Wilkinson complied although he protested that these documents were his "personal property, being mere matters of advice required in aid of my own judgement."[3] Armstrong also discussed with Morgan Lewis the letter written by Wilkinson to that officer the previous June, which in the secretary's opinion contained "a sentiment" that generals "were choice spirits" and "ought not to be exposed to the same hazards, as younger officers."[4] With his keen nose for trouble, Wilkinson attempted to forestall the secretary by requesting a court martial, ostensibly because of "slanders and misrepresentations" in the press, but Armstrong put him off.[5] By 24 March 1814 the secretary was ready and directed Colonel Henry Atkinson to take an order relieving Wilkinson of command, while at the same time warning Izard to be prepared to convene a court of inquiry into Wilkinson's conduct.[6]

It was unfortunate Armstrong did not take these steps earlier, for James Wilkinson got one last opportunity to take the field. On 19 March 1814, four days before the secretary signed the order relieving him of command, he marched out of Plattsburgh with three brigades of infantry and eleven pieces of artillery to attack the British post at Lacolle Mill, just inside the Canadian border, as a necessary first step for an assault on the enemy position at Isle aux Noix. If this latter objective could be taken, it would serve as the base for a renewed offensive against Montreal. It might also just salvage Wilkinson's career.

From first to last this operation went wrong. Bad guides and lack of proper reconnaissance resulted in part of Wilkinson's force getting lost and delayed the attack; the British post was more heavily fortified and garrisoned than had been assumed; the heavy guns needed to batter down the stone walls of the mill became mired along almost impassable roads, and those guns that did arrive were too light to have any useful effect; last, the tactical handling of the infantry was confused and at no time was Wilkinson's vastly superior strength used to advantage. In sum, the "battle" of Lacolle Mill, 30 March 1814, had all the hallmarks of Wilkinson's generalship, including the wholesale contempt directed against him by a demoralized army marching back to Plattsburgh.

Wilkinson now knew the game was up. When the order came for his relief he assured Armstrong he would "not lose time in obeying" but felt he would be acting "perversely and without due regard to the interests of the country and Government should I fly off in a tangent," leaving his successor "hood-winked, in respect to any plan of defence, and without the aid of my feeble judgement and my experience."[7] Fortunately for the northern army, Izard replaced Wilkinson on 12 April and the disgraced general commenced a leisurely journey south, staying some time with Lewis in New York. Having corresponded with the secretary about his court of inquiry during his journey, Wilkinson finally arrived in Washington at the end of June to discover that Armstrong was prepared to up the ante and that the War Department was going to court martial him on matters arising out his tenure in command in the north. There were four charges, and they were serious: neglect of duty and unofficer-like conduct; drunkenness on duty; conduct unbecoming an officer and gentleman; and countenancing and encouraging disobedience of orders. Wilkinson wanted the trial to begin as soon as possible, but since he also rightfully wanted the members of the court to be senior officers he was forced to wait until January 1815 when such men were available.[8]

Those seven months in between were eventful. In July Brown crossed to the Canadian side of the Niagara and commenced the longest and bloodiest campaign of the war. In early August a British expedition landed in the Chesapeake, swept aside a ragged army of American regulars and militia at Bladensburg, captured Washington and burned the White House before being rebuffed at Baltimore in early September. This calamity led to the demise of John Armstrong, who, preoccupied by the northern frontier, had ignored increasingly obvious signs that the British were going to attack in the Chesapeake and resisted entreaties from federal and state officials to improve the defences of the capital. Universally despised, Armstrong resigned in September, just as American and British diplomats were meeting in the Dutch city of Ghent to discuss a peace treaty. Also that month, Sir George Prevost, with an army of 8,000 of Wellington's regulars which had been shifted across the Atlantic following the downfall of Napoleon the previous spring, launched a major offensive in the Lake Champlain area. Prevost swept all before him until he came to Plattsburgh, where, following the defeat of the British naval squadron on the lake on 11 September, he decided to withdraw to Lower Canada. On Christmas Eve 1814, the War of 1812 officially ended when the Treaty of Ghent, based on the *status quo ante bellum*, was signed, but word of it did not reach North America in time to prevent one last major engagement being fought in Louisiana on 8 January 1815.

Five days before this battle – Andrew Jackson's victory at New Orleans – Wilkinson's court martial convened at Utica, New York. The president was Major General Henry Dearborn, his predecessor in command of the northern army, and one of the senior members of the board was Morgan Lewis. Shortage of accommodation led the venue being changed to Troy, New York, where for two months the court listened to evidence from Lewis, Swartout, Boyd, Ripley, Eustis, Walbach, Bissell and many junior officers. The only witness openly hostile to Wilkinson was Swartout although most officers who testified were very guarded, neither damning nor praising the man. Not called as witnesses were a number of officers who were now leading lights in the army, such as Brown, Scott, Gaines, Macomb and Swift, although Macomb did submit a written deposition.

The prosecution made a determined effort to show that the letter Wilkinson had written to Lewis in June 1813 suggesting that a general's role in battle was to direct not to expose himself was proof that Wilkinson advised coward-ice. The defence quickly turned it back on them by producing evidence that the letter had been sent through Armstrong, who had made a copy of this pri-vate communication for his own purposes. The charge of drunkenness on duty, stemming from Wilkinson's erratic behaviour while under the influence of laudanum, was easily disproved.

It was clear from the testimony that Wilkinson was a poor general, but it was also clear that on many occasions between August and December 1813 Armstrong had been disloyal and less than truthful to both him and Hamp-ton. Most of the senior members of the board, particularly Dearborn and Lewis, had suffered from the devious and meandering thought-processes of the former secretary of war, and there appears to have been some sympathy for Wilkinson as it seemed he was being made a scapegoat. Given the events of the intervening time, particularly the victories won by the army in 1814, the whole sad business had become an embarrassing episode many felt was best forgotten, and on 21 March 1815 the board honourably acquitted the accused of all charges. Their verdict was approved by the president and James Wilkin-son, "the general who never won a battle but never lost a court martial," es-caped once more.

The St. Lawrence campaign, the largest military operation mounted by the United States during the War of 1812, was an unmitigated disaster. Not one of the objectives approved by Madison's cabinet in February and July 1813 – the Niagara, Kingston or Montreal – was achieved and, worse still, at its end the Niagara and the vital St. Lawrence were under British control, which had not been the case when the campaign started. For the United States, the only high points in an otherwise dismal year came in the west, where Detroit was retaken, the threat of the native peoples was eradicated and American war-ships were victorious on Lake Erie. But these successes were illusory, for they occurred in a secondary theatre, and although they accomplished one of the political goals that had prompted the declaration of war, the crushing of the native nations of the Northwest, they did not offset the failures in the main theatre, nor did they affect the overall strategical picture on the northern fron-tier. In 1813 the major military effort of the republic had been on the St. Law-rence against Montreal, an operation that represented the best opportunity for the United States to conquer the Canadas – and it had failed. The responsibil-ity for that failure lies on the shoulders of Wade Hampton, James Wilkinson, John Armstrong and James Madison.

The faults of Wilkinson and Hampton have been discussed in detail above and it is not necessary to repeat them. The contrast between them and their British counterparts is striking and the 1813 campaign serves well as a case study of the military profession at its best and worst. It furnishes clear examples of leadership or the lack thereof, at all levels; of aggression opposed to passivity; of the willing assumption of responsibility set against abdication of the same; of attention to detail contrasted with a complete disregard of it; of motivation versus apathy; and, above all, of the importance of properly preparing troops for battle. In terms of their incapacity, there was not much to choose between Wilkinson and Hampton, who were, it should be remembered, the two senior officers of the peacetime American army. On balance, perhaps Hampton was marginally better, since he at least put some energy into training his troops, but he also displayed an arrogant insubordination which culminated in a refusal to obey either the spirit or the letter of his orders.

Responsibility must increase the higher one ascends the chain of command and next we come to Secretary of War John Armstrong. Most American historians who have analyzed the disaster of 1813 place blame for the disaster equally on Wilkinson and Armstrong and less on Hampton, but in general accept Armstrong's excuse that he had "to execute other men's plans and fight with other men's weapons" to lessen his culpability.[9] In doing this, they ignore the fact that Armstrong had a golden opportunity to remove both Wilkinson and Hampton before the 1813 operation started: Hampton was only too eager to resign in August and if he had would most likely have been replaced by the more competent Izard, while Wilkinson's dismal state of health provided a useful pretext to replace him with either Lewis or Boyd, who might not have performed better but certainly would not have performed worse. In this respect, therefore, the secretary's defence is not valid.

John Armstrong was a curious man, a compound of ambition, vanity, intelligence and energy. His tenure in the War Department compared well with that of his predecessor (which is not saying much), but his weaknesses far outweighed his strengths. An armchair strategist with a head full of book learning cribbed from European military writers whose maxims on the conduct of war were of limited value in North America, it is significant he liked to be addressed as "general," notwithstanding he had only served six months in that rank as the commander of the defences of New York City. Armstrong had the intelligence to choose the correct strategical objectives – particularly Kingston – but once having selected the aim lacked the will to maintain it. Even worse, some of his actions in the autumn of 1813 were nothing short of reprehensible. Armstrong went north to concert his two feuding generals, but having decided that the operation was at an end before it had commenced, did not possess the moral courage to terminate it. Instead he issued an order concerning the construction of winter quarters that had disastrous effects yet did not see fit to inform his senior general of the existence of this order. Deciding that the business would end badly, he then abandoned the northern army with the excuse that Washington called, although it took him nearly two months to get back to the capital. John Armstrong was basically a politician who wanted very much to be a general, but though he coveted the crown of command he was always unwilling to carry the heavy cross that must go with it.

And finally we come to President James Madison. A decent man, a man of principles, Madison had reluctantly decided that war was the only course by which the United States could resolve its grievances with Britain. Unfortunately, decency and principles are not high on the list of attributes necessary for the head of state of a nation at war, and Madison never seems to have made the transition from peacetime to wartime president, even as war was understood in the early 19th century. Given the context in which Madison had to operate, his options in strategy and the appointment of senior officials and military officers were limited but he might have displayed more vigour in his direction of the war and certainly should have paid closer attention to the actions of his secretary of war. As a result of poor health, the president remained aloof from the actual conduct of operations through much of 1813, and he would have great cause to regret that detachment. In the White House as on the frontier, it can only be said that in the autumn of 1813 there had been a complete failure in command.

In discussing the responsibility of senior American leaders for the defeat, it is easy to overlook what that failure cost and who paid it. The officers and men of the northern army footed the bill for the actions of their superiors, and to illustrate what that means, consider the Thirteenth Infantry Regiment – Mordecai Myers's "snorters." The Thirteenth had fought well at York in April and Fort George in May, and at Stoney Creek in June, but from that time until it embarked for Sackets Harbor in September, it was cooped up in Fort George, where it suffered much from sickness. It took the Thirteenth nearly four weeks to get by small boat first to Henderson Harbor, and then to Grenadier Island, during which time its men (with no outer clothing), were exposed (on Lake Ontario and on the shore) to heavy rain and snowstorms. It required another three days in a blowing snowstorm for the regiment to reach French Creek on 3 November, and of the following eight days the Thirteenth spent five in boats and two on the Canadian bank of the St. Lawrence under intermittent rain, snow and sleet storms. It should be noted that during these water voyages in crowded transport, approximately one-fifth of the men in each boat were so stricken with dysentery that they were on the sick list while at least two-fifths had the ailment to a lesser extent. After lying on its arms without shelter through the wretched wet night of 10 November and suffering through the rain of the morning of 11 November while waiting for its generals to make up their minds, the Thirteenth fought at Crysler's Farm, where it was hastily committed to battle under a brigade commander who had never before led a formation of that size in action against a well-trained and well-positioned enemy. Another wet and miserable night followed the action, as did two more days in the boats until the Thirteenth arrived at French Mills. Here it was put on half rations and ordered to build winter huts without proper tools, which it did, in several feet of snow and temperatures well below zero Fahrenheit. After twelve weeks at French Mills, a camp so cold that sentries froze to death at their posts, the Thirteenth made a fifty-mile march over wretched roads to Lake Champlain under the ubiquitous intermittent snow, sleet and rain, only to participate in Wilkinson's bungled attack on Lacolle Mill in April 1814. This is the price of a failure in command.

Turning to the British side, if the senior commanders were not inspired, they were at least competent. The essentially cautious Sir George Prevost had an easier task than his American counterparts; he fought primarily on the defensive and his logistical problems, although difficult, were not nearly as daunting. The British commander-in-chief missed a golden opportunity when he refused to mount a major attack on French Mills in November 1813, for this might have brought an otherwise successful operation to an outstanding conclusion. His principal subordinates, Major Generals Francis de Rottenburg and John Vincent and Commodore Sir James Yeo of the navy, did not perform as well. Vincent's withdrawal from before Fort George in early October was unnecessary and premature, while de Rottenburg and Yeo were rightly chastized by Prevost for their lack of aggression.

Unfortunately for the United States, any shortcomings on the part of the British senior commanders were more than balanced by the talents of the six officers primarily responsible for the successful defence of the Canadas in the autumn of 1813. Lieutenant Colonels John Harvey, George Macdonell, Joseph Wanton Morrison, Thomas Pearson and Charles de Salaberry, and Captain William Howe Mulcaster of the Royal Navy, exhibited initiative, willingness to assume responsibility, tempered aggression, personal leadership and technical proficiency throughout the campaign. In particular, Morrison and Mulcaster's decision to disobey a direct order to break off the pursuit of Wilkinson's army, an order they knew to be wrong, led to the victory at Crysler's Farm that blighted Wilkinson's dwindling hopes of a positive conclusion to his offensive.

With an average age of thirty-two, these six men were young, but with an average of fifteen years in service also experienced, and it is worth noting that three of them, Pearson, Macdonell and de Salaberry, possessed the light infantry background that provided them with tactical skills important for operations in North America, while Pearson, Macdonell and Harvey were veterans of the Egyptian campaign of 1800-1801, the operation that marked the comeback of the British army after a long period of decline. In the final analysis, well trained troops commanded by professionals such as these officers defeated opponents who, as one American historian has rightly remarked, were very much "amateurs at arms."[10]

The northern army, however, would not remain amateurs much longer. The cry that the "fault is with the generals, not the men" was a legitimate grievance, and it was heard. One of the positive results of the campaign was that it swept away an entire stratum of incompetent senior officers. Of the nine generals and one colonel who held brigade or higher commands during the operation, only Izard and Brown ever again saw active service, the rest being shuffled off to rear areas or retired. They were replaced by younger and more aggressive general officers such as Macomb, Ripley, Scott and Swift, while below them a cadre of excellent unit officers was coming to prominence, men like Pearce, Forsyth, Upham, Harris and Myers to name but a few, who had acquired their knowledge the hard way.

Foremost among this new breed of "war fighters" was Major General Jacob Brown. The only senior officer to come out of the St. Lawrence campaign with an enhanced reputation and one of the few generals on the frontier who understood what was necessary to campaign in that difficult theatre, Brown's brief experience as a regular had at least taught him what not to do and had underscored the problems needing correction if the northern army was to be victorious. Brown had learned some hard lessons in the autumn of 1813 and, as future events would show, he learned them well. Before he took the field again, he would ensure that his officers not only knew but performed their duty, his troops were properly trained and firmly disciplined, and careful attention was paid to their health.

But all that lay ahead. In February 1814 Jacob Brown and the men under his command (including young Drummer Hanks in his blanket breeches), splashing west through the mud to Sackets Harbor, had no idea that in the summer to come they would restore the reputation of the American soldier.*

---

* The story of the operations of Major-General Jacob Brown and his division during the sanguinary Niagara campaign of 1814 is contained in *Where Right and Glory Lead! The Battle of Lundy's Lane, 1814*, the companion book to *Field of Glory*.

What became of them all? Starting with John Armstrong, he retired with ill-concealed bad grace to his estate at Red Hook, New York, in September 1814. The following year he tried but failed to win a federal senate seat and thereafter he took no part in public life but devoted himself to agricultural pursuits. In 1836 Armstrong published a vindication of his wartime career, *Notices of the War of 1812*, which is remarkable for its vitriolic attacks on almost every major figure in the army, including not only such infamous officers as Wilkinson and Hampton but also such victorious commanders as Jackson, Brown and Scott. A man of many positive qualities, which unfortunately did not balance his many faults, John Armstrong died in 1843 at the age of eighty-four.[11]

Major General James Wilkinson was dropped from the rolls of the army in 1815. The following year he published a hefty autobiography entitled *Memoirs of My Own Times*, three confused and ill-organized volumes of documents in which he tried to justify his lengthy and disreputable career. Like Armstrong, Wilkinson reserved his most vicious remarks for successful commanders like Brown and Scott who gained victories in 1814 and also for the former secretary of war whom he had come to hate. Wilkinson later moved to a plantation near New Orleans but in 1821 travelled to Mexico City to obtain a grant of land in Texas (then a Mexican possession) and promote other schemes including, curiously enough, representing the American Bible Society. Before any of his plans came to pass he died in 1825 at the age of sixty-eight and was interred in the common vault of a Roman Catholic church in Mexico City. There is little good that can be said about James Wilkinson (one of his biographers described him as "a finished scoundrel," another a "tarnished warrior"), and he is perhaps most kindly summed up as an intelligent man of vaulting ambition, limited talents and no principles.[12]

Major General Wade Hampton retired to his estates in South Carolina and took no further part in public life. By the time of his death in 1835 at the age of eighty-three or eighty-four he was reputed to be one of the wealthiest men and the largest slave-owners in the United States. Unlike Armstrong and Wilkinson, Hampton had the good taste not to try to justify his actions in print and in fact never seems to have spoken or written a word on his wartime record. During the Civil War, his grandson of the same name rose to the rank of lieutenant general in the Confederate army and gained a reputation as one of the South's best cavalry commanders.[13]

Wilkinson's second-in-command, Major General Morgan Lewis, was appointed in 1814 to command the defences of New York City. He left the army at the conclusion of the war and his later years were devoted to freemasonry and good works; he served as president of the New York Historical Society and was one of the founders of New York University. Morgan Lewis died in 1844 at the age of ninety.[14]

Brigadier General John Parker Boyd was reassigned in 1814 to New York under Lewis's command. He never again held an active command in the field and was dropped from the rolls of the army during its reduction in 1815. Boyd tried to vindicate his wartime record, particularly his command at Crysler's Farm, in a pamphlet entitled *Documents and Facts Relative to the Military Events During the Late War* that appeared the following year and included a second report on the battle dated April 1815 in which he was critical of Lewis and Wilkinson. Boyd retired to Boston, where he served as a naval agent until his death in 1830 at the age of sixty-six.[15]

Jacob Brown assumed command of the Left Division of Military District No. 9 in February 1814. After properly training his division, he invaded Upper Canada in July 1814 to begin the most hard-fought campaign of the war. Brown gained a signal victory at the battle of Chippawa on 5 July and a tactical victory at Lundy's Lane on 25 July, and withstood a determined British siege of his position at Fort Erie in August and September. He proved that American soldiers were the equal of their opponents and in doing so removed the stain on the national military character left by Armstrong, Hampton and Wilkinson. He remained in the army after 1815, becoming general-in-chief in 1821, and was active in laying the foundations of a proper professional service. Jacob Brown died in 1828 having fought and won more pitched battles against British regular troops than any other American general. Sadly, he is all but forgotten today.

Brigadier General Robert Swartout, the quartermaster who wanted to be a general, reverted to his noncombatant role at the end of the 1813 campaign. He left the army in 1815 to reside in New York City, where he made a living as a merchant and a navy agent. Swartout was sixty when he died in 1838.[16]

The remains of Brigadier General Leonard Covington and Lieutenant Colonel Timothy Dix, who died from wounds received during the battle of Crysler's Farm, along with those of Colonel James Preston, who died from illness, were moved from Fort Covington to Sackets Harbor in 1820. They were re-interred at Madison Barracks, the peacetime military post established at that place, apparently near the remains of Brigadier General Zebulon Montgomery Pike, killed during the attack on York in April 1813. A wooden monument surmounted by a funereal urn was erected with the names of the officers carved on it, but by 1860 when Covington's son-in-law visited Sackets Harbor, this monument had almost distintegrated. In 1886, at the direction of General Phil Sheridan, an impressive stone monument to Pike and Covington was constructed in the new garrison cemetery but it is unclear whether the remains of the officers were actually transferred to this cemetery although some of the stone markers from the older cemetery appear to have been shifted. In 1943 the army left Madison Barracks, which passed into civilian hands. In 1989, a small memorial was erected near what may be the original site of the graves of the two generals but it does not bear their names, nor those of the officers who were buried with them. It is sad that two of the most meritorious generals of the northern army may be lying somewhere on the grounds of Madison Barracks in Sackets Harbor in what are virtually unmarked graves.[17]

Brigadier General George Izard, who fought at Châteauguay, was promoted major general and appointed to command the Right Division of Military District No. 9 in early 1814. He worked hard to improve the defences of Plattsburgh, but as a military commander Izard never had much luck. In August 1814 he was ordered to march to the Niagara to aid Brown's division, besieged at Fort Erie. Shortly after he moved out, Prevost launched his a major invasion down the Champlain valley which was halted on 11 September 1814 by an American naval victory and the resolute defence of Plattsburgh by Izard's subordinate, Brigadier General Alexander Macomb. Izard, meanwhile, arrived on the Niagara only to find that the British had lifted the siege of Fort Erie and withdrawn to a strong position behind the Chippawa River. Assuming command of the largest single force of American regular troops assembled during the war, Izard unsuccessfully tried to lure the British out of their defences. In a move that earned him much criticism, he withdrew to the United States in November and shortly thereafter resigned his commission. In 1825 Izard was named governor of the Arkansas Territory and he died there three years later at the age of fifty-two.[18]

Wilkinson's tough and profane artillery commander, Brigadier General Moses Porter, the source of such delight to the younger officers, was assigned to the command of the defences of Norfolk, Virginia, in the spring of 1814. He sat as a member of Wilkinson's court-martial board and ended the war commanding the defences of Boston. Moses Porter was still on active service when he died in 1822 at the age of seventy-two.[19]

Colonel Alexander Macomb, who commanded Wilkinson's "Elite" in 1813, was promoted brigadier general in 1814. When Izard marched to the Niagara in August, Macomb successfully defended Plattsburgh, gaining much acclaim and a promotion to major general. He remained in the army in 1815 and headed the Corps of Engineers until 1828 when, following the death of Jacob Brown, he was appointed general-in-chief, a position he held at the time of his own death in 1841 at the age of fifty-nine.[20]

Colonel Cromwell Pearce, who commanded the Sixteenth Infantry at Crysler's Farm, was sent on the recruiting service and did not return to the northern frontier until June 1814. He rejoined his regiment which formed part of Izard's Right Division and marched with it to the Niagara in the late summer. The Sixteenth fought at Lyon's Creek in Upper Canada in October but withdrew to the United States the following month. Pearce left the service in 1815 and returned to his home in Chester County, Pennsylvania, where he was elected sheriff the following year and, in 1825, an associate judge of the county court. In 1816, when Ripley published an inflated account of his own exploits at Crysler's Farm in the *Portfolio* magazine, Pearce took him to task in a carefully worded letter of rebuttal. Cromwell Pearce died in 1852 in his eightieth year.[21]

Colonel Robert Purdy, who commanded one of Hampton's brigades at the battle of Châteauguay, retired from the army in June 1815. Nothing is known about his postwar life.[22]

Colonel Thomas Mann Randolph, the commanding officer of the Twentieth Infantry during the campaign, resigned from the army in the spring of 1814 and returned to Monticello, the estate of his father-in-law, Thomas Jefferson. He served two terms in the Virginia House of Delegates but spent much of his time working in agriculture and became a respected botanist. Randolph died at the age of sixty in 1828 and is buried beside Jefferson.[23]

Colonel Eleazer W. Ripley, who commanded the Twenty-First Infantry at Crysler's Farm, was promoted brigadier general in early 1814 and assigned a brigade in Brown's Left Division. When both Brown and Winfield Scott were wounded at Lundy's Lane on 25 July, command of the division devolved on Ripley and, in a decision that was to cause him much trouble, he decided not to renew the battle but to withdraw. He was badly wounded during the sortie from Fort Erie on 17 September and saw no more active service in the war although he received a brevet promotion to major general. Ripley remained in the peacetime army and was the subject of a "biographical memoir" in the *Portfolio*, written by himself or an admirer, that exaggerated his role at Crysler's Farm. It was criticized by both Charles Gardner and Cromwell Pearce, who tried to set the record straight. Ripley resigned from the army in 1820 to practise law in Louisiana, served in the House of Representatives and died in 1839 in his fifty-seventh year.[24]

Colonel Winfield Scott, who fought at Hoople's Creek with Brown on 10 November 1813, was promoted to brigadier general in the spring of 1814 and given command of a brigade in Brown's Left Division. During a ten-week period of rigorous training at Flint Hill near Buffalo, he prepared that division for battle and his hard work paid off when it gained a major victory at

Chippawa on 5 July 1814. Badly wounded at Lundy's Lane three weeks later, Scott saw no further active service during the war, but he was to dominate the army for the following half century, although his arrogant personality made him many enemies. Scott led the army to victory in a brilliant and hard-fought campaign in Mexico in 1847-1848 and was commanding general when the Civil War broke out in 1861. He retired that year and died in 1866 in his eightieth year.[25]

Colonel Joseph Gardner Swift, Wilkinson's chief engineer and principal staff officer in 1813, was promoted brigadier general and appointed to command the Corps of Engineers in 1814. He resigned from the army in 1818 and became surveyor of the port of New York and was the chief engineer for all American ports on the Great Lakes from 1829 to 1845. Swift successfully carried out a diplomatic mission to settle border disputes with Canada and in his later years supervised railway construction in Louisiana, Maryland, Virginia and New York. He died at his home in Geneva, New York, in 1865 at the age of eighty-two.[26]

The man who ordered the cavalry charge at the battle, Colonel John de Barth Walbach, was retained in the postwar army. He was promoted a brevet major general in 1823, served for another two decades and was in his eighties when he finally retired. The old German warrior was much admired by his younger colleagues for his long service in the armies of at least three nations. After his retirement, Walbach attended a review as a spectator and the senior officer present, recognizing him, suggested that all the officers who had paraded should "proceed to that gallant old soldier (indicating Gen. W.) and pay our respects to him."[27] The group approached Walbach, "saluted him, and each offered a friendly hand." The "old gentleman was visibly moved, his eye filled with tears and he exclaimed: 'By Jove! By Jove!'" John Walbach was in his ninety-first year when he died at Baltimore in 1857.[28]

Lieutenant Colonel Thomas Aspinwall, who commanded the Ninth Infantry at Crysler's Farm, assumed command of Winfield Scott's brigade in July 1814 after Scott was wounded at Lundy's Lane. He was prominent during the siege of Fort Erie but lost his arm during the sortie of 17 September. Aspinwall left the army in 1815 to serve as the American consul in London, a position he held for thirty-seven years. During his tenure as consul Aspinwall became the director of one of the first trans-Atlantic steamship companies and had become wealthy by the time he returned to reside in Boston, where he became director of the Boston Board of Trade and a strong supporter of the Massachusetts Historical Society. When the Civil War began in 1861, the seventy-seven-year-old Aspinwall offered his services to the Union but they were politely declined. He died in 1876 at the age of ninety-one.[29]

Lieutenant Colonel Robert Carr of the Fifteenth Infantry left the army in 1815 to return to his prewar business as a printer and manager of the Philadelphia Botanical Garden. He was active in militia affairs, becoming adjutant general of Pennsylvania in the 1820s, and was also an alderman and justice of the peace. His later years were burdened by financial troubles after he lost control of the Botanical Garden and he had to accept a position as gatekeeper at the Asylum for the Insane. Carr was undaunted and remained vigorous to the end of his life – in 1861 he walked seventeen miles in one day while inspecting Union army camps in Virginia. In 1864, at the age of eighty-six, Robert Carr read Washington's Farewell Address to a reunion of War of 1812 veterans in Philadelphia.[30]

Lieutenant Colonel Benjamin Forsyth, the aggressive rifle regiment commander who fought at Hoople's Creek with Brown on 10 November, was killed in action in June 1814 in the Lake Champlain area during a skirmish with a raiding force from across the border. His piratical riflemen vowed revenge on the Canadian officer they held responsible for their beloved leader's death, Captain Joseph St. Valier Mailloux of the Frontier Light Infantry, and on 10 August set an ambush in which Mailloux was badly wounded and captured. Taken to the same house in Champlain, New York, from which Forsyth had been buried less than two weeks before, Mailloux was well treated but died five days later from his wounds.[31]

Lieutenant Colonel Timothy Upham of the Twenty-First Infantry, who commanded the boat guard at Crysler's Farm, assumed command of his regiment in 1814 and was prominent during the bloody sortie from Fort Erie on 17 September. His health ruined by active service, Upham left the army in 1815 and was appointed collector of customs at Portsmouth, New Hampshire, a post he held until 1829. He later served as the navy agent at Portsmouth and, later still, entered business at Charlestown, Massachusetts, but was not very successful. Upham's last years were marked by illness and he was in his seventy-second year when he died in 1855.[32]

Major William Clay Cumming of the Sixteenth Infantry was promoted colonel and appointed an adjutant general in 1814. When the war ended he returned home to Savannah, Georgia, and took no further part in public life, becoming somewhat of a recluse. Cumming died in 1863 in his seventy-fifth year.[33]

Major Charles Kitchell Gardner, who fought with the Twenty-Fifth Infantry during the battle, received a brevet promotion to lieutenant colonel in 1814 and served as Brown's chief of staff during the campaign of 1814. He resigned from the army in 1818 and moved to New York, where he served as a police magistrate and as the editor of a literary review and a newspaper. Gardner continued to be interested in military matters and published a number of drill manuals and a biographical dictionary. From 1824 onwards he held a series of minor government posts in the post office, Indian Department and Treasury Department. Gardner died in 1869 in his eighty-second year.[34]

Major Henry Lee, who served on Wilkinson's staff during the campaign, joined Izard's staff in 1814 but left the army at the end of the war to return to his estate in Westmoreland County, Virginia. He married in 1817, held minor government posts and became a writer, producing political pamphlets and three works of military history including a biography of Napoleon. Lee was a devoted follower of Andrew Jackson, arranged Jackson's military papers and wrote the 1829 inaugural address when Jackson was elected president. Lee's reward was an appointment as consul-general to Algiers but the senate refused to confirm him because of a scandal that arose when it became public knowledge that he was having an affair with his sister-in-law, his legal ward. Henry Lee spent his remaining years abroad and died in Paris in 1837.[35]

His younger half-brother restored the family name. He received an appointment to West Point in 1825 and, throughout his forty-year military career, served with veterans of the 1813 campaign. During this young man's time as a cadet, the superintendent of the academy was Colonel Sylvanus Thayer, who had been one of Hampton's engineer officers. Having seen the American officer at perhaps his worst, Thayer was determined that officers in any future conflict would know their responsibilities and instituted reforms at West Point that established it as one of the best military academies in the world. Thayer's assistant in this work was Major William Jenkins Worth, who been on Morgan Lewis's staff during the St. Lawrence campaign. Henry Lee's brother set an enviable record for scholastic achievement, graduated second in his class in 1829 and entered the Corps of Engineers, where his first superior was Colonel Abram Eustis, who had commanded the gunboats during the descent of the St. Lawrence. He was later appointed an assistant to the chief of the corps, Colonel Joseph Totten, who had kept Wilkinson's army journal in the autumn of 1813. When war with Mexico broke out in 1846, he joined the staff of Brigadier General John Wool, who, as a young major, had commanded a detachment of Hampton's light infantry at Châteauguay. His next assignment was to the headquarters of Major General Winfield Scott, who had commanded the Third Artillery in Macomb's brigade in 1813 before going on to greater things in the Niagara campaign of 1814. Among his comrades on Scott's staff were other promising young officers such as George B. McClellan, George G. Meade and Pierre T. Beauregard, but such were the talents of this Virginian that even Winfield Scott, a man not overly generous with praise, thought he "was the very best soldier I ever saw in the field." This was only the beginning for Robert Edward Lee, who went on to become one of America's greatest generals.[36]

Major Josiah Snelling, who served as a light infantry commander under Hampton during the 1813 campaign, joined the staff of Izard's Right Division in 1814 but later transferred to Brown's Left Division, where he participated in the sortie from Fort Erie in September and the battle of Lyon's Creek in October. Remaining in the army as a lieutenant colonel, Snelling was posted to the western territories, where he supervised the construction of a major post at the junction of the Mississippi and Minnesota rivers which was named in his honour. Snelling was the military commander of the Minnesota Territory when he died from illness in 1828 at the age of forty-five.[37]

Major John T. Woodford of the Second Light Dragoons, who gallantly led the cavalry charge at Crysler's Farm, resigned from the army in June 1814 and nothing is known of his later life.[38]

For Captain Mordecai Myers, who led his little command of "Jolly Snorters" into the closing stages of the battle of Crysler's Farm, the 1813 campaign brought a happy result. The wounded Myers went with the rest of the army to French Mills, where he was invited to lodge in the nearby house of a Doctor Mann until he recovered. Exhausted by the exertions of the campaign, he fell prey to a fever and his host despaired for his life but the young officer eventually recovered. During his stay Mordecai met the doctor's niece, a Miss Charlotte Bailey from Plattsburgh, and the couple married in March 1814. Promoted to major, Myers served at Plattsburgh in 1814 but saw no more fighting although he made a number of reconnaissance missions over the border in civilian clothes, where he "procured much valuable information at the risk of a halter for a neckcloth."[39]

In 1815 Myers was discharged from the army and settled in New York where he acted as an agent for former soldiers who had claims against the federal government for pay, allowances and land grants. He served several terms in the state legislature and, when he moved to Schenectady, two terms as mayor of that city. By the time of his death in 1871, at the age of ninety-five, Mordecai Myers was one of the leading citizens of Schenectady and the local paper eulogized him: "Major Myers was in many ways a remarkable man. He was possessed of a clear mind, strong will, and the fact that, with all the hardships incident to the life of a soldier in the war of 1812, he lived to be nearly ninety-six years of age, is proof that the possessed a strong and robust constitution." "No stranger," the newspaper said of Myers, "ever met him or passed him on the street without noticing his appearance; he was of very large proportions and had a clear and keen black eye, giving evidence of the strong intellectual power of the man."[40]

Captain Samuel Devins Harris of the Second Light Dragoons, who participated in the cavalry charge at Crysler's Farm, went on to greater glory as the cavalry commander of Brown's Left Division in 1814. He remained in the army until 1820 when he resigned to become U.S. Marshal in Boston and also served as the first chief engineer of the Boston Fire Department. Harris died in 1855 at the age of seventy-five.[41]

Lieutenant Henry Knox Craig, who commanded the American artillery at Crysler's Farm, was promoted captain in December 1813 and remained in the postwar army. By 1846, when he participated in Fremont's campaign in California, he was a major and later became chief of ordnance of the army from 1851 to 1861. He resigned in 1863 and was promoted a brigadier general "for long and faithful service." Craig died in 1869.[42]

Second Lieutenant Reynold M. Kirby of the Third Artillery, who caught up with the army in time to participate in the battle, fought in the Niagara campaign in 1814 and received brevet promotions to first lieutenant and captain for his gallantry during the siege of Fort Erie. Kirby remained in the army after 1815, fought in the Seminole War between 1836 and 1838 and participated in the "Aroostook War." As a brevet major in 1842 he was in command of Fort Sullivan at Eastport, Maine, when he took ill with a fever and died in his fifty-third year.[43]

Second Lieutenant Joseph Hawley Dwight of the Thirteenth Infantry, who thought his generals were "plow joggers," was transferred to the Thirty-First Infantry in January 1814 but resigned his commission the following month. Nothing is known about his later life.[44]

Sergeant Alexander Neef of the Fourth Infantry, who fought at Châteauguay, was commissioned an ensign in January 1814. He resigned from the army the following November and nothing is known about his later life.[45]

Corporal Richard Bishop of the Twenty-Ninth Infantry, who left a diary describing his experiences at the battle of Châteauguay, was killed in action in 1814.[46]

Drummer Jarvis Hanks, who saw his first combat at Crysler's Farm, would fight throughout the long and bloody Niagara campaign of the following summer. Hanks was discharged from the army in 1815 and became an itinerant teacher and artist. He wrote a lengthy memoir of his military experiences and died in Cleveland in 1858 at the age of fifty-seven.[47]

William Johnston, the Canadian who piloted Wilkinson's boat down the St. Lawrence, resided at French Creek after the war, where he operated as a smuggler between that place and Kingston. During the Patriot "troubles" of 1837-1838 along the border, Johnston, a fervent anti-monarchist and self-styled "commander in chief" of the patriot naval forces, led a group of these thugs who boarded and burned the Canadian steamer *Peel*. Both the British and American governments offered rewards for his arrest and, after a series of misadventures, periods of incarceration and escapes, Johnston was pardoned by President William Henry Harrison and appointed a lighthouse keeper on Rock Island in the St. Lawrence. He later kept a tavern in Clayton, as French Creek was renamed. When the Civil War broke out in 1861, William Johnston, aged seventy-nine, went to Washington and offered his services to President Abraham Lincoln but they were respectfully declined. The "pirate of the 1000 Islands" died at Clayton in 1870 in his eighty-eighth year.[48]

Lieutenant General Sir George Prevost continued to serve as commander-in-chief and governor-general of British North America until the end of the war. In command of the best army Britain ever sent to that continent, Prevost launched a major invasion of the United States in September 1814. It came to grief at Plattsburgh after the British naval squadron was defeated on Lake Champlain and, always cautious, Prevost made the controversial decision to retreat rather than continue with a land attack. It earned him a storm of censure and he was removed from his post in 1815 and returned to Britain, where he requested a court martial to clear his name, but shortly before it was to commence sitting in January 1816, he died suddenly at the age of forty-six.[49]

Major General Francis de Rottenburg served for the remainder of the war in a subordinate capacity to Prevost. He returned to Britain in July 1815, was knighted for his services and died in Portsmouth in 1832 at the age of seventy-five. De Rottenburg is remembered today as one of the officers responsible for the development of British light infantry tactics during the Napoleonic wars – few know of his service in North America.[50]

Lieutenant Colonel Joseph Wanton Morrison was justly feted for his victory at Crysler's Farm, collecting accolades and awards including one of the six officer's gold medals awarded for the battle, the thanks of the Legislative Assembly of Lower Canada and a sword from the Merchants Guild of Liverpool. Morrison met the American regular again at Lundy's Lane on 25 July 1814 but this time things went differently and he was badly wounded. He saw no more action during the war and was not fit for service again until 1821, by which time he had been promoted colonel and made a companion of the Order of the Bath. Morrison assumed command of the 44th Foot and sailed for India, where he was promoted brigadier general in 1824 and given command of a brigade organized for the invasion of Burma. Joseph Morrison's personality can best be judged from an order he issued shortly before his men went into action:

> The brigadier general, in promulgating the first arrangements for offensive operations, takes the opportunity to express his unbounded confidence, that every honourable achievement which zeal, discipline, and valour can effect, will be accomplished; and he humbly hopes that the Giver of all Victory will bless the united efforts of the division, to the glory of the British name, and the character of the Indian army.
>
> He at the same time begs the troops, when flushed with success, to remember that a vanquished foe ceases to be an enemy, and that mercy shown, though in some instance it may be abused ... yet can never fail of the best reward; while the example set must be productive of the ultimate good.[51]

The operation was successful but the forty-two-year-old Morrison was so severely stricken with malaria that he was sent home to recover. He died during the voyage on 15 February 1826 and was buried at sea.[52]

Lieutenant Colonel John Harvey, Morrison's chief of staff at Crysler's Farm, received a gold medal for the battle and held a similar appointment under Lieutenant General Gordon Drummond during the Niagara campaign of 1814. He remained on the staff in North America until 1817 when he returned to Britain, only to return to Upper Canada as the member of a government commission to regulate the sale price of Crown lands. In 1828 he was appointed inspector of police for Leinster in Ireland, a difficult position in harrowing times, but later held a series of colonial governorships in North America: Prince Edward Island (1836-1837), New Brunswick (1837-1841), Newfoundland (1841-1846) and Nova Scotia (1846-1852). Harvey was knighted for his services during the War of 1812 and at the time of his death in 1852 at the age of seventy-two held the rank of major general.[53]

Lieutenant Colonel Thomas Pearson, the bad-tempered veteran light infantryman, also received a gold medal for Crysler's Farm, the second such award of his career. He continued at Prescott until the spring of 1814 when he was transferred to Major General Phineas Riall's Right Division in the Niagara. On his way to take up that appointment, he participated as a volunteer in the amphibious attack on Oswego. Pearson performed brilliantly during the 1814 Niagara campaign, fighting a stubborn rearguard action against Winfield Scott and commanding a light infantry brigade at the battles of Chippawa and

Lundy's Lane, and was wounded in the arm at the latter action. He continued in the field but was again wounded at the sortie from Fort Erie on 17 September 1814, "when he received a musket ball in the upper part of the head which deprived him of hearing in the right side and caused several exfoliations of the skull."[54]

By late 1815 Pearson was fit for service again and assumed command of the 43rd Foot, an appointment he held for two years before taking over his own 23rd Foot. He remained with them for thirteen years but gave up command when promoted major general in 1830. By this time it would seem the irascible Pearson was starting to grow a bit soft – just before departing the 23rd, he addressed a letter to his officers, stating that "human nature is ever liable to err and in no situation more so than in the exercise of command," and apologizing for "those instances when in the execution of public duty I may unintentionally have given pain" as "the fault has proceeded from the head, and not from the heart."[55] Pearson was promoted lieutenant general in 1841, at which time he commanded a district in northern Ireland. By the time of his death in 1847, Thomas Pearson had served fifty-one years, fought in a dozen major battles and countless minor actions, suffered five wounds, and had collected two gold medals, a knighthood, a companionship in the Order of the Bath and a knight commandership in the Royal Hanoverian Order.[56]

Lieutenant Colonel Charles Plenderleath, who commanded the 49th Foot in the action of 11 November 1813, received a gold medal for Crysler's Farm. Suffering from the wound he received in the battle, which turned out be more serious than at first thought, Plenderleath went on half pay in 1814 and left the service in 1821 to retire to Tuscany, where he died in 1854.[57]

Lieutenant Colonel Charles d'Irumberry de Salaberry, the *Canadien* commander at Châteauguay, was so angered by Prevost's general order about the action that he sent in his resignation but it was intercepted by his patron, the Duke of Kent, and de Salaberry remained in service. He saw no further action during the war and gave up command of his Voltigeurs to Heriot in the spring of 1814. De Salaberry retired from the army in 1815 and settled on an estate near Chambly and, through conscientious management and inheritances from both his own and his wife's family, became a sizeable landowner with varied farming, business and transportation interests. De Salaberry was awarded a gold medal for Châteauguay and made a companion of the Order of the Bath. His later years were marked by public service as a member of the Legislative Council of Lower Canada and as a justice of the peace, but his military service had ruined his health and he was only fifty when he died in 1829.[58]

Lieutenant Colonel "Red George" Macdonell, the fiery Scot who rendered able support to de Salaberry at Châteauguay, also received a gold medal for that action. He was appointed an inspecting field officer of militia in 1814 and given command of the Cornwall district with responsibility for protection of the vital St. Lawrence communication line. Macdonell surveyed an alternate route along the Ottawa and Rideau rivers and through connecting lakes to Kingston, which was developed in the 1830s. He returned to England in 1816 and two years later married a wealthy heiress but his later years were marred by an obsession with gaining public recognition and financial compensation for his services during the War of 1812. "Red George" died at his wife's castle in Wiltshire in 1870 at the green old age of ninety.[59]

Captain William Howe Mulcaster, RN, the aggressive commander of the naval forces during the pursuit down the St. Lawrence, was appointed to command the 42-gun frigate HMS *Princess Charlotte*, launched at Kingston in April 1814. A few weeks later, he was badly wounded during the attack on Oswego, New York, and never fully recovered. Mulcaster married Sophie van Cordlandt, a Canadian woman, and for his services was made a companion of the Bath, naval aide-de-camp to the King and presented with an annual pension of £300. He died at his residence at Dover, Kent, in 1837 at the age of fifty-two.[60]

Major Miller Clifford, who commanded the 89th Foot at Crysler's Farm, received a gold medal for the action but was badly wounded at Lundy's Lane. He was knighted for his services during the war and continued in the army until 1836 by which time he had reached the rank of brevet colonel. Clifford died two weeks after his retirement.[61]

Major James Dennis of the 49th Foot, who defended Hoople's Creek with two regulars and a handful of militia against Jacob Brown on 10 November 1813, served on the staff in Lower Canada until the end of the war. He was made a knight commander of the Order of the Bath in 1844 and had reached the rank of major general when he died in London in 1852.[62]

Major Frederick George Heriot, who commanded the Canadian Voltigeurs at the battle, replaced de Salaberry in command of that regiment in April 1814 and held it until the end of the war. He received a gold medal for Crysler's Farm and, after the war, became the administrator of a veterans' land settlement on the south shore of the St. Lawrence in Lower Canada. Under Heriot's firm guidance, this settlement, named Drummondville after Lieutenant General Gordon Drummond, grew steadily. Heriot was made a companion of the Bath in 1822 and in 1840 reached the rank of major general. He also commanded the local militia during the troubles of 1837-1838 as well as serving two terms in the provincial Legislative Assembly. Although his name was often linked with Catherine Bowes, the attractive daughter of Sir John Johnson, the modest and well-liked Heriot died unmarried at his estate, "Comfort Cottage," near Drummondville in 1844 at the age of fifty-seven.[63]

Captain George West Barnes of the 89th Foot, who had erased the black mark on his record by his performance at Crysler's Farm, served on the staff of the army in the last year of the war as a brevet major. He went on half pay in 1816 and died on his native Isle of Man in 1820, survived by a wife and two children.[64]

Second Captain Henry George Jackson, the RA commander at the battle, received a gold medal for the action and later fought in the Plattsburgh campaign in 1814. He was promoted to full captain in 1827 and returned to Lower Canada as a major of artillery during the troubles of 1837-1838. Jackson was a lieutenant colonel by the time he died at Warley, England, in 1849.[65]

Lieutenant Charles Pinguet of the Canadian Fencibles light company, who fought at the abatis at Châteauguay, died of illness in 1814.[66]

Lieutenant John Le Couteur of the 104th Foot spent a pleasant winter in Kingston before fighting in the Niagara campaign of 1814. He was just twenty when the war ended and, returning to his native Jersey, resigned from the army to live a long and productive life devoted to improving his beloved island. Colonel Sir John Le Couteur died at his estate, Bellevue, at the age of eighty-five in 1872 surrounded by children and grandchildren.[67]

Lieutenant John Sewell of the 49th Foot remained in the army at the end of the war and eventually reached the rank of captain. He retired in 1829 and returned to his native Quebec City, where he was appointed gentleman usher of the Legislative Council and later municipal postmaster. Sewell married for the first time in 1815 and the union produced a son. His wife dying young, he was single for many years but married a second time in 1853. He was active in the militia and reached the rank of colonel, being disliked for his discipline but liked for his interest in the common soldier. When he lay on his deathbed at the age of eighty-one in 1875, Sewell asked "to be buried with full military honours" and his casket was escorted from the Anglican Cathedral at Quebec to Mount Hermon cemetery by a lengthy military procession.[68]

Surgeon William Dunlop of the 89th Foot fought in the Niagara campaign of 1814 and later published a witty and entertaining account of his services during the War of 1812. He returned to settle in Upper Canada in 1826, was elected to the Legislative Assembly and ended his career as the superintendent of the Lachine Canal. William "Tiger" Dunlop was fifty-six when he died in 1848.[69]

That intrepid border reiver, Canadian militia Captain Reuben Sherwood, purchased mills near Brockville in 1818 and continued to work as a land surveyor along the St. Lawrence. His first wife having died, Sherwood remarried in 1831 and died near Toronto at the age of seventy-six in 1851.[70]

In 1825 Sherwood's daughter, Clarissa, married Captain Richard Ferguson of the Canadian Fencibles, who had fought with his light infantry company and double-barrelled gun at Châteauguay. He was sixty-two, she was twenty-five and the ceremony took place at Ogdensburg in the United States possibly because Ferguson's first marriage, to Frederica Grant in 1784, was still legally valid although the couple had separated in 1799 under an agreement that Ferguson "was not to ever frequent her company or converse at any time with her and shall not sue or disturb any person or persons that shall receive her into their habitations." Ferguson died at the age of eighty in 1842 and his widows promptly got into a dispute over his military pension.[71]

Militia Captain John Crysler, on whose land the battle was fought, received £400 for the damage to his property caused by the fighting and the use of his buildings as military hospitals. He was appointed collector of customs at Cornwall in 1818. Bad luck or bad business decisions, exacerbated by his elegant life style and lavish hospitality, created financial problems for Crysler in the 1820s and he had difficulty in warding off the claims of numerous creditors. He continued to serve as a militia officer and was a lieutenant colonel by 1838 when he led men of the Dundas militia, including his son Pembroke, against the "patriots" at the battle of the windmill near Prescott. In 1843 Crysler moved to a smaller residence in the village of Crysler north of the St. Lawrence, where he died in 1852 aged eighty-four.[72]

Militia Lieutenant Christopher Hagerman, who was one of Morrison's aides during the battle, was appointed provincial aide to Lieutenant General Gordon Drummond and was on that officer's staff throughout the Niagara campaign of 1814. When peace broke out in 1815 Hagerman returned to his law practice in Kingston and served as a member of the Legislative Assembly of Upper Canada from 1821 to 1824 and later as a judge. Married three times, he died in Toronto in 1847 at the age of fifty-five.[73]

Lieutenant Duncan Clark of the Incorporated Militia, who brought the news of the American descent of the St. Lawrence on a borrowed plough horse, fought with his unit in the Niagara campaign of 1814. Awarded land at Edwardsburgh for his wartime service, Clark built a home in that area but in 1818 joined the Northwest Fur Trading Company and travelled in the western territories before returning to his home village and opening a store which he carried on until 1837. During the rebellion of 1837-1838 Clark was on active service as a major in the 1st Grenville Militia Regiment and later reached the rank of militia lieutenant colonel. Clark held a series of political appointments on various boards and commissions until his death in 1862 at the age of seventy-seven. He never married and "left no family to mourn his loss but many friends."[74]

Trooper John W. Loucks of the Canadian militia, who was cautioned by a British officer not to retreat too hastily in the face of the enemy, married Alta Mosely in 1817 and they had six children, who were raised on the Loucks farm by the banks of the St. Lawrence which John purchased from his father in 1824. Loucks served as clerk of the court for Stormont, Dundas and Glengarry counties and also as a justice of the peace. He continued in the militia and was present as an ensign when the 1st Dundas Regiment was called out under John Crysler's command to fight at the battle of the Windmill in 1838. John Loucks was a long-lived man – at the age of eighty-three he was described as "wonderfully well-preserved ... clear-headed and strong" and "elastic in body." In 1892, three years before a memorial was erected on the battlefield at Crysler's Farm, John W. Loucks, one of the last survivors of the engagement, passed away peacefully on his farm in his ninety-seventh year.[75]

Thomas Gibbs Ridout of the Commissariat Department, who narrowly escaped capture by Macomb's advance guard on the bank of the St. Lawrence on 7 November 1813, remained with the army until 1820 when he retired on half pay. Two years later he became the first general manager of the new Bank of Canada, a position he held until 1861, and commanded that institution's own militia unit during the troubles of 1837-1838. Through shrewd investment in the new railways and land speculation, Ridout became moderately wealthy and was prominent in social and public life in Toronto. He died in 1861 at the age of sixty-seven.[76]

Michael Cook, the owner of the land on which Wilkinson's army had camped the night before the battle, petitioned the Crown for £359 10s. 8d. compensation for loss of property during the American occupation. He received £197 7s. 6d. and used some of this money to build a larger, more substantial brick tavern that he operated into the 1840s and which can today be seen restored at Upper Canada Village near Morrisburg, Ontario. Michael Cook was eighty-six when he died in 1847; his wife, Abigail, survived him fourteen years to die in 1861 at the age of eighty-seven.[77]

"Lochaber No More"

THE FATE OF THE BATTLEFIELD

Farewell to Lochaber and farewell, my Jean,
Where heartsome with thee I have many days been.
For Lochaber no more, Lochaber no more,
We'll maybe return to Lochaber no more.
These tears that I shed they are all for my dear,
And nae for the dangers attending on war,
Though borne on rough seas to a far bloody shore,
Maybe to return to Lochaber no more.

Then glory, my Jean, maun plead my excuse,
Since honour commands me how can I refuse?
Without it I ne'er can have merit for thee,
And without thy favour I'd better not be.
I gae then, my lass, to win honour and fame,
And if should luck to come gloriously hame,
A heart I will bring thee with love running o'er,
And then I'll leave thee and Lochaber no more.[1]

For most of the people living along the St. Lawrence, it was a fairly easy matter to pick up the threads of their lives when peace returned in 1815. With the exception of Wilkinson's expedition and the occasional raid, the St. Lawrence area did not see heavy fighting during the war and those who resided on its banks did not suffer severely. In Upper Canada, the Crown promised reimbursement for wartime property damage caused either by American or friendly troops, although it took nearly a decade to do so.

In the immediate postwar decades, as succeeding waves of settlers flooded into Upper Canada, most moved west along the river, either by boat or on the King's highway. By 1820 the first steam vessel was plying the upper reaches of the river and the clumsy wartime batteaux and Durham boats gradually gave way to larger and more comfortable craft. All this was good news for the citizens of Williamsburgh Township who provided services for travellers, and Michael Cook and many of his neighbours became prosperous.

A few miles west of Cook's new brick tavern, John Crysler's yellow house became a landmark, sure to be pointed out to passing travellers. Inevitably visitors commented on the evidence of the fighting in the area, and the American historian Benson Lossing remembered on a visit in mid-century that one wartime barn "pierced and battered by bullets, was yet standing."[2] Not all tourists were entranced by the scene – one commented on the "vulgar flatness of the ground, the stagnant ditches, the mossy rotten fences, the dwarfed leafless trees, and the drowsy creaking of a pot house sign hard by" (probably swinging on Michael Cook's new tavern), all of which "indisposed" this visitor "for a patriot's death, there at least."[3] Neighbouring farms also exhibited signs of the battle; the Casselman barn had a roundshot lodged in it so the family dug it out, painted it red, white and blue, and proudly displayed it in their parlour for decades after the war. Musket balls were found by the hundreds, and sometimes more gruesome artifacts came to light. In 1861 James Croil noted that human remains "had been turned up by the plough" and that, during "the past year, two entire skeletons were thus rudely disinterred, at a depth of not more than nine or ten inches from the surface of the ground."[4]

There was another, more attractive, memento of the battle. In 1848 there was much general satisfaction in the Canadas when clasps for the battles of Châteauguay and Crysler's Farm were announced for the General Service Medal, 1793-1814. This decoration was awarded to all surviving officers and men who had participated in actions fought during the Napoleonic War and twenty-nine engagements were singled out by special clasps to be worn attached to the ribbon of the medal. Many of the local men who had fought at Crysler's Farm, including Captains John Crysler and Reuben Sherwood, Jacob and Peter Brouse, Sergeant Jacob Dulmage and John W. Loucks, made application, and in all twenty-nine members of the Upper Canada militia received it (see Appendix G).[5]

In the mid-19th century the steamboats began to give way to the railways. The Grand Trunk went through near the battlefield in 1854 and thirty years later the Canadian Pacific was constructed a short distance to the north. Travellers were able to cover the distance from Montreal to Kingston in hours rather than days but no longer had a ready opportunity to see the landmarks of the battle. Around the time the Crysler's Farm clasp to the General Service Medal was distributed there was some talk about building a monument to

It happened here – the battle memorial
Erected in 1895, the memorial is shown here in its original location on the banks of
the St. Lawrence near the high point of the action. It was moved in 1958 to Upper
Canada Village, where it is today positioned on a high mound overlooking the river.
(Archives of Ontario, Acc.9258 S14334)

mark the site but nothing came of it. James Croil, who lived near the battlefield, was a supporter of this idea and felt that Canadians had "long ago for-
given our enemy and that even now we love our neighbours as ourselves" but
"*forget* we never can the heroic deeds of our forefathers."[6]

By the time Croil wrote this, the War of 1812 had started to acquire a distinctly heroic sheen in Canada. One of his contemporaries, William Coffin,
commented that the very words "1812" serve to "quicken the pulse and vibrate
through the frame, summoning from the pregnant past memories of suffering
and endurance and honourable exertion."[7] Such emotions contributed to the
creation of a national myth that the war had been won by the heroism of the
Canadian militia with just a little occasional assistance from the British army.
Egerton Ryerson summed up this "militia myth" in 1880 when he wrote
(straight-faced) that "Spartan bands of Canadian Loyalist volunteers aided by
a few hundred English soldiers" had "repelled the Persian thousands of democratic American invaders and maintained the virgin soil of Canada unpolluted

339

by the foot of the plundering invader."[8] It was all untrue, of course, but it certainly made a good story and, if the imagery was going to be classical, there was no better battle than Crysler's Farm to serve as the Marathon of Canada. This being the case and this being the feeling, it was not long before a decision was made to formally mark the battlefield of 11 November 1813 to "teach the younger generation what patriotism and pluck can accomplish against great odds."[9]

The government of Canada provided the funds and a large crowd of dignitaries, invited guests and onlookers gathered on 25 September 1895 to witness the unveiling of the monument. Among them were three men in their nineties who had been children at the time of the action, including one of John and Nancy Crysler's sons. The obligatory speeches were made, the ribbon cut and the new monument dedicated. Located "in the centre of the farm" and occupying "a prominent spot, overlooking the river," it was "an obelisk of Stanstead granite, 38 feet high, resting on a base of cut stone, facing the river."[10] At about the same time a similar obelisk was erected near the site of the battle of Châteauguay.

Due respects having been paid, the crowds departed for home, but for one local historian the obelisk was only the first step. J. Smyth Carter, noting that

Not the real thing but close enough – the Governor-General's Foot Guards, 1913
There were no British regular troops at the battle centennial in August 1913 but these members of the Governor-General's Foot Guards, a militia regiment from Ottawa complete with bearskins and scarlet tunics, provided a reasonable facsimile. Within a year Canada was at war and fancy dress like this was put away for the duration. (Photograph by George Harold Van Allen, courtesy Dr. Traer Van Allen)

Pipe band, 59th Stormont and Glengarry Regiment, 1913
The direct descendants of the Canadian militia who participated in the St. Lawrence, the pipe band of this unit represented the many Scots settlers who fought for the Crown in 1813. (Photograph by George Harold Van Alllen, courtesy Dr. Traer Van Allen)

"familiarity breeds contempt," thought that people "in our little corner of Ontario are so intent on our daily pursuits that we can pass and repass the historic spot of Crysler's Farm without giving it a thought."[11] He urged his fellow citizens to hold "on the anniversary of the battle some kind of gathering" which "would bring together on this landmark the descendants of those worthy heroes of earlier days."[12]

Smyth Carter's wish was partially fulfilled on 27-28 August 1913 when a celebration was held on the battlefield to mark the centennial of Crysler's Farm. Organized by various local groups, this two-day event attracted nearly 5,000 people, special trains were arranged and a temporary wharf was constructed on the river bank near the memorial to accommodate charter steamers carrying those who chose to travel by water. The Women's Institute of nearby Morrisburg arranged a display of relics of the battle including a butter bowl that had actually been full of butter on the morning of 11 November 1813. A military presence was furnished by detachments from most of the eastern Ontario militia units. No British troops were present but the Governor General's Foot Guards of Ottawa, complete with bearskins and scarlet tunics, attempted to be a passable imitation.[13]

Bands played, patriotic songs were sung by "hundreds of school children who had been in training for months," and politicians made the usual lengthy speeches extolling the virtues of their forefathers. "The men of 1813," said one, "are like the men of 1913, they hold their heritage within the British Empire," and nothing will ever "tempt Canada to step out from under the protective folds of the Union Jack."[14] By this time, Crysler's Farm had become a Canadian battle and a Canadian victory and everyone praised the bravery of the militia who, it would seem, fought and won the battle, although no one mentioned that only one militiaman was wounded in the action. Crysler's Farm had also become the property of English Canada. Overlooked in the general feeling of self satisfaction evident during the 1913 centennial was the contribution made by the Tyendinaga Mohawks and the fact that nearly three-quarters of the Canadian regular or near-regular troops who fought at Crysler's Farm were French-speaking *Canadiens*.[15]

Less than a year later the world went to war and the anniversary date of Crysler's Farm, 11 November, ultimately became the solemn day throughout the English-speaking world when people would remember the death and wounding of not just hundreds but of millions. As the troop trains moved east along the St. Lawrence to Atlantic ports of embarkation during the long years of 1914-1918 and 1939-1945, they rolled past that obelisk of Stanstead granite on its bluff near the river.

It would perhaps have sat there forever but in 1958 both monument and battlefield fell victim to the most dangerous enemy of all, the relentless march of progress. From the late 18th century onwards, canals had been progressively dug to tame the rapids of the St. Lawrence and link the Atlantic with the upper Great Lakes, and in 1954 Canada and the United States began a massive and ambitious construction project that would permit ocean-going vessels to proceed inland as far as Lake Superior. The St. Lawrence Seaway, as it was called, changed the face of the river between Morrisburg and Cornwall irrevocably as it required the flooding of some twenty thousand acres on the Canadian bank. This meant that seven old waterfront communities, part of Iroquois, Moulinette, Mille Roches, Dickinson's Landing, Wales, Farran's Point and Aultsville – and much of the Crysler's Farm battlefield – were fated for inundation.

The disruption along the old "front" was total. Over a three-year period nearly five hundred buildings were relocated on massive house movers to new communities created on higher ground, but the majority of the structures in the threatened area were razed and new housing was built for those who had lost their property. A sensitive issue was the question of the estimated five thousand graves in cemeteries located in the areas slated for inundation. Some were transferred to new locations but most were left in place and only their headstones removed. By 1 July 1958, Dominion Day, Canada's birthday, all was ready, and as an estimated audience of thirty-five million watched on television, the explosives on the holding dams were detonated and the St. Lawrence gradually filled in a new man-made lake and destroyed much of the early history of Upper Canada.

It was 1958 and progress was king. The engineers were proud of their achievement and the politicians anticipated increased employment and happy voters. Unfortunately, what none of the people responsible for this gigantic project seems to have realized was that if you let ocean-going vessels into the Great Lakes you also allow ocean-going marine life into the same waters. In short order, the inland seas were invaded by foreign species such as the alewife and spiny water flea which caused devastating damage, both economic and ecological. The worst intruder is the zebra mussel, which has multiplied at an alarming rate, destroying traditional spawning grounds for native fish and clogging water intakes. If not checked it is estimated this species alone will inflict five billion American dollars of damage to the lakes' economy over the next decade. So much for progress.[16]

The politicians did have one good idea. To preserve the heritage of one of the older areas of Ontario they decided to create a ready-made historic site, a pioneer community composed of the houses, taverns, churches, shops, factories and mills saved from the river. Thus, Upper Canada Village was born and among its interesting collection of buildings are some from the farm of John W. Loucks, who fought at the battle; the fine brick mansion constructed by John Pliny Crysler, the son of the man over whose land the battle was fought; and the brick tavern erected by Michael Cook to replace the log structure occupied by Wilkinson's army the night before the battle. Separate and to the west of the Village are memorials to the Loyalists who first settled the Canadian bank of the St. Lawrence and the Crysler's Farm monument which was shifted east from its original location and positioned on top of a forty-foot mound next to the river. At the bottom, a battlefield memorial or museum was constructed to display a large panoramic mural of the high point of the action.

Upper Canada Village is a fascinating place to visit, and the best time to go is in the autumn after the leaves have started to turn and the surrounding woods are ablaze with colour. You can spend many enjoyable hours wandering about the streets of the village, and when you have had enough, you can make your way to the monument.

On the way, it is worth stopping at the pioneer memorial, as it contains the headstones of many local people connected with the battle. Here you can see the grave markers of Richard Loucks of Loucks's Tavern; Mary "Granny"

Hoople;[17] Thomas Nudel of "Nudel Bush" fame; Cephrenus (or is it Sephrenus or Sophrenus) Casselman of the Casselman family farm; Michael Mason Cook, who was sixteen years old when the Americans occupied his father's tavern on the night of 10 November 1813; and Trooper John W. Loucks. From the pioneer memorial it is but a short walk to the monument on its mound overlooking the St. Lawrence, but be careful not to stray off the path because successive generations of Canada geese have thoroughly mined the entire area.

So complete is the destruction wrought by the Seaway that it is difficult, if not impossible, to stand on that mound and get any sense of the ground as it was in 1813. Almost half the original battlefield is under water, while the remainder has been disturbed by massive "land forming" that includes the elevation on which you are standing. Somewhere beneath the water in front of you are the graves of about two hundred Americans, Britons and Canadians, who, in the words of the old soldier's song quoted above, will see "Lochaber no more." But it is still hard to comprehend that you are on a battlefield because everything has changed.

Except for one thing. As it did in 1813 and as it will forever, the St. Lawrence continues to flow down to the sea.

Weapons and Weapons Performance at Crysler's Farm

Infantry Weapons

British Short Land Musket, India Pattern

Furniture:	Brass
Calibre of bore:	.75 (.75 inch)
Calibre of projectile:	.71 (.71 inch)
Projectile:	Soft lead ball, just over an ounce in weight
Range – theoretical maximum:	250 yards

Range – effective maximum:

Volley (100 rounds):	150-200 yards
Single round:	100-150 yards
Favoured range:	Less than 100 yards

Weight:	9 pounds, 11 ounces
Optimum effect at 30 yards:	Penetrate 3/8 inch of iron or 5 inches of seasoned oak

Rate of fire by trained infantry:

Optimum:	4-5 rounds per minute
Actual:	2-3 rounds per minute
Rate of misfire:	20-40% depending on conditions

American 1795 Springfield Musket, or Later Variants

Furniture:	Steel
Calibre of bore:	.69 calibre
Calibre of projectile:	.65 calibre
Projectile	Soft lead ball just under 1 ounce or a "buck and ball" combination with one musket ball and three buckshot

Range (for ball ammunition):

Theoretical maximum:	less than 250 yards

Effective maximum:

Volley (100 rounds):	150-200 yards
Single round:	100-150 yards
Favoured range:	Less than 100 yards

Weight:	11 lb. with bayonet
Effect	Less than that of British ounce ball
Rate of fire and misfire:	Same as British musket

Note: When discussing the effectiveness of muskets, the target being fired at must be taken into account. The effectiveness of the weapon increased if the target was large bodies of formed troops and decreased if the target was smaller groups or individuals.

Depending on quality of powder and flint, the touch-holes of these weapons had to be manually cleaned every fifteen to twenty rounds and the flint replaced every ten to fifteen rounds. After fifteen or so repeated rounds the barrel became too hot to handle with comfort and, if the soldier did not have gloves, he usually wrapped the carrying strap around the barrel as a protection.

Artillery Weapons

British Light Brass 6-pdr. Gun

Weight of gun, carriage and limber: 3080 lb.

Number of horses in carriage team: 4-6

Service life:	500-600 rounds at service charge
Gun detachment	
Trained gunners:	2-4
Assistants:	3-5
Calibre	
Bore:	3.66 inches/ 83 mm.
Projectile (roundshot):	3.49 inches
Weight of projectile (roundshot)	6 lb./2.7 kg.
Range – roundshot	
Theoretical maximum:	1000 yards
Effective maximum:	800 yards
Favoured range:	600-800 yards
Range – canister (case shot):	200-600 yards
Range – shrapnel:	800-1000 yards
Effectiveness:	Under optimum conditions, a 6-pdr. roundshot could penetrate nineteen human beings or seven feet of compacted earth
Rate of Fire:	1-2 rounds per minute
Ammunition scales:	40 roundshot and 10 rounds of canister for ready-use with the gun and limber. A further 92 roundshot, 18 canister and 20 spherical case (shrapnel) rounds carried in the ammunition wagon.

American Light Iron 6-pdr. Gun

Weight of gun and carriage:	2000 lb.
Number of horses in gun team:	4-6
Service life:	Estimated 1000 rounds at service charge

Gun detachment:
    Trained gunners: 3
    Assistants: 6

Calibre:
    Bore   3.66 inches/83 mm
    Projectile (roundshot)   3.49 inches

Weight of projectile (roundshot)   6 lb./2.7 kg.

Range and effectiveness: Same as British light 6-pdr. gun except that the United States artillery did not have spherical case or shrapnel in 1813

Rate of fire: 1-2 rounds per minute

Ammunition scales: 18 roundshot carried in chest on carriage and 30 canister rounds in caisson

Sources

Muskets: Howard Blackmore, *British Military Firearms, 1650-1850* (London, 1961); René Chartrand, *Uniforms and Equipment of the United States Forces in the War of 1812* (Youngstown, 1992); William Duane, *American Military Library* (2 vols., Philadelphia, 1809); William Greener, *The Gun; or, A Treatise on the Various Descriptions of Small Fire Arms* (London, 1808); James Hicks, *Notes on U.S. Ordnance* (Mt. Vernon, 1940); B.P. Hughes, *Firepower, Weapons Effectiveness on the Battlefield, 1630-1850* (London, 1974).

Artillery: Ralph W. Adye, *The Bombardier and Pocket Gunner* (London, 1813); Henri Othon De Scheel, *Treatise on Artillery* (Philadelphia, 1800); Jean-Jacques Basilien de Gassendi, *Aide-Memoire, à l'usage des Officiers de l'artillerie de France* (2 vols., Paris, 1801); [Amos Stoddard], *Exercise for the Garrison and Field Ordnance, Together with Manoeuvres of Horse Artillery ...* (Philadelphia, 1812); and Louis de Tousard, *American Artillerist's Companion, or Elements of Artillery* (2 vols., Philadelphia, 1809).

Order of Battle and Strength

MAJOR GENERAL WADE HAMPTON'S DIVISION, UNITED STATES ARMY, 26 OCTOBER 1813

Commanding General: Major General Wade Hampton

Divisional Staff

Aide to General Hampton:	Lieutenant John Hoomes
Adjutant General:	Major William King
Inspector General:	Colonel Henry Atkinson
Chief Engineer:	Major William McRee
Assistant Engineer	Captain Sylvanus Thayer

First Brigade (est. 1677)

Commanding Officer:	Colonel Robert S. Purdy
Light Infantry Corps (est. 350)	Major Josiah Snelling
Fourth US Infantry Regiment (591)	Lieutenant Colonel John Darrington
Thirty-Third US Infantry Regiment (321)	Colonel Isaac Lane
Maine and New Hampshire Volunteer Regiment (Combined) (415)	Colonel Denny McCobb

Second Brigade (est. 1737)

Commanding Officer:	Brigadier-General George Izard
Aide:	Lieutenant Oldham D. Cooper
Battalion, Tenth US Infantry Regiment (250)	Major William S. Hamilton
Eleventh/Twenty-Ninth US Infantry Regiments (Combined) (762)	Colonel Melancthon Smith
Thirty/Thirty-First US Infantry Regiments (Combined) (700)	Colonel Daniel Dana
New York State Militia Volunteers (25)	Unknown

Cavalry (est. 150)

Commanding Officer:	Captain Henry Hall

company, Second US Light Dragoon
Regiment (75)   Captain Henry Hall

company, Second US Light Dragoon
Regiment (75)   Captain John Butler

Artillery (est. 200 gunners and 9 or 10 pieces of artillery)

Commanding Officer: Major William McRee

company, Third Artillery Regiment   Captain James McKeon

company, Light Artillery Regiment   Captain Mann Lomax

company, unidentified unit of artillery

8 x 6-pdr. guns
1 x 12-pdr. gun
1 x 5^1/$_2$-inch howitzer,

Recapitulation

Infantry
First Brigade   1677 of which 1677 saw action on 26 October 1813
Second Brigade   1737 of which 1737 saw action on 26 October 1813

Artillery   200 of which none saw action on 26 October 1813

Cavalry   150 of which 150 saw action on 26 October 1813

Total   3764 of which 3564 saw action on 26 October 1813

Notes

Note that strength figures above include *both* fit and sick and total just under 3,800 men. As Hampton estimated his strength at about 4,000 men, the discrepancy is due to the fact that accurate returns were not available for all the units in the division and, in this case, estimates by period witnesses had to be used and these may not have been completely accurate.

The artillery was nominally under the command of Major William McRee but, as he was also the chief engineer of the army, Captain Mann Lomax commanded it on campaign. There were three companies of artillery but the commander of one company, probably drawn from the Light or Third Artillery Regiments, cannot be identified from the sources. All sources agree that Hampton's artillery consisted of eight 6-pdr. field guns and one 5^1/$_2$-inch howitzer when the division advanced north toward Montreal on 21 October but one source states that, prior to this time, it also included a heavier 12-pdr. field piece. If this is true, it was possibly left behind at Four Corners due to the poor roads.

The "light infantry corps" attached to the First Brigade on 26 October 1813 consisted of nine companies drawn from all the infantry regiments organized into three "divisions" or detachments, each of three companies. The overall light infantry commander was Major Josiah Snelling, who also led one of the detachments, the other two being commanded by Majors John McNeil and John Wool.

As regards Hampton's infantry, the Tenth and Eleventh Infantry Regiments were originally raised on the two-battalion organization authorized at the outbreak of war. One battalion of the Tenth remained in Virginia while the other marched for the frontier in the summer of 1813, arriving with Hampton in late September or early October. The

Eleventh Infantry had one battalion serving with Wilkinson's army and a small four-company battalion with Hampton which was consolidated with the Twenty-Ninth Infantry. The Thirty and Thirty-First Infantry Regiments were consolidated as one unit while the Maine and New Hampshire Volunteers, units of volunteers in federal service, originally raised as separate organizations, were consolidated before the campaign began. The little band of New York militia consisted of one officer and twenty-four soldiers who volunteered to cross the international border.

Sources
United States National Archives: RG 92: Commissary General of Purchases: Letterbook, vol. 8, 19, Irvine to Langdon, 28 April 1813; Statement of Clothing for Third Artillery, 15 April 1813; RG 94: Adutant-General's Records: Box 321, 4th Regiment under arms, 31 August 1813; Morning Returns, 16 September 1813; War of 1812 Returns, Purdy's Brigade, 25 October 1813, 4 November 1813; Journal of General George Izard, 1813, 21-22 October, 26 October, 30 October, 6 November 1813; RG 98: vol. 495, General Orders, Wade Hampton, 1813: General Orders, 10 July, 15 July, 20 July and 3 August 1813; *American State Papers: Military Affairs*: 383, "Register and Rules and Regulations of Army for 1813," War Department, 27 December 1813; 460, Hampton to SW, 4 October 1813; *Documentary History* 8, 112, King to SW, n.d. (probably 30 October 1813); NYSL, Diary of Corporal Richard Bishop, 26 October 1813; John C. Fredriksen, ed., "A New Hampshire Volunteer in the War of 1812: The Experiences of Charles Fairbanks," *Historical New Hampshire*, 40, (1985), 156-178; James Wilkinson, *Memoirs of My Own Times* (3 vols, Philadelphia, 1816), Appendix 6, Returns of Troops, 2 August 1813; General Orders, 3 August 1813; Francis B. Heitman, *Historical Register and Dictionary of the United States Army* (2 vols., Washington, 1902).

Order of Battle and Strength

LIEUTENANT COLONEL CHARLES DE SALABERRY'S COMMAND, LEFT DIVISION, BRITISH ARMY IN NORTH AMERICA, 26 OCTOBER 1813

Forward Positions (408)

Commanding Officer:	Lieutenant Colonel Charles de Salaberry
Light Company, Canadian Fencible Regiment (72)	Captain George Ferguson
Canadian Voltigeurs, two companies (110)	Captain Michel-Louis Juchereau-Duchesnay
	Captain Narcisse Antoine Juchereau-Duchesnay

Select Embodied Militia (129)

Left Flank Company, 1st Battalion (69)	Captain George Godefroy de Tonnancour
Left Flank Company, 3rd Battalion (60)	Captain Charles Daly

Sedentary Militia (75)

Company, 2nd Battalion, Beauharnois Militia	Captain Joseph Longtin
Company, Chasseurs de Châteauguay	Captain Jean-Baptiste Brugière
Indian Department (22)	Captain Joseph-Maurice Lamothe
Abenaki and Nippissing warriors	

Rearward Positions (1369)

Commanding Officer:	Lieutenant Colonel George Macdonell
Canadian Voltigeurs, two companies (110)	Captain Benjamin Ecuyer
	Captain Jean-Baptiste Hertel de Rouville

Select Embodied Militia (712)

2nd Battalion, Select Embodied Militia (556)	Lieutenant Colonel Pierre Ignace Malhiot
2 companies, 5th Battalion, Select Embodied Militia (156)	Captain William B. Berczy
	Captain Marc-Antoine-Louis Levesque

Sedentary Militia (397)

5 companies, 1st Battalion, Boucherville Militia	Lieutenant-Colonel Louis Chaussegros de Lery
Indian Department (150)	Captain Dominique Ducharme

Recapitulation

Forward Positions: 408 of which 339 saw action on 26 October 1813

Rearward Positions: 1369 of which none saw action on 26 October 1813

Total: 1777 of which 339 saw action on 26 October 1813

Notes

The strength figures stated above are based on the calculations of Michelle Guitard, as contained in her work *The Militia of the Battle of Châteauguay*. Guitard has done the most thorough research into the British strength at the battle.

There were elements of five different types of military units at Châteauguay under de Salaberry and Macdonell. The Canadian Fencibles were, like all fencible units, indistinguishable (with the exception that they were not liable for service outside North America) from British regular infantry in equipment, weapons, training and discipline. The Canadian Voltigeurs were volunteers who enlisted for the duration of the war and were the same in quality as the fencible units being uniformed, armed, equipped and trained as regulars, while more than a fifth of their officers held commissions in the regular British army. The Select Embodied Militia units got their recruits (bachelors aged 18-30), either volunteers or conscripts, from the sedentary militia. Men in the SEM served varying terms from one to two years and were armed, uniformed, equipped and trained as regulars although only a few of their officers held regular commissions. From time to time, the flank companies of the SEM units were formed into light battalions under regular officers to work with the regiments of the line. Macdonell, an officer of the Glengarry Light Infantry Fencibles, commanded one of these *ad hoc* battalions and two of his companies fought at Châteauguay. The 2nd SEM Battalion was also present near the action as were two companies from the 5th Battalion. The sedentary militia were drawn from the entire male population of Lower Canada, aged 16-60, organized in geographical districts and areas. They were called out when needed and were armed and equipped but not issued uniforms. Two companies of sedentary militia took an active part in the battle of Châteauguay and a complete battalion was present near the scene of the action. The officers of the Indian Department commanded those native warriors from the Abenaki, Nipissing, Algonquin, Iroquois and Huron nations who chose to fight against the Americans.

Sources

Michelle Guitard, *The Militia of the Battle of Châteauguay: A Social History*, (Ottawa, 1983); Luc Lepine, *Lower Canada's Militia Officers, 1812-1815* (Montreal, 1996); L.H. Irving, *Officers of the British Forces in Canada During the War of 1812* (Welland, 1908); H. Michael O'Sullivan, "Eye Witness Account," *Gazette de Montréal*, 9 November 1813; Charles Pinguet to Louis Pinguet, 21 November 1813 in "Deux lettres écrites dan les tentes de Châteauguay," *Les Soirées canadiennes* (March, 1864); Victor Suthren, *The Battle of Châteauguay* (Ottawa, 1974); Stuart Sutherland, *His Majesty's Gentlemen* (Toronto, 1999); William C.H. Wood, ed., *Select British Documents of the Canadian War of 1812*, Volume I, 385-429 (Toronto, 1920) and "Canada in the War of 1812," in Adam Shortt and Arthur Doughty, *Canada and Its Provinces*, (Toronto, 1913), Volume 3.

Order of Battle and Strength

MAJOR GENERAL JAMES WILKINSON'S ARMY, UNITED STATES ARMY, NOVEMBER 1813

Commanding Officer:	Major General James Wilkinson
Second in Command:	Major General Morgan Lewis

Army Staff

Aides to General Wilkinson:	Major Henry Lee
	Major Ninian Pinckney
	Captain Charles Nourse
	Captain John Biddle
	Lieutenant John R. Bell
Aides to General Lewis:	Captain Daniel Baker
	Lieutenant William Jenkins Worth
Commander, Artillery:	Brigadier General Moses Porter
Quartermaster General:	Brigadier General Robert Swartout
Chief Engineer:	Colonel Joseph G. Swift
Assistant Engineer:	Major Joseph G. Totten
Topographical Engineer:	Major John Anderson
Adjutant General:	Colonel John de Barth Walbach
Assistant Adjutant Generals:	Colonel John Johnson
	Major Robert G. Hite
	Major Ebenezer Beebe
	Major Talbot Chambers
Inspector General:	Major James Gibson
Assistant Inspector General:	Lieutenant John R. Bell
Commissary General of Ordnance:	Colonel Decius Wadsworth
Chief Medical Officer:	Surgeon W.M. Ross
Medical Officer, Headquarters Staff:	Surgeon Ezekiel Bull
Contractor's Agent:	Mr. James W. Thorne

First Brigade (est. 1311)

Commanding Officer:	Brigadier General John Parker Boyd
Fifth US Infantry Regiment (551)	Colonel Daniel Bissell
Twelfth US Infantry Regiment (369)	Major Robert C. Nicholas
Thirteenth US Infantry Regiment (391)	Colonel James P. Preston

Second Brigade (est. 1294)

Commanding Officer:	Brigadier General Jacob Brown
Fifteenth US Infantry Regiment (457)	Colonel David Brearley
Twenty-Second US Infantry Regiment (469)	Colonel Hugh Brady
Sixth Infantry Regiment (368)	Lieutenant Colonel James Miller

Third Brigade (est. 1407)

Commanding Officer:	Brigadier General Leonard Covington
Ninth US Infantry Regiment (468)	Lieutenant Colonel Thomas Aspinwall
Sixteenth US Infantry Regiment (377)	Colonel Cromwell Pearce
Twenty-Fifth US Infantry Regiment (562)	Colonel Edmund P. Gaines

Fourth Brigade (est. 1348)

Commanding Officer:	Brigadier General Robert Swartout
Battalion, Eleventh US Infantry Regiment (449)	Lieutenant Colonel Timothy Upham
Fourteenth US Infantry Regiment (267)	Lieutenant Colonel Timothy Dix
Twenty-First US Infantry Regiment (632)	Colonel Eleazer Wheelock Ripley

Reserve Brigade or Elite (est. 1143)

Commanding Officer:	Brigadier General Alexander Macomb
Third Regiment of US Artillery (350)	Colonel Winfield Scott
Twentieth US Infantry Regiment (230)	Colonel Thomas Mann Randolph
Battalion, First US Rifle Regiment (263)	Lieutenant Colonel Benjamin Forsyth
Albany Volunteers (300)	Unknown

Cavalry (est. 460)

First Regiment of US Light Dragoons (249)	Lieutenant Colonel Nelson Luckett
Second Regiment of US Light Dragoons (211)	Major John T. Woodford

Artillery (est. 348) (See note below)

Commanding Officer:	Brigadier General Moses Porter
Regiment of US Light Artillery (264)	Lieutenant Colonel Abram Eustis
Second Regiment of US Artillery (78)	Captain Samuel B. Archer
Ordnance (see note below)	

Capitulation

First Brigade:	1311
Second Brigade:	1294
Third Brigade:	1407
Fourth Brigade:	1348
Reserve Brigade:	1143
Cavalry:	460
Artillery:	348
Total:	7311

Notes on the Strength of Wilkinson's Army

The strength figures above include *both fit and sick* troops. Wilkinson commanded a very unhealthy army: he estimated that fourteen hundred men were on the sick list during the movement down the river, or about 19 per cent of his total strength while other senior officers calculated the percentage of sick as even higher. The strength of Wilkinson's army has always been a subject of some uncertainty and this has not been helped by the poor records available for the period October-November 1813.

There are two relevant returns. The first, contained in the evidence presented at Wilkinson's court martial, is dated 9 October 1813 and titled "Order of Encampment," and was promulgated on the reorganization of the army undertaken when the divisions from Sackets Harbor and Fort George joined together. It lists and provides total strength figures for the units of the four infantry brigades but no numbers for the reserve brigade or the cavalry and artillery. The second return, furnished by Armstrong to Congress in January 1814 is dated 1 December 1813 and lists the units at French Mills on that date and their strengths giving a total of 8,143 men. Evidence presented at Wilkinson's court martial indicates that the figures in this return are inflated and Wilkinson's own calculation of his strength at French Mills in early December was 6,344 enlisted men of whom 4,482 were fit and 1,762 sick.

Wilkinson's assertion is borne out by a third return, "Abstract from the General Returns of Effective Force of the Following Corps," dated 1 January 1814, which was used as an additional check on numbers. This document lists not only all the infantry units known to have been on the river as being at French Mills but also a battalion of the Tenth Infantry. This battalion was formerly with Hampton's division and must have been transferred to French Mills sometime in November because it is not listed among the units of that formation at Plattsburgh in early January. Deducting these two units from those listed at French Mills on 1 January 1814, leaves a total of 3,514 men, much less than the 1 December return but this figure is for *effectives only and does not include the sick* nor does it include the two dragoon regiments who, by this time, had moved back to Sackets Harbor.

It would appear that the most reliable evidence for the strength of Wilkinson's army is that of the return dated 9 October and that document has been used as the basis for the strength in the above order of battle for those units for which it gives figures. The strengths of those units for which no figures were provided in this return was drawn from other evidence (listed below). The actual number of troops brought into battle by this army on 11 November 1813 is contained in Appendix E below.

Note on the Artillery of Wilkinson's Army, November 1813

Wilkinson's artillery was commanded by Brigadier General Moses Porter and comprised elements of three different units: the Light Artillery Regiment and the Second and Third Artillery Regiments. The Third Artillery acted mainly as infantry during the campaign, although one company served as gunners. The other two units functioned in their traditional role.

There is, unfortunately, no accurate information on the type and number of Wilkinson's artillery but, based on extant sources, it apparently consisted of between twenty and thirty-three weapons. Of these, the following types and calibres have been conclusively identified as having been with the army in November 1813:

1 x 24-pdr. gun	abandoned at Ogdensburg
4 x 18-pdr. guns	one abandoned at Ogdensburg, 3 landed on 1-2 and 10 November 1813
8 x 6-pdr. guns	landed and brought into action on 10-11 November 1813
1 x 13-inch mortar	abandoned at Ogdensburg
1 x 10-inch mortar	abandoned at Ogdensburg
2 x 5$^1/_2$-inch howitzers	identified by Porter during testimony at Wilkinson's court martial

The presence of such heavy weapons as the mortars and 24-pdr. gun is understandable as, when organizing the artillery, the three officers responsible, Porter and Colonels Decius Wadsworth and Alexander Macomb, would have calculated on having to attack some fortified positions during the course of the forthcoming operation. Wilkinson's artillery was divided into "field" and "siege or battering" pieces. The not altogether reliable return of 9 October 1813 shows, in visual form, the artillery of the army as being thirty-three weapons manned by ten symbols which appear (no further information is given) to be individual artillery half-companies, six of these manning twenty-two weapons attached to the four brigades of infantry and four manning seventeen weapons attached to the "Reserve" or "Park." If this depiction is accurate (and it may well not be), then Wilkinson's artillery consisted of six sub-units (probably half-companies) of field artillery with twenty-two guns and four sub-units (probably half-companies) manning seventeen heavy weapons. The names of five officers are identified with the field artillery symbols: Captains Robert Macpherson and Luther Leonard of the Light Artillery, Captains Samuel B. Archer and Spottswood Henry of the Second Artillery and Captain Alexander Brooks of the Third Artillery.

The question is – what type of ordnance equipped these two components of Wilkinson's artillery? Some idea of the composition of the field artillery can be gained from a "Project of Artillery" submitted by Colonel Decius Wadsworth, one of Wilkinson's senior artillery officers, to the secretary of war in 1812 which recommends that two-thirds be 6-pdr. guns while the remaining third be divided equally between 12 and 18-pdr. guns, and 5$^1/_2$-inch howitzers. Most period artillery authors recommend that the composition of a force of heavy or siege artillery be two thirds heavy 18 or 24-pdr. guns and the remaining third divided equally between between heavy mortars (10 and 13-inch) and howitzers (8-inch).

Taking all the above into consideration, a plausible breakdown of Wilkinson's artillery in November 1813 based on information in the 9 October return would be as follows:

Field artillery (3 companies)

6 x 12 or 18-pdr. guns

14 x 6-pdr. guns

2 x 5.5 inch howitzers

Siege artillery (2 companies)

12 x 18 or 24-pdr. guns

1 x 13-inch mortars

2 x 10-inch mortars

2 x 8-inch howitzers

Sources for Strength Figures
USNA, RG 107, Micro 222, Reel 8, Abstract from the General Returns of the Effective Force, 1 February 1814; *American State Papers: Military Affairs*, I, 481, Abstract ... showing the whole number of General Wilkinson's army, 1 December 1812; HSP, Carr Diary, Brigade Order, Second Brigade, 15 Sep. 1813: NAC, MG 23, F16, Walworth-Simonds Correspondence, Walworth to 9 Aug. 1813; John C. Fredriksen, ed., "The War of 1812 in Northern New York: The Observations of Captain Rufus McIntire," *New York History*, July 1987, McIntire to Holmes, 8 December 1813; Samuel Harris, "Service of Captain Samuel D. Harris," *Buffalo Historical Society Publications*, 24; Francis B. Heitman, *Historical Register and Dictionary of the United States Army* (2 vols., Washington, 1903); *Register, and Rules and Regulations of the Army for 1813* (Washington, December 1813); James Wilkinson, *Memoirs of My Own Times* (3 vols., Philadelphia, 1816), 3, General Order of Encampment, 9 October 1813.

Sources for Artillery of the Army
USNA, RG 107, Micro 221, Reel 49, Wadsworth to SW, 14 November 1812, Project of Artillery for an Army of 48 Battalions; Ralph W. Adye, *The Bombardier and Pocket Gunner* (London, 1813); Jean-Jacques Basilien de Gassendi, *Aide-Memoire, a l'usage des Officiers de l'artillerie de France* (2 vols., Paris, 1801); Henri Othon De Scheel, *Treatise on Artillery* (Philadelphia, 1800); W.L. Haskin, *The History of the First Regiment of Artillery* (Ft. Preble, 1879); Francis B. Heitman, *Historical Register and Dictionary of the United States Army* (2 vols., Washington, 1903); George Richards, Memoir of Alexander Macomb (New York, 1843); *New York Evening Post*, 29 November 1813, Letter from a gentleman in Hamilton village, 14 November 1813; *Register, and Rules and Regulations of the Army for 1813* (Washington, December 1813); [Amos Stoddard], *Exercise for the Garrison and Field Ordnance, Together with Manoeuvres of Horse Artillery ...* (Philadelphia, 1812); Louis de Tousard, *American Artillerist's Companion, or Elements of Artillery* (2 vols., Philadelphia, 1809); James Wilkinson, *Memoirs of My Own Times* (3 vols., Philadelphia, 1816), 3, testimony of Brooks, Eustis, Macpherson, Porter, Walbach, Wadsworth and Wilkinson.

Order of Battle and Strength

**BRIGADIER GENERAL JOHN BOYD'S COMMAND,
UNITED STATES ARMY, 11 NOVEMBER 1813**

Commanding Officer:	Brigadier General John Parker Boyd
Staff	
Aides to General Boyd:	Lieutenant Henry Whiting
	Lieutenant William Jenkins Worth
Chief of Staff:	Colonel Joseph G. Swift
Adjutant General:	Colonel John de Barth Walbach
Inspector General:	Colonel John Johnson
Assistant Adjutant Generals:	Major Ebenezer Beebe
	Major Talbot Chambers

First Brigade (est. 450)	
Commanding Officer:	Colonel Isaac Coles
Twelfth US Infantry Regiment (225)	Major Robert C. Nicholas
Thirteenth US Infantry Regiment (225)	Colonel James P. Preston

Third Brigade (est. 900)	
Commanding Officer:	Brigadier General Leonard Covington
Ninth US Infantry Regiment (300)	Lieutenant Colonel Thomas Aspinwall
Sixteenth US Infantry Regiment (225)	Colonel Cromwell Pearce
Twenty-Fifth US Infantry Regiment (375)	Colonel Edmund P. Gaines

Fourth Brigade (est. 850)	
Commanding Officer:	Brigadier General Robert Swartout
Eleventh US Infantry Regiment (300)	Lieutenant Colonel Timothy Upham
Fourteenth US Infantry Regiment (125)	Lieutenant Colonel Timothy Dix
Twenty-First US Infantry Regiment (425)	Colonel Eleazer Wheelock Ripley

Boat Guard (600)

Commanding Officer:	Lieutenant Colonel Timothy Upham, Twelfth US Infantry
Second-in-Command:	Major Richard Malcom, Thirteenth US Infantry

Cavalry (est. 150)

Second Regiment of US Light Dragoons	Major John T. Woodford

Artillery (est. 100)

Commanding Officer:	Lieutenant Henry Knox Craig, Second Artillery
detachment, Regiment of Light Artillery	Lieutenant Armstrong Irvine
detachment, Second Regiment of Artillery	Lieutenant Henry Knox Craig
6 x 6-pdr. guns	

Capitulation: American Troops in Action, 11 November 1813:

First Brigade:	450
Third Brigade:	900
Fourth Brigade:	850
Boat Guard:	600
Cavalry:	150
Artillery:	100
Total:	3050

Notes

The unit strengths of Boyd's infantry were arrived at by taking the unit totals in Appendix D and subtracting 19 per cent or one-fifth for the sick. From the remaining total, Upham's boat guard of six hundred was deducted to arrive at the figures provided above. The boat guard appears to have been drawn from every unit in the three brigades and it is likely that each regiment contributed one company or half-company to it.

The figure for Woodford's dragoons on 11 November 1813 comes from Captain Samuel Harris of the unit. He estimated that, of the two hundred sabres present with the squadron that morning, between fifty and seventy dragoons did not participate as combatants in the action because they were used as ammunition carriers or their horses were taken to mount senior officers and pull Craig's four artillery pieces.

There is no accurate information on the number of gunners in Craig's command – the figures stated above are an estimate based on the authorized size of gun detachments for American 6-pdr. field guns.

Sources

See sources for strength figures of the main army in Appendix D. Also, *Niles Weekly Register*, 5, 18 December 1813, Boyd to Wilkinson, 12 November 1813 plus attached casualty return dated same day; John P. Boyd, *Documents and Facts Relating to Military Events During the Late War* (Boston, 1816), 21, Boyd to SW, 29 April 1815.

Order of Battle and Strength

Commanding Officer: Lieutenant Colonel Joseph Morrison, 89th Foot

Staff

Chief of Staff: Lieutenant Colonel John Harvey

Aides to Colonel Morrison: Captain John Crysler, Militia of Upper Canada
Captain Reuben Sherwood, Militia of Upper Canada
Lieutenant Christopher Hagerman, Incorporated Militia

Quartermaster-General's Department Captain Edward Davis
Captain Robert Skinner
Lieutenant Andrew Bulger

49th Regiment of Foot (8 companies, 304)

Commanding Officer: Lieutenant Colonel Charles Plenderleath

89th Regiment of Foot (5 companies, 240)

Commanding Officer: Major Miller Clifford

The Advance (4 companies, 184)

Commanding Officer: Lieutenant Colonel Thomas Pearson
Grenadier company, 49th Foot (39) Lieutenant Samuel Holland
Light Company, 49th Foot (39)
2 companies, Canadian Fencibles (108)

Captain Barnes's Command, 89th Foot (3 companies, 144)

Commanding Officer: Captain George West Barnes, 89th Foot
Three companies, 89th Foot (144)

The Light Troops (192)

Commanding Officer:	Major Frederick G. Heriot
Canadian Voltigeurs (3 companies, 150)	Captain Jacques Adhémar
	Captain William Johnson
	Captain Jacques-Clément Herse
Provincial Light Dragoons (12)	Captain Richard D. Fraser
Mohawk Warriors (30)	Lieutenant Charles Anderson

Royal Artillery (est. 63)

Commanding Officer:	Captain Henry G. Jackson, RA
3 x 6-pdr. guns	

Capitulation

Infantry	1064
Cavalry	12
Artillery	63
Mohawk Warriors	30
Total	**1169**

Notes

Sixty officers and men of the Dundas militia were present at the action but there is no evidence they engaged in combat and they were probably used for such tasks as the evacuation of wounded and ammunition supply. One was wounded and twenty-nine received the Crysler's Farm clasp to the General Service Medal.

The figures for the remaining troops are for enlisted personnel only (sergeants, drummers, corporals and privates). Morrison estimated his own strength at eight hundred and many historians have relied on this statement but research for this book has revealed that there were more British and Canadians present at the battle and it is likely that, when Morrison made this statement, he was referring only to the "rank and file" (privates and corporals) strength of the troops he brought from Kingston and not including the detachment he picked up at Prescott.

The number of companies of the 49th and 89th Foot, and the Canadian Voltigeurs, at the action can be fairly accurately established from the sources below. The strength figure for these units was derived by taking the average strength (excluding sick) of a company in these units as contained in the monthly returns of 25 October 1813, the return closest to the date of the battle.

Ascertaining the size and composition of the detachment of Canadian Fencibles who fought in the battle has been a particular problem. It was either two companies with the strength stated above or a detachment in the strength of two companies with the strength listed above. It has not been possible to identify exactly which officers of the unit were present and who commanded this detachment.

The breakdown of Morrison's army by nationality is interesting. The vast majority (929) were British regulars while 270 were Canadian regulars (the Voltigeurs and dragoons have been included as regulars) and, of these, about three-quarters were French-speaking *Canadiens*.

Sources

Archives of Ontario, MU 1632, Kingsford papers, scrapbook 4, p. 117, Recollections of the Battle of Chrystler's Farm by an Eyewitness, Col. Sewell. Public Record Office: WO 17, General Monthly Returns of the Army, 25 September, 25 October, 25 November 1813; vol. 263, Return of the 49th Foot, 25 October 1813 and Monthly Return of the 49th Foot, 25 November 1813; vol. 266, Monthly Return, 2/89th Foot, 25 December 1813; vol. 269, Monthly Return of the Canadian Fencibles, 25 October 1813, Return of the Canadian Fencibles, 25 November 1813; WO 25: vol. 2187, Return of the Casualties of the Canadian Fencibles, 25 December 1813-25 January 1814; WO 44, vol. 248: Return of the Serviceable Brass, and Iron Ordnance on the several Batteries, Prescott, 30 June 1813; Return of Brass Ordnance, Travelling Carriages, etc., 30 June 1813. National Archives of Canada: CO 42, vol. 122, p. 291, Prevost to Bathurst, 30 October 1813. RG 8 I: vol. 681, p. 59, Corrected Return of the Killed, Wounded & Missing, 11 November 1813; vol. 681, p. 82, Morrison to de Rottenburg, 12 November 1813; vol. 1708, p. 60, General Monthly Return of the Sick, 24 September 1813.

Bath Archives, 393, Henry G. Jackson to George Jackson, 19 November 1813; E.A. Cruickshank, *Documentary History:* 7, 129, Return of the Troops at Prescott, 15 September 1813 and *Documentary History*, 8, 165, Memorandum of the Services of Lt. Colonel Charles Plenderleath; L.H. Irving, *Officers of the British Forces in Canada, 1812-1815* (Welland, 1908); Luc Lepine, *Lower Canada's Militia Officers, 1812-1815* (Montreal, 1996); Stuart Sutherland, *His Majesty's Gentlemen* (Toronto, 1999).

The Crysler's Farm and Châteauguay Medals and Recipients

BY STEPHEN PALLAS

Small Army Gold Medals

During the period of the Napoleonic Wars, officers of the British and allied armies who commanded units at "brilliant and distinguished events in which the success of His Majesty's arms has received the royal approbation" were eligible for gold medals. General officers received the Large Army Gold Medal and lower ranks received the Small Army Gold Medal. This medal carries on the obverse the figure of Britannia and on the reverse the name of the engagement wreathed in laurel and was worn suspended from a buckle with a red ribbon with blue edges.

In January 1814, Lieutenant-General Sir George Prevost was asked to provide the names of those officers under his command who had "been most distinguished" in actions "against superior numbers of the enemy." In his response he nominated nine officers who had fought at either Châteauguay or Crysler's Farm for gold medals which were later awarded. These officers were:

Châteauguay
Lieutenant Colonel George Macdonnell, Glengarry Light Infantry
Lieutenant Colonel Charles-Michel d'Irumberry de Salaberry, Canadian Voltigeurs

Crysler's Farm (Note: "Chrystler's Farm" is engraved on the medal)
Lieutenant Colonel John Harvey, 6th Garrison Battalion, acting on the staff
Lieutenant Colonel Joseph Wanton Morrison, 89th Foot
Lieutenant Colonel Thomas Pearson, 23rd Foot, acting on the staff (received a clasp to his Gold Medal awarded for Albuera)
Lieutenant Colonel Charles Plenderleath, 49th Foot
Major Miller Clifford, 89th Foot
Major Frederick George Heriot, Canadian Voltigeurs
Second Captain Henry George Jackson, Royal Artillery

(Left) Field officer's Small Gold Medal, Battle of Crysler's Farm, 1813

Awarded to unit commanders who participated in "brilliant and distinguished events in which the success of His Majesty's arms has received royal approbation," Colonels de Salaberry, Harvey, Macdonell, Morrison, Pearson and Plenderleath, Majors Clifford and Heriot, and Captain Henry Jackson received this medal for their efforts at Châteauguay and Crysler's Farm. This particular example belonged to Major George Heriot who commanded Morrison's light troops on 11 November 1813. (From *Canadian Antiquarian and Numismatic Journal*, 1911)

(Right) Military General Service Medal, 1793-1814, with Crysler's Farm clasp

The Military General Service Medal was instituted in 1847 for all surviving officers and soldiers who had participated in the Napoleonic Wars. Twenty-nine engagements, including Crysler's Farm and Châteauguay, were commemorated by a special clasp worn on the ribbon of the medal. (Benson Lossing, *Pictorial Field Book of the War of 1812*)

Military General Service Medal, 1793-1814, with Châteauguay and Chrysler's Farm Clasps

In 1847 it was decided to award medals to all surviving officers and soldiers who had participated in the battles of the Napoleonic period. It was also decided to issue clasps for each engagement that had been recognized by the previous award of an Army Gold Medal. A total of twenty-nine clasps were authorized including those for Châteauguay and Crysler's Farm. The medals and the relevant clasps were distributed to those eligible veterans who made application (and many did not bother) and approximately nine hundred medals were distributed to veterans of the fighting in Canada during the War of 1812.

The Military General Service Medal carries the head of Queen Victoria on the obverse and, on the reverse, the Queen seated on a dais holding a laurel wreath over the Duke of Wellington, who kneels before her. It is impressed on its edge with the name of the recipient and his regiment and was worn suspended from a red ribbon with blue edges.

The names of the British and Canadian applicants for the medal who received a clasp for Châteauguay or Crysler's Farm are as follows. Note that the ranks may not be those held by the officer or man at the date of actions but at the time the medals were distributed. The clasp for Crysler's Farm is embossed "Chrystler's Farm."

Although every effort has been made to ensure that the following information is as accurate as possible, there may be errors in it owing to inaccuracies in the original records and published sources from which this list was compiled. Those that have been identified to date are indicated by an endnote.

366

Châteauguay, 26 October 1813

British Army

Staff
Bourke, Major George Thew (also with clasp Egypt)
Freer, Captain Noah
Fulton, Lieutenant-Colonel James

Royal Artillery
Dougherty, Private James
Gibson, Gunner John
Purdie, Private John

Canadian Fencibles
OFFICERS
Delisle, Lieutenant Benjamin

ENLISTED MEN
Galarneau, Private Alexis
Germain, Private Pierre
Lamirande, Private Theodore
Oman dit Francoeur, Private

Canadian Units

Staff
de Boucherville, Lieutenant-Colonel Pierre

Artillery, Militia of Lower Canada
Barrette, Driver Joseph
Miclette, Private Joseph
Tome, Private Hugh (also with clasp for Crysler's Farm)

Canadian Chasseurs
Bouchard, Private Louis
Clouthier, Private Vincent
Gauthier, Private Damase
Labelle, Sergeant Charles
Lefebvre, Private Hyacinthe

Canadian Voltigeurs
OFFICERS
Clarke, Lieutenant William
Duchesnay, Lieutenant Narcisse
Globensky, Lieutenant Maxime
de Rouville, Captain Jean-Baptiste

ENLISTED MEN
Aljoe, Private John
Aubry, Joseph
Beaudoin, Private Andre
Billard, Private Benjamin
Brissette, Private Hypolite
Brown, Sergeant William
Claprood, Private Louis
Carrier, Private Toussaint
Charette, Private Jean-Baptiste
Daigneau, Private Charles
Dufour, Private Jean-Baptiste
Dugre, Private Olivier
Facette, Private Joseph
Fluet, Private Edouard
Gagnon, Private Augustin
Gaitors, Sergeant James
Grenier, Private Antoine
Helene, Private Simon
Hoyle, Private James R.
Jubb, Sergeant Major William
Julien, Private Joseph
Leduc, Private Pierre
Petitclair, Private Charles
Pigeon, Private Jean-Baptiste
Plante, Private Jean-Baptiste
Potvin, Private Jean-Baptiste
Proulx, Private Jacques
Richer dit Louveteau, Private Joseph
Rousseau dit Brook, Private Francis
Sharp, Private William
Tremblay, Sergeant Etienne
Tribot dit l'Afriquain, Private Edouard
Turcotte, Private Amable
Vincent, Private Louis
Vincent, Private Stanislas
Williamson, Private John

1st Battalion, Select Embodied Militia
OFFICERS
Burke, Ensign Charles
MacKay, Lieutenant Louis Eustache
Panet, Captain the Hon. Phillipe

ENLISTED MEN
Belanger, Private Guillaume
Benoit, Private Pierre
Berthiaume, Private Jean-Baptiste
Binet, Private Antoine
Boivin, Sergeant Elisee
Bouchard, Private Elie

Brown, Sergeant George Bess
Cloutier, Private Pierre
Cote, Private Jean
Courteau, Private Augustin
Desrochers, Private Jean
Doyer, Private Augustin
Duperre, Private Henri
Duseanme (Dumesne?), Private François
Filion, Private Olivier
Gagnon, Private Joseph
Gauthier dit Larouche, Private Augustin
Gonthier, Private Pierre
Hebert, Private Joseph
Lafontaine, Private Jacques
Lafrance, Private Louis
Langevin, Private Pierre
Lemieux, Private Michel
Lenseigne, Private Augustin
Lessard, Private Pierre
Mauricette, Private Joseph
Maye, Private Isidore
Paschal, Corporal Jean
Poulin, Private Jean-Baptiste
Proulx, Private Alexis
Robitaille, Private Etienne
Roy, Sergeant Jacques
Royer, Sergeant Lazard
Seguin, Sergeant Pierre
Terrien, Private Fereol
Vachon, Private Jerome
Vachon, Private Louis
Vezina, Private Joseph
Williams, Sergeant Olivier Robert

2nd Battalion, Select Embodied Militia

OFFICERS
Barbeau, Captain Louis
Dumont, Lieutenant Alphonse
Globensky, Lieutenant F.E.
de Labruere, Major Pierre René Boucherd
Laviolette, Lieutenant Jean-Baptiste
Leprohon, Lieutenant Edouard M.
MacKay, Captain Stephen

ENLISTED MEN
Arcand, Private Francis
Auger, Private Charles
Beaudry, Private Joseph
Bedard, Private Thomas
Belleau, Private Pierre
Blais, Private Joseph

Brisebois, Private François
Bureau, Private Joseph
Cloutier, Private Jean
Couture, Private Antoine
Degourdelle dit Lonchamps, Private
  Pierre
Drolet, Sergeant Jacques
Dubeau, Private François
Gauthier, Private Antoine
Gauvin, Private Ignace
Gauvreau, Private Louis
Gosselin, Private Joachim
Grenier, Private Olivier
Lacombe, Corporal Pierre
Laroche, Private François
Leclerc dit Francoeur, Private Joseph
Lefebvre, Private Alexis
Legare, Private Joseph
Legault, Private Jean-Baptiste
Monette, Private Joseph
Morin, Private Louis
Page, Private Louis Gonzague
Patris, Private Joseph
Petit dit St. Pierre, Private Jerome
Robert, Private Pierre
Robert, Corporal Pierre
Robitaille, Private Charles
Roy, Private Amable
St. Hilaire, Private Jean-Baptiste
Simard, Private Augustin
Vaillancourt, Private Charles
Verreault, Private Barthelemi

3rd Battalion, Select Embodied Militia

OFFICERS
Doucet, Major Nicolas B.
Goddu, Ensign Toussaint
Shuter, Captain Joseph

ENLISTED MEN
Berube, Private Joseph
Bouchard, Sergeant Elie
Courcy, Private Germain
Daigle, Private François
Dube, Private Magloire
Dufour, Private Alexis
Dumoulin, Private François
Emo, Private Henri
Gauthier, Private Joseph
Girard, Private Lambert
Guenette, Private Pierre

Lavasseur, Private Joseph
Lavoie, Private Joseph
Masse, Private Joseph
Mercier, Corporal Joseph
Ouellet, Private Antoine
Pilon, Sergeant Jean-Baptiste
Plourde, Private Prosper
Pradet dit St. Gelais, Private Jean-Baptiste
Robichaud, Private Germain
Simard, Private Vital
Simon, Private Hyacinthe
Tremblay, Private Christophe
Vanasse dit Vertefeuille, Private Pierre
Vaudal, Private Roger

4th Battalion, Select Embodied Militia
Cote, Private Jean-Baptiste
Dufresne, Private François
Foucher, Sergeant Jacques
Gendron, Sergeant Pierre
Hudon dit Beaulieu, Private Louis Paschal
Lacerte, Private Charles
Lesieur, Sergeant Joseph Madore
Morault, Private François
Robidas, Sergeant François
Veillet, Private Jean-Baptiste

5th Battalion, Select Embodied Militia

OFFICERS
Berczy, Captain William
Cuvillier, Captain Austin
Desfresne, Lieutenant Flavien
Larocque, Captain François A.
Rottot, Lieutenant Pierre
Tache, Lieutenant Etienne P.

ENLISTED MEN
Baillargeon, Private Joseph
Blanchet, Private Benjamin
Bock (Brock?), Private Charles
Brissette, Corporal Antoine
Cameron, Private Antoine
Clairmont (Clement?), Private François
Dostie, Private Joseph
Dupile, Private Michel
Godbout, Private Pierre
Goulet, Private Jean
Guibault, Private Hypolite
Laferte, Private Antoine
Latour dit Forget, Private Pierre
Leprohon, Private Joseph

Masse, Private Jean-Baptiste
Plante, Private Prisque
Proulx, Sergeant Joseph
Robert, Private Jean-Baptiste
Rousseau, Private François Jean
Tremblay, Private Flavien
Verret, Private Joseph

Militia of Lower Canada

OFFICERS
Mignault, Lieutenant Etienne (St. Denis Militia)

ENLISTED MEN
Aimond, Private Henri
Auclaire, Private Joseph
Bedard, Private Joseph
Belanger, Private Pierre
Belisle, Private Antoine
Berube, Private Jean-Baptiste
Boisvert, Private Pierre
Boucher, Private Pierre
Brogden, Sergeant François
Cimon, François
Corbeau, Private Louis
Daigneau, Private Antoine (Beauharois Militia)
Drolet, Private Pierre
Duchaine, Bruneau
Dupuis, Private François (Select Embodied Militia)
Fortier, Private Joseph
Gagnon, Private Jean-Baptiste
Garneau, Private Jacques
Julien, Private Louis (Beauharois Militia)
Lapierre, Private Jean-Baptiste (also clasps for Fort Detroit and Chrystler's Farm)
Leblond, Private Magloire
LeFrançois, Private Jean Heim
Lepart, Private Pierre
L'Esperance, Private Simon Telon
Marcot, Private Joseph
Marcotte, Private Joseph
Monpetit, Private Jean-Baptiste
Mousette, Private Jean-Baptiste
Naud, Private Jacques
Page, Private Olivier
Peltier, Private Jean-Baptiste
Poissant, Private Andre (Beauharnois Militia)

Potvin, Private Michel A.
Pradet dit St. Gelais, Private Bernard
Racine, Private Michel
Renaud, Private François
Robitaille, Private Olivier
St. Marie, Corporal Pierre (Beauharnois Militia)
Saumier, Private Louis
Surprenant, Private François (Canadian Guides)
Therien, Private François
Toussignant, Private Jerome
Tremblay, Private Edouard
Tremblay, Private Jean-Baptiste

Militia of Upper Canada
Jewell, Private Ebenezer

Indian Department

OFFICERS
Annance, Lieutenant Noel
Ducharme, Captain Dominique
Launiere, Lieutenant Legere
Maccomber, Lieutenant Jarvise
de Niverville, Lieutenant Joseph Boucher

CHIEFS
Katstirakeron, Saro
Metzalabanlette, Joseph
Picard, Laurent
Portneuf, Ignace
Romain, Andre
Sioui, Michel
Tekanasontie, Martin
Tiohatekon, Atonsa
Tomoquois, Louis

WARRIORS
Anaicha, Saro
Anionken, Sawatis
Annance Cadnash, Charles
Anontara, Saro,
Arenhoktha, Saro
Arosin, Wishe
Atenhara, Henias
Awachouche, Marie-Joseph
Awennaniio, Atonioa
Chouquelin, Louis
Honastiokon, Wishe
Honenharakete, Roren
Jahoaron, Rowi
Jakohate, Atonsa

Jasent
Kanenhariio, Rasar
Kanewatiron, Henias
Kaniakaroton, Saksarie
Karakontie, Arenne
Karenhoton, Atonsa
Kariwakeron, Sak
Karoniarakwen, Tier
Nikarakwasa, Atonsa
Sakahoronkwas, Triom
Sakoiatiiostha, Sose
Sakoratentha, Sawatis
Sakonentsiase, Sose
Sarenhowane, Arik
Sasennowane, Lazar
Saskwenharowane, Saro
Sawennowane, Atonsa
Shakarie, Antoine
Skaionwiio, Wishe
Soclan, Louis
Sononsese, Sose
Solaontion, Sak
Sowenhese, Tier
Taiakonentakete, Wishe
Taietakhenontie, Koi
Takontakete, Sak
Taratie, Sak
Tawentsiakwente, Saksarie
Tawesennenton, Saksarie
Tehaionwakhwa, Wishe
Tehiaase, Atonsa
Tekarihontie, Wishe
Tekaionwanhontere, Atonsa
Tewasarasere, Roiir
Tewaserake, Henias
Thanonianitha, Saro
Thasarenhawakwen, Sasatis
Thoientakon, Simon
Thomas, Noel
Thostosoroton, Saro
Tiakothare, Wishe
Tiohakwente, Tier
Tohesennenton, Tier
Tseoherisen, Tier
Tsiorakwisin, Rosi
Tsioriwa, Tier
Wawalomette, Antoine

Crysler's Farm, 11 November 1813

British Army

Royal Artillery
Gosling, Gunner Thomas
Martin, Private Dennis
Nuttall, Private Samuel
Sterland, Private Joseph[1]
Wells, Private Joseph

Royal Artillery Drivers
Boyle, Private John[2]

49th Regiment of Foot

OFFICERS
Morton, Lieutenant Harcourt
Munro, Lieutenant Hector
Ormond, Captain Harry Smith
Richmond, Lieutenant Sylvester
Sewell, Ensign John St. Alban[3]
Thompson, Ensign Augustus
Wrightwick, Captain Norman

ENLISTED MEN
Albert, Sergeant John
Booth, Sergeant William
Braithwaite, Private George
Brandon, Private Thomas
Brown, Private John
Brown, Corporal Josh
Brown, Private Thomas
Carthy, Private James
Comerford, Private Richard
Connelly, Private Matthew
Connelly, Private Michael
Conshay, Sergeant Joseph
Cronsby, Sergeant John
Dillon, Sergeant Frederick
Donnelly, Private William
Dooley, Private Lawrence
Fraser, Private John
Gardiner, Private Thomas
Gibson, Private Gideon
Gilstain, Q.M. Sergeant Arthur
Greenwood, Private Michael
Hawker, Drummer Charles
Hughes, Private William
James, Private John
Jamieson, Private Arthur
Keep, Private Arthur

Kerrigan, Private James
Kilgar, Private Miles
Laville, Private Michael
Lawlor, Private Nicholas
Leary, Private Thomas
Lees, Private John
Liston, Private Edward
Long, Sergeant John
Maunion, Private Thomas
McEnter, Sergeant Charles
McKeavor, Private Hugh
McLaughlin, Private John
Moore, Corporal Lawrence
Mordell, Private Robert
Murphy, Private Patrick
Newington, Private Abraham
Parsons, Private William
Plunkett, Sergeant Peter
Potter, Private Reuben
Roberts, Private Hugh
Rooke (or Roak), Private James
Rossiter, Private James
Rossiter, Private Thomas
Rougham, Private John
Scott, Private John
Shane, Private Michael
Shoreder, Private Alexander
Smith, Private Patrick
Staynes, Private Dennis
Thomas, Private George
Walsh, Private Anthony
Warren, Private Richard
Young, Private Robert

2nd Battalion, 89th Regiment of Foot

OFFICERS
Gore, Captain Henry Ross
Lewis, Lieutenant Henry Ogle
Shand, Captain John Muller

ENLISTED MEN
Baker, Sergeant John
Baylis, Private Francis
Billinger, Private John
Blane, Private Thomas
Burke, Private Thomas
Carroll, Private Patrick
Cassidy, Private John
Clarke, Private George
Cole, Sergeant William
Cosgrove, Sergeant Lawrence

Craigh, Sergeant William
Curley, Private Rich
Edwards, Private Joseph
Ferris, Private Thomas
Flinn, Private John
Flynn, Private William
Foster, Private John
Fricker, Private George
Garner, Private John
Gedding, Private James
Gibson, Private Absalom
Gillespie, Private James
Gordon, Private William
Hamilton, Private William
Hanfield, Private Lawrence
Harris, Private John
Hartland, Private John
Hasett, Private Michael
Hewson, Private Isaac
Hewson, Private John
Hill, Private Richard
Hines, Private John
Holland, Sergeant Patrick
Jordan, Private Edward
Kearns, Sergeant Marmaduke
Keating, Private John
King, Private William
Kirkham, Private John
Macalear, Private James
Mahon, Private John
Malone, Sergeant William
McCurry, Private Richard
McDonald, Private Richard
McDonald, Private Robert
McDonnell, Private John
McGurney, Private Terence
McKenzie, Private William
Mougan, Private John
Mulcravey, Private Patrick
Mulhall, Corporal Peter
Mullins, Private Patrick
Murphy, Private James
Murphy, Private John
Murray, Private Thomas
Naughton, Private Michael
Nowland, Private Richard
Parker, Private Phillip
Plumbley, Private John
Porch, Private Joseph
Price, Private Thomas

Rainey, Private William
Redshaw, Private Benjamin
Sedgwick, Private James
Sheridan, Private Philip[4]
Sibbald, Sergeant James
Silcock, Private James
Stevens, Private George
Sullivan, Private John
Swan, Private Samuel
Taylor, Private Abraham
Taylor, Private Benjamin
Thomas, Private John
Thomas, Private William
Thursday, Private George
Tone, Private Francis
Tracy, Private Patrick
Turner, Private James
Walsh, Private William
Ward, Sergeant Thomas
Wheatley, Private Benjamin
Whelan, Private Patrick

Canadian Fencibles

OFFICERS
Goodman, Captain Moses[5]

ENLISTED MEN
Brown, Sergeant Moses
Christy, Private John
Laporte, Sergeant Joseph
McLeod, Sergeant Daniel
Plamondon, Private Joseph

Others
Richardson, Private Bartholemew,
  Newfoundland Fencibles
Woodforde, Assistant Surgeon William,
  Medical Department[6]

Canadian Units

Canadian Voltiguers

OFFICERS
De Hertel, Lieutenant Daniel
Hebden, Lieutenant John[7]
Prendergast, Lieutenant James M.

ENLISTED MEN
Auge, Private Michel
Belinge, Private Antoine
Gadiva, Private Jean-Baptiste
Glass, Private George

Gouge, Private Charles
Grant, Sergeant John
Harkness, Corporal Andrew
Langevin, Private Joseph
Langevin, Sergeant Louis
Langevin, Private Regis
Leary, Private Thomas
McDougall, Bugler Duncan
Megre, Sergeant Jean-Baptiste
Morency, Private Marcel
Parent, Private Jean Olivier
Pelletier, Private Louis
Piche, Private Pierre
Portugais, Sergeant Jean-Baptiste
St.Etienne, Private John
Therien, Private François
Wagner, Corporal Frederick
Williamson, Sergeant John

1st Dundas Regiment, Militia of Upper Canada

OFFICER
Crysler, Captain John

ENLISTED MEN
Ault, Private Nicholas L.
Baker, Private Peter
Brouse, Private Jacob
Brouse, Sergeant Peter
Cook, Private George
Cook, Sergeant John
Doran, Private John
Kintner, Private Conrad
Lant, Private Frederick
Loucks, Sergeant John[8]
Loucks, Private Peter J.
McKay, Private Angus
Piller, Private John
Redman, Private Robert
Strader, Private John

Provincial (Fraser's) Light Dragoons

OFFICER
Fraser, Captain Richard Duncan

ENLISTED MEN
Brouse, Sergeant Nicholas G.
Dulmage, Sergeant Jacob
Freece, Private Peter
Shaver, Private Edward
Smyth, Private John R.

Canadian Chasseurs[9]

ENLISTED MEN
Morin, Private Barthelemi
Precour, Private Augustin
Proulx, Private Guillaume

Militia of Lower Canada

Desorme, Francis[10]
Gendron, Private Jacques (Colonel Robison's Battalion)[11]
Guibault, Private Hypolite, 5th Battalion, Select Embodied Militia[12]
Lapierre, Private Jean Baptiste (also with Fort Detroit and Châteauguay clasps)[13]
Paradis, Private Jacques[14]
Tome, Driver Hugh, Artillery (also with Châteauguay clasp)[15]

Militia of Upper Canada

OFFICER
Sherwood, Captain Reuben, 2nd Grenville Regiment

ENLISTED MEN
Acland, Private Charles, 1st Frontenac Regiment
Buell, Sergent William, 1st Leeds Regiment
Cameron, Private Hugh, 1st Stormont Regiment
Fraser, Private Simon, 1st Grenville Regiment
Read, Sergeant Guy, 2nd Grenville Regiment
Thompson, Robert, Militia of Upper Canada

Indian Department

WARRIORS
Keneguon, Joseph Skung (or Skunk)
Kenewe, John
Naliwhaquask King, James
Omeme, John Pigeon
Pahahiwickjecomwaby, Big Jacob
Pahguahjeneny, Old Peter
Patitickewa, John Snak (or Snake)
Powdash, George
Sasenowane, Tier (also with clasps "Fort Detroit" and "Châteauguay")
Shagaunnahquodwaby, Captain Jim
Shawindas, John Sunday

Notes

1. This man was also awarded the clasp for "Fort Detroit."
2. This man also received the clasp for "Corunna."
3. Although Sewell's clasp is engraved with the rank of ensign, he was actually a lieutenant at the time of the action.
4. This man also received the clasp for "Egypt."
5. Although Moses Goodman may have been an officer at the time the medal was awarded, in 1813 there is no record of him having been commissioned in the Canadian Fencibles.
6. This officer was actually attached to the 104th Foot, stationed at Kingston during November 1813. He must have volunteered to serve with Morrison.
7. This officer also received the clasp for "Martinique."
8. Loucks served with Fraser's dragoons during the action.
9. Although the following three soldiers received the Crysler's Farm medal as being members of the Canadian Chasseurs, this unit did not take part in the action of 11 November 1813. It is most probable that these men actually served with the Canadian Voltigeurs.
10. No unit was given for this man.
11. There was no battalion commander named Robison or Robinson in the militia of Upper or Lower Canada during the War of 1812. Given the man's surname, he is likely a *Canadien* and probably fought with the Canadian Voltigeurs during the action.
12. This unit was not present at the battle so this man must have been serving with another unit, probably the Canadian Voltigeurs.
13. Sources do not provide a unit for this man and to have been at both Châteauguay and Crysler's Farm would have taken some very tricky footwork.
14. The sources do not provide a unit for this man and he probably fought with the Canadian Voltigeurs.
15. As this man was an artillery driver, he may have had the opportunity to serve in both action but he would have been doing some hard travelling.

Sources

F.J. Blatherwick, *Canadian Orders Decorations and Medals* (Toronto, 1994); William Gray, *Soldiers of the King – The Upper Canadian Militia 1812-1815* (Boston Mills, 1995); R.W. Irwin, *War Medals and Decorations of Canada* (Toronto, 1969); A.L.T. Mullen, *The Military General Service Roll 1793-1814* (London, 1990); Stuart Sutherland, *His Majesty's Gentlemen* (Toronto, 1999); Ronald Way, "The Day of Crysler's Farm," *Canadian Geographical Journal*, 1961; Barbara Wilson, *Military General Service Medal 1793-1814 (Canadian Recipients), Egypt Medal 1882-1889 (Canadian Recipients) North West Canada 1885,* (London, 1975)

The Military Heritage of the Battles of Châteauguay and Crysler's Farm

The British Army

The 49th (or the Hertfordshire) Regiment of Foot is today, after many permutations, part of The Royal Anglian Regiment while the 89th Regiment of Foot is part of The Royal Irish Regiment. Thankfully, the Royal Artillery is still the Royal Artillery.

No battle honour was ever granted by the British army for Crysler's Farm although an attempt was made in 1819 by the commanding officer of the 89th Foot for "Christler's" to be borne on that unit's colours. Apparently, Sir George Prevost had declared to the officers of the 89th in 1815 that, as soon his court martial had finished, he would bring the matter before the proper authorities but unfortunately Prevost died before this could be done.

The response of the War Office to the request of the 89th Foot for a battle honour for Crysler's Farm was contained in a letter from the Duke of York, the commander-in-chief of the army, dated 25 July 1820. It is worth quoting at length because it is an indication of how the senior command of the British army viewed the war in North America, and it also serves as a sterling example both of the English penchant for calling a spade a digging implement used to excavate earth and a useful guide for the writing of lengthy but intelligible sentences that make correct use of subordinate clauses:

> His Royal Highness is perfectly sensible of the services of the late 2nd battalion 89th Regiment in Canada, which were very meritorious and such as might have been expected from the battalion, but as it did not happen to be the fortune of the battalion to be engaged in the description of actions, for which it has been usual to grant honorary distinction, His Royal Highness does not feel that he can consistently with the principles hitherto acted upon, recommend the request of the 89th Regiment to the favourable consideration of the Prince Regent.
>
> The Commander-in-Chief would at the same time regret if this decision should be thought in any degree to countenance the conclusion, that the action in which the 2nd battalion 89th Regiment bore a share in Canada, was under valued, because it happened to be of a less splendid character than others that occurred under different circumstances, and His Royal Highness would still further and more deeply regret, if ever the idea should go abroad or prevail in the army, that the gallantry of a regiment could be in any degree questionable, or its situation be considered irksome, because the fate of war had not afforded it equal opportunities of acquiring distinctions, and obtaining those Insignia of merit, which other more fortunate, but perhaps not more deserving corps, have become entitled to.

The Royal Artillery (who at this time did not report to the War Office) did better by its men. For its "gallantry and good conduct" at the capture of Fort Niagara on 19 December

1813 and during the fighting in the Niagara in 1812-1814, Captain William Holcroft's company, RA, was "permitted to bear the word 'Niagara' on its appointments." Today, that company is 52 ("Niagara") Battery, 4th Regiment, Royal Artillery, and as late as the 1960s its gunners were granted a holiday on 19 December, the anniversary of the fall of the fort.

The Canadian Forces

The three Canadian regular or near regular units (the Canadian Regiment of Fencible Infantry, the Canadian Voltigeurs and Fraser's Provincial Light Dragoons) that fought at the two actions were disbanded at the end of the war while the various militia units were either disbanded or lapsed back into peacetime somnolence.

None of these units have official successors in the modern Canadian Forces. This is because a decision was made in the early 1960s that no Canadian unit, with very few exceptions, would be allowed to trace its lineage back beyond 1855 or claim battle honours earned before that date. This idiotic *fiat* has effectively deleted the War of 1812 from the heritage of the Canadian Forces.

Nonetheless, there are a number of militia regiments on the present Canadian order of battle that can claim a traditional (if not official) connection based on their geographical location with those units that were present at the Crysler's Farm and Châteauguay campaigns. In Ontario (the former Upper Canada) the Brockville Rifles of Brockville and the Stormont, Dundas and Glengarry Highlanders of Cornwall would qualify, while in Quebec (the former Lower Canada) the 4ᵉ Bataillon of the Royal 22ᵉ Regiment (Châteauguay) at Montreal is directly descended from both the Canadian Voltigeurs and the men of the sedentary and embodied militia who fought in October 1813. Finally, the Royal Newfoundland Regiment can claim a connection with the battle because they had men present with the boat crews of Morrison's force.

The United States Army

Some of the American units that participated in the 1813 campaign were disbanded or amalgamated the following year. Following the end of the war in 1815 the regular United States army was drastically reduced and the existing infantry regiments, which numbered more than forty, were amalgamated into new infantry units with numbers based on the seniority of their colonels. The artillery and cavalry units were also amalgamated. The fates of the units that fought in the 1813 St.Lawrence Campaign were as follows

1813 Designation	Subsequent Fate
1st Regiment of Light Dragoons	Regiment of Light Dragoons in 1814, Corps of Artillery in 1815
2nd Regiment of Light Dragoons	Regiment of Light Dragoons in 1814, Corps of Artillery in 1815
Regiment of Light Artillery	Retained in 1815
1st Regiment of Artillery	Corps of Artillery, 1814
2nd Regiment of Artillery	Corps of Artillery, 1814
3rd Regiment of Artillery	Corps of Artillery, 1814
1st Rifle Regiment	Retained in 1815
4th Infantry	5th Infantry in 1815
5th Infantry	3rd Infantry in 1815

6th Infantry	2nd Infantry in 1815
9th Infantry	5th Infantry in 1815
10th Infantry	8th Infantry in 1815
11th Infantry	6th Infantry in 1815
12th Infantry	8th Infantry in 1815
13th Infantry	5th Infantry in 1815
14th Infantry	4th Infantry in 1815
15th Infantry	Regiment of Light Artillery in 1815
16th Infantry	2nd Infantry in 1815
20th Infantry	4th Infantry in 1815
21st Infantry	5th Infantry in 1815
22nd Infantry	2nd Infantry in 1815
23rd Infantry	2nd Infantry in 1815
25th Infantry	6th Infantry in 1815
29th Infantry	6th Infantry in 1815
30th Infantry	Regiment of Light Artillery in 1815
31st Infantry	Regiment of Light Artillery in 1815
33rd Infantry	Regiment of Light Artillery in 1815
Albany Volunteers	Disbanded in 1813
Maine Volunteers	Disbanded in 1814
New Hampshire Volunteers	Disbanded in 1814
Canadian Volunteers	Disbanded in 1815

The battles of the northern army in the autumn of 1813 are not specifically commemorated by the United States Army, which has never awarded a campaign streamer (the American equivalent of a battle honour) for the 1813 campaign. However, there is an authorized streamer, "Canada, 18 June 1812-17 February 1815," that includes all operations not otherwise commemorated by particular streamers in the northern theatre on either side of the border. The First through Seventh Infantry Regiments of the present American army carry this streamer on the staff of their regimental colours.

Sources
Marcus Cunliffe, *The Royal Irish Fusiliers, 1793-1950* (Oxford, 1952); M.E.S. Laws, *Battery Records of the Royal Artillery, 1716-1859* (Woolwich, 1952); Michael Mitchell, *Ducimus. The Regiments of the Canadian Infantry* (Ottawa, 1992); James Sawicki, *Infantry Regiments of the U.S. Army* (Dumfries, Va., 1981) and information provided by Lieutenant Colonel (Retd.) Joseph Whitehorne, formerly with the Office of the Chief of Military History in Washington, and Mr. Simon Bendall of London, formerly with 52 ("Niagara") Battery, Royal Artillery.

The Battle of Crysler's Farm
or Bush's Hill?

LOCATING THE BATTLE AND CRYSLER'S HOUSE

The battle fought on 11 November 1813 has always been known as the battle of Crysler's Farm after John Crysler, the most prominent man in the area, whose house in the west half of Lot 13, Concession 1, Williamsburgh Township, Dundas County, served as British headquarters before the action and the major hospital after it. Although Crysler gave his name to the engagement, the actual fighting took place some distance to the east in Lots 9, 10 and 11, an area local people called "Bush's Hill," after an early settler, William Bush, who owned property in Lot 10 from the early 1820s to the mid-1840s.

The actual area of the battle was owned by various people in 1813. The west half of Lot 9 was the property of Henry Casselman, the east was owned by Peter Loucks. Until 1854, when it was leased or purchased by the Grand Trunk, Lot 9 was mainly owned by members of the Casselman family (Martin, Cephrenus, Warner and Henry) and passed through that family. Lot 10 (the location of the second ravine) was owned partly in 1813 by Peter Fetterly (east half) and Anthony Atkinson (west half). It too had many owners after the war, most members of the Bush, Shaver, Casselman, Brouse or Beause, and Wells clans, until it too passed to the Grand Trunk in 1856. In November 1813, Lot 11 was owned partly by John Haines (east half) and Adam Bouck (west half). After the war it passed through various hands (Thomas, Henry, Warner and Cephrenus Casselman; Mary and Peter Brouse or Beause, Jeremiah Haines and Adam Baxter) until 1854 when it was leased or purchased by the Grand Trunk Railway. Although the railway acquired these properties in the 1850s, they shifted back to private hands about 1860, Lot 9 going to Henry Casselman, Lot 10 to Henry Wells and Lot 11 to John F. Brown.

Lot 12, somewhat to the west of the scene of the main fighting, is an interesting area because we have considerable information about its postwar history. In 1813 the entire lot was owned by Charles Jones, who sold it in 1818 to John Crysler, who held it until the early 1840s when it came into the possession of Joseph Schutter or Schuetter, who sold it in 1845 to James Croil. Croil passed it to George Doren or Doran in 1862, who sold it to Abraham Van Allen ten years later. In 1895, Abraham Van Allen donated the land for the site of the battlefield monument, which was located some distance to the east of his farmhouse. His descendants lived on Lot 12 until 1958 when forced off it by the Seaway Project.

The Van Allen farm contained many buildings that dated from the period of the battle but only one is definitely known to have been saved from the destruction wrought by the Seaway Project. This was a small frame house (possibly the early residence of one of the

The cottage – perhaps the only surviving building from the battle
This humble frame house was probably the early residence of the family which settled Lot 12 after the Revolutionary War. In 1872, it became the property of the Van Allen family and was used by them as the residence of their hired hands. In the 1920s, it was operated as a tearoom by Mary M. Van Allen, who used the proceeds to pay her way through university. In 1958 the Van Allen family saved it from the destruction caused by the Seaway and moved it to nearby Morrisburg where it can be seen today. (Photo by Mary M. Van Allen, courtesy of Dr. Traer Van Allen)

original settlers of Lot 12) located between the King's highway and the river, just east of the junction of the highway and the long farm lane that led north to the pine woods. The Van Allens called it "the cottage" and utilized it as the residence of their hired hands, and during the battle it would have been used, as were most buildings in the immediate area, as a makeshift hospital. In the 1920s, the cottage served briefly as a tea room catering to visitors to the nearby monument, and, in 1959, when the Van Allen family was forced to leave the river front, Mary M. and Blanche Van Allen moved it at their own expense to Morrisburg, where it can seen today at 84 Lakeshore Road.

In 1855 the American historian and artist Benson Lossing visited the battlefield and drew the sketch appended of what he thought was John Crysler's "Yellow House." In fact, it was not, and this error of identification was probably due to James Croil, a Scots immigrant and enthusiastic amateur historian, who purchased Lots 12 and 13 in 1845 and was proud to "be the owner of 500 acres of any kind of land, with all the historic associations thrown into the bargain." Croil recorded in his autobiography that the original house on his new property had "seen better days" and the "farm buildings and fences were in an advanced stage of decay." Croil moved onto his new purchase in 1847, but in 1855 had constructed a new and more spacious brick residence on the west half of Lot 13, the site of John Crysler's "Yellow House" at the time of the battle, which he called "Archerfield."

Croil is not very informative in his autobiography about the location of the house he lived in from 1847 to 1855 but other evidence suggests that it was on Lot 12, the site of the Jones farm in 1813 and the Van Allen farm after 1872. In 1855, the same year that "Archerfield" was either completed or in the final stages on the site of the original Crysler

379

A case of mistaken identity – what was thought to be Crysler's farmhouse
Illustrated as it appeared some forty years after the battle, this farmstead was mistakenly identified in 1855 as John Crysler's farmstead. In fact, it was probably Charles Jones's farm in Lot 12 and the sketch shows the junction of the Jones farm lane and the King's Highway, not the highway and the Nine-Mile Road. (Benson J. Lossing, *Pictorial Field Book of the War of 1812*)

house (which would have been torn down to make way for the new structure), Lossing visited the battlefield. He dined with the Croil family "at the Crysler mansion" which he sketched in the appended illustration. Note that this illustration illustrates a large frame house, not "Archerfield" which was brick structure. At the time of his visit, Lossing noted that one of the barns on the property, "pierced and battered by bullets, was yet standing and appears the larger (though the most remote) in the group of outbuildings" in his sketch.

It would appear from the evidence that the house where Croil was residing and which Lossing visited and sketched was on Lot 12, not Lot 13. If Lossing's 1855 drawing is compared with the 1949 photograph of the Van Allen farm reproduced here, a photo taken from almost the same spot the American drew his illustration, the similarities between the two properties become obvious. Note the resemblance of the small frame building at the right of the sketch to the similar structure in the 1949 photograph. Evidence from the Van Allen family is that this building was constructed in the 1930s on the site of a previous structure on the same spot. Behind the more modern brick Victorian Van Allen house in the photograph can be seen some of the same barns and outbuildings in the Lossing sketch. Perhaps the most important piece of evidence that the farmstead Lossing visited and drew in 1855 is not the Crysler farmstead of 1813 but the Jones (later Van Allen) property is the artist's own statement that one barn on the property displayed damage from the battle. The Jones farmstead on Lot 12 was just *within* range of American artillery; the Crysler farmstead on Lot 13 west was *out of range* of those weapons.

Croil was an enthusiastic amateur historian and it is curious why he would have made such a mistake in identification. It may be due to the fact that John Crysler purchased Lot 12 in 1818 and may have lived there for some years after the action. Crysler, at one time

The Van Allen farm in Lot 12, 1949

This 1949 photograph, shot from the east and from almost the same position where Lossing drew his 1855 sketch, shows a striking resemblance between the scene the American artist portrayed in 1855 and the Van Allen property in Lot 12. Notable is the similarity of the two small frame structures on the right of both illustrations. (Photo by Dr. Traer Van Allen)

or another, from the date of the battle to the time he left the river front in the early 1840s, either owned or leased property in Lots 9, 12 and 13, and over the years the entire area may have become associated with his name. Crysler's original "Yellow House" was probably torn down to make way for Croil's new "Archerfield." In 1870 William Mackenzie purchased Lot 13 and his descendants lived on it well into the present century, the nearby Nine-Mile Road being known locally as the "Mackenzie Road."

Sources

Family correspondence, records and photographs in the possession of Dr. Traer Van Allen of Morrisburg, Ontario; Queen's University Archives, Kingston, Ontario Land Registry 2784, Concession 1, Williamsburgh Township, Dundas County, Abstract Index of Deeds; *Canadian Military Gazette*, October 1895; James Croil, *Dundas, or, A Sketch of Canadian History* (Montreal, 1861) and *Life of James Croil. An Autobiography. 1821-1916* (Montreal, 1918); Benson Lossing, *Pictorial Field Book of the War of 1812* (New York, 1867); J. Smyth Carter, *The Story of Dundas, Being a History of the County of Dundas from 1784 to 1903* (Iroquois, Ontario, 1905).

I am indebted to Mr. George Henderson of Queen's University Archives, Kingston, and Dr. Traer Van Allen of Morrisburg for providing information for this appendix.

End Notes

Abbreviations Used in End Notes

Owing to their great number, highly abbreviated forms of the titles of published sources have been used in the notes. The full citation will be found in the bibliography which follows.

AO   Archives of Ontario, Toronto
ASPMA   United States, Congress. *American State Papers: Class V, Military Affairs*, Vol. 1. Washington: Gales & Seaton, 1832
BHL   Burton Historical Library, Detroit
DCL   Dartmouth College Library, Hanover, New Hampshire
CLUM   Clements Library, University of Michigan, Ann Arbor
CO   Colonial Office
DAB   *Dictionary of American Biography.* New York: Scribner, 1958-1964. 22 vols.
DCB   *Dictionary of Canadian Biography.* Volumes V-IX. Toronto: University of Toronto, 1976-1988.
Doc. Hist. Earnest A. Cruikshank, ed. *Documentary History of the Campaigns on the Niagara Frontier in 1812-1814,* Welland: Tribune Press, 1900-1908. Volume and page number cited first, followed by document.
HSP   Historical Society of Pennsylvania, Philadelphia
LC   Library of Congress, Washington
LLIU   Lily Library, Indiana University, Bloomington
MDHA   Mississippi Department of History and Archives, Jackson
MG   Manuscript Group
MHS   Massachusetts Historical Society, Boston
MsHS   Missouri Historical Society, St. Louis
MTPL   Metropolitan Toronto Public Library
NAC   National Archives of Canada, Ottawa
NAQ   National Archives of Quebec, Montreal
NYHS   New York Historical Society
NYSL   New York State Library, Albany
NWR   *Niles Weekly Register*
OHS   Oneida Historical Society, Utica
PRO   Public Record Office, Kew, United Kingdom
QU   Queen's University Archives, Kingston
RCMI   Royal Canadian Military Institute, Toronto
RG   Record Group
SW   Secretary of War
UCA   United Church Archives, Toronto
UCV   Upper Canada Village, Morrisburg
USMA   United States Military Academy, West Point
USNA   National Archives of the United States, Washington
WHS   Wisconsin Historical Society, Madison
WCM   James Wilkinson, *Memoirs of My Own Times* (3 vols, Philadelphia, 1816), vol. 3
WO   War Office

Prologue: A Miserable Night in November 1813

1. Cook and Vanderbaaren, "Descendants of John Cook, UEL."
2. *Ibid., Canadian Military Gazette,* 1 Oct. 1895.
3. NAC, RG 19 E5(a), Loss Claim, Michael Cook.
4. "First Campaign," no. 1, 155; no. 7, 173.
5. *Ibid.;* NAC, RG 8 I, vol. 681, 68, Statements of American deserters, n.d. [c. Jan. 1814].
6. NAC, MG 24, L8, Viger, "Ma Saberdache," vol. 3, Viger to wife, 12 May 1813.
7. MTPL, Hagerman Journal, 29 Nov. 1813; NAC, RG 8 I, vol. 1712, 56, Prevost to de Rottenburg, 11 Nov. 1813.
8. NAC, RG 19 E5(a), John Crysler loss claim.

Chapter 1: "Hark, now the drums beat…"

1. "Over the hills and far away" was apparently first heard in George Farquhar's play, "The Recruiting Officer" of 1706 and was included in Thomas D'Urfey's *Pills to Purge Melancholy* of 1707, see Winstock, *Songs,* 29-31. It then languished until the 1790s when it was revived to become one of the two traditional "loth-to-depart" marches of the British army (the other being "The Girl I Left Behind Me") played when a regiment left a station for the last time.
2. "First Campaign," no. 10, 440-441; *Register of the Army 1813.*
3. Macomb to Williams, 29 Apr. 1813, quoted in Skelton, *Profession of Arms,* 74.
4. Bissell to Kingsbury, 19 Sep. 1812, quoted in Skelton, *Profession of Arms,* 74.
5. Graves, *Right and Glory,* 7-12.
6. Greenhous, "A Note," 41.
7. Kimball, "Fog and Friction," 323-325.
8. *Ibid.,* 327-328.
9. Campbell to Worthington, 17 June 1812, quoted in Stagg, *Madison's War,* 163.
10. *Ibid.*
11. Stagg, *Madison's War,* 169-176. Stagg offers the best overview of the republic's problems in preparing for war.
12. Graves, *Right and Glory,* 7-12 and *Red Coats,* 3-4, 17-18; Myers, *Reminiscences,* 12-13.
13. *DCB,* 8, Prevost entry.
14. Glover, *Napoleonic Wars,* 148-157; Oman, *Peninsular War,* V, 136-156.
15. Prevost to Bathurst, 18 May 1812, quoted in Hitsman, *Incredible War,* 246-247.
16. NAC, RG 8 I, vol. 1218, 308, Prevost to Bathurst, 15 July 1812.
17. Graves, *Right and Glory,* 8-15.
18. Stagg, *Madison's War,* 282-284.
19. Flexner, *Washington,* 177.
20. *DAB,* Armstrong entry.

21. Skeen, *Armstrong,* 122-123. James Wilkinson, no friend of Armstrong, accused him of plagiarizing much of *Hints to Young Generals* from Jomini's *Traite de Guerre,* see *WCM,* defence of Wilkinson, 398.
22. Statement by Madison in 1824 quoted in Stagg, *Madison's War,* 283n. On Armstrong's appointment, see also Skeen, *Armstrong,* 121-125; and Stagg, *Madison's War,* 282-284.
23. Armstrong to Spencer, 25 Jan. 1813, quoted in Stagg, *Madison's War,* 284.
24. Skeen, *Armstrong,* 126-131, 135; Stagg, *Madison's War,* 278-288.
25. Gallatin to Madison, 5 Mar. 1813, quoted in Skeen, *Armstrong,* 131.
26. USNA, RG 107, Micro 6, SW to Swartout, 4 May 1813. On financial problems, see Skeen, *Armstrong,* 132-133.
27. Armstrong, *Notices,* 1, 234, Armstrong to Eustis, 2 Jan. 1812.
28. *ASPMA,* 439, Note Presented to Cabinet, 8 Feb. 1813.
29. *ASPMA,* 439, SW to Dearborn, 10 Feb. 1813.
30. USNA, RG 107, Micro 6, SW to Dearborn, 4 Mar. 1813.
31. *ASPMA,* 441, SW to Dearborn, 24 Feb. 1813; 441, Dearborn to SW, 26 Feb., 3 Mar., 9 Mar. 1813; Armstrong to Spencer, 28 Feb. 1813, quoted in Skeen, *Armstrong,* 148.
32. *ASPMA,* 441, Dearborn to SW, 3 Mar., 9 Mar. 1813.
33. *ASPMA,* 442, Dearborn to SW, 20 Mar. 1813.
34. USNA, RG 107, Micro 6, SW to Dearborn, 29 Mar. 1813.
35. *Doc. Hist.,* 6, 95, SW to Dearborn, 19 June 1813.
36. *ASPMA,* 451, SW to Dearborn, 6 July 1813.
37. *Doc. Hist.,* 6, 201, SW to Boyd, 7 July 1813.
38. NAC, CO 42, vol. 121, 194, Prevost to Bathurst, 21 Apr. 1813.
39. NAC, RG 8 I, vol. 678, 382, York to Prevost, 10 Aug. 1813; *DCB,* 6, de Rottenburg entry.

Chapter 2: "How uncomfortably like a civil …"

1. The "Anacreontic Song" or "To Anacreon in Heaven" was composed by a London club devoted to "wit, harmony and wine" who took as their patron the 5th Century Greek poet, Anacreon. As "Sung at the Crown and Anchor Tavern in the Strand," it exalted wine, song, fellowship and love. The song was very popular in the United States and its melody was used for a number of patriotic productions including Robert Paine's "Adams and Liberty" of 1798 and Francis Scott Key's "When the Warrior Returns" of 1806. On 3 September 1814 Key

witnessed the British attack on Fort McHenry and penned new lyrics for the "Anacreontic Song," – lyrics that opened with the line: "Oh, say can you see, by the dawn's early light, What so proudly we hailed at the twilight's last gleaming?" From Fort McHenry National Shrine Internet web page.

2. *DAB*, Wilkinson entry.

3. Quimby, *American Army*, 1, 303; also *DAB*, Wilkinson entry.

4. DAB, Wilkinson entry: Bidwell, *Swords for Hire*, 78.

5. Hampton to SW, 10 June 1811, quoted in Crackel, *Jefferson's Army*, 175.

6. Ellery, *Swift*, 96.

7. *Ibid.*, 97.

8. WCM, 342, SW to Wilkinson, 12 Mar. 1813, emphasis in the original. On distaste for Wilkinson in Louisiana, see Crawford to Madison, 3 March 1813, quoted in Skeen, *Armstrong*, 158.

9. WCM, 341, Wilkinson to SW, 23 May 1813. See also Jacobs, *Tarnished Warrior*, 284-285.

10. WCM, 115, Wilkinson to Lewis, 6 July 1813.

11. Stagg, *Madison's War*, 338.

12. ASPMA, 463, Precis submitted to Cabinet, 23 July 1813.

13. HSP, Parker Papers, Wilkinson to SW, 6 Aug. 1813, emphasis in the original.

14. ASPMA, 464, SW to Wilkinson, 8 Aug. 1813.

15. USNA, RG 107, Micro 222, reel 5, Hampton to Madison, 10 Nov. 1812.

16. DAB, Hampton entry; Scott, *Memoirs*, 1, 51-52.

17. Skeen, *Armstrong*, 160; USNA, RG 107, Micro 222, Hampton to SW, 13 July 1813.

18. HSP, Parker Papers, Wilkinson to SW, 6 Aug. 1813.

19. ASPMA, 464, SW to Wilkinson, 8 Aug. 1813.

20. WCM, App. 35, Wilkinson to Hampton, 16 Aug. 1813.

21. *Ibid.*

22. HSP, Parker Papers, Wilkinson to SW, 26 Aug. 1813.

23. HSP, Parker Papers, Wilkinson to SW, 30 Aug. 1813.

24. USNA, RG 107, Micro 222, Hampton to SW, 22 Aug. 13.

25. SW to Hampton, 25 August 1813, quoted in Skeen, *Armstrong*, 160.

26. USNA, RG 107, Micro 222, vol. 6, Hampton to SW, 31 Aug. 1813, emphasis in the original.

27. USNA, RG 107, Micro 222, Williams to SW, 3 Aug. 1813.

28. USNA, RG 107, Micro 222, Porter to SW, 27 July 1813.

29. Mann, *Medical Sketches*, 64.

30. Beaumont, *Medical Notebook*, 11.

31. Ashburn, "American Army Hospitals," 57.

32. USNA, RG 94, Micro 566, Johnson to Dearborn, 13 July 1813.

33. DAB, entry for Boyd; Heitman, *Historical Register*.

34. USNA, RG 107, Micro 222, Lewis to SW, 5 July 1813.

35. Scott, *Memoir*, 1, 93-94.

36. NAC, MG 24, F16, Walworth to Simonds, 19 Aug. 1813.

37. Fredriksen, "Georgia Officer," 681, Cumming to father, 20 November 1813.

38. "First Campaign," no. 10, 410.

39. Hughes, *Sketch*, 24.

40. Malcomson, *Sailors of 1812*, 39, Sinclair to Cocke, 4 July 1813.

41. O'Reilly, "Hero," 85, Macdonough to Parents, 4 Aug. 1813.

42. "First Campaign," no. 7, 173.

43. "First Campaign," no. 12, 191. From information contained in this anonymous officer's lengthy memoir, it is the author's opinion that the aide-de-camp was Lieutenant William Jenkins Worth of Albany who ended his military career as a general.

44. *Ibid.*, no. 10, 173-174.

45. *Ibid.*, no. 10, 174-175.

46. Myers, *Reminiscences*, 33.

47. *Ibid.*, 12-13.

48. *Ibid.*, 33.

49. "First Campaign," no. 9, 336.

50. Myers, *Reminiscences*, 34.

51. Norton, *Journal*, 334.

52. *Ibid.*, 335.

53. Graves, *Merry Hearts*, 127. The term "nitchie" was a corruption of the Ojibway "nii-jii" meaning friend or comrade.

54. Kirby, *Annals of Niagara,*, 198-199.

55. "First Campaign," no. 8, 338.

56. Norton, *Journal*, 338.

57. Graves, *Merry Hearts*, 136.

58. NAC, RG 8 I, vol. 680, 34, de Rottenburg to Prevost, 8 Sept. 1813.

59. Graves, *Merry Hearts*, 135.

60. *Ibid.*, 136.

61. Malcomson, *Lords*, 141-163.

62. NAC, CO 42, vol. 121, 158, Prevost to Bathurst, 25 Aug. 1813.

63. *Ibid.*; Graves, *Merry Hearts*, 132-133.

64. NAC, CO 42, vol. 121, 158, Prevost to Bathurst, 25 Aug. 1813.

65. WCM, 207, Testimony of Bull.

66. Spencer to SW, 20 February 1813, quoted in Stagg, *Madison's War*, 333. On Lewis, see *DAB*, Lewis entry.

67. USNA, RG 107, Micro 222, Porter to SW, 27 July 1813, emphasis in the original.

68. USNA, RG 107, Micro 222, Porter to SW, 27 July 1813, emphasis in the original.

69. *Appleton's Encyclopedia*, Swartout entry. On Wilkinson and Swartout, see *WCM*, 134, testimony of Lewis; 133-134, defence of Wilkinson.

70. Ellery, *Swift*, 113. On Brown, see Graves, *Right and Glory*, 18-19.

71. Wailes, *Covington*, 18-20; MDHA, Covington Papers, Covington to Alexander Covington, 31 July 1813; Heitman, *Historical Register*.

72. *WCM*, App 2, General Order, 23 August 1813.

73. MDHA, Covington Papers, Covington to A. Covington, 31 July 1813.

74. Malcomson, *Sailors of 1812*, 39, Sinclair to Cocke, 4 July 1813.

75. *WCM*, App. 2, General Order, 23 Aug. 1813. See also App. 2, General Order, 29 Aug. 1813.

76. Fredriksen, "War of 1812," 305, McIntire to Holmes, 11 Sep. 1813.

77. Fredriksen, "Kirby," 67.

78. Letter in *Ontario Repository*, 26 July 1814.

79. *WCM*, App. 9, Medical Report, Sackets Harbor, 11 Sep. 1813.

80. MDHA, Covington Papers, Covington to Alexander Covington, 31 July 1813.

81. *WCM*, App. 1, Minutes of a Council of War, 26 Aug. 1813; App. 6, Extracts from the Returns, 2 August 1813; *Register of the Army 1813*.

82. *WCM*, App. 1, Minutes of a Council of War, 26 Aug. 1813.

83. *WCM*, App. 30, Wilkinson to Brown, 29 Aug. 1813.

84. *ASPMA*, 465, Wilkinson to SW, 21 Aug. 1813. On preparations at Sackets Harbor for the forthcoming operation, see *WCM*, 51, Wilkinson to Swartout, 25 Aug. 1813, and App. 30, Wilkinson to Brown, 29 Aug. 1813.

85. *ASPMA*, 465, Wilkinson to SW, 21 Aug. 1813.

86. *WCM*, 348, Wilkinson to SW, 31 Aug. 1813.

Chapter 3: "Two heads on the same..."

1. The "Rogue's March" was the tune played in the British army when a soldier was found to be so worthless he was drummed out of his regiment and, given the need for manpower, a soldier would have to be pretty worthless to be drummed out, see Winstock, *Songs*, 95-97. The song quickly found its way into the American army, .

2. *ASPMA*, 458, SW to Hampton, 1 Sep. 1813.

3. Graves, *Merry Hearts*, 133.

4. NAC, CO 42, vol. 122, 158, Prevost to Bathurst, 25 Aug. 1813; Malcomson, *Lords*, 8-11.

5. *ASPMA*, 458, Hampton to SW, 7 Sep. 1813.

See also USNA, RG 107, Micro 221, reel 58, Hampton to SW, 20 Aug. 1813.

6. On Hampton's units, see USNA, RG 107, 221, Reel 53, Hampton to SW, 31 July 1813 and Hampton to Parker, 15 Aug, 1813; USNA RG 98, vol. 485, General Orders, 20 July and 3 Aug. 1813; Heitman, *Historical Register*; Lemmon, *Frustrated Patriots*, 58.

7. "Orders at Burlington," 86, General Order, 23 July 1813.

8. *ASPMA*, Purdy to Wilkinson, n.d., [c. mid-Dec. 1813]; "Orders at Burlington," 92, General Order, 27 July 1813; 93, General Order, 31 July 1813.

9. Parker, "Letters," 107.

10. "Orders at Burlington," 98, General Order, 1 Aug. 1813.

11. *Ibid.*, 88, General Order, 24 July 1813.

12. Penley, *Narrative*, 11.

13. USNA, RG 94, Journal of General George Izard, 21 Oct. 1813 (hereafter Izard Journal, and date).

14. Scott, *Memoirs*, 1, 50.

15. Eleazar Williams quoted in Bilow, *Chateaugay*, 78.

16. Sellar, *US Campaign*, 5.

17. *ASPMA*, 459, Hampton to SW, 25 Sep. 1813;

18. *Ibid.*

19. *ASPMA*, 479, Purdy to Wilkinson, n.d. [mid-Dec. 1813].

20. *ASPMA*, 460, Hampton to SW, 4 Oct. 1813; Izard Journal, 16 Oct. 1813.

21. *ASPMA*, 459, SW to Hampton, 25 Sep. 1813.

22. *ASPMA*, 460, SW to Hampton, 28 Sep. 1813, emphasis in the original.

23. *ASPMA*, 466, Wilkinson to SW, 11 Sep. 1813; *WCM*, 280, testimony of Hite.

24. "First Campaign," no. 10, 442. See also *WCM*, App. 30, Wilkinson to Brown, 29 Aug. 1813; App. 66, Wilkinson to Swartout, 25. Aug. 1813.

25. *WCM*, 280, testimony of Hite; also 487, defence of Wilkinson.

26. *ASPMA*, 467, Wilkinson to SW, 18 Sep. 1813.

27. *WCM*, 80, testimony of Boyd.

28. Armstrong to Madison, quoted in Skeen, *Armstrong*, 163, no date discernable but probably early October 1813.

29. *WCM*, 354, Defence of Wilkinson.

30. HSP, Parker Papers, Wilkinson to SW, 16 Sep. 1813.

31. HSP, Parker Papers, Wilkinson to SW, 18 Sep. 1813.

32. *WCM*, App. 12, Council of War, 20 Sep. 1813.

33. *ASPMA*, 468, SW to Wilkinson, 18 Sep. 1813.

34. MHS, Brown Papers, Wilkinson to Brown, 20 Sep. 1813.

35. MHS, Brown Papers, Wilkinson to Brown, 27 Sep. 1813.
36. USNA, RG 107, Micro 6, SW to Harrison, 22 Sep. 1813.
37. *ASPMA*, 468, Wilkinson to SW, 20 Sep. 1813.
38. *WCM*, App. 64, General Order, 23 Sep. 1813.
39. Graves, *Merry Hearts*, 135.
40. "First Campaign," no. 8, 265.
41. Malcomson, *Lords*, 203-205.
42. "First Campaign," no. 10, 441-442.
43. *Ibid.*, no. 10, 443.
44. *ASPMA*, 470, Wilkinson to SW, 2 Oct. 1813. On discussions and preparations for the defence of Fort George after the majority of the regular troops departed, see *WCM*, App. 12, Council of War, 20 Sep. 1813; App. 65, Wilkinson to Tompkins, 21 Aug. 1813; *ASPMA*, 467, Porter, Chapin and Holmes to Wilkinson, 17 Sep. 1813; 469, SW to Wilkinson, 22 Sep. 1813; 482, Scott to Wilkinson, 11 Oct. 1813; 483, Scott to Wilkinson, 31 Dec. 1813, SW to Cushing, 8 Feb. 1813; 484, Cushing to Dearborn, 8 Feb. 1813, Armistead to SW, 19 Jan. 1814, SW to McClure or officer commanding at Fort George, 4 Oct. 1813.

In early October 1813, Winfield Scott left Fort George with his regular regiment, turning the defence of that place over to New York militia Brigadier General George McClure. As will be seen below (Chapter 14), this decision was to have dire consequences and Scott has been criticized for this action, see Quimby, *American Army*, 1, 350-351, 360.
45. Myers, *Reminiscences*, 37-38.
46. NYHS, Goodell Papers, Goodell to father, 4 Oct. 1813.
47. *WCM*, 42, testimony of Swartout.
48. Description of watercraft in Wilkinson's flotilla from Pringle, *Lunenburgh*, 101-102. The provision of transport and supplies for the army undertaken between August and October 1813 was a herculean task, see *WCM*, 43-45, 50, 50, testimony of Swartout; 98-106, testimony of Thorne; 117, 127, 124, testimony of Lewis; 160-161, testimony of Wadsworth; 165-166, testimony of Macomb; 199, testimony of Lewis; 239, testimony of Bissell; 250-251, testimony of Brearly; 266, testimony of Camp; 276, testimony of Porter; 281, testimony of Hite; 290-291, testimony of Brooks; App. 30, Instructions to Brown, 29 Aug. 1813; App. 66, Wilkinson to Swartout, 25 Aug. 1813; App. 72, General Order, 21 Sep. 1813; App. 63, General Order, 22 Sep. 1813; App. 77, Return of Transports, Sackets Harbor, 25 Aug. 1813.
49. *WCM*, 141, testimony of Morgan Lewis.
50. OHS, Williams Papers, Brown to Nathan Williams, 7 Aug. 1813.
51. OHS, Williams Papers, Brown to Nathan Williams, 2 Sep. 1813.
52. *ASPMA*, 470, Journal of the SW, 4 Oct. 1813.
53. *ASPMA*, 470, Paper No. 1, emphasis in the original.
54. *ASPMA*, 470, Paper No. 2. There is disagreement between Armstrong and Wilkinson over whether the meeting of 4 October actually took place. The secretary claimed it did and produced the documents concerning it quoted above including an extract from his "daily journal," see *ASPMA*, 470, Journal of the Secretary of War, 4 Oct. 1813, and Papers 1 and 2. At his court martial and in his memoirs, Wilkinson disputed this assertion (see *WCM*, 350-353, defence of Wilkinson) and accused Armstrong of manufacturing evidence, as a reference to the secretary's journal entry for 4 October. Lewis had no recollection of any conference being held 4 October, see *WCM*, testimony of Lewis, 133-134.
55. Ellery, *Swift*, 114.
56. *WCM*, App. 24, Wilkinson to SW, 24 Aug. 1813.
57. Ellery, *Swift*, 115.
58. *WCM*, 153, Testimony of Walbach, emphasis in the original.
59. *ASPMA*, Hampton to SW, 12 Oct. 1813, emphasis in the original.
60. *ASPMA*, 471, Wilkinson to SW, 9 Oct. 1813; *WCM*, App. 15, Wilkinson to Chauncey, 9 Oct. 1813; App. 15, Chauncey to Wilkinson, 9 Oct. 1813; App. 17, Wilkinson to Chauncey, 9 Oct. 1813; App. 18, Chauncey to Wilkinson, 9 Oct. 1813.
61. *WCM*, 297, Testimony of Lee.
62. *WCM*, 353, defence of Wilkinson; see also, 207, testimony of Bull. On Boyd's movements, see 82, testimony of Boyd.
63. *WCM*, 82, testimony of Boyd.
64. *WCM*, 224-225, testimony of Totten; Malcomson, *Lords*, 210-214.
65. Fredriksen, "War of 1812," 304, McIntire to Holmes, 11 September 1813.
66. OHS, Williams Papers, Brown to Nathan Williams, 2 Sep. 1813.
67. "First Campaign," no. 11, 33-34.

Chapter 4: "God knows when we shall set out"

1. "The Bold Canadian," a ballad dating from the War of 1812, was written down by Robert Warner (1848-1924) who remembered his grandfather, Captain John Lampman

of the Upper Canada militia, singing it "when he drew his pension, and on the great battle dates of the war." See Zazlow, *Defended Border*, 303-305.

2. NAC, RG 8 I, vol. 1221, 56, Prevost to de Rottenburg, 3 Sep. 1813. On the sick of the army, see RG 8 I, vol. 1708, 60, General Monthly Return of the Sick in Upper Canada, 24 Sep. 1813.

3. NAC, RG8 I, vol. 680, 66, de Rottenburg to Prevost, 17 Sep. 1813.

4. NAC, RG 8 I, vol. 680, 119, de Rottenburg to Prevost, 28 Sep. 1813.

5. NAC, RG 8 I, vol. 680, 34, de Rottenburg to Prevost, 8 Sep.; 78, 17 Sep.; 123, 30 Sep.; 134, 3 Oct. 183; 196, de Rottenburg to Darroch, 28 Sep. 1813; 129, Darroch to Prevost, 2 Oct. 1813.

6. Graves, *Merry Hearts*, 136-137.

7. NAC, RG 8 I, vol. 680, 164, Darroch to Freer, 12 Oct. 1813.

8. Kingston *Gazette*, 9 Oct. 1813.

9. NAC, CO 42, vol. 122, 199, Prevost to Bathurst, 8 Oct. 1813. See also NAC, RG 8 I, 680, 151, Darroch to Prevost, 7 Oct. 1813. On the assessments of British senior commanders of American intentions, see NAC, RG 8 I, vol. 680, 134, de Rottenburg to Prevost, 3 Oct. 1813; 134, Darroch to Prevost, 3 Oct. 1813; 159, Darroch to Prevost, 8 Oct. 1813; 171, Pearson to Baynes, 12 Oct. 1813.

10. NAC, RG 8 I, vol. 680, 171, Pearson to Baynes, 12 Oct. 1813.

11. NAC, RG 8 I, vol. 1221, 179, Prevost to de Rottenburg, 12 Oct. 1813.

12. *Ibid.*

13. NAC, RG 8 I, vol. vol. 1221, 182, Prevost to Yeo, 12 Oct. 1813.

14. NAC, RG 8 I, vol. 731, 47, Yeo to Prevost, 17 Oct. 1813.

15. NAC, RG 8 I, vol. 680, 188, de Rottenburg to Prevost, 14 Oct. 1813.

16. AO, MS 537, Ridout to father, 16 Oct. 1813.

17. NAC, RG 8 I, vol. 680, 53, de Rottenburg to Prevost, 21 Oct. 1813. See also 266, de Rottenburg to Vincent, 23 Oct. 1813.

18. NAC, RG 8 I, vol. 73, 64, Prevost to de Rottenburg, 22 Oct. 1813.

19. SW to Madison, 19 Oct. 1813, quoted in Skeen, *Armstrong*, 163.

20. *ASPMA*, 461, SW to Hampton, 16 Oct. 1813.

21. Armstrong, *Notices*, 2, 406.

22. *WCM*, 70, SW to Swartout, 16 Oct. 1813, emphasis in original. Swartout passed this order on, see *WCM*, App. 7, Swartout to Baldwin, 20 Oct. 1813.

23. Armstrong to Madison, 11 Nov. 1813, quoted in Skeen, *Armstrong*, 164.

24. *WCM*, 123-125, testimony of Lewis and, 125, Order of Encampment, 9 Oct. 1813. See Appendix D for a discussion of the organization and strength of Wilkinson's army and units.

25. *WCM*, App. 21, Wilkinson to Chauncey, 16 Oct. 1813.

26. *ASPMA*, 471, Wilkinson to SW, 18 Oct. 1813.

27. *WCM*, App. 19, Chauncey to Wilkinson, 16 Oct. 1813; App. 21, Chauncey to Wilkinson, 16 Oct. 1813.

28. Armstrong, *Notices*, 2, 207, SW to Wilkinson, 19 Oct. 1813.

29. HSP, Parker Papers, Wilkinson to SW, 19 Oct. 1813, emphasis in original.

30. HSP, Parker Papers, SW to Wilkinson, 20 Oct. 1813, the emphasis is mine.

31. Adams, *History*, 182.

32. Stagg, *Madison's War*, 343.

33. Philadelphia *Aurora*, n.d. [early October 1813] quoted in Ingersoll, *History*, 1, 297.

34. Adams, *History*, 178-179.

35. HSP, Jones Papers, Chauncey to Jones, 27 Oct. 1813.

36. HSP, Jones Papers, Chauncey to Jones, 30 October 1813.

37. MDHA, Covington Papers, Covington to Lewis, n.d. [late October 1813].

38. Hough, *Jefferson County*, 117-118.

39. Myers, *Reminiscences*, 39.

40. *Ibid.*; *WCM*, 46-47, testimony of Swartout; 81-82, testimony of Boyd; 98-103, testimony of Thorne; 118-120, testimony of Lewis.

41. *WCM*, 200, testimony of Eustis.

42. *WCM*, 81-82, testimony of Boyd;, 98-103, testimony of Thorne; 118-120, testimony of Lewis; 425, defence of Wilkinson.

43. *Kingston Gazette*, 25 Dec. 1813, Extract of a letter from an Officer in the Army dated 26 Oct. 1813. On the movement to Grenadier Island, see *ASPMA*, 476, Army Journal, 23-30 Oct. 1813; *WCM*, 45, 50, 58, testimony of Swartout; 117-119, testimony of Lewis; 165-166, testimony of Macomb; 199-200, testimony of Eustis; 209, testimony of Bell; 224, testimony of Totten; 240-241, testimony of Bissell; 266-267, testimony of Camp; 281, testimony of Hite.

44. Ellery, *Swift*, 114.

45. *WCM*, App. 41, SW to Wilkinson, 27 Oct. 1813.

46. HSP, Parker Papers, Wilkinson to SW, 28 Oct. 1813.

47. HSP, Parker Papers, SW to Wilkinson, 30 Oct. 1813.

48. NAC, MG 24, F16, Walworth to Simonds, 8 Oct. 1813.
49. "First Campaign," no. 12, p. 91.
50. *Ibid.*, 90.
51. Graves, *Soldiers of 1814*, 26-27
52. Delafield, *Lewis*, 2, 93, Lewis to wife, 25 Oct. 1813. On movement off Grenadier, see HSP, Carr Diary, 27-30 Oct. 1813; LLIU, Orderly Book, Second Brigade, 27 Oct. - 1 Nov. 1813.
53. Graves, *Merry Hearts*, 145-146, 149.
54. *Ibid.*, 147, Le Couteur to Bouton, 24 October 1813.
55. NAC, RG 8 I, vol. 680, 188, de Rottenburg to Prevost, 14 Oct. 1813; 191, de Rottenburg to Prevost, 15 Oct. 1813; 193, de Rottenburg to Prevost, 15 Oct. 1813; 239, Information from Sackets Harbor, 17 Oct. 1813; 266, de Rottenburg to Vincent, 23 Oct. 1813; vol. 730, 51, A Scheme of Gunboat Squadron proposed for the St. Lawrence, 21 July 1813; vol. 731, Memorandum on Capture of Gunboat No. 1 off Gravelly Point, 11 Oct. 1813.
56. NAC, RG 8 I, vol. 681, 35, Harvey to Baynes.
57. NAC, RG 8 I, vol. 680, 226, Pearson to Baynes, 17 Oct. 1813; Fortier, "Dragoons," 44. Information on Sherwood from the files of the *Dictionary of Canadian Biography* project and I am indebted to Mr. David Roberts for communicating it to me.
58. NAC, RG 8 I, vol. 1221, 185, Prevost to de Rottenburg, 14 Oct. 1813; and vo. 680, 92, de Rottenburg to Prevost, 15 Oct. 1813. On the military build-up around Montreal in October 1813, see PRO, WO 17, General Return of the Army, 25 Oct. 1813; NAC, CO 42, vol. 122, Prevost to Bathurst, 30 Oct. 1813; RG 8 I, vol. 731, 56, Returns of the 1st Battalion, Royal Marines, 20 Oct. 1813; vol. 1171, 33, General Orders, 27 Sep. 1813; 58, General Order, 9 Oct. 1813; and 85, General Order, 8 Oct. 1813; Suthren, *Châteauguay*, 103-108; Cruikshank, "Isle aux Noix," 70-73; Hitsman, *Incredible War*, 162-163.
59. Guitard, *Militia*, 10-15; Suthren, *Châteauguay*, 103-108.
60. *Doc. Hist.*, 8, 75, Proclamation, 18 Oct. 1813.
61. NAC, RG 8 I, vol. 1171, 85, General Order, 8 Oct. 1813; 58, General Order, 9 Oct. 1813.
62. Suthren, *Châteauguay*, 103-107. On the build-up around Montreal, see sources for note 58 above.
63. Suthren, *Châteauguay*, 103-107; "Deux Lettres," 96, Charles Pinguet to L. Pinguet, 21 Nov. 1813.
64. AO, MS 537, Ridout to father, 14 Oct. 1813.
65. Diary of Anne Elinor Prevost, 163.
66. Suthren, *Châteauguay*, 112.

Chapter 5: "Le Diable au corps"

1. This song, sung by the Lower Canada militia during the War of 1812 had a number of variants – the lyrics that appear here were recorded in 1864 from a veteran militiaman, see Massicotte, "Chansons Militaires," 274-275. An approximate English translation would be as follows and, given its measure, it is probable that this song was sung to the drum signal for "reveille."

In the morning at the break of day,
We always hear those damned drums play,
Of those cursed drums and that cursed drill,
You, poor soldier, have had your fill.

They usually form us into a line,
Our sergeants and officers, so very fine,
Some shout "retreat!" while others shout "advance!"
You, poor soldier, haven't got a chance.

Our sergeants and officers live in style,
Drinking beer and wine, all the while,
Our captain has already ruined his liver,
You, poor soldier, must drink from the river.

Who is the man who composed this song?
Why it's a drummer of the battalion,
The same damned drummer who beats the retreat,
Dreaming of his mistress, so very sweet.

2. Fredriksen, "New Hampshire Volunteer," 167.
3. NYSL, Diary of Corporal Richard Bishop, Twenty-Ninth Infantry, 11 Oct. 1813 (hereafter Bishop Diary).
4. Bishop Diary, 15 Oct. 1813.
5. *ASPMA*, 460, Hampton to SW, 4 Oct. 1813.
6. *ASPMA*, 460, Hampton to SW, 4 October 1813; Walton, *Vermont*, 486, Clarke to SW, 15 Oct. 1813; *Kingston Gazette*, 6 Nov. 1813.
7. *ASPMA*, Hampton to SW, 12 Oct. 1813; Bishop Diary, 17 Oct. 1813, emphasis in the original.
8. *DAB*, Izard entry; Manigault, "Izard," 465-472.
9. For information on the organization and strength of Hampton's division, see Appendix B. The battalion of the Tenth Infantry left Virginia in early August, see Lemmon, *Frustrated Patriots*, 58.
10. *ASPMA*, I, Hampton to SW, 1 Nov. 1813; Armstrong, *Notices*, 2, 192, King to SW, 28 Oct. 1813.
11. *ASPMA*, 461, SW to Hampton, 16 Oct. 1813.

12. *ASPMA*, 461, SW to Hampton, 28 Sept. 1813, emphasis in the original.
13. *ASPMA*, 461, Hampton to SW, 1 Nov. 1813.
14. *Ibid.*
15. *Ibid.*; Izard, Journal, 21 Oct. 1813; Fredriksen, "New Hampshire Volunteer," 168.
16. Bishop Diary, 21 Oct. 1813.
17. *Ibid.*
18. CLUM, War of 1812 Manuscripts, Neef to Bell, 20 Dec. 1813.
19. Izard Journal, 21 Oct. 1813.
20. *ASPMA*, 461, Hampton to SW, 1 Nov. 1813.
21. Fredriksen, "New Hampshire Volunteer," 168.
22. Bishop Diary, 25 Oct. 1813.
23. Fredriksen, "New Hampshire Volunteer," 168.
24. *Ibid.*
25. *ASPMA*, 461, Hampton to SW, 1 Nov. 1813; Armstrong, *Notices*, 2, 192, King to SW, 28 Oct. 1813; Bishop Diary, 25 Oct. 1813; Izard, Journal, 25 Oct. 1813.
26. Izard, Journal, 22 Oct. 1813.
27. *ASPMA*, I, 461, Hampton to SW, 1 Nov. 1813.
28. *Doc. Hist.*, 8, 112, King to SW, n.d.
29. Wohler, *De Salaberry*, 17-53; *DCB*, 6, de Salaberry entry.
30. Song from Wohler, *De Salaberry*, 61, the translation is mine, see also 56, 59-65 and Guitard, *Militia*, 17-19.
31. Wohler, *De Salaberry*, 56.
32. *Montreal Gazette*, 9 Nov. 1813, Michael O'Sullivan, "An Eye-Witness's Account, (hereafter O'Sullivan, "Eye-Witness").
33. Shaw, "Remarks," 388.
34. Dunlop, *Tiger Dunlop*, 10.
35. For information on the organization and strength of de Salaberry's command, see Appendix C.
36. *DCB*, 9, Macdonell entry; Philatethes, "Last War," 274-275; NAC, RG 8 I, vol. 1170, 293, General Order, 30 June 1813.
37. Philatethes, "Last War," 274-275, emphasis in the original. On de Salaberry's defensive preparations, see Suthren, *Châteauguay*, 114-120.
38. "O'Sullivan, "Eye-Witness".
39. "Deux Lettres," 96, Charles Pinguet to L. Pinguet, 21 Nov. 1813.
40. *ASPMA*, 461, Hampton to SW, 1 Nov. 1813; Cruickshank, "Isle aux Noix," 83.
41. *ASPMA*, 479, Purdy to Wilkinson, n.d. [c. late Nov. 1813].
42. *ASPMA*, 461, Hampton to SW, 1 Nov. 1813; Izard, 26 Oct. 1813.
43. O'Sullivan, "Eye-Witness"; Philatethes, "Last War," 276.
44. O'Sullivan, "Eye-Witness"; Suthren, *Châteauguay*, 123-127.
45. *Ibid.*
46. Izard Journal, 26 Oct. 1813.
47. O'Sullivan, "Eye-Witness."
48. Izard Journal, 26 Oct. 1813.
49. CLUM, War of 1812 Manuscripts, Neef to Bell, 20 Dec. 1813.
50. Robert Morrison, "What an Eye-Witness said of the Engagement and What Followed It," *Montreal Gazette*, 11 May 1895 (hereafter Morrison, "Eyewitness").
51. Suthren, *Châteauguay*, 126-128; Morrison, "Eye-Witness."
52. *ASPMA*, 461, Hampton to SW, 1 Nov. 1813.
53. Bishop Diary, 26 Oct. 1813.
54. Morrison, "Eye-Witness".
55. "Deux Lettres,", C. Pinguet to L. Pinguet, 21 Nov. 1813.
56. Morrison, "Eye-Witness."
57. O'Sullivan, "Eye-Witness".
58. Bishop Diary, 26 Oct. 1813.
59. O'Sullivan, "Eye-Witness".
60. Philatethes, "Last War," 276.
61. *ASPMA*, 479, Purdy to Wilkinson, n.d.
62. CLUM, War of 1812 Manuscripts, Neef to Bell, 20 Dec. 1813.
63. Fredriksen, "New Hampshire Volunteer," 169.
64. Izard Journal, 26 Oct. 1813.
65. O'Sullivan, "Eye-Witness".
66. Suthren, *Châteauguay*, 130; CLUM, War of 1812 Manuscripts, Neef to Bell, 20 Dec. 1813.
67. CLUM, War of 1812 Manuscripts, Neef to Bell, 20 Dec. 1813.
68. O'Sullivan, "Eye-Witness".
69. *ASPMA*, 461, Hampton to SW, 1 Nov. 1813.
70. Izard Journal, 26 Oct. 1813.
71. Fredriksen, "New Hampshire Volunteer," 170.
72. CLUM, War of 1812 Manuscripts, Neef to Bell, 20 Dec. 1813.
73. *ASPMA*, 461, Purdy to Wilkinson, n.d.; Suthren, *Châteauguay*, 133.
74. Fredriksen, "New Hampshire Volunteer," 170.
75. Suthren, *Châteauguay*, 138.
76. NAC, MG 24, F96, Journal of Major General Louis de Watteville, 26 Oct. 1813.
77. *Ibid.*
78. NAC, CO 43, vol. 132, 255, Prevost to Bathurst, 30 Oct. 1813.
79. Suthren, *Châteauguay*, 133. See also Philatethes, "Last War," 276; Guitard, *Militia*, 84-85; NAC, MG 24, F95, De Watteville Journal, 26-27 Oct. 1813.
80. O'Sullivan, "Eye-Witness."
81. Izard Journal, 26 Oct. 1813; CLUM, War of

1812 Ms., Neef to Bell, 20 Dec. 1813; Suthren, *Châteauguay*, 137-138.

82. Quebec *Gazette*, 4 November 1813. See also "Deux Lettres," 96, C. Pinguet to L. Pinguet, 21 Nov. 1813.

83. De Salaberry to [probably Baynes], 1 Nov. 1813, in Wood, *Select Documents*, III, 396.

84. Guitard, *Militia*, 84-87.

85. Guitard, *Militia*, 84-87, 93-94; 1817; Philatethes, "Last War," 276-277; Wood, *Select Documents*, 3, 396, de Salaberry to [probably Baynes], 1 November 1813; 415, Kent to de Salaberry, 9 Mar. 1814; 481, Macdonell to de Salaberry, 2 Feb. 1817; 419, Macdonell to de Salaberry, 14 Jan. 1817; 420, Macdonell to de Salaberry, [n.d. but c. 1817].

86. *ASPMA*, 461, Purdy to Wilkinson, n.d.

87. Wool to Dawson, 26 Mar. 1860, in Hinton, "Wool," 31. The miscreant officers were disciplined – writing to Armstrong on 27 Feb. 1813, Wilkinson assured the secretary that "Several of the delinquent officers of Major General Hampton's Division, who were spared by that officer, had been brought to justice," see USNA, RG 107, Micro 221. Two of these officers, Lieutenant Richard Barrett of the Twenty-Ninth Infantry and Lieutenant William Morris of the Thirty-Third were dismissed the service, see *ibidem* and Bilow, *Chateaugay*, 72.

88. Suthren, *Châteauguay*, 137-138. The first American attempt to invade Lower Canada had come to grief the previous autumn at Lacolle Mill.

89. Izard Journal, 27-8 Oct. 1813; *Doc. Hist.*, 8, 112, King to SW, n.d.

90. *ASPMA*, 461, Hampton to SW, 1 Nov. 1813.

91. Diary of Eleazar Williams, 28 Oct. 1813, quoted in Bilow, *Chateaugay*, 78.

92. *ASPMA*, 461, Hampton to SW, 1 Nov. 1813.

93. Bishop Diary, 28 Oct. 1813.

94. CLUM, War of 1812 Manuscripts, Neef to Bell, 20 Dec. 1813.

95. USNA, RG 107, Micro 222, Hampton to SW, 1 Nov. 1813.

96. *WCM*, App. 69, Hampton to SW, 1 Nov. 1813.

Chapter 6: "The Yankees are coming"

1. "Canadian Boat Song" was written by the Irish poet and singer, Tom Moore (1779-1852) during a trip to Canada and first appeared in print in 1805. It was known to British soldiers as Lieutenant John Le Couteur of the 104th Foot was reminded of it when he travelled down the St. Lawrence by boat in 1815, see Graves, *Merry Hearts*, 235.

"Utawa" in the text is a reference to the Ottawa River, which joins the St. Lawrence west of Montreal.

2. *ASPMA*, 474, Wilkinson to SW, 1 November 1813.

3. *WCM*, App. 51, SW to Wilkinson, 30 Oct. 1813.

4. *ASPMA*, 474, Wilkinson to SW, 1 Nov. 1813.

5. *Ibid.*

6. Malcomson, *Sailors of 1812*, p. 66, Sinclair to Cocke, 30 Nov. 1813. On Chauncey's operations in October, see Malcomson, *Lords*, 212-220.

7. Delafield, *Lewis*, 2, 94, Lewis to wife, 2 Nov. 1813.

8. *WCM*, App. 38, Wilkinson to SW, 3 Nov. 1813.

9. Hough, *St. Lawrence*, 93, 97.

10. Burns, *Fort Wellington*, 1-7.

11. Lord Selkirk's Diary, 19 Jan. 1804, quoted in Harkness, *Stormont*, 80.

12. Pringle, *Lunenburgh*, 207, reproduces an Assessment of the Eastern District dated 1815 which contains information on the size and type of houses in the three counties that year.

13. Burns, *Fort Wellington*, 1-10.

14. Dunlop, *Tiger Dunlop*, 24.

15. NAC, MG 24, L8, Viger, "Ma Saberdache," Vol. 3, Viger to wife, 13 May 1813; Hough, *St. Lawrence*, 620; Pringle, *Lunenburgh*, 75.

16. R. Patterson, "Lieutenant Colonel Benjamin Forsyth," n.p.; Hough, *St. Lawrence*, 627.

17. Hough, *St. Lawrence*, 626.

18. *Ibid.*, 626; Heitman, *Historical Register*.

19. Boss, *Stormont*, 17. On the Ogdensburg action, see NAC, RG 8 I, vol. 678, 95, Macdonell to Prevost, 22 Feb. 1813; Philatethes, "Last War," 436-439; Boss, *Stormont*, 16-18; Hough, *St. Lawrence*, 627-635.

20. Boss, *Stormont*, 218.

21. BLC, Woolsey Papers, Logbook of US Schooner *Sylph*, 1-2 Nov. 1813.

22. On Mulcaster, see Malcomson, *Lords*, 118-120 and Morgan, *Sketches*, 226-227.

23. *Doc. Hist.*, 8, 123, Mulcaster to Yeo, 2 Nov. 1813.

24. HSP, Carr Diary, 1 Nov. 1813.

25. *WCM*, 200, testimony of Eustis.

26. LC, Brown Papers, Brown to SW, 10 Mar. 1815.

27. HSP, Carr Diary, 1 Nov. 1813.

28. *Doc. Hist.*, 8, 123, Mulcaster to Yeo, 2 Nov. 1813.

29. *Ibid.*

30. *WCM*, 200, testimony of Eustis.

31. *Doc. Hist.*, 8, 112, Mulcaster to Yeo, 2 Nov. 1813.

32. *Ibid.*; 125, Brown to Dennis, 2 Nov. 1813.

33. *WCM*, 201, testimony of Eustis.

34. *WCM*, 154, testimony of Walbach.

35. *WCM*, 379, defence of Wilkinson.
36. *Kingston Gazette*, 30 Dec. 1813, Extract of a letter from a gentleman, Ogdensburg, 23 Nov. 1813. Also, *WCM*, 379, Defence of Wilkinson.
37. *WCM*, 37, testimony of Eustis.
38. *WCM*, 318, testimony of Macpherson.
39. *WCM*, 50, 59, 62-65, testimony of Swartout; 98-106, testimony of Thorne.
40. *WCM*, 138, Testimony of Lewis; Fredriksen, "Plow Joggers," 22.
41. *Doc. Hist.*, 8, 133, After General Orders, 4 Nov. 1813 and Wilkinson to Chauncey, 4 Nov. 1813; 134, Chauncey to Wilkinson, 4 Nov. 1813.
42. "First Campaign," no. 13, 353.
43. HSP, Carr Diary, 4 Nov 13.
44. *Ibid.*, General Order, 4 Nov. 1813.
45. Hough, *St. Lawrence*, 639.
46. *WCM*, 138, testimony of Lewis; Fredriksen, "Plow Joggers," 22.
47. *WCM.*, 120, testimony of Lewis; 143, After General Orders, 4 Nov. 1813; Fredriksen, "Plow Joggers," 22-23.
48. *Doc. Hist.*, 8, 147, extract of a letter from an officer in the USN, n.d.; Malcomson, *Lords*, 220; BHL, Woolsey Papers, Log Book, US Schooner *Sylph*, 3 Nov. 1813.
49. Malcomson, *Lords*, 220.
50. Fredriksen, "Plow Joggers," 23; *WCM*, 120-121, testimony of Lewis; 144-145, testimony of Walbach; *DCB*, entry for William Johnston; NAC, MG 30, E66, 20, General Order, 11 Dec. 1813.
51. *WCM*, 82, testimony of Boyd; Fredriksen, "Plow Joggers," 23.
52. "First Campaign," no. 12, 53.
53. *WCM*, 139-141, testimony of Lewis.
54. Fredriksen, "Plow Joggers," 23.
55. Phillipart, *Royal Military Calendar*, 3, 339.
56. Obituary, *United Service Journal*, 1847, 2, 479.
57. NAC, RG 8 I, vol. 681, 323, Prevost to Brock, 19 Oct. 1812. On Pearson's life, see PRO, WO 47, vol. 747, 84, Statement of the Services of Major Thomas Pearson, 10 December 1809; Phillipart, *Royal Military Calendar*, 3, 339; and his obituary in *United Service Journal*, 1847, 2, 479.
58. Graves, *Merry Hearts*, 109, 113.
59. Dunlop, *Tiger Dunlop*, 27.
60. Graves, *Merry Hearts*, 113.
61. Dunlop, *Tiger Dunlop*, 14.
62. NAC, MG 19, A 39, Clark Papers, Garrison Order, 25 Apr. 1813.
63. Burns, *Fort Wellington*, 10-18; PRO, WO 44, vol. 248, Return of Brass Ordnance ... Travelling Carriages, etc., 30 June 1813; Return of the Serviceable Brass and Iron Ordnance, 30 June 1813; *Bath Archives*, 393, Henry Jackson to George Jackson, 19 Nov. 1813 (hereafter Jackson letter); NAC, MG 19, A39, Clark Papers, Brigade Order, Prescott, 1 Oct. 1813; Ellery, *Swift*, 116.
64. Hough, *St. Lawrence*, 635.
65. AO, MU 1054, A. Ford to D. Ford, 21 Oct. 1813.
66. *Ibid.*; also Hough, *St. Lawrence*, 635.
67. Croil, *Dundas*, 78.
68. LLIU, War of 1812 Ms., Order Book for 2nd Brigade, Aug.-Dec. 1813, General Orders, 6 Nov. 1813.
69. *WCM*, 73-74, testimony of King.
70. *WCM*, 121, testimony of Lewis.
71. *WCM*, 300, testimony of Lee.
72. HSP, Parker Papers, Wilkinson to Hampton, 6 Nov. 1813.
73. *Ibid.*
74. *WCM*, 73-74, testimony of King, 257, testimony of Lewis; Silver, *Gaines*, 31-33; Scott, *Memoirs*, 1, 107.
75. Myers, *Reminicences*, 40.
76. *WCM*, 210, testimony of Bull.
77. ASPMA, 477, Army Journal, 6 Nov. 1813.
78. ""First Campaign," no. 13, 256.
79. On lighting conditions at Prescott on the night of 6/7 Nov. 1813, see [Richardson], *Veritas*, 76.
80. Jackson letter.
81. ASPMA, 477, Army Journal, 7 Nov. 1813.
82. Scott, *Memoirs*, 1, 107.
83. Ellery, *Swift*, 116.
84. Jackson letter.
85. *WCM*, 202, testimony of Eustis; Ellery, *Swift*, 116.
86. Graves, *Merry Hearts*, 149.
87. *Doc. Hist.*, 8, 143, MacHahon to Powell, 8 Nov. 1813.
88. *Ibid.*
89. Patterson, "Forgotten Hero," 7-9.
90. NAC, RG 8 I, vol. 681, 29, de Rottenburg to Prevost, 11 Nov. 1813.
91. *DCB*, 8, Harvey entry.
92. Petre, *Royal Berkshire*, 1-104.
93. PRO, WO 27, vol. 96, quoted in Cunliffe, *Royal Irish Fusiliers*, 130.
94. Cunliffe, *Royal Irish Fusiliers*, 129-141.
95. James, *History*, 2, 331; USNA, RG 45, Logbook of HMS *Wolfe*, 6-7 Nov. 1813.
96. Dunlop, *Tiger Dunlop*, 10
97. *Quebec Mercury*, 16 Nov. 1813. The three American generals in captivity were Brigadier General James Winchester, captured at French Town in January 1813 and Brigadier Generals John Chandler and William Winder, captured at Stoney Creek in June 1813.

Chapter 7: "There is a spell on us"

1. "Pat's Observations on Harrison's Victory," a broadside dating from the autumn 1813 with a ballad, in an Irish style, celebrates Major General William H. Harrison's victory over the British army at the battle of the Thames, 5 October 1813. No tune has been discovered but the words go very well with the old Irish air, "Black Velvet Band."

2. Jackson letter; Hough, *St. Lawrence*, 640.

3. *ASPMA*, 477, Army Journal, 7 Nov. 1813.

4. *WCM*, 291, testimony of Brooks; 296, testimony of Nourse; *New York Evening Post*, 29 Nov. 1813, Extract of a letter from a gentleman in Hamilton, 14 Nov. 1813.

5. *ASPMA*, 477, Army Journal, 7 Nov. 1813.

6. *WCM*, 145, testimony of Walbach.

7. Ellery, *Swift*, 116.

8. *ASPMA*, 477, Army Journal, 7 Nov. 1813.

9. *WCM*, 284,, Wilkinson to Macomb, 7 Nov. 1813.

10. *WCM*, 168, testimony of Macomb.

11. Croil, *Dundas*, 78.

12. AO, MS 537, Ridout to father, 12 Nov. 1813; *WCM*, 303-304, testimony of Biddle.

13. AO, MS 537, Ridout to father, 12 Nov. 1813. See also Ridout to father, 20 Nov. 1813 and *WCM*, 303, Biddle.

14. *WCM*, 203, testimony of Eustis.

15. *ASPMA*, 477, Army Journal, 7 Nov. 1813.

16. Jackson letter.

17. Hough, *St. Lawrence*, 643; *WCM*, 303, testimony of Biddle.

18. NAC, RG 19 E5(a), Memorial of the Losses Sustained by Peter Shaver, 7th and 8th November 1813.

19. Malcomson, *Sailors of 1812*, 39, Sinclair to Cocke, 4 July 1813.

20. NAC, RG 19 E5(a), Memorial of the Losses Sustained by Peter Shaver, 7th and 8th November 1813.

21. *ASPMA*, 477, Army Journal, 8 Nov. 1813.

22. Smart, "St. Lawrence Project," 27; *ASPMA*, 477, Army Journal, 8 Nov. 1813; *WCM*, 178, testimony of Macomb; AO, MU 1054, A. Ford to D. Ford, 13 Nov. 1813.

23. *WCM*, 162-163, testimony of Wadsworth; 204, testimony of Eustis.

24. Fredriksen, "Georgia Officer," 681, Cumming to father, 20 Nov. 1813 (hereafter Cumming letter). Also *WCM*, 277, testimony of Porter; 319, testimony of Macpherson.

25. *WCM*, 122, testimony of Lewis.

26. HSP, Carr Diary, 8 Nov. 1813. Also *ASPMA*, 477, Army Journal, 8 Nov. 1813; *WCM*, 122, testimony of Lewis; 162, testimony of Wadsworth.

27. *WCM*, App. 24, Council of War, White House, 8 Nov. 1813. See also, 104, testimony of Thorne.

28. *WCM*, 162, testimony of Wadsworth.

29. *Kingston Gazette*, 1 Mar. 1814, letter from a gentleman, dated Ogdensburg, 23 Nov. 1813.

30. "First Campaign," no. 13, 259.

31. Izard Journal, 7 Nov. 1813.

32. *Ibid.*, 8 Nov. 1813.

33. USNA, RG 107, Micro 222, Reel 9, Hampton to Wilkinson, 8 Nov. 1813.

34. *Ibid.*

35. Bishop Diary, 8 Nov. 1813.

36. CLUM, War of 1812 Ms., Neef to Bell, 19 Dec. 1813.

37. Bishop Diary, 9 Nov. 1813.

38. Izard Journal, 15 Nov. 1813.

39. *Ibid.*

40. *Ibid.*

41. Fredriksen, "New Hampshire Volunteer," 171.

42. Smart, "St. Lawrence Project," 27.

43. *New York Evening Post*, 29 Nov. 1813, Extract of a Letter from a gentleman in Hamilton, 14 Nov. 1813; Hough, *St. Lawrence*, 641-642.

44. Jackson letter. On movements, see Smart, "St. Lawrence Project," 27-29.

45. *ASPMA*, 477, Army Journal, 8 Nov. 1813.

46. Loucks, "Battle of Crysler's Farm," (hereafter Loucks narrative).

47. "First Campaign," no. 13, 259.

48. *ASPMA*, 477, Army Journal, 8 Nov. 1813.

49. *ASPMA*, 477, Army Journal, 9 Nov. 1813; *WCM*, 301, testimony of Lee.

50. *ASPMA*, 477, Army Journal, 9 Nov. 1813.

51. NAC, MG 24, L8, Viger, Ma Saberdache," 3, Viger to wife, 13 May 1813.

52. *DCB*, 8, Crysler entry.

53. Frederiksen, "Kirby," 69.

54. Henderson, "A Winter Journey Long Ago."

55. On buildings, see Pringle, *Lunenburgh*, 207. The colour of Crysler's house was not unusual as deep yellow was the most popular covering at this time on the St. Lawrence, see Guillet, *Early Life*, 173.

56. Croil, *Dundas*, 79, 81.

57. NAC, RG 19 E5(a), Loss Claims of John Haines, Michael Ault, and Michael Cook.

58. "First Campaign," no. 13, 258-259.

59. HSP, Parker Papers, General Order, 10 Nov. 1813.

60. *Ibid.*

61. *Doc.Hist.*, 8, 148, Morning General Order, 10 Nov. 1813; also *WCM*, 89, testimony of Boyd; 301, testimony of Lee.

62. *WCM*, 301, testimony of Lee.

63. *WCM*, 324, testimony of Macpherson. On

Ingall's fort, see Hough, *St. Lawrence*, 643; *WCM*, 301, testimony of Lee; HSP, Carr Diary, 10 Nov. 1813.

64. *WCM*, 65, testimony of Swartout.

65. *WCM*, 82, testimony of Boyd.

66. Hough, *St. Lawrence*, 641-642.

67. *New York Evening Post*, 29 Nov. 1813, Extract of a Letter from a gentleman in Hamilton, 14 Nov. 1813.

68. *Ibid.*

69. NAC, RG 8 I, vol. 681, 74, Capitulation signed by David Ogden and Alexander Richards, Hamilton, 10 Nov. 1813.

70. Hough, *St. Lawrence*, 642; NAC, RG 8 I, vol. 642, p. 78, Morrison to de Rottenburg, 11 Nov. 1813.

71. Smyth Carter, *Dundas*, 238.

72. Jackson letter.

73. MTPL, Journal of Christopher Hagerman, 29 Nov. 1813 (hereafter Hagerman Journal).

74. NYSL, Gardner Papers, Gardner to Parker, 15 Nov. 1813 (hereafter Gardner letter).

75. *Quebec Mercury*, 23 Nov. 1813, Extract from an Officer of Rank with Colonel Morrison's army, Osnaburgh, 13 Nov. 1813.

76. *WCM*, 82, testimony of Boyd.

77. Jackson letter.

78. Gardner letter.

79. Hagerman Journal, 29 Nov. 1813.

80. *ASPMA*, 477, Army Journal, 10 Nov. 1813; *WCM*, 163, testimony of Walbach: 203, testimony of Eustis.

81. *WCM*, 130, testimony of Lewis.

82. *ASPMA*, 478, Army Journal, 10 Nov. 1813.

83. *WCM*, 141, testimony of Ripley.

84. *WCM*, 152, testimony of Walbach.

85. Dunlop, *Tiger Dunlop*, 14.

86. Fredriksen, "War of 1812," 306, McIntire to Holmes, 8 Dec. 1813. See also *WCM*, 297, testimony of Lee; 319, testimony of Macpherson.

87. NAC, RG 8 I, vol. 681, 41, Dennis to Scott, 11 Nov. 1813. On the cost of the bridge, see Pringle, *Lunenburgh*, 61.

88. Scott, *Memoirs*, 1, 108.

89. Fredriksen, "War of 1812," 306, McIntire to Holmes, 8 Dec. 1813.

90. NAC, RG 8 I, vol. 681, 41, Dennis to Scott, 11 Nov. 1813. See Pringle, *Lunenburgh*, 204, for names of casualties.

91. *WCM*, 319, testimony of Macpherson; HSP, Carr Diary, 15 Nov. 1813.

92. NAC, RG 8 I, vol. 681, 41, Dennis to Scott, 11 Nov. 1813; 31, Cochrane to Scott, 11 Nov. 1813; Croil, *Dundas*, 80.

93. *WCM*, 123, testimony of Lewis.

94. Cumming letter.

95. *ASPMA*, 477, Army Journal, 10 Nov. 1813.

96. *WCM*, 82, testimony of Boyd.

97. *WCM*, 47, testimony of Swartout.

98. *Doc. Hist.*, 8, 143, McMahon to Powell, 8 Nov. 1813.

99. James Croil, who lived on the Crysler property forty years after the battle and had the opportunity to talk to local men who fought in the action, maintained that Morrison held an orders group in the Crysler house during the evening of 10 November 1813, see Croil, *Dundas*, 83. It is very probable that this conference did take place as, at the very least, Morrison and Mulcaster had to confer and decide on their reponse to the order for them to break off contact and return to Kingston. If the two senior officers of the corps of observation had to meet, it would have made perfectly good sense to include other officers such as Clifford, Harvey, Heriot, Jackson, Pearson and Plenderleath to discuss plans and dispositions for the next day and the Crysler house would have provided an ideal meeting place.

100. *WCM*, 82, testimony of Boyd.

101. *ASPMA*, 477, Army Journal, 10 Nov. 1813.

102. *WCM*, 82, testimony of Boyd; also 145, testimony of Walbach.

Chapter 8: "Take the King's shilling!"

1. Sung to the tune of a traditional Scots air called "O Bonnie Wood O' Craigielee" or "Craigielee" (sometimes Craigielea) the words of "Who'll Be A Soldier?" date at least to 1715 as it is also known as "Who'll Be a Soldier with Marlboro and Me?" Other titles with varying words are "The Bold Fusilier" and "Marching through Rochester." The version here dates from 1809-1814 and can be sung as "Who'll Come to Spain with Wellington and Me?" The reason for this song's popularity may be its melody as "Craigielee" is a catchy, haunting tune. In 1894, a young Australian woman, Christina Macpherson, heard "Craigielee" being played by a military band at a race meeting and later played it on the autoharp for a visitor, A.B. "Banjo" Patterson, to her home. Patterson was entranced by the tune and wrote new words for it, calling the result "Waltzing Matilda."

A "fusilier" was, by 1813, an elite type of infantryman in the British army, and to "take the King's shilling" is to enlist in the army.

2. Graves, *Soldiers of 1814*, 27.

3. NAC, RG 19 E5(a), A Memorial of Losses Sustained by Jacob Sheaver.

4. Graves, *Where Right and Glory Lead*, 34-35.

5. William Napier quoted in Luvaas, *Education of an Army*, 24; Houlding, *Fit For Service*, 283-318. See also: Adjutant General, *Manual and Platoon Exercises*; Adjutant General, Lower Canada, *Rules and Regulations for the Militia Forces of Lower Canada*, Quebec, 1812.

6. The *Regulations for the Exercise of Riflemen and Light Infantry* published in 1798 with a second edition in 1802 was written by de Rottenburg and was shortly followed by the work of Francis Jarry, an expatriate officer of the French army and professor at the Royal Military College, who brought out *Instruction concerning the Duties of Light Infantry in the Field* in 1803. See also Cooper, *Practical Guide*, ix-xx.

7. Webb-Carter, "Letters of William Bell," 72, Bell to parents, 22 Sept. 1808.

8. Grattan, *Adventures*, 87.

9. PRO, WO 27, vol. 33, Inspection Report for the 2nd Battalion, 89th Foot, May 1815. The inspecting officer was being unduly critical – the 89th had not had time to carry out live fire practice during 1814 as, from July to October of that year, they were in combat.

10. Graves, "Dry Books," and "Steuben to Scott." On the origins of Steuben's *Blue Book*, see Peterkin, *Exercise of Arms*, 1-12.

11. Armstrong to Williams, 8 Feb. 1813, in United States Senate, *Report of the Committee on Military Affairs, 1813*.

12. General Order, 19 March 1813, contained in Duane *Hand Book*.

13. USNA, RG 107, Micro 6, SW to Duane, 5 Apr. 1814.

14. Graves, "Dry Books," 58-59.

15. Graves, "Dry Books," 58-59; Graves, *Right and Glory*, 34-35; HSP, Carr Diary, General Order, 3 Sept. 1813.

16. PRO, WO 27, vol. 33, Inspection Report for the 2nd Battalion, 89th Foot, May 1815

17. Nosworthy, *Battle Tactics*, 71-73; Duane, *American Military Library*, 1, 181-182.

18. *Quebec Mercury*, 17 Nov. 1812.

19. Nosworthy, *Battle Tactics*, 71-73.

20. Myers, *Reminiscences*, 12.

21. Nosworthy, *Battle Tactics*, 77-79.

22. Muir, *Tactics*, 86-89.

23. One of the outside readers of this book in manuscript queried me as to why I always object to the use of the word "cannon" to mean a smooth-bore artillery piece. The reason requires some explanation.

The word originates from the Italian *cannone* meaning an artillery piece, type unspecified. It passed into French as *canon* and was picked up by the Royal Navy which, prior to the 1780s, commonly used only one type of ordnance – the gun – and "cannon" and "gun" became synonymous in naval usage. Many of the naval ordnance terms used by the RN were adopted in the United States because manuals of naval gunnery, either military or merchant, were available at the time of Revolutionary War. The Royal Artillery did not publish an official manual dealing with technical terms until nearly the midpoint of the 19th century because education in that corps was based on personal notes made by officer cadets during their time at the Royal Military Academy at Woolwich and fleshed out on service by private publications such as Adye's popular *Pocket Gunner* series of handy reference works. In the Royal Artillery, the term "cannon" was never used as it was regarded as vague and incorrect. In the RA, the four types of smooth-bore ordnance – guns, mortars, howitzers and carronades – were always referred to by those designations.

Royal Navy terminology was taken over by the United States in the 18th century. Thus, American usage refers to a "gun captain" rather than a "gun commander," a "gun crew" rather than a "gun detachment," and an "artilleryman" instead of a "gunner." However, none of the documentation of the United States artillery of the War of 1812 written by officers of experience that I have examined ever uses the word "cannon;" the correct term "gun" is used instead.

In point of fact, the only time the word "cannon" can be used correctly in the English language during the smooth-bore period is if the weapon is mounted on board a ship. On land, the correct term is "gun" following RA practice. In modern times, a "cannon" is an automatic weapon, generally greater than 12 and less than 75 mm calibre.

24. Jackson letter; Graves, "Field Artillery"; Adye, *Bombardier and Pocket Gunner*; Hughes, *Firepower*; D'Antoni, *Treatise*.

25. Muir, *Tactics*, 47.

26. Hennell, *Gentleman Volunteer*, 91.

27. Hughes, *Firepower*, 166-167; Muir, *Tactics*, 41-50.

28. Bunbury, *Passages*, xv.

29. Glover, *Peninsular Reform*; Mackesy, *British Victory in Egypt*.

30. Information on the length of service of the officers of the 49th and 89th Foot have been extracted from Sutherland, *Majesty's Gentlemen* and the *Army Lists* for 1813 and 1814. Sutherland provides a succinct analysis of the complicated promotion system of the British officer during the War of 1812.

31. Cunliffe, *Royal Irish Fusiliers*, 134-135, General Orders, 10 July 1811; Sutherland, *His Majesty's Gentlemen*.

32. Sutherland, *His Majesty's Gentlemen*; Wrong, *Canadian Seigneury*, 125-165; *Doc. Hist.*, 8, 166, W. Claus to W. Claus, 11 May 114; *DCB*, 7, Jonathan Sewell entry; Howe, "Ormond."

33. Henderson, "Canadian Fencibles," 18-20; Sutherland, *His Majesty's Gentlemen*; Guitard, *Militia*; Lepine, *Militia Officers*; Heriot, "Frederick Heriot," 72; Thomas, *Johnson*, 158.

34. War Department, *Register of the Army 1813*; Heitman, *Historical Register*; *Appleton's Encyclopedia*, Walbach entry.

35. On enlistment periods of the northern army, see USNA, RG 107, Micro 222, Reel 9, Strength of the Army at French Mills and Chateaugay, 8 Dec. 1813. The infantry regiments of the American army during the War of 1812 can be divided into three distinct "waves." The first wave comprises the First through Seventh Infantry of the pre-war army; the second consists of eighteen regiments, numbered Eight through Twenty-Five, authorized just prior to the outbreak of war; and the third includes the Twenty-Sixth through Forty-Eighth Infantry which were raised after January 1813. Many of the units of this last wave were only partly raised or were combined with other units of the same wave. The best element in the northern army came from the first two waves which enlisted for five years or the duration of the war and all of Wilkinson's units were from these waves. Hampton only had three units from the first or second wave, the majority of his infantry were drawn from the third wave and had been in service less than six months when they went into action in the autumn of 1813.

36. Shaw, "Remarks," 392, emphasis in the original.

37. Stagg, "Enlisted Men," 645.

38. Graves, "Enlisted Men," 8.

39. Lerwill, *Personnal Replacement*, 39; Graves, "Enlisted Men," 8-10.

40. War Department, *Rules and Articles 1812*, 32, 94.

41. USNA, RG 107, Micro 221, reel 47, Old Soldier to SW, Nov. 1812.

42. War Department, *Army Register 1814*, 15, Recruiting Regulations, 2 May 1814.

43. *Ibid.*

44. Mann, *Medical Sketches*, 122.

45. Shipp, *Path of Glory*, 2-3

46. Glover, *Peninsular Preparation*, 214-254; Oman, *Wellington's Army*, 208-19.

47. Glover, *Peninsular Preparation*, 222-223.

48. The verse goes "Your sergeants and officers are very kind, If that you can flatter and speak to their mind, They will free you from duty and all other trouble, Your money being gone, your duty comes double." See Winstock, *Songs*, 38-39.

49. Harris, *Recollections*, 5.

50. Information on the place of enlistment, civilian occupation, age and length of service of the enlisted personnel of the 49th and 89th Foot abstracted from the records of the men of both units known to have been present at the battle of Crysler's Farm who later applied for pensions from the Chelsea Hospital. See Public Record Office, WO 97, vols. 629-634 and 979-981.

51. [Grose], *Advice to Officers*, 117.

52. Guitard, *Militia*; Henderson, "Canadian Regiment," 18-22, 24-28; Henderson, "Notes on Captain Hall's Company."

53. Lawrence quoted in Oman, *Wellington's Army*, 253.

54. Bell, *Soldier's Glory*, 97.

55. War Department, *Rules and Articles 1812*, 32, 94.

56. Desertion and casualty statistics for the British army in Canada extracted from PRO, WO 17, Monthly Returns of the Army, 25 June 1813 to 25 Dec. 1814. On the strength of the American army, see Kreidberg and Henry, *Military Mobilization*, 50 and on executions during the war, see Hare, "Military Punishments." Statistics for executions in Wellington's army from Oman, *Wellington's Army*, 243-245.

57. Graves, *Merry Hearts*, 157; *DCB*, 5, Deserontyon entry. What Le Couteur did not realize was that the Gospel of St. John was translated into the Iroquoian language by John Norton or the Snipe, the great Mohawk war chief.

58. AO, MS 35, Strachan Papers, List of Warriors, 1812; Graves, *Merry Hearts*, 126, Le Couteur to Bouton, 24 Oct. 1813. See Appendix G for the names of Mohawk warriors who fought at Crysler's Farm.

59. HSP, Carr Diary, 10 November 1813.

60. Smyth Carter, *Dundas*, 237.
61. NAC, RG 19 E5(a), Loss Claims of Michael Cook, Sophrenus Casselman and Peter Fetterly; Smith, *Makers of Old Ontario*, 57.
62. PRO, WO 42, vol. 59, 78, Petition of Louisa May de Lorimier; PRO, WO 55, vol. 1223, Glasgow to McLeod, 2 Dec. 1813.

Chapter 9: "Jack, drop cooking, the enemy..."
1. "Love, Farewell," though it has the flavour of the Emerald Isle and was a favourite of the many Irish soldiers in the British army during the Napoleonic wars, apparently originated in an English broadside ballad of the Revolutionary War period, see Winstock, *Songs*, 116-118. A firelock is a period term for a musket.
2. *WCM*, 84, testimony of Boyd.
3. Graves, *Soldiers of 1814*, 27.
4. Winstock, *Songs*, 45; *ASPMA*, I, 481, After General Order, 4 Nov. 1813; Fredriksen, "New Hampshire Volunteer," 163. I am indebted to Mr. Michael Putnam of Dundas and Mr. Nicko Elliott of Hamilton for information on military drumming of the Napoleonic period.
5. *WCM*, 48, testimony of Swartout.
6. *WCM*, 151, testimony of Walbach,
7. AO, MU 1032, Kingsford Papers, Recollections of the battle of Crysler's Farm by Colonel Sewell, 1869 (hereafter Sewell recollections).
8. For the strength and organization of Morrison's command, see Appendix F.
9. Croil, *Dundas*, 83.
10. The topography of the battlefield has been reconstructed from the description in Croil, *Dundas*, 83-85, the map sources listed in the bibliography, and the photographs of Dr. Traer Van Allen, whose family owned much of the battlefield for nearly a century.
11. *ASPMA*, 478, Army Journal, 11 Nov. 1813.
12. *WCM*, 85, testimony of Boyd; 130, testimony of Lewis; 243, testimony of Bissell;
13. *WCM*, 48, testimony of Swartout.
14. *WCM*, 130, testimony of Lewis.
15. Graves, *Soldiers of 1814*, 27; *WCM*, 130, testimony of Lewis; Boyd, *Documents*, 21, Boyd to SW, 29 April 1815 (hereafter Boyd, 1815 report).
16. Boyd, 1815 report.
17. Croil, *Dundas*, 83, 87; *St. Lawrence River Pilot*, 117.
18. Jackson letter.
19. Smith, *Makers of Old Ontario*, 56-57.
20. *WCM*, 130, testimony of Lewis. See also

WCM, 203, testimony of Eustis and, 285, testimony of Hite.
21. *WCM*, 164, testimony of Wadsworth.
22. *WCM*, 84, testimony of Boyd; 130, testimony of Lewis; 164, testimony of Wadsworth; 325, testimony of Pinckney.
23. Fredriksen, "Kirby," 69; Lossing, *Fieldbook*, 651n; Heitman, *Historical Register*.
24. HSP, Carr Diary, 11 November 1813.
25. *Ibid.*; Pringle, *Lunenburgh*, 76.
26. NAC, RG 8 I, vol. 681, 41, Dennis to Scott, 11 Nov. 1813.
27. NAC, RG 8 I, vol. 681, 70, Bouchette to Freer, 12 Nov. 1813.
28. NAC, RG 8 I, vol. 681, 33, Cochrane to Scott, 11 Nov. 1813; 41, Dennis to Scott, 11 Nov. 1813; 70, Bouchette to Freer, 12 Nov. 1813; Irving, *British Officers*; Gray, *Soldiers of the King*.
29. *WCM*, 243, testimony of Bissell.
30. Croil, *Dundas*, 80; *WCM*, 242-243, testimony of Bissell.
31. NAC, RG 8 I, vol. 681, 70, Bouchette to Freer, 12 Nov. 1813.
32. Pringle, *Lunenburgh*, 76-77.
33. *Ibid.*, 77.
34. *Ibid.*, 78. Also *WCM*, 242-243, testimony of Bissell; LLIU, Journal of Brown's Second Brigade, 11 Nov. 1813.
35. Croil, *Dundas*, 83.
36. Jackson letter.
37. Croil, *Dundas*, 94; USNA, RG 107, Micro 222, reel 9, Harvey to Wilkinson, 14 Nov. 1813; Oath of Parole signed by Young and Bruce, 11 Nov. 1813.
38. Fredriksen, "Kirby," 69.
39. *Ibid.*
40. Smyth Carter, *Dundas*, 238; Croil, *Dundas*, 95.
41. Gardner letter.
42. Boyd, 1815 report.
43. *Ibid.* This statement would seem to confirm that Porter and Wadsworth had been ordered away from the army although this is not clear from their testimony during Wilkinson's court martial.
44. *Ibid.*
45. Lossing, *Fieldbook*, 651.
46. *WCM*, 214, testimony of Bull.
47. *ASPMA*, 478, Army Journal, 11 Nov. 1813.
48. *WCM*, 82, testimony of Boyd; also 85 and 213, testimony of Bull.
49. Boyd, 1815 report.
50. *Ibid.*
51. *Ibid.* See also *WCM*, 89, testimony of Boyd; 207, testimony of Eustis; 311, testimony of Pinckney; Harris, "Service," 329; Heitman,

Historical Register. Porter's whereabouts on 11 November 1813 are very mysterious. It is known from the testimony of officers at Wilkinson's court martial that he received the order to position guns to drive off the British flotilla but, thereafter, he disappears and he is not mentioned by name in Boyd's report of the battle. The conclusion is that, after Mulcaster withdrew, Porter accompanied Wadsworth down the river.

52. WCM, 142, testimony of Ripley.

53. For information on the organization and strength of Boyd's force on 11 November 1813, see Appendix E.

54. Smyth Carter, *Dundas*, 238.

55. Hough, *St. Lawrence*, 647; NYSL, Gardner Papers, Charles Gardner, "Remarks on the Military Memoir of Major General Ripley published in the Portfolio".

56. On Ripley, see Fredriksen, *Officers of the Left Division*, 77-80 and on other officers, see Heitman, *Historical Register*. On the Eleventh Infantry, see USNA, RG 107, Micro 221, reel 43, Parker to Dearborn, 20 Nov. 1812 and Dearborn to SW, 24 Nov. 1812; *New York Evening Post*, 2 Nov. 1812; *NWR*, 2, 28 July 1812. On the Fourteenth Infantry, see USNA, RG 107, Micro 221: reel 52, Smyth to Dearborn contained in Dearborn to Monroe, 26 Dec. 1812; reel 54, Lewis to SW, 18 Apr. 1813; reel 55, Macomb to SW, 23 June 1813; Micro 222, reel 8, General Order, Buffalo, 19 Apr. 1813; *Buffalo Gazette*, 29 Sept. 1812; *Doc. Hist.*, 4, 265, Robinson to Van Rennsselaer, 2 Dec 1812; *NWR*: 2, 8 Aug. 1812; 3, 26 Sept. 1812, 17 Oct. 1812; 4, 29 May 1813; 5, 20 Nov. 1813. On the Twenty-First Infantry, see USNA, RG 107, Micro 221, reel 52, Dearborn to SW, 14 Mar. 1813; *NWR*, 4, 10 Apr. 1813; Hampton, *History*, 22, 30-35.

57. Gardner letter.

58. Gardner letter; Fredriksen, "Honest Sodger," 145.

59. On officers, see Heitman, *Historical Register*. On the Twelfth Infantry see USNA, RG 107, Micro 221: reel 43, Smyth to SW, 22 Sept. 1812; reel 47, Parker to SW, 27 Sept. 1812; reel 52, Smyth to Dearborn, 14 Dec. 1812; Micro 222, reel 8, General Order, Buffalo, 19 Apr. 1813; reel 9, Winder to illegible, 31 May 1813; *NWR*, 3, 12 Sept. 1812; 2 Jan. 1813; *Doc. Hist.*, 4, 159, Smyth to Dearborn, 24 Oct. 1812. On the Thirteenth Infantry, see *Doc. Hist.*, 3: 106, Wadsworth to Tompkins, 6 July 1812; 96, Hall to Tompkins, 4 July 1812; *NWR*, 2, 11 July 1812.

60. Fredriksen, "Plow Joggers," 24.

61. *Ibid.* Smyth, *Regulations*, 66. On Coles, see Heitman, *Historical Register*; Smyth, *Regulations*, 66.

62. Lepine, *Militia Officers*; Benn, *Iroquois*, 75.

63. Adjutant General, *Light Infantry Exercise*, 4-5.

64. *Ibid.*, 4-5, 10.

65. Chartrand and Summers, *Military Uniforms*, 68 and Blackmore, *British Military Firearms*, 137.

66. Benn, *Iroquois*, 77. Benn provides a well researched and lucid analysis of native tactics during the War of 1812.

67. Croil, *Dundas*, 95.

68. Dunlop, *Tiger Dunlop*, 48.

69. *NWR*, 5, 18 Dec. 1813, Boyd to Wilkinson, 12 Nov. 1813 (hereafter Boyd, 1813 report).

70. NYSL, Gardner Papers, "Remarks on the Military Memoir of Major General Ripley contained in the Portfolio."

71. *Ibid.*

72. Loucks narrative.

73. NAC, RG 8 I, Morrison to de Rottenburg, 12 Nov. 1813 (hereafter Morrison report).

74. AO, MS 537, Extract from a letter of Lieutenant Colonel Harvey, 12 Nov. 1813 (hereafter Harvey letter).

75. Morrison report; Harvey letter; Loucks narrative; Sewell recollections; Jackson letter.

76. Adjutant General, *Rules and Regulations*, 66-78, 144-145.

77. *Standing Orders, Ireland*, 35, Warrant for the Regulation of Clothing, Colours, etc., 19 Dec. 1786; Norman, *Battle Honours*, 95.

78. Haythornewaite, *Weapons and Equipment*, 142.

79. Sewell recollections.

80. *Standing Orders, Ireland*, 35, Warrant for the Regulation of Clothing, Colours, etc., 19 Dec. 1786.

81. Adjutant General, *Rules and Regulations*, 66-68; Adjutant General Lower Canada, *Rules and Regulations*, 25.

82. Adjutant General Lower Canada, *Rules and Regulations*, 39.

83. Harvey letter.

84. Morrison report.

85. Sewell, recollections.

86. Harvey letter, emphasis in the original.

87. Boyd, 1813 report.

88. WCM: 49, testimony of Swartout; 86, testimony of Boyd; 139, testimony of Ripley; 151, testimony of Walbach; Ellery, *Swift*, 116.

89. Cumming letter.

90. Trowbridge in Hough, *St. Lawrence*, 648.

Chapter 10: "They came on in a very gallant ..."

1. "A New Recruiting Song," one of the many variants of "Yankee Doodle" was published in the *Reporter*, a Pennsylvania newspaper in November 1812. Perhaps the best known of all American military marches, "Yankee Doodle" originated in the 1750s as a caustic satire by British soldiers of the amateurish pretensions of the American colonial militia. The joke backfired because the tune was adopted by the despised colonials themselves, who made it their anthem during the Revolutionary War. By the time of the War of 1812, "Yankee Doodle" was probably the most popular piece of music in the United States and American soldiers played it constantly – it was heard during the attack on York in April 1813, at the battle of Fort George in May 1813, during the Niagara campaign of 1814, at the battle of New Orleans in 1815 and probably every day in every camp of the United States Army during the war.

2. PRO, WO 55, vol. 1223, 347, Dickson to McLeod, 2 June 1813.

3. NAC, MG 19, A39, Clark Papers, General Order, 1 Oct. 1813.

4. Askwith, *List of Officers*; NAC, RG 8 I, vol. 1179, 283, General Order, 28 June 13.

5. Sewell recollections. Sewell is not saying here that Jackson's guns were behind the infantry and could fire over their heads but that they were beside the infantry and, if need be, might be able to fire across the infantry line.

   In his letter describing the battle, Henry Jackson displayed a maddening imprecision about the position of his three artillery pieces. Ronald Way, in his 1961 article on the battle, "The Day of Crysler's Farm," shows one 6-pdr. positioned at the left flank of Pearson's advance behind the first gully and a second weapon on the right flank of Plenderleath's eight companies of the 49th. Way gives no source for this positioning and Way seems to have been unaware of the existence of Jackson's letter describing the battle and that there were three, not two, 6-pdr. guns.

   The area of cleared fields was not completely level – it had small elevations and Jackson probably placed his two weapons on these little knolls which provided him with the ability, if necessary to fire across the main line. Unfortunately, there are no surviving maps with enough detail to show the exact location of these knolls, and as

the battlefield was destroyed by the Seaway Project in 1958, it is impossible to locate them accurately.

   In the absence of any more reliable information, the position of Jackson's three guns in the text and accompanying maps of *Field of Glory* is based on contemporary practice which was to position artillery so it would support, or cover the entire front of the infantry line without hampering it in its movement and fire. On the positioning of artillery, see Graves, *Right and Glory*, 37-38.

6. PRO, WO 55, vol. 1223, 227, Glasgow to McLeod, 30 June 1813.

7. On manning 6-pdr. guns, see Adye, *Bombardier and Pocket Gunner*, 142-145.

8. Adye, *Bombardier and Pocket Gunner*, 205-206; Hughes, *Firepower*, 41; RCMI, Paul Notebook.

9. *Ibid.*, 9; PRO, WO 44, vol. 248, Return of Brass Ordnance ... Travelling Carriages, etc., 30 June 1813; Return of the Serviceable Brass and Iron Ordnance, 30 June 1813; Jackson letter.

10. McConnell, *British Smooth-Bore*, 338-339; Hughes, *Firepower*, 33-35, and *Smooth-Bore*, 60.

11. Adye, *Bombardier and Pocket Gunner*, 98.

12. *Ibid.*, 97-98; NAC, MG 24, F 113, Shrapnel papers, poster, "Shrapnel's Shells," c. 1805-1809.

13. Jackson letter; NAC, MG 24, F 113, Shrapnel papers, poster "Shrapnel's Shells," c. 1805-1809.

14. *WCM*, 85, testimony of Boyd.

15. Boyd, 1813 report.

16. Croil, *Dundas*, 95.

17. William Patterson to author, 15 Aug. 1998.

18. Delafield, *Lewis*, 2, 96, Lewis to wife, 13 Nov. 1813.

19. *WCM*, 214, testimony of Bull.

20. Gardner letter.

21. DC, Weeks Papers, Weeks to Bliss, 18 Sept. 1836 (hereafter Weeks letter).

22. Myers, *Reminiscences*, 41. It may seem strange to the modern reader but in 1813 women and children accompanied armies on campaign. In the British army, twelve women were permitted for each company of a battalion embarked for foreign and six per company when that battalion went into the field. These women were to be the lawful wives of soldiers but the word "lawful" was often stretched and a simple verbal declaration by a couple was accepted as proof of the married state. Accompanying

the women were their children and, based on the information contained in the twice-yearly inspection reports (as the camp followers were counted), there were approximately 1.5 children for every woman, giving an average of 120 women and 180 children for each battalion of British infantry on foreign service. These were the legal camp followers, who received rations at a reduced rate from that of the soldiers, there were also many illegal camp followers. Regardless of their status, all camp followers were under military discipline. See Adjutant General, *Regulations 1811*, 124, 255, 375

The American army permitted four legal wives for every company of infantry to accompany it on campaign and they received a full ration although it does not appear that the American government made provision for the feeding of their children. The United States did however provide that the widow of a soldier who died in service would receive half his monthly pay for a period of five years. See *Articles of War 1816*, 38.

In North America in 1813, due to the shortage of foodstuffs in Upper Canada, all the legal camp followers of regular British and Canadian units were ordered out of that province to Lower Canada. Some managed to remain with their battalions although it is very doubtful that there were any with Morrison's command due to his limited transport. There were women with Wilkinson's army when in moved down the St. Lawrence as they are mentioned in a number of personal accounts. The soldiers' wifes served as laundresses and sometimes nurses in hospitals but, whatever their occupation, their lot and that of their children was not good.

23. Ellery, *Swift*, 117.
24. Lossing, *Fieldbook*, 629-630; Heitman, *Historical Register*.
25. Boyd, 1813 report and 1815 report; Haskin, *First Regiment*, 32-33.
26. Sewell, recollections.
27. Gardner letter.
28. *WCM*, 138, testimony of Ripley.
29. Salisbury, *Chrysler's [sic] Farm*, 7.
30. Ripley, "Memoir," 117.
31. Fredriksen, "Plow Joggers," 24.
32. *Ibid.*, 70-71; see also Fredriksen, "Honest Sodger," 145; Gardner letter; NYSL, Townsend Papers, Aspinwall to Townsend, 29 Nov. 1813 (hereafter Aspinwall letter).
33. *DAB*, Boyd entry. On Boyd's mercenary career and Karda, see Bidford, *Swords*, 78-80.
34. Boyd report, 1813.
35. Ripley, "Memoir," 117.; Harvey letter.
36. On the formation of close column, see Smyth, *Regulations*, 52-67. It is difficult to be more precise about these formations because one of the most important facts, the number of companies in Boyd's regiments is not known. On paper, each American infantry regiment possessed ten but it would be highly unusual, based on this author's experience, for all its companies to be present with a unit.
37. *Ibid*, 3.
38. Chartrand, *Uniforms*, 113-114.
39. Fredriksen, "Plow Joggers," 24.
40. Sewell, recollections.
41. Morrison report; Harvey letter; Adjutant General, *Rules and Regulations*, 200.
42. Adjutant General Lower Canada, *Rules and Regulations*, 25-27.
43. *Quebec Mercury*, 23 Nov. 1813, Extract from an Officer of Rank in Colonel Morrison's army, 13 Nov. 1813
44. Harvey letter.
45. Loucks narrative. See also Salisbury, *Chrysler's [sic] Farm*, 7.
46. Henegan, *Seven Years*, 1, 210.
47. Ajutant General Lower Canada, *Rules and Regulations*, 24-27; Adjutant General, *Rules and Regulations*, 43-47.
48. Sewell, recollections.
49. Morrison report; Harvey letter; *Doc. Hist.*, 8, 165, Memorandum of the Services of Lieutenant Colonel Plenderleath by Fitzgibbon (hereafter Plenderleath memorandum).
50. Harvey letter; Adjutant General, *Rules and Regulations*, 46-47.
51. Loucks narrative.
52. Gardner letter.
53. Salisbury, *Chrysler's [sic] Farm*, 7.
54. Harvey letter.
55. Adjutant General, *Rules and Regulations*, 202.
56. James, *History*, 2, 332.
57. Harvey letter.
58. Plenderleath memorandum.
59. Harvey letter.
60. Sewell, recollections.
61. Fredriksen, "Plow Joggers," 24.
62. Croil, *Dundas*, 95.
63. Morrison report; Harvey letter.
64. Salisbury, *Chrysler's [sic] Farm*, 7.
65. Boyd, 1813 report.
66. Fredriksen, "Honest Sodger," 145; Fredriksen, "Kirby," 71; and *WCM*, 139, testimony of Ripley.
67. *Quebec Mercury*, 23 Nov. 1813, Extract from

an Officer of Rank in Colonel Morrison's army, 13 Nov. 1813.

68. Fredriksen, "Honest Sodger," 145.

69. Van Allen Family Papers, George Salisbury Cook, "The American Lake Ontario Army;" Fredriksen, "Honest Sodger," 145. These buildings would have been on the property of either Adam Bouck or John Haines, see QU, Ontario Abstract Index of Deeds, Williamsburg Township, Concession 1.

70. *Ibid.*

71. Cumming letter. During the battle, most of the American brigade and regimental commanders were on foot, an unusual circumstance brought about by the shortage of horses. Contrary to legend, Covington was not riding a white horse when he was hit.

72. Pearce, "Honest Sodger," 145.

73. Cumming letter.

74. Fredriksen, "Honest Sodger," 131-133.

75. Jackson letter.

76. Fredriksen, "Honest Sodger," 145; Cumming letter; Fredriksen, "Kirby," 71; James, *History*, 2, 333.

77. Jackson letter.

78. On prisoners, see WO 17, vol. 269, Monthly Return, Canadian Fencibles, 25 Nov. 1813; WO 25, vol. 1829, Return of the 49th Foot, 25 Dec. 1813.

79. Cumming letter.

80. Gardner letter.

81. Aspinwall letter; Gardner letter; Fredriksen, "Honest Sodger," 145; Fredriksen, "Kirby," 71.

82. Fredriksen, "Kirby,"71.

83. Morrison report; Harvey letter.

84. Loucks narrative; Adjutant General, *Rules and Regulations*, 193-195.

85. Morrison report.

86. On position of surgeons, see Adjutant General, *Regulations*, 68.

87. Sewell, recollections.

88. Gassendi, *Aide-Memoire*, 1, 539; *DCB*, Johnston entry; Harris, "Service," 329.

89. Adye, *Bombardier and Pocket Gunner*, 96; Ajutant General, *Baggages and Marches*, 13-14.

90. Way, "Day of Crysler's Farm," 213.

91. Gardner letter.

92. Fredriksen, "Honest Sodger," 145.

93. Cumming letter.

94. Fredriksen, "Kirby," 71.

95. Jackson letter.

96. Aspinwall letter.

97. Fredriksen, *Officers*, 53-56.

Chapter 11: "Charge mit de dragoons!"

1. "Garryowen," an Irish drinking song that dates to 1770-1780 was the second most popular march in the British army during the Napoleonic wars after the ubiquitous "British Grenadiers," see Winstock, *Songs*, 102-104. It was adopted either then or later by American soldiers and sung during the Civil War but is today perhaps best known as the regimental march of George Armstrong Custer's Seventh Cavalry.

   "Spa" is a period term for mineral water and "garry" is Irish for garden. Garryowen was Owen Garden, a suburb of Limerick and a favourite hang-out for the monied young toughs who composed this song to accompany their drinking bouts.

2. On the low rate of sickness in the artillery, see Mann, *Medical Sketches*, 112. Three artillery officers – Izard, Macomb, and Scott – who started the war no higher than the rank of colonel, ended it as major generals and two, Macomb and Scott, went on in the prewar period to become the senior officers of the army.

3. Boyd, 1813 and 1815 reports; Haskin, *First Regiment*, 32-33; Heitman, *Historical Register*.

4. Senate, *Compendious Exercise*, 18-27; Adye, *Bombardier and Pocket Gunner*, 98.

5. Stoddard, *Exercises*, 31.

6. Trowbridge in Hough, *St. Lawrence*, 649.

7. *WCM*, 311, testimony of Pinckney.

8. *WCM*, 285, testimony of Hite.

9. Myers, *Reminiscences*, 41.

10. Harris, "Service," 329; Ellery, *Swift*, 117.

11. Boyd, 1813 report.

12. Sewell, recollections; Gassendi, *Aide Memoire*, 1, 536; James, *History*, 333.

13. Harvey letter.

14. *Ibid.*

15. Sewell, recollections.

16. *Ibid.* This is an exaggeration, only seven officers of the 49th Foot were killed and wounded on 11 Nov. 1813.

17. NAC, MG 23, GIII, vol. 1, Bowen to Le Coutoirs, 8 Dec. 1813.

18. *Doc. Hist.*, 8, 166, W. Claus to W. Claus, 11 May 1814.

19. Sewell, recollections.

20. *Ibid.* In many eyewitness accounts of War of 1812 actions, reference will be made to the use of "grape shot" by field artillery. In almost all cases, these statements are incorrect and what the witness is describing is actually canister or shrapnel bullets. The RA never used grape shot in its brass field artil-

lery pieces because it damaged the muzzles and the author has seen no documentation that the United States Artillery used it in its fieldpieces. Grape was a bulky projectile and the handier canister rounds were favoured instead. Grapeshot was used at sea or in large calibre garrison guns on land.

21. Plenderleath memorandum.
22. Harris, "Service," 329.
23. Sewell, recollections.
24. Sewell, recollections.
25. Morrison report.
26. Sewell, recollections.
27. Fredriksen, "Honest Sodger," 145.
28. *Ibid.*
29. Gardner letter.
30. Harris, "Service," 329; Ripley, "Memoir," 117.
31. *Appleton's Encyclopedia,* Walbach entry; Heitman, *Historical Register.*
32. Hunter, *Sketch,* 99.
33. Harris, "Service," 329.
34. *Appleton's Encylcopedia,* Walbach entry.
35. USNA, RG 107, Micro 221, reel 4, Poutingon to SW, 27 Oct. 1812.
36. *Ibid.*; see also Graves, "Second Regiment," 102.
37. Roach, "Journal," 148-149.
38. Fredriksen, "Honest Sodger," 145.
39. Graves, "Second Regiment," 101-104.
40. Harris, "Service," 329.
41. Duane, *American Military Library,* 2, 7.
42. Duane, *Hand Book for Cavalry,* 31, 109, 129.
43. Peterson, *American Sword,* 28-29; Chartrand, *Uniforms,* 97-98; Duane, *Hand Book for Cavalry,* 129.
44. Duane, *Hand Book,* 129-130. Elting, *Swords,* 538-541, is informative on the subject of a properly conducted cavalry charge.
45. Jackson letter.
46. Morrison report; and Sewell, recollections.
47. Sewell, recollections. On Ellis, see NAC, RG 8 I, vol. 924, 40, Memorial of Lt. Dixie Ellis, 18 Feb. 1814; and PRO, WO 27, vol. 98, Inspection Report, 49th Foot, 28 May 1810; Sutherland, *His Majesty's Gentlemen.*
48. Sewell, recollections.
49. Fredriksen, "Honest Sodger," 145.
50. Harris, "Service," 330.
51. *Biographical Notice of Smith,* 52-54.
52. Harvey letter.

Chapter 12: "Field of Glory"

1. "The British Bayoneteers," one of the many versions of "The British Grenadiers," perhaps the best known of all British military songs, was sung during the Napoleonic wars, see Winstock, *Songs,* 111. The term "horse" in the lyrics means cavalry and, thus, "light and heavy horse" are light and heavy cavalry.
2. Ellery, *Swift,* 117.
3. Morrison report; Adjutant General, *Rules and Regulations,* 34.
4. *WCM,* 91, testimony of Boyd.
5. Fredriksen, "Honest Sodger," 146.
6. Fredriksen, "Kirby," 71.
7. *WCM,* 152, testimony of Walbach.
8. *WCM,* 91, testimony of Boyd. When reproducing this testimony in his memoirs, Wilkinson noted that, in his report of the action dated 12 Nov. 1813, Boyd stated that he himself ordered the withdrawal.
9. Neither Wilkinson nor Lewis would admit to ordering a withdrawal. In November 1813, Boyd stated that he gave the order (see 1813 report); in his later report and in his testimony at Wilkinson's court martial, Boyd attributed the withdrawal order to Wilkinson but could not remember which officer delivered it to him.
10. Myers, *Reminiscences,* 42.
11. Weeks letter.
12. *New England Historical & Geneological Society,* 101.
13. Weeks letter.
14. Fredriksen, "Kirby," 71.
15. Jackson letter.
16. Weeks letter.
17. Myers, *Reminiscences,* 41.
18. Weeks letter.
19. Fredriksen, "Kirby," 69.
20. Morrison letter.
21. Harvey letter.
22. Morrison report.
23. Jackson letter.
24. Loucks narrative.
25. Smyth Carter, *Dundas,* 238.
26. On cheering, see AO MS 537, Ridout to father, 20 Nov. 1813.
27. Sewell, recollections.
28. NAC MG 23, GIII, 23, vol. 3, Bowen to Le Coutoirs, 27 Dec. 1813.
29. Croil, *Dundas,* 95.
30. MTPL, Hagerman Journal, 29 Nov. 1813.
31. Myers, *Reminiscences,* 42.
32. Trowbridge, in Hough, *St. Lawrence,* 649.
33. Weeks letter.
34. *WCM,* 91, testimony of Boyd.
35. *WCM,* 311, testimony of Boyd.
36. *WCM,* 311, testimony of Pinckney.
37. Fredriksen, "Kirby," 71.
38. *WCM,* 145, testimony of Walbach, emphasis in the original.
39. *Ibid.*

40. Cumming letter.
41. On Walbach's movements after the action, see HSP, Carr Diary, 12 Nov. 1813. On the wind and its effect on the flotilla, see Croil, *Dundas*, 83.
42. Fredriksen, "Kirby," 71.
43. Graves, *Soldiers of 1814*, 28.
44. Fredriksen, "Plough Joggers," 24.
45. Weeks letter.
46. NYSH, O'Connor Papers, O'Connor to wife, 15 Nov. 1813.
47. *WCM*, 311, testimony of Pinckney.
48. Delafield, *Lewis*, 2, 96, Lewis to wife, 13 Nov. 1813.
49. *Quebec Mercury*, 23 Nov. 1813, Extract from an Officer of Rank in Colonel Morrison's army, 13 Nov. 1813.
50. Harvey letter.
51. Sewell, recollections.
52. Hagerman Journal, 29 Nov. 1813.
53. *Kingston Gazette*, 13 Nov. 1813.
54. Croil, *Dundas*, 80.
55. NAC, RG 8 I, vol. 1221, 226, Prevost to Morrison, 11 Nov. 1813.

Chapter 13: "Beat the drums slowly…"
1. "The Soldier Cut Down in His Prime" is a hoary old piece that originates in the mid to late 18th century. There are many variants, the lyrics included here date at least from 1780 as the Lock Hospital in London was founded about that time. Other versions of this popular song are "The Trooper Cut Down in His Prime," "The Streets of Laredo," "I See By Your Outfit (That You Are A Cowboy)" and "St. James Infirmary Blues."
2. NAC, RG 8 I, vol. 681, 44, Morrison to Baynes, 15 Nov. 1813; Morrison report.
3. Harvey letter.
4. Morrison report; Harvey letter.
5. NAC, RG 8 I, vol. 694B, Prisoner of War Entry Book, October 1813; *Kingston Gazette*, 20 Nov. 1813.
6. NAC, RG 8 I, vol. 681, 59, Corrected Return of the Killed, Wounded and Missing, 12 Nov. 1813 (hereafter British casualty return).
7. PRO, WO 17, vol. 263, Monthly Return of the 49th Foot, 25 November 1813; PRO, WO 25, vol. 218, Return of the Casualties of the Canadian Fencibles, 25 December 1813.
8. NAC, RG 8 I, vol. 681, 77, Morrison to Baynes, 12 Nov 1813.
9. Boyd, 1813 report.
10. Return of the Killed and Wounded, 11 Nov. 1813, appended to Boyd, 1813 report (hereafter American casualty return).

11. Ellery, *Swift*, 117.
12. Fredriksen, "Kirby," 71.
13. Gardner letter.
14. American casualty return.
15. *NWR*, 5, 4 Dec. 1813, Wilkinson to SW, 18 Nov. 1813.
16. *ASPMA*, 475, Wilkinson to SW, 16 Nov. 1813.
17. *ASPMA*, 475, Wilkinson to SW, 16 Nov. 1813; *NWR*, 5, 4 Dec. 1813, Wilkinson to SW, 18 Nov. 1813.
18. *ASPMA*, 475, Wilkinson to SW, 16 Nov. 1813.
19. *ASPM*, 478, Army Journal, 11 Nov. 1813.
20. *ASPMA*, 475, Wilkinson to SW, 16 Nov. 1813.
21. *Ibid.*
22. AO, MS 537, Ridout to father, 20 Nov. 1813.
23. Croil, *Dundas*, 95.
24. Croil, *Dundas*, 95. Names of fatal casualties from British and American casualty returns and PRO, War Office 17: vol. 263, Monthly Return of the 49th Foot, 25 Nov. 1813; vol. 266, Monthly Return, 2/89th Foot, 25 Dec. 1813; vol. 26, Monthly Return, Canadian Fencibles, 25 Nov. 1813; WO 25, vol. 2187, Return of the Casualties of the Canadian Fencibles, 25 December 1813-25 January 1814.
25. Raney, *Gun-Shot Wounds*. Unless otherwise noted, the author's copy of this work, which has no page numbering, is the source of all quotations below on period medical practice.
26. Adjutant General, *Instructions for Regimental Surgeons 1808*, 49; NAC, RG 19E5(a) Loss Claim of John Crysler. Korb was the surgeon of the 49th Foot while Woodforde was an assistant surgeon of the 104th Foot. As there was no surgeon from the 89th Foot present with Morrison's force,, Woodforde must have been assigned to that unit when Morrison left Kingston. Morrison was much troubled by his shortage of medical personnel, see NAC, RG 8 I, vol. 681, 44, Morrison to Baynes, 15 Nov. 1813.
27. Raney, *Gun-Shot Wounds*; on the practice of military medicine in this period, see also Graves, *Right and Glory*, 197-208.
28. Mann, *Medical Sketches*, 212.
29. Guthrie, *Gun-Shot Wounds* quoted in Matheson, "Medical Aspect," 206.
30. Adjutant General, *Regulations for Regimental Surgeons 1799*, 57-59; *Doc. Hist.*, 8, 166, W. Claus to W. Claus, 11 May 1814.
31. *Kingston Gazette*, 1 Mar. 1814, Letter from a gentleman, dated Ogdensburg, 23 Nov. 1813.

32. Smyth Carter, *Dundas*, 237; Pringle, *Lunenburgh*, 79; *Doc. Hist.*, 8, 166, W. Clause to W. Claus, 11 May 1814; PRO, WO 42, vol. 59, D14, Petition of Louis May de de Lorimier, 27 Dec. 1814; PRO, WO 17, vol. 266, Monthly Return of 2/89th Foot, 25 Dec. 1813; NAC, RG 8 I, vol. 1221, 252, on Armstrong.

33. Dunlop, *Tiger Dunlop*, 16.

34. *Ibid.*

35. *Ibid.*, 17; Adjutant General, *Regulations for Regimental Surgeons 1799*, App. 6.

36. *ASPMA*, 475, Wilkinson to SW, 16 Nov. 1813.

37. HSP, Carr diary, General Order, 12 Nov. 1813.

38. *ASPMA*, 475, Wilkinson to SW, 16 Nov. 1813.

39. Lossing, *Fieldbook*, 655n, Swift to Armstrong, 17 June 1836.

40. *Ibid.* See also HSP, Parker Papers, Atkinson to Hampton, 13 Nov. 1813; *WCM*, App. 42, Declaration of Lee, 14 Mar. 1815.

41. Brannan, *Letters*, 263, Wilkinson to Hampton, 12 Nov. 1813, emphasis in the original.

42. Harris, "Service," 330. Apparently, many of the horses were left in Canada, see AO, MU 1054, A. Ford to D. Ford, 17 Nov. 1813.

43. *ASPMA*, 479, General Order, 13 Nov. 1813.

44. MDHA, Covington-Wailes Papers, Kean to A. Covington, 14 Nov. 1813.

45. HSP, Carr Diary, 13 Nov. 1813.

46. NAC, RG 8 I, vol. 681, 44, Morrison to Baynes, 15 Nov. 1813.

47. PRO, WO 55, vol. 1223, Glasgow to McLeod, 2 Dec. 1813.

48. USNA, RG 107, Micro 222, reel 8, Harvey to Wilkinson, 14 Nov. 1813, emphasis in the original.

49. USNA, RG 107, Micro 222, reel 9, Wilkinson to Harvey, 14 Nov. 1813.

50. NAC, RG 8 I, vol. 681, 135, Harvey to Baynes, 16 Nov. 1813.

51. Jackson letter.

52. NAC, RG 8 I, vol 681, 135, Harvey to Baynes, 16 Nov. 1813, emphasis in original.

53. NAC, RG 8 I, vol. 681, 135, Harvey to Baynes, 16 Nov. 1813.

54. Jackson letter.

55. *Ibid.*

56. NAC, RG 8 I, vol. 681, 304, Bathurst to Prevost, 27 Dec. 1813.

57. NAC, RG 8 I, vol. 681, 184, Mulcaster to Prevost, 2 Dec. 1813.

58. *Kingston Gazette*, 13 Nov. 1813.

59. *Doc. Hist.*, 8, 177, District General Order, 14 Nov. 1813.

60. NAC, MG 19, A39, General Order, 17 Nov. 1813.

61. Hagerman Journal, 17 Jan. 1814.

62. Prevost Diary, 15 Nov. 1813.

63. Prevost diary, 7 January 1814.

64. NAC, RG 8 I, vol. 1694, p. 48, General Order, 17 Nov. 1813.

65. Troop strength around Montreal taken from PRO, WO 17, General Return, 25 Nov. 1813 with the addition of the battalions of Select Embodied Militia.

66. NAC, RG 8 I, vol. 1712, 56, Prevost to de Rottenburg, 11 Nov. 1813. In fairness to de Rottenburg, he cancelled the order for Morrison and Mulcaster to withdraw as soon as it was confirmed that Wilkinson had bypassed Prescott and it was certain that the American objective was Montreal, see RG 8 I, vol. 681, 29, de Rottenburg to Prevost, 11 Nov. 1813.

67. NAC, RG 8 I, vol. 1171, p. 106, General Order, 20 Nov. 1813.

68. Julia de Rottenburg, née Orelli, the daughter of a Swiss general in the Neapolitan service, married her husband in 1802; she was fifteen, he forty-five. She was twenty-three when she arrived in Quebec in the summer of 1810 and seems to have entranced every man who met her. Prevost's adjutant general or chief of staff, Baynes, thought her "remarkable, handsome, both in face and figure, and her manners uncommonly pleasing, graceful and affable" and remarked that she had "made a complete conquest of all our hearts." Another military admirer described her as "fair, beautiful, – lively, discreet, witty, affable, – in short, so engaging, or rather so fascinating" that he could not do "her justice" and that wasn't just his "opinion alone but that of the public." Lieutenant John Le Couteur, a twenty-year-old lieutenant who knew nothing about women (but lived in hope) met Julia in 1815 and rather unkindly said she was "then about the period of Fat, Fair & Forty, scarcely a wrinkle on her lively, brilliant countenance." She was actually at that time just twenty-six years old. See Tupper, *Life of Brock*, 81, Baynes to Brock, 6 Sep. 1810; 84, Thornton to Brock, 4 Oct. 1810; and Graves, *Merry Hearts*, 224' DCB, de Rottenburg entry.

69. NAC, RG 8 I, vol. 1203 1/2J, 47, General Order, 28 Nov. 1813.

70. Prevost journal, 7 Jan. 1814.

71. On Christine Nairne and Nairne's burial, see Wrong, *Canadian Seigneury*, 166-167;

and NAC, MG 23, GIII, 23, vol. 1, Bowen to Le Coutoirs, 27 Dec. 1813.
72. Fredriksen, "Kirby," 73.
73. HSP, Carr diary, 17 Nov. 1813.
74. Wailes, *Covington*, 30.
75. Fredriksen, "Honest Sodger," 148.
76. HSP, Carr diary, 17 Nov. 1813.
77. Fredriksen, "Kirby," 73.
78. Graves, *Soldiers of 1814*, 28. On the weather of the winter of 1813, see James, *History*, 2, 7.
79. Fredriksen, "Honest Sodger," 148.
80. WCM, App. 43, Wilkinson to SW, 1 Dec. 1813.
81. WCM, 363-364, defence of Wilkinson.
82. NYSL, Gardner Papers, Gardner to Atkinson, 19 Jan. 1814.
83. Fredriksen, "Honest Sodger," 148.
84. LC, Madison Papers, Madison to Jefferson, 10 Mar 1813, quoted in Gaines, *Randolph*, 83.
85. Randolph to Campbell, 20 Nov. 1813 quoted in Gaines, *Randolph*, 91.
86. Wilkinson to Randolph, 18 Nov. 1813 quoted in Gaines, *Randolph*, 91.
87. LC, Madison Papers, Randolph to Madison, 11 December 1813, quoted in Gaines, *Randolph*, 91. On officers' salaries, see *Register of the Army 1813*.
88. HSP, Carr diary, 17 Nov. 1813.
89. Fredriksen, "Kirby," 75.
90. USMA, Miller Papers, Miller to wife, 8 Dec. 1813.
91. HSM, Smith Papers, Gardner to Smith, 4 Jan. 1814. Also WCM, 376, defence of Wilkinson; Mann, *Medical Sketches*, 120-123.
92. Mann, *Medical Sketches*, 123.
93. NYHS, George Howard Orderly Book, General Order, 23 Jan. 1814.
94. Graves, *Soldiers of 1814*, 28. See also, Mann, *Medical Sketches*, 119.
95. Fredriksen, "Kirby," 75, emphasis in the original.
96. Handbill in Lossing, *Fieldbook*, 658. Scott's idea did not entirely meet with Prevost's approval, see *Doc. Hist.*, 8, 239, Prevost to Scott, 27 Nov. 1813.
97. Jacobs, *Tarnished Warrior*, 301-302. On deserters, see NAC, RG 8 I, vol. 681, 68, Statements of American deserters [n.d., c. Jan. 1814].
98. *Doc. Hist.*, 9, 29, Mulcaster to Yeo, 20 Dec. 1813.
99. *Ibid.*
100. *Ibid.* On Harvey's promotion, see *Doc. Hist.*, 9, 30 General Order, 1 Jan. 1814.
101. AO, MS 537, Ridout to father, 20 Nov. 1813.
102. Dunlop, *Tiger Dunlop*, 22-23. See also AO, MS 537, Ridout to Ridout, 31 January 1814.

Chapter 14: "The fault is with the generals…"
1. "How Stands the Glass Around?" or "Why, Soldiers, Why?" appeared in the play, "The Patron," first performed in 1729 and was very popular during the Seven Years War, a popularity that increased during the Napoleonic period, see Winstock, *Songs*, 58.
2. WCM, App. 63, SW to Wilkinson, 15 Nov. 1813.
3. ASPMA, 480, SW to Wilkinson, 18 Nov. 1813.
4. ASPMA, 462, Hampton to Wilkinson, 12 Nov. 1813, emphasis in the original.
5. USNA, RG 107, Micro 222, Reel 7, Hampton to SW, 13 Nov. 1813, emphasis in the original.
6. USNA, Micro 222, Reel 9, Atkinson to Hampton, 12 Nov. 1813.
7. USNA, RG 107, Micro 222, Reel 8, SW to Hampton, 15 Nov. 1813.
8. ASPMA, 463, Hampton to SW, 12 Nov. 1813.
9. WCM, App. 69, Hampton to SW, 1 Nov. 1813.
10. Ellery, *Swift*, 120-121, Wilkinson to SW, 17 Nov. 1813.
11. USNA, RG 107, Micro 222, Reel 9, Wilkinson to Hampton, 26 Nov. 1813.
12. Ellery, *Swift*, 118, Wilkinson to Swift, 17 Nov. 1813.
13. *Ibid.*, 119, Swift to Wilkinson, 20 Nov. 1813.
14. *Ibid.*, 120, Swift to Wilkinson, 21 Nov. 1813.
15. Izard Diary, 5 Dec. 1813; Wilkinson to SW, 8 Dec. 1813, quoted in Jacobs, *Tarnished Warrior*, 300; USNA, Micro 222, Reel 9, Izard to Wilkinson, 3 Dec. 1813.
16. Fredriksen, "New Hampshire Volunteer," 171. See also USNA RG 107, Micro 222, Reel 9, Wilkinson to SW, 6 Dec. 1813 and Izard to Wilkinson, 3 Dec. 1813; Izard Diary, 5 Dec. 1813; Jacobs, *Tarnished Warrior*, 299.
17. ASPMA, 480, Wilkinson to SW, 24 Nov. 1813, emphasis in the original.
18. USNA, RG 107, Micro 222, Reel 9, Wilkinson to Hampton, 26 Nov. 1813.
19. Izard Diary, 5 Dec. 1813.
20. USNA, RG 107, Micro 222, Reel 9, Izard to Wilkinson,, 3 Dec. 1813.
21. USNA, RG 107, Micro 222, Reel 9, Wilkinson to SW, 6 Dec. 13; Izard to Wilkinson, 3 Dec. 1813.
22. Ellery, *Swift*, 120-121. Wilkinson's emissaries to Armstrong were Swift, Randolph, Lee and Walbach. On Lee, see WCM, App. 39, Lee to Wilkinson, 22 Dec. 1813; on Randolph, see Gaines, *Randolph*, 90-91; on Walbach, see USNA, RG 107, Micro 221, Reel 58, Wilkinson to SW, 20 Nov. 1813.

23. *WCM*, App. 39, Lee to Wilkinson, 22 Dec. 1813.
24. *WCM*, 77-78, testimony of King.
25. Hough, *Jefferson County*, 502.
26. OHS, Williams Papers, Brown to Williams, 11 Dec. 1813, emphasis in the original.
27. Smissaert to Parish, 25 Nov. 1813, quoted in Way, "Crysler's Farm," 212.
28. USMA, Miller Papers, Miller to wife, 8 Dec. 1813.
29. LC, Manuscripts Division, Amasa Trowbridge, A Description of Fort Erie with a History of its Siege.
30. NYSL, Gardner Papers, Gardner to Atkinson, 19 Jan. 1814.
31. Gaines to Campbell, 31 Jan. 1814, quoted in Silver, *Gaines*, 35.
32. Scott, *Autobiography*, 1, 111.
33. Fredriksen, "Plow Joggers," 24.
34. NYHS, O'Connor Papers, O'Connor to wife, 15 Nov. 1813.
35. HSW, Wood Papers, Wood to J. Wood, 14 Apr. 1814.
36. NYSL, Gardner Papers, Brown to Kent, 25 Feb. 1814.
37. *Ibid.*
38. Mann, *Medical Sketches*, 118-119.
39. Ellery, *Swift*, 122.
40. Christie, *Military Operations*, 153.
41. Boyd, *Documents*, 24, Glegg to a gentleman in Washington, 25 July 1815.
42. Dunlop, *Tiger Dunlop*, 12.
43. *WCM*, 65n.
44. Skeen, *Armstrong*, 138-139.
45. Adams, *History*, 364-390, 404-408, 411-414.
46. Ellery, *Swift*, 122.
47. HSP, Dallas Papers, Roberts to Dallas, 12 Dec. 1813, quoted in Stagg, *Madison's War*, 363.
48. Adams, *History*, 380-390; Stagg, *Madison's War*, 362-367; Skeen, *Armstrong*, 166.
49. LC, Madison Papers, SW to Madison, 25 Nov. 1813.
50. *Buffalo Gazette*, 19 Oct. 1813, Address to the Inhabitants of Upper Canada, 16 Oct. 1813. See also Graves, "Joseph Willcocks," 50-51.
51. Graves, "Joseph Willcocks," 51-52.
52. On the life and career of Joseph Willcocks, see Graves, "Joseph Willcocks".
53. USNA, RG 107, Micro 221, Harrison to McClure, 15 Nov. 1813.
54. Merritt, *Journal*, 42. See also Graves, "Joseph Willcocks," 54-56.
55. USNA, RG 107, Micro 222, Reel 9, Wilkinson to SW, 22 Nov. 1813.
56. Graves, "Joseph Willcocks," 56-62.
57. USNA, RG 107, Micro 6, Reel 7, SW to Commanding Officer at Fort George, 4 Oct. 1813.
58. Graves, "Joseph Willcocks," 62-63.
59. Hagerman Journal, 23 Dec. 1813.
60. NAC, RG 8 I, vol. 681, 217, Murray to Vincent, 12 Dec. 1813.
61. Dunnigan, *Forts*, 44-45.
62. NAC, RG 8 I, vol. 681, 258, Harvey to Morrison, 17 Dec. 1813.
63. Sutherland, *His Majesty's Gentlemen*; *Doc. Hist.*, 9, 6, Drummond to Prevost, 18 Dec. 1813; Dunnigan, *Forts*, 44-45.
64. National Archives of Quebec, Nowlan Papers, Nowlan to wife, 18 Dec 1813.
65. UCA, Journal of Reverend George Ferguson.
66. *Doc. Hist.*, 9, 19, Capture of Fort Niagara by Lt. Henry Driscoll.
67. Ferguson; See also NAC, RG 8 I, vol. 681, 249, Murray to Drummond, 19 Dec., 1813 and *Doc. Hist.*, 9, 19, Capture Fort Niagara by Lt. Henry Driscoll; Dunnigan, *Forts*, 45-49.
68. *Doc. Hist.*, 9, 19, Capture of Fort Niagara by Lt. Henry Driscoll.
69. NAC, RG 8 I, vol. 681, 249, Murray to Drummond, 19 Dec. 1813; Dunnigan, *Forts*, 46-48.
70. NAC, RG 8 I, vol. 681, 249, Murray to Drummond, 19 Dec. 1813; Dunnigan, *Forts*, 47-48.
71. *Doc. Hist.*, 9, 19, Capture of Fort Niagara by Lt. Henry Driscoll.
72. NAC, RG 8 I, vol. 681, 249, Murray to Drummond, 19 Dec. 1813; 257, Return of the Killed and Wounded and Prisoners, 19 Dec. 1813; 263, Memorandum of Captured Materiel. On flag, see Hagerman Journal, 26 Dec. 1813.
73. *Doc. Hist.*, 9, 86, A Statement of the Service of Major General R. A, Armstrong.
74. NAC, RG 8 I, vol. 682, 1, Drummond to Prevost, 2 Jan. 1814; 5, Riall to Drummond, 1 Jan. 1814.
75. NAC, RG 8 I, vol. 682, 3, Wilkinson to Prevost, 28 Jan. 1814.
76. *Doc. Hist.*, 9, 112, Proclamation, 12 Jan. 1814.
77. Adams, *History*, 340-363.
78. *WCM.*, 351, defence of Wilkinson, emphasis in the original.
79. *Annals*, 13th Congress, 2nd Session, 1521, quoted in Stagg, *Madison's War*, 140.
80. Skeen, *Armstrong*, 137-141.
81. USNA, RG 107, Micro 222, reel 8, Hampton to SW, 31 Dec. 1813.
82. *WCM*, App. 49, SW to Wilkinson, 20 Jan. 1814; Jacobs, *Tarnished Warrior*, 301-302; Croil, *Dundas*, 102-103.

83. NAC, RG 8 I, vol. 682, 114, Secret Information, 7 February 1814; vol. 695, 35, Scott to Prevost, 7 June 1814; vol. 1171, 276, General Order, 29 May 1814; *Doc. Hist.*, 9, 176, General Order, 13 Feb. 1814; Croil, *Dundas*, 102-103; Hough, *St. Lawrence*, 501-502, 651-652.

84. Hough, *St. Lawrence*, 641.

85. Hough, *St. Lawrence*, 641; Croil, *Dundas*, 102-103; Smyth Carter, *Dundas*, 244.

86. NAC, RG 8 I, vol. 682, 114, Secret Information, 7 February 1814; vol. 695, 35, Scott to Prevost, 7 June 1814; vol. 1171, 276, General Order, 29 May 1814; *Doc. Hist.*, 9, 176, General Order, 13 Feb. 1814; Croil, *Dundas*, 102-103; Hough, *St. Lawrence*, 501-502, 651-652.

87. Hough, *St. Lawrence*, 654-655.

Chapter 15: "And gentle peace returning"

1. "The Sodger's Return," set to a traditional Scots air, "The Mill, Oh!," but with new lyrics by Robbie Burns was a favourite of Scots soldiers in the British army and was also, according to Lieutenant-Colonel Cromwell Pearce of the Sixteenth Infantry, sung by American soldiers during the War of 1812, see Fredriksen, "Honest Sodger," 154.

2. USNA, RG 107, Micro 6, SW to Wilkinson, 27 Feb. 1814.

3. USNA, RG 107, Micro 221, reel 58, Wilkinson to SW, 27 Feb. 1814.

4. WCM, 115, Wilkinson to Lewis, 6 July 1813.

5. USNA, RG 107, Micro 221, reel 58, Wilkinson to SW, 20 Mar. 1814.

6. USNA, RG 107, Micro 6, SW to Izard, 24 Mar. 1814.

7. USNA, RG 107, Micro 221, Reel 58, Wilkinson to SW, 12 Apr. 1813.

8. Jacobs, *Tarnished Warrior*, 306-307. See also USNA, RG 107, Micro 6, SW to Wilkinson, 24 Mar. 1814.

9. Adams, *History of the Administration*, 197-204, attributes responsibility equally to Armstrong and Wilkinson while Stagg, *Mr. Madison's War*, 346-347, attributes less to Hampton but notes that Armstrong and Wilkinson's responsibility cannot be considered apart. Both Quimby, *United States Army*, 1, 344-347 and Mahon, *War of 1812*, 202-218, assign more blame to Wilkinson than Hampton but also question the conduct of Armstrong while Elting, *Amateurs to Arms*, 151-152, apportions equal responsibility to all three for the failure. It is significant that the biographers of both Armstrong and Wilkinson (Skeen, *Armstrong*, 166-167; and Jacobs, *Tarnished Warrior*,

296-297) feel their respective subjects must bear the major responsibility. Three authors of survey histories (Coles, *War of 1812*, 143-148; Jacobs and Tucker, *War of 1812* and Hickey, *War of 1812*) do not discuss or analyze the campaign at any length nor do they assess blame.

10. The phrase is Elting's and is the title of his 1986 book, *Amateurs, to Arms!: A Military History of the War of 1812.*

11. *DAB*, Armstrong entry; Skeen, *Armstrong*; John Armstrong, *Notices of the War of 1812* (2 vols., Wiley and Putnam, New York, 1836, 1840). The two editions vary slightly.

12. James Wilkinson, *Memoirs of My Own Times* (3 vols., Abraham Small, Philadelphia, 1816). A separate volume of plates was issued a year later.

13. *DAB*, Hampton entry.

14. *DAB*, Lewis entry.

15. *DAB*; John Boyd, *Documents and Facts Relative to Military Operations during the late War* (n.p.; 1816).

16. *Appleton's Encyclopedia*, Swartout entry.

17. Wailes, *Covington*, 32-35, 38-39, and information from Mr. Patrick Wilder of Oswego, N.Y.

18. *DAB*, Izard entry; Manigault, *Izard*; George Izard, *Official Correspondence with the Department of War* (T. Dobson, Philadelphia, 1816).

19. Putnam, "Porter," 22-25.

20. Heitman, *Historical Register*; *DAB*, Macomb entry; Richards, *Macomb*; Quaife, *Macomb*.

21. Fredriksen, "Honest Sodger," 161n.

22. Heitman, *Historical Register*.

23. *DAB*, Randolph entry; Gaines, *Randolph*.

24. *DAB*, Ripley entry. On Ripley and the Niagara campaign, see Graves, *Right and Glory*. The *Portfolio* article is "Biographical Memoirs of Major General Ripley," *Portfolio*, 15 (1815), 108-136.

25. On Scott in the Niagara campaign of 1814, see Graves, *Where Right and Glory Lead* and, on Scott's life and career, Johnson's *Winfield Scott* is a new, useful and critical biography.

26. *DAB*, Swift entry.

27. Churchill, *Churchill*, 99.

28. *Appleton's Encyclopedia*, Walbach entry.

29. Fredriksen, *Officers*, 53-56.

30. Lossing, *Fieldbook*, .

31. Patterson, "Forsyth."

32. *New England HIstorical and Geneological Register 1856*, 101-102.

33. Fredriksen, "Georgia Officer".

34. Fredriksen, *Officers*, 33-36.
35. *DAB*, Lee entry.
36. Freeman, *Lee*, 3-51.
37. Fredriksen, *Officers*, 41-44.
38. Heitman, *Historical Register*.
39. Myers, *Reminsicences*, 44, also 42-43.
40. *Ibid.*, 48.
41. Harris, "Services"; Fredriksen, *Officers*, 113-114.
42. Heitman, *Historical Register*.
43. Fredriksen, "Kirby."
44. Fredriksen, "Plow Joggers"; Heitman, *Historical Register*.
45. Heitman, *Historical Register*.
46. NYSL, Bishop Papers.
47. Graves, *Soldiers of 1814*, 6.
48. *DCB* 9, Johnston entry; Lossing, *Fieldbook*, 662-663.
49. *DCB*, 8, Prevost entry. Prevost's military career will shortly receive a fresh examination in Wesley Turner's book, *British Generals in the War of 1812. High Command in the Canadas*, to be published in 1999.
50. *DCB*, 6, de Rottenburg entry.
51. Order quoted in Morgan, *Sketches*, 226-227.
52. Patterson, "Forgotten Hero," 18-19.
53. *DCB*, 8, Harvey entry.
54. Obituary, *United Service Journal*, 1847, 479; PRO, WO 42, Bundle 37, P100, Oath by a widow of a general officer, 14 July 1847.
55. Holme and Kerby, *Medal Rolls*, 20, Pearson to Rowe, 3 Aug. 1830.
56. Obituary, *United Service Journal*, 1847, pt. 2, 479.
57. Sutherland, *His Majesty's Gentlemen*.
58. *DCB*, 6, de Salaberry entry; Wohler, *De Salaberry*, 97-140.
59. *DCB*, 9, Macdonell entry.
60. Morgan, *Sketches*, 226-227.
61. Sutherland, *His Majesty's Gentlemen*.
62. *Ibid.*
63. *DCB*, 7, Heriot entry; Heriot, "George Heriot," 71-72.
64. Sutherland, *His Majesty's Gentlemen*.
65. Askwith, *List of Officers of the Royal Artillery*; Leslie, "Chrysler's [Sic] Farm."
66. "Deux letters," 94.
67. Graves, *Merry Hearts*, 1-21.
68. Roy, *Fils de Québec*, 3, 65-66; *Quebec Morning Chronicle*, 20 Apr. 1853.
69. *DCB*, 7, Dunlop entry.
70. Files of the *DCB*, University of Toronto. I am indebted to Mr. David Roberts for this information.
71. PRO, WO 42, vol. 59, F, pp. 246-266. I am indebted to Mr. Robert Henderson for this information.
72. *DCB*, 8, Crysler entry; Neale, "John Crysler," 150-152. For the fate of John Crysler's farmstead, see Appendix I.
73. *DCB*, 7, Hagerman entry.
74. AO, MU 572, Clark Papers, Life of Duncan Clark.
75. Smyth Carter, *Dundas*, 432
76. *DCB*, 8, Ridout entry.
77. NAC RG 19E5(a), Loss Claim of Michael Cook; UCV, Cook and Vanderbaaren, "Descendants of John Cook."

Epilogue: "Lochaber no more"

1. "Lochaber No More," set to an old Scots air and also played as a lament on the pipes, was very popular with Scots soldiers during the Napoleonic wars and was still in service during the South African war of 1898-1900, see Winstock, *Songs*, 112, 262.
2. Lossing, *Fieldbook*, 666.
3. Bigsby, *Shoe and Canoe*, 47.
4. Croil, *Dundas*, 95-96.
5. See Appendix G for a list of the British and Canadian recipients of medals and clasps for the battles of Châteauguay and Crysler's Farm.
6. Croil, *Dundas*, 97.
7. Coffin, *The War and Its Moral*, 17.
8. Ryerson, *Loyalists*, 379
9. *Canadian Military Gazette*, 1 October 1895.
10. *Ibid.*
11. Smyth Carter, *Dundas*, 241.
12. *Ibid.*
13. *Cornwall Freeholder*, 29 Aug. 1913; *Brockville Evening Recorder*, 28 Aug. 1813.
14. *Cornwall Freeholder*, Speech by George Graham, 28 Aug. 1913.
15. See Appendix F.
16. "Counterattack: Great Lakes Panel Targets Aquatic Nuisance Species," Great Lakes Information Network, August 1992, Internet.
17. There is no name on Mary Whitmore Hoople's headstone which is in the west wall at the north end of the Memorial. Her death date, 2 October 1858, is inscribed on that of her husband, Henry Hoople.

Bibliography

PRIMARY SOURCES – ARCHIVAL

Archives of Ontario, Toronto
    MS 35, Strachan Papers
    MS 537, Ridout Papers
    MU 572, Clark Papers
    MU 1032, Kingsford Papers
    MU 1054, Ford Papers
Burton Historical Library, Detroit
    Melancthon Woolsey Papers
Clements Library, University of Michigan, Ann Arbor
    War of 1812 Manuscripts
Dartmouth College Library, Hanover, New Hampshire
    John W. Weeks Papers
Historical Society of Pennsylvania, Philadelphia
    Robert Carr Diary
    William Jones Papers
    Daniel Parker Papers
Library of Congress, Washington, D.C.
    Jacob Brown Papers
    James Madison Papers
    Manuscripts Division, Amasa Trowbridge, A Description of Fort Erie
Lily Library, Indiana University,
    War of 1812 Manuscripts
Massachusetts Historical Society, Boston
    Jacob Brown Papers
Metropolitan Toronto Reference Library, Toronto
    Journal of Christopher Hagerman
Mississippi Department of History and Archvives, Jackson
    Covington-Wailes Papers
Missouri Historical Society
    Smith Papers
National Archives of Canada, Ottawa
    Manuscript Group 11 (Colonial Office 42), Original Correspondence, Canada
    Manuscript Group 19
        A39, Duncan Clark Papers
    Manuscript Group 23
        G3, Murray Papers
    Manuscript Group 24
        F16, Walworth-Simonds Correspondence
        F96, De Watteville Papers
            Diary, October 1813

F113, Shrapnel Papers
G21, Muster Roll of Captain Hall's Company, Canadian Fencibles
L8, Viger Papers, "Ma Saberdache," Vols. 3-4
Manuscript 30
E 66, E.A. Cruikshank Papers
Record Group 8 I, British Military and Naval Records, 1757-1903
Record Group 9, Pre-Confederation Military Records
Record Group 10, Indian Department Records
Record Group 19, E5 (a), War of 1812 Loss Board Claims
National Archives of Quebec, Montreal
Nowlan Collection
National Archives of the United States, Washington, DC
Record Group 45
Micro 125, Logbook of HMS *Wolfe*
Record Group 92, Records of the Commissary General of Purchases
Record Group 94, Records of the Adjutant General
Micro 566, Letters Received
Journal of General George Izard
Record Group 98, Records of United States Army Commands
Record Group 107, Correspondence of the Secretary of War
Micro 6, Letters Sent
Micro 221, Letters Received, Registered Series
Micro 222, Letters Received, Unregistered Series
New York Historical Society, New York
Correspondence of Richard Goodell
New York State Library, Albany
Richard Bishop Diary
Charles Gardner Papers
John M. O'Connor Papers
David Townsend Papers
Oneida Historical Society, Utica
Jacob Brown Papers
Nathan Williams Papers
Prevost Family, London, United Kingdom
Diary of Anne Elinor Prevost
Public Record Office, Kew, Surrey, United Kingdom
War Office 17, Monthly Returns of the Army
War Office 25, Registers, Various
War Office 27, Inspection Returns
War Office 42, Pension Records
War Office 44, Ordnance Office, In-Letters
War Office 55, Ordnance Office, Out-Letters
War Office 97, Chelsea Hospital Records
Queen's University Archives, Kingston
Abstract Index of Deeds, Land Registry, Williamsburgh Township
Royal Canadian Military Institute, Toronto
Manuscript Notebook of Captain Abraham Paul, RA
United Church Archives, Toronto
Memoir of the Reverend George Ferguson
United States Military Academy Library, West Point
James Miller Correspondence
Van Allen, Dr. Traer, Morrisburg, Family Papers
Wisconsin Historical Society, Madison
Eleazar D. Wood Papers

PRIMARY SOURCES – PUBLISHED

Newspapers and Periodicals
Brockville Evening Recorder, 1913
Buffalo Gazette, 1813-1814
Canadian Military Gazette, 1895
Cornwall Freeholder, 1913
Kingston Gazette, 1812-1814
Montreal Gazette, 1895
New York Evening Post, 1813-1814
Niles' Weekly Register, 1812-1814
Ontario Repository, 1813
Philadelphia Aurora, 1813
Quebec Gazette, 1812-1813
Quebec Mercury, 1812-1813
Quebec Morning Chronicle, 1853
United Service Journal, 1847, 1848

Published Documents
Brannan, John, ed. *Official Letters of the Military and Naval Officers of the United States, during the War with Great Britain in the Years 1812, 13, 14 & 15*. Washington: Way & Gideon, 1823
Cruikshank, Ernest A., ed., *Documentary History of the Campaigns upon the Niagara Frontier in 1812-1814* [titles vary slightly]. Welland: Tribune Press, 1896-1908, 9 vols.
———., ed., *Records of Niagara. A Collection of Contemporary Documents and Letters. 1812*. Niagara-on-the-Lake: Niagara Historical Society, 1934.
"Garrison Orders, Burlington, Vermont, July 13–August 4, 1813," *Moorsfield Antiquarian*, 1 (1937), 79-103.
United States, Congress. *American State Papers: Class V, Military Affairs*, Vol. I. Washington: Gales & Seaton, 1832.
United States, Senate. *Report of the Committee on Military Affairs*. Washington: 1813
Wood, William C., ed. *Select British Documents of the Canadian War of 1812*. 4 vols. Toronto: Champlain Society, 1920-1928.

Published and Unpublished Maps and Plans
Hunter, W.S., *Hunter's Panoramic Guide from Niagara to Quebec*. Boston: J.P. Jewett & Co., 1857.
Illustrated Historical Atlas of the Counties of Stormont, Dundas and Glengarry. Toronto: H.P. Beldon, 1879. Map of Williamsburgh Township.
Melish, John. *A Military and Topographical Atlas of the United States; including the British Possessions and Florida*. Philadephia: G. Palmer, 1813. East End of Lake Ontario and River St. Lawrence from Kingston to French Mills, Reduced from an Original Drawing in the Naval Department.
National Archives of Canada
 Manuscript Group 24, A11, Murray Papers
  Map of the St. Lawrence, Prescott to Cornwall, 1815, by Reuben Sherwood, enclosed in Sherwood to Beckwith, 26 January 1815
 Record Group 8 I, British Military Records
  Volume 681, 58, Plan of the disposition of the Hostile forces in the action of the 11th November, 1813
 National Map Collection
  Morrisburg, Ontario, Geographical Section, Department of National Defence, 1905, 1913 and 1938.
Wilkinson, James. *Diagrams and Plans, illustrative of the Principal Battles and Military Affairs Treated of in Memoirs of My Own Times*. Philadelphia: Abraham Small, 1816. A Sketch of the Battle of Christlers Farm, Williamsburg, Upper Canada, 11th Novr. 1813.

Published Memoirs, Diaries, Journals and Correspondence

American
Anonymous. "First Campaign of An A.D.C.," *Military and Naval Magazine of the United States*, 1: 153-162, 257-267; 2: 10-20, 73-82, 200-211, 278-289; 3: 172-182; 258-266; 329-338; 437-447; 4: 26-34, 85-94, 253-261.
Armstrong, John. *Notices of the War of 1812*. New York: Wiley, 1840, 2 vols.

————. *Hints to Young Generals from an Old Soldier*. Kingston, N.Y.: Buell, 1812

Beaumont, William. *William Beaumont's Formative Years: Two Early Notebooks 1811-1821*. New York: Henry Schuman, 1946.

Boyd, John [First Brigade]. *Documents and Facts Relating to Military Events During the Late War*. Washington: n.p., 1816

Churchill, Sylvester. *Sketch of the Life of Bvt. Gen. Sylvester Churchill*. ed. Frank H. Hunter. New York: Willis, McDonald & Co., 1888

Cogswell, A.C. [Eleventh Infantry], "Letters of the War of 1812 in the Champlain Valley," ed. Wilmond Parker, *Vermont Quarterly*, 12 (April, 1944), 104-124.

Covington, Leonard [Third Brigade]. *Memoirs of Leonard Covington by B.C. Wailes, also some of General Covington's Letters*. eds., Nellie Wailes Brandon and W.M. Drake, eds. N.P., 1928.

Cumming, William Clay [Sixteenth Infantry]. "A Georgia Officers in the War of 1812: The Letters of Colonel William Clay Cumming," ed. John C. Fredriksen, *Georgia Historical Quarterly*, 71, (Winter, 1987), 668-691.

Dwight, Joseph [Thirteenth Infantry]. "Plow-Joggers for Generals: The Experiences of a New York Ensign in the War of 1812," ed. John C. Fredriksen, *Indiana Military History Journal*, 11 (1986), 16-27.h

Fairbanks, Charles [New Hampshire Volunteers]. "A New Hampshire Volunteer in the War of 1812: The Experiences of Charles Fairbanks," ed. John C. Fredriksen, *Historical New Hampshire*, 40 (1985), 156-157

Hanks, Jarvis [Eleventh Infantry]. *Soldiers of 1814: American Enlisted Men's Memoirs of the Niagara Campaign of 1814*. ed. Donald E. Graves. Lewiston, N.Y.: Old Fort Niagara Press, 1996.

Harris, Samuel D. [Second Dragoons]. "Service of Capt. Samuel D. Harris; A Sketch of His Military Career as a Captain in the Second Regiment of Light Dragoons during the War of 1812," *Publications of the Buffalo Historical Society* 24 (1920), 377-406.

Hughes, Matthew. *Sketch of the Life of Lieut. Matthew Hughes, Late of the U.S. Army*. Alexandria: n.p., 1815.

Izard, George. *Official Correspondence with the War Department*. Philadelphia: Thomas Dobson, 1816.

Kirby, Reynold M. [Artillery]. "Reynold M. Kirby and His Race to Join the Regiment: A Connecticut Officer in the War of 1812," ed. John C. Fredriksen, *Connecticut History* 32 (November 1991), 51-82.

Lewis, Morgan [Staff]. *Biographies of Francis Lewis and Morgan Lewis*. ed. Julia Delafield. New York: A.D.F. Randolph, 1877.

Macdonough, Patrick [Artillery]. "A Hero of Fort Erie. The Correspondence of Lt. P. McDonogh," ed. Isabell O'Reilly, *Publications of the Buffalo Historical Society*, 5 (1902), 63-93.

Mann, James [Surgeon]. *Medical Sketches of the Campaigns of 1812, 1813, and 1814*. Dedham, Mass.: H. Mann, 1816.

McClure, George. *Causes of the Destruction of the American Towns on the Niagara Frontier and the Failure of the Campaign of the Fall of 1813*. Bath, N.Y.: n.p., 1817.

McIntire, Rufus [Third Artillery]. "The War of 1812 in Northern New York: the Observations of Captain Rufus McIntire," ed. John C. Fredriksen, *New York History*, 73 (July 1987), 297-324.

Myers, Mordecai [Thirteenth Infantry]. *Reminiscences. 1700-1814. Including Incidents in the War of 1812-1814*. Washington: Crane, 1900.

Pearce, Cromwell [Sixteenth Infantry]. "'A Poor But Honest Sodger': Colonel Cromwell Pearce, the 16th U.S. Infantry and the War of 1812," ed. John C. Fredriksen, *Pennsylvania History*, 52 (1985), 131-161.

Penley, Joseph [Maine Volunteers]. *A Short and Thrilling Narrative of a Few of the Scenes and Incidents that Occurred in the Sanguinary and Cruel War of 1812*. Maine: the author, 1853.

Ripley, Eleazer W. [Twenty-First Infantry], "Memoirs of General Ripley," *Portfolio*, 14 (1815), 108-136.

Roach, Isaac, "Military Journal of the War of 1812," ed. A.M. Archer, *Pennyslvania Magazine of History and Biography*, 17 (1893), 129-158; 281-315.

Scott, Winfield [Third Artillery]. *Memoirs of Lieut-General Scott, LL.D. Written by Himself*. New York: Sheldon, 1864, 2 vols.

Sinclair, Arthur [United States Navy]. *Sailors of 1813. Memoirs and Letters of Naval Officers on Lake Ontario*, ed. Robert Malcomson. Lewiston, N.Y.: Old Fort Niagara, 1997.

Smith William [Artillery]. "Biographical Notice of Lieutenant W.W. Smith," *Analectic Magazine*, 8 (July 1816), 52-54.

Swift, Joseph Gardner [Staff]. *The Memoirs of Gen. Joseph Swift*. ed. Harrison Ellery, ed. N.P., 1890

Wilkinson, James [Staff]. *Memoirs of My Own Times*. Philadephia: Abraham Small, 1816, 3 vols.

British and Canadian

Bell, George. *Soldier's Glory. Being Rough Notes of an Old Soldier.* Tunbridge Wells: Spellmount, 1991

Bell, William [89th Foot]. "The Letters of William Bell, 89th Foot, 1808-1810," *Journal of the Society for Army Historical Research*, 48 (1970), 66-84.

Bunbury, Henry. *Narratives of Some Passages in the Great War with France (1799-1810).* London: Peter Davies, 1927.

Dunlop, William [Surgeon, 89th Foot]. *Tiger Dunlop's Upper Canada.* Carleton University, Toronto, 1967.

Grattan, William. *Adventures with the Connaught Rangers, 1809-1814.* London: Greenhill, 1989, original pub., 1902.

Harris, John. *The Recollections of Rifleman Harris.* London: Century, 1970.

Henegan, Richard. *Seven Years' Campaigning.* London: Coulbourn, 1846, 2 vols.

Hennell, George. *A Gentleman Volunteer. The Letters of George Hennell from the Peninsular War, 1812-1813.* ed. Michael Glover. London: Heineman, 1979.

Jackson, Henry G. [Royal Artillery]. *The Bath Archives. A Further Selection from the Diaries and Letters of Sir George Jackson, K.C.H., from 1809 to 1816.* ed., Lady Jackson. London: Richard Bentley, 1873, 2 vols.

Le Couteur, John [104th Foot]. *Merry Hearts Make Light Days: The War of 1812 Memoir of Lieutenant John Le Couteur, 104th Foot.* ed. Donald E. Graves. Ottawa: Carleton University Press, 1993.

Macdonell, George R. ("Philatethes") [Staff], "The Last War in Canada," *Journal of the United Service Institute*, 1848, 271-283, 425-441.

Merritt, William Hamilton [Provincial Light Dragoons]. *Journal of Events Principally on the Detroit and Niagara Frontiers during the War of 1812.* St. Catharines: Historical Society of British North America, 1863.

Morrison, Robert [Civilian], "What an Eye-Witness said of the Engagement and What Followed It," *Montreal Gazette*, 11 May 1895.

Norton, John. [Indian Department] *The Journal of John Norton 1816*, eds., J.J. Talman & C.F. Klinck. Toronto: The Champlain Society, 1970.

O'Sullivan, Michael [A Canadian Voltigeur]. "An Eye Witness's Account," *Montreal Gazette*, 9 November 1813.

Pinguet, Charles-Casimir [Canadian Fencibles]. "Deux lettres écrites dans les tentes de Châteauguay," *Les Soirées Canadiennes*, (March 1864), 94-96.

[Richardson, James]. *The Letters of Veritas.* Montreal: Gray, 1815.

Shipp, John. *The Path of Glory.* ed. C.J. Stranks. London: Chatto & Windus, 1969.

Period Military Regulations, Treatises and Technical Literature

Adjutant General, Great Britain. *Light Infantry Exercise: As ordered in His Majesty's Regulations for the Movements of the Troops.* London: 1797.

———. *Baggage and Marches of the Army.* London: Horse Guards, 1798.

———. *Regulations to Regimental Surgeons, for the Better Management of the Sick.* London: Horse Guards, 1798.

———. *Instructions to Regimental Surgeons for Regulating the Concerns of the Sick and of the Hospitals.* London: Horse Guards, 1808.

———. *Rules and Regulations for the Formation, Field-Exercise, and Movements of His Majesty's Forces.* London: T. Egerton, 1808.

———. *General Regulations and Orders for the Army.* London: T. Egerton, 1811

Adjutant General, Lower Canada. *Rules and Regulations for the Milita Forces of Lower Canada.* Quebec: Adjutant General of Militia, 1812.

Adjutant General, Ireland. *Standing Orders and Regulations for the Army in Ireland.* London: Mueller, 1969, original publication, 1794.

Adye, Ralph W. *The Bombardier and Pocket Gunner.* London:, T. Egerton, 1813.

Cooper, T.H. *A Practical Guide for the Light Infantry Officer.* London: Mueller, 1970, original publication 1806.

D'Antoni, Vittorio. *A Treatise on Gun-Powder … Fire-Arms … and the Service of Artillery.* Trans., Captain Thompson. London: n.p., 1789.

De Scheel, Henri Othon. *Treatise on Artillery*. Philadelphia: War Department, 1800, reprinted Museum Restoration Service, Bloomfield, 1984.

Duane, William. *American Military Library, or, Compendium of the Modern Tactics*. Philadelphia: Author, 1809. 2 vols.

———. *A Hand Book for Cavalry*. Philadelphia: author, 1813.

———. *Hand Book for Infantry*. Philadelphia: author, 1813.

Gassendi, Jean-Jacques Basilien de. *Aide-Memoire, à l'usage des Officiers d'Artillerie de France*. Paris: Magimel, 1801. 2 vols.

[Grose, Francis]. *Advice to Officers of the British Army*. London: G. Kearsley, 1783.

Raney, John. *The Nature and Treatment, of Gun-Shot Wounds. By John Raney, Esquire; Surgeon-General to the British Army*. Philadelphia, 1776

Tousard, Louis de. *American Artillerist's Companion, or Elements of Artillery*. Philadelphia, C. & A. Conrad, 1809. 2 vols.

United States, Senate. *Compendious Exercise of the Garrison and Field Ordnance as Practised in the United States*. Washington: R.C. Weightman, 1810.

United States, War Department. *An Act Establishing Rules and Articles for the Government of the Armies of the United States with the Regulations of the War Department*. Albany: 1812

———. *Register and Rules and Regulations of the Army for 1813*. Washington: 1813.

———. *The Army Register of the United States, Corrected Up to the 1st of June, 1814*. Boston: Chester Stebbins, 1814.

———. *Articles of War, Military Laws, and Rules and Regulations for the Army of the United States*. Washington: Adjutant and Inspector General's officer, 1816.

———. Smyth, Alexander. *Rules and Regulations for the Field Exercise, Manoeuvres and Conduct of the Infantry of the United States*. Philadelphia: T. & G. Palmer, 1812.

———. [Stoddard, Amos]. *Exercise for Garrison and Field Ordnance, Together with Manoeuvres of Horse Artillery, as altered from the Manual of General Kosciusko, and Adapted for the Service of the United States*. Philadelphia: A. Finlay, 1812.

Biographical Encyclopedias, Registers, Dictionaries, Military Unit and Medal Sources

Appleton's Encyclopedia of American Biography. eds., James Wilson & John Fiske. New York: Appleton, 1888. 7 vols.

Askwith, W.H. *List of Officers of the Royal Regiment of Artillery From the Year 1716 to the Year 1899*. London: Royal Artillery Institution, 1900.

Blatherwick, F.J. *Canadian Orders, Decorations and Medals*. Toronto: Unitrade, 1994.

Chichester, Henry and George Burgess-Short. *Records and Badges of the British Army*. London: Gale & Polden, 1902.

Dictionary of American Biography. New York: Scribner, 1958-1964. 22 vols.

Dictionary of Canadian Biography. Volumes V-IX. Toronto: University of Toronto, 1976-1988.

Fredriksen, John C. *Officers of the War of 1812 with Portraits and Anecdotes*. Lewiston: Edgar Mellen, 1989.

Gray, William, *Soldiers of the King. The Upper Canadian Militia 1812-1815. A Reference Guide*. Toronto: Boston Mills, 1995.

Great Britain, War Office. *A List of all the Officers of the Army and Royal Marines on Full and half-pay*. London: War Office, 1813, 1814.

Heitman, Francis B. *Historical Register and Dictionary of the U.S Army*. Washington: Government Printing Office, 1903. 2 vols.

Holme, Norman & E.L. Kerby. *Medal Rolls. 23rd Foot – Royal Welsh Fusiliers. Napoleonic Period*. London: Spink, 1978.

Irving, L. Homfray. *Officers of the British Forces in Canada during the War of 1812-15*. Welland: Canadian Military Institute, 1908.

Irwin, R.W. *War Medals and Decorations of Canada*. Toronto: n.p. 1969.

Laws, M.E.S. *Battery Records of the Royal Artillery, 1716-1859*. Woolwich: Royal Artillery Institute, 1952.

Lepine, Luc. *Lower Canada's Militia Officers, 1812-1815*. Montreal: Genealogical Society of Quebec, 1996.

Mitchell, Michael. *Ducimus. The Regiments of the Canadian Infantry*. Ottawa: Canadian War Museum, 1992.

Morgan, Henry J. *Sketches of Celebrated Canadians, and Persons Connected with Canada*. Quebec: Hunter, Rose, 1862.

Mullen, A.L.T. *The Military General Service Roll, 1793-1814*. London: Stamp Exchange, 1990.

National Cyclopedia of American Biography. Clifton, NJ: J.T. White, 1891, reprinted 1967. 63 vols.

New England Historical and Geneological Register .. for the Year 1856. Boston: Samuel Drake, 1856.

Norman, C.B. *Battle Honours of the British Army from Tangier 1662, to the Commencement of the Reign of Edward VII*. London: David & Charles, original publication 1911.

Phillipart, John. *The Royal Military Calendar, or Army Service and Commission Book*. London: T. Egerton, 1815. 5 vols.

Roy, Ferdinand. *Fils de Québec*. Lévis: 1933, 4 vols.

Sawicki, James. *Infantry Regiments of the US Army*. Dumfries, VA: Wyvern, 1981.

Sutherland, Stuart. *His Majesty's Gentlemen. A Directory of British Regular Army Officers of the War of 1812*. Toronto: author, forthcoming.

Swinson, Arthur. *A Register of the Regiments and Corps of the British Army*. London: Arms & Armour, 1972.

Wilson, Barbara. *Military General Service Medal 1793-1814 (Canadian Regiments), Egypt Medal 1882-1889 (Canadian Recipients), North West Canada 1885*. London: Spinks, 1975.

SECONDARY SOURCES

Books

Adams, Henry. *History of the United States during the Administration of James Madison*. New York: A.C. Boni, 1930. 4 vols.

Benn, Carl. *The Iroquois in the War of 1812*. Toronto: University of Toronto, 1998.

Bidwell, Shelford. *Swords for Hire. European Mercenaries in Eighteenth Century India*. London: John Murray, 1971.

Bigsby, John J. *The Shoe and the Canoe, or, Pictures of Travels in the Canadas*. London: Chapman & Hall, 1850.

Bilow, John. *Chateaugay, N.Y., and the War of 1812*. N.p., 1984.

Blackmore, Howard. *British Military Firearms, 1650-1850*. London: Herbert Jenkins, 1961.

Boss, W. *The Stormont, Dundas and Glengarry Highlanders, 1783-1951*. Ottawa: Runge Press, 1952.

Burns, Robert J. *Fort Wellington; A Narrative and Structural History, 1812-1838*. Ottawa: Parks Canada Manuscript Report No. 296, 1979.

Canadian Hydrographic Service. *St. Lawrence River Pilot. Quebec Harbour to Kingston Harbour*. Ottawa: Queen's Printer, 1953.

Chartrand, René. *Uniforms and Equipment of the United States Forces in the War of 1812*. Youngstown: Old Fort Niagara Association, 1992.

—— and Jack Summers. *Military Uniforms in Canada, 1665-1970*. Ottawa: National Museums, 1981.

Christie, Robert. *The Military and Naval Operations in the Canadas, During the Late War with the United States*. New York: Oram & Mott, 1818.

Coffin, William F. *1812. The War and Its Moral: A Canadian Chronicle*. Montreal: Lovell, 1864.

Coles, Harry. *The War of 1812*. Chicago: University of Chicago Press, 1965.

Crackel, Theodore. *Mr. Jefferson's Army. Political and Social Reform of the Military Establishment, 1801-1809*. New York: New York University Press, 1987.

Croil, James. *Dundas, or, A Sketch of Canadian History*. Montreal: Dawson, 1861.

——. *A Life of James Croil, Montreal. An Autobiography. 1821-1816*. Montreal: Mitchell & Wilson, 1918.

Cunliffe, Marcus. *The Royal Irish Fusiliers, 1793-1950*. London: Oxford University Press, 1950.

Dunnigan, Brian L. *Forts within a Fort. Niagara's Redoubts*. Lewiston, N.Y.: Old Fort Niagara, 1989.

Elting, John. *Amateurs, to Arms! A Military History of the War of 1812*. Chapel Hill, N.C.: Algonquin, 1991.

——. *Swords Around a Throne. Napoleon's Grande Armée*. New York: Free Press, 1988.

Erney, Richard A. *The Public Life of Henry Dearborn*. New York: Arno, 1979.

Everest, Alan S. *The War of 1812 in the Champlain Valley*. Syracuse: Syracuse University Press, 1981.

Flexner, James. *Washington. The Indispensable Man*. New York: Little, Brown, 1969.

Freeman, Douglas S. *Lee: An Abridgement in One Volume by Richard Harwell*. New York: Collins, 1961, 1991.

Gaines, William H. *Thomas Mann Randolph, Jefferson's Son-in-Law*. Baton Rouge: Lousiana State University Press, 1966.

Glover, Michael. *The Napoleonic Wars. An Illustrated History, 1792-1815*. New York: Hippocrene, 1978.

Glover, Richard. *Peninsular Preparation. The Reform of the British Army, 1795-1809.* Cambridge: Cambridge University, 1963.

Graves, Donald E. *Redcoats and Grey Jackets. The Battle of Chippawa, 1814.* Toronto: Dundurn, 1994.

———— *Where Right and Glory Lead! The Battle of Lundy's Lane, 1814.* Toronto: Robin Brass Studio, 1997.

Greener, William. *The Gun; or, A Treatise on the Various Descriptions of Small Fire-Arms.* London: Longman, Rees, Orme, Brown, Green, and Longman, 1835.

Guillet, Edwin. *Early Life in Upper Canada.* Toronto: Ontario Publishing Co., 1933.

Guitard, Michelle. *The Militia of the Battle of Châteauguay. A Social History.* Ottawa: Parks Canada, 1981.

Hampton, Celwyn E. *History of the Twenty-First U.S. Infantry, from 1812 to 1863.* Columbus, Ohio: Edward T. Miller Co., 1911.

Harkness, John. *Stormont, Dundas and Glengarry. A History, 1784-1945.* Oshawa: Mundy-Goodfellow, 1946.

Haskin, William L. *The History of the First Regiment of Artillery, From Its Organization in 1821 to January, 1876.* Portland, Maine: Thurston, 1879.

Haythornewaite, Philip. *Weapons and Equipment of the Napoleonic Wars.* Poole: Blandford, 1979.

Hickey, Donald R. *The War of 1812. A Forgotten Conflict.* Chicago: University of Illinois, 1989.

Hicks, James. *Notes on U.S. Ordnance.* Green Farms, Conn.: Modern Books & Craft, 1971, reprint of 1940 edition. 2 vols.

Hitsman, J.M. *The Incredible War of 1812.* Toronto: University of Toronto, 1965.

Hough, Franklin B. *A History of Jefferson County.* Albany: Little, 1854.

————. *A History of St. Lawrence and Franklin Counties, New York.* Baltimore: Regional Publishing, 1970, original publication 1853.

Houlding, John. *Fit for Service: The Training of the British Army, 1715-1795.* Oxford: Clarendon, 1981.

Hughes, B.P. *British Smooth-Bore Artillery. The Muzzle-Loading Artillery of the 18th and 19th Centuries.* London: Arms & Armour Press, 1969.

————. *Firepower. Weapons Effectiveness on the Battlefield, 1630-1850.* London: Arms and Armour, 1974.

Ingersoll, Charles J. *Historical Sketches of the Second War between the United States of America and Great Britain.* Philadelphia: Lee, Blanchard, 1849. 2 vols.

Jacobs, James R. *Tarnished Warrior. Major General James Wilkinson.* New York: MacMillan, 1938.

———— and Glen Tucker. *The War of 1812.* New York: Alfred Knopf, 1969.

James, William. *A Full and Correct Account of the Military Occurrences of the Late War between Great Britain and the United States.* London, Black, 1818. 2 vols.

Johnson, Timothy D. *Winfield Scott. The Quest of Military Glory.* Lawrence: University of Kansas, 1998.

Kirby, William. *Annals of Niagara.* Niagara Falls: Lundy's Lane Historical Society, 1896, 1972.

Kreidburg, John. *History of Military Mobilization in the United States Army, 1775-1845.* Washington: Department of the Army, 1958.

Lemmon, Sarah McCullough. *Frustrated Patriots: North Carolina and the War of 1812.* Chapel Hill: University of North Carolina, 1977.

Lerwill, Leonard. *The Personnel Replacement System in the United States Army.* Washington: Department of the Army, 1954.

Lossing, Benson J. *Pictorial Field Book of the War of 1812.* New York: Harpers, 1869.

Luvaas, Jay. *The Education of An Army. British Military Thought, 1815-1940.* Chicago: University of Chicago Press, 1964.

Mackesy, Piers. *British Victory in Egypt, 1801. The End of Napoleon's Conquest.* London: Routledge, 1995.

Mahon, John K. *The War of 1812.* Gainesville: University of Florida, 1972.

Malcomson, Robert. *Lords of the Lake. The Naval War on Lake Ontario, 1812-1814.* Toronto: Robin Brass Studio, 1998.

McConnell, David. *British Smooth-Bore Artillery: A Technological Study.* Ottawa: Environment Canada, 1988.

Muir, Rory. *Tactics and the Experience of Battle in the Age of Napoleon.* New Haven, CT.: Yale University Press, 1998.

Nosworthy, Brent. *Battle Tactics of Napoleon and His Enemies.* London: Constable, 1995.

Oman, Charles. *Wellington's Army, 1809-1814.* London: Greenhill, 1986, original publication, 1912.

————. *A History of the Peninsular War. V. December 1810 to December 1811.* London: Greenhill, 1996, original publication, 1911.

Peterkin, Ernest W. *Exercise of Arms in the Continental Infantry*. Alexandria Bay, N.Y.: Museum Restoration Service, 1989.

Peterson, Harold L. *The American Sword, 1792-1945*. Philadelphia: Ray Riling Books, 1970.

Petre, Francis L. *The Royal Berkshire Regiment (Princess Charlotte of Wales). Vol. 1, 1743-1914*. Reading: The Barracks, 1925.

Pringle, J.F. *Lunenburgh, or the Old Eastern District*. Cornwall: Standard Printing House, 1890.

Quimby, Robert S. *The U.S. Army in the War of 1812. An Operational and Command Study*. East Lansing, Michigan: Michigan State University Press, 1997, 2 vols.

Richards, George. *Memoir of Alexander Macomb*. New York: McElrath and Bangs, 1843.

Ryerson, Egerton. *The Loyalists of America and Their Times, from 1620 to 1816*. Toronto: Briggs, 1880, 2 vols.

Salisbury, George Cook. *The Battle of Chrysler's [sic] Farm, War of 1812-1814*. n.p., n.d. [c. 1955].

Sellar, Gordon. *The U.S. Campaign of 1813 to Capture Montreal*. Huntington, Quebec: Gleaner Office, 1913.

Shortt, Adam and Arthur Doughty. *Canada and Its Provinces. A History of the Canadian People*. Toronto: Constable, 23 vols., 1914-1917.

Skeen, Edward C. *John Armstrong Jr., 1758-1843: A Biography*. Syracuse: University of Syracuse, 1981.

Skelton, William. *An American Profession of Arms. The Army Officer Corps, 1784-1861*. Louisiana: University of Kansas, 1992.

Smith, W.L. *The Makers of Old Ontario*. Toronto: G.N. Monroe, 1928.

Smyth Carter, J. *The Story of Dundas, Being a History of the County of Dundas from 1784 to 1903*. Iroquois, Ontario: St. Lawrence News, 1905.

Stagg, John. *Mr. Madison's War: Politics, Diplomacy, and Warfare in the Early American Republic*. Princeton: Princeton University, 1983.

Suthren, Victor J. *The Battle of Châteauguay*. Ottawa: Parks Canada, 1974.

Thomas, Earle. *Sir John Johnson, Loyalist Baronet*. Toronto: Dundurn, 1986.

Tupper, Ferdinand B. *Life and Correspondence of Major General Sir Isaac Brock*. St. Peter's Port, Guernsey, Burbet, 1847.

Walton, E.P. *Records of the Governor and Council of the State of Vermont. Vol. VI. Vermont in the War of 1812*. Montpelier, Vermont: n.p. 1878.

Winstock, Lewis. *Songs and Music of the Redcoats, 1642-1902*. London: Leo Cooper, 1972.

Wohler, Patrick. *Charles de Salaberry. Soldier of the Empire, Defender of Quebec*. Toronto: Dundurn, 1984.

Wrong, George. *A Canadian Manor and Its Seigneurs*. Toronto: Macmillan, 1926.

Zazlow, Morris. *The Defended Border. Upper Canada and the War of 1812*. Toronto: Macmillan, 1964.

Articles

Ashburn, P.M., "American Army Hospitals of the Revolution and the War of 1812," *Bulletin of the Johns Hopkins Hospital*, 46 (1920), 47-60.

Chartrand, René, "Canadian Voyageurs During the War of 1812," *Journal of the Society for Army Historical Research*, 1994, 184-186.

Cruikshank, Ernest A., "From Isle au Noix to Chateauguay. A Study of Military Operations on the Frontier of Lower Canada in 1812 and 1813," *Transactions of the Royal Society of Canada*, 1 (1913), 129-173; 2 (1914), 25-102.

Duncan, Louis, "The Days Gone By. Sketches of the Medical Service in the War of 1812," *Military Surgeon*, 71 (1932), 436-542.

Fortier, Paul, "Fraser's Troop. Incorporated Provincial Light Dragoons in Upper Canada During the War of 1812," *Campaigns*, 47 (1984), 42-48.

Graves, Donald E., "From Steuben to Scott: The Adoption of French Infantry Tactics by the U.S. Army, 1807-1816," *Acta* No. 13, International Commission on Military History, Helsinki, 1991, 223-235.

————, "American Ordnance of the War of 1812: A Preliminary Investigation." *Arms Collecting*, Volume 31, No. 4 (November 1993): 111-120

————, "Field Artillery of the War of 1812: Equipment, Organization, Tactics and Effectiveness," *Arms Collecting*, 30 (1992) No. 2, 39-48.

————, "Dry Books of Tactics. Infantry Manuals of the War of 1812 and After," Part I, *Military Historian*, 38 (1986), 50-61.

————, "The Second Regiment of United States Light Dragoons," *Military Historian*, 1982 Fall, 101-108.

————, "The Enlisted Men of the Left Division, 1814," in Donald E. Graves, ed., *Soldiers of 1814: American Enlisted Men's Memoirs of the Niagara Campaign.* Youngstown, N.Y.: Old Fort Niagara Press, 1996.

Greenhous, Brereton, "Western Logistics in the War of 1812," *Military Affairs*, 34 (1970), 41-44.

Hare, John S. "Military Punishments in the War of 1812," *Journal of the American Military Institute*, 4 (Winter 1940), No. 4, 225-239.

Henderson, Robert, "His Majesty's Canadian Regiment of Fencible Infantry, 1803-1816," *Military Illustrated*, No. 37 (June 1991), 18-25; No. 38 (July 1991), 27-33.

Heriot, J.C.A. "Major General, The Hon. Frederick George Heriot, C.B.," *Canadian Antiquarian and Numismatic Journal*, 8 (April 1911), 49-72.

Howe, Jonas, "Colonel Henry Ormond: The Career of a New Brunswick Soldier," *Acadiensis*, 2 (1902), 19-23.

Howell, H.A.L., "The British Medical Arrangements during the Waterloo Campaign," *Proceedings of the Royal Society of Medicine*, 17 (1923-1924), 39-50.

Kimball, Jeffrey, "The Fog and Friction of Frontier War: The Role of Logistics in American Offensive Failures during the War of 1812," *Old Northwest*, 5 (Winter 1979-1980), 323-343.

Leslie, J.H., "Chrysler's [sic] farm, 11 November, 1813," *Journal of the Royal Artillery*, 63 (1936), 188-199.

Manigault, Gabriel, " Military Career of General George Izard," *Magazine of American History*, 20 (1888), 465-472.

Massicotte, Etienne-Zodiac, "Chansons militaires de 1812," *Bulletin des Récherches Historiques*, 25 (1911), 188-191.

Matheson, J.M., "Comments on the Medical Aspect of the Battle of Waterloo, 1815," *Medical History*, 10 (1960), 52-58.

Neale, Graham, "Colonel John Crysler of Crysler's Farm," *Journal of the Orders and Medals Research Society*, 21 (Autumn 1982), 50-54.

Patterson, Richard. "Lieutenant Colonel Benjamin Forsyth," *North Country Notes*, November 1974.

Patterson, William, "A Forgotten Hero in a Forgotten War," *Journal of the Society for Army Historical Research*, 78 (1990), 7-21.

[Pearson, Thomas], Obituary, *United Service Journal*, 2, (1847), 479.

Putnam, Alfred, "General Moses Porter," *Historical Collections of the Danvers Historical Society*, 15 (1927), 1-25

Quaife, Milo. "Detroit Biographies: Alexander Macomb," *Burton Historical Collection Leaflet*, 10, No. 1, 1931.

Shaw, Claudius, "Remarks on the Defences and Resources of Canada in the Event of War," *United Service Journal*, 1845, 244-399.

Stagg, John. "Enlisted Men in the United States Army, 1812-1815: A Preliminary Survey," *William and Mary Quarterly*, 3rd Series, 43 (1986), 616-645.

Way, Ronald. "The Day of Crysler's Farm," *Canadian Geographical Journal*, 62 (1961), 184-217.

SECONDARY SOURCES – UNPUBLISHED

Cook, George Salisbury, "The American Lake Ontario Army – 1813," typescript in possession of Dr. Traer Van Allen, Morrisburg.

Cook, Lynne and K. Vanderbaaren, "Descendants of John Cook, U.E.L.," typescript, archives of Upper Canada Village, Morrisburg.

Graves, Donald E., "Joseph Willcocks and his Canadian Volunteers. A Study of Political Disaffection in Upper Canada During the War of 1812." M.A. Thesis, Carleton University, Ottawa, 1982.

Henderson, Robert. "Notes on Captain Hall's Company, Canadian Fencibles," 1990.

Hinton, Harwood, "The Military Career of John Ellis Wool, 1812-1863," PhD. Thesis, University of Wisconsin, 1960.

Loucks, John W., "Battle of Crysler's Farm – November 11, 1813, as personally related to his grandson, Arthur M. Loucks," typescript, n.d. [c. 1960], archives of Upper Canada Village.

"The Loucks Family and the Loyalist Farm," typescript, n.d., [c. 1960], Upper Canada Village.

Smart, James, "St. Lawrence Project. Events in Military History of the St. Lawrence River Valley, 1760-1814," typescript, n.d. [c. 1960], archives of Upper Canada Village, Morrisburg.

Stokes, Peter, "Cook's Tavern Research," typescript, 1959, archives of Upper Canada Village.

Index

Eight months after the disastrous St. Lawrence campaign
of 1813, a renewed American army led by Major General Jacob Brown took
the field again. The story of the campaign that followed is told in *Where
Right and Glory Lead! The Battle of Lundy's Lane, 1814* by Donald E. Graves.

The centrepiece of *Where Right and Glory
Lead!* is a detailed analysis of the battle of Lundy's
Lane, one of the most hard-fought military actions to take place in North America. On a summer evening in July, five thouand American, British and Canadian soldiers struggled desperately
within sight of Niagara Falls in a stubborn close-
range battle that raged on into the dark. The two
armies fought each other to a standstill, and the
victor has long been a matter of dispute.

In his analysis of this still-controversial action,
Donald E. Graves narrates the background and
events of the 1814 Niagara campaign, the longest
and bloodiest military operation of the War of 1812, and provides a thorough examination of the weaponry, tactics and personalities of the opposing armies. The result is possibly the most thorough analysis of a musket-
period action to appear in print, and an engrossing sequel to *Field of Glory.*

Fought near Niagara Falls, it was the most
bitterly contested battle of the War of 1812.

Where
Right and
Glory Lead!

THE BATTLE OF LUNDY'S LANE, 1814

Donald E. Graves

"Donald Graves's brilliant and exciting and sometimes surprising interpretation
of the greatest battle ever to have taken place on Canadian soil."
Michael Power, Brock Review

"Where Right and Glory Lead! is how military history should be written –
deeply and carefully researched, salted with common sense, and put into a prose
that stands you in a firing line that is fraying thinner by the minute...."
**John Elting, author of *Swords Around a Throne: Napoleon's Grand Armée*
and *Amateurs to Arms: A Military History of the War of 1812***

"... a vivid and scholarly account of ... a desperate and extraordinary night
battle, written by a master of the military techniques of the day. ...
an enjoyable and compelling read."
**Piers Mackesy, author of *The War for America, 1775-83*, *War Without
Victory: The Downfall of Pitt* and *British Victory in Egypt, 1801***

"Read Donald Graves's brilliant and exciting and sometimes surprising
interpretation of the greatest battle ever to have taken place on Canadian soil."
Michael Power, *Brock Review*

Donald E. Graves is an internationally recognized expert on the War of 1812 and has written four previous books on that conflict. His study of the bloody 1814 battle of Lundy's Lane, *Where Right and Glory Lead!* (Robin Brass Studio, 1997), has been called "an exercise in military history at its best" and is regarded as a minor classic. Don Graves's other War of 1812 titles are: *Redcoats and Grey Jackets: The Battle of Chippawa, 1814; Merry Hearts Make Light Days: The War of 1812 Memoir of Lieutenant John Le Couteur, 104th Foot;* and *Soldiers of 1814: American Enlisted Mens' Memoirs of the Niagara Campaign.* He has also served as an historical consultant for the War of 1812 segment of the Canadian Broadcasting Corporation's forthcoming "Millenium History of Canada" to be televised in the year 2000.

Donald Graves's most recent book is *South Albertas: A Canadian Regiment at War* (Robin Brass Studio, 1998) and he is currently writing a biography of Joseph Willcocks, the worst traitor in Canadian history and the man who bears the greatest responsibility for the burning of Washington in 1814. Donald Graves is the director of Ensign Heritage, a company specializing in heritage consulting and travel, and lives with his author wife, Dianne, near Almonte, the only municipality in Canada named after a Mexican general.

Peter Rindlisbacher, who painted the cover art and contributed a number of sketches to the book, is a full-time marine artist specializing in War of 1812 subjects. Museums and historic sites in the U.S. and Canada have purchased many of his oil paintings, while prints of his work are sold as fundraisers for various historical groups. His images have appeared on book and magazine covers and in a number of public television programs. He lives in Amherstburg, Ontario, with his wife and two children.